Lecture Notes in Artificial Intelligence   1688

Subseries of Lecture Notes in Computer Science
Edited by J. G. Carbonell and J. Siekmann

Lecture Notes in Computer Science

Edited by G. Goos, J. Hartmanis and J. van Leeuwen

T0217374

Springer

*Berlin
Heidelberg
New York
Barcelona
Hong Kong
London
Milan
Paris
Singapore
Tokyo*

Paolo Bouquet   Luciano Serafini
Patrick Brézillon   Massimo Benerecetti
Francesca Castellani (Eds.)

Modeling and Using Context

Second International and
Interdisciplinary Conference, CONTEXT'99
Trento, Italy, September 9-11, 1999
Proceedings

 Springer

Series Editors

Jaime G. Carbonell, Carnegie Mellon University, Pittsburgh, PA, USA
Jörg Siekmann, University of Saarland, Saarbrücken, Germany

Volume Editors

Paolo Bouquet
Massimo Benerecetti
University of Trento, DISA
5, via Inama, I-38050 Trento, Italy
E-mail: {bouquet,bene}@unitn.it

Luciano Serafini
IRST-ITC
Pante di Povo, I-38050 Trento, Italy
E-mail: serafini@irst.itc.it

Patrick Brézillon
University Paris VI, LIP6
4, Place Jussieu, F-75252 Paris Cedex 05, France
E-mail: Patrick.Brezillon@lip6.fr

Francesca Castellani
University of Trento
26, via Verdi, I-38050 Trento, Italy
E-mail: francesca.castellani@soc.unitn.it

Cataloging-in-Publication data applied for

Die Deutsche Bibliothek - CIP-Einheitsaufnahme

Modeling and using context : second international and
interdisciplinary conference, context '99, Trento, Italy, September 9 -
11, 1999 ; proceedings / Paolo Bouquet ... (ed.). - Berlin ; Heidelberg
; New York ; Barcelona ; Hong Kong ; London ; Milan ; Paris ;
Singapore ; Tokyo : Springer, 1999
  (Lecture notes in computer science ; 1688 : Lecture notes in artificial
intelligence)
  ISBN 3-540-66432-7

CR Subject Classification (1998): I.2, F.4.1, J.3, J.4

ISBN 3-540-66432-7 Springer-Verlag Berlin Heidelberg New York

© Springer-Verlag Berlin Heidelberg 1999
Printed in Germany

Typesetting: Camera-ready by author
SPIN 10704444   06/3142 – 5 4 3 2 1 0   Printed on acid-free paper

Preface

This volume contains the papers presented at the *Second International and Interdisciplinary Conference on Modeling and Using Context* (CONTEXT'99), held in Trento (Italy) from 9 to 11 September 1999. CONTEXT'99 is the second in the CONTEXT series. The first was held in Rio de Janeiro (Brazil) in 1997.

The CONTEXT conference series is meant to provide an interdisciplinary forum where researchers can exchange ideas, methodologies, and results on context, and is increasingly becoming an important reference for all people doing research on context. This is testified by the larger number of research areas that are represented at CONTEXT'99 (in particular, Philosophy and Cognitive Psychology were not significantly present at the first conference), and by the number and quality of submitted papers. Specifically, we received 118 papers, mostly of good or excellent quality. Among them, 33 (28%) have been accepted as full papers, and 21 as short papers. We think it is fair to say that the 54 papers collected in this volume provide a significant picture of the international research on context currently going on.

The notion of context plays an important role in many areas, both theoretical and applied, such as Formal Logic, Artificial Intelligence, Philosophy, Pragmatics, Computational Linguistics, Computer Science, Cognitive Psychology. If, on one hand, this provides a promising ground for interdisciplinary events such as the CONTEXT conference series, on the other hand it does not mean *per se* that there is a general agreement on a unique, shared notion of context. Depending on the research goals and on the different conceptual tools and methods, various – and apparently quite heterogeneous – notions of context are introduced and used. Indeed, they diverge on several crucial issues, such as: is context internal (part of the state of the mind) or external (part of the state of the world)? Is context explicitly represented in the human mind or just implicitly? Is context to be thought of as a collection of parameters (such as time, location, speaker, ...) which affect the meaning of a linguistic expression, or rather as a collection of propositions which belong to a conceptual/mental/logical space?

This situation, however, is not hopeless. On the contrary, cross-fertilization among the various disciplines has just started, and we believe that the papers presented in this volume provide a good example of the results we may expect from such an interaction. We are extremely confident that the results will become even more apparent and significant in the near future.

We would like to express our gratitude to the five keynote speakers: A. Bonomi (Department of Philosophy, University of Milan), who spoke on *Fictional Contexts*; G. Fauconnier (Cognitive Science Department, University of California, San Diego), on *The Dynamics of Meaning Construction*, F. Giunchiglia (University of Trento and ITC-IRST, Italy), on *Local Models Semantics, or Contextual Reasoning = Locality + Compability*, D. Lenat (CYCorporation, Austin, Texas), on *The Dimensions of Context-Space*, and F. Récanati (Centre de Recherche en

Epistémologie Appliquée, École Polytechnique, Paris), on *Are 'Here' and 'Now' Indexicals?*

We would also like to thank the many people who made CONTEXT'99 possible. First of all, the program committee members and all the additional reviewers for all they did to ensure the high quality of accepted contributions. Second, Massimo Benerecetti and Francesca Castellani. They not only helped us to edit this volume, but also served as publicity chair and local chair, respectively. We thank Igino Fagioli, Head of the *Department of Theory History and Social Research* (University of Trento); Alessandro Zorat, Head of the *Department of Computer and Management Sciences* (University of Trento); Enrico Zaninotto, Dean of the *Faculty of Economics*; the administrative staff of the University of Trento, coordinated by Stefano Mariucci, who safely led us across the "bureaucracy jungle"; and Elisabetta Nones (Office for Public Relations, University of Trento). Finally, we would like to thank Valeria Ascheri and Ilaria Cecot for their help as volunteers in the local organization.

September 1999

Paolo Bouquet
Luciano Serafini
Patrick Brézillon

Organization

CONTEXT'99 was organized by the *Department of Theory History and Social Research* and the *Department of Computer and Management Sciences* at the University of Trento. The former also partially funded the conference. CONTEXT'99 was hosted by the *Faculty of Economics* (University of Trento).

Organizing Committee

Conference Chair	Patrick Brézillon (University Paris VI, Paris)
Program Co-Chairs	Paolo Bouquet (University of Trento)
	Luciano Serafini (ITC-IRST, Trento)
Local Chair & Treasurer	Francesca Castellani (University of Trento)
Publicity Chair	Massimo Benerecetti (University of Trento)

Program Committee

Aamodt, A. (Norway)
Abu-Hakima, S. (Canada)
Akman, V. (Turkey)
Bonzon, P. (Switzerland)
Castelfranchi, C. (Italy)
Cavalcanti, M. (Brazil)
Chandrasekaran, B. (USA)
Dichev, C. (Bulgaria)
Edmonds, B. (UK)
Fauconnier, G. (USA)
Fisher, M. (UK)
Frasson, C. (Canada)
Gabbay, D. (UK)
Gaines, B. (Canada)
Giunchiglia, E. (Italy)
Giunchiglia, F. (Italy)
Guha, R. (USA)
Hayes, P. (USA)
Hayes-Roth, B. (USA)
Hollnagel, E. (Denmark)
Iwanska, L. (USA)

Kodratoff, Y. (France)
Kokinov, B. (Bulgaria)
Maybury, M.T. (USA)
Moulin, B. (Canada)
Noriega, P. (Spain)
Paris, C. (Australia)
Penco, C. (Italy)
Perry, J. (USA)
Pomerol, J.-Ch. (France)
Raccah, P.Y. (France)
Rastier, F. (France)
Shahar, Y. (USA)
Sharma, N. (USA)
Singh, M. (USA)
Thomason, R.H. (USA)
Tiberghien, G. (France)
Turner, R. (USA)
Widmer, G. (Austria)
Wilson, D. (UK)
Young, R. (USA)
Young, R. (UK)

Additional Reviewers

Aguzzoli, S.

Barnden, J.

Bazzanella, C.

Benerecetti, M.

Benzi, M.

Blanzieri, E.

Bonatti, P.

Bonomi. A.

Bresciani, P.

Brevik, O.A.

Caprile, B.

Castellani, F.

Cesta, A.

D'Aloisi, D.

Dell'Acqua, P.

Dragoni, A.

Falcone, R.

Fetzer, A.

Franconi, E.

Frixione, M.

Fuernkranz, J.

Furlanello, C.

Gherardi, S.

Ghidini, C.

Giboin, A.

Giorgini, P.

Greco, A.

Holme, A.

Lavelli, A.

Magnini, B.

Marconi, D.

Montecucco, L.

Musso, P.

Nossin, M.

Origgi, G.

Ozturk, P.

Pasquier, L.

Pianesi, F.

Rizzo, P.

Sbisà, M.

Sebastiani, R.

Sparzani, A.

Tovena, L.

Varzi, A.

Viezzer, M.

Virbel, J.

Sponsoring Institutions

The following institutions have generously contributed to the organization of
CONTEXT'99:

- *Dipartimento di Teoria Storia e Ricerca Sociale* (University of Trento).
- *Comprensorio della Valle dell'Adige – C5* (Trento)
- *Federazione Trentina delle Cooperative – Casse Rurali Operanti Società di Trento.*
- *Provincia Autonoma di Trento.*

Table of Contents

Full Papers

Short Papers

Strawson on Intended Meaning and Context

Varol Akman[1] and Ferda Nur Alpaslan[2]

[1] Department of Computer Engineering and Information Science,
Bilkent University, 06533 Ankara, Turkey
akman@cs.bilkent.edu.tr
http://www.cs.bilkent.edu.tr/~akman
[2] Department of Computer Engineering,
Middle East Technical University, 06531 Ankara, Turkey
alpaslan@ceng.metu.edu.tr
http://www.ceng.metu.edu.tr/~alpaslan

Abstract. Strawson proposed in the early seventies an attractive three-fold distinction regarding how context bears on the meaning of 'what is said' when a sentence is uttered. The proposed scheme is somewhat crude and, being aware of this aspect, Strawson himself raised various points to make it more adequate. In this paper, we review the scheme of Strawson, note his concerns, and add some of our own. However, our main point is to defend the essence of Strawson's approach and to recommend it as a starting point for research into intended meaning and context.

> 'That is not it at all,
> That is not what I meant, at all.'
> T. S. Eliot, *Prufrock and Other Observations* (1917)

1 Introduction

The following anecdote comes from the first author [3]:

> Not long ago, I was visiting Boston for a small workshop on context. After a demanding morning session I got into the MIT Bookstore for a bit of shopping. Walking along the isles I noticed on a crowded shelf a sign which read:

> | ← NOAM CHOMSKY'S SECTION IS A LITTLE TO THE LEFT |

> I found this fairly clever! In fact, my expectation that the workshop audience might also like the tongue-in-cheek message of it was fulfilled. When I showed a copy of the sign at some point during my talk I got quite a few chuckles.

Leaving aside whatever that left arrow contributes to the meaning of the sign—for it indeed seems to add something, doesn't it?—what kind of understanding did the author of the sign expect the reader to have as a result of his[1]

---

[1] In this paper "he" is used as a shorthand for "he/she."

seeing it? In treating this question in any detail, it is unavoidable, we think, to notice the interaction of authorial intentions and context. And it turns out that in his most recent volume of essays, Strawson had considerable things to say on this very question, or more generally, the issue of intended meaning.

Strawson's book is entitled *Entity and Identity*, and the essays which treat the afore-mentioned question at some length appear as Chapters 11 [26] and 12 [27]. It must be observed that the original versions of the essays were published considerably earlier. Thus, Chapter 11, "Austin and 'locutionary meaning'," first appeared in I. Berlin et al., eds., *Essays on J. L. Austin*, Oxford: Oxford University Press (1973). A partial translation of Chapter 12, "Meaning and context," appeared in *Langages* 17 (March 1970), with the title "Phrase et acte de parole."

In these essays Strawson advances a particularly attractive threefold distinction regarding how context bears on the meaning of 'what is said' when a sentence is uttered [28]. But he also remarks that the proposed scheme "may be held to be too simple, since the situation is, or may be, more complex than the scheme suggests" [27, p. 216], and raises various points to make it more adequate. Here, we will (i) review the scheme of Strawson, (ii) summarize his ameliorations, and (iii) add some of our own. (These three activities will not always be separated by careful boundaries.) However, our main purpose will be to defend the versatility of his approach. As a result, the reader will hopefully appreciate why a Strawsonian look at context may be useful for forming realistic models of how intended meaning is achieved.

An explanation regarding the motivations of the two essays is in order. As is well known, Austin [4] distinguished between the *meaning* and *force* of an utterance. He associated the former with the 'locutionary' act performed in making the utterance, and the latter with the 'illocutionary' act. In his chapter on Austin, Strawson *uses* the threefold distinction to examine Austin's work; his standpoint is that what Austin means by locutionary meaning is not very clear. On the other hand, in "Meaning and context" the threefold distinction *itself* is examined in detail. In the light of this fact, our remarks will generally bear on the contents of that essay (Chapter 12).

2   The Problem and Strawson's Scheme

"A friend of mine [...] once told me [...] that the way to write a paper in philosophy was to begin by asking a question that anybody could understand or by posing a problem in such a way that anyone would see that it was a problem." In the spirit of these words of Davidson [17], Strawson tackles the riddle of how context influences intended meaning by first proposing a simple question and an economic answer, and then attending to the complications which seem not to be easily resolvable by the latter.

Assume that a certain sentence S of a language L (e.g. English) was seriously uttered on some occasion. (N.B. The adverb "seriously" plays a crucial role, as we'll see in the sequel.) Assume further that X, the hearer, possesses only that much information, i.e. X knows that S was uttered but knows nothing about the identity of Y, the speaker, or the nature or date of the occasion. (In various places in the sequel, this restriction will be relaxed.) Let us grant X full mastery of the syntax and semantics of L; thus, X is assumed to have ideally complete knowledge of L (lexicon plus grammar). The question is as follows [26, p. 192]:

> [I]s there any sense in which X can be said to know *the meaning of precisely what was said on the occasion in question*?[2]

Strawson's proposed scheme to investigate this problem is a fine example of the principle of 'separation of concerns'. It consists of erecting three progressively richer senses of meaning which he dubs sense-A-meaning, sense-B-meaning, and sense-C-meaning. We now explain these.

According to Strawson, sense-A-meaning is *linguistic* meaning. Suppose S is free of ambiguity, or more realistically, X is informed which of the alternative readings of S is the right one, i.e. the one meant by Y. (It is beside the point, for the time being, *how* X could be told which of the possible lexical items or syntactic constructions Y actually had in mind in uttering S.) We then say that X knows the *sense-A-meaning* of what is said. An important characteristic of such meaning is that if he has access to it, then X can give a correct translation of S into another language L' (e.g. French), which X, once again, is assumed to know perfectly well. In other words, when sense-A-meaning is under consideration, X basically knows neither more nor less than he needs to know in order to translate S into a sentence S' of L'. Consider the following example (due to Strawson) as S: "The collapse of the bank took everyone by surprise." The designation of the word "bank" varies with different uses. But once the intended designation is clarified, then the translation of S from L to L' proceeds smoothly. Also witness Perry's similar remarks [21]: "An ambiguous expression like 'bank' may designate one kind of thing when you say 'Where's a good bank?' while worried about finances, another when [you] use it, thinking about fishing. [...] Is the speaker holding a wad of money or a fishing pole?"

To summarize the preceding paragraph, we can write

$$\text{sense-A-meaning} = S + \text{A-knowledge} + \text{disambiguating knowledge},$$

where *A-knowledge* is the ideally complete knowledge of the lexicon and grammar of L. In this mock equation, the interpretations of "=" and "+" are somewhat

---

[2] Modern literary theory famously distinguishes between an author's intended meaning and whatever *significances* a reader finds in the text. Obviously, not all patterns and relationships found by the reader in a text can be attributed to authorial intention [2]. The meaning/significance contrast, first formulated by E. D. Hirsch, is accepted by Eco. The producer of a text, Eco claims [8, p. 7], "has to foresee a model of the possible reader [...] supposedly able to deal interpretatively with the expressions in the same way as the author deals generatively with them." This possible reader Eco calls the *model reader*. Eco's proposal is that to make his text communicative, the author has to make sure that the totality of 'codes' upon which his work is built is the same as that shared by the model reader.

procedural; that is, the equation states that sense-A-meaning is obtained by just understanding S in the light of A-knowledge and disambiguating knowledge (and with a propensity toward accurate translation of S into any other, equally rich language).

Strawson's sense-B-meaning is *linguistic-cum-referential* meaning. X will learn the *sense-B-meaning* of S if he has access to the references of proper names or indexicals which may be contained in S.[3] An example might illustrate the difference between sense-A- and sense-B-meanings. If S is the sentence "He stood on his head since then," and if X is further told that this potentially ambiguous sentence has its natural reading where "his" is coindexed with "he," then X can easily translate S to say, French. When X does that accurately, it would show that X understood the sense-A-meaning of S. Now suppose X has no idea who "he" stands for and which time point "then" denotes. This would certainly not pose a problem for the translation. But if X additionally learns the reference of "he" (say, J. L. Austin) and "then" (say, New Year's Day, 1955) then X would know a richer meaning, the sense-B-meaning of S.[4]

In a style suggested by the earlier equation, we can write

$$\text{sense-B-meaning} = \text{sense-A-meaning} + \text{B-knowledge},$$

where *B-knowledge* includes—in addition to A-knowledge—the knowledge of the reference of proper names and indexical expressions that might be occurring in S. Again, this mock equation can be interpreted as follows: sense-B-meaning is obtained by scrutinizing sense-A-meaning in the light of B-knowledge.

Finally, Strawson offers sense-C-meaning as *complete* meaning of a message. *Sense-C-meaning* is obtained by adding to sense-B-meaning the illocutionary force (à la Austin) of what was said, together with a complete grasp of how what was said is intended (by Y) to be understood (by X). Thus,

$$\text{sense-C-meaning} = \text{sense-B-meaning} + \text{C-knowledge},$$

where *C-knowledge* consists of—in addition to B-knowledge—the illocutionary force of S plus the true intent of Y. For instance, if S is the sentence "Don't sign that contract yet," then X needs to know whether this was issued as a request, a command, a piece of advice, or what have you. This is the dimension of meaning Austin captured with the phrase 'illocutionary force'.[5] There is a related but distinct notion: it may be that Y intends to be taken to be implying

---

[3] The reader is referred to [20] for a recent account of problems raised by names and indexicals.

[4] One may object to the preceding analysis by noting that there are naturally occurring contexts in which the particular S of this example might have metaphorical meaning. Or at least, this is exactly what happens when one replaces S with a similar sentence "He stood on his own feet since then," meaning he thought and acted independently since then. We agree and just note that this is precisely the point of what Strawson imposes on S, viz. S is uttered 'seriously'. More on this later.

[5] An anonymous referee rightly pointed out that Strawson understands illocutionary force as having to do simply with what the speaker means. However, illocutionary

by S something which does not ensue from S's sense-B-meaning alone. Assume that both X and Y know (and know each other to know) that their mutual friend Z declined an honor conferred upon him by a church. When Y says "It is the sign of a feeble mind to turn down a gift from God," the meaning of what he said would not be fully understood by X if X fails to recognize that Z is being labeled as the decrepit one by Y. Grice [9] was in some sense the first to produce an elucidation of how a speaker can communicate more than what his words explicitly say [5]. Since Strawson does cite Grice, it is safe to predict that he has in mind the same kind of systematic Gricean principles underlying pragmatic 'implication'.

With the preceding three equations at hand, we can write the mock inequality

$$\text{sense-A-meaning} < \text{sense-B-meaning} < \text{sense-C-meaning},$$

where progressively 'richer' senses of meaning are obtained by moving from left to right in the inequality. Since X employs (in proceeding from S to sense-A, sense-A to sense-B, and sense-B to sense-C) A-knowledge, B-knowledge, and C-knowledge, respectively, the progression in meaning will in general be *additive*. However, sometimes the move from one sense to another is really no move at all. A fitting example comes from mathematics: let S be a sentence expressing a proposition of arithmetic, e.g. "There is always a prime number greater than a given natural number." In this case, the move from sense-A to sense-B is no move at all because the sentence is completely general and explicit. (Clearly, the tense of "be" lacks any temporal significance.)

How about C-knowledge? Can its additional contribution also be null sometimes?[6] The answer is not obviously in the affirmative, despite what Strawson thinks. Take an explicitly performative statement such as "I order you to drop that gun." Together with Strawson, we may, at first, be inclined to accept that knowledge of the force of this S can be taken to belong to the sense-A-meaning. However[7], this is not really to follow Austin [4]. To give an example, if a mutinous private in the British army purported to order his sergeant to drop his gun and the cowardly sergeant did so, then a court martial would definitely rule that there was no order (or nothing with the force of an order), because a private cannot give an order to a sergeant. In other words, it is one thing for a type to be meant to be tokened in an act with a certain force and another thing for the token *actually* to realize an act with that force.

---

force has to do with what is conventionally constituted by the locutionary act being performed in context. Witness the following caveat of Austin [4, pp. 116–117]: "I cannot be said to have warned an audience unless it hears what I say and takes what I say in a certain sense. [...] So the performance of an illocutionary act involves the securing of *uptake*." In a nutshell, then, one decides on what interpretation to accept by examining uptake—the (conversational) process through which lines of reasoning are developed/modified [12].

[6] In which case the move from B to C might still be regarded as an addition, even if it is the minimal addition that *there is nothing to be added* to the B-meaning.

[7] We owe the rest of this paragraph to an anonymous referee.

3 A Striking Similarity

We believe that Strawson's distinction is a natural one. To support this premise, another threefold distinction due to Leech is worth indicating at this point. Leech states that specification of context has the effect of narrowing down the communicative possibilities of a message. He says that in particularizing meaning, context helps in the following ways [18, p. 67]:

- (A) Context eliminates certain ambiguities or multiple meanings in the message (e.g. lets us know that *page* in a given instance means a boy attendant rather than a piece of paper).
- (B) Context indicates the referents of certain types of word we call DEICTIC (*this, that, here, there, now, then*, etc.), and of other expressions of definite meaning such as *John, I, you, he, it, the man.*
- (C) Context supplies information which the speaker/writer has omitted through ellipsis (e.g. we are able to appreciate that *Janet! Donkeys!* means something like 'Janet! Drive those donkeys away!' rather than 'Janet! Bring those donkeys here!', or any other of the indefinitely many theoretical possibilities).

Clearly, (A) states the so-called *disambiguating role* of context and immediately brings to mind Strawson's sense-A-meaning. Likewise, (B) is along the lines of Strawson's sense-B-meaning. Finally, although the singling out of ellipsis might at first sight seem way too specific, it is clear that Leech is talking in (C) about a particular way of how speaker's intention is to be inferred. His example has the same import as Strawson's sense-C-meaning, viz. the requirement that the reader must be aware of all that was intended by the speaker.[8]

4 A-, B-, C-Meanings and Their Dependence on Context

Having defined the three senses of meaning, A-, B-, and C-, Strawson turns to the following question: what specific differences are there in the ways in which the meaning of 'what is said' depends on context in the three cases? In particular, in which cases and to what degree can this dependence be itself represented as governed by *linguistic rule* or *convention*?

Obviously, context bears on determination of sense-A-meaning in just those situations where S suffers from syntactic and/or lexical ambiguity. However, disambiguation of S by context at this level is not in general a matter of linguistic rule or convention. Rather, it is a matter of general relevance, cf. the earlier example of Perry regarding which meaning of "bank" might be more plausible. In the same vein, Leech [18, p. 69] states that it is relevant to the interpretation of "Shall I put the sweater on?" to know whether sweaters heated by

---

[8] "Janet! Donkeys!" is recurrently used by aunt Betsey Trotwood in *David Copperfield*; it is an order to her maid to carry out the routine task of driving donkeys off the grass.

electric power are on the market. This shows, in a rather strong sense, that the study of meaning- or interpretation-in-context is closely tied to the *encyclopedic knowledge* about the world.

Context bears on the determination of sense-B-meaning in all cases except those where B-knowledge adds nothing to A-knowledge. And surely there are some semantic rules of natural language moderating such contextual dependence. Here's what Perry [19] says about indexicals:

> There is an intimate connection between the meanings of "I" and "the person who utters this token," even if it falls short of synonymy. The second phrase does not have the meaning of "I," but it gives part of the meaning of "I." It supplies the condition of designation that English associates with "I." [...] Here are the conditions of designation for some familiar indexicals [...]:
> - I: u [an utterance of "I"] designates x iff x is the speaker of u
> - you: u [an utterance of "you"] designates y iff $\exists x(x$ is the speaker of u & x addresses y with $u)$
> - now: u [an utterance of "now"] designates t iff $\exists x(x$ is the speaker of u & x directs u at t during part of $t)$
> - that Φ: u [an utterance of "that Φ"] designates y iff $\exists x(x$ is the speaker of u & x directs u towards $y)$

It is noted, however, that B-knowledge is not wholly under the governance of language rules (cf. Perry's caveat above: "... part of the meaning..."). For instance, with the demonstrative "here" there arises the question of how large a region to consider: "It is always very hot here at this time of the day" ("here" = in this room/in this town?). Similarly, an utterance of "We must sell those HAL stocks now" would signify different time points when it is made by a portfolio manager sitting at his on-line terminal ("now" = in a couple of seconds) and by an executive during a luncheon with his assistants ("now" = in a couple of days).

5 Amendments to the Above Scheme

Strawson enumerated several points at which his threefold distinction is too crude to provide for all the complexities of language use. As a matter of fact, and despite what the title of this section says, he did not always suggest these as amendments to his scheme; sometimes he was content with just jotting them down.

5.1 Semantic Creativity

This refers to the following problem. According to the inequality given earlier, some sense-A-meaning is always included in the complete meaning of what is said. This is due to the nature of construction of sense-C-meaning. However, isn't it unrealistic to suppose that all meanings of a particular word are listed priorly in X's ideal lexicon? Consider the interpretation of a morphologically complex word w. Word formation rules might constrain but do not fully determine the interpretation of w. To put it mildly, the linguistically specified meaning of w may and frequently does go beyond what is available from its compositional subparts [6, pp. 366–370].

On a related note, Aitchison [1, pp. 16–17] remarks that newspapers can popularize new words such as *yomp* and *wimp*. For instance, yomp (to march with heavy equipment over difficult terrain) was a military term used frequently during the Falklands War. Wimp (a feeble or ineffectual person) originated in the U.S.—remember those White House correspondents reporting "President Bush has finally shaken off his wimp image," etc.—and also became popular in the U.K.

Récanati uses the term *contextual sense construction* to refer to the general problem. He notes that sometimes the conventional sense of the subparts of a complex phrase and the way they are syntactically brought together is insufficient to evaluate the semantic value of the complex phrase. His examples are particularly forceful [23, p. 343]:

> Thus 'he finished the book' can mean that he finished reading the book, writing it, binding it, tearing it into pieces, burning it, and so forth [...]; 'finger cup' will mean either 'cup having the shape of a finger' or 'cup containing a finger of whisky' or 'cup which one holds with one finger', or whatever [...]; 'John's book' can mean 'the book that John owns, wrote, gave, received', or whatever [...]. In all such cases there is not a 'selection' from a *limited* range of *preexisting* interpretations for the complex phrase. Rather, an indefinite number of possible interpretations can be constructed in a *creative* manner. [our italics]

Strawson finds his scheme too simple when it comes to such matters of semantic creativity. He first suggests a compromise can be made by allowing that X's ideal dictionary is updated by adding the new (extended) meaning of a new (complex) word. However, he sees this as a sacrifice of his ground rules, viz. when we do this, we make X's dictionary follow his understanding rather than his understanding obey his dictionary.

5.2 Seriousness

Let us return to a crucial proviso in the original formulation of our question, i.e. that a certain sentence S of a language L must be *seriously* uttered. This implies that an *ironical utterance* of S is regarded as non-serious. However, ironical utterances make up quite a large crowd and cannot be so easily dismissed as aberrations.

The essential problem posed by ironical utterances is that a declarative sentence uttered ironically may express an idea that contradicts the idea which it professes to express. Consider saying "Oh, you are always so tidy!" to a janitor and meaning that he has made a mess again. Or consider related variants such as *understatements*, e.g. saying "It was rather concise" and meaning that it (e.g. a televised speech by the president) was extremely terse. As Strawson notes [27, p. 222], in these cases "we cannot say that the C-meaning includes and adds to the B-meaning, but only that the C-meaning *contradicts* the *apparent* B-meaning."

5.3 Reference

Reference has always been a grand issue in studies of contextualism in the philosophy of language [22], and it is only normal that Strawson notes that sometimes a given S admits different interpretations where in one interpretation a certain constituent of S (e.g. a definite description) has a referential use whereas in some other interpretation it doesn't. Take as S the sentence "The next parliamentary elections will resolve the matter." The descriptive phrase may be used to refer to a definite event (say, the elections scheduled to April 23, 2000) or S may be used with the intention of saying "Whensoever the parliamentary elections are carried out, the matter will be resolved."

6 Further Points

The following are not so much weaknesses of Strawson's scheme as possible avenues of research for streamlining it. Due to space limitations they are sketchy and would deserve to be enlarged in a more substantive version of this paper.

6.1 Radical Interpretation

Regarding sense-A-meaning, the following singularity (overlooked by Strawson) needs to be noticed: if his A-knowledge is null then X cannot even set himself to the study the question properly. Obviously, this remark should not be taken as an avowal of the impossibility of radical interpretation. When X is a *radical interpreter* who must interpret L from scratch, he must do so in the absence of any antecedent understanding of L, and only using evidence which is plausibly available to him, cf. Davidson [7]. That this is difficult, on the other hand, is something even Davidson himself accepts to a large extent [17]: "It would beg the question, in trying to study the nature of interpretation, to assume that you know in advance what a person's intentions, beliefs, and desires are. [. . .] There is no master key or framework theory that you can have prior to a communicative interaction or situation."

6.2 Presemantic Uses

Sometimes context is used to figure out which language is being spoken. Consider the following example due to Perry [21]:

> Ich! (said by several teenagers at camp in response to the question, "Who would like some sauerkraut?")

Perry notes that knowing that this took place in a German rather than an American camp might help one to see that it was made by eager German teenagers rather than American teenagers repelled by the very idea. In this case, context (or rather its *presemantic* use) is pertinent to figuring out which language is being used.

6.3 Contextual Domains

This problem has been discussed most recently in [24]. In a nutshell, it refers to the fact that natural language quantifiers often seem implicitly restricted. When S is the sentence "The president shook hands with everyone," X is inclined to think that "everyone" must range over the domain of people who attended the press conference or the reception or the fund-raising dinner or whatever—not everyone in the whole world. Along similar lines, when Y utters "Most beggars attended the bash" he is likely to allude to a particular group of beggars (say, those in his neighborhood); it is from this group that many joined the festivities.

6.4 Subjective Adjectives

In dealing with *subjective* (a.k.a. *relative* in linguistics literature) adjectives such as "large," the context contributes to meaning in a decisive way. Consider an example attributed to Hans Kamp and Barbara Partee [6, p. 374]: "Lee built a large snowman." If Lee is a toddler playing in the backyard of his house, the snowman is probably at most as big as Lee himself. On the other hand, if Lee is a teenager competing in a snow carnival, the snowman is probably much bigger than Lee. One way of dealing with the context-dependent nature of relative adjectives is to assume that the context provides us with a set of comparison classes. Still, with sentences like "A large tadpole is not a large animal" the situation is tricky; in the *same* context different comparison classes are needed for the first and second occurrences of the adjective.

Perry [19] gives "It is yea big" as another example. Here, the object of conversation is as big as the space between the outstretched hands of the speaker. But then this space is a contextual factor on which the indexical "yea" crucially depends.

6.5 Context-Renewal

Consider an on-going conversation between X and Y. Y utters S, X in return utters S', Y in return utters S", and so on and so forth. In order to understand say, S", X would need to use the previous discourse, or the meaning of 'what was said earlier'.

That an interactional context is continually being developed with each successive utterance is an observation Heritage [15] has made in his work on ethnomethodology. According to him, utterances and the social actions they embody are treated as doubly contextual. First, utterances and actions are *context-shaped*. This means that their contributions cannot be adequately appreciated unless the context in which they operate is taken into account. Second, utterances and actions are *context-renewing*. Every utterance will form the subsequent context for some following action in a sequence; it will thus contribute to the contextual framework which lets one understand the next action. Additionally, each action will function to renew context, where 'renewal' is understood as one or more of the processes of maintaining, adjusting, altering, and so on.

In the remainder of this section we look at contributions similar in nature to Heritage's. Our general point is that at the level of sense-C-meaning Strawson's scheme would benefit from enhancements of sociocultural nature.

6.6 Context of Situation

J. R. Firth introduced the term *sociological linguistics* in 1935. His goal was to discuss the study of language in a social perspective; he derived two important notions, context of culture and context of situation, from B. Malinowski. Firth's key observation is that language is a range of possibilities (options) in behavior that are available to an individual in a social setting. The *context of culture* refers to the environment for the entire collection of these options. The *context of situation* refers to the environment of a particular member that is drawn from the context of culture [13]. To make a rough analogy, the context of culture resembles the possible worlds; it defines the potential—the totality of options that are available. A given context of situation is simply the actual choice among these options. Firth's research program aspired to describing and classifying typical contexts of situation within the context of culture, and clarifying the types of linguistic function in such contexts of situation [18, p. 61].

6.7 SPEAKING

Hymes developed his celebrated *SPEAKING* model [16] to encourage a cultural approach to the analysis of discourse. His model is not an explanatory theory; rather, it is a descriptive attempt aimed at producing a taxonomy of languages. Viewed as a linguistic checklist, it advocates that the ethnographer should basically record eight elements which are briefly explained in what follows.

[S]etting and scene refer to the time and place of a speech act, and the psychological setting or 'cultural definition' of a scene, respectively. *[P]articipants* include the speaker and audience (addressees plus other hearers). *[E]nds* concern the purposes of the discourse. *[A]ct sequence* is the format and order of the series of speech events which make up the speech act. *[K]ey* denotes the cues that establish the tone (manner, spirit) of the speech act. *[I]nstrumentalities* are the forms and styles of speech, including channels (oral, written, etc.) and forms of speech (language, dialect, code, variety, register[9]). *[N]orms* refer to the

---

[9] Halliday [14, p. 142] defines *register* as "the theoretical construction that relates the situation simultaneously to the text, to the linguistic system, and to the social system," and asserts that language is the ability to 'mean' in the social contexts generated by the culture.

social rules governing the event and the participants' actions. *[G]enre* includes assorted categories such as poem, myth, tale, proverb, riddle, prayer, oration, lecture, etc.

6.8 Communicative Competence

As is well-known, N. Chomsky's notion of *linguistic competence* consists of the knowledge of the grammatical rules of a language by an idealized speaker (hearer). Hymes coined the more general notion of *communicative competence* to go beyond mere description of language usage patterns and to focus on varieties of shared knowledge and cognitive abilities.

Citing J. Habermas's thoughts on 'trouble-free communication' and 'the universal conditions of possible understandings', Gumperz [12, pp. 40–41] regards communicative competence as "the knowledge of linguistic and related communicative conventions that speakers must have to initiate and sustain conversational involvement." This requires a knowledge of social and cultural rules of a language (in addition to a knowledge of grammatical) and preferably addresses the competences of actual speakers, not an idealized standard.

Another contribution of Gumperz is a *contextualization cue* [10]. He confirmed that a given aspect of linguistic behavior (e.g. lexical, prosodic, phonological, etc.) can function as a cue, indicating those aspects of context which are to be taken into account to interpret what is said by a speaker. Contextualization cues hint at relevant aspects of the social context (via particular codes, styles, and dialects), thus enabling participants in a discourse to reason about their respective communicative intentions and purposes.

Gumperz notes that because of its cultural base, the meaning of a conversation is frequently different for different participants if they are not members of the same speech community. He [11] offers a case study of how differences in the use of contextualization cues between a native speaker of English and a non-native yet fluent speaker of English cause a serious breakdown in communication. As another example of a cross-cultural (mis)communicative event, Saville-Troike [25, pp. 131-132] observed the following exchange in a kindergarten on a reservation:

> A Navajo man opened the door to the classroom and stood silently, looking at the floor. The Anglo-American teacher said 'Good morning' and waited expectantly but the man did not respond. The teacher then said 'My name is Mrs. Jones,' and again waited for a response. There was none. [...]

The whole exchange is even more interesting and enlightening but this brief excerpt will serve to illustrate our point. The man's silence is appropriate from a Navajo perspective; it shows respect. (What is more, a religious Navajo taboo prohibits individuals from saying their own name!) Mrs. Jones's expectation is also reasonable from an Anglo-American perspective; the man must have returned her greeting, identified himself, and stated his reason for being there. (It turns out that he was there to take his son.)

7 Conclusion

The originator of a message (S) usually assumes quite a bit of background knowledge on the part of an addressee [18]. The task of the addressee is to narrow down the list of meanings available to him and attain the intended meaning of S. Originally, S may be replete with several potential meanings. By 'enveloping' it in increasingly narrower contexts, the number of meanings is reduced. Eventually, it is hoped that just one meaning is isolated as *the* meaning of S. This paper argued that there is a certain persuasive approach to studying the feasibility of this problem, first spelled out in "Austin and 'locutionary meaning' " and later taken up in detail in "Meaning and context," two early papers by Strawson. The approach is both simple and elegant, and we believe that future studies of context might profit from it. Interestingly, we have not come across any mention of it in the recent literature on contextual reasoning in artificial intelligence, and while we, along with Strawson, have proposed certain enrichments, our central goal has been to advocate its general legitimacy and efficacy.

Acknowledgments. The first author thanks Paolo Bouquet and Patrick Brézillon for their invaluable support and leniency. The perceptive comments of the anonymous referees of *CONTEXT'99* have been utilized (almost verbatim) in a couple of places in the paper. Other than these, the views expressed herein are our own; we especially take full responsibility for our reconstruction of Strawson's ideas.

References

1. Aitchison, J., *The Language Web: The Power and Problem of Words (The 1996 BBC Reith Lectures)*, Cambridge: Cambridge University Press (1997).
2. Akman, V., "Ripping the text apart at different seams," *Stanford Humanities Review* 4(1): 31–34 (1994). Special Supplement, Bridging the Gap (Where Cognitive Science Meets Literary Criticism), G. Güzeldere and S. Franchi, eds. [Available at http://shr.stanford.edu/shreview/4-1/text/akman.commentary.html]
3. Akman, V., "Rethinking context as a social construct," *Journal of Pragmatics* (1999, to appear).
4. Austin, J. L., *How to Do Things with Words (The William James Lectures delivered at Harvard University in 1955)*, J. O. Urmson and M. Sbisà, eds., Oxford: Oxford University Press (1976). [Second edition]
5. Bach, K., "The semantics-pragmatics distinction: what it is and why it matters," *Linguistische Berichte*: 33–50 (1997). Sonderheft 8/1997, Pragmatik: Implikaturen und Sprechakte, E. Rolf, ed. [Available at http://userwww.sfsu.edu/~kbach/semprag.html]
6. Chierchia, G. and S. McConnell-Ginet, *Meaning and Grammar: An Introduction to Semantics*, Cambridge, Mass.: MIT Press (1990).
7. Davidson, D., "Radical interpretation," pp. 125–139 in *Inquiries into Truth and Interpretation*, Oxford: Clarendon Press (1984). [Paper originally appeared in 1973]
8. Eco, U., *The Role of the Reader: Explorations in the Semiotics of Texts*, Bloomington, Ind.: Indiana University Press (1984).
9. Grice, P., *Studies in the Way of Words*, Cambridge, Mass.: Harvard University Press (1989).

10. Gumperz, J., "Contextualization and understanding," pp. 229–252 in A. Duranti and C. Goodwin, eds., *Rethinking Context: Language as an Interactive Phenomenon*, Cambridge: Cambridge University Press (1992).

11. Gumperz, J., "Culture and conversational inference," pp. 193–214 in W. Foley, ed., *The Role of Theory in Language Description*, Berlin: Mouton De Gruyter (1993).

12. Gumperz, J., "Communicative competence," pp. 39–48 in N. Coupland and A. Jaworski, eds., *Sociolinguistics: A Reader*, New York: St. Martin's Press (1997). [Abridged version of a paper which originally appeared in 1981]

13. Halliday, M. A. K., "Language in a social perspective," pp. 48–71 in *Explorations in the Functions of Language*, London: Edward Arnold (1973).

14. Halliday, M. A. K., *Language as Social Semiotic: The Social Interpretation of Meaning*, London: Edward Arnold (1978).

15. Heritage, J., *Garfinkel and Ethnomethodology*, Cambridge: Polity Press (1984).

16. Hymes, D., "Models of interaction of language and social life," pp. 35–71 in J. Gumperz and D. Hymes, eds., *Directions in Sociolinguistics: The Ethnography of Communication*, Oxford: Blackwell's (1986).

17. Kent, T., "Language philosophy, writing, and reading: a conversation with Donald Davidson," *JAC: A Journal of Composition Theory* **13**(1) (1993). [Available at http://www.cas.usf.edu/JAC/131/kent.html]

18. Leech, G., *Semantics: The Study of Meaning*, Harmondsworth, Middlesex: Penguin (1981). [Second edition]

19. Perry, J., "Indexicals and demonstratives," pp. 586–612 in C. Wright and R. Hale, eds., *A Companion to Philosophy of Language*, Oxford: Blackwell's (1997). [Available at http://www-csli.stanford.edu/~john/PHILPAPERS/shortind.pdf]

20. Perry, J., "Reflexivity, indexicality, and names," pp. 3–19 in W. Kunne et al., eds., *Direct Reference, Indexicality, and Propositional Attitudes*, CSLI Lecture Notes No. 70, Stanford, Calif.: CSLI Publications (1997). [Available at http://www-csli.stanford.edu/~john/PHILPAPERS/names.pdf]

21. Perry, J., "Indexicals, contexts, and unarticulated constituents," in *Proceedings of the 1995 CSLI-Amsterdam Logic, Language, and Computation Conference*, Stanford, Calif.: CSLI Publications (1998). [Available at http://www-csli.stanford.edu/~john/PHILPAPERS/context.pdf]

22. Récanati, F., "Contextualism and anti-contextualism in the philosophy of language," pp. 156–166 in S. L. Tsohatzidis, ed., *Foundations of Speech Act Theory: Philosophical and Linguistic Perspectives*, London: Routledge (1994).

23. Récanati, F., "Processing models for non-literal discourse," pp. 343–356 in R. Casati et al., eds., *Philosophy and the Cognitive Sciences*, Vienna: Hölder-Pichler-Tempsky (1994).

24. Récanati, F., "Contextual domains," pp. 25–36 in X. Arrazola et al., eds., *Discourse, Interaction, and Communication*, Dordrecht, The Netherlands: Kluwer Academic (1998).

25. Saville-Troike, M., *The Ethnography of Communication: An Introduction*, Oxford: Basil Blackwell (1989). [Second edition]

26. Strawson, P. F., "Austin and 'locutionary meaning'," pp. 191–215 in *Entity and Identity (and Other Essays)*, Oxford: Clarendon Press (1997). [Paper originally appeared in 1973]

27. Strawson, P. F., "Meaning and context," pp. 216–231 in *Entity and Identity (and Other Essays)*, Oxford: Clarendon Press (1997). [A partial translation into French originally appeared in 1970]

28. Ziff, P., "What is said," pp. 709–721 in D. Davidson and G. Harman, eds., *Semantics of Natural Language*, Dordrecht, The Netherlands: D. Reidel (1972).

Epistemic Context, Defeasible Inference and Conversational Implicature

Horacio Arló Costa

Carnegie Mellon University, Pittsburgh PA 15213, USA
hcosta@andrew.cmu.edu

Abstract. Recent foundational work on the nature of *defeasible* inference has appealed to an *epistemic context principle* (ECP): β follows defeasibly from α ($\alpha \mathrel{|\!\sim} \beta$)if and only if β follows classically from $C(\alpha)$, where $C(\alpha)$ is the given epistemic context for α. Since nothing requires that $C(\alpha) \subseteq C(\alpha \wedge \gamma)$, the induced notion of consequence is non-monotonic. We will focus on a particular manner of articulating ECP where $C(\alpha)$ is an *autoepistemic* (AE) extension of $\{\alpha\}$.

Robert Stalnaker proposed in [25] a substantial way of understanding this defeasible notion of AE-consequence. The gist of the proposal is: (P) what is non-monotonically entailed by a sentence α is what is meant or implicated, but not explicitly said by uttering α. He suggested that a defeasible notion of consequence (explicated via ECP) could be used to formally encode Grice's notion of *conversational implicature* - and to understand its context-dependent behavior.

This article makes three main contributions. First, we will focus on the tenability of (P). Paul Grice considered in [10] some minimal constraints on implicature needed in order to handle G.E. Moore's paradox of 'saying and disbelieving'. We will show that (P) is incompatible with those constraints. Secondly we will offer an alternative account of AE consequence based on several remarks made by Grice in [10]. According to this account $C(\alpha)$ encodes the body of full beliefs to which someone is *committed* after uttering α. Thirdly we will offer a preliminary account of the formal properties of this new notion of consequence.

AE logic assumes that introspective reasoners do not subscribe to the alethic principle (T) - establishing that the AE-operator L obeys $L(A) \rightarrow A$. This is due to a tacit interpretation of L as an operator of 'weak' belief. This is done even when (T) is satisfied *post hoc* in every AE-extension. The price paid by this maneuver is that AE logic, unlike most defeasible logics, is not *cumulative* - although (T) is satisfied in every extension, the principle cannot be used in the reasoning to arrive at the extension (see [13], page 228). We verify that our notion of AE-consequence is not affected by this problem by showing that (with certain provisos) the notion is cumulative.

1 Introduction

Standard logic is monotonic. Increasing the amount of information available as premises never leads to losses of correctly drawn conclusions. Nevertheless, computer scientists have been interested (at least during the last two decades) in studying reasoning systems where the law of monotonicity fails [7], [15], [19], [8]. These systems can infer B when A is taken as a premise, but they might fail to infer B when additional premises supplement A. In the late 80's it began to be evident to many researchers that there were salient similarities between the behavior of the non-monotonic inference relations induced by these systems and the conditionals studied by philosophers one decade before [18]. Failure of monotony is reflected in those conditionals by the failure of the strengthening of the antecedent.

The subtleties of this comparison have, nevertheless, misled researchers in the past and they continue to be puzzling for many. The problem is that there are *many* conditional (and modal) systems whose non-nested fragments reflect the non-monotonic systems. Initially researchers focused on *counterfactual* systems [9]. Nevertheless the *minimal* conditional systems reflecting general patterns of non-monotonic reasoning are not counterfactual systems [4], [14], [20]. Today the formal relationships between defeasible inference and conditional reasoning are better understood (see [5] for a book-length analysis of the problem).

Some philosophers and computer scientists interested in foundations have recently offered more substantial accounts of the nature of nonmonotonic inference. Independently of the tight relationships between certain conditional logics and defeasible inference, one can ask as Robert Stalnaker did in [25]: what is a non-monotonic consequence relation? Two main answers have been offered in [25] to this foundational question. These answers are representative of recent foundational efforts in the field and we will take them here as our point of departure.

According to the first response defeasible inference should be seen as a form of pragmatic inference. B is a non-monotonic consequence of A if B is a consequence in the classical sense of the *implicit content* of A. Non-monotonic consequences of A are then understood as a formalization of what is implicitly meant but not explicitly stated by A. Robert Stalnaker is the first researcher who clearly articulated this way of interpreting defeasible inference.

The underlying idea is to see defeasible inference as a formalization of Grice's notion of *conversational implicature* (see [10], essays 2 and 3). If successful, this move can be used to accomplish two important theoretical goals: to formalize implicatures and to understand their contextual behavior via a relatively well known form of non-standard inference, and (2) to explain what non-monotonic inference is in terms of a well known, but poorly formalized, pragmatic phenomenon. So, in many senses Stalnaker's idea is quite attractive. In this article we will focus on some problems related to the existing articulation of the proposal, and we will only sketch possible ways out. But obviously Stalnaker's idea deserves further scrutiny. A first attempt to circumvent the main problems elaborated in this article is offered in [1].

Stalnaker has proposed to study some particular non-monotonic theories from this point of view. The general tool used in his analysis is an *epistemic context principle* according to which β follows defeasibly from α if and only if β follows classically from $C(\alpha)$, where $C(\alpha)$ is an epistemic context for α. A full-fledged presentation of ECP requires of course to explain how to construct $C(\alpha)$, for a given arbitrary α. Stalnaker investigated a particularly interesting (as well as elusive) case when $C(\alpha)$ is constructed as an *autoepistemic extension* of α. Informally the idea can be presented as follows:

(P) B is an autoepistemic consequence of A if and only if logically omniscient knowers who have introspective access to their epistemic states can infer B from A.

The basic idea is that the full implicit meaning of a set of premises S is now constructed in terms of the epistemic state of an autoepistemic agent, when S is, in a relevant sense, the basis of everything that the agent knows or believes. Section 2 will be devoted to making precise this relevant sense. Section 3 will then be devoted to some objections against (P) and to consider viable alternatives.

What about Stalnaker's second response to his question about non-monotonic inference? This second answer is a more popular answer. The basic idea is that non-monotonic inference is inductive inference. Authors might differ as to the nature of the induction performed when agents 'jump to conclusions' non-monotonically. Nevertheless there is a growing consensus about the fact that non-monotonic inference is *some* kind of inductive inference ([17], [12], are examples of (non-necessarily compatible) attempts to characterize non-monotonic inference this way).

In this essay we will focus on the first response rather than the second, although something will be said about the need of making (ECP) more context-dependent, and these arguments will apply to both construals of defeasible inference.

2 Autoepistemic logic: some background

First some clarifications about the underlying language. Let L_0 be a Boolean language and let L be the language formed inductively from L_0 by adding the formation rule:

$$\text{If } A \in L, \text{ then } L(A) \in L.$$

L's intended interpretation will be left open for the moment. The notation is reminiscent of the one used in modal logic for the necessity operator. This is basically the idea behind the operator although the emphasis in autoepistemic logic is, of course, epistemic rather than ontologically related.

The following notation will be useful later on (Γ here could be either a theory defined on L_0, L, or languages of intermediate complexity):

$$L\Gamma = \{L(A) : A \in \Gamma\}$$
$$\neg L\Gamma = \{\neg L(A) \; ; \; A \in L, \text{ and } A \notin \Gamma\}$$

A crucial concept is the notion of *stable* set:

DEFINITION 1: A stable set Γ satisfies the following properties: (1) Γ is closed under logical consequence, (2) If $A \in \Gamma$, then $L(A) \in \Gamma$, (3) If $A \notin \Gamma$, then $\neg L(A) \in \Gamma$.

Stable sets are sometimes also called AE theories. Robert Moore proposed (see [22]) the idea of a *stable extension* of a premise set Γ. The gist of his proposal is to represent an agent whose epistemic state is both stable and *grounded* in Γ. The basic idea is to characterize a set T containing at most the consequences of $\Gamma \cup LT \cup \neg LT$.

DEFINITION 2: A set T_Γ is a stable expansion of the premise set Γ if and only if it satisfies:

$$T_\Gamma = \{A : \Gamma \cup LT_\Gamma \cup \neg LT_\Gamma \vdash A\}$$

A set Γ_0 of non-modal sentences has exactly one AE extension, but modal sets might have various or no extension (for example, $\{L(A)\}$ lacks extensions and $\{L(A) \to A\}$ has two).

Now we have enough background to define a non-monotonic notion of AE consequence:

DEFINITION 3: $\Gamma \mathrel{|\!\!\sim} A$ means A is contained in every AE extension of Γ.

Of course, $\Gamma_0 \mathrel{|\!\!\sim} A$ means that A is contained in *the* AE extension corresponding to Γ_0. Therefore it is easy to see how to understand ECP for modal-free sets of premises. In fact, $T_{\Gamma_0} = C(\Gamma_0)$. For modal Γ one needs to consider all possible epistemic contexts induced by Γ, i.e. all the AE extensions of Γ.

The previously defined notion of consequence does not enforce the inference from L(A) to A. In other words the pattern:

(P2) $L(A) \mathrel{|\!\!\not\sim} A$

does not hold. Nevertheless the pattern:

(P1) $A \mathrel{|\!\!\sim} L(A)$

is indeed enforced, because every autoepistemic extension of $\{A\}$ contains L(A). The rationale behind this asymmetry is that most autoepistemic theories intend to model a notion of 'weak belief', rather than a notion of certainty or 'full belief'. [1] Rational agents should be self-aware of the facts they (firmly) hold

---

[1] Autoepistemic logicians have not paid much attention to similarly motivated notions of consequence where the L-operator is informally interpreted as a notion of certainty, full belief or holding true. This is an unfortunate situation taking into account the centrality of this notion in decision theory and pure epistemology (as well as metaphysics). Preliminary considerations concerning the properties of the autoepistemic closure of sets of full beliefs are presented below. See also [26], [11], [16].

as true. Nevertheless agents might believe facts that they are not willing to hold as true.

Stronger notions of consequence have been also considered in the literature. For example Kurt Konolige proposed the following alternative:

DEFINITION 4: $\alpha \Rightarrow \beta$ iff whenever α is in an AE extension, so is β.

This notion is certainly stronger. As a matter of fact it is monotonic. For assume that A $\Rightarrow$ B. Then assume by contradiction that A $\wedge$ C $\not\Rightarrow$ B. Then there is an AE extension E such that A $\wedge$ C $\in$ E and B $\notin$ E. But if this is so A $\not\Rightarrow$ B. For there is an extension (E) containing A that does not contain B.

3 Implicature and non-monotonic inference

The inference from A to L(A) is a very robust pattern enforced by all the notions of consequence considered above (and some alternatives considered below). In fact,

$$(\text{P1}) \ A \mathrel{\vdash\mkern-7mu\sim} L(A) \ \text{and} \ (\text{P1'}) \ A \Rightarrow L(A)$$

The intended epistemological interpretation of these patterns was discussed at the end of the previous section (the idea being that agents should be self-aware of the facts they (firmly) hold as true).

It is less clear how these patterns can be interpreted when we take into account Stalnaker's pragmatic reading of $\mathrel{\vdash\mkern-7mu\sim}$ as a notion of (generalized) implicature. One might perhaps try to accommodate (P1) by arguing that part of the implicit speaker's meaning of every utterance A is determined by the speaker's belief in A. After all, if the utterance of A is sincere (and we can restrict our attention to this case) the main *reason* for the utterance is the speaker's belief in A. Nevertheless the grounds on which a sincere utterance is performed should not be confused with what is entailed or implicated by the utterance in question. Implicatures are calculated in terms of the suppositions needed in order to maintain the assumption that the so-called Cooperative Principle is observed (see essay 2 in [10]).

At this juncture it seems appropriate to quote Grice extensively about this point. His 'further notes' on his seminal article *Logic and Conversation* are highly relevant for the issue at hand:

> When I speak of the assumptions required in order to maintain the supposition that the Cooperative Principle and maxims are being observed on a given occasion, I am thinking of assumptions that are non-trivially required; I do not intend to include, for example, an assumption to the effect that some particular maxim is being observed. This seemingly natural restriction has an interesting consequence with regard to Moore's 'paradox'. *On my account, it will not be true that when I say that p, I conversationally implicate that I believe that p*; for to suppose that I

believe that p (or rather think of myself as believing that p) is just to suppose that I am observing the first maxim of Quality on this occasion. I think that this consequence is intuitively acceptable; *it is not a natural use of language to describe one who has said that p as having, for example, 'indicated', 'suggested' or 'implied' that he believes that p, the natural thing to say is that he has expressed the belief that p. He has of course committed himself, in a certain way, to its being the case that he believes that p*, it is bound up, in a special way, with saying that p.[Italics are mine, [10], pages 41-42.]

The moral of the passage seems to be that Grice strongly opposes any possible formalization of his notion of implicature capable of sanctioning (P1). Therefore an important epistemological obstacle against reading AE-inference as a notion of implicature is that such reading does induce (P1).

The problem reappears if we consider some of the features needed for an implicature to qualify as a *conversational implicature*. One of these features is *cancelabilty*.

[...] a putative conversational implicature that *p*, is explicitly cancelable if to the form of words of the utterance of which putatively implicates that *p*, it is admissible to add, *but not p*, [...]

So, if we focus on *generalized implicature*, anyone who says *Pete is meeting a woman tonight* normally implicates that Pete is meeting someone other than Pete's spouse, sister or mother (Grice adds close Platonic friends to the list). The fact that this putative implicature does indeed qualify as a bona fide implicature is corroborated by the fact that it is perfectly proper to say:

Pete is meeting a woman tonight, but the woman is none other than his wife.

Notice that it is also perfectly possible for Pete himself to cancel the generalized implicature carried by the form of words: 'I am meeting a woman tonight'. In fact, Pete can felicitously say:

I am meeting a woman tonight, who does not happen to be anyone other than my own wife.

Nevertheless it seems that accepting (P1) as a constraint on a formalization of implicature will force us to say that the implicatures sanctioned by (P1) are cancelable by speakers only on pain of incurring G. E. Moore's paradox (see [21]). In fact, say that X says 'It is raining'. If the putative implicature is that X believes that it is raining, then it should not be felicitous for X to say:

(M) It is raining, but I do not believe it.

Which is a form of Moore's paradox (usually called a paradox of 'saying and disbelieving').

The problem seems difficult to avoid because (P1) is a very robust AE inference preserved under different variants of AE logic. In particular the inference is granted by the type of AE theory envisaged by Stalnaker in [25].[2] One possible way out could be to deny Grice's own thoughts about implicature and epistemic paradox, but this way out does not seem feasible. In fact, Grice's arguments are quite persuasive and they seem corroborated by other considerations (like the argument in terms of cancelability offered above). Another possibility could be to remark that (M) requires an indexical use of the belief operator that might not be encoded in the autoepistemic operator L. This way of circumventing the problem does not seem available either. This is so for several reasons. Perhaps the more obvious line of response can be based on the fact that several authors have suggested that AE-operators can indeed be interpreted in a multi agent context as indexical doxastic operators. We will not analyze nevertheless this issue in detail here (see [2] for a preliminary consideration on this problem).

There is also a second obvious line of response for the indexical problem. Even if one does not interpret L indexically, the argument in terms of cancelability can be run for the speaker. Perhaps it is a little bit odd for a third person to say: 'It is raining, and Pete just sincerely and accurately said so, but nevertheless he does not believe it'. Nevertheless this is perhaps not fully paradoxical. But when it comes to Pete himself, he can only cancel the putative AE-implicature by uttering (M). And this is a fully paradoxical.

My suspicion is that what we are beginning to uncover by analyzing this problem has wider repercussions than the ones which have explicitly surfaced above. In fact, my impression is that the moral of this story is that pragmatic phenomena related to assertabilty, 'saying that', and conversational implicature conform a family of notions that are constantly in danger of being conflated with other pragmatic phenomena related to a different (and better understood) family of mental acts (rather than speech acts). I am thinking of the family of notions related to belief, acceptance and some non-standard form of doxastic entailment whose main function is to make explicit the *doxastic commitments* contracted by speakers who decide to accept some piece of information. The last part of Grice's quote elaborates on this idea and we will pay some attention to it in a moment. But before abandoning the topics sketched in this paragraph, let me offer some preliminary thoughts which intend to explain why these two families of notions tend to be conflated. Speech acts like assertion are usually formalized in terms of their epistemic consequences. For example, Stalnaker has proposed to think about assertions in terms of the changes that such an act induces in a presupposition set. The problem with this strategy (which can indeed be successfully exploited in many concrete cases) is that there are many

---

[2] [25] sketches a theory according to which the epistemic context induced by A (in a non-monotonic inference from A to B) is determined by 'all that the agent knows' at certain instant. The L-operator is, in turn, interpreted as a third-person operator of (weak)-belief. Without entering into the details of the proposal, it is intuitively clear that, as long as one endorses the idea that knowledge entails belief, the inference from A to L(A) should be made valid in Stalnaker's framework.

other mental acts capable of producing the same epistemic effects. Moreover if we think of asymmetric contexts of communication (the so-called *defective* contexts) agents are constantly processing messages received from interlocutors and considering whether to input the information and update their own views about what the presupposition set for the current exchange is. This activity requires them to evaluate speech acts, but ultimately the change in the presupposition context is a mental act of rejection or acceptance (or the decision to ignore the message and remain open about it). Calculating an implicature requires a much more complicated mental process involving some form of hypothetical reasoning (one has to take into account the suppositions needed in order to maintain the assumption that the so-called Cooperative Principle is observed). AE reasoning does not seem to have the representational power to capture this subtle form of pragmatic inference. Of course, one also has the strong feeling that there is nevertheless *something* pragmatically entailed by accepting a piece of information (or even by sincerely saying that one accepts the information in question).

The interest of Grice's insights is that they also give us an idea of how to understand this pragmatic entailment. In fact, Grice remarks that anyone uttering p also has 'committed himself, in a certain way, to its being the case that he believes that p.' In other words, it is perhaps plausible to say that what follows (classically) from the AE-extension of (a purely Boolean) premise set Γ_0 formalizes the *epistemic commitments* contracted by accepting Γ_0.[3]

This interpretation of AE-inference can make sense of the problematic inference pattern (P1). We can paraphrase Grice and say that any rational agent who accepts A should 'commit himself to its being the case that he believes that A'. And this commitment is the reason stopping him from canceling a putative implicature induced by A. Since the agent is committed to L(A), denying L(A) will put him in an incoherent scenario.

3.1 Certainty and belief

In the previous section we sketched an alternative to Stalnaker's account of AE inference. The idea (inspired by Grice's remarks on commitment) is that the AE consequences of a premise set A make explicit the doxastic commitments contracted by agents holding A true (or accepting the premise set A as given). We also considered above some possible objections to this interpretation. In this section we will focus on some residual problems importantly related to open foundational problems in AE logic.

It is easy to see that:

(A) $\emptyset \hspace{0.2em}\vdash\hspace{-0.6em}\sim\hspace{0.3em}$ (T), where (T) is the alethic axiom L(A) → A

---

[3] Similar ideas have been defended by other authors in different contexts. For example see [16] or [26]. The notion of acceptance (and full belief) is central in the theory of games and decisions as well as the normative perspective that focus on modeling the commitments of rational agents rather than the performance of bounded agents.

This follows from the fact that every AE extension of a set A is a stable set containing A and that every stable set is a S5 theory. Should we then say that every rational agent is committed to the 'alethic' axiom (T)? Remember that so far we are simultaneously maintaining that the L-operator encodes a notion of weak belief (instead of a notion of certainty or full belief). A negative answer to the former question is part of the philosophical folklore.

Kurt Konolige puts the problem in the following terms:

> AE logic assumes that agents are ideal introspective reasoners who do not subscribe to the principle T. [...] It is troubling, however, that the schema T is satisfied *post hoc* in any extension, but cannot be used in the reasoning to arrive at the extension. In metatheoretic terms, AE logic is not *cumulative* ([13], pp. 228-229).

A cumulative logic is one obeying the principle also called *cautious monotonicity* stating that A, B $\vdash$ C holds whenever A $\vdash$ B and A $\vdash$ C hold. But it is clear that cautious monotonicity fails when A is $\emptyset$, α is a non-tautological formula, C is $\neg L(\alpha)$ and B is the following instance of schema T: $L(\alpha) \to \alpha$.[4] To be sure there might be good reasons to construct inductive machines which are not cumulative, but the failure of cumulativity in AE logic seems to appear rather artificially as the result of forcing a particular doxastic interpretation on the L-operator used to build AE extensions. This interpretation is forced on L in spite of basic logical aspects of stable theories (the fact that they are S5 theories). Autoepistemic logicians have managed to implement smart moves in order to circumvent this mismatch of intuitions, but, as Konolige makes clear in his remark, the problem persists. The problem also is an epistemological obstacle against our 'commitment view' about the nature of AE inference.

In this article we will consider the following solution. We will define an alternative notion of AE inference, which obeys cumulativity and fits our 'commitment account' of AE inference. In addition we will propose a different presystematic understanding of 'L' as an operator of full belief or certainty. Pros and cons of this approach will be discussed below. But first we need some basic definitions used in AE logic.

DEFINITION 5: A stable set S is *minimal for a premise set A* if S contains A and there is no other stable set S' containing A such that S' $\cap L_0 \subset$ S $\cap L_0$.

Minimal stable sets have been considered in the recent literature in AE logic (see for example [13] pp. 234-5). To be a minimal stable set for A (MSS for A) is a necessary condition for a set of modal sentences to qualify as the set of introspective epistemic commitments associated with A. So a natural application of the ECP in this situation will lead to the construction of a notion of inference such that B follows defeasibly from A whenever B is in all the MSSs for A.

---

[4] To see that the conclusion of cautious monotony fails it is useful to keep in mind that $\{L(\alpha) \to \alpha\}$ has two extensions: one including α and another which does not contain α. Therefore it is not true that $\neg L(\alpha)$ is in every AE extension of $\{L(\alpha) \to \alpha\}$.

DEFINITION 3: $\Gamma \mathrel{\mkern-3mu\vdash\mkern-10mu\approx} A$ means A is contained in every minimal stable set for Γ and there is at least a stable S such that $\Gamma \subseteq S$.

This notion is obviously non-monotonic (consider the case when Γ is empty A is $\neg$ L(A), A is a propositional atom not included in ST(), and Γ is augmented with A). This notion of consequence obeys cautions monotony. To establish this fact we need some previous definitions.

Let me first consider a class of *normal form* formulae. Consider the language L_D such that non-modal (purely Boolean) formulae are in L_D, if $\alpha \in L_D$ and $\beta \in L_D$, then $\alpha \vee \beta \in L_D$, and both L($\alpha$) and $\neg$ L(α) are in L_D, when α is Boolean. We are basically focusing on formulae of the form:

$$\neg \, L(\alpha) \vee L(\beta_1) \vee L(\beta_2) \vee ... \vee L(\beta_n) \vee w$$

where α, β_i and w are all non-modal sentences.

It can be established as a lemma that every consistent and stable A-theory K (where $A \in L_D$) is such that there is a minimal stable set for K. This lemma can, in turn be generalized with the help of the fact (proved in [13], page 230) establishing that every set of modal sentences (containing the L-operator) is K45-equivalent to one in normal form.

Consider now Cautious Monotony. Assume that both A $\mathrel{\mkern-3mu\vdash\mkern-10mu\approx}$ B and A $\mathrel{\mkern-3mu\vdash\mkern-10mu\approx}$ C - where $A \in L_D$. We have to check that $C \in K$ where K is a MSS for A $\wedge$ B. Notice that (in the presence of the assumptions) every MSS for A $\wedge$ B is also a MSS for A. For pick an arbitrary MSS for A $\wedge$ B, say K, and assume by contradiction that it is not a MSS for A. Then (since K is an A-theory) there is a stable set K' such that $A \in K'$ and $K' \cap L_0 \subset K \cap L_0$. Now, in virtue of the previous lemma, either K' is itself a minimal A-set or there is K" (such that $A \in K"$ and $K" \cap L_0 \subset K' \cap L_0$). Since A $\mathrel{\mkern-3mu\vdash\mkern-10mu\approx}$ B, $B \in K'$ (or K"), which contradicts the assumption that K is a MSS for A $\wedge$ B. Now, since K is a MSS for A, and we assumed that A $\mathrel{\mkern-3mu\vdash\mkern-10mu\approx}$ C, $C \in K$, which suffices to complete the proof. Almost identical strategy can be applied to establish that $\mathrel{\mkern-3mu\vdash\mkern-10mu\approx}$ obeys CUT and other basic properties of non-monotonic inference.[5]

Of course, $\mathrel{\mkern-3mu\vdash\mkern-10mu\approx}$ obeys the pattern (P1):

$$\text{(P1) A} \mathrel{\mkern-3mu\vdash\mkern-10mu\approx} \text{L(A)}$$

It is also the case that $\mathrel{\mkern-3mu\vdash\mkern-10mu\approx}$ obeys:

$$\text{(P2) L(A)} \mathrel{\mkern-3mu\vdash\mkern-10mu\approx} \text{A}$$

This second pattern, according to our understanding of $\mathrel{\mkern-3mu\vdash\mkern-10mu\approx}$, indicates that every agent who accepts L(A) is committed to hold A true. We understand here (tacitly) that the occurrence of non-modal sentences in a stable set represents the fact that the agent in question (firmly) holds (or takes as) true the sentence in question. On the other hand we are leaving open which is the intended meaning of the L-operator compatible with our characterization of $\mathrel{\mkern-3mu\vdash\mkern-10mu\approx}$. Nevertheless it

---

[5] Cut establishes that A $\mathrel{\mkern-3mu\vdash\mkern-10mu\approx}$ C follows from A $\mathrel{\mkern-3mu\vdash\mkern-10mu\approx}$ B and A, B $\mathrel{\mkern-3mu\vdash\mkern-10mu\approx}$ C.

is not difficult to elicit this meaning taking (P2) into account. L cannot be understood as a notion of weak belief. It should be understood as the strongest doxastic attitude of which the agent is capable. Basically L in this context should be understood as a notion of certainty or full belief.

In this context the troublesome inference $\emptyset \mathrel{\vdash\!\!\!\sim} (T)$, ceases to be problematic. In fact, such a pattern only says (in this context) that every agent who fully believes A is committed to the truth of A. It is important to realize that the pattern $\emptyset \mathrel{\vdash\!\!\!\sim} (T)$, should not be interpreted as saying that AE agents are committed to a principle of 'arrogance'[6] legislating that full beliefs are true. What the schema T says in this context is that agents are committed to *accept* that fully believed items are true. In other words, form the point of view of the agent, every item of which he is certain is an item such that he should be willing to (firmly) hold as true. Of course, the item might be false (objectively), but all that counts for AE inference are the introspective obligations of the agent in question (at a certain instant). Therefore rational agents should accept schema T as a coherence principle in charge of maintaining an equilibrium between the items held as true (non-Boolean sentences in his stable theory) and his certainties (sentences prefixed by L-operators in stable sets).

Of course the inference (T) is problematic if L is not pre-systematically understood as a notion of full belief. Why a rational agent should be committed to (firmly) hold as true items which are only (weakly) believed? In contrast it seems reasonable to require that rational agents should be committed to hold as true every item of which (s)he is certain of (or which (s)he fully believes).

AE logicians seemed to have paid attention only to either a variety of notions of weak belief or to the strong notion of knowledge, somewhat neglecting the intermediary notion of full belief. Such a notion is widely used in many fields where doxastic representation matters (the theory of games and decisions is an obvious example of a field where the notion plays a crucial role). This section has been devoted to define a cumulative notion of AE inference which seems optimally understood when the intended interpretation of the L operator is as an operator of full belief. The interpretation has the independent virtue of offering an unified explanation of the role of schema T. The schema is indeed satisfied in every stable theory (as a matter of fact in every AE extension) and the principle can be cumulatively used in AE reasoning.

In addition the picture fits Grice's account of pragmatic inference in terms of commitments, and it circumvents the previous criticisms to the idea of seeing non-monotonic inference as the encoding of pragmatic implicatures. Finally, our definition of $\mathrel{\vdash\!\!\!\approx}$ satisfies several of the widely accepted properties of non-monotonic inference (like cumulativity) in a rather natural manner.

4 Future work

Recent work in several areas of conditional logic suggests the interests of providing an account of expressions of the form: 'If A, then B, given evidence e' - see for

---

[6] The terminology is used in [13].

example [24]. Because of space constraints we cannot fully consider this matter in this article. Here is nevertheless a natural idea that seem worth entertaining:

$A >_e B$ is accepted with respect to e if and only if $c(e, A)$ entails classically B

where, in order to make things simpler, e is purely Boolean and $c(e, A)$ is understood as follows,

$$c(e, A) = C(Cn(e)^*A)$$

and where * is a binary revision function mapping prior epistemic contexts to posterior contexts. As long as A is Boolean, the C function is understood, as before, as the unique minimal stable theory for $Cn(e)^*A$. The details of the theory generated by the former constraints seem still unknown. It will also be interesting to know how ECP should be applied in the more complex case where the background e contains modal information and when modal formulae are learnt.

The notion of *common ground* (see [3]) has been extensively used in computational linguistics. As Patrick Hayes has noted in an unpublished manuscript[7] several important distinctions have been blurred, or deliberately ignored, in concrete uses of this theoretical construal. On the one hand one has the ambivalence between ontological, linguistic and epistemic contexts. The previous arguments intend to establish that, even if one sticks to a purely epistemic account of this common ground, there are important distinctions to be made concerning the attitudes that are commonly held. These distinctions are perhaps familiar to epistemologists or philosophers of science. Nevertheless linguists seem to have developed their notions by paying attention to previous discussions in philosophy of language, and these discussion tend to be heavily motivated by ontological, rather than epistemological, concerns. It seems central to the task of representing knowledge in context to re-direct this discussion by making it more amenable to the epistemological tasks that seem involved in (at least) some of the aspects of representing attitudes in context.

Acknowledgments: I would like to thank Isaac Levi, Rohit Parikh, and an anonymous referee for several useful comments.

References

1. Arló-Costa, H., 'Assertion, acceptance and defeasible inference,' manuscript, CMU, March 1999.
2. Arló-Costa, H., 'Qualitative and probabilistic models of full belief,' Proceedings of the Logic Colloquium '98, ASL European Summer Meeting, Springer Verlag, 1999.
3. Clark, H. H.; Carlson, T. B., 'Context for comprehension, in *Attention and Performance*IX, ed. Long and Baddeley, Erlbaum, 1981, 313-330.

---

[7] Context in context.

4. Arló-Costa, H., Shapiro, S. (1992) "Maps between non-monotonic and conditional logics," *Principles of Knowledge Representation and Reasoning: Proceedings of the Third International Conference* (eds.) Nebel,B., Rich, C., Swartout, W.: 553-564.

5. L. Fariñas del Cerro, G. Crocco, A. Herzig, (eds.), *Conditionals, from Philosophy to Computer Science* , Oxford University Press, Oxford, 1995.

6. Fitting, M. 'Moore's nonmonotonic logic and S5,' manuscript, CUNY, November 1983.

7. Gabbay, D. "Theoretical foundations for non-monotonical reasoning in expert systems" *Logics and Models of Concurrent Systems*, K.R. Apt., ed., 1985.

8. Gabbay, D.M., Hogger, C.J., Robinson, J.A., (eds.) *Handbook of Logic in Artificial Intelligence and Logic programming*, Volk. 3 Nnonmonotonic reasoning and uncertain reasoning, Oxford Science Publications, Oxford, 1994.

9. Ginsberg, M., 'Counterfactuals,' *Artificial Intelligence* 30, 1986, 35-79.

10. Grice, P., Studies in the way of words, Cambridge, Mass., Harvard University Press, 1989.

11. Hild, M., 'The diachronic coherence of ungraded beliefs,' manuscript, Christ's College, Cambridge, November, 1998.

12. Kelly, K., 'The learning power of belief revision,' TARK VII, *Theoretical Aspects of Rationality and Knowledge*, Morgan Kaufman, 1998.

13. Konologige, K., 'Autoepistemic Logic,' in *Handbook of Philosophical Logic, second edition*, Vol III Extensions of Classical Logic (eds.) D. Gabbay and F. Guenthner, Reidel, Dordrecht, 1998.

14. Lamarre, P., "S4 as the conditional logic of nonmonotonicity" *Proceedings KR'91*, 1991.

15. Lehmann, D., Magidor, M., "Rational logics and their models; A study in cumulative logics." *Technical Report TR 88-16 of the Dept. of Computer Science, Hebrew University of Jerusalem*, November 1988.

16. Levi, I., 'The logic of full belief,' in *The Covenant of Reason: Rationality and the Commitments of Thought*, CUP, 1997, 40-69,.

17. Levi, I., *For the Sake of Argument: Ramsey Test Conditionals, Inductive Inference, and Nonmonotonic Reasoning.* Cambridge University Press, Cambridge, England, 1996.

18. Lewis, D. *Counterfactuals* (1973).

19. Makinson, D., "General Theory of Cumulative Inference" *Non-Monotonic Reasoning*, M. Reinfrank, J. de Kleer, M. Ginsberg, and E. Sandewall eds., 1988.

20. Makinson, D., 'Five faces of minimality,' *Studia Logica* 52, 1993, 339-379.

21. Moore, G.E., 'Russell's 'Theory of Descriptions,' in *Philosophical Papers* by G.E. Moore, ed. H.D. Lewis, London: Muirhead Library of Philosophy, 1959, [2nd ed. 1963].

22. Moore, R., *Logic and Representation*, CSLI Lecture Notes No. 39, 1995.

23. Stalnaker, R., 'A note on non-monotonic modal logic,' *Artificial Intelligence* 64, 1993, 183-196.

24. Pearl, J., 'Probability of causation: Three counterfactual interpretations and their identification,' Technical Report R-261, UCLA, 1998.

25. Stalnaker, R., 'What is a non-monotonic consequence relation? *Fundamenta Informaticae* 21, 1994, 7-21.

26. van Fraassen, B., 'Fine-grained opinion, probability, and the logic of full belief,' *Journal of Philosophical Logic* **24**, 1955, 349-377.

An Implemented Context System that Combines Belief Reasoning, Metaphor-Based Reasoning and Uncertainty Handling

John A. Barnden and Mark G. Lee

School of Computer Science, The University of Birmingham
Birmingham, B15 2TT, United Kingdom
{J.A.Barnden,M.G.Lee}@cs.bham.ac.uk

Abstract. An implemented context-based reasoning system called ATT-Meta is sketched. The system can perform both reasoning about beliefs of agents and metaphor-based reasoning. In particular, it can perform metaphor-based reasoning about beliefs and reasoning acts. The metaphor-based reasoning and belief reasoning facilities are fully integrated into a general framework for uncertain reasoning. This framework allows for uncertain reasoning and conflict resolution within individual contexts, uncertainty in individual inter-context bridging rules, conflict resolution between the effects of different bridging rules, and conflict-resolution across context boundaries when argumentation inside a context conflicts with argumentation outside.

1 Introduction

We have developed and implemented a context-based mechanism for belief reasoning, in our ATT-Meta system (Barnden 1998, Barnden *et al.* 1994), mainly for the purposes of natural language pragmatics. However, we have also taken the unusual step of developing, within the very same system, a context-based mechanism for metaphor-based reasoning—the reasoning needed during the understanding of metaphorical utterances. ("ATT-Meta" = "[propositional] ATTitudes" and "Metaphor.") Use of contexts for handling metaphor is a central part of the work of Fauconnier & Turner (1998). However, that work has not led to an implemented metaphor-processing system, does not combine belief reasoning and metaphor-based reasoning, and does not address uncertainty issues in any detail.

Indeed, belief reasoning and metaphor are almost always studied separately. But metaphorical utterances can be about the mental states and processes of agents. ATT-Meta was originally focused only on that type of metaphor, though in fact its metaphor mechanisms are in no way confined to it. Metaphorical utterances about mental states lead to the need to combine belief reasoning and metaphor-based reasoning in intimate ways, one of which we will detail.

A third prominent strand in our work is qualitative uncertainty-handling. This is important both for useful, common-sensical belief reasoning and useful, common-sense reasoning based on metaphor. Although belief reasoning is occasionally combined with uncertainty handling (e.g., in Parsons, Sierra & Jennings 1998), the only previous metaphor research that devotes extensive technical attention to uncertainty appears to be that of

Hobbs (1990). One goal of the ATT-Meta research is for the system to perform uncertain belief reasoning and uncertain metaphor-based reasoning in a systematic and uniform way, doing more justice to uncertainty than has heretofore been seen.

Although we have only studied contexts for belief reasoning and metaphor-based reasoning, our work on uncertainty should be generalizable to contexts much more generally. The mechanisms we have developed allow for uncertain reasoning and conflict resolution within individual contexts, uncertainty in individual inter-context bridging rules, conflict resolution between the effects of different bridging rules, and conflict-resolution across context boundaries (e.g. to handle conflict between what it seems an agent believes according to simulation of the agent's reasoning, and what it seems the agent believes according to "external" information, such as statements by other people about the agent). The mechanisms have been designed to work with unlimited nesting of contexts, where contexts of different types can occur in a nesting.

The remainder of the paper addresses the following topics, in sequence. the type of metaphorical utterance we address; ATT-Meta's basic reasoning facilities and uncertainty-handling; ATT-Meta's facilities for reasoning about agents' beliefs and reasoning; ATT-Meta's metaphorical reasoning; and one type of interaction of belief reasoning and metaphor-based reasoning. Our presentation will be informal, as it is the general issues that our work has addressed and the inference strategies that we have used that are important, not their precise clothing in formal terms.

2 Metaphor in ATT-Meta

A metaphorical utterance is one that *manifests* a metaphorical view, where a *metaphorical view* is a conceptual view of one topic or domain as another that is judged qualitatively different from it. Here we broadly follow Lakoff (e.g., Lakoff 1993). An example of a metaphorical view is the view of MIND AS PHYSICAL SPACE. A natural-language manifestation of this view might be "John believed in the recesses of his mind that ...." In a manifestation, the topic actually being discussed (John's mind, in the example) is the *target* topic or domain, and the topic that it is metaphorically cast as (physical space, in the example) is the *source* topic or domain.

The ATT-Meta system does not currently deal with novel metaphorical *views* that can appear in natural language utterances. Rather, it has pre-established knowledge of a specific set of metaphorical views, including MIND AS PHYSICAL SPACE. But it is specifically designed to handle novel *manifestations* of those views, or, more precisely and generally, manifestations which cannot immediately be handled by the known mappings from source to target that constitute the metaphorical view. Such manifestations are common in ordinary discourse (see, e.g., Martin 1994).

Mundane types of discourse, such as ordinary conversations and newspaper articles, often use metaphor in talking about mental states/processes of agents. There are many mental-state metaphorical views apart from MIND AS PHYSICAL SPACE. Some are as follows: IDEAS AS PHYSICAL OBJECTS, under which ideas are cast as physical objects that have locations and can move about, as in "He pushed these ideas to one side;" COGNITION AS VISION, as when understanding, realization, knowledge, etc. is cast as vision, as in "His view of the problem was blurred;" and MIND PARTS AS PERSONS, under which a person's mind is cast as containing several sub-agents with their own thoughts, emotions, etc., as in "One part of him was convinced that he should go to the party."

3 ATT-Meta's Basic Reasoning

ATT-Meta is a rule-based reasoning system. Reasoning (sub)goals, provided facts and derived propositions are all called *hypotheses* for convenience. Hypotheses are actually (Barnden *et al.* 1994) terms in a first-order, episode-based logic akin to that of, say, Hobbs (1990), but for simplicity of presentation they will be portrayed here as formulas in a first-order modal logic.

For our present purposes a fact contains no variables, and if a goal contains variables then the only quantification is implicit existential quantification of all those variables, prefacing the entire formula. A fact or goal can involve negation, conjunction and disjunction, but in this paper we will only touch on negation. The reader may assume that for each ground (i.e., variable-free) hypothesis entertained, the *complement* is also entertained, even though this is only roughly true. Two variable-free hypotheses are complementary when one is the negation of the other. This paper largely omits explicit consideration of variables in hypotheses from now on.

At any time any particular hypothesis is tagged with a *qualitative certainty level,* one of `certain`, `presumed`, `suggested`, `possible` or `certainly-not`. The intuitive meanings are as follows:

> `certain`: The hypothesis is true without reservation.
> `certainly-not`: The complement is `certain`.
> `presumed`: the hypothesis is a *default*: i.e., it is taken as a working assumption, pending further evidence.
> `suggested`: there is evidence for the hypothesis, but it is not (yet) strong enough to enable the hypothesis to be `presumed`.
> `possible`: No evidence at all has yet been found for the hypothesis, but the negation is not `certain`.

(The level `certainly-not` is included for practical reasons, even though it is redundant.) If a hypothesis is at a level less than `certain` at some moment it can potentially achieve a higher level later. However, each hypothesis also has an upper bound that can limit the rise of its certainty level. Our current system of levels is no doubt simplistic compared to what may ultimately be required, but it is complex and powerful enough for substantial advances to be made in our areas of interest.

A rule in ATT-Meta is of largely traditional form, having an *antecedent* and a *consequent*, but it also has a *qualitative certainty level*. We will display rules in the following format:

> IF <antecedent component 1> AND <antecedent component 2> .... AND <antecedent component N>
> THEN [<certainty level>] <consequent>

The consequent is of the same form as a goal, and may therefore contain variables. Each component of the antecedent is an expression in goal form. Implicitly, all variables in the rule are universally quantified, outside the whole rule. The certainty level of a rule is one of `suggested`, `presumed`, `certain`.

ATT-Meta applies its rules in a backchaining style. It is given a reasoning goal by a user, and uses rules to generate subgoals in the normal way. Goals can of course also be satisfied by provided facts. When a rule application successfully supports a goal, it supplies a level of certainty to it, calculated as the minimum of the rule's own certainty level and the levels picked up from the hypotheses satisfying the rule's antecedent.

The rule's certainty level thus acts as an upper bound on the certainty that the rule can supply to its conclusion. The rule only supplies support to the goal in this way if all those certainty levels are at least suggested (because every hypothesis starts off as possible anyway). When several rules support a hypothesis, the maximum of their certainty contributions is taken. Currently, ATT-Meta tries to apply all rules to all goals, though an important future research goal is to refine this procedure by the use of heuristics.

The system contains a modified type of justification-based truth-maintenance mechanism for propagating levels of certainty around via rule-applications. There are often cycles in the *hypothesis graph* (which is essentially a dynamically changing AND/OR graph defined by the rule-applications that have been created). As a result, in general the system iteratively settles to a consistent set of hypothesis certainty levels. The process is guaranteed to terminate.

4 Basic Conflict Resolution

When both a hypothesis and its complement are supported to level at least presumed, conflict-resolution will take place. The most interesting case is when both hypotheses are exactly presumed. In this case, the system attempts to see whether one hypothesis has *more specific* evidence than the other. The former is then the "winner." If the system determines a winner, it downgrades the certainty level of the loser to suggested, keeping the winner's at presumed. If it cannot determine a winner, it downgrades both to suggested. It is therefore conservative in its conflict resolution, avoiding arbitrary decisions between hypotheses. For instance, in the Nixon diamond it will end up attaching level suggested to the hypotheses that Nixon is and is not a pacifist.

Specificity comparison is a commonly used heuristic for conflict-resolution in AI (see, e.g., Loui *et al.* 1993) although serious problems remain in coming up with adequate and practical heuristics. ATT-Meta's specificity comparison depends on what facts the two conflicting hypotheses rely on and on derivability relationships between the hypotheses supporting the conflicting hypotheses. The derivability aspect is analogous to derivability aspects of other schemes for specificity, and has as a special case the ancestor-closeness heuristic central to most semantic networks. The fact aspect relies on the intuition that if one of the conflicting hypotheses relies on more facts than the other then it has more specific evidence ("more" in a set-inclusion sense).

The following is a simple example of specificity comparison is sufficient for the purposes of this paper. It illustrates only the derivability aspect. Suppose the system has rules saying that students are presumably not rich, medical students are presumably rich, but English medical students are presumably not rich. Thus the second rule overturns the first and the third overturns the second. Suppose there is fact saying that Bill is an English medical student. Then the system concludes that Bill is presumably not rich, defeating the line of evidence from the second rule mentioned. The system can deal with any number of levels of overturning in a scenario of this sort.

5 ATT-Meta's Reasoning about Agents' Beliefs and Reasoning

ATT-Meta has facilities for reasoning non-metaphorically about the beliefs and reasoning acts of agents, where those beliefs and acts may in turn be about the beliefs and reasoning for further agents, and so forth. Although ATT-Meta can reason about beliefs in an ordinary rule-based way (e.g. using rules such as "if X is English then X presumably believes cricket is interesting"), its main tool is *simulative reasoning* (e.g., Creary 1979). Roughly, in attempting to show that agent X believes P, the system puts P as a goal in a *simulation context* for X, which is a special environment which is meant to reflect X's own reasoning processes. If P is supported within the simulation context by hypotheses Q, where the system takes X to believe the Q, then the reasoning from the Q to P in the context is alleged (by default) to be reasoning by X. The reasoning within the context can involve ordinary rule-based reasoning and/or simulation of further agents. Currently, ATT-Meta can use any of its rules within any simulation context, so that all rules are effectively treated as common knowledge. Of course, this needs to be modified in future research.

The picture just given of simulative reasoning needs to be greatly complicated because of uncertainties. First, the reasoning within the simulation context can be uncertain. Also, the information about X resulting from a simulation of X is itself uncertain: even if the reasoning *within* the simulation context supports P with absolute certainty, ordinary rule-based reasoning outside the context may support the proposition that it is *not* the case that X believes P. Also, there is always the possibility that (a) X may not in fact have done some of the alleged reasoning steps, and (b) even if X has done them, it may be that X has also done steps that support the negation of P (when P is uncertain within the context).

An *atomic belief hypothesis* is a formula of the form $B(a, \phi, \lambda)$, where B is a modal operator, a is a term denoting the agent, ϕ is a hypothesis-like formula, and λ is a certainty level greater than or equal to possible. Intuitively the hypothesis means that the agent believes ϕ with certainty AT LEAST λ. Because of the λ argument, the system expresses uncertainty in every layer of belief. Hypotheses involving belief take part in rule-based reasoning just as other hypotheses do (subject to a rather complicated optimization concerning the λ arguments in belief hypotheses). Notice that because of the "AT LEAST λ" provision, if $B(a, \phi, \lambda)$ holds then so does every $B(a, \phi, \lambda')$ for lesser certainty levels λ.

Ordinary rule-based reasoning involving belief hypotheses is not intended to cater for reasoning that is alleged to be performed by other agents. Simulative reasoning is implemented for this purpose. Whenever a hypothesis that is an atomic belief hypothesis is created, the hypothesis formed by stripping off the application of the belief operator B is also formed (unless it already exists), and placed inside the "simulation context," or "reasoning space," for the agent in question (similar to the belief spaces and contexts in many other authors' work). This happens recursively in the case of nested belief hypotheses, so that we get nested reasoning spaces (nested contexts). Conversely, whenever a goal is created inside an agent's reasoning context, an application of B is wrapped around it and placed in the immediately surrounding context (which may be the system's own).

The support for an atomic belief hypothesis can come from: ordinary rule-based reasoning in the layer (i.e., reasoning context) it lies in; from simulative reasoning resulting from stripping off the B; and from rule-based reasoning at higher levels resulting from adding further B applications. One of our foci in this paper is on matters of conflict resolution, discussed below. For this purpose, a technicality needs to be explained. Each rule-application within a non-system reasoning context is "lifted" to the next reasoning-context out. That is, consider a hypothesis $B(a, \phi, \lambda)$ within a reasoning context R, and hypothesis ϕ within R_a, the reasoning context for a nested within R. For each rule-application α supporting ϕ, a "lifted rule application" $\Lambda(\alpha)$ is created as a support for $B(a, \phi, \lambda)$. Let $\Delta(\alpha)$ be the set of hypotheses directly used by application α.

Then, the set of hypotheses directly used by $\Lambda(\alpha)$ formed by wrapping B(a, ...) around each member of $\Delta(\alpha)$, plus an extra "agent-inference hypothesis" that will be explained in the discussion of metaphor. The system always uses presumed as the strength of the imaginary rule of which $\Lambda(\alpha)$ is an application.

Such lifted rule applications account for almost all the direct effect that the simulation of a (i.e., the reasoning within R_a) has on the reasoning about B(a, ϕ, λ) within context R. Importantly, *lifted rule applications for a hypothesis are treated in the same way as ordinary rule applications for the hypothesis in respect of certainty-value accumulation and conflict resolution involving the hypothesis.* This principle supplies a valuable amount of modularity in the design of the system.

6   Conflict Within and Across Belief Layers

Consider the hypothesis B(a, ϕ, presumed) within a reasoning context R, and hypothesis ϕ within R_a. Also consider the following related hypotheses: the complement ϕ' of ϕ within R_a, the hypothesis B(a, ϕ', presumed), and the complements of the two B hypotheses. (For simplicity, we will not discuss here the matter of other B hypotheses of the form B(a, ϕ, ...).) All six hypotheses can have independent rule-based argumentation supporting them, and we are therefore faced with the problem of there being potential conflict-resolution within R_a between ϕ and ϕ', and within R between B(a, ϕ, presumed) and its complement, and between B(a, ϕ', presumed) and its complement. In two special cases it is clear what to do.

(a): when there is no evidence for the four hypotheses in R other than what arises within R_a, conflict resolution should occur within R_a, between the inside hypotheses ϕ and ϕ'. As a result, the certainty levels of some or all of the four outside hypotheses, as well as of one or both of the inside hypotheses, will be adjusted.

(b): This special case is the opposite of case (a) — that is, no rule-based reasoning inside R_a supports ϕ or ϕ' to level presumed. Then, conflict resolution should not be done within the simulation, but should occur outside.

The difficult case is when there is (non-lifted) rule-based support, either directly or indirectly, for at least one of the four outer hypotheses, as well as rule-based support (lifted or otherwise) for at least one of ϕ and ϕ'. This case is made to look like special case (b) by means of the lifting mechanism. That is, the rule-based argumentation within context R_a is lifted to the outer context, and combines with the rule-based argumentation in that context. Thus, conflict-resolution is performed in the normal way in that context, in an attempt to find a winner between B(a, ϕ, presumed) and its complement, and between B(a, ϕ', presumed) and its complement.

However, a special provision helps this process. Any rule-applications directly supporting B(a, ϕ', presumed) are copied to become rule applications directly supporting the complement of B(a, ϕ, presumed) as well. Conversely, applications directly supporting B(a, ϕ, presumed) are copied to become ones for the complement of B(a, ϕ', presumed) as well. This is necessary so as to allow conflict within the simulation to be reflected as conflict in outer contexts, because B(a, ϕ', presumed) and B(a, ϕ, presumed) are not complements of each other, and because specificity-comparison depends in part on *direct* support relationships between hypotheses.

Since the cross-context considerations we have been discussing can apply at any context boundary in a nesting of reasoning contexts, the following recursive process is defined. Starting at the top reasoning context (i.e., the system's), the system works down through contexts. If it hits an atomic belief hypothesis and its complement that are in conflict, and where at least one has non-lifted rule-based support (either directly or indirectly), it applies the basic conflict-resolution procedure to those hypotheses. The system now descends to the inner context, and so forth. If the conflicting belief hypotheses do not have non-lifted rule-based support, then the system just goes down to the inner context.

7 Metaphor-Based Reasoning in ATT-Meta

ATT-Meta is merely a reasoning system, and does not deal with natural language input directly. Rather, a user supplies hand-coded logic formulae that are intended to couch the literal meaning of small discourse chunks. The system does reasoning on the basis of these formulae. Consider the following metaphorical sentence:

(1) "The two ideas were in different store-rooms in John's mind."

The sentence manifests two metaphorical views: MIND AS PHYSICAL SPACE and IDEAS AS PHYSICAL OBJECTS. We assume that the understander is familiar with both metaphorical views. We assume that the understander only has a physical sense for "store-room" and that the notion of physical store-room is not *map-enshrined* for the understander by either of the metaphorical views: that is, the notion is not mapped by either metaphorical view to any target-domain notion. We say the sentence is an *exploitation* of the two metaphorical views, because of this use of a non-map-enshrined notion. Such exploitative sentences are a major issue, because they appear to be common in discourse. However, existing implemented system for metaphor other than our own are largely not directed at them, with two main exceptions: Martin (1994) and Narayanan (1997). These systems are more restricted in scope than ours specialised aims than ours and do not deal with the uncertainty-handling issues that we address.

In our approach to exploitative metaphorical utterances, we try to avoid discovering or inventing mappings for non-map-enshrined notions such as STORE-ROOM. Rather, we rely on *on-the-fly source-based inference*—inference conducted, during understanding, within the terms of the source domain(s) of the metaphorical view(s) involved—to link the utterance's use of the notions to notions that *are* map-enshrined by the views. By this means, the understander can infer connotations of the utterance such as the following:

Connotation
> *The mentioned ideas were involved in John's mind in such a way that John was NOT in a position to mentally operate upon them conjointly—for instance, to compare them or to perform an inference that directly relied on both of them.*

The desirability of deriving the connotation could arise from a belief-reasoning episode, but we defer this matter to Section 3.8. In the present section we explain, with the aid of Fig. 1, how the connotation can be derived, as an *uncertain* inference obtained by usage of

A. the information in the utterance *taken literally*, i.e. taken to say that John's mind literally has physical store-rooms as parts and that the ideas are in those store-rooms;

B. general knowledge about real physical store-rooms and other physical objects, locations and interactions;

C. *conversion rules* associated with MIND AS PHYSICAL SPACE and IDEAS AS PHYSICAL OBJECTS, where a conversion rule is a type of *context bridging rule* that maps information between the source domain and the target domain of a metaphorical view.

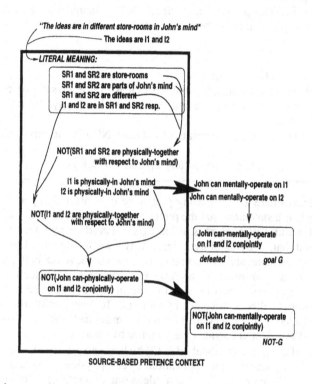

Fig. 1. *Part of the reasoning in store-room example.* The literal meaning of the sentence is shown in the topmost part of the large box. The processing shown within the large box is source-based inference. The processing outside the box is reasoning within the terms of the target domain. The arrows from within the box to outside depict applications of conversion rules.

The reasoning, apart from the application of the conversion rules, occurs within a special context that we call a *source-based pretence context*. (Elsewhere we have uses the word "cocoon" instead of "context.") Within this context, the *literal* information from the sentence—(A) above—is taken to be true, no matter how absurd. This meaning, being literal, is in the terms of the source domains of the metaphorical views used the sentence, that is the domains of PHYSICAL SPACE and PHYSICAL OBJECTS in our example. ATT-Meta can use any of its reasoning rules within the source-based pretence context to try to infer propositions that can be used by the conversion rules to generate propositions about the target domain. The propositions thus generated are in the system's top reasoning context, not the pretence context. The reasoning within the pretence context is what we called above the on-the-fly source-based reasoning. Because of the nature of the conversion rules and information (A), this reasoning is largely or wholly conducted using rules about the source domains, but we allow it to involve other rules also, such as rules about the target-domain itself.

The main conversion rule used maps inability of someone to *physically* operate on two ideas conjointly (where the ideas are viewed metaphorically as a physical object) to that person's inability to operate *mentally* on the two ideas conjointly. (We emphasize that the word "operation" here is used loosely in both its physical and mental sense. Physical operation includes perception, comparison, etc; mental operation similarly includes noticing, comparison, etc.) The rule is actually as follows:

---

(2)

IF J is an idea AND K is an idea
AND it is being pretended that, presumably at least, J is a physical-object
AND it is being pretended that, presumably at least, K is a physical-object
AND X is a person
AND it is being pretended that, presumably at least, NOT(X can-physically-operate-on {J,K})
THEN [presumed] NOT(X can-mentally-operate-on {J,K}).

A hypothesis glossed here as "it is being pretended that, presumably at least, H" for some hypothesis H is a statement that the pretence context contains H and that the level of certain for H within that context is at least presumed. A hypothesis of form "it is being pretended that, with certainty at least λ, H" is a highly analogous to a belief hypothesis. Using the same style of notation as we used above for belief hypotheses, it can be expressed as a formula of the form pretend (H, λ). Such a formula is outside the pretence context. The formula H is within the context. A formula using the pretend operator is called a "pretence hypothesis." To oversimplify this, every such hypothesis is reflected within the context by its "H" argument, and every hypothesis H within the context is reflected outside by a pretence hypothesis.

Conjointness of operation is modelled in (2) by having a set of objects, rather that a single object, as an argument in the applications of can-physically-operate-on and can-mentally-operate-on. The above conversion rule is one of a set of related rules. Others include a converse, a contrapositive and a converse-contrapositive for the above. (Two of these map from the target domain to the source domain, rather than the reverse. This is another unusual feature of our approach with respect to to other approaches to metaphor.) Also, there are rules dealing with single objects, rather than non-singleton sets.

The connotation shown above arises by an application of (2). This is because it can be shown that, by default, NOT(X can-physically-operate-on {I1,I2}), where I1 and I2 are the ideas mentioned in the sentence, from the premise that I1 and I2 are literally in different store-rooms in John's mind. This is because (a) store-rooms are rooms, (b) different rooms in a building are usually do not spatially overlap, (c) objects in non-overlapping subregions of a physical region R are, by default, not spatially-together with respect to the scale of R, and (d) in the common-sense physical world, a person who can operate in a physical region R cannot, by default, physically operate on two physical objects in R conjointly if they are not spatially together with respect to the scale of R. In our example, R is instantiated John's mind. But note that (a) to (d) are just pieces of common-sense information about the physical world. The only properly metaphorical processing is the application of rule (2). Principles (a) to (d) are couched as ATT-Meta rules that we do not detail here.

The reasoning using (a–d) occurs within the source-based pretence context. Into that context is inserted (at the appropriate moment in the backwards rule-based reasoning) the facts that I1 is in a store-room SR1, I2 is in a store-room SR2, SR1 is part of John's mind, and SR2 is part of John's mind. From these facts, ATT-Meta can infer, within the source-based pretence context, that John's mind is a building and therefore a physical region, and I1 and I2 are physical objects. These inferences use further common-sense rules about the ordinary physical world.

Note that the above reasoning requires it to be shown that John can physically operate within his mind. This is shown by a rule associated with MIND AS PHYSICAL SPACE that says that if a person X's mind is pretended to be a physical region then X can physically operate within it.

The key point is that this reasoning from the *literal* meaning of the utterance, conducted within the pretence context, link up with the knowledge displayed as (2). That knowledge is itself of a very fundamental, general nature, and does not, for instance, rely on the notion of store-room. *Any* line of within-pretence inference that linked up with that knowledge could lead to a conclusion that the person in question could not mentally operate on some ideas conjointly.

Recall that ATT-Meta applies rules in a backwards, goal-directed way. So, we need a goal to start the process off. For the moment, let us somewhat artificial assume the goal is

(G)   **John can-mentally-operate-on {I1, I2}.**

In fact, the system will conclude with a certainty of presumed for the *negation* of (G), thereby drawing the Connotation displayed above. Below we will show how the need to establish the Connotation could arise naturally and implicitly in belief reasoning.

8   A Case of Metaphorical Conflict

Notice the uncertainty in the system's conclusion about the negation of (G)—it is only presumed. The uncertainty arises partly from the fact that conversion rules, such as (2), have a certainty level only of presumed, not certain. Indeed, ATT-Meta allows the possibility that there is evidence for (G) itself that outweighs the evidence for its negation. In our actual implementation of the store-rooms example, we do have a further rule, operating entirely within the target domain of mental states:

---

(3)

IF X can-mentally-operate-on J AND X can-mentally-operate-on K
THEN [presumed] X can-mentally-operate-on {J,K}.

This supports (G), because of a MIND AS PHYSICAL SPACE conversion rule that says that if an idea J is in a mind that is viewed as physical region then the agent can mentally operate on the idea. Thus, there is a real conflict between (G) and its negation.

Our general-purpose, specificity-based conflict-resolution mechanism is adequate for establishing that the evidence supporting goal (NOT-G) above it be more specific than the evidence supporting (G) itself. The argumentation for the negation of (G) ultimately relies on all the facts that (G) relies on together with an extra one, namely that it is pretended that SR1 and SR2 are *different*. Therefore, merely by the fact-based aspect of specificity comparison, (NOT-G) is regarded as having more specific support.

(G) and (NOT-G) are both supported directly or indirectly by conversion rules (for different metaphorical views). However, (G) could potentially be supported by information that is entirely derived in the target domain. For instance, the understander might know a fact F from previous non-metaphorical discourse that allows it to be concluded that John is entertaining I1 and I2, and therefore can mentally operate on I1 and I2 individually, so that by target-domain rule (3) we get further support for (G). However, although we do not show here how this happens, (NOT-G) would still win against (G), again just by the *general-purpose* conflict-resolution mechanism.

9   Uncertainty in Metaphor

ATT-Meta includes the following types of uncertainty handling in its metaphor-based reasoning.

(1) Given an utterance, it is often not certain what particular metaphorical views or variants of them are manifested. Correspondingly, ATT-Meta may merely have presumed, for instance, as a (tentative) level of certainty for a pretence hypothesis, such as that the pretence that idea I1 is a physical object, in the store-room example. This hypothesis is then potentially subject to defeat. Indeed, note that, in the example the pretence hypothesis just alluded to only arises in the middle of reasoning: the system does *not* start with a premise that some idea is being viewed as physical object.

(2) Knowledge about the source domain of the metaphorical view is itself generally uncertain. Correspondingly, in ATT-Meta the hypotheses and reasoning within the pretence context are usually uncertain, and can involve the use of the conflict-resolution mechanism described above. For instance, it is not *certain* that a person cannot physical operate conjointly on two objects if they are physically separated from each other. There could be evidence in a particular case that the person can indeed operate conjointly on them.

(3) Conversion rules like (2) are merely default rules. There can be evidence against the conclusion of the rule. Whether the conclusion survives as a default (presumed) hypothesis depends on the relative specificity of the evidence for and against the conclusion. Thus, whether a piece of metaphorical reasoning overrides or or is overridden by other lines of reasoning about the target is matter of the peculiarities of the case at hand. However, many researchers (e.g., Lakoff 1993) appear to assume that, in cases of conflict, target information should override metaphor-based inferences, and thus do not fully address the potential uncertainty of target information. It must be realized that, just as with literal utterances, a metaphorical utterance can express an exception to some situation that would *normally* apply in the target domain. To metaphorically say "The company nursed its competitor back to health" contradicts default knowledge that companies do not normally help their competitors, and should override that knowledge.

(4) Different conversion rules working may create propositions that lead to conflict. We saw this in the discussion of (G) and its negation in the store-room example. Such conflict can also occur between the conversion rules for just a single metaphorical view. For example, in uses in real discourse of the metaphorical view of ORGANIZATIONS AS PHYSICAL OBJECTS, companies are often cast as eating things, such as other companies. Eating actions by companies might be mapped to *legal* company-acquisition

be default, but there could be a more specific mapping that says that eating by a Mafia-run company maps (by default) to *illegal* company acquisition.

10 Importation-Based Conflicts

By default, a pretence context is taken to contain as a fact any fact sitting immediately outside. The store-room example provides an illustration of the need for this *importation* of facts. One of the rules applied within the pretence context needs to establish that John is a person. That John is a person is given only outside the context, however.

Importation can lead to reasoning conflicts. In brief, within the pretence context, the imported facts may support the complement of a presumed hypothesis that derives indirectly from the special metaphorical facts inserted into the context at the start (e.g., the fact that idea I1 is in store-room SR1). That fact leads to the conclusion that I1 is a physical object. But the fact outside the context that I1 is an idea leads by a rule about mental entities that I1 is *not* a physical object. To cater for such situations, *certain* facts outside the pretence context are downgraded to presumed on importation, and a simple modification is made to the conflict-resolution scheme as described so far: within a metaphorical pretence context, specificity-comparison is first attempted in a mode where all reasoning lines partially dependent on imported facts are thrown away. Only if this does not yield a winner are those lines restored, and specificity-comparison is attempted again. This preference against imports needs to be reflected out to higher levels via lifting. The preference can naturally be regarded as an additional specificity principle.

11 Combining Metaphorical and Belief Reasoning

Here we present one type of interaction that is possible between metaphorical and belief reasoning in ATT-Meta. Other types not addressed here include reasoning about other agents' metaphorical reasoning and reasoning about the alleged reasoning of personified non-agents.

The store-room example as presented so far is does not address the question of why understanders would try to establish the above Connotation, or how understanders would make use of that connotation if they spontaneously derived it. But suppose that the two ideas (I1, I2) mentioned in the store-rooms sentence (1) are stated (elsewhere in the discourse) to be believed by the agent, John, and suppose that they lead by some fairly direct, natural reasoning to some conclusion C. Then, if (1) had not been uttered, it would have been reasonable to ascribe by default to John a belief in the conclusion C. But this ascription relies on a default assumption that John does mentally operate conjointly on I1 and I2. If there is evidence that this is not the case, then the ascription should be abandoned. Sentence (1) provides just such evidence against John's mentally operating conjointly on I1 and I2. We just mention briefly here what happens, with the aid of Fig. 2. We suppose the user supplies the goal

(K)   John believes C to level at least presumed

and also the facts that John believes I1 to level certain and that John believes I2 to level certain. Without any further information, ATT-Meta would proceed as follows, on the simplifying assumption that C can be derived to level presumed by just one rule application from I1 and I2. ATT-Meta would open a simulation pretence context in which I1 and I2 are set up as facts and C is set up as a goal. An attempt would be made to establish C within the simulation context. We assume that this attempt is successful because of the mentioned rule application, giving some certainly level for C. For definiteness, let us say that this level is certain. As a result, the hypothesis (K) in the top context is supported. The level to which it is currently supported is also presumed, according to a general policy regarding simulation of reasoning.

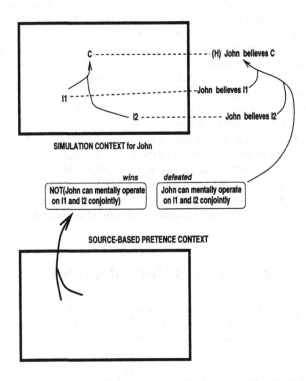

Fig. 2. *Combining belief reasoning and metaphorical reasoning.*

But, the system notes that hypothesis (K) depends not only on John's belief in I1 and I2 but also on the assumption that John mentally operates on I1 and I2 conjointly. Such notes are established in all cases of belief reasoning, not just when metaphorical reasoning is in the offing: there may, in principle, be non-metaphorical evidence that the assumption is wrong. Because of the note, the assumption is set up as a goal, namely goal (G) of the previous section. Such goals are the "agent-inference hypotheses" mentioned in an earlier section. They are given an initial certainty level of presumed, and this level stays if there is no counter-evidence. In our example, the evidence for (NOT-G) prevails. Because (G) is defeated, the support for the hypothesis that John believes C to at least level presumed collapses. (And as a result, the inference step within the simulation pretence context is deleted.)

12 Conclusion

ATT-Meta embodies a unique, implemented application of context-handling. It incorporates belief reasoning, metaphor-based reasoning and uncertainty-handling in a unified framework. In addition, the uncertainty-handling could be generalized to work with types of context other than those needed for belief reasoning and metaphor. We have paid much attention to the need for conflict resolution to be handled correctly within different contexts at any depth of nesting, and across the boundaries of contexts. Also, different bridging rules working from one context to another may lead to conflict. We saw a case of this in metaphor-based reasoning.

ATT-Meta's metaphorical reasoning in all its aspects (reasoning within contexts, application of conversion rules, etc.) uses the same general-purpose rule-based reasoning provisions as for any other reasoning within the system. The only thing special about it is the type of knowledge used (mainly in the form of conversion rules), fine detail of the handling of the contexts, and the special conflict-resolution provisions concerning importation of facts into metaphorical pretence contexts.

We do not claim that ATT-Meta can deal with all the subtleties of the types of metaphorical utterance it is directed at. In particular, ATT-Meta currently lacks a proper treatment of change and time, and so cannot do justice to the processual quality of many metaphorical descriptions. But one issue partially addressed is the context-sensitivity of what particular connotations are drawn, because the metaphorical reasoning (as with all other reasoning in the system) is goal-driven and therefore responsive to the particular "issues" raised by surrounding sentences.

References

1. Barnden, J.A. (1998). Uncertain reasoning about agents' beliefs and reasoning. Technical Report CSRP-98-11, School of Computer Science, The University of Birmingham, U.K. Also in *Artificial Intelligence and Law,* in press.
2. Barnden, J.A., Helmreich, S., Iverson, E. & Stein, G.C. (1994). An integrated implementation of simulative, uncertain and metaphorical reasoning about mental states. In J. Doyle, E. Sandewall & P. Torasso (Eds), *Principles of Knowledge Representation and Reasoning: Proceedings of the Fourth International Conference,* pp.27–38. San Mateo, CA: Morgan Kaufmann.
3. Creary, L. G. (1979). Propositional attitudes: Fregean representation and simulative reasoning. *Procs. 6th. Int. Joint Conf. on Artificial Intelligence* (Tokyo), pp.176–181. Kaufmann.
4. Fauconnier, G. & Turner, M. (1998). Conceptual integration networks. *Cognitive Science,* 22(2), pp.133–187.
5. Hobbs, J.R. (1990). *Literature and cognition.* CSLI Lecture Notes, No. 21, Center for the Study of Language and Information, Stanford University.
6. Lakoff, G. (1993). The contemporary theory of metaphor. In A. Ortony (Ed.), *Metaphor and Thought,* 2nd edition, pp.202–251. Cambridge, U.K.: Cambridge University Press.
7. Loui, R.P., Norman, J., Olson, J. & Merrill, A. (1993). A design for reasoning with policies, precedents, and rationales. In *Fourth International Conference on Artificial Intelligence and Law: Proceedings of the Conference,* pp.202–211. New York: ACM.
8. Martin, J. (1994). Metabank: A knowledge-base of metaphoric language conventions. *Computational Intelligence, 10* (2), pp.134–149.
9. Narayanan, S. (1997). KARMA: Knowledge-based action representations for metaphor and aspect. Ph.D. thesis, EECS Department, U. of California, Berkeley, August 1997.
10. Parsons, S., Sierra, C. & Jennings, N. (1998). Multi-context argumentative agents. In *Working Papers of the 4th Symp. on Logical Formalizations of Commonsense Reasoning,* London.

Pragmatic Reasoning: Inferring Contexts

John Bell

Applied Logic Group
Department of Computer Science
Queen Mary and Westfield College
University of London
London E1 4NS
jb@dcs.qmw.ac.uk

Abstract. Pragmatic reasoning is defined as the process of finding the intended meaning(s) of the given, and it is suggested that this amounts to the process of inferring the appropriate context(s) in which to interpret the given. This suggestion is illustrated by examples from natural language understanding and visual object recognition. A formal, model-theoretic, definition of pragmatic reasoning is then presented and discussed.

1 Pragmatic Reasoning

The semantics-pragmatics distinction is common in Linguistics and in the Philosophy of Language, however it is not altogether clear; see, for example, the discussion in [8, Ch. 1]. For present purposes we will say that semantics is concerned with context-free meaning, while pragmatics is concerned with context-dependent meaning. Moreover, this distinction is not restricted to the meaning of language, and may include the meaning of perceptions, events, actions, etc. In each case, the semantic or literal or context-free meaning of the phenomenon in question is contrasted with its pragmatic or appropriate or context-dependent meaning or meanings. This liberal view is supported by the definition of context given in the *Concise Oxford English Dictionary*:

> **1** the parts of something written or spoken that immediately precede and follow a word or passage and clarify its meaning. **2** the circumstances relevant to something under consideration. □ **in context** with the surrounding words or circumstances (*must be seen in context*). □ **out of context** without the surrounding words or circumstances and so not fully understandable.

The distinction extends to reasoning. Semantic reasoning, traditionally called deductive reasoning, aims at certainty. It is concerned with what follows from the given by virtue of its semantic meaning alone, with what follows from the given regardless of the context in which it occurs. By contrast, pragmatic reasoning is concerned with drawing reasonable or appropriate conclusions on the basis of the given. It thus depends on finding appropriate interpretation(s) of the given. And this, it is suggested, amounts to progressively inferring the appropriate context(s) in which to interpret the given. The process of inferring a context involves making assumptions about what is normal or typical or conventional on the basis of the given context, and using pragmatic (context-sensitive) rules to extend the given context on the basis of these assumptions. In order to elaborate these ideas, four examples are now discussed.

The suggestion that finding the pragmatic meaning(s) of the given amounts to inferring context(s) seems to be anticipated by the following passage from Wittgenstein [17, I 525]:

> "After he had said this, he left her as he did the day before." — Do I understand this sentence? Do I understand it just as I should if I heard it in the course of a narrative? If it were set down in isolation I should say, I don't know what it's about. But all the same I should know how this sentence might perhaps be used; I could myself invent a context for it.
> (A multitude of familiar paths lead off from these words in every direction.)

Wittgenstein seems to be distinguishing between the semantic meaning of the sentence (its meaning if it were set down in isolation) and its pragmatic meaning (the meaning which would satisfy someone who asked about it) and suggests that the pragmatic meaning can be obtained by inventing a context in which the sentence might be used. His final remark can perhaps be understood as suggesting that the sentence evokes many typical contexts. Note that the contexts we infer when interpreting the sentence are not arbitrary. For example, lacking any information to the contrary, it seems reasonable to conclude that each occurrence of the pronoun 'he' in the sentence refers to the same individual.

It is important to stress that pragmatic reasoning involves inferring contexts, rather than simply making assumptions. Inferring a context can be thought of as a "bootstrapping" process. A given partial context suggests appropriate assumptions which are then used with pragmatic rules to extend it. The extended context then suggests further assumptions, leading to further extensions, etc.

The dual role of (partial) contexts in suggesting and constraining assumptions is illustrated by the use of context in human and artificial visual object recognition as described by Ullman [15]. In the artificial case, models of the objects to be recognized are learned and stored in memory. For current purposes, object models can be thought of as standard, or prototypical, or "canonical" representations of the objects. The recognition task is then to match given unknown objects with appropriate stored models. When a large number of models are stored it is important to examine the more likely ones first. One method of model selection suggested by Ullman involves the use of context. In support of this method, he discusses psychological studies on the role of context in human object recognition. Familiar objects can often be recognized in the absence of context. However when dealing with less familiar objects, or with complex scenes, or when viewing conditions are degraded, the role of context increases in importance and can become indispensable. There are strong correlations between objects found in typical scenes. The presence of an object in a scene can therefore be used to make some objects more likely to appear in the same scene than others; a pair of similar elongated blobs in the image may be ambiguous, but in the appropriate context, for instance under a bed, they may be immediately recognized as a pair of slippers. The recognition of an object in a scene can not only suggest other probable objects, but also their expected location, size and orientation; for example, the slippers should be of an appropriate size, are more likely to be under the bed than on top of it, etc. The powerful effects of object configurations of this kind are illustrated by Figure 1.

Fig. 1. Object recognition in context. Drawing by W.E. Hill, [4].

The figure is Boring's famous illusion, which can be interpreted as depicting either an old woman or a young woman. Many of the objects in the scene are schematic and ambigous and cannot be interpreted without context, however they are easily recognized in a (partial) context. For example, the object which is interpreted as the young woman's ear can also be interpreted as the old woman's right eye, but once the young woman's profile is recognized so is her ear, or once the old woman's profile is recognized so is her right eye. In looking at the figure it seems that our visual recognition systems progressively infer two likely contexts in which to interpret it.

This example illustrates how a partial context can suggest and constrain assumptions. The following two examples are more formal, and make the reasoning process more explicit.

Kamp and Reyle [7] aim to show how discourses (sequences of English sentences) can give rise to semantic representations which they call discourse representation structures (DRSs). The construction of a DRS proceeds sentence by sentence, each sentence being interpreted in the context of the existing DRS. This incremental nature of interpretation reflects what they call the "semantic cohesiveness" of discourse. The sentences of a coherent discourse are typically connected by various kinds of cross-reference, so it is often impossible to analyse the meaning of the discourse as a simple conjunction of the separate meanings of individual sentences that make it up, "The meaning of the whole is more, one might say, than the meaning of its parts". In order to understand what information is added by the next sentence of a discourse to what has been learned already, the interpreter must relate the sentence to the DRS, the context, that has already been constructed. This is done by means of construction rules which are triggered by the syntactic structure of the sentence and which extend the DRS in an appropriate way. The analysis of pronomial anaphora exemplifies discourse cohesion and the need for incremental interpretation. An introductory example in [7] is the analysis of the discourse: 'Jones owns a Porsche. It fascinates him'. The natural interpretation of this discourse, in the absence of further contextual information, is that the pronouns 'him' and 'it' refer back to Jones and his Porsche respectively. The construction rules should thus use the input sentence and the existing DRS, the existing context, to relate the pronouns with the correct antecedents. The construction of the complete DRS is illustrated by the sequence of DRSs in Figure 2.

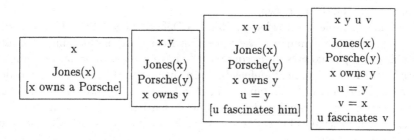

Fig. 2. Construction of a discourse representation structure

The first NP of the first sentence, represented in simplified linearized form as [Jones owns a Porsche], triggers the construction rule for proper names, which constructs the first DRS in the sequence. This consists of a new discourse referent, 'x', and two discourse conditions; 'Jones(x)' and '[x owns a Porsche]'. The NP of the latter condition again triggers the construction rule for proper names, which results in the second DRS in the sequence. This cannot be reduced further and so represents the semantic meaning of the first sentence and the context it gives rise to. The interpretation of the second sentence is then begun in this context. The first pronoun triggers the construction rule for pronouns, which constructs the third DRS in the sequence. A new discourse referent, 'u', is added and identified with a suitable element chosen from those already in the universe of the DRS, in this case with 'y'. The pronoun in the final condition of this DRS again triggers the construction rule for pronouns, and this results in the final DRS in the sequence. Once again, a new discourse referent, 'v', is added and is identified with a suitable element from the universe of discourse, in this case with 'x'.

As Kamp and Reyle note, their construction rule for pronouns is vague in that it requires that the new discourse referent is identified with a "suitable" element chosen from those already in the universe of the DRS, but does not specify what "suitable" means. For the example, they suggest that gender information could be added to the DRS and then used to identify the objects appropriately ('he' is male, 'it' is not human).

This example illustrates the cohesiveness of meaningful discourse in two ways. First, the predication in the first sentence and the predication in the second sentence must be understood as referring to the same pair of individuals. This is made explicit by the equational conditions of the final DRS, and reflected in its truth condition. Informally, the final DRS is true iff there are individuals a and b such that a is Jones, b is a Porsche, a owns b and b fascinates a. Second, the existential element of the truth condition makes it clear that the predications of the two sentences refer to the same Porsche. This interpretation depends on there being a single representation that captures the joint content of the two sentences together, rather than a pair of unconnected representations, one for each of the sentences on its own.

The final example is provided by Reiter's Default Logic [12], which was developed to formalize common sense reasoning Reasoning of this kind typically takes place in a partial epistemic context. We have limited information and are required to draw reasonable, if defeasible, conclusions on the basis of it. In order to represent inferences of this kind, default rules (defaults), are added to classical first-order logic. Default rules are context-sensitive in that their premises may refer both to what is known and to what is not known. A default rule is an expression of the form:

$$\frac{\alpha(\overline{x}) : \beta_1(\overline{x}), \ldots, \beta_n(\overline{x})}{\omega(\overline{x})}$$

where $\alpha(\overline{x})$, the $\beta_i(\overline{x})$, and $\omega(\overline{x})$ are all formulae whose free variables are among those in $\overline{x} = x_1, \ldots, x_m$, and α, the β_i, and ω are called the prerequisite, the justifications, and the consequent of the default respectively. Defaults are rules of conjecture (pragmatic rules). If their prerequisites ae known and their justifications are "consistent" (i.e. their negations are not provable), then their consequences can be inferred. A default theory is a pair $\langle D, W \rangle$ where D is a set of default rules and W is a set of first-order formulae. Intuitively, W can be thought of as representing a partial description of the world (a partial context), and the defaults in D are used to extend W in appropriate way(s). For example, if $D_1 = \{ \frac{Student(x) : \neg Married(x)}{\neg Married(x)} \}$ and $W_1 = \{ Student(Jones) \}$, then we can conclude $\neg Married(Jones)$ from the default theory $\langle D_1, W_1 \rangle$; Jones is a student, students are not normally married so, by default, Jones is not married. Similarly if $D_2 = \{ \frac{Adult(x) : Married(x)}{Married(x)} \}$ and $W_2 = \{ Adult(Jones) \}$, then we can conclude $Married(Jones)$ from the theory $\langle D_2, W_2 \rangle$; Jones is an adult, adults are normally married so, by default, Jones is married. Moreover, the combined theory $\langle D_1 \cup D2, W_1 \cup W2 \rangle$ has two extensions, depending on which of the two defaults is considered first. If the default in D_1 is considered first, it is applicable, as $\neg Married(Jones)$ is consistent, and so $\neg Married(Jones)$ is added to the extension, and this has the effect of "blocking" the application of the conflicting default in D_2. Likewise, if the default in D_2 is considered first it is applicable so its consequent, $Married(Jones)$, is added to the extension thereby blocking the application of the other default. If the default rules of a theory are all normal, if the rules are all of the form $\frac{\alpha:\beta}{\beta}$, its extensions can be constructed inductively. However when this is not the case it is necessary to ensure that the justifications of the defaults used in constructing an extension are jointly consistent and so do not undermine each other. For example, [3], the theory $\langle\{\frac{:\neg\beta}{\neg\beta}, \frac{:\beta}{\alpha}\}, \emptyset\rangle$ does not have an extension containing α. If the second default is considered first, it seems that β is consistent and hence that α can be added. However, the first default is also applicable, so $\neg\beta$ would also be added, thereby undermining the justification for the second default. Reiter shows that the extensions of a (closed) default theory $\langle D, W\rangle$ can be defined quasi-inductively.[1] Let:

$$E_0 = W, \text{ and for } i \geq 0$$
$$E_{i+1} = Th(E_i) \cup \{\omega : \frac{\alpha:\beta_1,\ldots,\beta_n}{\omega} \in D, \alpha \in E_i, \neg\beta_j \notin E\}.$$

Then $E = \bigcup_{i=0}^{\infty} E_i$ is an extension of $\langle D, W\rangle$. While normal defaults can be considered in isolation, coherence requires that the whole context (extension) is considered when a non-normal default is applied.

The last two examples have illustrated in detail how syntactic representations of contexts can be inferred. The following section is concerned with the model-theoretic representation of contexts and pragmatic reasoning.

2 Pragmatic Entailment

In what follows, let $\mathcal{L}$ be a language, a set of sentences determined by a grammar, and $\mathcal{L}^*$ be the set of all sequences of sentences of $\mathcal{L}$. We begin by generalizing Tarski semantics to sequences in a straightforward way.

Definition 21 *A semantics for $\mathcal{L}^*$ is a pair $S_{\mathcal{L}} = \langle I, [\![\,]\!]\rangle$ where:*

I is a set of models of $\mathcal{L}$, and
$[\![\,]\!] : \mathcal{L} \to \mathcal{P}I$ is a semantic interpretation function.

For each $\phi \in \mathcal{L}$, $[\![\phi]\!]$ is the set of semantic models of ϕ, the set of models in which ϕ is semantically true. The semantic interpretation function is naturally extended to sequences: for each Γ in $\mathcal{L}^*$, $[\![\Gamma]\!] \stackrel{def}{=} \bigcap\{[\![\phi]\!] : \phi \text{ in } \Gamma\}$.

---

[1] In practice a closed theory can be formed from an open theory by replacing open defaults (defaults containing free variables) by appropriate ground instances. The definition is quasi-inductive (a term due to David Makinson) because E is mentioned in the "inductive step" of its definition. In the definition, $Th(S)$ denotes the deductive closure of the set S.

Intuitively $[\![\phi]\!]$ represents the semantic, or literal, or context-free meaning of ϕ. This intuition is captured by the defined extension of $[\![]\!]$; which has the consequence that, for any sequences Γ and Δ, $[\![\Gamma, \phi, \Delta]\!] = [\![\Gamma]\!] \cap [\![\phi]\!] \cap [\![\Delta]\!]$.[2] Thus the semantic meaning of ϕ is independent of the sequence in which it occurs.

In what follows, contexts are represented as sets of models.[3] A sentence ϕ is semantically true in a context if it is true in all models in the set. Thus $[\![\phi]\!]$ can be considered to be the *semantic context* for ϕ, $[\![\phi]\!]$ represents what is (semantically) true on all semantic interpretations of ϕ.

As a simple example of the semantics, if $\mathcal{L}$ is the language of classical first-order logic, then the Tarski semantics for $\mathcal{L}$ define a truth relation $\models \subseteq I \times \mathcal{L}$. The semantic meaning function of $S_{\mathcal{L}}$ is thus defined by putting $[\![\phi]\!] = \{i \in I : i \models \phi\}$.

Each semantics determines a semantic logic.

Definition 22 *Let $S_{\mathcal{L}} = \langle I, [\![]\!]\rangle$ be a semantics for $\mathcal{L}^*$. The* semantic logic *determined by $S_{\mathcal{L}}$, S, is defined by its* semantic entailment relation:

$$\Gamma \models_S \phi \quad \text{iff} \quad [\![\Gamma]\!] \subseteq [\![\phi]\!]$$

Thus Γ semantically entails ϕ in S iff all semantic models of Γ are also semantic models of ϕ.

Note that, as the semantic interpretation function is context free, $[\![\Delta, \Gamma, \Delta']\!] \subseteq [\![\Gamma]\!]$. So any semantic logic is monotonic.

We can now define the pragmatics for $\mathcal{L}^*$.

Definition 23 *A* pragmatics *for $\mathcal{L}^*$ is a triple $P_{\mathcal{L}} = \langle I, [\![]\!], [\,]\rangle$ where:*

$\langle I, [\![]\!]\rangle$ *is a semantics for $\mathcal{L}^*$, and*
$[\,] : \mathcal{L}^* \to \mathcal{PPI}$ *is a* pragmatic interpretation function.

For each sequence Γ, $[\Gamma]$ is the set of pragmatic contexts *for Γ, the set of contexts which are inferred when interpreting Γ.*

Note that we did not start with a pragmatic function of type $\mathcal{L} \to \mathcal{PI}$ as it is not assumed that, for any sequence Γ, $[\Gamma] = \bigcap\{[\phi] : \phi \text{ in } \Gamma\}$. Indeed it may well be the case that there are sequences Γ and Δ such that $[\Gamma, \phi, \Delta] \neq [\Gamma] \cap [\phi] \cap [\Delta]$. The pragmatic interpretation of ϕ may thus depend on the sequence in which it occurs.

Note also that, as a sequence Γ may be (pragmatically) ambiguous, there may be several pragmatic contexts for it. Each of these can be called a *credulous* pragmatic context for Γ. As contexts are represented by sets of models, it is also

---

[2] For convenience we use customary abbreviations when writing sequences. Thus the concatenation of the sequences Γ and Δ is written simply as Γ, Δ and the sequence consisting of the single sentence ϕ is written simply as ϕ.

[3] Similarly, Stalnaker argues that contexts can be represented as sets of possible worlds [14].

possible to define the *sceptical* pragmatic context for Γ to be the union of the credulous contexts; $\bigcup [\Gamma]$. Intuitively, $\bigcup [\Gamma]$ represents what is semantically true on all pragmatic interpretations of Γ.

For example, Kamp and Reyle's work can be seen as defining a pragmatic function for a subset of English discourses. Thus the semantic interpretation of the Jones-discourse can be represented as:

$$[\![\exists x (Porsche(x) \wedge Owns(j,x)) \wedge \exists x, y Fascinates(x,y)]\!],$$

where 'j' denotes Jones, etc., While the pragmatic interpretation of the discourse, the context corresponding to the final DRS for it, can be represented as:

$$[\![\exists x (Porsche(x) \wedge Owns(j,x) \wedge Fascinates(x,j))]\!].$$

The possibility of ambiguity in pragmatic interpretation admits of (at least) two notions of pragmatic consequence.

Definition 24 *Let $P_{\mathcal{L}} = \langle I, [\![\,]\!], [\,] \rangle$ be a pragmatics for $\mathcal{L}^*$. The credulous pragmatic logic determined by $P_{\mathcal{L}}$, P_c, is defined by its credulous pragmatic entailment relation:*

$$\Gamma \mathrel{\approx^c_P} \phi \text{ iff for some } c \in [\Gamma],\ c \subseteq [\![\phi]\!]$$

Thus Γ credulously entails ϕ in P_c iff ϕ is semantically true in some pragmatic context for Γ.

The sceptical pragmatic logic determined by $P_{\mathcal{L}}$, P_s, is defined by its sceptical pragmatic entailment relation:

$$\Gamma \mathrel{\approx^s_P} \phi \text{ iff for every } c \in [\Gamma],\ c \subseteq [\![\phi]\!]$$

Thus Γ sceptically entails ϕ in P_s iff ϕ is semantically true in every pragmatic context for Γ.

Note that both forms of pragmatic inference are nonmonotonic, as it need not be the case that $[\Delta, \Gamma, \Delta'] \subseteq [\Gamma]$.

All pragmatic interpretation functions satisfy the following conditions:

Tautologies: For any sequence Γ and tautology $\top$, $\bigcup [\Gamma] \subseteq [\![\top]\!]$.
Weakening: For any sequences Γ and Δ and Σ, and context c,
if $c \in [\Gamma]$ and $c \subseteq [\![\Delta]\!]$ and $[\![\Delta]\!] \subseteq [\![\Sigma]\!]$, then $c \subseteq [\![\Sigma]\!]$.

All tautologies of $\mathcal{L}$ according to the semantics in question (if indeed there are any) are pragmatically inferrable, so is any semantic consequence of what is pragmatically inferrable.

Sceptical entailment also satisfies the following condition:

Scepticism: For any sequences Γ and Δ,
$\bigcup [\Gamma] \subseteq [\![\Delta]\!]$ iff for every sentence ϕ in Δ, $\bigcup [\Gamma] \subseteq [\![\phi]\!]$.

Many other conditions can be imposed, for example:

Inclusion: For any sequence Γ, $\bigcup [\Gamma] \subseteq [\![\Gamma]\!]$.
Equivalence: For any sequences Γ and Δ,
if $[\![\Gamma]\!] = [\![\Delta]\!]$ then $\bigcup [\Gamma] = \bigcup [\Delta]$.

Inclusion has the effect that the pragmatic consequence relation in question is ampliative, the pragmatic consequences of Γ include the semantic consequences of Γ. Recall Kamp and Reyle's comments on semantic cohesion: the meaning of the whole (the pragmatic meaning of the discourse) is more than the meaning of its parts (the semantic meaning of the discourse). However, this condition may not always be wanted. For example, people do not always say what they mean or mean what they say, while illusions (such as the Muller-Lyer arrows illusion) show that one cannot always believe what one literally sees.

Equivalence is a strong condition. For example, it implies:

Permutation: For any sequences Γ and Δ, and sentences ϕ and ψ,
$\bigcup [\Gamma, \phi, \psi, \Delta] = \bigcup [\Gamma, \psi, \phi, \Delta]$.

Permutation has the effect of reducing sequences to sets. It is thus not appropriate, for example, when attempting to represent the sequence-based cohesiveness of discourse.

By way of illustrating pragmatic entailment, some well known nonmonotonic logics are discussed briefly, all of which satisfy Inclusion, Equivalence and a number of further conditions; see, e.g. [1].

Pragmatic entailment has its origins in McCarthy's model theory (pragmatics) for Predicate Circumscription [10], and in the notion of preferential entailment defined by Shoham [13]. Predicate Circumscription is designed to represent the common sense inference that the objects which are required to satsify a predicate P given an axiom A are the only objects which satisfy P. The model theory is based on the idea of P-minimal entailment. Let I be the set of all models of classical first-order logic and, for $i, j \in I$, let:

$$i <_P j \quad \text{iff} \quad Ext(P, i) \subset Ext(P, j);$$

that is, $i <_P j$ iff the extension of P in i is a proper subset of the extension of P in j. A model i is said to be a P-minimal model of A if i is a model of A and there is no model j of A such that $j <_P i$. Then A P-minimally entails B iff B is true in all P-minimal models of A. This idea is generalized by Shoham. Given the set of models I of a logic L, and an arbitrary (strict) partial ordering $<$ of I, the preference logic $L_<$ is determined by its preferential entailment relation. A model $i \in I$ is said to be a preferred model of a sentence A iff i is a model of A and there is no model j of A such that $j < i$. Then a sentence A preferentially entails a sentence B (written $A \models_< B$) iff the preferred models of A are all models of B. Clearly Predicate Circumscription is a preference logic; the preferred models of A are just the P-minimal models of A. Clearly also any preference logic is a (sceptical) pragmatic logic; the pragmatic models of A are just the preferred models of A. However, the converse is not the case. Preference logics satisfy the following property:

Cautious Monotony: If $A \models_< B$ then $A \wedge C \models_< B$ provided that $A \models_< C$

However, pragmatic logics need not satisfy the counterpart of this property; as pragmatic functions need not satisfy the corresponding condition. Makinson [5] gives an example which shows that Cautious Monotony does not hold for Default Logic and hence that it cannot be a preference logic. His example can also be applied to show that Autoepistemic Logic [9]. Makinson also shows that the property fails for Logic Programs with negation as failure. However, these logics are readily shown to be pragmatic logics. This will be shown for Default Logic.[4] Before doing so however, it is worth noting that it is possible to define credulous preferential entailment by defining an equivalence relation on the set of preferred models of a theory. For example in the case of the circumscription of a predicate P given an axiom A, the models in each equivalence class are those in which P holds for the same individuals. Intuitively the models in an equivalence class are those in which the same assumptions are made.

Etherington [6] gives a pragmatics for Default Logic which is based on classical first-order semantics. In what follows, his notation is changed slightly and contexts are used to provide an alternative motivation. The basic idea is as follows: given a default theory $\Delta = \langle D, W \rangle$, the world description W is represented as (the partial context) $[\![W]\!]$ and the default rules in D are used to produce refinements of this set by eliminating models from it, resulting in the set of extensions (inferred contexts) $[W]$. Defaults thus induce a partial ordering on sets of models. Let $\delta = \frac{\alpha : \beta_1, \dots, \beta_n}{\omega}$ be a default, I be a set of models (of classical first-order logic), and $I_1, I_2 \in \mathcal{P}I$. Then:

$$I_1 \leq_\delta I_2 \quad \text{iff} \quad \forall i \in I_2 . i \models \alpha, \exists i_1, \dots, i_n \in I_2 . i_j \models \beta_j, \text{ and}$$
$$I_1 = I_2 - \{i \in I_2 : i \models \neg \omega\}.$$

Thus if $I_1 \leq_\delta I_2$ then I_2 can be regarded as a (partial) context in which the default δ is applicable and I_1 can be regarded as the context which results from applying δ in I_2. So, if $I_1 \neq I_2$, applying δ in I_2 extends I_2 by eliminating those models in which the consequent of δ is false. The ordering is extended to a set of defaults, D, by taking the union of the partial orders given by the defaults in D:

$$I_1 \leq_D I_2 \quad \text{iff} \quad \exists \delta \in D . I_1 \leq_\delta I_2.$$

For a normal default theory $\Delta = \langle D, W \rangle$ it is sufficient to consider the $\leq_D$-minimal elements of $\mathcal{P}[\![W]\!]$, as each of these corresponds to the set of all models

---

[4] The case for Autoepistemic Logic is discussed in [1]. The case for Logic Programs with negation as failure has similarities with the case for Default Logic. A preference ordering can be defined on Herbrand interpretations of the logic program [11] which minimizes the degree of truth of the atoms in them. The unique well-founded model of the program is then a minimal model in the ordering. However, as it need not be the minimum model, the ordering is not sufficient as a preference criterion and "post-filtering" may again be required.

of an extension of Δ, and vice versa. However for non-normal theories, such as the example given earlier, it is necessary to ensure that the application of each default does not violate the justifications of already-applied defaults. Thus, for a non-normal theory $\Delta = \langle D, W \rangle$, we should consider only those $\leq_D$-minimal elements of $\mathcal{P}[\![W]\!]$ which are stable for Δ in that they do not refute any of the justifications in any of the defaults used in extending $[\![W]\!]$:

$$I \text{ is stable for } \Delta \text{ iff } \text{ there is a } D' \subseteq D \text{ such that } I \leq_{D'} [\![W]\!],$$
$$\text{and for each } \tfrac{\alpha:\beta_1,\dots,\beta_n}{\omega} \in D', \exists i_1,\dots,i_n \in I \,.\, i_j \models \beta_j.$$

Etherington proves that the pragmatics is sound and complete; that is, that a set of models I is stable for a default theory Δ iff I is the set of all models of some extension of Δ. As with preference logics a partial order is defined. However unlike preference logics the ordering is on sets of models and, more significantly, the partial ordering is insufficient as "post-filtering" may be required in order to determine the appropriate elements in the ordering. By contrast, a default theory $\Delta = \langle D, W \rangle$ can readily be seen as a pragmatic logic in which $[\![W]\!]$ is the set of $\leq_D$-minimal models of $\mathcal{P}[\![W]\!]$ which are stable for Δ.

3 Concluding Remarks

The contributions of this paper are twofold: the notion of pragmatic reasoning has been clearly defined and argued for, and a general model-theoretic formalization has been given of it. This work thus represents a significant improvement of earlier versions of some of these ideas [1, 2].

Clearly this formalization of pragmatic inference is general enough to include any nonmonotonic logic which has an appropriate model theory. More generally, pragmatic entailment includes what has traditionally been called inductive reasoning in Philosophy; in a forthcoming paper it is argued that both inductive reasoning and abductive reasoning can be seen as forms of ampliative context-dependent reasoning, and therefore as forms of pragmatic reasoning.

In related work [2, 16] it is suggested that reasoning of this kind can be implemented by building computational counterparts of pragmatic contexts.

Acknowledgements

I am grateful to the referees for their comments.

References

1. J. Bell, Pragmatic Logics, in: Proc. KR'91, pp. 50-60.
2. J. Bell, Pragmatic Reasoning; a model-based theory. In: *Applied Logic: How, What and Why?*, L. Polos and M. Masuch (eds.), Kluwer Academic Publishers, Amsterdam, 1995, pp. 40-55.

3. G. Brewka, *Nonmonotonic Reasoning: Logical Foundations of Commonsense*, Cambridge University Press, Cambridge, 1991.
4. K. Campbell, *Brainspotting*, Channel 4 Television Publications, London, 1996.
5. D. Makinson, General Patterns in Nonmonotonic Reasoning. In: *Handbook of Logic in Artificial Intelligence and Logic Programming*, D.M. Gabbay, C.J. Hogger and J.A. Robinson (eds.), Vol. 3, pp. 35-110.
6. D.W. Etherington, A Semantics for Default Logic, in Proc. IJCAI'87, pp. 495-498.
7. H. Kamp and U. Reyle, *From Discourse to Logic; Introduction to Modeltheoretic Semantics of Natural Language, Formal Logic and Discourse Representation Theory*, Kluwer Academic Publishers, Dordrecht, 1993.
8. S.C. Levinson, *Pragmatics*, Cambridge University Press, Cambridge, 1983.
9. R.C. Moore, Semantical considerations on nonmonotonic logic. Proc. IJCAI'83, pp. 272-279.
10. J. McCarthy, Circumscription–A Form of Nonmonotonic Reasoning, *Artificial Intelligence* 13, 1980, pp. 27-39.
11. T. Przymusinski, Three-valued nonmonotonic formalisms and semantics of logic programs, *Artificial Intelligence* 49, 1991, pp. 309-343.
12. R. Reiter, A Logic for Default Reasoning, *Artificial Intelligence* 13, 1980, pp. 81-132.
13. Y. Shoham, Nonmonotonic Logics: Meaning and Utility. In: Proc. IJCAI'87, pp. 23-28 .
14. R. Stalnaker, On the Representation of Context, *Journal of Logic, Language and Information*, 7(1), 1998, pp. 3-19.
15. S. Ullman, *High-Level Vision; Object Recognition and Visual Cognition*, MIT Press, Cambridge Massachusetts, 1996.
16. G. White, J. Bell and W. Hodges, Building Models of Prediction Theories. In Proc: KR'98, pp. 557-568.
17. L. Wittgenstein, *Philosophical Investigations*, translated by G.E.M. Anscombe, Blackwell, Oxford, 1953.

A Model of Context Adapted to Domain-Independent Machine Translation

Cathy Berthouzoz

[1] University of Texas at Austin, Department of Philosophy, Campus mail code
C3500, Austin/TX 78712, USA
cathyb@cs.utexas.edu
[2] Université de Genève, Laboratoire d'Analyse et de Technologie du Language, Rue
de Candolle 2, 1203 Genève, Suisse
berthouzoz@lettres.unige.ch

Abstract. In this paper, we explore the integration of context into
domain-independent machine translation based on a pseudo-semantic
approach. We choose a theory of discourse structure (SDRT) to provide the model of context. The incompatibility between the knowledge
poor translation model with the knowledge rich discourse theory leads to
supplement the first with some basic lexical semantics, and to replace the
specific rules of the second with more general pragmatic principles. How
contextual information is used to choose the preferred interpretation of
globally ambiguous sentences is then described with two examples.

1 Introduction

Language is a means of communication. As speaker/writer of a language we use
our linguistic and world knowledge to choose words that best express what we
mean – or do not mean. Words are then combined into bigger units to form sentences, which in turn are combined into texts. As hearer/reader, we use the same
knowledge to infer what the speaker/writer intended to communicate. The task
of translation involves yet one more step: expressing within the target language
what was communicated in the source language.

It is a matter-of-fact that machine translation is not yet equipped with the
necessary tools to adequately translate real texts in unrestricted domains. Such a
task will become feasible once we will be able to come up with interpretation and
disambiguation models that can cope with huge amounts of linguistic and extra-
linguistic knowledge, while minimizing computational costs. However, a small
step toward this idealistic, long-term goal is to switch from sentence translation
to *sentence-in-context* translation.

The sentence-in-context translation approach follows a pseudo-semantic transfer model as proposed by Etchegoyen and Wehrli in [7] and [8]: the functional
words (prepositions, determiners, conjunctions), along with the aspectual information, are given a full semantic interpretation, while the open class words
(nouns, adjectives and verbs) are lexically transferred. However, it departs from

the pseudo-semantic transfer approach in the sense that contextual information is integrated into both the analysis and transfer processes.

During source analysis, the need for contextual information is twofold. First, to achieve a full interpretation of the source sentence, antecedents need to be attributed to anaphora. Second, to resolve global ambiguity, the most appropriate interpretation of the current sentence in the current context need to be selected. As a result, the selected interpretation is included into the current context.

During transfer, contextual information is needed to disambiguate multiple bilingual choices. The use of contextual information leads to another augmentation of the pseudo-semantic approach, in the sense that the pseudo-semantic representation of the sentences will include some semantic information for the open class words. The integration of the context into the translation process is shown in Fig. 1 below.

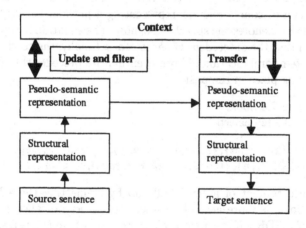

Fig. 1. Model of sentence-in-context translation. ↑= analysis, ↓= generation

The context is heterogeneous – various types of information come into play during the interpretation of a sentence. Moreover, since it grows as the discourse goes on, a theory of dynamic discourse interpretation is chosen as framework, namely the *Segmented Discourse Representation Theory* (SDRT) proposed by Asher in [1]. Thus, the model of context is provided by the theory. However, the standard theory has to be adapted to the needs of domain-independent machine translation on the one hand, to the specific model assumed here on the other hand. These adaptations will be described in Sect. 2. Two examples of global disambiguation within this model will then be discussed in Sect. 3.

2 Adaptation of SDRT to Machine Translation

2.1 Standard SDRT

SDRT constructs the discourse structure incrementally, by connecting each new sentence to the structure already built, by means of discourse relations. Although this theory is based on *Discourse Representation Theory* (DRT) as defined by Kamp and Reyle in [10], it is better suited to machine translation, since the structure of the text is reflected in the representation of the discourse. It is not the case in DRT, where the whole discourse ends up with one huge flat structure. From the generation point of view, we need to have clues on the source text structure, because the target text should reflect the source structure as much as possible, within the target language adequacy, as defined by Doherty in [6].

Within SDRT, the semantic content of a clause is represented by a *Discourse Representation Structure* (DRS). A DRS k is a pair $< U_k, Con_k >$ where U_k is the set of discourse entities – called *discourse referents* – denoting individuals, eventualities and times, and Con_k is the set of conditions on those entities. To illustrate these notions, the semantic represention of the two simple sentences (1a-b) is given in (2a-b), where x and y are discourse referents denoting individuals, u is a discourse referent representing a pronoun, e_1 and e_2 denote eventualities, and n denotes the speech time, now. The equation $u = x$ represents the information that the antecedent of *she* is *Mary*. Finally, the condition $e_x < n$ states that the temporal location of both eventualities precedes the speech time, *i.e.* that they took place in the past.

(1)a. Mary read a book.
   b. Then, she fell asleep.

(2)a. $k_1 :=< \{x, y, e_1, n\}, \{Mary(x), book(y), e_1\text{-}read(x, y), e_1 < n\} >$
   b. $k_2 :=< \{u, e_2, n\}, \{u = x, e_2\text{-}fell\text{-}asleep(u), e_2 < n\} >$

The semantic content of a text, built up by connecting these DRSs with rhetorical relations, is represented by a recursive structure called a *Segmented DRS* (SDRS). An SDRS K is a pair $< U_K, Con_K >$, where U_K is a set of DRSs or SDRSs, and Con_K a set of conditions on those (S)DRSs, that is, a set of discourse relations. New material can be attached only to *open* constituents, *i.e.* constituents on the *right frontier* of the discourse, as defined by Asher, and Grosz and Sidner in [1] and [9]. As an illustration, (3) is the representation of (1), which is a simple narrative text.

(3) $K :=< \{k_1, k_2\}, \{ Narration (k_1, k_2)\} >$

Discourse relations are usually signalled by syntactic markers such as *then, as a result, however*, as demonstrated by Knott in [11]. In the absence of such cue phrases, discourse relations need to be inferred from the reader's knowledge base, especially world knowledge, as noted by Asher and Lascarides in [1], [4] and [12]. Section 2.3 defines the conditions under which discourse relations can be inferred without resorting to world knowledge.

2.2 Foreground and Background Contexts

When inferring a relation, the reader's knowledge base contains the SDRS of the text so far, the logical form of the current sentence, the assumption that the text is coherent, all the pragmatic and world knowledge[1], and all the laws of logic. Within standard SDRT, the knowledge base is thus unstructured. Intuitively, however, the contextual information can be partitioned into *foreground* and *background* information, the former being expressed in the discourse, the latter not[2]. Thus, the foreground context contains the SDRS of the text so far, while the background context is made up of the pragmatic and world knowledge[3]. The foreground context is domain-independent, and (partly) language-independent, while the background context is (partly) domain-dependent. If the discourse relations are introduced by syntactic markers, no inferences are to be made, thus it is not necessary to resort to the background context at this stage of processing. However, it still needs to be accessed during the disambiguation phase.

In order to infer the discourse relations, SDRT strongly relies on world knowledge. This is incompatible with a domain-independent translation system, since it would amount to implementing vasts amounts of knowledge. Moreover, the translation model assumed here does not derive a semantic representation for the open class words. Hence, in order for SDRT to be meaningful within this model, a compromise has to be reached. Therefore, the pseudo-semantics will be supplemented with some lexical semantics necessary to infer the most important discourse relations. As a result, the background context will be kept as general as possible.

2.3 Discourse Relations

Another departure from standard SDRT is that not all the relations defined in the theory are inferable from the discourse. In the absence of syntactic markers that introduce discourse relations, the only relations that are inferred without resort to world knowledge are *Narration*, *Background* and *Elaboration*.

Let $< \tau, \alpha, \beta >$ express the fact that the clause β is to be attached to the clause α in the context τ, and $R(\alpha, \beta)$ that β is connected to α by the relation R. Then, the discourse relations and their entailments are defined by the following pragmatic rules, adapted from [2], [4], and [12]:

Narration If $< \tau, \alpha, \beta >$, then, in the absence of any other information, *Narration* (α, β) holds.

Background If $< \tau, \alpha, \beta >$, and the eventuality of β is a state, then *Background* (α, β) holds.

Elaboration If $< \tau, \alpha, \beta >$, and the event of β is negated, then *Elaboration* (α, β) holds.

---

[1] The distinction between defeasible and indefeasible knowledge is not at issue here.

[2] This distinction is also made by Buvač in [5] between discourse contexts and knowledge base contexts.

[3] The assumption of coherence and the laws of logic are not contextual information.

As an illustration, instances of *Narration, Background,* and *Elaboration* are presented in the simple discourses (4a-c) below. Although some sequences of sentences may suggest other rhetorical relations – for instance in (4c), the second sentence is more likely understood as the result of the argument – the proposed relations can be inferred without resort to deep semantic or world knowledge.

(4)a. John went home directly after work. He cooked a delicious dinner for Mary.
   b. She arrived home very late that night. The dinner was burned.
   c. They had a big argument. They did not speak to each others for several days.

Narration being the default relation, incoherence arises when two clauses related by a *Narration* do not elatorate a common topic. However, incoherence does not block the translation, since even an incoherent source text should be translated into the target language. I will therefore assume a weak notion of *Narration,* in the sense that it does not trigger the creation of a topic constituent, even in the cases of coherent text. As for *Elaboration,* the elaborated constituent serves as topic for the continuating constituent(s), allowing new material to be attached to it, although it is normally closed for further attachments.

The *Background* relation leads to the creation of a *Foreground-Background Pair* (FBP) as defined in [2]: the information contained in α and β is combined into a new constituent, noted here $\alpha + \beta$, which becomes the new site for further combinations. Although β remains an open constituent, new attachments are constrained by the following rules:

Constraint 1 on Background If *Background*(α, β) holds, then β is closed for *Narration.*

Constraint 2 on Background If *Background*(α, β) holds, then *Background* (γ, β) holds only if $\gamma = \alpha$.

The first constraint rules out, for instance, the attachment of the first sentence of (4c), α, to the last sentence of (4b) with *Narration.* The only possible attachement for α is thus *Narration*$(FBP(4b), \alpha)$. The second constraint simply forbids the attachment of the same background information to two different constituents. Section 3.1 provides an example of the application of these constraints.

I define a third rule that constrains the attachment of two *Background* relations to the same constituent:

Constraint 3 on Background If *Background*(α, β) holds, then *Background* (α, γ) holds only if γ is consistent with α.

Without going into details – consistency will be defined in Sect(s). 2.4 and 2.5 – let simply say that this constraint rules out attachments that lead to contradictory DRS conditions. An example of the application of this constraint is given in Sect. 3.2.

The temporal implications that the discourse relations entail about the eventualities they connect are defined by the following rules:

Axiom on Narration If *Narration*(α, β) holds, then the event of α precedes the event of β.

Axiom on Background If *Background*(α, β) holds, then the state of β overlaps the eventuality of α.

The causal implications that the discourse relations entail about the eventualities they connect are defined by the next rules:

Axiom on Explanation If *Explanation*(α, β) holds, then the event of β caused the event of α.

Axiom on Result If *Result*(α, β) holds, then the event of α caused the event of β.

Note that causality have also temporal implications, since the cause must have occurred before the effect. This is stated by the following rule:

Causes precede Effects If the event e_1 causes the event e_2, then e_1 precedes e_2.

Although temporal entailments are of no use during disambiguation, they will be of importance during generation, in order to produce the adequat sequence of tenses, thus improving the quality of the translation.

2.4 General Pragmatic Rules

Discourse relations associated with specific lexical rules are used by Asher and Lascarides to disambiguate word senses in [4]. In the pseudo-semantic approach word senses are expressed only in the bilingual lexicon. Thus, disambiguation will take place during transfer. This is not a matter at issue here, although it is crucial to translation. On the contrary, global ambiguity has to be resolved before transfer, since it leads to more than one pseudo-semantic representation, and only one is transferred, the preferred one, if possible. To resolve this ambiguity with contextual information without relying on world knowledge is possible only with general pragmatic principles.

Preferred Interpretation. The first general principal states that the preferred interpretation is the one that is connected with the strongest discourse relation.

Definition 1. *Let x be an open constituent, α an ambiguous clause, $i_1, \ldots, i_n, n$ possible interpretations of α, $R_{ij}(x, i_i) for i = 1, \ldots, n, j = 1, \ldots, m$, the discourse relations connecting an interpretation to an open constituent in the context, and $str(R_{ij})$ the strength of relation R_{ij}. Then, the preferred interpretation is i_i such that $\forall k, 1 \leq k \leq n$, and $\forall l, 1 \leq l \leq m, str(R_{ij}) > str(R_{kl})$.*

Strengthening Discourse Relations. The second principle states that a discourse relation is strengthened by anaphoric links. Anaphoric links hold between a pronoun and its antecedent, or between a referential expression and its antecedent. Referential expressions trigger presuppositions about the existence of their antecedent in the discourse universe. While antecedents of pronouns have to be expressed in the discourse, antecedents of referential expressions may be implicit: they are part of the meaning of the words without being expressed themselves (see Sect. 3.2 for an example of implicit antecedent). Another difference between the two kinds of anaphora is that the discourse interpretation fails if a pronoun lacks its antecedent, while this is not the case for referential expressions.

Definition 2. *Let α and β be two DRSs, x an individual discourse referent in α, u a discourse referent representing an anaphor in β, and $R(\alpha, \beta)$ a discourse relation holding between α and β. Then, if $u = x$ is a condition of β, set $str(R) := str_1(R)$, with $str_1(R) > str(R)$.*

Inconsistency. The third general principle states that there is inconsistency between two representations if they contain antynomic DRS conditions holding at the same time.

Definition 3. *Let α and β be two DRSs, x a discourse referent of α, u a discourse referent of β, con_x a condition on x in α, con_u a condition on u in β, and $R(\alpha, \beta)$ a discourse relation holding between α and β. Then, if $u = x$ is a DRS condition of β, and $con_u = \sim con_x$, then β is inconsistent with α.*

In Sect. 3, we will see how these principles work during disambiguation of globally ambiguous sentences.

2.5 Basic Lexical Semantics

Although the pragmatic principles defined in the previous section are meant to be applied on pseudo-semantic representations, *i.e.* representations that do not include a semantic interpretation for the open class words, they have indeed lexical semantics consequences. First, the anaphoric link between a referential expression and its antecedent should hold even if the antecedent is not expressed in the discourse, but it is implicit to its meaning. For instance, in Sect. 3.2 below, the expression *the water* in sentence *I didn't stay long in the water* refers to the water that is implicit to the activity of swimming introduced by the previous sentence *I went to swim*.

The proposed solution is to supplement the lexical entry of the verbs of activity with the usual location of the activity. For example, swimming is normally done in water, flying is normally performed in the air, and running is normally done on earth. This can be represented as a kind of *shadow* argument as defined by Pustejovsky in [13], which is then accessible for presupposition binding in case of referential expression/antecedent linking, but not for pronoun/antecedent linking. This implies the development of a more general theory of argument structure representation, which falls outside the scope of this article.

Second, inconsistency between DRSs can be signalled by structural clues like negation: the same condition holds in both DRSs, but it is negated in one of them. In the absence of such a clue, the semantic features of the conditions themselves have to be checked. In the absence of a full semantic representation for open class words, inconsistency may be signalled by the relation of antonymy holding between lexical items. Therefore, the lexicon needs to include this relation between antonymic pairs of words such as *cold/hot, big/small, love/hate*, etc...

3 Contextual Resolution of Global Ambiguity

Natural language interpretation requires contextual information because ambiguity is one of the pervasive characteristics of natural language. Global ambiguity, for instance, arises when the analysis of a sentence generates more than one interpretation. Within a translation system, one interpretation has to be selected for further processing. Therefore, contextual information is used as a filter on the set of hypotheses. This role will be described with two examples, an instance of literal/idiomatic interpretation, and an instance of anaphoric/expletive interpretation.

3.1 Example 1: He kicked the bucket

Even if the context is an essential part of natural language interpretation, it is not an inherent characteristic of natural language: words and expressions do actually have a meaning by themselves. We all know what the expression *He kicked the bucket* means outside any context. Our lexical knowledge tells us that *he* refers to a male individual that was previously introduced in the discourse, *kick* describes an action performed with one's foot toward a physical object, and that *the bucket* is a physical object, used as a container. Our grammatical knowledge tells us that the agent of the action is the male individual referred to by *he*, that the object on which the kicking was done is the specific object referred to by *the bucket*, and that this action was performed in the past, and is actually completed.

We can use this sentence to describe a specific man performing this physical action as expression of his anger, as in discourse (5) below. But *kick* and *the bucket* together form an idiomatic expression meaning *to die*. Thus, we can use the same sentence to express the fact that a specific man has died, as in discourse (6).

(5)a. Mary came into the room with a bucket of water.

    b. John was angry.

    c. He kicked the bucket.

d. As a result, the water spilled over the floor.

(6)a. Max had a car accident last week.
  b. He was dead drunk.
  c. He kicked the bucket.
  d. As a result, his wife is staying alone with four kids.

When translating this sentence into French, the right interpretation has to be picked up in order to generate the correct target expression: the idiomatic expression *Il a cassé sa pipe* (7d) is not appropriate in discourse (7), and the literal expression *Il donna un coup de pied dans le baquet* (8c) has nothing to do with the story in (8).

(7)a. Marie entra dans la pièce avec un baquet d'eau.
  b. Jean était en colère.
  c. Il donna un coup de pied dans le baquet.
  d. ? Il a cassé sa pipe.
  e. $$ En conséquence, l'eau s'est renversée sur le sol.

(8)a. Max a eu un accident de voiture la semaine passée.
  b. Il était ivre mort.
  c. ? Il donna un coup de pied dans le baquet.
  d. $$ Il a cassé sa pipe.
  e. En conséquence, sa femme reste seule avec quatre gamins.

How to rule out the wrong interpretation? Let α, β, and δ be the representations of the sentences (5a-b,d), γ_l and γ_i be the literal and idiomatic representations of sentence (5c), and τ the representation of the context, $\tau = \emptyset$ before processing (5a), and $\tau = \{\alpha\}$ after. When processing (5b), α is the only attachment point, thus we try to attach β to α, so we have the hypothesis $< \alpha, \alpha, \beta >$. The main eventuality of β being a state, we infer that β forms a background to α i.e. the relation $Background(\alpha, \beta)$. This relation leads to the creation of the FBP $\alpha + \beta$.

When processing (5c), there are two possible attachment points, $\alpha + \beta$, and β, so we have the four hypotheses $< \tau, \alpha + \beta, \gamma_l >$, $< \tau, \alpha + \beta, \gamma_i >$, $< \tau, \beta, \gamma_l >$, and $< \tau, \beta, \gamma_i >$. In the case of $< \tau, \alpha + \beta, \gamma_l >$, the only relation that can be inferred is $Narration(\alpha + \beta, \gamma_l)$, and the anaphor *he* can be resolved with *John*. The presupposition triggered by the referential expression *the bucket* can be bound within $\alpha + \beta$, thus strengthening the discourse relation $Narration(\alpha + \beta, \gamma_l)$.

$Narration(\beta, \gamma_l)$ and $Background(\beta, \gamma_l)$ are ruled out by Constraints 1 and 2 on Background respectively. $Result(\beta, \gamma_l)$, would hold if we had a law establishing the causality between being angry and kicking something. This is a far too specific law to be included in the knowledge base of the system as presented here.

In the case of the idiomatic interpretation, the same line of reasoning leads us to infer $Narration(\alpha + \beta, \gamma_i)$, and to reject any attachment to β. In that case, however, there is no discourse referent for the referential expression, since it has no meaning outside the verb meaning, there is thus no anaphoric link. Therefore γ_l is the preferred interpretation, since it is connected to the context with the strongest relation.

This prediction is confirmed by sentence (5d). Contrary to the previous sentences, the discourse relation is given by the syntactic marker *as a result*. As the only attachment point is γ, we infer $Result(\gamma_l, \delta)$ and $Result(\gamma_i, \delta)$ for the literal and idiomatic interpretation respectively. The referential expression *the water* triggers a presupposition that can be bound within γ_l through a referential chain linking *the bucket* in γ_l and *a bucket of water* in $\alpha + \beta$, in case of the literal expression, strengthening $Result(\gamma_l, \delta)$. It cannot be bound in case of the idiomatic expression. The preferred interpretation is still γ_l.

As for discourse (6), the discourse structure is the same, but in this case, the presupposition triggered by the referential expression *the bucket* in the literal interpretation cannot be bound. The preferred interpretation is then γ_i. The discourse structures of discourses (5) and (6) are given in (9a) and (9b) respectively.

(9)a. $K_{(5)} :=< \{\alpha, \beta, \gamma_l, \delta\}, \{ Background\,(\alpha, \beta),\ Narration\,(\alpha+\beta, \gamma_l),\ Result\,(\gamma_l, \delta)\} >$

b. $K_{(6)} :=< \{\alpha, \beta, \gamma_i, \delta\}, \{ Background\,(\alpha, \beta),\ Narration\,(\alpha+\beta, \gamma_i),\ Result\,(\gamma_i, \delta)\} >$

3.2 Example 2: It was too cold

Outside any context, the pronoun *it* is ambiguous between its expletive and anaphoric uses in the simple sentence (10a) below. Therefore, the three sentences in (10b) are possible translations into French. Adding context allows us to reduce the ambiguity. For instance, in discourse (11), both anaphoric and weather interpretations are possible, but the preferred interpretation seems to be that the water was too cold (12c).

(10)a. It was too cold.

b. Il faisait trop froid/ Il était trop froid/Elle était trop froide.

(11)a. Yesterday, I went to swim.

b. I didn't stay long in the water.

c. It was too cold.

(12)a. Hier je suis allée nager.

b. Je ne suis pas restée longtemps dans l'eau.

c. $$ Elle était trop foide.

d. Il faisait trop froid.

Let α, and β, be the representations of the sentences (11a-b), γ_e and γ_a be the expletive – in this case the weather use – and anaphoric representations of sentence (11c), and τ the representation of the context, as in previous example.

When processing (11b), α is the only attachment point, thus we have the hypothesis $< \alpha, \alpha, \beta >$. From the negation in β, we infer $Elaboration(\alpha, \beta)$, and α serves as topic for β.

When processing (11c), both α and β are open constituents, so we have the four hypotheses $< \tau, \alpha, \gamma_e >$, $< \tau, \alpha, \gamma_a >$, $< \tau, \beta, \gamma_e >$ and $< \tau, \beta, \gamma_a >$. The eventuality in γ being a state, we can infer the four relations $Background(\alpha, \gamma_e)$, $Background(\alpha, \gamma_a)$, $Background(\beta, \gamma_e)$ and $Background(\beta, \gamma_a)$. In the case of the anaphoric interpretation, the anaphor it can be resolved with $water$ in β, but not in α: the relation $Background(\beta, \gamma_a)$ is strengthened, while the relation $Background(\alpha, \gamma_a)$ is ruled out. In the case of γ_e, the relations $Background(\alpha, \gamma_e)$ and $Background(\beta, \gamma_e)$ hold, but as they are not strengthened by anaphoric links, the preferred interpretation is γ_a.

If no mention of water is made, as in discourse (13), there is no antecedent, the anaphor cannot be resolved, thus ruling out the anaphoric interpretation (14). In that case, both relations $Background(\alpha, \gamma_e)$ and $Background(\beta, \gamma_e)$ hold. The discourse structures of (11) and (13) are given in (15a) and (15b) respectively.

(13)a. Yesterday, I went to swim.
  b. I didn't stay long.
  c. It was too cold.

(14)a. Hier, je suis allée nager.
  b. Je ne suis pas restée longtemps.
  c. Il faisait trop froid.
  d. # Elle était trop froide.

(15)a. $K_{(11)} :=< \{\alpha, \beta, \gamma_a\}, \{$ $Elaboration$ (α, β), $Background$ $(\beta, \gamma_a)\} >$
  b. $K_{(13)} :=< \{\alpha, \beta, \gamma_e\}, \{$ $Elaboration$ (α, β), $Background$ (α, γ_e), $Background$ $(\beta, \gamma_e)\} >$

If we change the context by adding some information about the weather as in (16a), the preferred interpretation is the anaphoric one (17). Let α, β, γ, δ_a and δ_e be the representations of the sentences of discourse (16). The main eventuality in α being a state, $Background(\beta, \alpha)$ is inferred, leading to the creation of the FBP $\alpha + \beta$. γ can be attached to $\alpha + \beta$ and δ with $Elaboration$, giving the hypotheses $Elaboration(\alpha + \beta, \gamma)$, and $Elaboration(\beta, \gamma)$. For both hypotheses, δ_a can be attached with $Background$ only to γ in order for the anaphor it to be resolved with $water$. As for δ_e, its attachment to $\alpha + \beta$ is ruled out by the Constraint 3 on Background and the Principle of Inconsistency, since the weather cannot be hot and cold at the same time, but it can be attached to γ with $Background$. $Background(\gamma, \delta_a)$ being the strongest relation, the preferred interpretation is δ_a (17d).

(16)a. Yesterday, it was really hot.
  b. I went to swim.
  c. I didn't stay long in the water.
  d. It was too cold.

(17)a. Hier, il faisait très chaud.
  b. Je suis allée nager.
  c. Je ne suis pas restée longtemps dans l'eau.
  d. Il faisait trop froid.
  e. $$ Elle était trop froide.

Note that if the relation between γ and δ is *Narration*, as this is the case in (18), the weather interpretation is the preferred one (19c). To treat discourse like this one requires a law stating that the water in a pool does not suddenly become cold. It is a far too specific world knowledge to be included in the system, which will make the wrong prediction. The discourse structures of discourses (16) and (18) are given under (20a) and (20b) respectively.

(18)a. Yesterday, it was really hot. I went to swim.
  b. I stayed in the water for a couple of hours.
  c. Then, it got cold.

(19)a. Hier, il faisait très chaud. Je suis allée nager.
  b. Je suis restée dans l'eau pendant plusieurs heures.
  c. $$ Puis, il a fait froid.
  d. Puis, elle s'est refroidie.

(20)a. $K_{(16)} :=< \{\alpha, \beta, \gamma, \delta_a\}, \{$ *Background* (β, α), *Elaboration* $(\alpha + \beta, \gamma)$, *Elaboration* (β, γ), *Background* $(\gamma, \delta_a)\} >$
  b. # $K_{(18)} :=< \{\alpha, \beta, \gamma, \delta_a\}, \{$ *Background* (β, α), *Narration* $(\alpha + \beta, \gamma)$, *Narration* (β, γ), *Narration* $(\gamma, \delta_a)\} >$

4 Concluding Remarks

In this paper, it has been proposed to supplement a domain-independent translation system with the context provided by a theory of discourse structure, namely SDRT. However, the context as provided by SDRT is dependent on world knowledge, while the pseudo-semantic approach of the translation system does not provide the necessary semantics. It has thus been proposed to replace the specific rules of SDRT with more general pragmatic principles, and to augment the lexicon with some basic lexical semantics. The applicability of these principles has been shown by two examples of disambiguation of globally ambiguous sentences, according to different contexts.

The generality of the background context is meant to facilitate its integration into the domain-independent translation system. However, it has been pointed out that without resort to some world knowledge, the system cannot make the right prediction for every cases. Further research will tell how much world knowledge can be added to the system without compromising its domain-independence.

Lexical semantics proved to be crucial. Pseudo-semantics alone is not powerful enough for disambiguation. There is a need for an adequat representation of the semantics of the the open class words. Again, further research will tell how much details this representation should include in order to be useful for disambiguation, not only of source interpretations, but also of bilingual correspondences.

Acknowledgments. The author gratefully acknowledges the Swiss National Science Foundation fellowship 81GE-54587. Many thanks go to Eric Wehrli, for steady encouragement, and to Ana Alves, Nicholas Asher, Tim Fernando, and Isabel Gomez Tzurruka for helpful discussions.

References

1. Asher, N.: Reference to Abstract Objects in Discourse. Studies in Linguistics and Philosophy. Kluwer Academic Publishers (1993)
2. Asher, N., Aurnague, M., Bras, M., Sablayrolles, P., Vieu, L.: De l'Espace-Temps dans l'Analyse du Discours. Sémiotiques **9**: Théories Sémantiques et Modélisation, Didier-Érudition, CNRS, France (1995) 11-62
3. Asher, N., Morreau, M.: Commonsense Entailment: a Modal Theory of Nonmonotonic Reasoning. Proc. of the 12th Int. Joint Conf. on Art. Int. (IJCAI'91) (1991) 387-392
4. Asher, N., Lascarides, A.: Lexical Disambiguation in a Discourse Context. J. Semantics **12** (1995) 69-108
5. Buvač, S.: Resolving Lexical Ambiguity Using a Formal Theory of Context. In K. Van Deemter and S. Peters (eds), Semantic Ambiguity and Underspecification. Cambridge University Press: CSLI Lecture Notes **55** (1996)
6. Doherty, M.: Textual Garden-Paths – Parametrized Obstacles to Target Language Adequate Translations. In C. Hauenschild and S. Heizmann (eds), Machine Translation and Translation Theory. Berlin, New York: Mouton de Gruyter (1997) 69-89
7. Etchegoyen, T.: Génération Automatique de Phrases. Le système GBGen. Notes Tech. 98-1, Université de Genève (1998)
8. Etchegoyen, T., Wehrli, E.: Traduction Automatique et Structures d'Interface. Proc. Trait. Aut. du Lang. Nat. (TALN 98), Paris, France (1998) 2-11
9. Grosz, B.J., Sidner, C.L.: Attention, Intentions, and the Structure of Discourse. Computational Linguistics **12(3)** (1986) 175-204
10. Kamp, H., Reyle, U.: From Discourse to Logic. Dordrecht: Kluwer (1993)
11. Knott, A.: A Data-Driven Methodology for Motivating a Set of Coherence Relations. PhD diss., University of Edinburgh (1995)
12. Lascarides, A., Asher, N.: Temporal Interpretation, Discourse Relations and Commonsense Entailment. Linguistics and Philosophy **16(5)** (1993) 437-493
13. Pustejovsky, J.: The Generative Lexicon. Cambridge: The MIT Press (1995)

Three Forms of Contextual Dependence

Claudia Bianchi

Università del Piemonte orientale (Vercelli, Italy) & Crea (Paris, France)
bianchi@poly.polytechnique.fr

Abstract. The paper emphasizes the inadequacy of formal semantics, the classical paradigm in semantics, in treating contextual dependence. Some phenomena of contextual dependence threaten one central assumption of the classical paradigm, namely the idea that linguistic expressions have a fixed meaning, and utterances have truth conditions well defined. It is possible to individuate three forms of contextual dependence: the one affecting pure indexicals, the one affecting demonstratives and "contextual expressions", and the one affecting all linguistic expressions. The third type of dependence is top-down: context, and not only linguistic material, shows which variables must be instantiated, relying on context itself. The generalization of underdetermination to all linguistic expressions is in fact a kind of meta-dependence: the mode of dependence itself depends on context.

Introduction

The main purpose of my paper is to emphasize the inadequacy of formal semantics - the classical paradigm (CP) in semantics - in treating contextual dependence. Some phenomena of contextual dependence threaten one central assumption of CP - namely the idea that linguistic expressions have a fixed meaning and utterances have truth conditions well defined. It is possible to individuate three forms of contextual dependence, to which correspond three categories of linguistic expressions.

1. Pure indexicals show a form of dependence that CP can handle without modifying its general structure. Determination of the truth conditions of an utterance containing an indexical expression, although indirect, is mechanical, functional, hence semantic.
2. Demonstratives and "contextual expressions" show a form of dependence more threatening for CP: the functional solution at work for pure indexicals cannot be applied to those kinds of expressions. A pragmatic processor is brought into play to identify the proposition expressed, i.e. the semantic level. Therefore, linguistic meaning *underdetermines* truth conditions of an utterance containing a demonstrative or a contextual expression.

3. Authors like John Searle or Charles Travis point out a form of contextual dependence affecting all linguistic expressions, even after disambiguation and saturation of the variables corresponding to pure indexicals, demonstratives and contextual expressions. This kind of underdetermination is top-down: context, and not only linguistic material, shows which variables must be instantiated, relying on context itself.

Top-down dependence generalizes the underdetermination - which becomes a *property* of linguistic meaning in general: linguistic meaning underdetermines truth conditions of any utterance. In the last section of my paper I show that the generalization of underdetermination to all linguistic expressions is in fact a kind of *meta-dependence*: the idea is that the mode of dependence itself depends on context.

1 The First Form of Contextual Dependence

Pure indexicals[1] show a form of dependence that CP can handle without modifying its general structure. CP identifies meaning and truth conditions: the existence of expressions as *I* or *today* in natural language obliges CP to rectify this identification. The *linguistic meaning* of an indexical expression (kaplanian *character*) determines its semantic value (kaplanian *content*): it is a function from contextual factors to semantic values. Determination of the truth conditions of an utterance containing an indexical expression, although indirect, is mechanical, functional, hence semantic. The truth conditions of an indexical sentence as

I am tired

are determined indirectly, by the linguistic meaning of the sentence and a local and precise aspect of the context – fixed by the character of *I*. The *mode of dependence* itself is determined by the conventions of the language: the character of *I* specifies *how* the content of the expression is determined by the context – in other words, character specifies which particular feature of the context fixes the referent.

2 The Second Form of Contextual Dependence

Demonstratives show a form of dependence more threatening for CP: the functional solution at work for pure indexicals cannot be applied to demonstratives.

The truth conditions of a demonstrative sentence like

She is tired

depend on a contextual factor (the referent of *she*) which is part of the truth-conditional content of the sentence.[2] The linguistic meaning of *she* does not specify this aspect of the content – which the addressee must determine independently,

---

[1] On the distinction between pure indexicals and demonstratives the canonical reference is [12].
[2] Cf. [22], p.5.

reconstructing the speaker's communicative intentions.[3] Therefore semantic reference is determined trough the determination of pragmatic reference: a pragmatic processor is brought into play to identify "what is said" - the proposition expressed, i.e. the semantic level.

"Contextual expressions"[4] (possessive constructions as *John's book*, name-name constructions as *apple-juice chair*, some adjectives like *fast*, or *easy*) are in many respects similar to demonstratives: they can take an indefinite number of senses depending on the context of use. For example, the possessive construction *John's book* indicate the existence of a relation between John and the book, but this relation must be contextually determined for each occurrence of the construction. So *John's book* could refer to the book written by John, or read by John, or bought, burnt, lost, imagined, etc., by John. There is neither a rule, nor an automatic linguistic procedure that could identify the nature of the relation independently of any context.

Demonstratives and contextual expressions have neither a pre-assigned value (as the non contextual expression) nor a mechanical rule of saturation (as the indexical expressions): their semantic value is fixed by the speakers intentions. The linguistic meaning of those kinds of expressions *locate* the underdetermination, pointing out the presence of a variable which must be instantiated: but linguistic meaning does not state *how* the variable must be instantiated.

Therefore, the linguistic meaning of a sentence containing a demonstrative or a contextual expression underdetermines the truth conditions of the sentence.

Against this refutation, CP can follow two types of strategies:

☐ a. the first one concerning the *extension* of underdetermination: the phenomenon is real, but restricted to only a few categories of expressions, fully specifiable;

☐ b. the second one concerning the *form* of underdetermination: for those categories there is still a bottom-up determination, i. e. a determination constrained by linguistic meaning for all tokens of the expression type; therefore a mandatory determination.

3 The Third Form of Contextual Dependence

Authors like John Searle[5] and Charles Travis[6] point out a form of contextual dependence affecting *all* linguistic expressions. This kind of underdetermination is *top-down*: context, and not only linguistic material, determines which variables must be instantiated relying on context itself.

For Searle and Travis the existence of this generalized form of contextual dependence is an empirical hypothesis, rather than a conclusion following from a genuine argument. Their examples *show* the underdetermination affecting sentences

---

[3] See [13], [3] and [4].
[4] I borrow the term from [7].
[5] Cf. [23], [24] and [25].
[6] Cf.[27], [28] and [29.

apparently without any possibility of variation in truth conditions. In their well known thought experiments for sentences like

The cat is on the mat
Bob cut the grass
Bill opened the door,

Searle and Travis set up anomalous or strange contexts: the cat and the mat travelling in interstellar space, people cutting grass as a cake, people opening doors with a scalpel. The examples show that every sentence has a literal meaning only against a Background of contextual assumptions fixing its truth conditions: the Background states, for example, that gravitation is, or is not, effective, or the way people "normally" cut things, and grass in particular, or open doors. And the examples show easily that the Background is not unique, constant, fixed once and for ever.[7]

To understand which kind of contextual dependence Searle and Travis are pointing out, let us examine some of Searle's examples containing the verb *cut:*[8]

(1) *Bill cut the grass*
(2) *The barber cut Tom's hair*
(3) *Sally cut the cake*
(4) *I just cut my skin*
(5) *The tailor cut the cloth.*

In (1) – (5) the linguistic meaning of *cut* does not change, but its interpretation is different in each utterance: so one could ask oneself if the sentence (3) is true, if Sally starts mowing Mary's cake. What constitutes satisfying the truth conditions of *cut* is different in each case: the linguistic meaning of the verb determines a different contribution to the truth conditions of each sentence.

3.1 The Indexical Conception

The indexical conception (the First Form of Contextual Dependence) applied to examples (1) – (5) generalizes the idea of linguistic meaning as a function, and allows CP to maintain the idea of a conventional meaning which is fixed: the function associated to *cut* is always the same, and its different values depend on the different arguments it can take (grass, hair, cake...).

Searle rejects the indexical conception: one can always obtain for (1) the interpretation of *cut* which is normally obtained for (3). It is easy to build up an appropriate context: just imagine that (1) is uttered in a firm selling strips of grass turf to people who want an instant lawn, where *cutting grass* means "slicing" it into strips, as with a cake.[9]

---

[7] See [23].
[8] [24], p.221.
[9] See [25], pp.24-25.

3.2 The Demonstrative Conception

Let us see if the Second Form of Contextual Dependence would do for *cut*. Searle defends the idea that the linguistic meaning of (1) specifies a set of truth conditions which is different in different contexts. Let us examine two possible contexts for (1): in C_1, ("Gardening") the appropriate set of truth conditions will be something like: "Bob cut the grass with a lawnmower". In C_2 ("Selling instant lawns") the appropriate set of truth conditions will be something like: "Bob cut the grass with a knife". Let us assume that the element differentiating the two sets of truth conditions is the "way of cutting" grass – a contextual feature responsible for the variation in truth conditions. The feature "way of cutting" has to be specified in order for (1) to have determined truth conditions – as it was for contextual expressions. It looks like the verb contains a *variable* (here the "way of cutting") which must be instantiated for *every* occurrence of the verb, in *every* context.

3.3 Top-down Dependence

Searle's argument (and Travis's) is still more radical. As a matter of fact, one can imagine contexts where the feature "way of cutting" has no relevance at all in determining the truth conditions of (1). Hence the "way of cutting" is not a feature of the context that the addressee *must necessarily* specify in every context – as it happens for a contextual expression or a possessive construction, where saturation is mandatory, forced by linguistic material, therefore necessary for the expression in order to have a determined semantic value. Imagine a group of botanists studying a new variety of transgenetic grass, extremely resistant (C_3): Bob has tried for months to cut just a blade of grass, or even to stab the lawn once. In this context the relevant contextual feature is the *variety* of grass that Bob has, or has not, cut – it doesn't matter if with a lawnmower, or a knife, or scissors or a scalpel. This sort of examples is different from the examples of underdetermination of demonstratives and contextual expressions – where the feature that had to be specified *was always the same*. The context specifies which variable must be instantiated - "way of cutting", or "variety" or "quantity". On the one hand, the linguistic meaning of *cut* doesn't impose a particular instantiation of the feature "way of cutting": it is the context which impose it. On the other hand, even when this particular feature is specified, it is still possible to modify the truth conditions of (1), modifying other features of the context: those features will then be responsible for the underdetermination of (1).

3.4 Unarticulated Constituents

The analysis of contextual dependence, as I have exposed it, is in many ways comparable to the one held by John Perry in many papers in the 80's and in the 90's. "Thought Without Representation", in particular, can be viewed as an attack to CP, and its central thesis of *homomorphic representation*[10] – namely isomorphism between constituents of the proposition expressed by a statement and articulated components of the statement. Statements like

(6) *It rains,*

lacking a component designating the *place* where it is raining, are a counterexample to such a thesis. In this case the place is an *unarticulated component* of the statement, a component which is not designated by any part of the statement, but determined by the context.

Now, at what type of contextual dependence do unarticulated constituents correspond? It looks to me that they are examples of the second type of contextual dependence. Perry says that, as far as

(7) *It rains here,*

is concerned, because the addressee knows the meaning of *here*, he "knows exactly what fact is relevant" for the determination of the truth conditions of (7).[11] As far as (6) is concerned, on the other hand, the semantics of the words does not provide a guide: the interpretation is a pragmatic work, just as for demonstratives.

In fact the type of contextual dependence that I have underlined in § 3.3 goes further. In Perry's example, it is the linguistic meaning that indicates the existence of a free variable (the existence of an unarticulated constituent); it is the use of the predicate *Rain* that indicate the existence of two arguments - place and time - that the addressee must identify: here saturation is mandatory.

Of course if we consider Z-land and Z-landish practices or linguistic games, saturation *is not* a mandatory process; still, even in this case, context has the only function of modifying the relevance for the truth conditions of an utterance, of *always the same* variable – the place for *rain*, or for reports of time, the world for a contingent relation, etc.[12] In the third form of contextual dependence, on the other hand, context (being a Z-lander, for example) can, not only *neutralize* the relevance of those variables for the determination of the truth conditions of the utterances (neutralize the relevance of the variable "place" for (6)), but also *activate* other variables, which become relevant to the truth conditions of the same utterances in different contexts.

4 Contextual meta-dependence

4.1 Distal Context and Proximal Context

In analyzing Searle's examples, I have used the distinction between a notion of context (e. g. C_1, C_2, or C_3), basically corresponding to Searle's Background – and

---

[10] [17], p.208.
[11] [19], p. 6.
[12] See the section "When Things Are Not Worth Mentioning" in [19].

which I call *Distal Context* – and local features of the context, corresponding to the variables of the examples (e. g. "way of cutting", variety", "quantity") – which I call *Proximal Context*. Given a particular Distal Context for a sentence, some specific features become relevant to the determination of the truth conditions of the sentence: Distal Context determines the relevant contrast set, the set of salient alternatives.

This determination is not automatic: C_2 does not impose, *per se*, neither the interpretation "slice" of *cut*, nor the relevance of the feature "way of cutting". As I anticipated in § 3, as far as the third form of contextual dependence is concerned, the *mode* of dependence is not given, fixed independently of any context whatever. Distal Context will set the relevant dimensions of dependence, while giving birth to a form of *contextual meta-dependence*.

In specifying the truth conditions of an utterance, only a few features are mentioned. Features belonging to the Distal Context can be ignored as long as they are present in all contexts that may be taken into consideration (the set of alternatives). Those features do not allow to discriminate between contexts. Borrowing the expression from Amos Tversky, features in Distal Context have no *diagnostic value*: the diagnostic factors refer to the classificatory significance of features.[13] Context – and in particular the contrast set – affects the diagnostic value and the salience of features.

Let's go back to Searle: the Distal Context of a sentence represents features having a weak degree of diagnosticity – features appearing in all contexts, information weakly manifest.[14] A classification cannot be based on such features: therefore those features do not appear in the truth conditions of the sentence. The presence of a gravitational field, for example, is not part of the truth conditions of

(8) *The cat is on the mat*

if all the situations taken into consideration are on the Earth. Although they are extremely stable, those features can always be suspended: a variation in the Distal Context itself can modify their diagnostic value. If we consider contexts as "Interstellar space", the feature "presence of a gravitational field" looses its status of feature of the Distal Context of (8) – and becomes a feature of the Proximal Context of the sentence. That feature will then affect the application conditions of the predicate *being on*, and the truth conditions of the sentence (8).

4.2 Contextualism

An alternative approach to CP must then be defended: for reasons of space, in this paper I shall limit myself to a quick exposition of this approach, the contextualist approach. Contextualism is, more than a real paradigm, a research program[15], which

---

[13] [30], p.342: "For example the feature 'real' has no diagnostic value in the set of actual animals since it is shared by all actual animals and hence cannot be used to classify them. This feature, however, acquires considerable diagnostic value if the object set is extended to include legendary animals, such as a centaur, a mermaid, or a phoenix"; cf. [22], pp. 9-10.

[14] For this notion, see [26].

[15] For a detailed exposition, see [6].

can be reconstructed within the cognitive current, in the models and the observations of linguists, psychologists or philosophers, like David Rumelhart, George Dunbar, Charles Fillmore, Lawrence Barsalou, Ronald Langacker, François Récanati and Douglas Hintzman.

The application of the contextualist approach in semantics blurs the semantics/pragmatics distinction: subjects make use of the pragmatic processor to determine the semantic core itself, i. e. to determine the truth conditions of any utterance. Two ways of integrating pragmatics to semantics are possible:

☐ *Weak Contextualism* maintains the notion of the linguistic meaning of an expression, but stresses the distinction between this meaning and the semantic value that the expression takes in context;

☐ *Strong Contextualism* abandons the very notion of linguistic meaning.

Weak Contextualism can be seen as the generalization of contextual expressions model to all linguistic expressions. In this model a verb like *open* or *cut* is assimilated to a contextual expression. A frame is associated to the verb, a frame specifying several roles, namely the agent, the object, the instrument, etc. The structure of the frame represents the *semantic* component: a fixed meaning, although a complex one. On the other hand, determination of the values of the roles is a *pragmatic* procedure, relying on linguistic and encyclopedic knowledge.

As far as a contextual expression is concerned, the addressee must instantiate always *the same variable*, encoded in the linguistic meaning of the expression; in Searle's examples, on the other hand, it is the context that points out the roles that the addressee must instantiate. The mode of dependence depends on context: Strong Contextualism develops the thesis of a contextual meta-dependence.

Operating a focalization in the frame associated to a verb like *cut*, context can activate roles which are unarticulated constituents of the utterance: a specific schema is then put in the foreground. This focalization is not necessarily constrained by linguistic material (the articulated constituents): the same linguistic material can force to instantiate - in different contexts - different variables, corresponding to different semantic roles belonging to the frame associate to the verb.

The main thesis of Strong Contextualism is that a word is not associated in a primitive way to a set of application conditions (as in a fregean model) – its conventional meaning – but to a *set of applications*: meaning is built up from contexts of use. The semantic potential of a word w is the set of applications of w to situations, or objects, or contexts, applications accepted by the linguistic community. This set can be interpreted in different ways: set of objects[16], set of real situations[17], or of schemas of situations[18], set of traces of cognitive episodes stored in the memory.[19]

---

[16] For Putnam: see [20].
[17] For Récanati: see [22].
[18] For Fillmore: see [9] and [10], or Langacker: see [14].
[19] For Hintzman: see [11].

5 Conclusion

Pure indexicals show a form of dependence that CP can handle without modifying its general structure. Determination of the truth conditions of an utterance containing an indexical expression, although indirect, is mechanical, functional, hence semantic.

Demonstratives and "contextual expressions" show a form of dependence more threatening for CP: the functional solution at work for pure indexicals cannot be applied to those kinds of expressions. A pragmatic processor is brought into play to identify the semantic level itself. Therefore, linguistic meaning *underdetermines* truth conditions of an utterance containing a demonstrative or a contextual expression.

I said that CP can follow two types of strategies of self defense:

☐ a. the first one concerning the extension of underdetermination;
☐ b. the second one concerning the form of underdetermination.

I hope I have shown that both strategies are wrong. Searle and Travis point out a form of contextual dependence affecting *all* linguistic expressions (contra a.), even after disambiguation and saturation of the variables corresponding to pure indexicals, demonstratives and contextual expressions. This kind of underdetermination is *top-down* (contra b.): context, and not only linguistic material, shows which variables must be instantiated, relying on context itself. The instantiation is here facultative, because linguistic meaning does not impose it in all contexts.

Top-down dependence generalizes the semantic underdetermination - which becomes a *property* of linguistic meaning in general: linguistic meaning underdetermines the truth conditions of any utterance.[20]

References

1. Almog, Joseph, Perry, John & Wettstein, Howard (eds) [1989] *Themes from Kaplan*, Oxford, Oxford University Press.
2. Austin, John L. [1961] *Philosophical Papers*, Oxford, Clarendon Press, 1979, Third edition.
3. Bach, Kent [1992a] "Paving the road to reference", *Philosophical Studies*, 67.
4. Bach, Kent [1992b] "Intentions and Demonstrations", *Analysis*, vol. 52, n°3.
5. Bianchi, Claudia [1995] "Osservazioni sulla teoria dell'indicalità di John Perry", *Pratica Filosofica*, 5.
6. Bianchi, Claudia [1998] *Flexibilité sémantique et sous-détermination*, PHD thesis, Ecole Polytechnique, Paris.
7. Clark, Herbert H. [1992] *Arenas of Language Use*, Chicago, The University of Chicago Press & CSLI.
8. Dunbar, George [1991] *The Cognitive Lexicon*, Tübingen, Gunter Narr Verlag.
9. Fillmore, Charles J. [1982] "Frame Semantics" in *Linguistics in the Morning Calm*, The Linguistic Society of Korea (ed), Seoul, Hanshin Publishing Co.

---

[20] This kind of dependence corresponds to the "open texture" of empirical terms pointed out in the '40s by ordinary language philosophers, like Waismann or Austin: see [31] and [2].

10. Fillmore, Charles J. [1992] "'Corpus linguistics' or 'Computer-aided armchair linguistics'", *in* Jan Svartvik, *Directions in Corpus Linguistics*, Berlin, Mouton de Gruyter.
11. Hintzman, Douglas L. [1986] "'Schema Abstraction' in a Multiple-Trace Memory Model", *Psychological Review*, vol.93, n°4.
12. Kaplan, David [1977] "Demonstratives" *in* [1].
13. Kaplan, David [1989] "Afterthoughts" *in* [1].
14. Langacker, Ronald W. [1987] *Foundations of Cognitive Grammar, vol.I: Theoretical Prerequisites*, Stanford, California, Stanford University Press.
15. Lewis, David [1970] "General Semantics", *Synthese*, 22.
16. Lewis, David [1980] "Index, Context, and Content, in Kanger & Ohman [1980] *Philosophy and Grammar*, Reidel Publishing Company.
17. Perry, John [1986] "Thought Without Representation", in [18].
18. Perry, John [1993] *The Problem of the Essential Indexical and Other Essays*, New York, Oxford University Press.
19. Perry, John [1998] "Indexicals, Contexts and Unarticulated Constituents", forthcoming.
20. Putnam, Hilary [1975] *Mind, Language and Reality. Philosophical Papers Vol. 2*, Cambridge, Cambridge University Press.
21. Récanati, François [1993] *Direct Reference: From Language to Thought*, Oxford, Blackwell.
22. Récanati, François [1997] "Déstabiliser le sens", *Rapport du CREA* n° 9714.
23. Searle, John R. [1979] *Expression and Meaning*, Cambridge, Cambridge University Press.
24. Searle, John R. [1980] "The Background of Meaning" in Searle, Kiefer & Bierwisch [1980].
25. Searle, John R. [1992] *The Rediscovery of the Mind*, Cambridge (Mass.), MIT Press.
26. Sperber, Dan & Wilson, Deirdre [1986] *Relevance. Communication and Cognition*, 1995².
27. Travis, Charles [1975] *Saying and Understanding*, Oxford, Blackwell.
28. Travis, Charles [1981] *The True and the False: the Domain of Pragmatics*, Amsterdam, Benjamins.
29. Travis, Charles [1985] "On What Is Strictly Speaking True", *Canadian Journal of Philosophy*, vol. 15, n°2.
30. Tverski, Amos [1977] "Features of Similarity", *Psychological Review*, vol.84, n°4.
31. Waismann, F. [1940] "Verifiability", in A. Flew (ed), *Logic and Language*, Oxford, Basil Blackwell, 1951.

Context Representation for Dialogue Management

Harry Bunt

Computational Linguistics and Artificial Intelligence Group
Tilburg University,
P.O. Box 90153, 5000 LE Tilburg, The Netherlands
bunt@kub.nl

Abstract. There are many different kinds of context information, with different demands on representation. In this paper we discuss the representation of the context information needed to support intelligent dialogue management in interactive speech systems. We argue that simple types of context information should be represented in a very simple form to allow efficient processing, while other types of context information require sophisticated logics for articulate representation and reasoning. For dialogue management in spoken natural language dialogue systems, a complication is that some types of context information most of the time have a very simple structure, but occasionally may be quite complex, and require articulate representation. We will propose a way to handle this problem, and show how a dialogue manager can operate on elements of context information that may be represented in different formalisms.

1 Introduction

Dialogue management is the process of deciding what to do next in a dialogue. In human communication, dialogue management is a process that seems to go unnoticed much of the time; only rarely are we aware of having to make a decision on what to say next, or on whether to say anything at all. When designing a computer dialogue system, however, we either have to pre-program the possible dialogues according to certain fixed sequence of utterances, or else we have to define a 'dialogue manager', who decides what the system should do next, based on a model of the current dialogue context.

Investigations of human dialogue management, partly inspired by research on the design of intelligent computer dialogue systems, have made it clear that human dialogue management is highly complex and sophisticated, and suggests that one of the stumbling blocks for the development of high-quality speech dialogue systems is the design of dialogue managers that have some of the sophistication and subtlety of human dialogue management.

In this paper, we examine the notion of 'dialogue context' in the sense of the information that is relevant for deciding what to do next in a dialogue. We will model the communicative behaviour of dialogue participants using *Dynamic Interpretation Theory*, a theoretical framework for dialogue analysis that views communication in terms of actions, intended to change the context in certain ways.

This paper is organized as follows. We first consider the basics of dialogue management within the framework of Dynamic Interpretation Theory. We then turn to an analysis of the types of information needed to support effective dialogue management. We identify some of the most important logical and computational properties of these information types and consider the consequences of these properties for computer representations of dialogue contexts. We argue that each type of context information should be represented in a way that optimally supports efficient reasoning. Finally we show how a dialogue manager can operate on the basis of a context model that includes different representation formalisms, by carefully relating context information types to types of communicative acts and dialogue management mechanisms.

2 Dialogue management in DIT

Dialogue management, as we said above, is the process of deciding what to do next in a dialogue. This decision must take a lot of considerations into account. Often, participating in a dialogue goes hand in hand with some noncommunicative activity. For instance, the information service representative engaged in a dialogue with a client alternates talking to the client with consulting her computer information system, and the client may be taking notes and consulting his agenda while talking to the information service. A computer dialogue system playing the part of one of the participants also has to perform both kinds of action, and the dialogue manager of such a system therefore has to interact closely with other processes, in particular with processes that gather and combine pieces of information, i.e., with *reasoning* processes. Some of this information may be highly complex, as we will see, and require sophisticated logics and inference procedures. For effective dialogue management, it is vital to keep the representation and processing of conceptually simple context information simple, rather than casting all types of information into a single, powerful formalism for the sake of uniformity.

The two kinds of activity that a dialogue partner is typically engaged in, communicative and noncommunicative, can both motivate a contribution to the dialogue. In Dynamic Interpretation Theory two classes of communicative acts are distinguished, corresponding to these two underlying motivations: *task-oriented* acts and *dialogue control* acts. Task-oriented acts are motivated by the non-communicative purpose or 'task' underlying of the dialogue; dialogue control acts monitor the interactive process, helping to create and maintain the conditions for smooth and successful communication.

2.1 Dialogue acts

Dynamic Interpretation Theory (DIT) defines both task-oriented and dialogue control acts as context-changing operations. We have defined the concept of a *dialogue act* as the functional units used by dialogue participants to change the context ([6]). A dialogue act has a *semantic content*, formed by the information the speaker introduces into the context, and a *communicative function* that defines the significance of this information by specifying how the context should be updated with the information. By saying that dialogue acts are units 'used by dialogue participants', we mean that every communicative function corresponds to a particular set of features of the communicative behaviour that dialogue participants display.

Communicative functions can be divided into three categories: those specific for dialogue control, those specific for a particular type of task domain, and those that have a general use for exchanging any kind of information. Task-specific communicative functions are for instance OFFER, ACCEPTANCE and REFUSAL in negotiation dialogues (see [11], [1]).

For dialogue control acts we have proposed a classification into three subsystems, concerned with *feedback, interaction management,* and *social obligation management* ([6]). Feedback acts provide information about the processing of partner inputs, reporting or resolving problems (negative feedback), or reporting successful processing (positive feedback). Social obligation management acts deal with socially indicated obligations such as welcome greeting, thanking, apologizing, and farewell greeting. Interaction management acts handle various aspects of the interactive situation, such as taking turns; pausing and resuming; monitoring attention and contact; and structuring the discourse explicitly.

In [5] we have presented a hierarchical system of general information-exchange functions, where at the top of the hierarchy we find two subclasses of dialogue acts, those concerned with *information seeking* and those with *information providing*. Figure 1 provides a schematic overview of these subsystems.

A general information-exchange function, such as INFORM, can be combined with discourse domain information as semantic content, and form a task-oriented dialogue act, as in (1a), or it may combine with interaction-related information and form a dialogue control act, as in (1b).

(1) a. The next train to Amsterdam leaves at 9.05.
    b. I didn't hear you what said.

Both dialogue control acts and task-specific dialogue acts can thus be formed in two ways from a communicative function and a semantic content. This is summarized in Table 1. Example (2) illustrates the two ways of forming a task-specific dialogue act, and (3) the two ways of forming a dialogue control act.

(2) a. Twenty-five thousand.
    b. I am willing to offer twenty-five thousand.

(3) a. Thank you.
    b. I am extremely grateful for your help.

2.2 Dialogue management mechanisms

As mentioned above, communicative acts may be motivated either by the underlying purpose of the dialogue or by the purpose of securing the conditions for

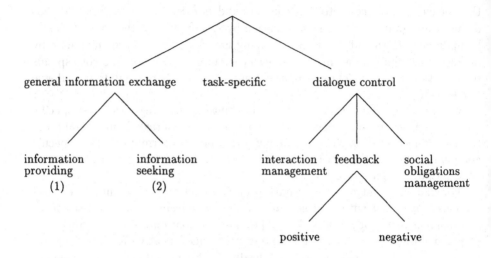

(1), (2): Hierarchies of communicative functions defined in [5].

Fig. 1. *Subsystems of communicative functions.*

effective communication. These motivations form the basis of dialogue mechanisms if we make the following idealizing assumptions:

Rationality Communicative agents act in order to achieve something. They form communicative goals to fulfill their underlying goals and desires; choose their communicative actions so as to optimally further their communicative goals, and organize the interaction so as to optimize the chances of success of their communicative actions.

Sociality Communication is a form of social behaviour, and is thus subject to cultural norms and conventions. An important aspect of this is **Cooperativity**, i.e. the disposition to act so as to be optimally helpful for the dialogue partner, taking his goals, interests and abilities into account.

From these assumptions, the motivations of the various types of communicative act can be derived as follows.

– Task-oriented acts are motivated by the speaker's underlying task goals (Rationality) or by his knowledge of the partner's goals (Cooperativity).
– Dialogue control acts:
  - *Interaction management* acts and *negative feedback* acts are motivated by the drive to communicate successfully (Rationality);
  - *Positive feedback* acts are motivated partly by Rationality and partly by Sociality (see below).
  - *Social obligation management* acts are motivated by the desire to honour social obligations (Sociality).

comm. function	semantic content	dialogue act type
general info. exchange	task domain information interaction information	task-oriented dialogue control
task-specific	(task domain information)	task-oriented
dialogue control	(interaction information)	dialogue control

Table 1. Possible constructions of dialogue act types

These motivations can all be construed as relations between dialogue acts and aspects of dialogue context. In the next section we consider these aspects of context.

3 Types of dialogue context information

We will follow the division of dialogue acts into task-oriented (TO-) acts and dialogue control (DC-) acts, with the further distinctions indicated in Fig. 1 and below, to consider the types of context information that a dialogue manager needs to generate the various types of acts.

Task-oriented dialogue acts The generation of a TO-act, being motivated by the underlying dialogue purpose or 'task', depends on the state of the task that the speaker is trying to accomplish. For instance, suppose the speaker is planning a trip, and contacts an information service to obtain travel information. In order to obtain specific information, a question is the appropriate act; the primary condition for asking a question being that the speaker wants to know the information he asks for. Additional conditions for the generation of this act will include the assumption that the information service does have the information requested (which may not be obvious, depending for instance on where the trip is going) and a number of seemingly trivial assumptions, such as Searle's 'preparatory conditions' ([17]). All information-seeking acts share these assumptions. Finer distinctions within the class of information-seeking acts correspond to additional assumptions, such as the CHECK having the condition that the speaker weakly believes the semantic content to be true (see further [5]).

While information-*seeking* TO-acts nearly always have their origin in information needs that the speaker experiences in trying to achieve the underlying task, information-*providing* acts often derive from cooperativity: the speaker believes it to be in the hearer's interest to obtain certain information. This requires the speaker to have beliefs about the underlying task and its current state, from the hearer's point of view. For a dialogue manager to generate TO-acts, it must have information about the underlying task and the task domain, as well as about the dialogue partner's information (and this recursively).

Dialogue control acts The generation of a *feedback act* is triggered by difficulties that thespeaker encounters in processing an utterance (negative feedback) or by successful completion of such processing (and positive feedback). The decision to generate a negative feedback act seems relatively easy for a dialogue manager, provided that it receives sufficiently clear failure messages from modules that run into difficulties; depending on the seriousness of a difficulty, the dialogue manager should generate a feedback act with the appropriate priority.

The generation of positive feedback acts is more difficult to regulate (except when they have been elicited), since it is conceptually not very clear why and when such acts should be produced. An efficient dialogue strategy might be one that assumes communication always to be successful, unless there is evidence to the contrary; positive feedback would then never be necessary. Natural human dialogue, especially spoken dialogue, is full of positive feedback, however, and complete absence of it is experienced as uncomfortable. Some spoken dialogue systems follow another extreme position and provide positive feedback all the time, reporting what they have recognized at every turn. This introduces too much redundancy, and slows the interaction down too much. Positive feedback seems desirable to have some of the time, but not all the time.

Three reasons for performing positive feedback acts:

1. The speaker assesses the dialogue context as 'risky': he has reason to believe that the hearer might think that something in the speaker's processing went wrong, where this is in fact not the case.
2. The speaker has not contributed anything to the dialogue quite a while; 'it is about time to say something'.
3. It is the speaker's turn to contribute to the dialogue, but he cannot immediately come up with something to say. In that case, a positive feedback act can be used as a 'filler'.

Whatever precisely the mechanisms for generating feedback acts may be, they clearly require a speaker's context to contain knowledge of his own processes of recognition, interpretation, evaluation and execution, what we call his *own processing status*, as well as knowledge of the dialogue partner's processing status (for corrective feedback).

It may be noted that the reaction to a negative feedback act often requires knowledge of the preceding discourse; for instance, *"Did you say Thursday?"* and *"Do you mean Friday April the second or Thursday April the first?"* require knowledge of what was said and what was meant, respectively.

Interaction management (IM) acts, at least in spoken dialogues, are primarily concerned with turn-taking, timing, contact, dialogue structuring, and the utterance formulation process. In a corpus of 111 naturally occurring spoken information dialogues (see [3]) the most important cases of *turn management* were (TURN-GIVING, TURN-KEEPING and (INTERRUPTION). Dialogue participants apparently have a view on who is having the main speaker role ('the turn').

Time management acts are concerned with the amount of time that various activities may take. When a speaker needs some extra time to formulate his contribution, he may produce a STALL act (*"Ehm"*, *"Let's see"*,..); when he needs more time, for instance to collect some information or to deal with an interfering activity, he is likely to produce a PAUSE act, to prevent his dialogue partner from worrying about the reasons of a prolonged silence. The generation of such acts depends on speakers having an estimate of the time needed to perform various activities.

Contact management acts are used by speakers to monitor contact with the dialogue partner both in the 'physical' sense, as when checking someone's presence at the other end of a telephone line *"Hello?"*), and in the sense of giving and having attention. The generation of these acts thus depends on the speaker having beliefs about the physical/perceptual dialogue context and about whether attention is being paid.

Own communication management acts (borrowing a term from [2]) are used by a speaker to deal with disfluencies in his contribution to the dialogue; what is in the literature also referred to as 'self-repair'. The generation of such acts by a dialogue manager depends on the availability of information about difficulties in the output generation processes, which is very similar to the kind of information we have seen for the generation of feedback acts.

Discourse structuring acts are used to explicitly structure the interaction, indicating for example that a certain topic is being closed, that a new topic is going to be addressed, or that the speaker wants to ask a question. The generation of discourse structuring acts is based on the speaker's view of the current context and on his plan for continuing the dialogue. We have argued elsewhere ([8]) that a separate representation of topics is not necessary if there is an articulate representation of goals and related aspects of the state of information, especially if the dialogue history keeps a record of goals that have been achieved earlier in the interaction.

Social obligations management (SOM) acts reflect that natural language communication between human partners is subject to conventions of social behaviour; for instance, when one does something wrong, or is unable to help, one is expected to apologize. And when meeting an acquaintance, one is supposed to greet.

For dealing with such 'social obligations', languages have closed classes of utterances with the property that their use puts a pressure on the addressee to react with an utterance from a related class. For example, *Thank you"* creates a pressure to say something like *"You're welcome"*, and a greeting creates a pressure to respond with a return greeting. SOM acts characteristically come in pairs, of what in the terminology of the Geneva School is called an 'initiative' and a 'reaction' (see [12],[16]).

In [6] we have introduced the notion of *reactive pressures* (RPs) to capture this phenomenon: an 'initiative' SOM-act has as part of its definition a description of the reactive pressure it introduces into the context. To account for the occurrence of initiative SOM-acts, we have further introduced the concept of *interactive pressures* ([7]). An interactive pressure (IP) differs from an RP in that it is created not by a particular SOM-act, but by properties of the context that are created in the course of the dialogue.

RPs and IPs lead to the generation of SOM-acts if we assume that communicative agents always aim at resolving such pressures. This is a way of turning the observation made above that speakers have "the desire to honour social obligations" into a mechanism for dialogue act management.

In sum, this analysis leads us to distinguish the following types of context information:

1. (a) Knowledge of the task and the task domain. We call this the *semantic context*.
   (b) Knowledge of the dialogue partner's semantic context (and this recursively).
2. (a) Knowledge of one's own processing status.
   (b) Knowledge of the partner's processing status.
3. Knowledge of the preceding discourse; we call this the *linguistic context*.
4. Knowledge for IM-acts:
   (a) Knowledge of the allocation of turns. This can be considered part of the linguistic context.
   (b) Knowledge of the time needed by various processes. This can be considered part of the processing status.
   (c) Knowledge of the physical and perceptual/cognitive 'contact' between speaker and hearer. We call this the *physical/perceptual* context.
   (d) Knowledge of one's own contribution production processes. This can be considered part of one's processing status.
   (e) Knowledge of the discourse structure. This can be considered part of the linguistic context.
5. Interactive and reactive pressures. We call this the (local) *social* context.

It is worth noting that all types of dialogue context information consist of beliefs, knowledge, goals, obligations ('pressures'), and other attitudinal elements. When we speak of 'the dialogue context', we mean in fact always the dialogue context *according to the speaker*. What a speaker does next in a dialogue depends only on how *he* views the context; for the purpose of dialogue management, dialogue contexts are always subjective.

The importance of identifying the above types of context information is that the various information types have different logical properties, and the recognition of these properties allows us to design effective and efficient inference systems to support dialogue management. We now turn to a brief discussion of these properties.

3.1 Logical properties of information types

For computationally adequate modeling of dialogue contexts, the crucial issue is how the context information can be exploited in reasoning processes. Logically complex information should be represented in an articulate way, allowing inference procedures to exploit the logical significance of the articulation, while logically simple information should be represented in a simple way, allowing fast, simple calculations like checking the value of a parameter, rather than requiring expensive computations such as searching and reasoning. We therefore consider the information types distinguished above with the following two questions:

1. To what extent is the information complex and logically articulate?
2. Do communicating agents use the information in full-blown inferential processing or in simpler, special-purpose processing?

Full-blown inferential processing naturally goes hand in hand with articulate expression of information, while simpler processing is appropriate for information with little internal structure. The articulation of information types and the complexity of the associated processing can be investigated empirically by examining the semantic content of the dialogue acts addressing the various information types, and by investigating the complexity of subdialogues where the various kinds of context information are the topic of conversation.

Semantic context The semantic content of task-oriented dialogue acts can be quite articulate, reflecting the complexity of the task domain. It is the subject of the most elaborate discussions in a dialogue, that dialogue participants reason about, make plans about, and use to guide their communicative activity in a rational way.

Semantic context information, moreover, is often embedded within recursive belief attitudes as part of an agent's information about his dialogue partner. As such, it is the most complex kind of context information, combining the inherent complexity of the task domain with that of nested propositional attitudes. An adequate representation of this information therefore calls for a logically sophisticated formalism with inference machinery.

Processing Status Processing status information is needed by a dialogue manager for the generation of feedback acts, time management acts, and own communication management acts. This means that an agent's processing status should contain the following elements per process: (1) state of progress; (3) difficulties encountered; (2) results obtained; (4) estimated time to completion.

In natural information dialogues the estimated completion time of a process is never expressed in precise terms; we will therefore consider only the representation of time estimates in the same crude way people do. This can be accomplished with a simple parameter-value pair. The same holds for feedback acts about reporting the state of progress of a process and for inarticulate own communication management acts.

In negative feedback acts, when processing difficulties are reported, the speaker signals the overall failure of a process, as in *"I beg you pardon?"*, or asks for clarification of a particular item, as in *"You mean this Tuesday?"*. This may be represented with two parameters: one representing overall success or failure, and one that may have a problematic item as its value. In the case of negative feedback w.r.t. evaluation, an agent reports conflicts between new information and previously available information. To detect such conflicts may require full-blown inferential processing. It is therefore not surprising that such feedback acts tend to be expressed not with dedicated feedback functions, but with a general information-exchange function, using a full sentence with articulate semantic content. In such a case a parameter-value representation would be inadequate. We will deal with this in the next section.

Linguistic context and dialogue memory Linguistic context, a recording of what has happened in the dialogue, can serve as a *memory*. This has the advantage that all other components of dialogue context do not need to have a memory! Consider, for example, the modelling of a participant's beliefs and intentions relating to the underlying task. It would not suffice to only model the *current* beliefs and intentions, for an agent may sometimes discover that something went wrong, and should then be able to return to a previous state of beliefs and intentions. By associating with each utterance in the linguistic context the changes that the utterance has brought about in the semantic context, we obviate the need to 'remember' these changes in the semantic context; any previous state of the semantic context can be reconstructed from its current state plus the changes recorded in the linguistic context. The same goes for other context components.

The information that participants have about turn allocation is conveniently integrated with the linguistic context, which can be seen as a 'dialogue history' (cf. [14]). In order to take the participants' anticipations as to how the dialogue will continue into account, we extend the dialogue history with a planned 'dialogue future', which can include the representation of the present and future allocation of turns. This view on the linguistic context has been implemented in the linguistic context model of the PLUS dialogue system; see [9].

Physical/perceptual context Of the physical and perceptual context, which characterizes the ways the dialogue participants can interact with their environment, including each other, the only aspects that can be changed by the dialogue are the effective availability of communication channels and whether the participants are paying attention to each other.

In the case of a telephone dialogue we thus need to represent in the speaker's physical and perceptual context his assumptions about the current availability of the telephone line. Whether the participant who is not speaking is paying attention, is indistinguishable form the availability of the communication channel. The contact management acts we have found in telephone information dialogues confirm this; physical and cognitive 'availability' are not addressed separately. A single parameter is thus sufficient to represent assumed physical and mental 'presence'. When the participants can see each other, additional parameters will be needed to make finer distinctions.

Social context The local social context consists of the 'pressures' to perform SOM-acts. Such pressures are created either by IP rules expressing the conditions under which a certain 'initiative' SOM-act is appropriate, or by the reactive pressure of a preceding SOM-act. These 'pressures' are in fact partical specifications of dialogue acts, typically containing a communicative function and a context-dependent semantic content, and possibly some constraints on the linguistic surface realization. As such, these pressures are represented by substructures of the data structures that are used for the linguistic context.

3.2 Information types and reasoning

This brief analysis of the logical properties of the various dialogue context information types leads to the conclusion that a computational model of dialogue context should distinguish the following kinds of structures:

1. formulas in an expressive logical language, like typed lambda calculus with propositional attitude operators for two agents;
2. parameters with simple, unstructured values;
3. nested feature structures, or something equivalent for representing linguistic information.

Parameters may be considered a special case of feature structures, so this may boil down to just two kinds of representational structure. Also, typed lambda calculus or another formalism in that league is powerful enough to represent virtually any kind of information, including the linguistic information that is often represented in nested feature structures. So in principle, all context information can be represented in one such very powerful language. However, the more expressive a logical language is, the more cumbersome are the reasoning procedures with expressions in the language. First-order logic has for this reason generally be preferred in language-understanding systems (see e.g. [13].)

Of the three kinds of structure mentioned above, simple attribute-value pairs allow computationally trivial processing; nestead feature structures, if well-designed (cf. [10]), allow more efficient reasoning than first-order logic; for typed lambda calculus (extended with belief operators) the design of effective reasoning systems is currently an area of active research (see e.g. [4]). In view of this, it is important for effective dialogue management to keep the representation of the various kinds of context information as simple as possible, and let the dialogue manager invoke sophisticated reasoning processes only when necessary for dealing with logically complex information.

A problem for this approach is that some information, notably dialogue control information, which is usually of the logically simplest type, occasionally may become the topic of conversation, become quite complex, and require sophisticated reasoning. This would seem to undermine the idea of designing a dialogue manager that invokes different reasoning processes for different types of context information. We consider this problem in the next section.

4 Dialogue control with articulate information

The representation of processing status, perceptual/physical context, and interactive/reactive pressures by simple parameter-value structures has computational advantages; it also has limitations. Consider, for instance, a dialogue system that supplies travel information, and a traveller who asks for departure times of KLM flights from Amsterdam to Beijing on Monday. It so happens that there are no such flights on Monday. The system should then produce a negative feedback act containing that information, like (4b)

(4) a. What are the departure times of KLM flights to Beijing next Monday?
     b. There are no KLM flights to Beijing on Monday.

but this semantic content is too complex to be represented by a parameter-value structure; it is in fact a piece of task domain information, and is thus represented like all semantic context. How can the dialogue manager generate such a feedback act? The answer depends on the difference between the two ways to construct a dialogue control act, noted before and indicated in Table 1.

Compare the feedback example (4b) with one where the speaker's utterance was unintelligible for the system. In that case the system's processing status will contain something like `Recognition:[PROGRESS:fail]`, and from this the dialogue manager will generate a negative feedback act that might be phrased as *"Please repeat"*. In the case of (4), we assume that a system component that is called to find departure times of flights to Beijing is unable to process a request, and something like `Execution:[PROGRESS:fail]` is recorded in the processing status. On the basis of that information, the dialogue manager might generate a feedback message such as *"Execution of request impossible."* But there is more, for the search for flights to Beijing was initiated by the system trying to construct an answer to (4a), an answer which it is unable to construct. Now one of the IP rules expressing cooperativity says that if the system is unable to perform a requested action or to answer a question, it should explain the reason why. If the reasoning process, involved in constructing the answer to the user's question 'knows' that there are no flights to Beijing on Monday, it will be able to conclude that for this reason no pertinent departure times can be found, and the dialogue manager will generate an explanatory INFORM act with that content. So the dialogue manager will generate two dialogue acts, to be phrased e.g. as:

(5) a. Execution of request impossible.

    b. There are no KLM flights from Amsterdam to Beijing on Monday.

The dialogue manager should be sophisticated enough to schedule these acts in the right order, or even to note that in this case (5b) alone is to be preferred, since it implies (5a).

We started out by considering the generation of an articulate negative feedback act like (4b) - but the question might well be raised whether (4b) is actually a feedback utterance. In its appearance, it is simply an INFORM act. Indeed, there is little reason to consider the utterance in any other way than an INFORM; like other INFORMs, it is generated on the basis of a cooperativity principle expressing that, when an agent has information available that he thinks is in the interest of the partner and which the partner does not have, than this information should be provided.

Similar analyses may be applied to other cases of dialogue control acts with articulate semantic content. Such dialogue acts are invariably constructed with the help of general information-exchange functions (see Table 1), and can be generated as well as interpreted by the dialogue manager simply by taking their communicative functions at face value, rather than looking for an interpretation as a dialogue control act. Our solution is then to treat the semantic content of the act in this case in the same way as when the same communicative function is combined with another type of semantic content, and represent the content in the same way as when it is semantic context information. Note that this corresponds with the view that, when dialogue control information is discussed in an articulate manner, then the domain of discourse is temporarily shifted from the underlying task to the interactive process. This in contrast with the use of special-purpose DC functions plus marginal content, where the domain of discourse remains that of the underlying task.[1]

5 Conclusions

We have argued that effective dialogue management in mixed-initiative spoken dialogue systems relies on taking a variety of types of context information into account with different degrees of logical complexity, whose representation requires different formalisms and reasoning processes. For the generation of a dialogue act, the dialogue manager should then invoke the most efficient reasoner, appropriate for the type of context information under consideration. This approach is threatened by the phenomenon that some context information is most of the time logically simple, but occasionally complex and requiring articulate representation. We have indicated how this problem can be resolved by distinguishing the different ways in which dialogue acts may be constructed, and taking the construction into account when dealing with the semantic content of a dialogue act.

---

[1] This view is supported by the study of topic shifts in spoken information dialogues by [15].

References

1. J. Alexandersson. Some ideas for the automatic acquisition of dialogue structure. In *Proc. 11th Twente Workshop on Language Technology*, Enschede, University of Twente, 1996. 149-158.
2. J. Allwood, J. Nivre & E. Ahlsén. On the semantics and pragmatics of linguistic feedback. *Journal of Semantics*, 9(1): 1-29, 1992.
3. R.J. Beun. *The recognition of declarative questions in information dialogues.* PhD thesis, Tilburg University, 1989.
4. T. Borghuis. *Coming to Terms with Modal Logics.* PhD thesis, Eindhoven University of Techology, 1994.
5. H. Bunt. Information dialogues as communicative actions in relation to user modelling and information processing. In M. Taylor, F. Néel & D. Bouwhuis (eds.) *The Structure of Multimodal Dialogue*, North-Holland Elsevier, Amsterdam, 47-73, 1989.
6. H. Bunt. Context and dialogue control. *THINK Quarterly*, 3(1): 19-31, 1994.
7. H. Bunt. Dynamic interpretation and dialogue theory. In M. Taylor, F. Néel & D. Bouwhuis (eds.) *The Structure of Multimodal Dialogue, Vol. 2.* Benjamins, Amsterdam, 1996.
8. H. Bunt. Iterative context specification and dialogue analysis. In H. Bunt & W. Black (eds.) *Abduction, Belief and Context: Studies in Computational Pragmatics*, 73-129, London, UCL Press, 1999.
9. H. Bunt, & W. Black. The ABC of computational pragmatics. In H. Bunt & W. Black (eds.) *Abduction, Belief and Context: Studies in Computational Pragmatics*, 1-35, London, UCL Press, 1999.
10. R. Carpenter. *The Logic of Typed Feature Structures.* Cambridge University Press, 1992.
11. S. Jekat, A. Klein, E. Maier, I. Maleck, M. Mast, & J. Quantz. Dialogue acts in Verbmobil. *Verbmobil Report*, 65, 1995.
12. J. Moeschler. *Argumentation et conversation, éléments pour une analyse pragmatique du discours.* Hatier, Paris, 1985.
13. R. Moore. A formal theory of knowledge and action. In J. Hobbs & R. Moore (eds,), *Formal Theories of the Commonsense World*, Norwood (NJ), Ablex, 1985.
14. V. Prince & D. Pernel. Several knowledge models and a blackboard memory for human-machine robust dialogues. *Natural Language Engineering*, 1(2): 113-145, 1995.
15. M. Rats. *Topic management in information dialogues.* PhD thesis, Tilburg University, 1996.
16. E. Roulet. *L'articulation du discours en francais contemporain.* Lang, Bern, 1985.
17. J.R. Searle. *Speech Act Theory.* Cambridge University Press, 1969.

Ecological Interfaces:
Extending the Pointing Paradigm by Visual Context

Antonella De Angeli[1], Laurent Romary[2] and Frederic Wolff[2]

[1]Department of Psychology, University of Trieste,
Via dell'Università, 7, I-34123, Trieste, Italy
deangeli@univ.trieste.it
[2]Laboratoire Loria
BP 239, 54506 Vandoeuvre-Les-Nancy, France
{deangeli, romary, wolff}@loria.fr

Abstract. Following the ecological approach to visual perception, this paper presents an innovative framework for the design of multimodal systems. The proposal emphasises the role of the visual context on gestural communication. It is aimed at extending the concept of *affordances* to explain referring gesture variability. The validity of the approach is confirmed by results of a simulation experiment. A discussion of practical implications of our findings for software architecture design is presented.

1. Introduction

Natural communication is a continuous stream of signals produced by different channels, which reciprocally support each other to optimise comprehension. Although most of the information is provided by speech, semantic and pragmatic features of the message are distributed across verbal and non-verbal language. When talking, humans say words with a particular intonation, move hands and body, change facial expressions, shift their gazes. Interlocutors tend to use all the modalities that are available in the communicative context. In this way, they can accommodate a wide range of contexts and goals, achieving effective information exchange. As a new generation of information systems begins to evolve, the power of multimodal communication can be also exploited at the human-computer interface. Multimodal systems have the peculiarity of extracting and conveying meanings through several I/O interfaces, such as microphone, keyboard, mouse, electronic pen, and touch-screen. This characteristic applies to a number of prototypes, varying on the quantity and the type of implemented modalities, as well as on computational capabilities. The design space of multimodal systems can be defined along two dimensions: Use of modalities and Fusion [10]. Use of modalities refers to the temporal availability of different channels during interaction. They can be used sequentially or simultaneously. Fusion refers to the combination of data transmitted from separate modalities. They can be processed independently or in a combined way. The two dimensions give rise to four classes of systems (see Table 1).

Table 1. The design space of multimodal systems, adapted from [10].

		Use of modalities	
		Sequential	Parallel
Fusion	Combined	Alternate	Synergistic
	Independent	Exclusive	Concurrent

This paper addresses synergistic systems, combining simultaneous input from speech and gesture (from now on, simply, multimodal systems). Speech refers to unconstrained verbal commands, gesture to movements in a 2-d space (the computer screen). The focus is on the use of contextual knowledge for disambiguating spatial references (communicative acts aimed at locating objects in the physical space). The ecological approach to multimodal system design is presented. Its innovative aspect regards the importance given to visual perception as a fundamental factor affecting the production and the understanding of gesture. The basic assumption is that referring acts can rely both on explicit information, provided by intentional communication (verbal language and communicative gesture), and on implicit information, provided by the physical context where communication takes place (objects visual layout). The validity of the approach is confirmed by empirical results from a Wizard of Oz study and by the satisfactory performance of a prototype basing gesture analysis on anthropomorphic perceptual principles.

2. Towards a natural interaction

Enlarging the bandwidth of the interaction, multimodal systems have the potential for introducing a major shift in the usability of future computers. Users can express their intentions in a spontaneous way, without trying to fit to the interface language. They can also select the most appropriate modalities according to the circumstances. In particular, multimodal systems were found to be extremely useful whenever the task was to locate objects in the physical space [14]. Users were faster, less error prone and less disfluent, when interacting via pen and voice, than via voice only or pen only [12]. The advantage was primarily due to verbal-language limitations in defining spatial location [5], [1], [14]. Gestures, on the contrary, are efficient means for coping with the complexity of the visual world. As an example, referring to a triangle in Fig. 1 by verbal language alone produces a complex utterance describing the spatial position of the target. A much easier solution is to directly indicate the target, integrating a pointing gesture into the flow of speech. From a linguistic point of view, this communication act is called gestural usage of space deixis. It is a canonical example of semantic features distribution across different modalities: the final meaning results from the synchronisation of a space deictic term ("this-that"; "here-there") and a deictic gesture (mainly pointing).

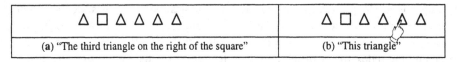

(a) "The third triangle on the right of the square"	(b) "This triangle"

Fig. 1. Facilitating effect of gesture in referring to visual objects

Deixis production and understanding are mediated by cross-modal-integration processes, where different information channels are combined in modality-independent representations. Exploiting the perceptual context, verbal language is amplified by essential information provided by gesture. Localisation is directly achieved by selecting the object from the visual representation, so it is independent of the symbolic mental representation used by interlocutors. On the contrary, the pure linguistic expression must rely on implicit parameters of the symbolic representation (e.g., left or right of the observer).

The way communication is produced depends on the complexity of extracting the target from the visual context [1], [19]. Psychological studies showed how gesture is adapted to the perceptual context during both planning and production [8]. Various criteria, intrinsic to perceptual features of the target, determine gesture configuration (e.g., trajectory, granularity and shape of the movement). Visual attention is a fundamental precondition for gestural communication. Although a form of spontaneous gesticulation is always present during speech (e.g., facial and rhythmic movements), communicative gestures are effective only if interlocutors face each other and are exposed to the same image. Perceptual cues allow the speaker to monitor listener comprehension: in correspondence to a referential gesture, the hearer turns his/her own gaze following the speaker's movement. So, the speaker is provided with an immediate non-verbal feedback (gaze movement) which anticipates and supports the delayed verbal one. Despite the importance of perception to resolve references, multimodal interfaces have usually been kept blind. They do not consider the visual context in which the interaction takes place. The first design approaches have been mainly verbal-language driven [6], treating gesture as a secondary dependent mode and completely ignoring other information sources. Co-references were resolved by considering the sole dialogue context: looking for a gesture each time a term in the speech stream required disambiguation. Usually, the only triggers were deictic terms. When applied to real field applications, these specialised algorithms for processing deictic to pointing relations have demonstrated limited utility [14]. There are several reasons to such failure. First, some deictic terms can also be used as anaphors and text deixis, which obviously require no gestural support. Secondly, empirical research shows that under particular circumstances (such as the presence of a visual feedback to the user gesture), Human-Computer Interaction (HCI) favours the elision of the verbal anchor [14], [1].

Another fundamental limitation of previous approaches has been the reduction of the gestural vocabulary to a simple pointing which had to be situated within the visual referent. Even though a lot of studies have aimed at improving the understanding and also the computation of verbal utterances, only a few works have dealt with gesture variability [14] and flexibility [15]. This lack has led to a weakness in the understanding of and thus in the ability to process complex gestures. The pointing paradigm is in sharp contrast with natural communication where gestures are often inaccurate and imprecise. Moreover, referring gestures can be performed by a great flexibility of forms [2], such as directly indicating the target (typically, but not only, extending the index finger of the dominant hand towards the target) or dynamically depicting its form (indicating the perimeter or the area of the target).

Nowadays, the design of effective multimodal systems is still hampered by many technical difficulties. The major one is connected to constraining the high variability of natural communication inside system capabilities. Historically, researchers designing language-oriented systems have assumed that users could adapt to whatever they built. Such system-centred approach has generated low usable systems, because it stems from a basic misunderstanding of human capabilities. Indeed, although adaptation is a fundamental aspect of communication, the usage of communicative modalities conforms to cognitive and contextual constraints that cannot be easily modified [1]. Communication involves a set of skills organised into modality-specific brain centres. Some of these skills escape conscious control and involve hard-wired or automatic processes (e.g., intonation, spoken disfluencies, kinaesthetic motor control, cross-modal integration and timing). Automaticity occurs over extensive practice with a task, when specific routines are build up in the memory. Being performed beyond conscious awareness, automatic processing is effortless and fast, but it requires a strong effort to be modified. Moreover, even when people learn new solutions (i.e., set up new routines in their memory), as soon as they are involved in demanding situations, they tend to switch back to their old automatism, thus leading to potential errors. Given the automatic nature of communication, it is unrealistic to expect that users will be able to adapt all parts of their behaviour to fit system limitations. On the contrary, effective interaction should be facilitated by architectures and interfaces respecting and stimulating spontaneous behaviour. The ecological approach to multimodal system design moves from this user-centred philosophy.

3. The ecological approach

The ecological approach to multimodal system design is both a theoretical and a methodological framework aimed at driving the design of more usable systems. The name is derived from a psychological approach to perception, cognition and action, emphasising the mutuality of organism-environment relationship [4]. It is based on the validity of information provided to perception under normal conditions, implying as a corollary that laboratory study must be carefully designed to preserve ecological validity. Thus, our approach is ecological in a double sense. Claiming that technology should respect user limitations, the approach is aimed at preserving the ecological validity of human-computer interaction. Claiming that perception is instrumental to action, the approach tries to extend the original ecological theory to explain referring actions variability in HCI.

In our approach, referring gestures are considered as virtual actions, intentional behaviours affecting only the dialogue context, not the physical environment. The appropriate unit of analysis to investigate multimodal actions is therefore the perception-action cycle [9]. This is a psychological framework explaining how action planning and execution is controlled by perception and how perception is constantly modified by active exploration of the visual field. In other words, while acting on the environment, we obtain information; this information affects our set of expectations about the environment, which then guides new actions. The cyclic nature of human cognition provides a powerful framework for understanding gesture production. According to ecological psychology, perception and action are linked by affordances [4], optic information about objects that convey their functional properties. Affordances provide cues about the actions an object can support, as if the object suggested its functionality to an active observer. For example, a hammer usually induces us to take it by the handle and not by the head, because the handle is visually more graspable. An extension of the concept of affordances to the world of design was initially proposed by [11], but its potentialities in the domain of natural communication is still little understood. The ecological approach to multimodal systems attempts to extend the concept of affordances to explain gesture production. As such, it is based on the assumption that gestures are determined by the mutuality of information provided by the object, and the repertoire of possible human actions. Then, through empirical investigations it tries to identify the visual characteristics affording specific referring gestures.

4. Empirical study

To evaluate the validity of the ecological approach, an empirical study was carried out. The aim of the research was twofold.

- At an exploratory level, it was aimed at collecting a large corpus of spontaneous multimodal gestures produced in the context of different visual scenarios. This part provided us with a gesture taxonomy and some interesting examples of how gesturing is adapted to the visual context;
- At an experimental level, it was aimed at measuring the effect of visual perception on referring gestures. This part provided a preliminary quantification of the strength of the perception-gesture cycle.

The grouping effect of visual perception was investigated. According to the psychological theory of Gestalt [7], [17], perceivers spontaneously organise the visual field into groups of percepts. Stimulus simplification is necessary since human capabilities to process separate units are limited. Gestalt laws describe the principles underlying grouping. The main principle (*prägnanz* law) states that elements tend to be grouped into forms that are the most stable and create a minimal of stress. The other principles describe how stability is achieved. Here, we focus on similarity (objects are grouped on the basis of their physical salient attributes, such as shape and colour), proximity (objects are grouped on the basis of their relative proximity), and good continuation (shapes presenting continuous outlines have a better configuration than those with discontinuous ones).

4.1. Method

Participants. Seven students from the University of Nancy participated in the simulation as volunteers. All of them were native French speakers.

Procedure. Working individually, participants were asked to perform a typical computer-supported task: placing objects into folders. Interaction was based on speech and gesture, mediated by a microphone and an electronic pen. The user screen displayed a collection of objects and 8 boxes. Targets were groups of identically shaped stimuli that had to be moved into the box displaying their figure. Engaging a dialogue with the system, participants had to identify targets and tell the computer where to move them. To inhibit pure verbal references, targets were abstract-shape figures [1]. At the beginning of the interaction, the system welcomed the user and explained task requirements. After each successful displacement, the interface was refreshed and the system prompted a new action (Fig. 2).

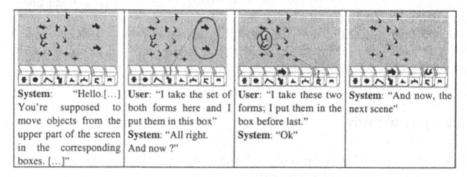

| System: "Hello.[...] You're supposed to move objects from the upper part of the screen in the corresponding boxes. [...]" | User: "I take the set of both forms here and I put them in this box" System: "All right. And now ?" | User: "I take these two forms; I put them in the box before last." System: "Ok" | System: "And now, the next scene" |

Fig. 2. Example of dialogue

Thirty different visual scenes were presented. At the end of the session each participant filled in a satisfaction questionnaire and was debriefed.

Design. The experimental part was based on 14 visual scenes. Group Salience (High vs. Low) was manipulated in a within-subject design. In the High-salience condition, targets were easily perceived as a group clearly separated by distractors. Proximity and good continuation supported similarity. In the Low-salience condition, targets were spontaneously perceived as elements of a broader heterogeneous group that included distracters. Proximity and good continuation acted in opposition to similarity. Table 2 summarises the experimental manipulation.

Table 2. Experimental manipulation.

	Similarity	Proximity	Good continuation
High-salience	+	+	+
Low-salience	+	-	-

Semi-automatic simulation. The system was simulated by the Wizard of Oz technique [3], in which an experimenter (the wizard) plays the role of the computer behind the human-machine interface. A semi-automatic simulation was supported by Magnetoz, a software environment for collecting and analysing multimodal corpora [18]. The Wizard could observe user's action on a graphical interface, where he also composed system answers. The simulation was supported by interface constraints and prefixed answers. These strategies have been found to increase simulation reliability by reducing response delays and lessening the attention demanded upon wizards [13]. Three types of information (speech signals, gesture trajectories, task evolution) were automatically recorded in separate files, allowing to replay the interaction and perform precise automatic analysis on dialogue features.

4.2. Results and discussion

As expected given the particular shapes of the stimuli, users were naturally oriented towards multimodal communication. With only a few exceptions (N=3), displacements were performed incorporating one or more gestures inside the verbal command. Most inputs were group oriented (92%): all the elements of the group were localised and then moved together to the box. Analysing the whole corpus, a taxonomy of referring gestures in HCI was developed. Gestures performed to identify targets were defined as trajectories in certain parameter space and classified in four categories:

- Pointing (0-d gesture, resembling to a small dot),
- Targeting (1-d gesture, crossing targets by a line),
- Circling (2-d gesture, surrounding targets by a curved line),
- Scribbling (2-d gesture, covering targets by meaningless drawing).

Examples and percentages of each category are reported in Fig. 3. Reading these data, one should carefully take into account the very exploratory nature of the study and the reduced size of the sample. Although preliminary, these results urge us to rethink the traditional approach to gesture recognition. Indeed, limiting interaction to pointing actually appears to be in sharp contrast with spontaneous behaviour.

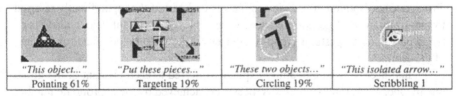

"This object..."	*"Put these pieces..."*	*"These two objects..."*	*"This isolated arrow...."*
Pointing 61%	Targeting 19%	Circling 19%	Scribbling 1

Fig. 3. Gesture taxonomy (Percentages are computed considering groups as the unit of analysis)

The predominance of pointing can be partially explained by the high inter-individual variability affecting gestures. Two major categories of users were identified: persons performing almost only pointing and others with a richer gestural dictionary.

Consistently with the basic assumption of the ecological approach, gestures appear to be determined by the mutuality of information coming from the object and the repertoire of actions available to users. Different users can perform different gestures on the same referent. An informal investigation concerning computer literacy supports the idea that beginners prefer pointing only, whereas experts take advantage of more complex forms. This hypothesis is consistent with previous results [1] showing a strong effect of computer literacy on multimodal production. The existence of different users categories stresses the importance of designing adaptive systems, capable of respecting personal strategies, but also to suggest more efficient behaviours. Moreover, it requires testing large samples of users to avoid biasing experimental results.

Free-form gestures (i.e., targeting, circling and scribbling) were strongly influenced by the visual context. Even at the cost of producing very unusual movements, users adapted to visual layout. Prototypical examples are reported in Fig. 4a. The form of the gesture can be explained by visual affordances: e.g., a triangular layout of referents is likely to stimulate a triangular gesture. The size of the gesture may vary relatively to surrounding objects location (Fig. 4b). Gesture precision depends on the pressure of the perceptual context. Finally, a strong perceptual influence arises on the number of gestures performed to indicate a group (Fig. 4c).

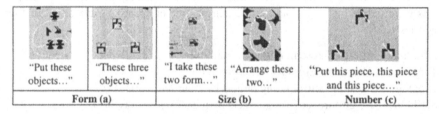

"Put these objects…"	"These three objects…"	"I take these two form…"	"Arrange these two…"	"Put this piece, this piece and this piece…"
Form (a)		Size (b)		Number (c)

Fig. 4. Examples of visual perception effect on gesturing

The effect of visual perception on multimodal communication was further investigated in the experimental part of the study. Each displacement was tabulated into one of the following categories (Fig. 5).

- Group-access. Both the linguistic and the gestural part of the input directly referred to the group. Verbal group-references were achieved by plural deictic anchors or target descriptions; gestural group-references by showing the perimeter or the area of the group.

- Individual-access. Both modalities explicitly referred to each element of the group one by one. Verbal individual-references were achieved by the appropriate number of singular anchors; gestural individual-reference by singularly indicating all the elements.

- Mixed-access. This is an interesting case of asymmetry between modalities, one referring to the group as a whole, the other to individual targets. In the sample, all mixed-accesses were composed by verbal group-references amplified by gestural individual-references. Therefore, mixed-access can be misunderstood if multimodal constructions are resolved without considering the visual context. Indeed, the deictic "these" has to be associated to n gestures (n corresponding to the number of elements composing the group), but not to other eventual gestures that indicate different elements (in our case boxes) and that are associated to separate linguistic anchors.

Group access (28%)	Mixed access (32%)	Individual access (40%)
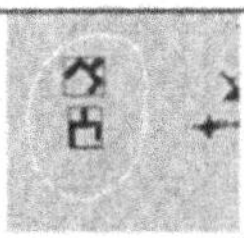 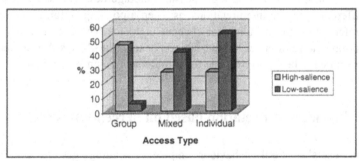		
"Move these 2 objects..."	"These objects..."	"This figure and this figure..."

Fig. 5. Examples and percentages of referring strategies.

To test the effect of Group Salience on multimodal production, the occurrence of referring strategies in the two experimental conditions was compared ($\chi^2 = 18.38$, d.f.=2, $p< .001$). As illustrated in Fig. 6, the two patterns clearly differed. Group-access occurred almost only when the group was visually salient. On the contrary, individual and mixed-access were predominant in the Low-salience condition. Analysing the two modalities separately, we discovered that the perceptual effect was stronger with respect to the gestural part of the input ($\chi^2 = 14.96$, d.f. = 1, $p< .001$), than to the verbal one ($\chi^2 = 6.68$, d.f. = 1, $p< .01$). All in all, these findings confirm the ecological hypothesis that perceptual organisation is a powerful cue for predicting a user's input, particularly regarding his motor-behaviour.

Fig. 6. Percentage of referring strategies in the two experimental conditions.

The occurrence of different access strategies gave rise to a number of gestural ambiguities. Although pointing was the prototypical form for referring to individual objects, and circling for referring to groups, this distinction was not straightforward (Fig. 5 and 7). All gestures were used both for individual and for group access. Therefore, knowledge about the visual context was instrumental to disambiguate movement meaning. Analysing the whole corpus, two main types of imprecision were identified: granularity and form ambiguities. The first derives from a non 1-to-1 relation between referred area and gesture extent. As shown in Fig. 7a, the group salience can be sometimes so strong that users reduce their gestural expression to a small gesture, such as a single pointing. Note that the gestural simplification is accompanied by a detailed verbal description, eliciting the number of referred objects. The co-reference can be properly disambiguated only taking into account the perceptual context that discriminates the intended objects from all the others displayed on the user screen. In such cases, perceptual groups become the main criteria to determine the "three objects" within the surrounding ones.

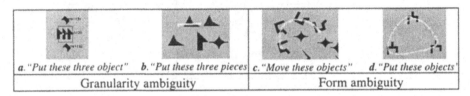

a. "Put these three object"	b. "Put these three pieces	c. "Move these objects"	d. "Put these objects"
Granularity ambiguity		Form ambiguity	

Fig. 7. Referring ambiguities

Free form gestures also introduced form ambiguities. Observe the example in Fig. 7c. Taking into account only the trajectory, the gesture can be considered as a free form targeting or as an incomplete circling. In the two cases, the referential candidates are different (only the U shaped percepts, or also the star shaped percept). Again, the verbal language is not sufficient to disambiguate it and only the perceptual context drives our choice towards the U-shaped solutions.

To conclude, the empirical study showed that it is necessary to extend the pointing-inclusion paradigm for allowing users to express their communicative intentions in a natural way. The extension has to consider the variability of gesture forms and meanings, as well as their possible ambiguities. The same gesture can convey different semantic interpretations, as when a pointing action is performed in order to refer either to an individual element or to the whole group; and when a circling is drawn to refer either to inner objects or to strike objects. Visual perception was demonstrated to be a powerful cue for communication understanding.

5. Referring act interpretation based on perceptual context

Respecting users' natural behaviour implies designing gesture interpretation components that are able to cope with flexibility and ambiguity. As previously shown variability emerges from the perceptual context: when users are involved in the perception-action cycle, their expression is continuously adapting to the environment variability. To interpret natural gestures, a dialogue system thus has to integrate knowledge from the visual environment. Indeed, reproducing human perceptual capabilities allows users to anticipate the system's capabilities by transposing their own. In this way, users express their intention in a simpler way as in normal dialogue. They do not need anymore to learn a new communication style or to reflect on their expressions and they can rely on implicit information received from the perceptual context to build up their expression.

5.1. Gesture interpretation process

On the basis of the experimental data, two main points have been considered in the operational model of gesture understanding. The ecological approach offers freedom of gestural expression by allowing flexibility concerning production (e.g. precision, type, form etc...) and by coping with simplifications based on perceptual organisation (e.g., granularity ambiguities).

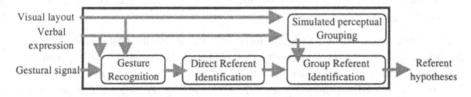

Fig. 8. Ecological approach: gesture analysis based on perceptual context

Flexibility modelling is aimed at understanding the way users arrange their gestures among the percepts. Such knowledge related to affordances is used to recognise the gesture category and intention. Once the referring type has been identified, referents can be retrieved among the percepts by employing the appropriate heuristics. However, such rules not only have to consider standard locations of referents according to the trajectory, but also to integrate implicit perceptual grouping information for understanding simplified expressions. Indeed, resolving granularity ambiguity introduces implicit information conveyed by a third modality: visual perception. Perception is introduced firstly by affordances during gesture recognition and secondly at the simulated grouping stage.

5.2. Gesture recognition

The first step consists in determining gesture type, and then deducing the corresponding referring intention. Recognition considers the production context to predict how visual space is accessed by gestural action. By basing gesture recognition on visual layout, the analysis can cope with variability sources. Gesture is no longer understood on the unique basis of its morphological structure as an out-of-context process but as a contextual phenomena described by the perception-action cycle. Therefore, the visual environment is structured to anticipate possible forms of gestural access. Each percept defines an access area whose extent depends on the proximity of surrounding percepts (Fig. 9). This approach allows to reproduce the phenomena of visual pressure presented above and contributes to cope with some variability features such as:

- **Imprecision.** Users can access to percept through whatever location in the defined area. Moreover this area is determined according to the local perceptual context. This allows users to be more or less precise in referring according to the proximity of the surrounding visual elements.

- **Partial, complete or repetitive trajectory**. Reducing gesture identification by only considering those trajectory elements which belong to a defined area avoids examining numerous dynamic and morphological factors (speed, acceleration, curvature..). The static analysis allows modelling more or less entire movements (partial, complete and repetitive gestures) as a continuum of a single trajectory.
- **Free form gesture**. The main interpretation criteria concerns the crossed areas independent of the movement itself. In this way, referents configuration affording adapted trajectories can directly be understood, no matter the complexity of the free form gesture is.

Once areas involved in the process have been identified, the gesture recognition is performed and the corresponding intention deduced. On the basis of experimental trajectories and their relative location to surrounding percepts, particular sub-areas have been identified as supporting special intentions (Fig. 9): elective area for central ballistic accesses (pointing, targeting, or scribbling) and separative area for peripheral accesses (circling).

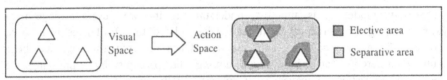

Fig. 9: Action oriented space partitioning

Intention is deduced from space partitioning, by explaining how gestures focus interlocutor attention. Performing a gesture in separative areas indicates the user's intention to isolate, separate a certain sub-space from the remaining scene in which referents have to be found. On the contrary, using elective areas by passing through percepts (independently from the trajectory form) contrasts crossed elements with surroundings. This ecological analysis, based on the perception-action cycle, allows one to cope with form variability and ambiguity.

5.3. Referent retrieval.

The second step in the gesture interpretation process consists in determining the referents among the percepts. Our approach relies upon perceptual considerations to remove granularity ambiguity: a simple trajectory can indeed refer to either one or more objects. But instead of directly trying to resolve such cases by deciding on the access type, two kinds of referent hypotheses are generated:

- Direct referent hypotheses which correspond to an individual access
- Group referent hypotheses which suggest the most appropriate perceptual groups for group access strategy.

The choice between these two hypotheses is carried out afterwards by the dialogue manager that is able to correlate them with linguistic intentions. Determining direct referents corresponds to producing individual access hypotheses. This step relies on the detected gestural intention. Either the trajectory is recognised as an elective gesture and the referents are deduced from used areas, or the gesture mainly occurred in the separative area and referred objects are located on the concave side of the corresponding circling. At this point, the model still needs to remove the granularity ambiguity. Therefore, a group access hypothesis is generated by choosing the most salient perceptual group containing the direct referents. Simplified gestures, such as unique pointing to group, can then be understood and treated. Introducing knowledge on the perceptual context corresponds to structure the visual flow as a third modality. In this way, organising visual context reduces scene complexity and offers abstract information available for simplified referring expressions To reproduce perceptual groups, Gestalt principles and in particular the proximity and similarity laws are used as shown in Thorisson's algorithm [16]. More precisely, between each couples of percepts different scorings are computed according to spatial proximity and feature similarity (colour, size, type, brightness). Groups are then deduced by considering differences of scores in a descending order. Resulting sets of couples build groups with decreasing salience.

Conclusion and perspectives

In this paper, we have tried to show the strategy that has to be followed to design multimodal systems which do not simply rely on the individual selection of objects through a pointing gesture, with the high constraint it imposes on users. On the contrary, we want to allow spontaneous expression and we have seen that it is only possible to do so by taking into account the perceptual context within which a given speech + gesture utterance has been expressed. This suggestion is presented with the larger proposal of an ecological approach to multimodal system design, which positions the perception-action cycle at the center of the multimodal process. In particular, we think that this approach is a good candidate to cope with the high variability of gestural expression that has been observed in the experiment we have conducted.

From the point of view of multimodal system design, this implies that such systems should comprise perceptual mechanisms extending the traditional notion of context that they are to deal with, i.e. a pure dialogic one. However, even if the first implementation of these principles is promising, it is still necessary to generalize our approach so that it can be considered by other multimodal system designers independently of the specific task to be handled. Such a perspective is related to the possibility of defining generic perceptual components which are still to be modeled.

References

1. De Angeli A., Gerbino W., Cassano G., Petrelli D.: Visual Display: Pointing, and Natural Language: The power of Multimodal Interaction. In proceedings of Advanced Visual Interfaces Conference, L'Aquila, Italy (1998)

2. Feyereisen, P.: La compréhension des gestes référentiels. In Nouveaux Actes Semiotiques, Vol. 52-53-54 (1997) 29-48.

3. Fraser, N. M. and Gilbert, G. N.: Simulating speech systems. Computer, Speech and Languages, Vol. 5 (1991) 81- 99.

4. Gibson, J.J.: The Ecological Approach to Visual Perception. Boston: Houghton Mifflin (1979)

5. Glenberg, A. and McDaniel, M.: Mental models, pictures, and text: Integration of spatial and verbal information. Memory and Cognition, Vol. 20(5) (1992) 158-460

6. Johnston M., Cohen P.R., McGee D., Oviatt S., Pittman J.A. e Smith I.: Unification-based multimodal integration. In Proceedings of the 35 th Annual Meeting of the Association for Computational Linguistics, Madrid, Spain (1997) 281-288

7. Kanizsa, G.: Organization in vision. Praeger New York (1979)

8. Levelt, W. J., Richardson, G., & La Heij, W.: Pointing and voicing in deictic expressions. Journal of Memory and Language, Vol. 24 (1985) 133-164

9. Neisser, U.: Cognition and Reality. San Francisco: Freeman & Co (1976)

10. Nigay, L. and Coutaz, J.: A design space for multimodal systems: Concurrent processing and data fusion. In Proceedings of INTERCHI'93 (1993) 172- 178

11. Norman, D. A. and Draper, S. W.: User Centered System Design: New Perspectives on Human-Computer Interaction. Hillsdale, New Jersey: Lawrence Erlbaum Associates (1986).

12. Oviatt, S.: Multimodal interactive maps: Designing for human performance. Human-Computer Interaction, Vol. 12 (1997) 93-129

13. Oviatt, S., Cohen, P. R., Fong, M. and Frank, M.: A Rapid Semi-automatic Simulation Technique for Investigating Interactive Speech and Handwriting. In Proceedings of the International Conference on Spoken Language Processing, Vol. 2 (1992) 1351-1354

14. Oviatt, S., De Angeli, D., Kuhn, K.: Integration and synchronization of input modes during multimodal human-computer interaction. In: Conference on Human Factors in Computing Systems, CHI97, New York, ACM Press (1997)

15. Streit, M.: Active and Passive Gestures - Problems with the Resolution of Deictic and Elliptic Expressions in a Multimodal System. In Proceedings of the Workshop on Referring Phenomena in a Multimedia Context and Their Computational Treatment, ACL-EACL, Madrid, Spain (1997)

16. Thorisson K.R.: Simulated perceptual grouping : an application to human-computer interaction, 16th annual conference of cognitive science society (1994).

17. Wertheimer, M.: Untersuchungen zur Lehre von der Gestalt I. Psychologische Forschung, (1922) 47-58.

18. Wolff, F.: Analyse contextuelle des gestes de désignation en dialogue Homme-Machine. PhD Thesis, University Henri Poincaré, Nancy 1, LORIA, Laboratoire Lorrain de Recherche en Informatique et ses Applications (1999).

19. Wolff, F., De Angeli, A. , Romary , L.: Acting on a visual world : The role of perception in multimodal HCI. Workshop Representations for Multi-Modal Human-Computer Interaction , AAAI Press (1998).

Formal Context and Morphological Analysis[1]

Anna-Maria Di Sciullo

Université du Québec à Montréal

Abstract. This paper presents a definition of context for the interpretation of word-structure that is based on the formal relation of asymmetry. We provide evidence that morpho-conceptual complexity is optimally tractable in terms of local asymmetrical relations in formal context. We present the main features of a morpho-conceptual parser implementing our proposal. We show, on the basis of the comparison with existing morphological parsers, that the accuracy of the analysis increases when the operations of the parser are oriented by the recognition of local asymmetries in formal contexts. We predict that the inclusion of modules scanning local asymmetries in information processing systems will increase their precision

Introduction

This paper deals with our knowledge of word-internal context.[2] We refer to this under-the-word-level context as formal context and differentiates it form the world-theoretical context. We take the formal context to be defined in terms of a model of formal grammar and the world-theoretical context to be defined in terms of a model of the world (or possible worlds). The formal and the world-theoretical contexts in conjunction provide the basis upon which the linguistic expressions are analyzed and interpreted, as well as they make learning and reasoning possible.

[1] We thank the four anonymous reviewers for their comments and suggestions on an earlier version of this paper. This work is supported in part by the Social Sciences and Humanities Research Council of Canada to the Major Collaborative Research Project on Asymmetries in Natural Languages and their Treatment by the Performance Systems (Grant no. 412-97-0016).

[2] We relate our notion of formal context to a broader notion of context, according to which context is an entity about which inferences can be made and propose that morphological expressions present a context for grammatical reasoning. The notion of context is central in current research on the modelization of the cognitive system. Advances in different fields indicate that progress is achieved in our understanding of what makes it possible to reason, learn and, more basically in our perspective, to use our knowledge of language in an optimal way. Advances in AI with respect to the formalization of context bares on the simulation of human methods for the acquisition and application of knowledge and reasoning, such as the formulation of multi-agent models for the representation of belief contexts (Cimatti and Serafini, 1995; Benerecetti and al., 1996). Advances in NLP with respect to the formalization of context bare on the integration of formal principles in natural language generation and parsing systems (Berwick, 1991; Fong, 1991, and retated works). We come back to this point below.

The basic idea underlying our notion of formal context is that the derivation of complex morphological structures is achieved via formal asymmetries.

The articulation of this paper is the following. In the first section, we propose a definition of formal context and we present empirical evidence to support. The second section outlines the general properties of an integrated model of grammar knowledge and use where the proposed notion of formal context is central. The third section presents a computational implementation of the basic idea for the analysis of complex morphological expressions. In the last section, we consider some consequences for the inclusion of language-dependent modules based on formal context in information processing systems.

1.   Context

We approach the question of the modelization of the context in a perspective that has not yet been explored to our knowledge. We take a dynamic approach to morphological analysis according to which lexical items are constructed on the basis of the properties of the formal context the morphemes are a part of, the latter having no full feature structure specifications to begin with.

More precisely, we assume that the categorial and conceptual feature structures of the morphemes is not fully specified in the lexicon but constructed in the derivation of the expressions they are a part of. We are thus taking a constructivist view of lexical items as opposed to a projectionist view, according to which the feature structure of lexical items is fully specified in the lexical entries and is projected in the derivation of linguistic expressions.

We propose that the categorial and the conceptual feature structures spelled-out by morphemes, roots and affixes, are constructed in the derivation of lexical items on the basis of formal context.

1.1   Hypothesis

In order to make precise the notion of formal context, we posit the hypothesis in (1) and the definitions in (2)-(4).

(1) **Feature Structure Derivation**
   The feature structures of morphemes are derived in formal contexts.

(2) **Formal Context**
   The formal context of a feature structure F is the context that includes F itself and another feature structure I, where F and I are in local asymmetrical relation.

(3) **Asymmetrical Relation**
   Two elements x and y are in asymmetrical relation, iff there is a formal relation r that is true for the pair (x, y) and false for the pair (y, x).

(4) **Locality**

The local domain of a relation r is the smallest domain where r applies.

There is empirical evidence, to which we now turn to, that indicates that the notion of formal context is in effect operative in the derivation of lexical items.[3]

1.2 Evidence

Empirical evidence in favor of our proposal, specifically that morphological analysis is dependent on formal context, comes from the fact that the relative position of singular morphemes in morphological structure determines their feature structures.

Thus, a sub-set of morphemes in natural languages, in English for instance, may either be spelled-out at the left edge or the right edge of a word. This is illustrated in (5) with different sorts of morphemes.

(5)   a. *en*bark, light*en*, *en*bold*en*   b. *arch*etype, matri*arch*   c. *a*social, magnesi*a*

In (5a), the categorial features (preposition or verb) and the conceptual features (directional aspect or inchoative) of the affix *en* is a function of the formal context it is a part of. The feature structures vary according to the adjunct or head position[4] of the affix. In (5b), the categorial feature structure of the affix *arch* is constant (numeral), while its conceptual features (scalar or goop) is a function of its formal context, here again adjunct or head position. In (5c), the categorial (negation or noun) and conceptual features (negation or reference) of the affix *a* is also a function of the formal context it is a part of.

It is assumed that the morphological context of affixes is modelized in terms of subcategorization features (See Lieber (1992) among others). However subcategorization frames are partial description of the formal context in which

---

[3]

There is evidence to the effect that it is the formal context also determines the full feature structure of the syntactic phrases in the derivation of the linguistic expressions they are a part of Facts from nominal and verbal modification are relevant in this respect. In cases where there is more than one interpretation for the adjective or the adverbial modifier, as it is the case with adjectives that can have both a descriptive/result and an attributive/event interpretation, such as *beautiful*, as well as with adverbs such as *again*, which can have both a iterative and a restitutive interpretation. The difference of interpretation of the derived modified phrase is a function of the local asymmetrical relation that holds between the adjectival or adverbial phrase and the related nominal or the verbal phrase. Thus in *Luc is a beautiful dancer*, the descriptive/result interpretation is derived via a local asymmetrical relation that holds between the adjective and the nominal head *–er*, the feature structure of which includes an *r* variable; whereas the attributive/event interpretation is derived via a local asymmetrical relation relating the adjective and the verbal head included in the derived nominal *dancer*, as the verb *dance* has an event *e* variable in its feature structure. Thus, semantic compositionality is derived via the formal context in syntactic analysis. See Di Sciullo (in press) for a detailed discussion of the facts.

An adjunct differs from a headas follows. The, categorial features of a head are the categorial features of the constituent it is a part of, whereas, this is not the case for an adjunct. Furthermore, a head is dominated by the projections that contains it; whereas this is not the case for an adjunct, which is dominated by a segment of a category and not by a category. Moreover, the semantic feature structure of a head include the semantic feature structure of its complement; whereas this is not the case for an adjunct, the semantic feature structure of which modify the semantic feature structure of the constituent it is adjoined to.

morphemes are licensed and interpreted. Conditions, such as the Adjunct Identification Condition (Di Sciullo, 1997a) determine the full feature structure of morphemes. This is illustrated by cases where the subcategorization of the affix is constant, but not its categorial and its conceptual features.

(6)　a.　think*er*, great*er*　b.　*dis*please, *dis*embark　c.　*re*write, *re*inforce

In (6a), the difference in category (noun or degree) and semantic (agent/instrument or superlative) of the suffix could be attributed to a difference in the subcategorization feature of that affix, viz., [V__] or [A__]. However, a difference in subcategorization does not cover the facts in (6b) and (6c). In (6b), the prefix *dis-* has negative evaluative features in the first case and prepositional directional features in the second case. In (6c), the prefix re- has adverbial iterative features in the first case and degree intensifier features in the second case. The differences in categorial and conceptual features do not follow from subcategorization, as the prefixes in (6b) and (6c) both compose with verbs and thus would have the same subcategorization feature, viz., [__V]. Contrastingly, the Adjunct Identification Condition. determines the feature structure of the affixes on the basis of the feature structure of the category they compose with. Thus, the prefix *dis-* in *displease* is a degree modifier, as it identifies an unspecified feature of the psychological predicate it is adjoined to; the prefix *dis-* in *disembark* is a directional preposition, as it identifies a orientation to the event denoted by the projection it is a part of, which includes a locative endpoint. Likewise, the prefix *re-* in *rewrite* is an iterative adverb, as it identifies an unspecified feature to the activity it modifies, while the prefix *re-* in *reinforce* is a degree modifier.

Thus, formal context is more accurate than subcategorization for the analysis of complex words.

2.　Model

We present the main features of an integrated competence-performance model where the notion of formal context, based on asymmetry plays a central role.

We assume that singular grammars are the instantiation of Universal Grammar (UG) parameters in terms of differences in the projection or non-projection of morpho-functional features (Chomsky, 1998, and related works) and that parsing singular languages is performed by the processing of specific UG parametrizations. We posit that as UG is designed to optimally derive linguistic expressions in terms of asymmetrical relations, Universal Parser (UP) is designed to optimally process natural language asymmetries.

Given the modular architecture we take the sub-systems of the grammar to be based on the elemental relations of UG and to instantiate specific formal relations. Our model includes a lexicon, the general properties of which are limited at the initial state and are enriched during the acquisition process. The lexicon includes for every underived lexical item, a set of minimal feature structures, formal (categorial) and semantic (conceptual, aspectual, argumental). These feature structures are further specified in the derivation of the linguistic expressions, and used (visible/interpreted) compositionally at the interfaces of the grammar with the performance systems, the cognitive-intentional system and the acoustic-perceptual system. The model includes a computational space where the derivations of the different sorts of linguistic expressions, words (Xo) and phrases (XP), take place under the control of constraints applying in the course of the derivation as well as at the interfaces (Di Sciullo, 1966). In this model, the components, even though autonomous, interact in the derivation of the linguistic expressions.

2.1 Grammar

It is assumed that asymmetrical relations are central in UG, as they offer an explanation to the existence of constraints on the fusion of the linguistic categories, their dependency, and their linear order (Chomsky, 1995, 1998; Kayne, 1984, 1994).

Current works indicate that what has been taken to be the basic asymmetrical relation of the grammar, viz. asymmetrical c-command (Reinhart,1983; Chomsky 1981), is derived from independently needed formal relations (Reuland, 1998; Epstein, 1995, Robert & Vijayashankar 1995). The generic definition of asymmetry given in (3) above constitutes a more basic relation of asymmetry than asymmetrical c-command. It contributes to the identification of the formal context for the derivation of feature structures under the word-level as well as in phrasal syntax.

In our model, the derivation of linguistic expressions is driven by the conceptual necessity to obtain what we call canonical target configurations at the interfaces with the performance systems (Di Sciullo, 1996). These configurations are restricted to elemental asymmetrical relations, mainly the specifier-head relation, the complement-head relation and the adjunct-head relation. We propose that these relations are distinct with respect to feature structure relations in the following way. The features of a complement are properly included in the feature structure of the head, the features of a specifier are included in the feature structure of the category it is the specifier of, and the feature structure of an adjunct are excluded from the features of the category it is adjoined to. Let us refer to these relations as configurational asymmetries.

(7) **Configurational Asymmetries**

Head-Complement $(x > y)$; Adjunct-Head $(x < y)$; Specifier-Head $(x \wedge y)$

Confirming evidence for the existence of such elemental asymmetrical relations comes from the fact that semantic compositionality cannot be obtained via adjunct-head configurations, while it may be obtained via spec-head-complement configurations. Thus, the difference in compositionality of Xo vs XP expressions follows as a consequence in our model, the canonical target configuration for Xo expressions is the adjunct-head configuration, whereas the canonical target configuration for XP expressions is the spec-head-complement configuration.

Furthermore, the feature systems defining the different categories of the grammar are also organized in terms of asymmetrical relations, providing a rationale to the restrictiveness of their paradigms, as discussed in Di Sciullo (to appear). Confirming evidence comes from the conceptual restrictiveness of derivational affixes, as derivational prefixes and suffixes may conceptually affect roots under a limited set of relations, the Predicate-Argument relation, the Modifier-Modifee relation and the Operator-Variable relation. Let us refer to these relations as semantic asymmetries.

(8) **Semantic Asymmetries**

Predicate-Argument $(P(x))$; Modifier-Modifiee $(MOD(x))$;

Operator-Variable $(OP(x))$

These semantic asymmetries are supported by the Head-Complement, the Adjunct-Head and the Specifier-Head relations defined above. In our model, conceptual features are visible in formal contexts under the word-level as well as in phrasal syntax, even though under different locality conditions, see Di Sciullo (1999).

Under the word-level, the Predicate-Argument asymmetry is instantiated in the relation between directional affixes and roots; the Modifier-Modifiee asymmetry is licensed in the relation between scalar affixes and roots; the Operator-Variable relation is licensed in the relation between comparative and superlative affixes and roots.

To illustrate the complementation-predication vs the adjunct-modification differences consider the verbal forms in (9), where (9a) instantiate the first relation and (9b) instantiate the second. Empirical evidence that this is the case comes from the fact that separability of the prefix from the root is excluded in the first case, but not in the second. This indicates that the prefixes in (9a) are part of the categorial/semantic make-up of the projection they are part of, whereas they do not affect the /semantic structure of the verbal projection they modify in the second case.

(9) a. en-chain, de-plain   b. un-fold, re-write

In our model, the configurational asymmetries are paired with the semantic asymmetries. Thus, the iterative prefix re- is in Adjunct-Head and in Modifier-Modifiee relations. It is an adjunct to the verbal projection it is a part of and it modifies the sequenciality of the terminative event denoted by the verbal predicate it is adjoined to. We correctly predict that the iterative prefix may not adjoin to/modify a verbal projection the aspectual structure of which does not have sub-internals, such as verbs denoting bare states and achievements. This prediction is borne out.

(10)	a.	Paul knows French	(state)
	b.	??Paul reknows French.	
	c.	Mary sang La Walli.	(activity)
	d.	?Mary resang La Walli.	
	e.	Paul died.	(achievement)
	f.	??Paul redied.	
	g.	John constructed the structure.	(accomplishment)
	h.	John reconstructed the structure.	

Moreover, only given asymmetrical relations can be visible/interpreted at a given interface with the performance system. Empirical evidence that this is the case comes from the interpretation of compounds vs the interpretation of phrases. In effect, contrary to what is observed in phrasal syntax, a nominal expression, say a DP in a Romance compound, neither has specific reference nor affects the delimitedness of the event denoted by the projection it is a part of (see Di Sciullo and Tenny, 1998).

In our model, the Interpretability Under Asymmetry Condition, defined in (11), drives the derivations and ensures optimal interface interpretation.

(11) Interpretation Under Asymmetry

An interpretation is optimally obtained under a unique local asymmetrical relation.

A local asymmetrical relation optimally supports a unique interpretation.

The Interpretation Under Asymmetry Condition subsumes the set of heterogeneous principles proposed in the literature to account for construction specific properties, such as the First Sister Principle for compounds. In our model, the singular constraints are the effects of the basic asymmetry of the grammar. Local asymmetry defines the formal context within which the operations and the conditions of the grammar apply in an optimal way.

2.2 Processing

A typical computational model includes the axiomatization of a grammar and a set of heuristics that associate one or more formal representations to the expressions submitted to processing.[5] Asymmetrical relations are central in computational models integrating linguistic theory (Berwick, 1991, and related works). We propose an integrated knowledge-use theory of language, where the performance system (UP) is designed to use the asymmetrical properties of the linguistic expressions generated by the grammar (parametrized UG) in an optimal way. Let us take the general principles underlying asymmetry-based parsing to be the following.

(12) **Asymmetry-Based Parsing**

   The parser makes an optimal use of the asymmetrical relations of the grammar.

   The operations of the parser are controlled by the Interpretability Under Asymmetry Condition.

   The parser provides an incremental analysis of the linguistic expressions on the basis of formal context.

We thus propose a direct implementation of asymmetry in the computational model: the properties of the competence grammar are directly used by the processor. The asymmetrical relations of the grammar are implemented directly in the parser. That is, the system integrates the universal asymmetric relations as well as the grammar specific parametric values. The lexical database includes the idiosyncratic properties of underived items, couched in terms of elemental asymmetrical relations. The actions of the parser are oriented by the identification of local asymmetrical relations at each step of the parse, including categorization, attachments and dependencies between categories. In our model, the computational operations are oriented by natural language asymmetries and not by language independent heuristics. The Interpretation Under Asymmetry Condition is used as a control mechanism devise that legitimizes of the choices undertaken by the parser at each step of the parse.

The generality, modularity and lack of directionality of asymmetry-based parsing, as it is the case more generally for principle-based parsing, allow for a wider range of computational strategies. However, our model presents a practical solution to the difficult search control problems typical of principle-based parsing, as the control strategies are unified and restricted by asymmetry.

(13) **Control**

   Search until an asymmetrical relation is identified.

   Search for formal and semantic asymmetry at each step of the parse.

   In case of multiple choice, choose the more local asymmetrical relation rather than a non-local one.

---

[5] There has been important changes in NLP with respect to the recovering of the structures underlying the generation and the analysis of linguistic expressions. The transition from case-based to principled-based approach (Berwick, 1991) is one of the most important change of perspective in NLP. These changes are parasitic on theoretical advances. In linguistic theory, the formulation of the Principle and Parameter framework, giving rise to a family of related theories and frameworks, such as the Government and Binding Theory (Chomsky 1981, and related works), and more recently, the Minimalist framework (Chomsky, 1998, and related works).

Our integrated model keeps maximally simple the relation between the theory of grammar and the theory of parsing. Nevertheless, it keeps constant the specificity of each system and identifies their point of juncture. It relies on the central relation of asymmetry that is part of the definition of the formal context required to the processing of linguistic expressions.

3. A Prototype for morpho-conceptual parsing

We present the main features of a prototype implementing the asymmetry-based grammar for the analysis of morphological structure in formal context. We will refer to this prototype as CONCE-MORPHO-PARSE.[6]

The morphological parsing is performed by a Unification grammar incorporating a LR(1) control structure. The prototype builds morphological trees for words (W), providing a structure to the morphemes (Head (H), External Prefix (EP), Internal Prefix (IP), Suffix (S), Root (R)) they are composed of. A unification-based chart parser, the general properties of which are described in Shieber (1986), provides parse trees with "categorial" and conceptual feature structures.[7] Unification is useful in implementing an asymmetry-based grammar, as asymmetry holds primarily for pairs of feature structures in our model. Thus, feature unification under head-complement asymmetry is possible only when the features of the complement are properly included in the features of the head; feature unification under adjunct-head relation is possible only if the features of the adjunct are not included in the features of the head; feature unification under specifier-head asymmetry is possible only if the features of the head are included in the feature structure of its head. The LR(1) grammar controls Unification and implements the Interpretability Under Asymmetry Condition, as the operations of the grammar apply only if the relevant symmetrical relation between two features structures is obtained. The prototype builds trees on the basis of the recognition of Head-Complement (HC), Adjunct-Head (AH) and Specifier-Head (SH) relational categories, as only these asymmetrical relations are accepted by the parser. These relations are paired with the semantic asymmetrical relations Predicate-Argument, Modifier-Modifiee and Operator-Variable relations

(14) **Part of the LALR(1) grammar**

---

[6] CONCE-MORPHO-PARSE is a refinement of MORPHO-PARSE (Di Sciullo, 1989, 1997b), which was designed to analyze the categorial and argument-structure properties of complex words. While MORPHO-PARSE implemented the morphological theory of Di Sciullo and Williams (1987), CONCE-MORPHO-PARSE implements the theory of asymmetry of Di Sciullo (1998, 1999). It analyzes word-internal configurational and semantic asymmetries. The prototype is implemented by Christian Thérien in the Asymmetry project at the Université du Québec à Montréal.

[7] Unification is defined as an operation that merges the information of two feature structures. The concept of Unification grammar refers to complex feature structures which are used as partial descriptions of linguistic objects. The information that is contained in these descriptions is combined through a monotonic operation, the operation of unification (Uszkoreit, 1990).

a.	W -> AH	e.	HC -> HC S
b.	AH -> PE AH	f.	HC -> R S
c.	AH -> P R	g.	HC -> PI R
d.	AH -> HC S		

A description of the morpho-conceptual parsing of the right edge of words is detailed in Di Sciullo (1989, 1997b). We discuss here the analysis of the left edge of words with CONCE-MORPHO-PARSE, which incorporates the morpho-conceptual specifications of prefixes within the asymmetry-based grammar.

While category-changing suffixes are part of the Predicate-Argument asymmetry, derivational prefixes also participate in modification and Operator-Variable asymmetry. The prototype analyses the different asymmetrical relations, given the Unification grammar, the control structure and the information encoded in the lexicon, an extract of which is given below.

(15) **Extract from the lexicon**

a.	re-:	RelF (x),	MOD (s/t),	AGAIN (e)
b.	un-:	RelF (x),	MOD (s),	INVERSE (e)
c.	de-:	Rel (x),	PRED (r),	OUT OF (loc)
d.	en-:	Rel (x),	PRED (r),	IN (loc)

MORPHO-PARSE licenses Head-Complement, Specifier-Head as well as Adjunct-Head structures. The Head-Complement relation is licensed when categorial selection holds for a pair of items, while the Adjunct-Head relation is licensed when there is no categorial selection, but a modification relation between two items, the Specifier-Head relation is licensed when an operator binds a variable in its local domain. The parser analyses a string of morphemes from left to right and assigns, for every word (W), a parse tree which correctly differentiates between external prefixes (PE), basically modifiers, from internal prefixes (PI), basically predicate. This makes the correct predictions with respect to the argument structure properties of prefixed words (Di Sciullo, 1997a), as well as it accounts for their aspectual structure properties. This is not the case for current morphological analyzers, where all prefixes are treated on a par.

The parse tree derived by CONCE-MORPHO-PARSE presents a finer-grained analysis of complex words, such as prefixed denominal verbs, as depicted in (16). This is not the case for other morphological analyzers, such as PC-KIMMO 2 with Englex 2 (Karttunen, 1983; Antworth, 1990, and related works),[x] which would assign the parse tree in (17) to these expressions.

```
(16)      W                (17)      Word
          !                           !
          AH                         Stem
      PE----!----AH                   !
      re+      HC--!--S           ---------
     [RelF]    !   [V]          Prefix   Stem
```

[x] PC-KIMMO has two analytical components: the rules component and the lexical component. The rules component consists of the two-level rules that account for phonological or orthographic alternations. The lexicon lists all morphemes, including prefixes and suffixes, in their lexical form, and specifies the morphotactic constraints. The two components work together to perform both recognition and generation of word forms, on the basis of the tokenization of words into a sequence of tagged morphemes.

```
[AGAIN]    !    [e]              re+         ----!-----
      PI--!--R                    ORD5    Prefix  Stem
   en+       bottle                      en+        !
   [ P ]                               REV2+     Root
   [ IN ]                                        bottle
```

The superiority of (16) over (17) is both categorial and conceptual, as we will see immediately. CONCE-MORPHO-PARSE assigns an adverbial feature (RelF) to the prefix *re-*, which is the adjunct in the asymmetrical adjunct-head relation formed by the prefix and the rest of the structure. This asymmetrical relation cannot be accepted however at this point of the parse, as there is no such relation between the iterative prefix *re-* and the directional prefix *en-* which is the second prefix analyzed by the parser. As there is no asymmetry between the first and the second prefix, they do not form a constituent. There is however an asymmetry between the directional prefix *en-* and the root *bottle*, it is a Head-Complement relation, given the lexical specification of the prefix *en-* and the root *bottle*. Thus, the Unification grammar controlled by the LR(1) grammar correctly parse the Head-Complement relation. This relation, being more local, is parsed before the adjunct-head relation, connecting the already parsed Head-Complement structure to the suffixal head of the structure. Finally, the Unification grammar controlled by the LR(1) grammar attaches the external prefix to the lastly parsed Adjunct-Head relation. The category of the suffixal root is derived by the parser. As the prefix *re-* locally selects a bare event (e) category, thus a verb.

The configurational as well as the conceptual distinctions between complementation-predication and adjunction-modification, are not expressed by current morphological parsers, such as PC-KIMMO. Moreover, there is no way for a parser that is not fully specified for the categorial and conceptual features of derivational affixes to escape from the ambiguity arising form the phenomenon of conversion. That is, the fact that in English bare nouns can also be verbs according to their syntactic context, as it is the case with our example above, *bottle*, viz., *a bottle* and *to bottle*. CONCE-MORPHO-PARSE correctly assigns the category noun to *bottle* in the configuration at hand, given the local asymmetry between the prepositional prefixal head *en-* and the root *bottle*, viz, the co-extensive categorial Head-Complement asymmetry and the semantic Predicate-Argument asymmetry, where the internal prefix is a head-predicate and the root is a complement-argument.

Summing up, our prototype assigns the correct categorial and semantic feature structures to complex words on the basis of the recognition of co-extensive configurational and semantic asymmetries in formal context. Moreover, it is able to resolve categorial ambiguities on the basis of decisions taken locally.

4. Consequences for information processing

Our proposal has consequences for information processing systems. In particular, we expect the notion of formal context based on local asymmetries to enhance the precision of information extraction as well as information retrieval systems based on natural language processing.

We predict that the integration of CONCE-MORPHO-PARSE in information extraction systems will contribute to their optimization. Stemming algorithms, such as Porter (1980) and Antworth (1990), do not fully rely on word internal information. In our model, parts of words provide "categorial" and conceptual feature structures that determine the information provided by words in formal contexts. The processing of these features is necessary for information processing in more than one way.

Morpho-conceptual features are part of the feature structures of singular words and they constitute the base upon which decisions about the properties of the local syntactic context of words can be anticipated. These predictions are not based on statistical calculi, but rather on morpho-conceptual knowledge. Interestingly, this knowledge is not analogical in nature, it is not part of semantic nets, and governed by IS A and AS A relations. It is a part of the knowledge of language, as it is couched in terms of elementary asymmetrical relations according to our model. This knowledge is used when performing the task of extracting information from texts or retrieving texts from collections.

In our view, information processing reduces to one case of grammar use by a performance system. That is, we take the performance system to be capable to use the formal properties of the grammar to extract specific information from texts or retrieve the relevant documents satisfying a specific query.

A query or a template present partial symbolical properties of a referent, the subject of the search. In our view, an information processing system is an automated simulation of the performance system that interprets the linguistic expressions it is exposed to on the basis of the asymmetrical properties of these expressions. We take these properties to be mainly grammatical in nature and not exclusively statistical.

However, most functioning automatic information processing systems are exclusively based on stochastic methods, such as the Boolean search criterion in information retrieval systems. In these systems, the indexing of the query consists in its translation into Boolean proper forms, while the indexing of the documents consists in the identification of document profiles by means of the selection of descriptors (significant word) for document profiles using a descriptor dictionary. The use of Boolean algebra for query formulation and of descriptor dictionaries for the identification of document profile are based on the view that the representation of the meaning of the objects they manipulate is independent of the very properties of these objects. In effect, Boolean algebra and equivalence classes are natural language independent representations.

On the other hand, morpho-conceptual systems are natural language dependent. Even though, as it is the case for any system, they constitute a simplification of the object they define, they are similar to their object, in such a way as to allow one to obtain new knowledge about it.

The probability-statistical theory of information, and the subsequent approaches to the measurement of information, including the combinatorial approach, the topological approach and the algorithmic approach, are mathematical manipulations of the information conveyed by natural languages. It is acknowledged that information extraction systems based on strictly probabilistic methods achieve high levels of performance, it is generally admitted that these systems have now met their limits.

Several works indicate that the use of natural language processing methods in IR systems contribute to improve the performance of these systems (Savoy, 1993; Arampatzis, Tsaris et Koster, 1997; Pohlmann et Kraaij, 1997). Different factors contribute to the non-optimality of IR systems operating on strictly probabilistic methods. One factor is that stemming algorithms, such as Porter (1980) algorithm, do not remove affixes on the basis of natural language asymmetries, they do not always have a positive effect on the quality of the retrieval, in particular on the precision of the retrieval. Contrastingly, information extraction systems based on natural language asymmetries may improve precision.

We expect that information-processing systems will gain in optimality if they include contextual search based on asymmetry. The optimization covers different modules of information processing systems including stemmers identifying the canonical form of words, morphological analysis, identifying word-internal structure, part-of-speech taggers, identifying the category of lexical items and post-taggers, identifying the constituent structure of phrases. We expect the optimization to achieve the following results:

(18) a.　　fine-grained categorial analysis of word-structure
　　　b.　　fine-grained conceptual analysis of word-structure
　　　c.　　disambiguation in part-of-speech tagging
　　　d.　　greater precision in super-tagging

In the following, we outline the main features of an information processing system incorporating morpho-conceptual parsing. Assuming that information processing systems are series of texts (documents and queries) filters. The first filter submits a text to morphological and lexical analysis, assigning tags, including morpho-conceptual feature structures to words. In this system, the dictionary plays an important part in tagging. In particular, the lexical entries for derivational affixes, as well as functional categories, carry important information about the syntactic and the semantic structure of the linguistic expressions. Initial tagging is performed on the basis of a limited dictionary consisting of function words. The functions words are specified in the dictionary in our features under asymmetrical relations format, as shown in part in (19) for the functional category one, which is either a numeral (as in *one, two, three,...*) or a quantifier (as in *(some)one never knows,...*) according to the syntactic context.

(19)　one:　NUM (x),　PRED (x)
　　　　　　Q (x),　OP (x)

A comparison of the text words against the dictionary is performed, a sentence at the time, by a sequential merging process. As a result of the look-up process, any word found in the text will have received one or more tags. The majority of content words not listed in the dictionary are tagged using morphological information about the suffixes, as in the following entries.

(20) a.　-al: Thi(x),　PRED (p),　RESULT $(EVENT (t))$
　　　　　　　Prop(x),　MOD (r),　PROPERTY $(THING (abs))$
　　　b.　-er: Thi(x),　PRED (e),　RESULT $(EVENT (orig))$
　　　　　　　Prop$_F$ (x, y),　OP (r),　HAVE (x) MORE $(PROPERTY$ THAN $(y))$

Contrary to the vast majority of information extraction systems incorporating NLP (Briscoe, 1997; Basili & al., 1997), our lexicon does not include sub-categorization frames, given that, we have shown above, sub-categorization does not qualify as a proper context for the interpretation of morphological expressions. Sub-categorization frames are partial descriptions of the categorial context within which full lexical items can be analyzed and interpreted. In contrast, the representations in (20) includes the properties of the predicate denoted by the affix, be it nominal (Thin), adjectival (Prop) or functional (Prop$_F$), its argument structure properties depicted in terms of argument variables $(x, y,...)$ and constants (predicate (p), referent (r), event (e)), as well as the roles of the affix in local asymmetrical relation, be they predicate-argument relations (PRED), modifier-modified relation (MOD) or operator variable relation (OP). The selectional properties of affixes are derived from their conceptual structure, where the embedded (italicized) conceptual categories may have one or more categorial realization.

Each one of the examples in (20) present a case of polysemic morpheme. Each affix is associated with more than local asymmetrical relation, be it categorial or semantic. Thus, as they stand in the lexicon, each affix may virtually compose with more than one categorial type of expression, as well as more than one semantic type of expression. Disambiguation is performed by the analysis of local asymmetries in formal context, using a bottom-up chart parser and a Unification grammar to form constituents and to compositionally derive the features of constituents from the features of their parts.

The formalization of context in terms of asymmetrical relations renders superfluous the need for an information processing language that represents the objects of extraction (fragments of documents) or retrieval (documents in a collection) as well as the search requests (the user's queries). Moreover, the use of a dictionary the lexical entries of which are based on natural language asymmetries and a parser to disambiguate tags renders a corpus for statistical analysis not necessary in information processing systems, an improvement with respect to stochastic methods (Church, 1988; Derose, 1988; Marken, 1990).

References

1. Antworth, E., PC-KIMMO: A Tow Level Processor for Morphological Analysis. Dallas, TX: Summer Institute of Linguistics (1990)
2. Arampatzis, A.T., Tsoris, T., Koster, C.H.A.: IRENA: Information Retrieval Engine Based on Natural Language Analysis. RIAO 97 Proceedings, McGill University (1997)
3. Basili, R., Vindigni, M., M. T. Pazienza.: Corpus-driven unsupervised learning of verb subcategorization frames. In Proc. Of the Italian Association for Artifical Intelligence, AI*IA 97, Rome (1997)
4. Berwick, R.: Principle-Based Parsing . Dordrecht: Kluwer Academic Publishers (1991)
5. Benerecetti, M., Cimatti, A., Giunchiglia, F., Serafini, L.: Context-Based Formal Specification of Multi-Agent Systems. In: proceedings of the Third International Workshop on Agent Theories, Architectures, and Languages (ATAL-96), ECAI-96, Budapest (1996)
6. Chomsky, N.: Lectures on Government and Binding . Foris Publications (1981)
7. Chomsky, N.: The Minimalist Program. Cambridge: The MIT Press (1995)
8. Chomsky, N.: Minimalist Inquiries. Ms. MIT (1998)
9. Church, K.: Stochastic Parts Program and NP Parser for Unrestricted Text, Proceedings of the Second Association of Computational Linguistics Conference on Applied Natural Language Processing (1988)
10. Cimatti, A., Serafini, L.: Multi-Agent Reasoning with Belief Contexts III: Towards Mechanization. In : Brezillon, P., Abu-Hakim, S. (eds.): Proceedings (1995) of the IJCAI-95 Workshop on "Modelling Context in Knowledge Representation and Reasoning" (1995) 35-45
11. Derose, S. J.: Grammatical Category Disambiguation by Statistical Optimization, Computational Linguistics, Vol. 14.1 (1988)

12. Di Sciullo, A.M.: Modularity and Xo/XP Asymmetries. Linguistic Analysis Vol. 26 (1996)
13. Di Sciullo, A.M. : Prefixed verbs and Adjunct Identification. In A.M. Di Sciullo (ed) Projections and Interface Conditions. Oxford University Press. (1997a)
14. Di Sciullo, A.M.: Argument Structure Parsing. In: Ralli, A., Grigoriadou, M., Philokyprou, G., Christodoulakis, D., Galiotou, E. (eds.) Papers in Natural Language Processing. (1997b) 55-77
15. Di Sciullo, A.M.: Features and Asymmetrical Relations in Morphological Objects. GLOW Newsletter (1998)
16. Di Sciullo, A.M.: The Local Asymmetry Connection. Penn/MIT Workshop on The Lexicon. MIT (1999)
17. Di Sciullo, A.M.: Conceptual Knowledge and Interpretation. In: ICCS/JICSS, Chukyo, Japan (In press)
18. Di Sciullo, A.M.: Asymmetries, Morphological Configurations and Paradigms. In: Acta Linguistica Hungarica, Hungarian Academy of Sciences and Kluwer Academic Publishers (to appear)
19. Di Sciullo, A.M., Tenny, C.: Modification, Event Structure and the Word/Phrase Asymmetry. NELS 18, (1998)
20. Di Sciullo, A.M., Williams, E.: On the Definition of Word. Cambridge: The MIT Press (1987)
21. Epstein, S.: The Derivation of Syntactic Relations. Ms. Harvard University (1995)
22. Fong, S.: The Computational Implementation of Principle-Based Parsing. In Berwick, R. and al. (eds.) Principle-Based Parsing. Dordrecht: Kluwer Academic Publishers (1991) 65-83
23. Kartunnen, L.: KIMMO : A General Morphological Processor in Texas Linguistic Forum 22 (1983) 163-186
24. Kayne, R.: Connectedness and Binary Branching. Dordrecht: Foris (1984)
25. Kayne, R.: The Antisymmetry of Syntax. Cambridge, MA.: MIT Press (1994)
26. Lieber, R.: Deconstructing Morphology. Chicago University Press. (1992)
27. Marken, C.G.: Parsing the LOB Corpus. Association of Computational Linguistics Annual Meeting (1990)
28. Pohlmann, R., Kraaij, W.: The Effect of Syntactic Phrase Indexing on Retrieval Performance for Dutch Texts. RIAO 97 Proceedings. McGill University, Montreal (1997)
29. Porter, M.F.: An Algorithm for suffix Stripping in Program 14.3 (1980)
30. Reinhart, T.: Anaphora and Semantic Interpretation. Croom Helm, London (1983)
31. Robert, F., Vijayashankar, K.: C-command and Grammatical Primitives. GLOW Newsletter (1995)
32. Reuland, E.: Deriving C-command in Binding. NELS 18 (1998)
33. Savoy, J.: Stemming of French Words Based on Grammatical Categories in Journal of the American Society for Information Sciences 44.1 (1993)
34. Uszkoreit, H.: Unification in Linguistics. Class Lectures, 2nd European Summer School in Language, Logic and Information, Leuven (1990)

The Pragmatic Roots of Context[1]

Bruce Edmonds

Centre for Policy Modelling,
Manchester Metropolitan University,
Aytoun Bbuilding, Aytoun Street, Manchester, M1 3GH, UK.

b.edmonds@mmu.ac.uk http://www.cpm.mmu.ac.uk/~bruce

Abstract. When modelling complex systems one can not include all the causal factors, but one has to settle for partial models. This is alright if the factors left out are either so constant that they can be ignored or one is able to recognise the circumstances when they will be such that the partial model applies. The transference of knowledge from the point of application to the point of learning utilises a combination of recognition and inference – a simple model of the important features is learnt and later situations where inferences can be drawn from the model are recognised. Context is an abstraction of the collection of background features that are later recognised. Different heuristics for recognition and model formulation will be effective for different learning tasks. Each of these will lead to a different type of context. Given this, there two ways of modelling context: one can either attempt to investigate the contexts that arise out of the heuristics that a particular agent actually applies or one can attempt to model context using the external source of regularity that the heuristics exploit. There are also two basic methodologies for the investigation of context: a top-down approach where one tries to lay down general, a priori principles and a bottom-up approach where one can try and find what sorts of context arise by experiment and simulation. A simulation is exhibited which is designed to illustrate the practicality of the bottom-up approach in elucidating the sorts of internal context that arise in an artificial agent which is attempting to learn simple models of a complex environment.

1 Introduction

Frequently at workshops and conferences on context, one finds that the emphasis is on drawing distinctions between different types of context and illustrating how little

[1] Thanks to Scott Moss, Varol Akman and Helen Gaylard for comments on these ideas, to Pat Hayes for stimulating arguments about context and related matters and Steve Wallis for writing SDML. SDML has been developed in VisualWorks 2.5.1, the Smalltalk-80 environment produced by ObjectShare. Free distribution of this for use in academic research is made possible by the sponsorship of ObjectShare (UK) Ltd.

each type has to do with the others. If this trend continues it will quickly become impossible to use the term "context" at all. Now it is certainly the case that naively conflating different usages of the term can cause confusion, but I wish to claim that there is a good reason that we use the same term for these different entities. The reason, I claim, is that context arises from a study of the *pragmatics* of learning and applying knowledge. These roots of context explain why and how the different types of context and approaches to studying them arise. This account centers on the *transference* of knowledge between learning and application. If this is the case, then accounts of context which capture either *only* context-dependent learning or *only* context-dependent inference will be inadequate.

2   Causal Structure

In any but the simplest (e.g. linear) systems, effects can have a great many causes (when modelled in absolute terms). In most systems, the web of causation is so dense that the number of factors that could be included in a model of an event is limited only by the resources we put into it. This is what has been called "causal spread" by Wheeler and Clarke in [19]. It has led some philosophers to argue that many (i.e. non-statistical) notions of causality are only meaningful for simple systems (e.g. [18]). This causal spread makes the *complete* modelling of an event impractical – we are forced to concentrate only on a small subset of possible factors. Of course, this omission of factors in our models is only effective if *either* they are so reliable that their omission is unimportant for practical purposes *or* if we are able to recognise when our restricted model is likely to be applicable. In either case we will not attempt to use the model when it is inapplicable.

Formalisations of causality always involve assumptions about the set of possible factors. Usually they merely present a test which can be used to reject the hypothesis that a given factor or variable is causally irrelevant. The strongest formulation I have found is that of Pearl [15]. He presents an algorithm for finding all the factors that *are* causes, but under the assumption that *no causally relevant factor has been omitted* from the initial set of possible factors.

I will illustrate this "causal spread" with two examples, which will be used to motivate the approach that follows. The first is the causation involved in a man breaking a leg and the second the inference involved in interpreting an utterance.

Example 1. A man is distracted and falls off a small ledge onto a pavement. When he lands his leg breaks. What caused his leg to break? It could be attributed to many things: the hardness of the pavement; the weakness of his femur; the way he landed on the leg; gravity; the mass of his body; him falling off the ledge; the ledge itself; the height of the ledge; the distraction; or even the man's distractability. There seems to be no end to the number of factors one *could* include as causes of the fracture. Whether one *does* count each of these as causes is arbitrary from an absolute external viewpoint. It can depend on the extent to which we judge each of them as *unusual*. For example, if the ledge was there due to a freak subsidence we might say that this subsidence was the cause – if the ledge was normal (the side of some steps) but the distraction was exceptional (there was a couple making love in the middle of the street) we would say the distraction was the cause.

Example 2. Two people, Joan and Jill, are talking: Joan says "We'll go and have a friendly chat in a bar."; Jill replies "Yeah, right!" which is (correctly) taken to mean by Joan that Jill thinks that this is a *bad* idea and does *not* want to go. In what way was the negative message conveyed? In other words, what allowed Jill to infer the meaning of Joan's utterance? There could be many such factors: the tone of Jill's voice; that the peer group to which Jill and Joan belong always say "Yeah, right!" when they disagree; that Jill is pointing a gun at Joan; that they are both are locked away in jail and so the suggestion was impossible to carry out; that Jill had been neurotically repeating "Yeah, right!" over and over for the past two years since her sister died etc. The answer could have been any one of these or any combination of them. Even if many of these factors *were* present Joan may have only used one or two of them in her inference, the rest being redundant.

Our models of the world (physical or social) are distinctly limited constructs. We could not possible learn useful models of our world if we had to include all the *possible* causes. In practice, we have to restrict ourselves to but a few causes that we *judge* to be the significant. The means by which we reach such judgements can vary greatly depending on the circumstances (including our knowledge etc.).

In general (as developing human beings) we start by learning simple models of our world, i.e. those with only a few explicated causes and only introduce more causes as we need to. The more causes we include in our model the more generally applicable, but also the more unwieldy, it becomes. If we are lucky, the natural world is so structured as to allow us to abstract away some of this detail and find a more generally applicable model for certain aspects that are relevant to us. Sometimes we can construct models that have sufficiently wide conditions of application that it is convenient for us to *consider* them as general truths. However, such cases, are exceptional – they tend to be highly abstract and so to apply them one typically has to bring the cluttering detail back in to the model in the process of applying it to a particular situation. In many models in the field of physics, this detail is frequently bought in as either initial conditions or auxiliary hypotheses.

In this paper I want to consider aspects of the more usual models we learn and apply, not the exceptional ones that are we consider as generally applicable. There is a view that somehow more general models are *better*, because they are not restricted to particular domains of applicability, and hence should be the focus of our study. According to this view more specialised knowledge *should* be represented as specialisations of these 'general' models. I dispute this – I contend that although there is great theoretical economy of representation in the more abstract and generally applicable models, the huge difficulties of applying them to common situations often precludes them as a sensible way to proceed. It would be incredible indeed if it just so happened that the world was constructed so that it was *always* sensible to work via the most general structures possible!

3   Contexts emerge from Modelling Heuristics

The efficacy of our limited learning and inference in dealing with our complex world is dependent on the presumption that many of the possible causes of events that are important to us remain relatively constant. Otherwise we would need to include all the possible causes in our models and decision making processes, which would not be feasible. This relative constancy is what makes our limited modelling ability useful: we can learn a simple model in one circumstance and successfully use it in another circumstance that is sufficiently similar to the first.

Roughly, I am going to attribute the label of 'context' as a stand-in for those factors that are *not* explicitly included in the simple models we learn, or, to put it positively, those factors that we use to recognise when a model is applicable. This is similar to Zadrozky's approach:

"...*for any procedure we can divide its parameters into two sets: those that change with each invocation of the procedure and those that are there but remain constant. The latter set will be called its content and the former its focus.*" [21]

It is the possibility of the transference of knowledge via fairly simple models from the circumstances where they are learnt to the circumstances where they are applied which allows the emergence of context. The utility of 'context' comes from the possibility of such transference. If this were not feasible then 'context', as such, would not arise. This process of transference is illustrated below in figure 1.

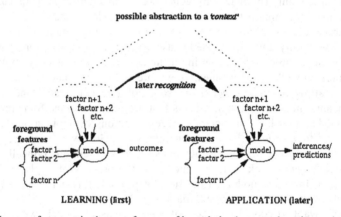

Fig. 1. The use of context in the transference of knowledge between learning and application

For such a transference to be possible a number of conditions need to be met, namely:
- that some of the possible factors influencing an outcome are separable in a practical way;
- that a useful distinction can be made between those factors that can be categorised as foreground features (including 'causes') and the others;
- that the background factors are capable of being *recognised* later on;
- that the world is regular enough for such models to be at all learnable;
- that the world is regular enough for such learnt models to be at all useful when applied in situations where the context can be recognised.

While this transference of learnt models to applicable situations is the basic process, observers and analysts of this process might identify some of these combinations of features that allow recognition and abstract them as a 'context'. This usually is possible because the transference of knowledge as models requires that the agent doing the transference can recognise these characteristic combinations, so it is possible that an observer might also be able to do so and give these combinations names. Note that it is not *necessarily* possible that such an observer will be able to do this as the underlying recognition mechanism may be obscure. Of course, it may be that the agent doing the transference *itself* analyses and abstracts these features, and thus makes this abstract available for reflective thought.

Given the above conditions are possible, I am defining 'context' as:

the abstraction of those elements of the circumstances in which a model is learnt, that are not used explicitly in the production of an inference or prediction when the model is later applied, that allow the recognition of new circumstances where the model can be usefully applied.

Due to the fact that context is characterised as an abstraction of an aspect of a heuristic for the learning *and* application of knowledge, the properties of such contexts can not be meaningfully analysed if one only considers *either* the learning *or* the application of such knowledge. If one did this one would not only be missing out on over half of the story but also undercutting the reasons for its very existence. If the problems of learning are ignored then there is no reason not to encode such models without context – the non-causal factors can be treated as either given or the same as the other features of the model, de-contextualising them. If the problems of inference are ignored then there is no reason to separate the recognition of an appropriate context from that of recognising the correct prediction in that context.

4   Internal and External Conceptions of 'context'

Given the above picture of context and ignoring, for the moment, the effect that different heuristics will have in different domains, there are at least two ways in which we (as people discussing the idea of context) can make a reference to this process. I will call these the 'internal' and 'external' ways of referring to context. The distinction drawn here is not new (e.g. [10]), but I wish to re-tell it in terms of the picture presented herein.

We can refer to the context as that which an individual (or group of individuals) actually uses as a result of their learning. This has the disadvantage that different individuals or groups will develop different constructs as a result of their circumstances and the heuristics they happen to use. On the other hand these can be empirically investigated.

It is not clear that the contextual mechanism that an individual uses to remember and recognise a situation will be best represented by symbolic inference. For it may be that one such 'context' isn't *clearly* separable from another. Deciding which context is relevant may be more of a process of recognition than an inferential process. If this is the case the recognition might be better modelled by something like a neural network than using a logic-based system. It may be that there isn't sufficient continuity for the results of the recognition process to be meaningfully ascribed separate identities. But even if this *is* the case, it does not mean that it is useful for *us* to analyse and model these mechanisms using computational, symbolic or other reified terms.

Alternatively, we could try to abstract from the concrete manifestation of individual's constructs outwards to the regularities and features these constructs rely on in order for their modelling heuristics to be useful (or even possible). Thus we have talk of context-as-a-resource in NL [11], or the context-we-inhabit in AI [3].

The problem with this approach is that the number of possible outward features that *might* be useful can be large. In order to focus on the parts that might actually be useful for an intelligence that is attempting to exploit them one has to consider (maybe implicitly) the internal construct of a context anyway. There may be some good grounds for identifying some relevant regularities on a priori grounds (for example, temporal context) but even in these cases it is hard to see how the properties of such contexts could be deduced for *actual* agents in real examples, without some validation that the presumed a priori grounds were *actually* used by the agent.

Thus in each case the pragmatics of learning, transferring and applying knowledge creeps in. The only escape from the relevance of these pragmatic roots of context is if one is not considering an *actual* or *applicable* rationality and reasoning but only some artificial rationality for use on problems in restricted domains (e.g. a heavily idealised or purely normative rationality).

5   Context in Different Domains

Different modelling heuristics will be useful in different domains, which explains why different sorts of context arise in these different domains. The modelling heuristics typically exploit some sort of commonality. This commonality ensures that some of an event's features will remain constant from the time of learning a model to its application. This commonality makes the modelling of events feasible by limiting the number of features have to be explicitly included in the model, under the conditions that the commonality is either pervasive or recognizable.

Sometimes these common features can be identified, and the external approach to context adopted (as discussed in section 4.2 above), but at other times this may not be obvious so that one is forced to indentify the heuristics that happen to be used by the agent, leading to the internal approach (section 4.1). I list three broad areas of commonality below, and discuss the likely tractability of the contexts that may arise from them as an objects of study.

One of the most obvious and straight-forward commonalities is a shared spatial location or time. This can either mean that a model is learned at a particular location and time and then applied at similar location or time (e.g. on Sunday in church), or it can mean that there is a spatial and temporal commonality between conversers allowing a listener to infer the meaning of indexicals. Such physical commonalities are, by their nature, readily indentifiable. This means that laws of spatial and temporal context are among the most amenable of all contexts to analyse. For an introduction to the situation calculus approach for this type of commonality see [2].

The richest source of commonality we have as humans, arises from our shared culture, in particular our language. In fact the trouble is that often, this source is *too* rich for us as academics. As Graeme Hirst points out there are often *no* external features that are identifiable as the commonality, since the commonality may be a purely social construct with no accompanying external markers [11]. This would mean that the external approach would not be viable. Of course, in such situations the internal approach is almost as difficult, since the heuristics used by individuals may vary amoung individuals at the same time and over time for one individual the same. This embarrassment of riches may well mean that there are no *general* characteristics that can be abstracted from the multitude of heuristics used to model these social constructs, and hence no generally applicable characteristics of social context *per se*.

This does not mean that the relevant commonalities and heuristics can not be discovered in *particular instances*. For example, if a set of social norms has been established within a certain social group, then it might be sensible (in circumstances where one recognises that the situation lies within that grouping) to model others' behaviour in terms of deviations from these norms. If these norms have been sufficiently externalised into an explicitly expressed set of rules this will be identifiable as a source of social context. Akman outlines some other feasible approaches to aspects of social context in [1].

A third area of commonality is our shared biology. This may provide a shared experience of emotions, experience of inhabiting a body, experience of consciousness and other shared knowledge (e.g. basic language structure). These may be very important in a child's early development but are complicated and 'masked' with cultural overlays in later life. However their relative constancy across humans and their pervasiveness may allow for studies of context arising from these commonalities in a way that is difficult with commonality based in social constructions. Apart from linguists who apply the concept of deep-structure, I do not know of any studies of context which focus in these biological areas (Although Drescher's 'schema' touch on this area [5].).

6   Bottom-up and Top-down Approaches to Modelling Context

In addition to the differences in context resulting from the heuristics relevant to a domain and whether an 'internal' or 'external' approach is taken, there are also differences that are imposed by us as modellers due to the different approaches we use for investigating these situations. One of the most important (in terms of contrasts in approach) is whether one attempts to formulate one's models using a 'top-down' or 'bottom-up' approach. A top-down approach is where one attempts to lay down general principles (encoded variously as axioms, rules, algorithms, etc.) based on current or *a priori* thought. A bottom-up approach would involve attempting to induce models of context from the details of the learning and inferential processes as they might occur in practice, and later seeing if any appropriate abstractions or generalisations suggest themselves.

The approach to modelling context most frequently taken in AI, and perhaps epitomised by the approach of John McCarthy [12], which is to specify a general structure for representing statements concerning contextual reasoning and then to investigate some of the possible axiomatisations of logics that encapsulate principles that are thought desirable. Thus the general principles are formulated first and the properties emerging from these are investigated later. The initial standard for judging such constructs is the plausibility and generality of the abstract principles – thus like mathematics this is a foundationalist approach. Of course, the *ultimate* judgement comes from the usefulness of the approach in formalising or implementing actual systems. This approach is partly a result of a desire to elucidate generally applicable AI principles and partly a bias resulting from the selection of formal logics as a tool for modelling practical reasoning.

Of course, some work in AI takes a less general approach than this, especially where the work is focused towards a specific problem or problem domain.

In other domains it is much more difficult to establish general principles for learning and inference. Here a more bottom-up approach needs to be taken. A small sub-domain is typically chosen and then relevant examples considered to establish the likely heuristics involved. In this approach the specific data and facts come first and the more abstract principles and theories come second. The models are formulated to capture or explain observed processes and will be judged in this light. Later more abstract models (or laws) might be posited from testing against these models and the data. Thus this approach could be dubbed the 'scientific' approach.

The bottom-up approach is perhaps taken most seriously by those who advocate a constructivist approach to AI. Here care is taken to assume *as little as possible* in advance so that as much as possible of the behaviour is available for capture in the models induced [17].

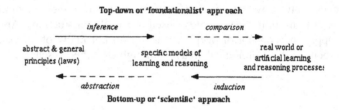

Fig. 2. Top-down and bottom-up approaches to the investigation of context

The community interested in context is unevenly split into these two approaches. The 'foundationalists' are searching for a sort of *mathematics* of context, their approach is principle-based and has a potentially general applicability. However they are dogged by problems of scalability from the toy-problems they are tested on and will only be as strong as their *a priori* principles turn out to be. The 'scientists' are typically working in a specific domain with more realistic processes and problems, they face the same difficulties of generalisation as other scientists – it is a slow and difficult process to discover successful theories. On the other hand any progress they make will be strongly grounded in real processes and have clear conditions of applicability. In other sciences both kinds of approach have turned out to be useful, the foundationalists have typically had a role in producing a palate of formalisms, a few of which turn out to be useful to the scientists who use them for describing or modelling the actual phenomena. The high odds against a particular type of formalism turning out to be useful means that it is vital that the *maximum possible* variety of approaches be developed. The scientists have the job of finding the mappings from the phenomena concerned to models expressed in these formalisms. This job is harder, which possibly explains why they are in the minority.

7   A Bottom-up Investigation of Internal

To illustrate how a bottom-up investigation of context might proceed, I exhibit a simulation which allows the analysis of the emergence of context in the knowledge learned by an artificial agent in a controlled environment. The model and results are preliminary and are intended to be more suggestive of future methodology than significant in detail.

The idea is to place an artificial agent in a environment that is well beyond its capacity to model but one which exhibits some regularities. The agent is designed to learn about its environment using feedback from its attempts to predict outcomes in that environment. It learns using a method that allows the development of pattern-recognition, inference and context-like constructs. I then study the structure of the knowledge that the agent learns in order to identify whether context-like constructs emerged.

The learning algorithm is based upon the neural network invented by Chialvo and Bak in [4]. This algorithm learns a set of mappings between single inputs and single outputs using purely negative feedback. The information is stored as the set of weights associated with the arcs connecting a set of nodes. The algorithm works as follows: an input node is fired, then the arc from this node with the greatest weight fires which fires the node it leads to; this carries on until an output node is fired; if the output is correct then nothing happens but if it is wrong all the weights on fired arcs are depressed and this change in weight is redistributed to other arcs.

This 'learning by mistakes' algorithm is very efficient to train and use. Also, due to the fact that successful associations are not positively reinforced, the network remains in a critical state so that if the environment it is learning about returns to a previous state, the associations it had learned are relatively quickly re-established. In other words, since an arc either fires or it does not, the network only needs to marginally depress previously correct associations and hence does not totally 'forget' them. The topology of the network turns out not to be critical for the working of this algorithm. This algorithm is illustrated in section 3.

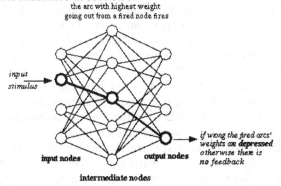

Fig. 3. Chialvo and Bak's learning algorithm

I have adapted this algorithm in two ways: *firstly*, to allow the network to learn mappings from combinations of inputs to combinations of outputs and, *secondly*, to add 'switching' arcs that can turn other arcs on or off.

The first adaption was achieved by introducing a global critical level for the network. Arcs leading from a fired node can only fire if their weight is greater than the critical level. The critical level is gradually changed so as to ensure that the appropriate level of firing occurs. As before, all fired arcs that cause output nodes to fire when they should not have are depressed.

Secondly, arcs are of two kinds: switched and unswitched. Unswitched are as already described, switched arcs are enabled by an arc that leads to them (an *enabling* arc)– they can only fire if: (1) the nodes they come from have fired; (2) their weight is greater than the critical level; *and* (3) the arc that leads to them has fired. If the firing of an enabling arc leads to the over-firing of an output node then it is depressed in a similar manner to other arcs but to a lesser degree (e.g. depressed by 25% of the value by which the other arcs are depressed). This algorithm is illustrated in figure 4.

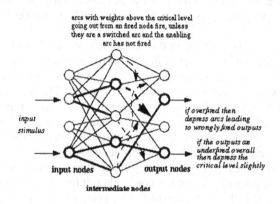

Fig. 4. Generalised version of the algorithm

This generalised version of Caviallo and Bak's algorithm is *not* designed to be a particularly effective learning mechanism but rather a tool for investigating what sort of rules are learnable in an environment. It is particularly appropriate for this task for two reasons: *firstly*, because the network can be readily analysed since the arcs that have weights greater than the critical level can be interpreted as implications; and *secondly*, because the switched arcs allow the emergence of nodes that act as contexts, in that they do not directly cause the firing of further nodes but *enable* a set of other implications without this being imposed.

The network is designed so that it can learn the structures of directed arcs described in [9]. It is designed to be as free from assumptions about the structure of the contexts as possible – thus it is ideal for this kind of investigation where the purpose is to investigate *what the appropriate assumptions are* in a particular environment. Broadly speaking, a context is represented by one (or more) nodes that develop a role of 'switching' sets of associations, whilst other nodes represent facts about the environment. There is, of course, no hard and fast distinction between context nodes and other nodes but more that in some circumstances some nodes act more *as* contexts and others act more *as* the content of the model in context. The difference is illustrated in figure 5.

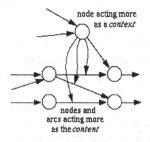

Fig. 5. Nodes acting as contexts and other nodes

If the structure of the network allows it, there is nothing in the algorithm that prevents the network: learning in a context-free way; having contexts imply other contexts, developing hierarchies of contexts, having nodes acting as contexts in some situations and not in others etc. It can be interpreted as implementing both inferential and pattern recognition processes: whether a node is fired is a matter of pattern recognition as a result of the learning done by the network, but the resulting firable arcs can be analysed in terms of (possibly context-dependent) implications about its environment.

The environment is a small artificial stock market. Broadly it is an extension of [14]. There is a small population of artificial traders who are each attempting to predict the next day's stock prices based on data from the recent past. Each trader has a small population of candidate models of the price behaviour in terms of past movement, dividends, comparisons against historical levels etc. Each agent is continually: generating new variations of past models; evaluating them as to how well they would have predicted prices in the recent past; choosing the best of its models; using this model to predict future prices and taking an action to buy or sell dependent on this prediction. It is doing this in parallel to the other agents – essentially each is trying to 'out-think' the other traders by predicting the effect of each other's predictions. The price series that results are weakly related to the fundamentals of the stocks (e.g. the dividend to price ratio) but this is 'masked' by self-reinforcing patterns of speculation among the traders.

I enhanced this model by substituting a genetic programming algorithm for the classifier system. This enables the traders to develop their internal models in a more open-ended and creative way using a much wider range of strategies, including imitation. I also introduced a round of communication between traders before each session of buying and selling. The details of the traders and their interactions can be found in [6, 7], but they are not critical here. What is important here is that it provides: an environment that is beyond the capacity of agent to completely model [8]; that displays distinct phases to which learning heuristics might apply; and that is tunable in the level and type of learning difficulties it presents. To give an idea of the level of difficulty, figure 6 shows a typical example of the price series that the agent is trying to learn. Although it is fairly unpredictable *in detail*, there are distinct and recognizable phases of buying and selling indicated by the cyclical nature of price swings and the clear negative correlation between the prices of the two stocks.

The whole model was implemented in SDML, a declarative modelling language developed at the Centre for Policy Modelling for social simulation. For details of SDML see [13] and http://www.cpm.mmu.ac.uk/sdml.

Preliminary Results

Since the purpose of this model is merely to demonstrate the feasibility of a bottom-up approach, this description of the results will be cursory. Those who want more detail will either have to imitate the techniques or wait for a fuller investigation of the subject by me.

Two runs were performed with the same learning agent but different environmental set-ups. The first run's environment consisted of a market with 5 traders, each of which had 20 models of initial depth 5, while the second had only 2 agents each with 10 models of initial depth 4. The first will be called the 'harder' and the second the 'easier' learning task. The 'harder' series change more abruptly and exhibit a more complex cycle than the 'easier' series.

For each task the agent was given an identical network structure of: 23 input nodes, 20 intermediate nodes; and 11 output nodes. The input nodes were randomly connected to an average of four intermediate nodes each, which were connected with 3 output nodes and switching 3 other arcs using enabling arcs as described above. The agent then runs through the dates once, hence it is a one-shot incremental learning task. The network is deliberately limited in order to simulate the sort of learning a real agent might attempt in a similar situation.

Despite the considerable difficulties it was faced with the agent did manage to induce some effective (but, of course, fallible) rules about the prices series. For both tasks the agent specialised some of the nodes to act as indications of context, that is it learnt arc weights such that these nodes acted to 'switch' other arcs and did not imply any of the output nodes directly themselves. In figure 8 I have plotted the number of these 'context' nodes as the simulation progressed for both learning tasks. It can be seen that the agent induced more contexts for the 'easier' task than the 'harder' one.

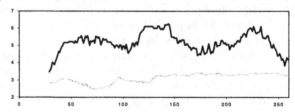

Fig. 6. (smoothed) Number of nodes acting as contexts – both learning tasks (the 'hard' learning task in bold)

In figure 9 I have summarised the contexts developed by the agent at the end of the 'harder' learning task. These were constantly being selected in and out, due to the nature of the learning algorithm. The underlined headings indicate the conditions under which the context is recognised and the implications under them are the rules that are hold in that context (i.e. are enabled by them). Thus the consequent of one of these rules will only be inferred if the context is fired as well as the antecedent, but this does not mean that the context is functionally the same as the antecedent as they are reinforced by the learning algorithm in different ways. The enabling arcs' weights are changed at a slower rate than the node-node arcs (one quarter as slowly). Thus it will take many more occasions of negative feedback to change a context node's associations than one of the implicational arcs in that context. This allows learnt contexts to last longer. Likewise the arcs that lead to the contextual node (i.e. those representing the conditions which the context is recognised) can change more quickly than the 'membership' of that context.

In this way I have allowed the emergence of context-like behaviour without imposing the sort of two-tier structures that have been employed in other machine learning algorithms (e.g. [16, 20]). If I had a network with more than one intermediate layer we could allow the emergence of contexts within contexts etc. but this would take longer runs in order for any results to emerge.

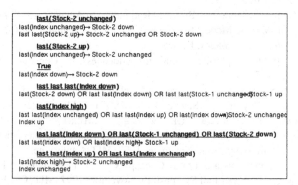

Fig. 7. The 'contexts' induced by the agent by the last 10 dates – harder learning example

Future work with this model will involve attempting more runs of the current model; runs with a more intricate network topology and runs on data generated by real-world processes. The idea is not to discover any 'golden rules' for these domains but to start to tease out how and in what way different contextual structures can arise from different sorts of regularity (or lack of it) in the data.

8   Conclusion

If one only studies *either* the learning of context-dependent knowledge *or* context-dependence inference then one may well be missing the essence of context. I suggest that context only makes complete sense when considering the *transference* of knowledge from point of learning to point of application. Identifiable contexts arise from *our modelling* of those features that allow the recognition of a situation in which an inferential model can be applied. If this is correct then a successful study of context may need the *combined* expertise of the AI and Machine Learning communities.

References

1.   Akman, V. (1997). Context as a Social Construct. Context in Knowledge Representation and Natural Language, AAAI Fall Symposium, November 1997, MIT, Cambridge.

2. Akman, V. and Surav, M. (1996). Steps Towards Formalizing Context. *AI Magazine*, 17:55-72.

3. Barwise, J. and Perry, J. (1983). Situations and Attitudes. Cambridge: MIT Press.

4. Chialvo, D. R. and Bak, P. (1997). Learning by Mistakes. Sante Fe Working Paper 97-08-077.

5. Drescher, G. L. (1991). *Made-up Minds – A Constructivist Approach to Artificial Intelligence*. Cambridge, MA: MIT Press.

6. Edmonds, B. (1998). Modelling Socially Intelligent Agents. *Applied Artificial Intelligence*, 12: 677-699.

7. Edmonds, B. (in press). Modelling Bounded Rationality In Agent-Based Simulations using the Evolution of Mental Models.In Brenner, T. (ed.), *Computational Techniques for Modelling Learning in Economics*, Kluwer.

8. Edmonds, B. (1999). Capturing Social Embeddedness: a Constructivist Approach. *Adaptive Behaviour*, 7(3/4).

9. Edmonds, B. A Simple-Minded Network Model with Context-like Objects. European Conference on Cognitive Science (ECCS'97), Manchester, April 1997. (http://www.cpm.mmu.ac.uk/cpmrep15.html)

10. Hayes, P. (1995). Contexts in Context. Context in Knowledge Representation and Natural Language, AAAI Fall Symposium, November 1997, MIT, Cambridge.

11. Hirst, G. (1997). Context as a Spurious Concept. Context in Knowledge Representation and Natural Language, AAAI Fall Symposium, November 1997, MIT, Cambridge.

12. McCarthy, J. (1996). A logical AI approach to context. Unpublished note, 6 February 1996. http://www-formal.stanford.edu/jmc/logical.html

13. Moss, S., Gaylard, H., Wallis, S. and Edmonds, B. (1998). SDML: A Multi-Agent Language for Organizational Modelling. *Computational and Mathematical Organization Theory*, 4, 43-69.

14. Palmer, R.G. et. al. (1994). Artificial Economic Life – A Simple Model of a Stockmarket. *Physica D*, 75:264-274.

15. Pearl, J. (forthcoming). An Axiomatic Characteriztion of Causal Counterfactuals. *Foundations of Science*.

16. Trun S. and Mitchell, T. M. (1995). Learning One More Thing. Proceedings of the 14th International Joint Conference on Artificial Intelligence (IJCAI'95). San Mateo, CA: Morgan Kaufmann, 1217-1223.

17. Vaario, J. (1994). Artificial Life as Constructivist AI. *Japanese Society of Instrument and Control Engineers, 33:65-71.*

18. Wagner, A. (1997). Causality in Complex Systems. Sante Fe Working Paper 97-08-075.

19. Wheeler, M. and Clark, A. (forthcoming). Genic Representation: Reconciling Content and Causal Complexity. *British journal for the Philosophy of Science*.

20. Widmer, G. (1997). Tracking Context Changes through Meta-Learning. *Machine Learning*, 27:259-286.

21. Zadrozny, W. (1997). A Pragmatic Approach to Context. Context in Knowledge Representation and Natural Language, AAAI Fall Symposium, November 1997, MIT, Cambridge.

Non-acceptances: Re- or Un-creating Context?

Anita Fetzer

University of Stuttgart
Institute for English Linguistics
D-70174 Stuttgart
Germany
e-mail: anita@ifla.uni-stuttgart.de

Abstract

Non-acceptances are discussed in *speech act theory, logic & conversation* and *conversation analysis* with special reference to *how* context is accommodated. The results are systematized in the framework of *plus/minus-validity claims* based on the contextualization of Habermas's *theory of communicative actions* [18], defined as minus-validity claims anchored to an interactive tripartite system of *objective, subjective* and *social worlds* subdivided into further *textual, interpersonal* and *interactional* sub-systems.

Non-acceptances of the objective world are represented explicitly (syntactic, semantic negation), non-acceptances of the subjective world represented non-linearly (negative non-verbal behaviour), and non-acceptances of the social world explicitly *and* implicitly (denials, rejections, negative contextualization cues).

Context is both *micro & institutional*, and *process & product*. Minus-validity claims are not only calculated in a bottom-up manner with regard to their references to the three worlds, but also with regard to institutional contexts. Before this type of presupposed context may be rejected, it is re-created by being made explicit. Only then is it possible to reject and un-create it.

1 Introduction

If natural-language discourse consisted of the transmission of information only, both saying NO and interpreting the communicative meaning of NO would be a rather straight-forward matter, as the communication act NO would present explicit information, such as *I do not agree with you, I reject your invitation* or *you are not telling the truth*. However, in real-life discourse the communication act NO is hardly ever performed baldly on record, but frequently mitigated in order to avoid potential threats to the participants' face-wants / needs [5]. However, the appropriate degree of mitigation required is not universal, but depends on the socio-cultural context in which the non-acceptance is produced. As a consequence, an investigation of non-acceptances, such as the speech acts rejection and denial, or the conversation-analytic moves rejection and disagreement, has to account for the relationship between *what is said* and *what is meant* by accommodating not only *linguistic* and *speaker-intended meaning*, but also their explicit and implicit linguistic representation(s) in discourse. More precisely, in natural-language communication denials and rejections may not only realize the non-acceptance of a speech act's propositional content and/or illocutionary force, but also the non-acceptance of a speech act's sequential status, or the non-acceptance of participant-oriented presuppositions, such as face-wants or participant status. Generally, these language-external phenomena have been attributed to the fields of *background assumptions*, *felicity conditions*, *pragmatic presuppositions* or *context*.

External context is thus of immense importance in the fields of pragmatics, discourse analysis and conversation analysis because of its decisive influence on the communicative meaning of an utterance with regard to both production and interpretation. That is to say, natural-language communication never takes place in a void because the participants of a communicative encounter produce, i.e. encode and/or conversationally implicate, and interpret, i.e. decode and/or infer, their utterances in already existing linguistic and extra-linguistic contexts which are embedded in institutional contexts, thus anchoring their utterances to these linguistic and extra-linguistic contexts. More precisely, utterances are not only embedded in context, but interact with context. The acceptance of an utterance does not only accept the utterance-as-such, but it also accepts the implicitly represented contextual information and its presuppositions. However, there is a crucial difference between acceptances and non-acceptances in discourse, since the former accepts both utterance and its constitutive contextual presuppositions whereas the latter only rejects the utterance-as-such, because contextual presuppositions have to be made explicit and thereby be attributed a determinate status. And it is this determinate status, which has to be ratified, before it may be rejected. Since contextual presuppositions are indeterminate to some extent, their non-acceptance requires two moves, at least.

Part I of this contribution investigates the interdependence of non-acceptances and context in the frameworks of *speech act theory*, H. P. Grice's *logic and conversation*, and *conversation analysis*. Part II systematizes the results obtained in the framework of the contextual function *plus/minus-validity claim*, which is based on the contextualization of Jürgen Habermas's *theory of communicative actions* [18] and his notion of communication as a process of negotiating validity claims. In this setting, validity claims are anchored to an interactive tripartite system of objective, social and subjective worlds and their respective presuppositions, thus allowing for the accommodation of linguistic code, social context and socio-cultural practice.

2 Non-Acceptances in Speech Act Theory, *Logic and Conversation*, and Conversation Analysis

2.1 Non-Acceptances in Speech Act Theory

Speaking a language is engaging in a (highly complex) rule-governed form of behavior [25,12] - and this applies to non-acceptances, i.e. rejections and denials, too. Speech act theory has paved the way for investigating both linguistic and speaker-intended meaning by explicitly referring to the dichotomy of *what is said* and *what is meant* thereby attributing relevance to both linguistic and extra-linguistic contexts.

Speech act theory's basic unit of investigation is the speech act, and depending on the frameworks employed, speech acts divide into locutionary, illocutionary and perlocutionary acts [2], or propositional and illocutionary acts [25], and their respective sub-acts. In authentic discourse, these acts are performed simultaneously and may be represented linguistically in both direct and indirect modes, i.e. as direct and indirect speech acts. Direct speech acts are more explicit and therefore less context-dependent. However, they still require speech-act-specific felicity conditions, i.e. specified contexts, in order to be felicitous. Indirect speech acts, on the other hand, are less explicit and therefore more context-dependent. They generally refer to one specific felicity condition and query or state its validity thereby triggering a process of inferencing in order to retrieve the speaker's communicative intention. Rejections may, for instance, be represented directly by *I hereby reject your offer* or they may be represented indirectly by *your offer seems very generous, but ...* . With regard to the explicitly represented rejection, the hearer has to retrieve quite a lot of contextual information from the socio-cultural context, such as the content of the offer-in-question and the speaker=s identity, i.e. whether the speaker refers to herself as an individual or speaks on behalf of some institution. The implicitly represented rejection, however, requires the hearer to do even >more inferencing work= since s/he is confronted with a positive evaluation and a negative evaluation: there is the intensified positive evaluation >very generous= which seems to indicate that the offer-in-question was received favourably, and there is the connective >but=, which functions as a corrective discourse marker signalling non-acceptance. It is the hearer=s task to >come to terms= with this inconsistency, i.e. the intensified positive evaluation and the negative discourse marker, and search for further evidence in order to be more precise. That is to say, the predication >seems very generous= does not only consist of the positive evaluation >very generous=, but also the modality marker >seems= which reduces the degree of certainty about the positive evaluation. As a result, the hearer comes to the conclusion that >your offer seems very generous, but ...= represents an implicit rejection.

While rejections realize a non-acceptance of a speech act=s illocution, denials do not accept a speech act=s propositional content. Denials may be realized directly by *what you've been saying is not true*, and indirectly by *could you supply further evidence*. Both utterances require the hearer to retrieve contextual information: the former requires the hearer to infer the reference of >what=, while the latter requests the hearer to >supply more evidence= thus representing a rather straight-forward request which is attributed the communicative function of an indirect denial. More precisely, the hearer is requested to >supply further evidence=, to attribute a >determinate status= to her/his implicitly represented contextual presuppositions, i.e. to be more explicit and initiate a process of ratification. Despite the fact that rejections and denials differ with regard to *what is not accepted* [28], both may employ explicit and implicit modes of representation: the former rejects the speech act's illocution based on the proposition, which is defined in the framework of social conventions, whereas the latter denies a speech act's proposition, which is either true or false.

Speech act theory combines language-internal and language-external factors by systematizing them in the framework of a speech act's felicity conditions, which are classified with regard to propositional content conditions, preparatory conditions, essential conditions and sincerity condition. While propositional content conditions generally specify restrictions on the content of the proposition, preparatory, essential and sincerity conditions explicate language-external and thus contextual phenomena concerning the language game as well as speaker- and hearer-specific requirements. That is to say, rejections and denials restrict the propositional content condition to an un-acceptable past act A of the hearer, which generally is not represented explicitly, but implicitly and therefore attributed to the rejection=s contextual presuppositions. The sincerity condition of a rejection expresses the belief that the illocution is inappropriate, while the sincerity condition of a denial states the belief that the propositional content is false. The preparatory conditions of denials and rejections state that the speech act, which is rejected or denied, must have been felicitous, while their essential condition state an attempt to make the hearer nullify or modify the speech-act-in-question and /or its contextual presuppositions. In general, direct speech acts express speaker-intended and linguistic meaning explicitly while indirect speech acts express speaker-intended meaning implicitly by stating or questioning the speech acts= felicity conditions, such as *are you seriously suggesting, is it the case that, are you sure* or *wouldn't you rather*. Since indirect speech acts have both a *primary* and a *secondary illocutionary point* [26], they are, to some extent, vague or indeterminate, thus allowing the speaker to leave their speaker-intention in-context.

Speech act theory has had a tremendous effect on linguistics as it offers a frame-of-reference which accounts for both linguistic and so-called non-linguistic or contextual phenomena. Furthermore, natural-language communication is attributed a social-action status and therefore represents a speaker-, respectively hearer-intended action [16] embedded in context. However, there is more to natural-language communication than the exchange of micro speech acts in micro contexts, for there are further requirements, such as coherence, sequentiality and institution.

2.2 Non-Acceptances in Logic and Conversation

The differentiation of direct and indirect speech acts cannot be investigated in the framework of speech act theory only, but requires an extended frame-of-reference, which may accommodate both background assumptions and social context in order to account for the presupposed mutual knowledge. In his work on indirect speech acts, Searle [26] explicitly refers to the phenomenon of common ground and conversation.

H.P. Grice bases his approach to natural-language communication on the premise of rationality, which is manifest in intentionality and cooperation. More precisely, communication is guided by the *cooperative principle* (CP): *Make your conversational contribution such as is required, at the stage at which it occurs, by the accepted purpose or direction of the talk exchange in which you are engaged.* [15, 45], which holds for every rational interaction, and the maxims of quantity: *The category of QUANTITY relates the quantity of information to be provided, and under it fall the following maxims: 1. Make your contribution as informative as is required (for the current purpose of the exchange). 2. Do not make your contribution more informative than is required.* [15, 45], quality: *Under the category QUALITY falls a supermaxim - "Try to make your contribution one that is true"- and two more specific maxims: 1. Do not say what you believe to be false. 2. Do not say that for which you lack adequate evidence.* [15, 46], relation: *Under the category of RELATION I place a single maxim, namely, "Be relevant".* [15, 46] and manner: *Finally, under the category of MANNER, which I understand as relating not (like the previous categories) to what is said but, rather, to HOW what is said to be said, I include the supermaxim- "Be perspicuous"- and various maxims such as: 1. Avoid obscurity of expression. 2. Avoid ambiguity. 3. Be brief (avoid unnecessary prolixity). 4. Be orderly.* [15, 46]. If one or more of the maxims are violated or exploited, the speaker communicates a *conversational implicature:*

> *The presence of a conversational implicature must be capable of being worked out; for even if it can in fact be intuitively grasped, unless the intuition is replaceable by an argument, the implicature (if present at all) will not count as a CONVERSATIONAL implicature; it will be a CONVENTIONAL implicature. To work out that a particular conversational implicature is present, the hearer will rely on the following data: (1) the conventional meaning of the words used, together with the identity of any references that may be involved; (2) the CP and its maxims; (3) the context, linguistic and otherwise, of the utterance; (4) other items of background knowledge; and (5) the fact (or supposed fact) that all relevant items falling under the previous headings are available to both participants and both participants know or assume this to be the case.* [15, 50]

In his definition of conversational implicature, H.P. Grice explicitly refers to >context=, which is specified as *linguistic* and *otherwise*, as well as >background knowledge=, which is required for the calculation of the conversational implicature. That is to say, the cooperative principle, the maxims, context and background knowledge are the foundations, on which the conversational implicature is calculated. As a result, conversational implicatures are characterized by some degree of indeterminateness, since they are, by definition, *defeasable*, *non-detachable*, *calculable* and *non-conventional* [22]. Yet speech acts and conversational implicatures are not produced at random in natural-language conversation, but expected to be *dovetailed*, i.e. linked by one or more common goals manifest in prior and succeeding talk [15, 48]. The resulting interrelatedness or coherence [3; 19] holds for both local and global coherence, which may be interpreted from an interactional-organization viewpoint with regard to sequential phenomena, such as turn-taking or adjacency, and from micro- and macro-semantic viewpoints with regard to discourse-topic and sub-topics, and cataphoric and anaphoric reference.

Grice=s cooperative principle is based on the premise that conversations are rational endeavours, i.e. cooperative efforts, in which participants realize and recognize a common purpose or set of purposes, or, at least, some mutually accepted direction. But how are rejections or denials and their references to context and background knowledge accounted for in this framework? Is it possible to reject or deny the cooperative principle and / or the maxims? Do context and background knowledge represent contextual presuppositions?

The cooperative principle is the solid base of any rational interaction and is therefore, by definition, not open for negotiation. A speaker may, however, violate or exploit a maxim or be faced with a clash, which does not mean that one or more maxims are not accepted, but that s/he got in a conversational implicature and thereby communicated something *beyond what has been said*, which, of course, has to be calculated, i.e. inferred from the utterance=s contextual presuppositions. In other words, it is only possible to reject a maxim, if the speaker explicitly opts out. But is it possible to reject or deny conversational implicatures? Conversational implicatures may be rejected, if their calculation seems inconsistent, but their rejection requires two moves, at least: firstly, the explication and determination of the conversational implicature=s relevant contextual presuppositions, which is required because conversational implicatures are indeterminate by definition. Secondly, the reconstruction of the respective argumentation and the rejection of one or more invalid arguments and/or conclusions.

To conclude, conversational implicatures are calculated through a process of inferencing, in which the relevant contextual presuppositions are explicated in order to re-create the type of context required for the reconstruction of the speaker=s communicative intention. If the conversational implicature is not accepted, the context re-created in and through the inferencing processes is being un-created.

In the following section, the interdependence of non-acceptances and context is investigated in the field of conversation analysis, a predominantly structurally oriented framework.

2.3 Non-Acceptances in Conversation Analysis

Conversation analysis investigates longer stretches of institutional and non-institutional discourse by classifying conversation with regard to its constituitive sections. Two of its most important premises are *sequentiality* and *adjacency* manifest in the *turn-taking system* and *preference organization*. Levinson defines adjacency pairs as follows:

> *Adjacency pairs are sequences of two utterances that are: (i) adjacent, (ii) produced by different speakers, (iii) ordered as a **first part** and a **second part**, (iv) typed, so that a particular first part requires a particular second (or range of second parts) - e.g. offers require acceptances or rejections, greetings require greetings, and so on and there is a rule governing the use of adjacency pairs, namely: (19) Having produced a first part of some pair, current speakers must stop speaking, and the next speaker must produce at that point a second part to the same pair. [22, 303/4]*

However, S. Levinson also explicitly refers to the manifestation of adjacency with regard to adjacency positions, adjacency relations and adjacency pairs.

Preference organization categorizes adjacency pairs in a preferred and dispreferred format [23], which is also referred to as the unmarked and marked format [22]. In general, non-acceptances are attributed to the second parts of adjacency pairs and are frequently realized in the dispreferred or marked format [21; 22] and characterized by *plus-language* [8; 9]. Which function does plus-language have with regard to creating, re-creating or un-creating context?

In a functional-grammar-oriented framework [13], the marked format is defined by structural complexity, less frequent distribution, cognitive salience and therefore requires longer processing for the retrieval of the speaker intention. As stated above, non-acceptances are generally marked by plus-language, which is attributed the function of an inference trigger signalling a dispreferred move, a non-acceptance feature par excellence. The contextualization and determination of plus-language thus indicates firstly, a dispreferred move, and secondly, a non-acceptance. As a result, the interpretation of an implicitly represented non-acceptance cannot be achieved by references to linguistic meaning or to >what-is-said= only, as the hearer has to retrieve the speaker-intended meaning of the implicitly represented non-acceptance through a process of inferencing.

Non-acceptances with regard to the turn-taking system are manifest in interruptions, overlaps and simultaneous talk. These instances of discontinued talk indicate a mismatch of the respective contextualization procedures employed with regard to local management and institutional prerequisites. More precisely, interruptions stop and thus un-create the context which is created in and through the process of communication, while overlaps and simultaneous talk might both re-create and un-create context. A re-creation of context occurs if a high involvement style [4] is employed, whereas the phenomenon of un-creating context is achieved if interruptions and simultaneous talk are employed in order to gain the floor.

In the following section the results obtained in the investigation of speech act theory, logic & conversation, and conversation analysis are adapted to Jürgen Habermas=s *theory of communicative actions* [18], in which speakers and hearers do not only produce and interpret speech acts, but postulate and ratify validity claims. That is to say, communicative meaning - and thus context - are not given per se, but negotiated in discourse. If a validity claim is accepted, it is attributed the status of a *plus-validity claim*, if rejected, it represents a *minus-validity claim* and initiates a process of negotiation, in which the participants of a communicative encounter negotiate the communicative status of their utterance(s) with regard to their references to the three worlds and their respective presuppositions.

3 Non-Acceptances and Minus-Validity Claims

An investigation of authentic discourse requires a frame-of-reference which may account for the interaction of language-internal and language-external factors with regard to *how* linguistic code is employed in social contexts and social practice. In other words, this framework has to accommodate the interdependencies between firstly, speech acts and adjacent speech acts, i.e. immediate linguistic and extra-linguistic contexts, secondly, speech acts and participation framework, i.e. speaker as *principal* or *originator, emittor, strategist* and *figure*, hearer as *addressee, over-hearer* or *target*, and *(un)ratified* audience [14], and thirdly, speech acts and less immediate contexts. As a result, the investigation of natural-language communication requires a theoretical framework which may accommodate both bottom-up and top-down approaches in order to account for the interactions between macro and micro phenomena, such as discourse genre and felicity conditions, and their manifestations in micro settings.

The contextual function *plus/minus-validity claim* is based on Habermas's *theory of communicative actions* [18] and supplemented by *discursive* and *ethnomethodological* perspectives on communication [12]. It systematizes the results obtained from the investigations of non-acceptances in speech act theory, logic & conversation, and conversation analysis. It is based on the premise that the linguistic representation of speech acts can no longer be restricted to so-called objective information represented in the *propositional format* (true/false), since speech acts cannot be separated from the agent who produces them. Futhermore, agents cannot exist in isolation and are thus influenced by conventions and norms, i.e. by social and cultural phenomena. This interactive relationship of internal and external factors indicates that there is not only one external representation of one validity claim, but that alternative surface-structures exist, since there is a continuum on the scale of explicit vs. implicit modes of representation. Adapting the sociolinguistic and functional-grammar principle of *linguistic variation* [13; 20; 29], validity claims can be realized in more or less explicit surface-structures, which depend on the communicative intention of the speaker.

As a consequence, there are two sides to the coin >validity claim=, i.e. its surface-structure representing the speaker's communicative intention, and the so-called deep-structure, which explicates the surface-structure=s references to the three worlds and their underlying presuppositions. But how are rejections, denials and other non-acceptances accounted for in this framework?

Validity claims are anchored to an interdependent tripartite system of *objective*, *subjective* and *social worlds* as schematized in figure I.

figure I:

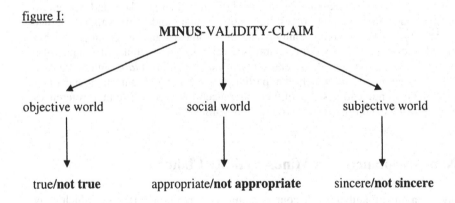

MINUS-VALIDITY-CLAIM

objective world   social world   subjective world

true/**not true**   appropriate/**not appropriate**   sincere/**not sincere**

The *objective world* is determined by the dichotomy of *true/false* and thus represents a denial-feature par excellence. References to this world are characterized by *theoretical claims* represented in the *propositional format* (reference & predication) and their mode of representation is *direct / explicit*. Denials are thus represented by semantic and syntactic negation.

The *subjective world* is determined by the premise of *sincerity*, i.e. speaker=s communicative intention meant as uttered. References to this world represent *emotive information* and their mode of representation is *non-linear*, i.e. simultaneously explicit / implicit, e.g. non- or paraverbal behaviour. References to this world cannot be denied or rejected, and the non- and paraverbal realization of a non-acceptance is extremely context-dependent since it depends on socio-cultural conventions, such as shaking one=s head versus nodding.

The *social world* is determined by the paradigm of *appropriateness*, which is calculated with regard to its constituitive tripartite system of textual (Gricean CP), interpersonal (participation format; face) and interactional (sequential status; adjacency) subsystems, as schematized in figure II.

figure II:

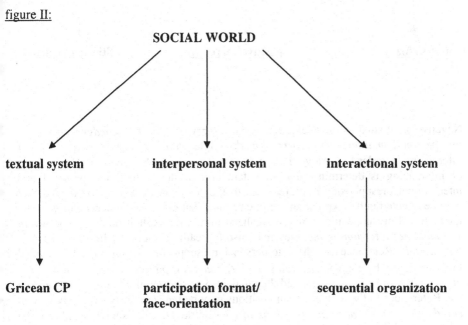

The social world can be realized in both *direct* and *indirect* modes. Direct / explicit references to this world are realized by direct or on-record speech acts [5], whereas the indirect / indexical mode is represented by indirect or off-record speech acts and subsystem-specific contextualization cues, as schematized in figure III.

<u>figure III:</u>

social world: indexical representation

n e g a t i v e c o n t e x t u a l i z a t i o n c u e s

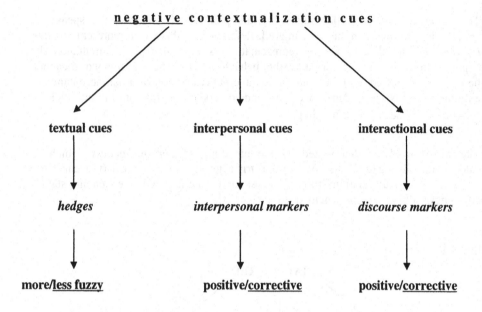

textual cues	**interpersonal cues**	**interactional cues**
hedges	*interpersonal markers*	*discourse markers*
more/<u>less fuzzy</u>	positive/<u>corrective</u>	positive/<u>corrective</u>

Negative contextualization cues, such as *more-fuzzy* and *less-fuzzy hedges, corrective interpersonal markers* and *corrective discourse markers* trigger a process of inferencing in order to retrieve the speaker=s communicative intention. This process of inferencing is determined by the interaction of the textual, interpersonal and interactional presuppositions. References to the social world cannot be denied, but only be rejected in the explicit and implicit / indexical modes. Non-acceptances of the interactional presuppositions may be realized in a fairly explicit mode by e.g. *would you mind not interrupting me*, they may also be realized implicitly by the indexicals *but* or *well*. References to the interpersonal presuppositions may also be realized fairly explicitly by e.g. *why are you so rude?*, *I don=t want to be unreasonable, but ...* or *you have no right to do that* and they may also be realized implicitly by e.g. *excuse me*. References to the textual presuppositions may be realized fairly explicitly by e.g. *could you be a bit more precise* or *be brief*. Additionally, the social world may be rejected, e.g. *a quite inappropriate remark*.

The investigation of the interdependence of minus-validity claims and context has focussed on the micro level. However, the contextual function plus/minus validity claim may also accommodate macro-features, such as genre-specific requirements of institutional and non-institutional discourse by specifying the contextual presuppositions of the social world accordingly and thus representing a filter which canalizes what-has-been-said accordingly.

4 Conclusion

In natural-language communication speakers do not only encode messages and send out signals - to employ different terminologies, produce speech acts or postulate validity claims - but also anchor their utterances to the immediate and remote contexts of the communicative encounter. Natural-language discourse therefore requires an analytic framework which goes beyond the investigation of paired utterances. The results of the investigation of rejections, denials and other non-acceptances are systematized in the framework of the contextual function *plus/minus validity claim* based on the contextualization of Jürgen Habermas's approach to communication and his premise of negotiating validity claims, which may be represented in the explicit and / or implicit modes. The resulting interactive framework may not only account for the interdependence of linguistic and non-linguistic meaning in different social settings, such as institutional and non-institutional discourse, but also for the natural-language specific process of negotiation of meaning by classifying language-external and language-internal domains in a tripartite system of objective, subjective and social worlds and their respective presuppositions. In this setting, the non-acceptance of a validity claim requires the re-creating of context before it may be un-created.

References

1. Atkinson, J.M., Heritage, J. (eds.): Structures of social action. CUP, Cambridge (1984)
2. Austin, J.L.: How to do things with words. CUP, Cambridge (1980)
3. de Beaugrande, R., Dressler, W.: Einführung in die Textlinguistik. Niemeyer, Tübingen (1981)
4. Biber, D: Variations across Speech and Writing. CUP, Cambridge (1988)
5. Brown, P., Levinson, S.: Politeness. Some universals in language usage. CUP, Cambridge (1987)
6. Duranti, A., C. Goodwin (eds.): Rethinking Context. CUP, Cambridge (1992)
7. Fetzer, A.: Negative Interaktionen: kommunikative Strategien im britischen Englisch und interkulturelle Inferenzen. Peter Lang, Frankfurt/Main (1994)
8. Fetzer, A.: Konversationsanalyse und Konversationsunterricht. Zeitschrift für Interkulturellen Fremdsprachenunterricht [online], **2**,1 (1997) http://www.ualberta.ca/~german/ejournal/ejournal.html, pp.29
9. Fetzer, A.: Negative contextualization: a socio-semiotic approach to language teaching. In Pütz, M. (ed).: The cultural context in foreign language teaching. Peter Lang, Frankfurt/Main (1997) 85-109
10. Fetzer, A.: NEIN-SAGEN. In: Pittner, R., Pittner, K. (eds.): Beiträge zu Sprache & Sprachen, 5. Münchner Linguistik Tage. Lincom Europa, München (1998) 183-191
11. Fetzer, A.: Validity claims: assigning contextual information. In: Wilson, T.D., Allen, D. (eds.): Information seeking in context: proceedings of the 2nd ISIC conference, Sheffield, 1998. Taylor Graham Publishing, London (1999)
12. Garfinkel, H.: Studies in ethnomethodology. Polity Press, Cambridge (1994)
13. Givón, T.: English Grammar: a function-based introduction. Benjamins, Amsterdam (1993)
14. Goffman, E.: Frame analysis. North Eastern University Press, Boston (1974)
15. Grice, H.P.: Logic and conversation. In: Cole, M., Morgan. J.L. (eds.): Syntax and semantics, Vol. III. Academic Press, N.Y. (1974) 41-58

16. Grimshaw, A.D.: Mishearings, misunderstandings, and other nonsuccesses in talk: a plea for redress of speaker-oriented bias. Sociological Inquiry 50 (1980) 31-74
17. Gumperz, J.J.: Sociocultural Knowledge in Conversational Inference. In: Saville-Troike, M. (ed.) Linguistics and Anthropology. Georgetown University Press, Washington DC (1977) 191-211
18. Habermas, J.: Theorie des kommunikativen Handelns. Suhrkamp, Frankfurt (1987)
19. Halliday, M.A.K., R. Hasan: Cohesion in English. Longman, London (1976)
20. Halliday, M.A.K.: An introduction to functional grammar. Arnold, London (1994)
21. Lauerbach, G.: Conversation analysis and its discontent. In: Goebel, W., Seeber, H.U. (eds.) Anglistentag 1992. Niemeyer, Tübingen (1993) 427-436
22. Levinson, S.: Pragmatics. CUP, Cambridge (1983)
23. Pomerantz, A.: Agreeing and disagreeing with assessments: some features of preferred/ dispreferred turn shapes. In: Atkinson, J., Heritage, J.M. (eds.) Structures of social action. CUP, Cambridge (1984) 57-101
24. Schiffrin, D.: Discourse markers. CUP, Cambridge (1987)
25. Searle, J.: Speech acts. CUP, Cambridge (1969)
26. Searle, J. : Indirect speech acts. In: Cole, M., Morgan, J.L. (eds.): Syntax and semantics, Vol. III. Academic Press, N.Y. (1974) 59-82
27. Sperber, D., Wilson, D.: Relevance. Blackwell, Oxford (1996)
28. Tottie, G.: Negation in English speech and writing. Blackwell, Oxford (1991)
29. Wardhaugh, R.: An introduction to sociolinguistics. Blackwell, Oxford (1998)
30. Watts, R.W., Ide, S. , Ehlich, K. (eds.): Politeness in Language. de Gruyter, Berlin (1992)

Modelling (Un)Bounded Beliefs

Chiara Ghidini*

Dept. of Computation and Mathematics
Manchester Metropolitan University
Manchester M1 5GD, United Kingdom
C.Ghidini@doc.mmu.ac.uk

Abstract. This paper is concerned with providing a context based logic (language + semantics) for the representation of agents's beliefs. While different approaches that make use of a single theory have been proposed in order to model agent's beliefs, such as modal logics, these often suffer from problems, as lack of modularity, logical omniscence, and dissimilarity with implementations. A partial solution to these problems is to distribute the agent's knowledge into different and separated modules which interact each others. Our approach is to provide these modules, but in the form of (multi) contexts, each one with its own *local* language and semantics, and to model the relations among modules as *compatibility* relations among contexts. We extend here this approach to capture important aspects of "ideal" agents, namely their logically omniscent nature, and of "real" agents, namely their non logically omniscent nature due to some resource-boundedness. The logic we use is based on a logic for contextual reasoning, called *Local Models Semantics*, which allows a (multi) context-based representation of agent's belief. A tableau system for a simple instance of such a logic is also presented.

1 Introduction

Reasoning about their own and other agents' beliefs is an important capability inside complex reasoning programs, e.g. knowledge representation systems, natural language understanding systems, or multi-agent systems. Despite the pervasiveness of the notion of belief and the apparent easiness for humans to deal with it, representing beliefs and formalizing reasoning with and about beliefs has raised very difficult problems. Modal logics [2] are the well known formalism for representing beliefs and, more generally, propositional attitudes, the one which has been most widely proposed and studied in the logic and philosophical literature (see [13]). Following the analisys of [10, 11], the approaches that make use of a single theory suffer from many problems:

- *lack of modularity.* In a unique theory it is very hard to represent all the agents' knowledge, their – usually very different – reasoning capabilities, the – usually very complicated – interactions among them;

---

* Visiting Research Fellow from University of Trento, Italy, supported by the Italian National Research Council (CNR)

146

- *logical omniscence.* The approaches which make use of a single theory have been mainly exploited to model "ideal" agents which suffer the "logical omniscence problem" (first pointed out by Hintikka in [13]), that is agents (are forced to) believe all the logical consequences of their own beliefs;
- *dissimilarity with implementations.* From the point of view of implementors, it is very hard to codify in a unique theory all the needed information about agents and their beliefs so has to have efficient easy-to-develop and to-maintain implementations.

A partial solution to these problems is to distribute the knowledge into different and separated modules which interact each others. A first attempt to distribute knowledge into different modules is due to Fagin and Halpern [4]. Fagin and Halpern define logics for general awareness and limited reasoning in which knowledge and beliefs of an agent refer to different states (or agent's frames of mind), and different kinds of knowledge (e.g. *implicit, explicit, local* knowledge) are represented by different modal operators added to the language. Another attempt is due to Giunchiglia et al. [10, 11, 7] and is based on the notion of context. Giunchiglia et al. present formal systems for the representation of propositional attitudes and multi-agent systems based on the framework of ML systems[1]. Such systems provide the expressibility of normal modal logics [10] and of the most common non normal modal logics [7]. The main idea is to represent an agent (a set of agents) as a set of (belief) contexts, also called *views*, each context representing the point of view that the agent has about its own beliefs, about the beliefs about its own beliefs, the beliefs about another agent, and so on. Every context is a formal theory. The basic feature of these systems is their modularity. Knowledge can be distributed into different contexts. For instance, the belief of an agent can be represented with one or more contexts, distinct from the ones representing the beliefs of other agents; furthermore different contexts can be used to represent the beliefs of an agent in different situations. Interaction between contexts might be used in order to express the effect of communication between agents, and the evolution of their beliefs. The context-based treatment of agents who are not logically omniscent, given in [11, 7], is based on the fact that different contexts may have different structural properties and may be related in different ways with other contexts.

Inspired by the same intuitions as ML systems, a semantics for contextual reasoning, called Local Models Semantics (LMS), has been defined in [9]. LMS is based on the ideas that (i) each context has its own *local semantics* and (ii) relations between different contexts are *compatibility relations*. In [8] the authors apply LMS in order to model agent's beliefs and to provide the semantics for MBK, a ML system which has a standard formulation in modal K. The local semantics allows us to model the different points of view of an agent about its own (other agents') beliefs, whereas compatibility relations provide enough modularity and flexibility to model the relations between different contexts which correspond to modal K. While [8] provides the basic ideas for modelling agent's

[1] The idea of using multiple distinct theories has been exploited in much applied work in the area multi-agent systems [12, 15, 17, 3]

beliefs using LMS, and claims that a semantics based on local semantics + compatibility relations provides enough modularity and flexibility to model different relation between contexts, corresponding to different aspects of agents, it deals mainly with the basic relations among contexts corresponding to modal K.

The goal of this paper is to show that the representation of an agent's beliefs based on the notion of context (view) and formalized with Local Models Semantics allows us to model, in a uniform way, different aspects of (ideal and real) agents. In particular, in Section 3 we apply LMS to model logically omniscent agents, which have been formalized using normal modal logics, in Section 4 we show that the classes of models defined in Section 3 can be easily modified in order to treat an important aspect of "real" agents, namely their resource-bounded nature [1]. We show, by mean of two simple examples that, differently from Kripke semantics, where agents are modelled as "ideal" reasoners "forced" to believe (and compute) all the logical consequences of their own beliefs, LMS allows us to explicitly represent agents' resource bounds. Finally (Section 5) we modify the tableau systems defined in [16] in order to provide tableaux for the logics defined in Section 3 and Section 4. We use the tableau as a simple mechanism for building models for "ideal" and "real" agents and to emphasize the difference existing among them in a very simple case.

2 Beliefs and Logical Onmiscence

In the paper we will consider the situation of a single agent a (usually thought of as the computer itself or as an external observer) who is acting in a world, who has both beliefs about this world and beliefs about its own beliefs and it is able to reason about them. There has long been interest in both philosophy and AI in defining a logic for a's beliefs. The standard approach is basd on modal logics and Kripke semantics. The basic idea underlying Kripke semantics is that besides the true state of the world, there are a number of other possible states of the world. An agent is said to *believe* ϕ if ϕ is true in all the worlds he think possible.

As has been frequently pointed out in the literature (see, for instance, [14]) Kripke semantics assumes an "ideal" rational agent, with infinite computational power and which suffers from the problem of what Hintikka calls *logical onmiscence*. Logical onmiscence means that agents are assumed to be so "clever" that (i) they must know all the valid formulae, and that (ii) their beliefs are closed under implication, i.e. if an agent believes ϕ and believes that ϕ implies ψ, then he must believe ψ as well. Unfortunately, in many cases (applications) we cannot assume that the agent a is logically omniscent. In particular, the resource-bounded nature [1] of many "real" agents, prevents them to have an infinite computational power, and therefore to be able to compute (believe) the closure under implication of their own beliefs. In this cases a logic that provides a more realistic representation of resource-bounded agents must be used.

3   Local Models Semantics for "Ideal" Agents

Let's consider again our basic situation of a single agent a who is acting in a world, who has both beliefs about this world and beliefs about its own beliefs and it is able to reason about them. The first step in our work is to extend the logic presented in [8] in order to obtain a (multi) context-based logic equivalent to the most common normal modal logics. In order to do this, we formalize the notion of beliefs, and beliefs about beliefs by exploiting the notion of *view*. By a view we formalize the mental images that a has of itself, i.e., the set of beliefs that a ascribes to itself.

Views are organized in a chain depicted in Figure 1. We call a the root view,

Fig. 1. The chain of views

representing the point of view of the agent a; we let the view aa formalize the beliefs that the agent a ascribes to itself. Iterating the nesting, the view aaa formalizes the view of the agent a about beliefs about its own beliefs, and so on[2].

In this section we are principally interested in applying propositional Local Models Semantics, introduced in [9], in order to define the classes of models for the belief systems defined in [10] which have a "standard" formulation using normal modal logics. In order to achieve this, we focus our attention on single agent beliefs in which a is "on top" of an infinite chain of views. The infinite chain reflects the fact that using modal logics, people model a as an ideal agent able to express and reason about beliefs of arbitrary nesting, e.g. sentences like "I believe that I believe that I believe that ... I believe that ϕ" with arbitrary nested belief operator, and having arbitrary deep views of its own beliefs.

The first step in defining the logic is to recall a particular class of languages (introduced in [10]) used to describe what is true in every view.

---

[2] For a more detailed description of the structure, a good reference is [3]

3.1 HMB Languages

Notationally we use the natural numbers 0, 1, 2, ... to refer to the infinite sequence $a, aa, aaa, \ldots$ of views. $\mathbb{N}$ refers to the set of natural numbers. We define a countable sequence of different languages $L_0, L_1, \ldots, L_n, \ldots$, where the language L_0 is the language of a, the language L_1 is the language of aa, the language L_n is the language of $aa \ldots a$ $(n + 1$ times), and so on. To express statements about the world, every L_n contains a set P of propositional constants. To express beliefs about beliefs described with L_{n+1}, L_n contains a predicate B which intuitively stands for belief and the name "ϕ" for each formula ϕ in L_{n+1}.

For obtaining the equivalence with modal logics, we have considered an agent a "on top" of an infinite chain of views. As each view is "above" an infinite chain and each level corresponds to a level of nesting of the belief predicate, all the languages L_i, with $i \in \mathbb{N}$, must have the same expressibility. I.e., they are the same language $L(B)$ containing all the propositional formulae ϕ, the formulas $B("\phi")$, $B("B("\phi")")$, $B("B("B("\phi")")")$, and so on.

Formally, $L(B)$ is defined as follows. Let L be a propositional language containing a set P of propositional letters, the symbol for falsity $\bot$, and closed under implication[3]. Then for any natural number $i \in \mathbb{N}$, L_i is defined as follows:

- if $\phi \in L$, then $\phi \in L_i$;
- $\bot \in L_i$;
- if $\phi \in L_i$ and $\psi \in L_i$ then $\phi \supset \psi \in L_i$;
- if $\phi \in L_i$ then $B("\phi") \in L_{i+i}$;
- nothing else is in L_i

$L(B)$ is the union of all the L_n, i.e. $L(B) = \bigcup_{n \in \mathbb{N}} L_n$.

We may now define the class of languages associated to the chain of views in Figure 1.

Definition 1 (HMB language). *Let L be a propositional language. An* HMB *language (where* HMB *stands for Hierarchical Multilanguage Belief) is a class of languages $\{L_i\}$ over the set of indexes $\mathbb{N}$ such that for every $i \in \mathbb{N}$, $L_i = L(B)$.*

Notationally, we write $i : \phi$ to mean ϕ and that ϕ is a formula of L_i. We say that ϕ is an L_i-formula, and that $i : \phi$ is a formula or, also, a labelled formula. This notation and terminology allows us to keep track of the language (view) we are talking about. Given a set of labeled formulae Γ, Γ_j denotes the set of formulae $\{\gamma \mid j : \gamma \in \Gamma\}$.

3.2 HMB Models

The semantics for HMB languages we present in this section is a slightly simplified version of Local Models Semantics for reasoning about beliefs presented in [9]. The main idea of Local Models Semantics is to model an agent having

---

[3] We use the standard abbreviations from propositional logic, such as $\neg \phi$ for $\phi \supset \bot$, $\phi \vee \psi$ for $\neg \phi \supset \psi$, $\phi \wedge \psi$ for $\neg(\neg \phi \vee \neg \psi)$, $\top$ for $\bot \supset \bot$.

beliefs about its own beliefs based on (i) the local semantics of every language L_i used to describe what is true in in the view i it is associated with, and (ii) compatibility relations formalizing different relation between the views in the chain in Figure 1.

An HMB language $\{L_i\}$ can be considered as a family of propositional languages containing the propositional letters in P used to express statements about the world, and "special" propositional letters $B(\text{"}\phi\text{"})$ used to express beliefs about beliefs. Let $\overline{P}$ be the new set of propositional constants such that, $\overline{P} = P \cup \{B(\text{"}\phi\text{"})|B(\text{"}\phi\text{"}) \in L(B)\}$. A *local model* for L_i is a set $m \subseteq \overline{P}$. Notice that that m is a propositional model for L_i, therefore the definition of *local satisfiability* of a formula of L_i in a model m is the usual definition of satisfiability for propositional models.

A *compatibility sequence* $\mathbf{c}$ for $\{L_i\}$ is a sequence

$$\mathbf{c} = \langle \mathbf{c}_0, \mathbf{c}_1, \mathbf{c}_2, \ldots \rangle$$

where, for each $i \in \mathbb{N}$, $\mathbf{c}_i$ is either a set containing a local model for L_i or the empty set. We call $\mathbf{c}_i$ the i-th element of $\mathbf{c}$.

Intuitively, a compatibility sequence $\mathbf{c} = \langle \mathbf{c}_0, \mathbf{c}_1, \ldots, \mathbf{c}_n \rangle$ is a possible state of the world (i.e. a possible chain in Figure 1) in which, from the point of view of a:

(0) the world is $\mathbf{c}_0$;
(1) a believes that the world is $\mathbf{c}_1$;
(2) a believes that he believes that the world is $\mathbf{c}_2$;

$$\vdots \quad \vdots$$

This notion is formalized by the definition of satisfiability of a formula by (the appropriate element of) a compatibility sequence. Let $\mathbf{c}$ be a compatibility sequence. $\mathbf{c}_i$ *satisfies a formula* $\phi \in L_i$ (in symbols $\mathbf{c}_i \models \phi$) if all the local models in it satisfy ϕ. $\mathbf{c}_i$ satisfies a set of formulae $\Gamma_i \in L_i$ (in symbols $\mathbf{c}_i \models \Gamma_i$) to mean that $\mathbf{c}_i \models \gamma$ for every $\gamma \in \Gamma_i$.

A *compatibility relation* $\mathbf{C}$ for $\{L_i\}$ is a non empty set of compatibility sequences. A set of compatibility sequences formalizes different states of the world from the point of view of a. For instance, the fact that $\mathbf{C}$ is composed by two sequences $\mathbf{C} = \{\mathbf{c}, \mathbf{c}'\}$, intuitively means that (from the point of view of a) either the world is $\mathbf{c}_0$, a believes that the world is $\mathbf{c}_1$, and so on, or the world is $\mathbf{c}'_0$, a believes that the world is $\mathbf{c}'_1$, and so on. Figure 2 gives a graphical representation of the structure of a generic model for $\{L_i\}$.

A model of an HMB language is a set $\mathbf{C}$ of different states of the world from the point of view of a, i.e. a compatibility relation. Since we are interested here in defining models for belief systems which have a "standard" formulation using normal modal logics, we focus on special classes of compatibility relations which express the relations among views imposed by such logics.

Definition 2 (HMB Model). *An HMB model is a compatibility relation* $\mathbf{C}$ *such that each* $\mathbf{c} \in \mathbf{C}$ *satisfies a set of properties* HMB$\subseteq\{$MBK, D, T, 4, 5, Fun$\}$, MBK $\in$ HMB, *defined as follows*

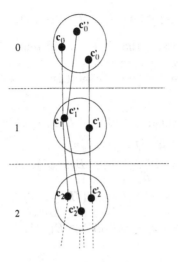

Fig. 2. A model for the single agent scenario

MBK : (1) $c_i \models B(\text{``}\phi\text{''})$ *implies* $c_{i+1} \models \phi$

    (2) *for each* $c' \in C$ *s.t.* $c_i = c'_i$, $c'_{i+1} \models \phi$ *implies* $c_i \models B(\text{``}\phi\text{''})$

D: *for each* $c' \in C$ *s.t.* $c_i = c'_i$, $c'_{i+1} = \emptyset$ *implies* $c_i = \emptyset$

T: *for each* $c' \in C$ *s.t.* $c_i = c'_i$, $c'_{i+i} \models \phi$ *implies* $c_i \models \phi$

4: $c_i \models B(\text{``}\phi\text{''})$ *implies* $c_{i+1} \models B(\text{``}\phi\text{''})$

5: $c_i \models \neg B(\text{``}\phi\text{''})$ *implies* $c_{i+1} \models \neg B(\text{``}\phi\text{''})$

Fun: $c_i = c'_i$ *implies for all* $j \in \mathbb{N}, c_j = c'_j$

Notice that each HMB model is an MBK model. From the definition of MBK model it follows that for all compatibility sequences c in an HMB model if $c_i \neq \emptyset$ then $c_j \neq \emptyset$ for all $j \geq i$. Therefore, all the compatibility sequences in a HMB model are of the form $\langle m_0, m_1, \ldots, m_k, \emptyset, \ldots \emptyset, \ldots \rangle$ (we omit {} for singleton sets). Therefore a model for an HMB system can be thought as a set of compatibility sequences starting from the "top" view a and descending along the chain in Figure 1 until the agent a is able to have a model of the views of its own belief about beliefs. Since we are considering here ideal agents, able to express and reason about beliefs of arbitrary nesting, compatibility sequences are potentially infinite.

Definition of satisfiability and logical consequence follow from [9]. Namely. let C be an HMB model and $i : \phi$ a formula. C *satisfies* $i : \phi$, in symbols $C \models i : \phi$, if for all sequences $c \in C$, $c_i \models \phi$. A formula $i : \phi$ is *valid* in the class of HMB models, in symbols $\models_{\text{HMB}} i : \phi$, if all HMB models satisfy $i : \phi$. A formula $i : \phi$ is a *logical consequence* of a set of formulae Γ, in symbols $\Gamma \models_{\text{HMB}} i : \phi$, if for all HMB models C, every sequences $c \in C$ satisfies:

$$\text{if for all } j \in \mathbb{N}, \mathbf{c}_j \models \Gamma_j \text{ then } \mathbf{c}_i \models \phi$$

Some of the basic theorems that hold in different HMB models are listed below. Notice that they correspond (using the mapping between L_i-formulae and modal formulae defined in [10]) to the theorems characterizing the main normal modal logics.

Theorem 1. *For any formulae ϕ and ψ in $L(B)$ and any $i \in \mathbb{N}$.*

1. $\mathbf{C} \models i : B(\text{``}\phi \supset \psi\text{''}) \supset (B(\text{``}\phi\text{''}) \supset B(\text{``}\psi\text{''}));$
2. $D \in \text{HMB}$ *implies* $\mathbf{C} \models i : B(\text{``}\phi\text{''}) \supset \neg B(\text{``}\neg\phi\text{''});$
3. $T \in \text{HMB}$ *implies* $\mathbf{C} \models i : B(\text{``}\phi\text{''}) \supset \phi;$
4. $4 \in \text{HMB}$ *implies* $\mathbf{C} \models i : B(\text{``}\phi\text{''}) \supset B(\text{``}B(\text{``}\phi\text{''})\text{''});$
5. $5 \in \text{HMB}$ *implies* $\mathbf{C} \models i : \neg B(\text{``}\phi\text{''}) \supset B(\text{``}\neg B(\text{``}\phi\text{''})\text{''});$
6. $\text{Fun} \in \text{HMB}$ *implies* $\mathbf{C} \models i : \neg B(\text{``}\neg\phi\text{''}) \supset B(\text{``}\phi\text{''});$

Proof *(Sketch)*

1. We need to prove that all the compatibility sequences in $\mathbf{C}$ satisfy $i : B(\text{``}\phi \supset \psi\text{''}) \supset (B(\text{``}\phi\text{''}) \supset B(\text{``}\psi\text{''}))$. Suppose that $\mathbf{c}_i$ satisfies both $B(\text{``}\phi \supset \psi\text{''})$ and $B(\text{``}\phi\text{''})$. From condition (1) in the definition of MBK model every $\mathbf{c}'_{i+1}$ such that $\mathbf{c}_i = \mathbf{c}'_i$ satisfy both $\phi \supset \psi$ and ϕ. Being all the $\mathbf{c}'_{i+1}$ propositional models, they satisfy also ψ. Therefore, from condition (2) of MBK model $\mathbf{c}_i$ satisfies $B(\text{``}\psi\text{''})$.

2. Suppose that $\mathbf{c}_i$ satisfies $B(\text{``}\phi\text{''})$ and that $\mathbf{c}_i \neq \emptyset$ (otherwise the proof is done). From the definition of D model there is at least a $\mathbf{c}'_{i+1}$ with $\mathbf{c}'_i = \mathbf{c}_i$ such that $\mathbf{c}'_{i+1} \neq \emptyset$. From condition (1) in the definition of MBK model $\mathbf{c}'_{i+1}$ satisfies ϕ. This fact prevents $\mathbf{c}_i$ from satisfying $B(\text{``}\neg\phi\text{''})$, and therefore $\mathbf{c}_i$ satisfies $\neg B(\text{``}\neg\phi\text{''})$.

3. Suppose that $\mathbf{c}_i$ satisfies $B(\text{``}\phi\text{''})$. From the definition of MBK model (condition (1)) all the $\mathbf{c}'_{i+1}$ such that $\mathbf{c}_i = \mathbf{c}'_i$ satisfy ϕ. Therefore, from definition of T model $\mathbf{c}_i$ satisfies ϕ as well.

4. Suppose that $\mathbf{c}_i$ satisfies $B(\text{``}\phi\text{''})$. From the definition of 4 model, all the $\mathbf{c}'_{i+1}$ such that $\mathbf{c}_i = \mathbf{c}'_i$ satisfy $B(\text{``}\phi\text{''})$ as well. Therefore, from condition (2) in the definition of MBK model $\mathbf{c}_i$ satisfies $B(\text{``}B(\text{``}\phi\text{''})\text{''})$.

5. Suppose that $\mathbf{c}_i$ satisfies $\neg B(\text{``}\phi\text{''})$. From the definition of 4 model, all the $\mathbf{c}'_{i+1}$ such that $\mathbf{c}_i = \mathbf{c}'_i$ satisfy $\neg B(\text{``}\phi\text{''})$ as well. Therefore, from condition (2) in the definition of the MBK model $\mathbf{c}_i$ satisfies $B(\text{``}\neg B(\text{``}\phi\text{''})\text{''})$.

6. Suppose that $\mathbf{c}_i$ satisfies $\neg B(\text{``}\neg\phi\text{''})$. From the definition of Fun model, there is no other compatibility sequence $\mathbf{c}'$ with $\mathbf{c}'_i = \mathbf{c}_i$. Therefore $\mathbf{c}_{i+1}$ must satisfy $\phi$ (otherwise from condition (2) in the definition of MBK model $\mathbf{c}_i$ must satisfy $B(\text{``}\neg\phi\text{''})$) and applying condition (2) in the definition of MBK model $\mathbf{c}_i$ satisfy $B(\text{``}\phi\text{''})$.

3.3 An Axiomatization of HMB Models

[8] shows that the MultiLanguage system (ML system) MBK [10], a formal system allowing multiple languages and equivalent to modal K, provides a sound

and complete axiomatization of the HMB model MBK . An ML system is a triple $\langle \{L_i\}, \{\Omega_i\}, \Delta \rangle$ where $\{L_i\}$ is a family of languages, $\{\Omega_i\}$ is a family of sets of axioms, and Δ is the deductive machinery. Δ contains two kinds of inference rules: *i rules*, i.e., inference rules with premises and conclusions in the same language, and *bridge rules*,i.e., inference rules with premises and conclusions belonging to different languages. Notationally, we write inference rules, with, e.g., a single premise, as follows:

$$\frac{i : \psi}{i : \phi} \; ir \qquad\qquad \frac{i : \psi}{j : \phi} \; br$$

ir is an *i* rule while *br* is a bridge rule. Derivability in a ML system is defined in [10]; roughly speaking it is a generalization of the notion of deduction in natural deduction. The ML system MBK is a triple $\langle \{L_i\}, \{\Omega_i\}, \Delta \rangle$ where $\{L_i\}$ is a family of HMB languages, there are no axioms, and Δ contains the ND inference rules for propositional calculus:

$$\frac{\begin{array}{c}[i : \phi]\\ i : \psi\end{array}}{i : \phi \supset \psi} \; \supset I_i \qquad \frac{i : \phi \quad i : \phi \supset \psi}{i : \psi} \; \supset E_i \qquad \frac{\begin{array}{c}[i : \neg\phi]\\ i : \bot\end{array}}{i : \phi} \; \bot_i$$

and the following bridge rules:

$$\frac{i : B(\text{``}\phi\text{''})}{i+1 : \phi} \; \mathcal{R}dw_i \qquad\qquad \frac{i+1 : \phi}{i : B(\text{``}\phi\text{''})} \; \mathcal{R}upr_i$$

RESTRICTIONS: $\mathcal{R}upr_i$ is applicable if and only if $i + 1 : \phi$ does not depend on any assumption $j : \psi$ with index $j \geq i + 1$.

The idea underlying MBK is straightforward. Every view in Figure 1 is formalized by a propositional theory in the language L_i. The (compatibility) relation existing between different views are formalized by bridge rules. In particular $\mathcal{R}dw_i$ and $\mathcal{R}upr_i$ formalize conditions (1) and (2), respectively, in the definition of a MBK model. The axiomatization of the remaining HMB models is obtained adding the following bridge rules (introduced in [10]), which correspond to the properties D, T, 4, 5, and Fun of compatibility relations in Definition 2.

$$\frac{i+1 : \bot}{i : \bot} \; D_i \quad \frac{i+1 : \phi}{i : \phi} \; T_i \quad \frac{i : B(\text{``}\phi\text{''})}{i+1 : B(\text{``}\phi\text{''})} \; 4_i \quad \frac{i : \neg B(\text{``}\phi\text{''})}{i+1 : \neg B(\text{``}\phi\text{''})} \; 5_i \quad \frac{i+1 : \phi}{i : \neg B(\text{``}\neg\phi\text{''})} \; Fun_i$$

RESTRICTIONS: D_i, T_i and Fun_i are applicable if and only if $i + 1 : \phi$ does not depend on any assumption $j : \psi$ with index $j \geq i + 1$.

The proof of soundness and completeness of these ML systems with respect to the corresponding classes of HMB models is very similar to that of ML system MBK shown in [8].

4 Local Models Semantics for Resource-bounded Agents

We consider here an agent a unable to reason about all the belief formulae of $L(B)$. The reasons why a is not able to use belief formulae with arbitrary nested belief predicates B can be different. In this paper we consider two very natural bounds of a's resources which prevent it from using all the belief formulae of $L(B)$.

1. *Bounded languages.* a is able to (interested in) use only the initial part of the chain of views depicted in Figure 1. This intuitively means that a is able to (interested in) express and reason about beliefs with at most, e.g., n nested belief predicates.
2. *Bounded reasoning capabilities.* The reasoning process of a involves a finite sequence of views of depth (at most) $n + 1$. This intuitively means that a is able to use, in the reasoning process, a finite (and usually not very deep) sequence of views about its own beliefs. Notice that such a sequence is not necessarily the one composed by the initial $n + 1$ views in Figure 1.

4.1 Bounded Languages

HMB languages can be easily modified to formalize bounded beliefs with bounded languages. Let n be the maximum degree of nested belief predicates B in a formula. We replace the definition of $L(B)$ in Section 3.1 with the following definition

$$L(B) = \bigcup_{i \in \{0, 1, \ldots, n\}} L_i$$

The definition of HMBB language(s) for belief systems with bounded languages, where HMBB stands for *Hierarchical Multilanguage Bounded Belief*, follows Definition 1 in Section 3.1.

The semantics for HMBB languages is a straightforward modification of that for HMB languages. Indeed we modify the definition of HMB models in order to consider a set of indexes $I = \{0, 1, \ldots, n\}$ instead of $\mathbb{N}$. An HMBB *model* is a compatibility relation $\mathbf{C}$ containing compatibility sequences of the form

$$\mathbf{c} = \langle c_0, c_1, \ldots, c_n \rangle$$

such that each $\mathbf{c} \in \mathbf{C}$ satisfies a set of properties HMBB$\subseteq\{$MBK, D, T, 4, 5, Fun$\}$, MBK $\in$ HMBB, where MBK , D, T, 4, 5, and Fun are obtained from those in Definition 2 adding the constraint $i < n$.

HMBB models formalize real agents which do not suffer of the logical omniscence problem because of "lack of language". Indeed a cannot believe a sentence, e.g., $0 : B^k(``\phi \vee \neg\phi")$, with $k > n$, because such a sentence is not in its own language.

4.2 Bounded Reasoning Capabilities

Suppose that a is able to express all the formulae in $L(B)$ but that he is not able to use all its basic facts or capabilities in reasoning. In this case $L(B)$ remains the one defined in Section 3 and many different classes of models can be defined, depending on the form of lack reasoning capabilities of a. A lot of work can be found in literature about this issue. Most of this work is based on the use of modal logics (see [5] for a survey), whereas a context-based characterization can be found in [7,11]. We consider here a very simple class of model, where Definition 2 is modified in order to consider compatibility sequences of depth $n + 1$. Future work is to apply LMS in order to give a uniform representation of the different forms of lack of reasoning capabilities studied in the literature. An HMBR *model* is a compatibility relation $\mathbf{C}$ containing compatibility sequences of the form

$$\mathbf{c}_{h,h+n} = \langle \mathbf{c}_h, \mathbf{c}_{h+1}, \ldots \mathbf{c}_{h+n} \rangle$$

where each $\mathbf{c}_{h,h+n} \in \mathbf{C}$ satisfies a set of properties HMBR$\subseteq$\{MBK, D, T, 4, 5, Fun\}, MBK $\in$ HMBR, where MBK , D, T, 4, 5, and Fun are obtained from those in Definition 2 adding the constraint $i < h + n$.

HMBR models formalize an agent a which is able to express all the formulae in $L(B)$. Differently from the case presented in Section 3 a suffers from a form of limitation in its resources and its is not able to describe (and reason about) possible states of the world involving more than $n + 1$ views. The structure of a HMBR model is depicted in Figure 3, with $n = 2$. A particular instance of this

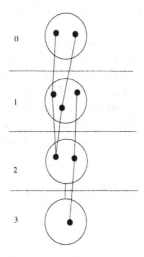

Fig. 3. A model with $n = 2$

class of models is obtained considering compatibility sequences are of the form $\mathbf{c}_{0,n}$. This case is similar that in Section 4.1, except for the fact that we do not impose any restriction on the language $L(B)$. In this case a might not believe $0 : B^k(\text{``}\phi \vee \neg\phi\text{''})$, with $k > n$, because the view $k$ representing the beliefs in $B^k$ does not exists. Therefore $a$ is not able to "look inside" $B^k(\text{``}\phi \vee \neg\phi\text{''})$, and the the truth value of $0 : B^k(\text{``}\phi \vee \neg\phi\text{''})$ can be either true of false. Notice that the reason why we can easily define a model which does not satisfy $0 : B^k(\text{``}\phi \vee \neg\phi\text{''})$ is that (differently from modal logics) a belief formula $B(\text{``}\phi\text{''})$ is an atomic formula and its truth value is local, i.e. it is not defined in terms of any other formulae. Therefore the fact that $B(\text{``}\phi\text{''}) \in L_n$ does not imply the existence of a view $n+1$ in Figure 1 such that $\phi \in L_{n+1}$.

5 A Simple Tableau System

We briefly show in this section how to construct HMB models using tableaux. Due to the lack of space we consider here only MBK models. Due to the equivalence with modal logics, we can apply the same ideas in order to construct tableaux for the other HMB systems.

The tableau both models the multicontext aspect of MBK and reflects its modal behaviour. The multicontext aspect is modelled in that each prefix in the tableau contains a "location" which establishes the context the formula belongs to. The modal behaviour is modelled by using a "prefixed tableau" style similar to that presented in [16].

The tableau uses prefixed formulae. We introduce a new definition of prefix which takes into account the multi-language aspect of our system. A *prefix* is an expression of the form i/s where i is a natural number in I, the *level*, and s is a finite sequence of natural numbers, the *point*. A *prefixed formula* is an expression of the form $i/s : \phi$ with $\phi \in L_i$.

A *tableau* $\mathcal{T}$ is a (binary) tree whose nodes are labelled with prefixed formulae. A *branch* $\mathcal{B}$ is a path from the root to the leaf. A prefix is *present* in a branch $\mathcal{B}$ if there is a prefixed formula in $\mathcal{B}$ with that prefix and it is *new* if it is not present. A tableau branch $\mathcal{B}$ is closed if it contains $i/s : \phi$ and $i/s : \neg\phi$. A tableau $\mathcal{T}$ is i-closed if it every branch is closed. A tableau proof for $i : \phi$ begin with a root $i/1 : \neg\phi$. A closed tableau for $i/1 : \neg\phi$ is a proof for $i : \phi$.

Tableau rules are the multi-language version of prefixed rules in [16].

$$\frac{i/s : \neg(\phi \supset \psi)}{\begin{array}{c} i/s : \phi \\ i/s : \neg\psi \end{array}} \; \alpha \qquad\qquad \frac{i/s : \phi \supset \psi}{i/s : \neg\phi \quad i/s : \psi} \; \beta \qquad\qquad \frac{i/s : \neg\neg\phi}{i/s : \phi} \; dneg$$

$$\frac{i/s : \neg B(\text{``}\phi\text{''})}{i+1/sn : \neg\phi} \; \pi \qquad\qquad \frac{i/s : B(\text{``}\phi\text{''})}{i+1/sn : \phi} \; \nu$$

Restrictions: In π the prefix i/sn must be new. ν is applicable only if i/sn is present in the branch.

Imposing restrictions on the level, we can obtain a tableau system for the HMBR models. For instance, imposing that π and ν are applicable only if $i \leq n$, we can define a tableau for the HMBR models containing only compatibility sequences of the form $c_{0,n}$. It is easy to see that imposing these restriction prevents us from proving the formula $0 : B("B("\phi \supset \psi")") \supset (B("B("\phi")") \supset B("B("\psi")"))$, which is easily proved using the non-restricted rules for MBK . The different proof trees are showed below. Notice that the second tableau shows us an HMBR model satisfying $0 : \neg B("B("\phi \supset \psi")") \supset (B("B("\phi")") \supset B("B("\psi")"))$.

(1)	$0/1 : \neg(B(B(\phi \supset \psi)) \supset (B(B(\phi)) \supset B(B(\psi))))$	
(2a)	$0/1 : B(B(\phi \supset \psi))$	α rule at (1)
(2b)	$0/1 : \neg(B(B(\phi)) \supset B(B(\psi)))$	
(3a)	$0/1 : B(B(\phi))$	α rule at (2b)
(3b)	$0/1 : \neg B(B(\psi))$	
(4)	$1/11 : \neg B(\psi)$	π rule at (3b)
(5)	$1/11 : B(\phi \supset \psi)$	ν rule at (2a)
(6)	$1/11 : B(\phi)$	ν rule at (3a)
(7)	$2/111 : \neg\psi$	π rule at (4)
(8)	$2/111 : \phi \supset \psi$	ν rule at (5)
(9)	$2/111 : \phi$	ν rule at (6)
(10)	$2/111 : \neg\phi \qquad 2/111 : \psi$	β rule at (8)
	Contradiction	tableau closes

(1)	$0/1 : \neg(B(B(\phi \supset \psi)) \supset (B(B(\phi)) \supset B(B(\psi))))$	
(2a)	$0/1 : B(B(\phi \supset \psi))$	α rule at (1)
(2b)	$0/1 : \neg(B(B(\phi)) \supset B(B(\psi)))$	
(3a)	$0/1 : B(B(\phi))$	α rule at (2b)
(3b)	$0/1 : \neg B(B(\psi))$	
(4)	$1/11 : \neg B(\psi)$	π rule at (3b)
(5)	$1/11 : B(\phi \supset \psi)$	ν rule at (2a)
(6)	$1/11 : B(\phi)$	ν rule at (3a)
	No more rules applicable	tableau doesn't close

6 Conclusions and Future Work

We have considered the extension of Local Models Semantics defined in [9, 8] to model different aspects of "ideal" and "real" agent's beliefs. In particular, we have introduced HMB models for the representation of agent's beliefs which have a standard formulation in normal modal logics and we have modified such classes of models in order to deal with some forms of resource-boundedness. It is important to note that we considered here very simple cases of resource-bounded agents. However they allow us to exploit the use of modularity and flexibility of Local Models Semantics in order to model different aspects of agent's beliefs. Future work include applying LMS in order to give a uniform representation of the different forms of lack of reasoning capabilities present in the literature as well as investigating the addition of temporal aspects, e.g. bounded forms of temporal reasoning capabilities studied in [6].

References

1. M. E. Bratman, D. J. Israel, and M. E. Pollack. Plans and Resource-Bounded Practical Reasoning. *Computational Intelligence*, 4(4), 1988.
2. B. F. Chellas. *Modal Logic – an Introduction*. Cambridge University Press, 1980.
3. A. Cimatti and L. Serafini. Mechanizing Multi-Agent Reasoning with Belief Contexts. In *Practical Reasoning, International Conference on Formal and Applied Practical Reasoning, FAPR'96*, number 1085 in Lecture Notes in Artificial Intelligence, pages 694–696. Springer, 1996.
4. R. Fagin and J.Y. Halpern. Belief, awareness, and limited reasoning. *Artificial Intelligence*, 34:39–76, 1988.
5. R. Fagin, J.Y. Halpern, Y. Moses, and M. Y. Vardi. *Reasoning about knowledge*. MIT Press, 1995.
6. M. Fisher and C. Ghidini. Programming Resource-Bounded Deliberative Agents. In *Proceedings of the Sixteenth International Joint Conference on Artificial Intelligence (IJCAI'99)*, 1999. To appear.
7. E. Giunchiglia and F. Giunchiglia. Ideal and Real Belief about Belief. In *Practical Reasoning, International Conference on Formal and Applied Practical Reasoning, FAPR'96*, number 1085 in Lecture Notes in Artificial Intelligence, pages 261–275. Springer Verlag, 1996.
8. F. Giunchiglia and C. Ghidini. A Local Models Semantics for Propositional Attitudes. In *Proceedings of the 1st International and Interdisciplinary Conference on Modeling and Using Context (CONTEXT-97)*, pages 363–372, Rio de Jeneiro, Brazil, 1997.
9. F. Giunchiglia and C. Ghidini. Local Models Semantics, or Contextual Reasoning = Locality + Compatibility. In *Proceedings of the Sixth International Conference on Principles of Knowledge Representation and Reasoning (KR'98)*, pages 282–289, Trento, 1998. Morgan Kaufmann.
10. F. Giunchiglia and L. Serafini. Multilanguage hierarchical logics (or: how we can do without modal logics). *Artificial Intelligence*, 65:29–70, 1994.
11. F. Giunchiglia, L. Serafini, E. Giunchiglia, and M. Frixione. Non-Omniscient Belief as Context-Based Reasoning. In *Proc. of the 13th International Joint Conference on Artificial Intelligence*, pages 548–554, Chambery, France, 1993.
12. A. R. Haas. A Syntactic Theory of Belief and Action. *Artificial Intelligence*, 28:245–292, 1986.
13. J . Hintikka. *Knowledge and Belief*. Cornell University Press, Ithaca, NY, 1962.
14. J. Hintikka. Impossible possible worlds vindicated. *Journal of Philosophical Logic*, 4:475–484, 1975.
15. I.A. Langevelde, van, A.W. Philipsen, and J. Treur. A Compositional Architecture for Simple Design Formally Specified in DESIRE. In J. Treur and T. Wetter, editors, *Formal Specification of Complex Reasoning Systems*. Ellis Horwood, 1993.
16. F. Massacci. Strongly analytic tableaux for normal modal logics. In *Proc. of the 12th Conference on Automated Deduction*, 1994.
17. J. Treur. On the Use of Reflection Principles in Modelling Complex Reasoning. *Internation Journal of Intelligent Systems*, 6:277–294, 1991.

A Context-Based Logic for Distributed Knowledge Representation and Reasoning

Chiara Ghidini[1]* and Luciano Serafini[2]

[1] Department of Computation and Mathematics
Manchester Metropolitan University, Manchester M1 5GD, U.K.
[2] ITC–IRST, 38050 Povo, Trento, Italy
C.Ghidini@doc.mmu.ac.uk   serafini@itc.it

Abstract. This paper is concerned with providing a logic, called *Distributed First Order Logic (DFOL)*, for the formalization of distributed knowledge representation and reasoning systems. In such systems knowledge is contained in a set of heterogeneous subsystems. Each subsystem represents, using a possibly different language, partial knowledge about a subset of the whole domain, it is able to reason about such a knowledge, and it is able to exchange knowledge with other subsystems via query answering. Our approach is to represent each subsystem as a context, each context having its own language, a set of basic facts describing what is "explicitly known" by the subsystem, and a set of inference rules representing the reasoning capabilities of the subsystem. Knowledge exchange is represented by two different relations on contexts: the former on the languages (query mapping) and the latter on the domains (answer mapping) of different contexts. DFOL is based on a semantics for contextual reasoning, called *Local Models Semantics*, which allows to model contexts having different languages, basic knowledge, and reasoning capabilities, as well as relations between contexts. An axiomatization of DFOL is also presented.

1 Introduction

In distributed knowledge representation and reasoning systems, knowledge is not organized in a monolithic and homogeneous system, it is rather composed of a set of heterogeneous subsystems, each subsystem representing a certain subset of the whole knowledge. Analogously distributed reasoning is not a single process which involves the whole knowledge; it is rather a combination of various reasoning processes, autonomously performed by the subsystems on different subsets of the global knowledge.

Well known formalisms for the representation and integration of distributed knowledge and reasoning systems are based on Multi Modal Logics [7], Labelled Deductive Systems [8] and Labelled Deductive Systems for Modal Logics [4, 2], Annotated Logics [16], and Cooperative Information Systems [3]. The underlying

---

* Visiting Research Fellow from University of Trento, Italy, supported by the Italian National Research Council (CNR)

idea of these formalisms is that the truth values of different formulae in different subsystems are related one another. In modal logics truth values of different formulae in different worlds are related imposing axioms connecting different modal operators and constraints between different accessibility relations. Labelled deductive inference machine and fibred semantics relate the truth values of formulae with different labels. In annotated logics, annotated clauses enable to relate truth values of formulae with different labels. Finally, in cooperative information systems an inclusion between concepts belonging to different databases is specified by mean of interschema assertions.

In many cases stating relations between truth values of different formulae is not enough. Consider an example from the Electronic Commerce scenario: a buyer agent asks a vendor agent for the price list of different fruits. The vendor returns a list of pairs ⟨fruit, price⟩. This list might contain fruits which are "unknown" to the buyer, fruits known with different names, and so on. In order to formalize this simple example we need to represent and reason about the relations existing between terms for fruits in the languages of the vendor and terms for fruits in the languages of the buyer.

The definition of a formalism for representing and reasoning about relations between terms in different languages is a challenging issue in the development of distributed systems. The goal of this paper is twofold. First, we extend the ideas and the formal work on contextual reasoning described in [10], in order to define a logic for distributed knowledge and reasoning systems, called *Distributed First Order Logic (DFOL)*. DFOL must formalize relations among objects as well as relations among formulae of different subsystems. Second, we provide a context-based calculus for DFOL, based on the ML systems introduced in [12].

The main idea of DFOL is to represent each subsystem as a context, each context having its own language, used to describe a piece of knowledge, a set of facts, describing what is true in the subsystem, and an inference engine, expressing the reasoning capabilities of the subsystem. Following this idea DFOL syntax is composed of a family of first order languages, each language describing a piece of the global knowledge contained in a subsystem. DFOL semantics is an extension of Local Models Semantics [11]. It is defined in terms of sets of first order interpretations for the languages of the different subsystems and relations between domains of interpretation of the different languages. DFOL calculus is based on ML systems [12]. It is composed of a set of first order natural deduction systems, connected by a set of inference rules, called *bridge rules* . Bridge rules export theorems among different theories, each theory representing the piece of knowledge contained in a subsystem. Notice that we restrict ourselves to first order languages as they are powerful enough to represent most of the knowledge representation formalisms currently used. The same ideas can be extended to other logical languages.

This paper is organized as follows. Section 2 gives a list of desiderata for DFOL. In Section 3 we introduce the logic and we we show (Section 4) that it enjoys the desiderata defined in Section 2. In Section 5 we define a calculus for DFOL. Then we compare DFOL with similar approaches in Section 6.

2 Requirements

Our requirements for a logic for distributed knowledge and reasoning systems are grouped in two different sets: representational requirements and structural requirements. A close look to the literature on context (see [1] for a survey on this field) shows that most of these requirements are among the reasons for which contexts have been used in knowledge representation. This fact motivates our context-based approach to the definition of a logic for distributed knowledge representation and reasoning systems.

Representational requirements These requirements concern the ability of a formal logic to represent a set of aspects which are relevant in a distributed knowledge representation systems.

- *different languages.* This is necessary as different subsystems might represent knowledge using different languages.
- *different domains.* This is necessary as different subsystems might represent knowledge about different domains at a different level of abstraction.
- *different (local) semantics.* This is necessary as each representational language has its own autonomous semantics. The meaning of a symbol in a subsystem should be distinct from that of the same symbol in another subsystems.
- *directional relations among objects in different (sub)domains.* Relations among objects are necessary as objects in a (sub)domain of a subsystem S might correspond to one or more objects in a (sub)domain of another subsystem S'. Since the capability of S to represent object of the domain of S' might differ from the capability of S' to represent the objects of the domain of S, relations among objects are directional, i.e., the relation from the domain **dom** of S into the domain **dom'** of S' is not the inverse of that from **dom'** into **dom**.
- *directional relations among formulae* in different languages. This is necessary as the meaning of a formula in a subsystem might depend on the meaning of one or the combination of more formulae in different subsystems. Since the information flows in input to two different subsystems S and S' are independent, the relation from tuples of formulae of $S_1, \ldots, S_n$ to formulae of S is independent from the relation from tuples of formulae of $S'_1, \ldots, S'_n$ to formulae of S'.
- *partial information.* This is necessary as subsystems might contain incomplete information. Therefore the logic can't force a formula to be either true or false in a local interpretation.
- *local inconsistency.* This is necessary as inconsistent information is often not propagated across subsystems. Therefore the logic must formalize that an inconsistent set of formulae in a language, corresponding to an inconsistent set of facts in a subsystem, might not imply inconsistency in other subsystems.
- *preventing hypothetical reasoning across subsystems*, i.e., the logical consequence relation $\models$ between formulae in different subsystems is not closed under the rule

$$\frac{\phi_1 \models \psi \quad \phi_2 \models \psi}{\phi_1 \vee \phi_2 \models \psi}$$

This is necessary as this kind of reasoning might not be allowed. Consider, for instance, the knowledge bases of two agents *John* and *Sue*. If John communicates either $phone(Mary, 1234)$ or $phone(Mary, 1235)$, then *Sue* can infer $knows(John, phone(Mary))$. However $knows(John, phone(Mary))$ can't be inferred by *Sue* if *John* communicates $phone(Mary, 1234) \lor phone(Mary, 1235)$.

Structural requirements These are requirements on *how* the logic represents the characteristics of a distributed knowledge representation system.

- *Modularity* and *compositionality*. Modularity means that each representational property described above is formalized by a formal component in the logic (an axiom schema, an inference rule, an applicability condition, and so on.). Compositionality means that the formalization of a distributed knowledge representation system with a specific set of representational properties P must be obtained by combining the formal components of the logic which formalize the single properties in P. Compositionality makes the logic flexible enough to formalize a wide range of distributed knowledge representation systems.
- *Incrementality* w.r.t. the formal logics for the representation of non-distributed reasoning systems. I.e., the logic must be based on well established and well studied logics. This requirement is necessary as we want to exploit all the previous formal results, especially the results obtained in the area of automated reasoning and knowledge representation.

3   The Logic

The goal of this section is to define the main components of a DFOL. These components are the family of languages, the interpretation, the satisfiability relation, possible constraints on the interpretations, and logical consequence.

3.1   Languages and Semantics

Let $\{L_i\}_{i \in I}$ (in the following $\{L_i\}$) be a family of first order languages defined over a set I of indexes. Each language L_i partially describes the world from a certain perspective (i's point of view). For instance in the formalization of multi-agent propositional attitudes described in [12] I is a set of names for agents and each L_i is the language adopted by agent i to express its beliefs about the world. In the formalization of federated databases described in [15] I contains the indexes associated to the databases of a federated database and each L_i is the language which describes the logical schema of the i-th database in the federation.

Languages L_i and L_j are not necessarily disjoint and the same formula ϕ may occur in different languages. As L_i and L_j describe the world from different point of view, the meaning of a formula ϕ in L_i and in L_j might be different. Suppose for instance that two agents i and j "live" in different places. Then the formula *it-is-raining* in the language of agent i means that it is raining where i lives, whereas the same formula in the language of agent j means that it is raining where j lives. Similarly, the same symbol, occurring in two different databases in a federation, may have different semantic interpretations in each database. In order to distinguish occurrences of the same formula in different languages we annotate in which language a formula is to be considered. A *labeled formula* is a pair $i : \phi^1$. It denotes the formula ϕ and the fact that ϕ is a formula of the language L_i. When no ambiguity arises, labeled formulae are called formulae. Given a set of labeled formulae Γ, Γ_j denotes the set of formulae $\{\gamma \,|j : \gamma \in \Gamma\}$. From now on, a formula ϕ of the language L_i is called *i-formula* .

The semantics for $\{L_i\}$ is an extension of Local Models Semantics defined in [11]. The languages $\{L_i\}$ are interpreted in a structure which consists of two components: (i) a local interpretation for each L_i, and (ii) a binary relation between the interpretation domains of each pair of languages L_i and L_j.

Let M_i be the set of all the first order models of L_i on a given domain **dom**. $m \in M_i$ is a *local model* (of L_i). Each first order model m is a pair $\langle \mathbf{dom}, \mathcal{I} \rangle$ where **dom** is the *domain* of interpretation (or *universe*) of L_i and $\mathcal{I}$ is the the *interpretation* function. The *local satisfiability relation* is the usual satisfiability relation $\models$ between first order models and first order formulae with an assignment to the free variables. The set M_i of local models and the local satisfiability relation define the *local semantics* of L_i. The fact that that i-th subsystem contains partial knowledge about facts in L_i is represented associating each L_i to a set of *possible models* $S_i \subseteq M_i$ on the domain $\mathbf{dom}_i$. The satisfiability of a formula in a a set of possible models is defined as follows:

Definition 1 (Satisfiability of a formula). *Let $\{S_i\}$ be a family of set of possible models for $\{L_i\}$; let an assignment a be a family $\{a_i\}$ of assignments a_i to the variables of L_i. A formula $i : \phi$ is satisfied in $\{S_i\}$ by an assignment a, in symbols $\{S_i\} \models i : \phi[a]$, if for all $m \in S_i$ $m \models \phi[a_i]$. For any set of i-formulae Γ_i, $S_i \models \Gamma_i[a]$ means that $S_i \models \gamma[a]$ for all $\gamma \in \Gamma_i$.*

The second component of a model for $\{L_i\}$ is a family of *domain relations* from the domain of L_i to the domain of L_j. A domain relation r_{ij} from $\mathbf{dom}_i$ to $\mathbf{dom}_j$ is a subset of $\mathbf{dom}_i \times \mathbf{dom}_j$, and represents the capability of subsystem j to map the objects of $\mathbf{dom}_i$ into its domain $\mathbf{dom}_j$. A pair $\langle d, d' \rangle$ being in r_{ij} means that, from the point of view of j, d in $\mathbf{dom}_i$ is the representation of d' in $\mathbf{dom}_j$. Notice that r_{ij} formalizes j's subjective point of view of the relation between domains and not an absolute objective point of view. Therefore $\langle d, d' \rangle \in r_{ij}$ must not be read as if d and d' represent the same object in a domain shared by i and j. This facts indeed would be formalized from a point of view which is external (above, meta) of both i and j. Consider the example of the vendor and the buyer presented in Section 1. The vendor and the buyer represent a "piece of world", i.e. the fruits, at two different approximation levels. Suppose that the vendor is interested in dealing with *lemons, red apples, green apples,* and *pineapples,* whereas the buyer deals with *lemons* and *apples.* From the point of view of the buyer, *lemons* in the domain of the vendor and *lemons* in its own

---

[1] Similar notations have been introduced by [8, 16, 5, 13].

domain represent the same object of the real world, both *red apples* and *green apples* in the domain of the vendor represent the real world object it represents with the object *apples*, and finally *pineapples* in the domain of the vendor doesn't correspond to any object in its own domain. This is formalized by defining the domain relation r_{vb} (where v stands for the vendor and b stands for the buyer) as the set of pairs $\{\langle lemons, lemons \rangle, \langle red\ apples, apples \rangle, \langle green\ apples, apples \rangle\}$. This translation from vendor's domain to buyer's domain does not tell us much on how the vendor maps the object of the domain of the buyer. Indeed it might be the case that the vendor is not interested in receiving any communication from the buyer, and therefore, from its point of view, there is no relation from the buyer's domain to its domain i.e., r_{bv} is empty.

Notice that we are not imposing that the point of view of i is always different from the point of view of j. In many cases it is plausible that r_{ij} and r_{ji} are such that $\langle d, d' \rangle \in r_{ij}$ if and only if $\langle d', d \rangle \in r_{ji}$.

Definition 2 (Model). *A model $\mathcal{M}$ (for $\{L_i\}$) is a pair $\langle \{S_i\}, \{r_{ij}\} \rangle$ where, for each $i, j \in I$, $S_i \subseteq M_i$ is a set of possible models over the same domain of interpretation dom_i and r_{ij} is a domain relation from dom_i to dom_j.*

3.2 Compatibility Constraints

One of the main purposes of DFOL is enabling a formal reasoning among different first order theories. To do this we need a way for specifying constraints on DFOL models. Being a DFOL model composed of a family of possible models and a family of domain relations, the constraints on DFOL models we consider in this paper are (a) constraints on the domain relation, and (b) constraints on the possible models. We call the former *domain constraints* and the latter *interpretation constraints*.

Definition 3 (Domain Constraint). *Let L_i, L_j be two first order languages. A domain constraint from L_i to L_j is an expression of the form T or S.*

Intuitively T from L_i to L_j captures the fact that, from j perspective, dom_i is contained in dom_j. Conversely S from L_i to L_j captures the fact that, from j perspective, dom_j is contained in dom_i. Consider the example of a mediator M [17], i.e., a database which integrates the information of n databases. The mediator collects all the information about the individuals contained in the n databases. The fact that the domain dom_i of each database must be embedded by M into its own domain dom_M can be formalized by imposing the domain constraint T from each database to the mediator M.

The set of domain constraints from L_i to L_j is denoted by DC_{ij}.

Definition 4 (Interpretation Constraint). *Let L_i and L_j be two first order languages. An interpretation constraint from L_i to L_j is an expression of the* *form $i : \phi(x_1, \ldots, x_n) \to j : \psi(x_1, \ldots, x_n)$ where $\phi(x_1, \ldots, x_n)$ and $\psi(x_1, \ldots, x_n)$ are formulae of L_i and L_j, respectively[2].*

Intuitively $i : \phi(x_1, \ldots, x_n) \to j : \psi(x_1, \ldots, x_n)$ captures the fact that, from the point of view of j, the set of tuples of objects of $\mathbf{dom}_i$ which satisfy $\phi(x_1, \ldots, x_n)$ in L_i corresponds (is mapped via r_{ij} into) to a set of tuples which satisfy $\psi(x_1, \ldots, x_n)$ in L_j. Let us consider the example of the mediator given above. Suppose that the i-th database contains data about the telephone numbers of a town (say Roma) and a relation $phone(x, y)$ stating that x has telephone number y. Suppose that $phone(x, y)$ is mapped by the mediator into its relation $telno(x, 39, 6, y)$, with the addition of international and area code. This mapping is represented by the interpretation constraint:

$$i : phone(x, y) \to \text{M} : telno(x, 39, 6, y) \tag{1}$$

The set of interpretation constraints from L_i to L_j are denoted by IC_{ij}. A *compatibility constraint* C_{ij} from L_i to L_j is a pair $C_{ij} = \langle DC_{ij}, IC_{ij} \rangle$.

Definition 5 (Satisfiability of Compatibility Constraints). *Let $\mathcal{M} = \langle \{S_i\}, \{r_{ij}\} \rangle$ be a model and $C = \{C_{ij}\}$ be a family of compatibility constraints. $\mathcal{M}$ satisfies a domain constraint $\mathsf{T} \in DC_{ij}$ if for any $d \in \mathbf{dom}_i$ there is a $d' \in \mathbf{dom}_j$ such that $\langle d, d' \rangle \in r_{ij}$. Analogously $\mathcal{M}$ satisfies $\mathsf{S} \in DC_{ij}$ if for any $d \in \mathbf{dom}_j$ there is a $d' \in \mathbf{dom}_i$ such that $\langle d', d \rangle \in r_{ij}$. $\mathcal{M}$ satisfies an interpretation constraint $i : \phi(x_1, \ldots, x_n) \to j : \psi(x_1, \ldots, x_n) \in IC_{ij}$ if for any $\langle d_k, d'_k \rangle \in r_{ij}$ ($1 \le k \le n$), $S_i \models \phi(d_1, \ldots, d_n)$ implies that $S_j \models \psi(d'_1, \ldots, d'_n)$. $\mathcal{M}$ satisfies the family of compatibility constraints C if for each $i, j \in I$, it satisfies all the domain constraints in DC_{ij} and all the interpretation constraints in IC_{ij}.*

3.3 Logical Consequence

Compatibility constraints imply that certain facts in a language are necessarily true as consequence of other facts being true in, possibly distinct, languages. The formal characterization of such a relation is crucial as it allows us the detection of inconsistencies in the languages and to understand how information propagates through languages. In this section we formalize this relation among facts by means of the notion of *logical consequence w.r.t. a set of compatibility constraints* (or more simply logical consequence).

Before defining the logical consequence we extend the set of variables of each L_i to a set of what we call *extended variables*. For each $j \in I$ and each variable x in L_i, $x^{j\to}$ and $x^{\to j}$ are variables of L_i. Intuitively a variable x (without indexes) occurring in $i : \phi$ is a place-holder for a generic element of $\mathbf{dom}_i$; the extended variable $x^{j\to}$ occurring in $i : \phi$ is a place-holder for an element of $\mathbf{dom}_i$ which

---

[2] For the sake of simplicity we define interpretation constraints as pairs of formulae with the same set of free variables. Interpretation constraints can be easily generalized by dropping this requirement.

is an image, via the domain relation r_{ji}, of the element of $\mathbf{dom}_j$ denoted by x; analogously $x^{\rightarrow j}$ occurring in $i : \phi$ is a place-holder for an element of $\mathbf{dom}_i$ which is a pre-image, via r_{ij}, of the element of $\mathbf{dom}_j$ denoted by x. We also extend the assignment a to all extended variables. a is an *admissible assignment* if for any variable x and any variable $x^{i\rightarrow}$ and $x^{\rightarrow i}$

1. if $\mathsf{T} \in DC_{ij}$, then $\langle a_i(x), a_j(x^{i\rightarrow}) \rangle \in r_{ij}$
2. if $\mathsf{S} \in DC_{ji}$, then $\langle a_j(x^{\rightarrow i}), a_i(x) \rangle \in r_{ji}$.

For any set of i-formulae Γ, ϕ, $\Gamma[a] \models_{S_i} \phi[a]$ if and only if for all $m \in S_i$, $m \models \Gamma[a]$ implies $m \models \phi[a]$.

Definition 6 (Logical Consequence). *Let Γ be a set of formulae. A formula $i : \phi$ is a logical consequence of Γ w.r.t. a set of compatibility constraints C, in symbols $\Gamma \models_C i : \phi$, if for all the models $\langle \{S_i\}, \{r_{ij}\} \rangle$ satisfying the compatibility constraints C and for all the admissible assignments a, if for all $j \neq i$, $S_j \models \Gamma_j[a]$, then $\Gamma_i[a] \models_{S_i} \phi[a]$.*

4 Fulfillment of the Requirements

DFOL satisfies the representational and structural properties introduced in Section 1 (Proofs of theorems are reported in [9]). The capability of DFOL to cope with different languages, interpretation domains, and semantics is a consequence of how we define DFOL syntax and semantics. Directional relations between objects in different domains are represented by mean of domain relations. Directionality is guaranteed as both domain relation and domain constraints from L_i to L_j do not depend on these from L_j to L_i. The basic relations of totality and surjectivity are formalized by imposing domain constraints T and S. Other relations between domains can be expressed using suitable combinations of domain constraints and interpretation constraints on the equality predicate:

Embedded domains From the point of view of j the domain of i is isomorphic to a subset of its domain. This can be represented by imposing the domain constraint T and the interpretation constraint $i : x \neq y \rightarrow j : x \neq y$ from L_i to L_j. The domain relations from $\mathbf{dom}_i$ to $\mathbf{dom}_j$ satisfying these constraints are the total injective relations from $\mathbf{dom}_i$ to $\mathbf{dom}_j$. Moreover, for any $n \geq 1$ Equation (2) can be proved. (2) means that $\mathbf{dom}_j$ contains at least as many elements as $\mathbf{dom}_i$.

$$i : \exists x_1, \ldots x_n \bigwedge_{i \neq j} x_i \neq x_j \models_C j : \exists x_1, \ldots x_n \bigwedge_{i \neq j} x_i \neq x_j \qquad (2)$$

Abstracted domains From the point of view of j each object of its domain is an abstraction of a set of objects of the domain of i. This can be represented by imposing the domain constraint S and the interpretation constraint $i : x = y \rightarrow j : x = y$ from i to j. The domain relations that satisfy these constraints are the surjective functions from $\mathbf{dom}_i$ to $\mathbf{dom}_j$. Under these constraints Equation (3) can be proved for any $n \geq 1$. (3) means that $\textbf{dom}_j$ contains at most as many objects as $\textbf{dom}_i$.

$$i : \forall x_1, \ldots x_n \bigvee_{i \neq j} x_i = x_j \models_C j : \forall x_1, \ldots x_n \bigvee_{i \neq j} x_i = x_j \qquad (3)$$

Isomorphic domains From the point of view of j, its domain is isomorphic to the domain of i. This is obtained by combining embedding and abstraction. The domain relations that satisfy both the constraints of embedding and abstraction are the isomorphisms from $\textbf{dom}_i$ to $\textbf{dom}_j$.

Directional relations among formulae in different languages are represented by mean of interpretation constraints. An interpretation constraint from L_i to L_j affects the logical consequence from i-formulae to j-formulae, and it does not impose any relation in the opposite direction. This result is expressed by the following theorem.

Theorem 1. *Let $i : \phi$ and $j : \psi$ be closed formulae such that ψ is classically satisfiable. There is a set of compatibility constraints C such that $i : \phi \models_C j : \psi$ and $j : \neg\psi \not\models_C i : \neg\phi$.*

As the model associates to each language L_i a set S_i of possible models, partiality is represented. Complete distributed knowledge is represented by defining a model for $\{L_i\}$ as a pair $\langle \{m_i\}\{r_{ij}\} \rangle$, where each m_i is a (single) local model for the language L_i. The capability of DFOL to cope with local inconsistency is a consequence of the fact that $i : \bot \models_C j : \bot$ does not hold unless the interpretation constraint $i : \bot \rightarrow j : \bot$ is added to C. Finally Theorem 2 guarantees that hypothetical reasoning across subsystems is, in general, not allowed.

Theorem 2. *Let $i : \phi_1$, $i : \phi_2$, and $j : \psi$ be classically satisfiable closed formulae. There is a set of compatibility constraints C such that $i : \phi_1 \models_C j : \psi$, $i : \phi_2 \models_C j : \psi$, and $i : \phi_1 \vee \phi_2 \not\models_C j : \psi$.*

5 The Calculus

Providing a calculus (axiomatization) for DFOL is a necessary step to show that DFOL derivability relation is semi-decidable and to give the main hints for the definition of decision algorithms for decidable subclasses DFOL models. We adopt Multilanguage Systems (ML systems) [12], which are formal systems designed to formalize contextual reasoning. Soundness and completeness theorems can be found in [9].

An ML system is a triple $\langle \{L_i\}, \{\Omega_i\}, \Delta \rangle$ where $\{L_i\}$ is a family of languages, $\{\Omega_i\}$ is a family of sets of axioms, and Δ is the deductive machinery. Δ contains two kinds of inference rules: *i rules*, i.e., inference rules with premises and conclusions in the same language, and *bridge rules*, i.e., inference rules with premises and conclusions belonging to different languages. Notationally, we write inference rules, with, e.g., a single premise, as follows:

$$\frac{i : \psi}{i : \phi} \; ir \qquad\qquad\qquad \frac{i : \psi}{j : \phi} \; br$$

ir is an i rule while br is a bridge rule. Derivability in an ML system, defined in [12], is the obvious generalization of derivability in a natural deduction system.

An ML system for a DFOL with languages $\{L_i\}$ and compatibility constraints C is composed of the same family of languages, a sets of axioms corresponding to the basic facts of the subsystem, a set of i rules for local reasoning, and a set of bridge rules which formalize the compatibility constraints.

Definition 7 (First Order ML system). *The ML system for the DFOL with languages $\{L_i\}$, basic facts $\{\Omega_i \subseteq L_i\}$, and compatibility constraints $C = \{\langle DC_{ij}, IC_{ij} \rangle\}$ is the tuple* $\mathrm{MC} = \langle \{L_i\}, \{\Omega_i\}, \Delta \rangle$, *where Δ contains:*

1. *for each $i \in I$ the natural deduction inference rules for propositional calculus and equality (see [14] and [12]) and the following rules for quantifiers:*

$$\frac{i : \phi_x^y}{i : \forall x \phi} \; \forall\mathrm{I} \qquad \frac{i : \forall x \phi}{i : \phi_x^t} \; \forall\mathrm{E} \qquad \frac{i : \phi_x^t}{i : \exists x \phi} \; \exists\mathrm{I} \qquad \frac{i : \exists x \phi \quad \overset{[i : \phi_x^y]}{i : \psi}}{i : \psi} \; \exists\mathrm{E}$$

2. *for each interpretation constraint $i : \phi(x_1 \ldots, x_n) \to j : \psi(x_1, \ldots x_n) \in IC_{ij}$ the bridge rule C*

$$\frac{i : \phi(x_1, \ldots, x_n)}{j : \psi(y_1, \ldots, y_n)} \; C$$

where if $n \neq 0$, for each k, either y_k is $x_k^{i \to}$ and $\mathsf{T} \in DC_{ij}$ or x_k is $y_k^{\to j}$ and $\mathsf{S} \in DC_{ij}$;

3. *the bridge rules for equality:*

$$\frac{i : e_1 \vee e_2 \quad \overset{[i : e_1] \; [i : e_2]}{j : \phi \quad j : \phi}}{j : \phi} \; \vee\mathrm{E}_= \qquad\qquad \frac{i : \exists x e \quad \overset{[i : e_x^y]}{j : \psi}}{j : \psi} \; \exists\mathrm{E}_=$$

where e, e_1, e_2 are pure equality formulae, i.e., formulae whose only predicate is the equality predicate.

RESTRICTIONS C *and bridge rules for equality are applicable only if the premise in i does not depend on assumptions in j. $\forall\mathrm{I}$ is applicable only if neither y nor $y^{\to i}$ occur in any assumptions which ϕ_x^y depends on. $\exists\mathrm{E}$ and $\exists\mathrm{E}_=$ are applicable only if neither y nor $y^{\to i}$ occur in $\exists x \phi$ and $\exists x e$ respectively, in ψ, and in any assumption which ψ depends on. Derivability in MS is denoted by $\vdash_C$.*

Rules for quantifiers defined above are similar to the natural deduction rules for quantifiers introduced in first order logic. The only difference is that the applicability of $\forall\mathrm{I}$ and $\exists\mathrm{E}$ depends also on the occurrence of variables in other languages. This fact is formalized by restrictions on $\forall I$ and $\exists E$. The bridge rule C formalizes the effects of the interpretation constraint $i : \phi(x_1 \ldots, x_n) \to j : \psi(x_1, \ldots x_n) \in IC_{ij}$ on the logical consequence relation $\models_C$, in presence of domain constraints from i to j. Notice that if the interpretation constraint does not contains free variables, then C can be instantiated as a propositional bridge rule

$$\frac{i : \phi}{j : \psi} \ C$$

and it is independent from the domain constraints in DC_{ij}. If the interpretation constraint contains free variables, then the bridge rule C depends on the domain constraints in DC_{ij}. The the four possible cases are: $DC_{ij} = \emptyset$, $DC_{ij} = \{T\}$, $DC_{ij} = \{S\}$ and $DC_{ij} = \{T, S\}$. If $DC_{ij} = \emptyset$, then the interpretation constraints from i to j are not enough for i to affects j. Indeed there are no constraints on the mapping (correspondence) from the elements in $\mathbf{dom}_i$ and the elements in $\mathbf{dom}_j$. Therefore no bridge rule is imposed from i to j. In the other three cases the bridge rule C is instantiated as the following bridge rules T, S, and TS, respectively:

$$\frac{i : \phi(x_1, \ldots, x_n)}{j : \psi(x_1^{i \to}, \ldots, x_n^{i \to})} \ T \qquad \frac{i : \phi(y_1^{\to j}, \ldots, y_n^{\to j})}{j : \psi(y_1, \ldots, y_n)} \ S \qquad \frac{i : \phi(x_1, \ldots, x_h, y_{h+1}^{\to j}, \ldots, y_n^{\to j})}{j : \psi(x_1^{i \to}, \ldots, x_h^{i \to}, y_{h+1}, \ldots, y_n)} \ ST$$

$\lor E_=$-rule and $\exists E_=$-rule state that we can perform reasoning by case across different theories on equality. Reasoning by case allows to infer a fact, say ϕ, from a disjunction, say $\psi \lor \theta$, by deriving ϕ from ψ and θ separately. The basic assumption of reasoning by case is that, if a model satisfies a disjunction, then it must satisfy at least one of the disjunct. In general this is not true in our logic as there are DFOL models S such that $S \models i : \psi \lor \theta$ and neither $S \models i : \psi$ nor $S \models i : \theta$. Equality formulae however constitute an exception since the equality predicate $=$ has a unique interpretation on any domain. Therefore it can be proved that, if $S_i \models e_2 \lor e_2[a]$, then either $S_i \models e_1[a]$ or $S_i \models e_2[a]$. Analogous observations hold for the $\exists E_=$-rule.

As an explanatory example consider the deduction of property (2).

$$\frac{i : \exists x_1, \ldots x_n \bigwedge_{h \neq k} x_h \neq x_k \qquad \dfrac{\dfrac{\dfrac{[i : \bigwedge_{h \neq k} x_h \neq x_k]^{(1)}}{i : x_h \neq x_k} \ \land E}{j : x_h^{i \to} \neq x_k^{i \to}} \ T}{\dfrac{j : \bigwedge_{h \neq k} x_h^{i \to} \neq x_k^{i \to}}{j : \exists x_1, \ldots x_n \bigwedge_{h \neq k} x_h \neq x_k} \ \exists I} \ \land I}{j : \exists x_1, \ldots x_n \bigwedge_{h \neq k} x_h \neq x_k} \ \exists I_= \text{(discharging }^{(1)})$$

In the above deduction we start by taking n distinct individuals $x_1, \ldots x_n$ in the domain of i (assumption $^{(1)}$). Totality from i to j implies that each individual x_h in the domain of i is mapped in an individual $x_h^{i \to}$ in the domain of j. Interpretation constraint $i : x \neq y \to j : x \neq y$ implies that if x_h is distinct from x_k in i then $x_h^{i \to}$ is distinct form $x_k^{i \to}$ in j (application of T). We repeat the previous reasoning for each $h \neq k$ and apply $\land I$ in j. We then introduce the existential quantifier in j and eliminate the existential quantifier in i by the $\exists E_=$

bridge rule. Another example comes from the mediator example described above. Suppose that the i-th database contains the fact $phone(John, 12345)$. Then we want to infer $telno(John, 39, 6, 12345)$ in M. This, however, is not possible using only constraint (1), as this inference is based on the assumption that $John$ and 12345 denote the same person and number in i and M. This assumption should be made explicit as, i and M might adopt different encoding for person names and telephone numbers. What we are allowed to infer in M, however, is that there is a person from Rome who has a telephone number, i.e. $\exists xy.telno(x, 39, 6, y)$. The deduction follows:

$$\cfrac{i : \exists xy, x = John \land y = 12345 \quad \cfrac{\cfrac{i : phone(John, 12345) \quad [i : x = John \land y = 12345]^{(1)}}{\cfrac{i : phone(x, y)}{M : telno(x^{i\rightarrow}, 39, 6, y^{i\rightarrow})} C}{M : \exists xy.telno(x, 39, 6, y)} \exists I}}{M : \exists xy.telno(x, 39, 6, y)} \exists I_= (\text{discharging } ^{(1)}) =$$

6 Related Work

We consider here four state of the art classes of formal systems for distributed knowledge and reasoning: Labelled Deductive Systems, Modal Logics, Annotated Logics, and Cooperative Information Systems.

Labelled Deductive Systems (LDS) [8] are very general logical systems. We compare DFOL with LDSs for Quantified Modal Logics (LDSQML) [2]. LDSQMLs deal with domains and relations between domains, as well as relations between formulae. LDSQMLs provide a formalization for modal logics with varying, increasing, decreasing, and constant domains. The main analogies between DFOL and LDSQML is that they both allow for distinct domains and basic relations between them. The main differences concern:

- *Reasoning on labels.* In LDSQML (and in LDS in general) it is possible representing and reason about properties of labels (represented by *relwffs*). This is not possible in DFOL.
- *Reasoning on term existence.* In LDSQML the literal $w : t$ represents the fact that a term t denotes an individual in the domain of a world w. We cannot represent this fact in DFOL since we adopt first order semantics and each term of the language L_i denotes an object in $\mathbf{dom}_i$.
- *Reasoning about relation between individuals of different domains.* LDSQML allows for representing only few relations between domains: containment and equivalence. In DFOL the equality interpretation constraint $1 : x = t \rightarrow j : x = u$ represents the fact that a certain individual t in $\mathbf{dom}_i$ corresponds to another individual u in $\mathbf{dom}_j$. This fact allows DFOL to cope with more complex domain relations.
- *Inconsistency propagation.* The $\bot E$ rule of LDSQML enables the propagation of false across worlds. This prevents LDSQML to represent local inconsistency.

A comparison of DFOL with quantified Modal Logics leads to the same observations given above.

Annotated Logic [16] is a formalism that has been applied to a variety of situations in knowledge representation, expert systems, quantitative reasoning, and hybrid databases. In annotated logics a set of logical theories is integrated in a unique amalgamated theory. The amalgamated theory is the disjoint union of the theories plus a set of amalgamated clauses which resolve conflicts due to inconsistent facts and compose uncertain information of different theories. As DFOL, annotated logics have the capability to cope with inconsistent knowledge bases. They provide also an explicit way to solve conflicts. The main difference between annotated logics and DFOL concerns the ability to represent different interpretation domains. Annotated logics have a unique logical language, and the same symbol in different knowledge bases is interpreted in the same object. This might be solved by indexing the constant with the name of the knowledge base and by introducing explicit relational symbols between objects of different knowledge bases.

A Cooperative Information System (CIS) is a formal system based on description logics [6]. A CIS copes with the semantics for heterogeneous information integration. A CIS is quite similar to a theory in DFOL. A CIS is composed of a set of description languages, a T-BOX for each language, and a set of so-called interschema assertions. Under the usual translation of description logics in first order logics and the translation of interschema assertion into DFOL compatibility constraints, it can be shown that a CIS can be embedded into DFOL. The main difference between CIS and DFOL concerns the semantics. A model for a CIS is defined over a "global" domain Δ which is the union of the domains Δ_i of the models of each description language. This implies that a constant c in different languages is interpreted in the same object c in the CIS. As a consequence various forms of relation between domains, e.g., abstraction, cannot be represented in CIS. A second difference is that CIS models complete databases and cannot express partiality. Totality affects directionality. Indeed in CIS every interschema assertion $L_1 \leq_{ext} L_2$ ($L_1 \leq_{int} L_2$) from a description language to another entails the converse interschema assertion $\neg L_2 \leq_{ext} \neg L_1$ ($\neg L_2 \leq_{int} \neg L_1$) in the opposite direction.

7 Conclusions

In this paper we have introduced a context-based logic, called *Distributed First Order Logic* for the formalization of distributed knowledge representation and reasoning systems. First we have defined a class of representational and structural requirements which must be satisfied by a logic formalizing distributed knowledge representation. These requirements are our motivation for the use of contexts in representing the different subsystems of a distributed knowledge representation system. Second we have defined a model theoretic semantics for a family of languages based on the notions of possible model and of domain relation. This semantics provides an extension to first order logics to the semantics for contextual reasoning proposed in [11]. Finally we have defined a sound and complete calculus for DFOL based on ML systems and we have compared our logic with other formalisms for the representation and integration of distributed knowledge and reasoning systems.

References

1. V. Akman and M. Surav. Steps toward Formalizing Context. *AI Magazine*, pages 55–72, FALL 1996.
2. D. Basin, S. Matthews, and L. Viganò. Labelled Modal Logics: Quantifiers. *Journal of Logic, Language and Information*, 7(3):237–263, 1998.
3. T. Catarci and M. Lenzerini. Representing and using interschema knowledge in cooperative information systems. *International Journal of Intelligent and Cooperative Information Systems*, 2(4):375–398, 1993.
4. M. D'Agostino. Are tableaux an improvement on truth-tables? Cut-free proofs and bivalence. *Journal of Logic, Language and Information*, 1:235–252, 1992.
5. J. Dinsmore. *Partitioned Representations*. Kluwer Academic Publisher, 1991.
6. F. Donini, M. Lenzerini, D. Nardi, and A. Schaerf. Reasoning in description logics. In G. Brewka, editor, *Principles of Knowledge Representation and Reasoning*, Studies in Logic, Language and Information. CLSI Publications, 1996.
7. R. Fagin, J.Y. Halpern, Y. Moses, and M. Y. Vardi. *Reasoning about knowledge*. MIT Press, 1995.
8. D. M. Gabbay. *Labelled Deductive Systems; principles and applications. Vol 1: Introduction*, volume 33 of *Oxford Logic Guides*. Oxford University Press, 1996.
9. C. Ghidini. *A semantics for contextual reasoning: theory and two relevant applications*. PhD thesis, Department of Computer Science, University of Rome "La Sapienza", March 1998.
10. F. Giunchiglia. Contextual reasoning. *Epistemologia, special issue on I Linguaggi e le Macchine*, XVI:345–364, 1993.
11. F. Giunchiglia and C. Ghidini. Local Models Semantics, or Contextual Reasoning = Locality + Compatibility. In *Proc. of the 6th Int. Conference on Principles of Knowledge Representation and Reasoning (KR'98)*, 1998. Morgan Kaufmann.
12. F. Giunchiglia and L. Serafini. Multilanguage hierarchical logics (or: how we can do without modal logics). *Artificial Intelligence*, 65:29–70, 1994.
13. A. Masini. 2-Sequent calculus: a proof theory of modalities. *Annals of Pure and Applied Logic*, 58:229–246, 1992.
14. D. Prawitz. *Natural Deduction - A proof theoretical study*. Almquist and Wiksell, Stockholm, 1965.
15. L. Serafini and C. Ghidini. Context Based Semantics for Federated Databases. In *Proceedings of the 1st International and Interdisciplinary Conference on Modeling and Using Context (CONTEXT-97)*, pages 33–45, Rio de Jeneiro, Brazil, 1997.
16. V.S. Subrahmanian. Amalgamating Knowledge Bases. *ACM Trans. Database Syst.*, 19(2):291–331, 1994.
17. G. Wiederhold. Mediators in the architecture of future information systems. *IEEE Computer*, 25(3):38–49, 1992.

Independence from Context Information Provided by Spatial Signature Learning in a Natural Object Localization Task

Guillaume Giraudet and Corinne Roumes

Institut de Médecine Aérospatiale du Service de Santé des Armées
Département Sciences Cognitives
BP73 - 91223 Brétigny-sur-Orge, France
ggiraudet@imassa.fr

Abstract. Although computational sciences have made considerable progress, artificial systems have not yet managed to duplicate the efficiency of human perceptive systems. This superiority may come from the human capacity to integrate world knowledge within perceptive processes. This study assesses the importance of context in a task where a target is to be located within a natural image. The use of context information is probably not the only reason for the high performance level of our perceptive system. Context information is modified using a jumbling process. Image quality is altered by blur or time constraint. The results show that, even if subjects are disturbed by image modifications, they are able to develop perceptive strategies used to selectively extract object distinctive features helping differentiate it from its surrounding.

1   Introduction

Research in vision sciences increasingly aims at finding how perception really works and at understanding the links between perception and cognition. One question keeps springing up: given the recent progress in computational sciences, why is it that the human visual system remains so greatly superior to artificial vision? The efficiency of human vision may lie in the additional data provided by scene context. We are well aware that objects in a scene are not randomly laid out, but are connected by spatial relationships determined by their nature. Context information, as defined here, is related to the "logical" spatial relationships existing between various elements in a scene. These logical relationships come from perception and depend on world knowledge and on the various rules governing proper spatial organization. The superiority of the human visual system over any artificial system probably comes from the integration of context data into the perception process, in order to optimize low-level computations. According to this operating model of the visual system, perception is organized along two processing routes: bottom-up, where data is collected at eye sensor level and taken towards high level visual areas, and top-down, where information originates from other cortical areas (essentially memory areas) and is mainly derived from our knowledge of the world. A great number of researchers studied how context information is involved in achieving complex perception-related tasks. However, the subject remains controversial.

Some scientists believe context plays a leading and early role in perception mechanisms, whereas others consider it to be only a post-perception and supplementary input, playing an optional role in most cases.

It is easier to recognize or identify an object when it is placed in its "usual" surroundings, i.e. when it meets our expectations and world knowledge. Carr and Bacharach [8] suggest that high-level conceptual information (such as world knowledge stored in long term memory) is available early in the process, and that it helps guide low-level information processing (color, spatial frequency, contours, orientation, etc.). Biederman, in a nearly similar functional architecture design of the visual system allocates a prominent role to context information in the process of object perception. He suggests that a simple glance is sufficient to trigger early on a specific schema containing the knowledge available on scene elements and typical scene content (according to the subject's perceptive experience). Activating this schema generates expectations which in turn, via the top-down route, influence the extraction of characteristics relevant to the objects included in the scene [3], [4].

These studies, aimed at assessing the relative weight of context knowledge in the perception process, address tasks such as object identification or recognition. The question is the following: does the information connected to the scene's meaning have any influence on the process employed to recognize objects included in this scene? Various conflicting theories try to answer this question [10]. They differ on the actual place occupied by cognitive information within the perception process.

According to the *perceptual schema model*, meaningful scene information plays an early role in the analysis of stimulation, by facilitating the processing of scene consistent objects. This model provides no separation between perceptive and cognitive processing [3], [4]. This theory is essentially derived from the experimental results obtained with the object detection paradigm.

Severe reservations have recently been expressed on the relevance of this assessment method. The object detection paradigm, as specified by Biederman, is suspected of not effectively controlling the subject's response biases; furthermore, given that the target object is cued beforehand, this paradigm is suspected of generating expectations which could provide additional information, and eventually influence detection performance levels, that is the so-called priming effect. Hollingworth and Henderson [11] reproduced Biederman et al's experiments [4] and showed once again that scene context indeed does influence the performance achieved by subjects.

However, by adapting the original paradigm in order to remedy the two bias-inducing factors mentioned above, they also showed that scene consistency effect no longer exists.

Hollingworth and Henderson's objections lead to developing another approach of the influence played by cognitive information in the perceptive process. This model, called *functional isolation model*, assumes a strict separation between the perceptive and the cognitive aspects of visual information processing involved in object recognition. These two authors, as well as Thorpe [20] or Pylyshyn [17], believe that an object in a scene can be identified without the involvement of any top-down information connected to meaning or to scene context. Context information remains merely optional, as long as the object stands out sufficiently in its environment; in such a case, the decision is only influenced by the analysis of bottom-up data coming directly from sensors [5], [13].

But what happens when the bottom-up information is of poor quality? Context information may usually not be required in "normal" perceptual conditions, but these conditions can change. They may be degraded naturally (fog, blinding light, etc.), or artificially (various optic devices, poorly compensated ametropia, etc.). It is therefore necessary to assess the capacities of the visual system when signals are degraded. Since the late 60's, and Campbell and Robson's work, spatial frequency is known as an essential parameter in human vision. So, modifications in the resolution quality of visual stimulation can alter perception [7].

Few studies have directly assessed the influence of context information according to the frequency content of images. Oliva and Schyns's experiments must be mentioned here, since the frequency content of stimulations is a variation parameter. Through a unique approach, using hybrid images, they demonstrated that low spatial frequency signals, extracted early on in the process and providing spatial organization data, activate an entire range of representations linked to the category of scene under consideration. In turn, these representations are handled as constraints imposed on the processing of higher spatial frequency information, involving the specific identity of the stimulation [14], [18].

The *Coarse-to-Fine* model defined here is close to the *perceptual schema model* described earlier. However, this work does not specifically assess the influence of context on perception.

The purpose of this study is to assess the role played by scene context in a task where objects are to be located within natural scenes. Furthermore, a new approach is suggested, where results are no longer expressed in terms of the influence of context data on the perceptive process but in terms of the co-operation between the two processing routes.

Co-operation assumes that a relative weight will be allocated to bottom-up and top-down processing. No information route strictly dominates the other, but their synergy is adapted according to the task at hand. It is difficult to imagine a visual system as frozen. Indeed, many studies show that perceptive processes use a high degree of flexibility and plasticity in responding to the infinite number of possible visual and visuomotor tasks.

It is possible to assume that the perceptive system uses only a small amount of context data in the case of pictures with a clear and unequivocal physical outline. However, our assumption is that, in specific conditions where the quality and quantity of bottom-up information is deficient, the visual system compensates for these deficiencies by giving more importance to top-down information derived from context knowledge. The assumption is that the perception system reacts to external constraints like any living system. Similarly to most human functions, after this first reaction, if constraints are repeated, the visual system adapts to degraded conditions. We expect top-down cognitive information to lose its relevance as the subject becomes increasingly familiar with experimental conditions.

2 Experiment n°1

The purpose of this first experiment is to assess the role played by context information in a task where an object must be located within a natural scene. This first experiment aims at determining the relative importance of bottom-up and top-down information in performing the required visual task. The principle adopted is to change the quantity of bottom-up information by altering the data intake through various factors (frequency filtering or exposure time); the next step is to verify the importance of top-down information in task performance; this is achieved by controlling the relevance of context information through the jumbled image technique developed by Biederman [1], [2].

2.1 Method

Subjects. 5 subjects, 2 women and 3 men, took part in the study. They were 23 to 29 years old, their eyesight was at least 10/10, and their sensitivity to contrast was normal for the entire spectrum of spatial frequencies under study.

Apparatus. Test images are presented to subjects on a 21" Hitachi colour monitor. Presentation sequencing and data collection is managed by a RE2 Silicon Graphics workstation. The monitor is equipped with a touch screen to collect the subjects' responses. Subjects sit 50cm from the screen, head resting on a chinrest, with their hand 40 cm from the screen, on the keyboard spacebar.

Stimuli. Visual stimulations used are natural pictures, coming from a database and representing scenes from everyday life, in the countryside, from city life or inside homes. Eight pictures were selected, according to criteria of size, location and environment of objects. The target object is located in the central block of a grid, made up of 5 x 3 blocks - 5 horizontal and 3 vertical blocks (Fig. 1).

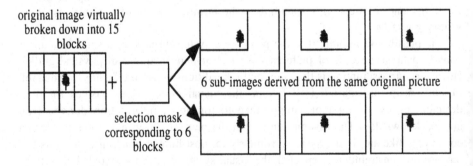

Fig. 1. Method used to create the images presented

Objects or semantic elements are evenly distributed throughout the entire surface of the picture. Each picture is defined by 1705 x 1152 pixels. On a virtual 15 block matrix, a selection mask corresponding to 6 blocks (3x2) is used to extract 6 sub-images of 1074 x 768 pixels, making up the initial image base displayed on the screen. The target-object has a different position on the screen in each of these sub-images. Given the homogeneous presence of elements all-over the original pictures, it is assumed that the semantic information provided by the environment does not change from one sub-image to the next.

In experimental conditions, monitor screen subtends 39° horizontally and 31.5° vertically of visual angle. The image is centrally displayed with a viewing angle of 31° x 23.7°. The blank part of the screen and the entire screen when no image is displayed make up a uniform area, with the following colorimetric co-ordinates: x = 0.276 and y = 0.311, corresponding to the uniform distribution of luminance on all three luminophores) with an average luminance of 35 cd.m^{-2}. This luminance corresponds to the average luminance of all images. The average luminance of original images varies from 21.6 cd.m^{-2} to 40.3 cd.m^{-2}. Stimulations are therefore at photopic luminance level.

Three factors are controlled in this experiment to study their impact on target object recognition: frequency content, exposure duration and context content of stimulation.

Three spatial frequency filtering levels are selected. The filtering is achieved by breaking down the original picture through a wavelet analysis [12], with a base profile of analyzing functions corresponding to a DOG (Difference Of Gaussians). This image analysis method extracts, at each scale, a spatial frequency image content similar to the selectivity of spatial frequencies encountered in the visual system [16]. Experimental images then result from a partial reconstruction process, depending on the filtering level desired. Filtering is low-pass. Three cut-off frequencies ensure a variation in the image detail level: 6, 3, 1.5 cycles/degree (cpd). Therefore, the various filtering levels correspond to an increasingly extended amputation of the frequency spectrum of original images along high spatial frequencies. In other words, more filtering results in increasingly blurred images. The various filtering levels are referred to as fs0 for the unfiltered images, as fs1, fs2 and fs3 for increasingly blurred images.

Four exposure times are selected: 100, 200, 400 and 800 ms. This viewing time constraint is a way to measure the time required for the task to be accessible; it also limits the visual information intake.

The principle of modifying the context content of an image is derived from Biederman's work [1], [2]. The image is cut into 6 blocks (3 x 2), and these six blocks are randomly mixed. This transformation of the original picture breaks all consistent spatial relationships existing between various scene elements (Fig. 2). The informative weight of context varies between the unjumbled image and its jumbled complement. In order to compare performance levels obtained for both kinds of images, the target object is systematically located in the same place in the unjumbled as well as in the jumbled image (Fig. 2). Furthermore, all blocks neighboring the target object's block are systematically moved in the jumbled image.

Fig. 2. Principle of context modification derived from Biederman's work [1], [2]. The jumbled image (*right*) is created by cutting and mixing the original image (*left*)

The position of the object on the screen is also controlled: it appears once on the left, once in the center and once on the right, for each experimental condition.

All possible conditions are combined for each image, generating 96 configurations (4 spatial frequency filtering levels x 2 context level x 4 viewing times x 3 positions). The 8 original images thus result into 768 different viewings (8 x 96 configurations per image).

Procedure. The experiment is broken down into several sessions. The 768 viewings are divided into two even sets and are presented in a random and different order to each viewer. Each set of 384 images is used for a single experimental session. Each subject views the 768 images three times, in the same order (i.e. 6 sessions per subject), called R1, R2 and R3. Before recording data, a preliminary training session helps the subject get accustomed to the experimental setup and to the task, which is to manually locate the target object cued beforehand.

Before each viewing trial, the name of the object is displayed for 1 second. After this semantic priming, a focus-square is immediately displayed in the middle of the screen; its purpose is to provide the subject with a reference for fixation. The focus square remains on display until the subjects triggers the rest of the sequence by pressing on the keyboard spacebar. The test image is then displayed for 100, 200, 400 or 800 ms. After viewing, a grid comes on the screen, displaying the six theoretical blocks in the image.

The instruction is to point as quickly as possible on the right location of the target-object, while giving priority to response accuracy. As soon as the touch screen registers the subject's answer, the next sequence is activated. Object localization and response time are stored. The latter is defined in terms of the time elapsed between pressing the space bar and pointing the touch screen.

2.2 Results

The analysis of results mainly addresses the error rate (i.e. failing to correctly achieve the task) expressed as a percentage. A data variance analysis (ANOVA) shows that the overall rate of errors gradually increases as further spatial frequencies are deleted from the spectrum, or as exposure time decreases (Spatial frequency effect: $F^3_{1276}= 54.064$; $p < 0.0001$ – Viewing time effect: $F^3_{1276}= 8.998$; $p < 0.0001$). The main results first deal with the variations observed in the context effect (i.e. disturbance of performance linked to image jumbling) according to the frequency content (Fig. 3, left); they also provide information on the evolution of variations as the experiment goes on (Fig. 3, right).

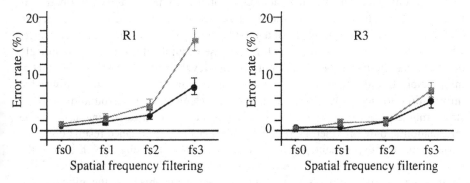

Fig. 3. Changes in performance between unjumbled images (*circles*) and jumbled images (*squares*) according to the spatial frequency content. In the first experimental sequence (*left*), the effect of scene jumbling increases as the filtering level increases. On the other hand, the effect of scene jumbling is almost non-existent in the third repetition.

In the case of a first exposure to stimulations, the performance difference between unjumbled and jumbled images is significant (Context effect: $F^1_{1272}= 14.413$; p= 0.0002) and increases with the blurring of the image (Context*Filtering effect: $F^3_{1272}= 6.272$; p= 0.0003). On the contrary, when the viewing is repeated for the third time, the effect of jumbling is almost non-existent (Context effect: $F^1_{1272}= 1.820$; p= 0.1775) and no longer varies according to frequency content (Context*Filtering effect: $F^3_{1272}= 1.073$; p= 0.3593).

2.3 Discussion

The data collected during this first experiment seem to confirm our early assumptions of a possible co-operation between perceptive and cognitive routes during visual information processing in object localization tasks. However, the relative importance of one route vs. the other varies. Results point out that context has an influence on subject performance only when the bottom-up sensory signal is degraded. This result agrees with the assumption that a normal subject placed in optimal perception conditions (in terms of image resolution quality) can disregard context information to achieve a complex visual task [20]. This varying importance of context according to the image frequency content also confirms the "Coarse to Fine" model developed by Oliva and Schyns [14], [18]. In the case of degraded images, the subject only obtains coarse information on the scene's spatial organization. Performance is supposed to be strongly affected by the jumbling of scene organization. This corresponds exactly to the results obtained in our study, where the negative effect of a jumbled context on performance is compounded by the increasing degradation of images. These results are compatible with the idea that preliminarily processed low spatial frequencies provide information of the scene's spatial organization. This information in turn influences, via the top-down link, the processing of higher spatial frequencies, essential to element identification [14], [18].

The results also indicate that the weight of the scene's context information is limited in time. Indeed, during the third sequence of experiments, difference in performance between unjumbled and jumbled images has no statistical relevance, whatever the frequency filtering level. In the case of jumbled images, it is intuitively obvious that there can be no learning at the level of the scene's global spatial information. In order for learning to happen, images must provide sufficiently stable information to serve as a visual landmark, whatever the surrounding scene's structuring level. Information on the scene's global context varies continuously. Stable information is only provided more locally. Changes in performance results observed during this first experiment probably come from local learning, which allows the subject to extract constant relevant information, while variations in the scene's global environment occur. Subjects were asked to locate an object in the picture. The learning observed probably comes from the subject's capacity to isolate the object's distinctive features (its spatial signature) separating the object from its background, whatever the visual aspect of the image displayed. In order to verify this assumption, a second experience is carried out, in which the object and the scene's spatial signals vary. The object's physical content also changes during the experiment, so it can be assumed that the learning encountered during the first experiment will probably be greatly reduced, if not totally cancelled out.

3 Experiment n°2

Biederman's jumbling process is once again used to modify the scene and the object's spatial signatures. The initial procedure used in the first experiment to break-down and jumble images is modified and adapted to meet the requirements of this new experiment. The target object's spatial signature is modified by using the edge effects induced by image jumbling. Indeed, the object in the middle of a block is relatively undisturbed by edge effects. But the closer the object is to the edge of the block, the more its frequency content changes, in relation to the frequency content of the neighboring block. If the target object is close to the edge of the block, its spatial signature changes continuously according to the different image layouts.

3.1 Method

Subjects. 5 subjects, different from those having taken part in the first experiment. This group was made up of 1 woman and 4 men, 18 to 28 years old.

Selected subjects had normal eyesight, in terms of sharpness and sensitivity to contrast.

Apparatus. Same setup as in the first experiment.

Stimuli. The four images presented to subjects are natural images, different from those presented during the first experiment. Initial images are first broken down into blocks according to the same procedure as in the first experiment. Then, in order to shift the target object towards the edge of a block or to center it, the original image is either shifted to the side or not (Fig. 4).

Fig. 4. Sliding the original image (*left*) to the right allows to shift the target object towards the edge of a block (*right*)

A new variation factor (centering or shifting the target object) is now added to the three other factors previously assessed in the first experiment: spatial frequency content, exposure time and context content of stimulation.

Procedure. The experiment is broken down into several sessions. The 768 viewings are divided into 2 equal sets, each set of images representing one experimental session with 384 viewings. The 768 viewings are repeated three times for each subject, in the same order (i.e. 6 sessions per subject), and called R1, R2 and R3. Before data recording, subjects undergo a training trial, to get used to the experimental setup and the task, which is to manually locate the target object cued beforehand. The course of a viewing is identical to conditions prevailing in the first experiment. Data collected is expressed, once again, in terms of success/failure in pointing the target object on time, and of the time elapsed before touching the screen in response to the viewing.

3.2 Results

A data ANOVA is used to determine the changes in performance levels between unjumbled and jumbled images, at first for centered objects (Fig 5, left) and then for shifted objects (i.e. close to block edge, Fig 5, right).

Subjects are disturbed by scene jumbling, whether the object is centered (Context effect F^1_{1914}=59.375 ; p<0.0001) or shifted (Context effect F^1_{1914}= 53.098 ; p<0.0001). However, the Context effect (i.e. disturbance linked to jumbling) does not vary with the repetition of viewings, either for centered objects (Context*Repetition effect: F^2_{1914}= 0.766 ; p=0.3593) or for shifted objects (Context*Repetition effect : F^2_{1914}=2.654 ; p=0.0706).

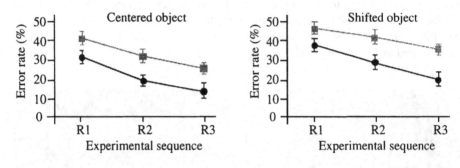

Fig. 5. Changes in performance level as viewings are repeated, according to scene jumbling (*circles correspond to original or unjumbled images and squares correspond to jumbled images*). Cases of centered object (*left*) and shifted object (*right*)

3.3   Discussion

According to results obtained in experiment 1, it is assumed that the visual system, once accustomed to the various stimulations, only uses local information to distinguish the object from its immediate surroundings. It seems therefore that context information is not inhibited, but that its relative weight vs. bottom-up information related to the object's spatial signature becomes minimal.

The results of the "shifted object" category seem to confirm this assumption. When object-related local spatial information changes continuously, subjects can probably no longer isolate the object's specific features to distinguish it readily from its environment. Since learning cannot occur, subjects must remain acutely sensitive to the scene's global aspect. This is exactly confirmed by the results observed. In the situation of shifted objects, the disturbance induced by scene jumbling remains constant throughout the entire experiment.

Conversely, when the object is centered, learning is expected. In other words, the influence of scene jumbling should decrease as subjects become more familiar with the various experimental conditions. However, results do not confirm this expectation. These results, which seem paradoxical at first, can however be explained in terms of the learning process.

In order to isolate the object's distinct features, there is a need for stability of the object's spatial signature on the one hand; but this relevant information must also be stable over time so that, through reinforcement, it can root itself sufficiently deeply to be used in an automatic processing. In our experiment, the results obtained can be explained by the lack of stability over time of the object's specific visual features vs. background features, due to randomization of experimental conditions. So the shifted viewings collapsed the object's spatial signature learning that might emerged from centered object viewings.

4   General Discussion

Since the middle of this century, our understanding of the processes involved in perception has increasingly improved. However, it is still impossible to develop an artificial system as powerful and effective as the human visual system. The use of context in perceptive processing may be a reason for this superiority. However, given the results obtained in this study, another explanation may be envisaged; it explores the flexibility of processing strategies used by our visual system. More and more surveys are being conducted to highlight the formidable adaptation capabilities of the human visual system. Single and rigid information processing organization models are outdated. People are increasingly aware that the response provided by the human visual system is highly dependent on the task required.

Oliva and Schyns's studies also underscore the flexibility of perceptive strategies. They point out that a short period of sensitization can bias processing towards the information best suited to meet the demand [15]. Thus, instead of "Coarse to Fine" processing, a reorganization can be made to opt for "Fine to Coarse", according to available information best suited to perform the task. The results of our first experiment seem to confirm Oliva and Schyn's conclusions. As the experiment goes on, the subjects are not longer penalized by scene jumbling, whatever frequency degradation is applied to the image. Since context information is no longer relevant to perform the task, the visual system seems to simply disregard it during processing. The question now is whether the learning involved consists in inhibiting non-relevant information or in actively selecting relevant information. Oliva and Schyns clearly opt for this second solution. They show that even if the visual system is sensitized by clearly specifying that only one type of information is relevant to achieve the task, the non-relevant information is still integrated, although it has no influence on decision-making. The hypotheses developed out of the results obtained in our first experiment go in the same direction. It is assumed that after a period of time used to get accustomed to the various types of stimulation, the visual system manages to isolate the local distinctive features of the object, so as to easily separate it from its immediate surroundings. Context information is not inhibited, but the relative weight of this information vs. bottom-up data on the object's spatial signature is greatly reduced. This hypothesis is confirmed by our second experiment. Indeed, it shows that if the visual system is prevented from extracting the object's distinctive invariant features from its background by destabilizing this information in space or time, the learning process observed in our first experiment no longer exists.

These data highlight that the influence of context can only be assessed if space and time-related aspects of the stimulations presented are taken into account. The perspective here is not the influence of top-down context information on the bottom-up processing of sensor-acquired data, but rather the co-operation between these two processing routes. Other studies also point out this synergy in processing. Boucart and Bruyère tested the effect of physical similarity in a task where fragmented objects were to be categorized. They pointed out that even though subjects mainly use the object's physical attributes to categorize it, they also use semantic information when the physical information is insufficient to make a decision [6]. Stanovich, observing more or less fluent young readers, assumed the existence of a "compensatory interactive process" helping account for context facilitator effects. This top-down process, supported by other knowledge sources (notably context information) is of increasing importance when the bottom-up information prove to be ineffective [9], [19].

The results of our study point out the co-operation between bottom-up and top-down information routes in visual processing, but they also highlight the ever changing relative weight assumed by both co-operating routes according to the physical content of stimulations, and the familiarity of the subject with these stimulations. For relatively unfamiliar images, when sensorial data are of good quality, context information plays a minor role in achieving the experimental task (locating the object). However, the cognitive route plays a relatively greater role when bottom-up information becomes so degraded that it no longer allows for the decision to be made on the basis of this sole information. As degraded images become more familiar, subject performance is no longer penalized by jumbling. With training, subjects can characterize the target object's spatial signature. This information is then sufficient to make a decision, whatever the degradation and jumbling of the scene. The subject can, once again, successfully perform the task, only using bottom-up information pertaining to the object's spatial signature.

References

1. Biederman, I.: Perceiving real-world scenes. Science 177 (1972) 77-80

2. Biederman, I., Glass A.L., Stacy E.W.: Searching for objects in real-world scenes. Journal of Experimental Psychology 97 (1973) 22-27

3. Biederman, I.: On the semantics of a glance at a scene. In: Pomerantz, J.R., Kubovy, M. (eds): Perceptual organisation. LEA, Hillsdale (1981) 181-211

4. Biederman, I., Mezzanotte, R.J., Rabinowitz, J.C.: Scene perception: detection and judging objects undergoing relational violations. Cognitive Psychology 14 (1982) 143-177

5. Biederman, I.: Recognition by components: a theory of human image understanding. Psychological Review 94 (1987) 115-147

6. Boucart, M., Bruyère, R.: Influence of physical and semantic information in a categorisation task of fragmented forms. Perception 20 (1991) 403-414

7. Campbell, F.W., Robson, J.G.: Application of Fourier Analysis to the visibility of gratings. J. Physiol. 197 (1968) 551-566

8. Carr, T.H., Bacharach, V.R.: Perceptual tuning and conscious attention: systems of input relation in visual information processing. Cognition 4 (1976) 281-302

9. Dubois, D., Sprenger-Charolles, L.: Perception/interprétation du langage écrit: Contexte et identification des mots au cours de la lecture. Intellectica (1988) 113-146

10. Henderson, J.M., Hollingworth, A.: High-level scene perception. Annual Review of Psychology (in press)

11. Hollingworth, A. & Henderson, J.M.: Does consistent scene facilitate object perception ? Journal of Exp. Psychol. : General (in press)

12. Mallat, S.: Multifrequency channel decomposition of images on walvelet models. I.E.E.E. Transaction on acoustic speech and signal processing 37 (1989) 2091-2210

13. Marr, D., Nishihara, H.K.: Representation and recognition of the spatial organisation of three-dimensional shapes. Proc. Royal Soc. Lon. B200 (1978) 269-294.

14. Oliva, A., Schyns, P.G.: Analyse multi-échelle de la perception de scènes. NSI. Chamonix (1994) 15-18

15. Oliva, A., Schyns, P.G.: Coarse blobs or fine edges ? Evidence that information diagnosticity changes the perception of complex stimuli. Cognitive Psychol. 34 (1997) 72-107

16. Plantier, J., Menu, J-P.: Analyse des contrastes locaux de luminance dans les images complexes. Rapport de recherche IMASSA-CERMA 93-12 (1993)

17. Pylyshyn, Z.: Is vision continuous with the cognition ? The case for cognitive impenetrability of visual perception. Behav. Brain Sci. (in press)

18. Schyns, P.G., Oliva, A.: From blobs to boundary edges: evidence for time- and spatial-scale-dependent scene recognition. Psychological Science 5 (1994) 195-200

19. Stanovich, K.E.: Toward an interactive compensatory model of individual differences in the development of reading fluency. Reading Research Quaterly 16 (1980) 32-71

20. Thorpe, S.: La reconnaissance visuelle: de la rétine au cortex inféro-temporal. Revue de Neuropsychologie 5 (1995) 520-522

Contextual Dependence and the Epistemic Foundations of Dynamic Semantics

Wolfram Hinzen

New York University, 10003 New York, USA
wh12@is9.nyu.edu

Abstract. Three accounts relating meaning and context are compared: a classical or *static* one as proposed by Stalnaker, a contextual or *dynamic* one as proposed in Dynamic Semantics, and a *massively contextual* one, defended here. On the last view, meaning and interpretation is a matter of a change of an epistemic context by means of an inductive inference, thus of pragmatics. As in dynamic semantics, meaning is a matter of epistemic state change. But now it is construed normatively, and it is the contextual change that explicates meaning, not meaning that explicates why a context changes in the way it does. Meaning is contextual on this approach because the justification of inductive inferences depends on contextual parameters (such as a partition of answers, or a degree of caution with respect to the risk of incurring error, etc.) for whose assessment no objective standards can be given. Contextuality is not a feature of language per se, and questions of contextual change are not primarily linguistic ones.

1 Introduction

Semantics, the study of linguistic meaning, often makes language-world relations its topic, but has also tried to explicate meaning in terms of the relation of a sentence to the mind of a speaker who is using it. In some sense, dynamic semantics (see [5] for one version) falls into the latter "epistemic" tradition. At the same time, it remains firmly rooted in a broadly Fregean approach to language. Thus, e.g., "mind" is not primarily regarded as a psychological category, and the focus has been rather on the model-theoretic study of epistemic states to which objective propositional contents are attributed. But the idea of content is given a dynamic twist in that the semantic value of a sentence uttered in conversation is defined as an update function that expands the body of shared presuppositions of the participants into a new such body.

In this model content and context are unified. A formal semantic representation of a discourse can be looked at as a conten*t* (a set of truth conditions) as well as a con*text* (for the interpretation of further input). What a sentence is said to "do" is to update the semantic representation generated by the previous sentences, giving a new content as well as context as result. Naturally, this new perspective on meaning involves an increased involvement with pragmatics within semantics. A sentence meaning now itself is said to consist in a dynamic potential for changing a context. It is not merely a semantic content, kept free of the pragmatic elements governing such changes.

1.1 Stalnaker's Critique

Dynamic semantics is often said to have one of its origins in Stalnaker's work on assertion (cf. [10]). Nonetheless Stalnaker has recently criticized it precisely for taking the pragmatics of contextual change to define *semantic* content (cf. [11]). The attack is Gricean in spirit and recommends separating a purely semantic core notion of meaning from pragmatic aspects of meaning having to do with the *use* of expressions that *have* that semantic content. Linguistic phenomena that supposedly motivate the introduction of dynamic (functional) semantic values, Stalnaker argues, can be accounted for just as well with classical, less-structured models of contexts and propositions (sets of possible worlds). It is the *point* of a meaningful speech act to change a context; but this is not what defines the *meaning* of a sentence.

It is essential to Stalnaker's argument that the proposition that is asserted ("proposed for acceptance" as Stalnaker says) is fixed before we look at the contextual dynamics that the assertion of the sentence expressing that proposition affects. Specifically, if a context changes through the assertion of a sentence, it does so in two ways: first the set of mutually shared assumptions adjusts to the fact that a *particular sentence with a particular content* has been asserted (first context change); secondly, the proposition proposed for acceptance is either accepted or rejected (second context change) (cf. [11], p.8). Semantics is dealt with when the first change has happened. Pragmatic principles control the second. Both changes are formally modelled as modifications of sets of possible worlds modelling the information that is compatible with the shared assumptions of a group of speakers at a particular moment of their discourse.

To see how Stalnaker suggests to circumvent arguments to the effect that dynamic semantic values are needed, consider the following well-known pair of examples, said in the same initial context:

(1) Exactly nine of the ten balls are in the bag.

(2) Exactly one of the ten balls is not in the bag.

If their contents are modelled as sets of possible worlds, their contents will come out as exactly the same. This, dynamic semantics has claimed, is a problem since if we continue a discourse started with either (1) or (2) with

(3) It is under the sofa,

the pronoun 'it' acquires a different referent in the two cases.

The problem vanishes, Stalnaker argues, if the first of the above kinds of context changes is taken seriously. For since a different sentence is used in two utterances of the respective sentences (1) and (2) to get the same content across, the context will change in different ways. The set of possible worlds compatible with the information that (1) has been uttered must be compatible with the fact that a reference that *nine* balls took place, while after an utterance of (2) there is a different such constraint, namely that an act of reference to *one* missing ball was made. The utterance events thus lead to different modifications of the contextually given set of worlds: the pragmatics of language use explains the difference in content of (1) and (2), not a difference in their content.

1.2 Outline

Stalnaker's second step of contextual change involves adopting or not adopting a belief that will in general not be a logical consequence of what is believed already. In this sense the inference that is drawn to its truth is ampliative and raises issues of justification. It will by necessity involve, from the agent's point of view, a risk of error. An inference that proceeds from a body of beliefs that are held true to a new such body, and hence involves a risk of error from the viewpoint of what is currently held true, I shall call an *inductive inference*(cf. [7]).

My claim against Stalnaker will be that the determination of the proposition proposed for acceptance in a speech act itself requires making reference to pragmatic principles for changing one's context or doxastic dispositions. Truth-conditional content is then itself largely a matter of pragmatics and inductive inference, not given independently (analytically) by "language" itself. Contextuality enters because of subjective factors controlling the justification of inductions, hence not for linguistic reasons. If a model of "meaning" is wanted, one may read off the meaning of an input from the ways in which agents change their minds. How this happens is a normative and non-linguistic matter, a point that seems to contravene the idea in Discourse Representation Theory that interpretation can be modeled in terms of changes in semantic representations within a computational theory of meaning.

2 Discourse in a Descriptive and in a Normative Perspective

2.1 Common Ground Construction

A common empirical hypothesis under which the modelling discourses in dynamic semantics proceeds, is that

> speaker and hearer engage in constructing a common ground, maybe from an already existing common ground constructed in earlier conversations ([13], p.25).

The meaning of an uttered sentence is typically regarded as

> an instruction to carry out a series of actions on a given database, with the end effect of incorporating the information given in the sentence into the database (ibid., p. 22).

In accordance with such assumptions, an assertion is described as a transition from one common ground to another. But the scope of such assumptions is unclear. Far from being a condition for the possibility of communication, the shared common ground is what participants in a conversation form more or less well-supported hypotheses about. Common purpose inquiries with shared preference structures are rare, and common grounds may have to be negotiated. Agents do not exclusively or mainly strive for the truth, and for getting their findings as effectively as possible across to their fellows.

It is also argued that for asserting, requesting, promising etc. to take place, interlocutors must attempt to recognize the speaker's intentions, and that this can only be if they cooperate. Speakers, as Grice put it, must

> make their contribution such as is required, at the stage at which it occurs, by the accepted purpose or direction of the talk exchange in which (they) are engaged ([3] 45).

But there may not be such an "accepted purpose or direction", and although an agent may assume or come to the conclusion that there is, he may at any time become uncertain about whether unanimity really prevails. Even if he does act cooperatively, we may ask why, and construct an explanation that makes it come out as an optimal decision in its own best interest.

Thus a hearer may have good reasons not to dispute the proposition whose truth he regards his interlocutor to commit himself to. He may enter into a political agreement; or it may not be useful to weigh the views of others and to start an inquiry as to whether they are correct. But it will be some such reasons, which may or may not be there, which explain the fact, if it is one, that a conversation steers towards a common ground, a political agreement or an actual shared agreement at the end of a common inquiry.

I seems we make sense of acts of uses of linguistic competence in the same way in which we make sense of other kinds of actions, such as the action of playing the piano, which involves use of a musical competence. Musical competence might be scientifically studied, or naturalistically. A decision to do what we call "play the piano" will likely not, and belongs to the theory of rational action.

The act we call "speaking" hardly is a causal process: consciousness and deliberate choice enters into a speaker's using a particular form of expressions in a particular context of his beliefs and desires. We may observe that a *question* is something that an addressee tends to *answer*, although some agents do not. Or that agents take turns in conversation according to some order. But if we want to understand what is the driving force behind phenomena that structure discourse, we may have to look at the theory of rational decision.

2.2 Attitudinal Commitments

An *agent* I shall here understand to be whatever does not frustrate our attempts to characterize it in terms of a set of more or less coherent propositional attitudes. Forming an attitude is what makes an agent committed to make judgements that correspond to this type of attitude. For example, if an agent comes to the conclusion that a proposition is fully (i.e., non-conditionally, non-partially) true, he undertakes a rational commitment to a disposition to assent to it as well as its logical consequences when prompted to do so.[1]

---

[1] The extent to which such commitments are actually fulfilled is an empirical matter.

Judgements corresponding to the various attitudes allow us to make distinctions between propositions, on any chosen level. For present purposes we will distinguish

- propositions that are judged fully true, forming a background for reasoning and inquiry that is not now questioned;
- propositions that are, relative to this background, judged uncertain or probable to some degree, where the probability is subjective, and
- propositions that are judged valuable, in accordance with one or the other system of value commitments.

The first propositions I will call (full) *beliefs*, the second *potential beliefs* or *states*, and the third *outcomes*. We identify the commitment (to the truth of) a proposition **A** with the set of the commitments generated by it, its consequences. I will reserve the term *proposition* for consequence sets. Thus propositions that are judged fully true are full beliefs, and the notion of a potential full belief is just the same notion as that of a proposition.

Although there is a reasonable question how we should define propositions, it is not reasonable to inquire into the nature of propositions. The term proposition has exactly the meaning we give it, and what meaning we give it depends on our purposes: on what propositions we decide to distinguish, and how we distinguish them: in terms of their truth alone, of their probability alone, or both their truth and probability, for example.

It is often asked how fine-grained our notion of proposition should be, or when two propositions are identical. But independently of given interests and concerns that define what the propositions are that are the objects of deliberation, and thus when two of them are identical, the question does not seem meaningful. There may not be general rules for partitioning the space of propositions; just as there may be no general rules for determining questions and abducing a set of potential answers for them. The interrogative

(4) Do you accept Credit Cards?

used by me calling a restaurant does not come with a partition of potential answers, nor does it determine, by itself, what the question is in the first place. It may not in fact be a question. If it is a question, it may be inferred that I want to know whether one of the accepted Credit Cards is the one I own; whether I can pay with one of my Credit Cards, which are most probably among those accepted in a restaurant; whether I can patronize this restaurant; etc.[2]

Having inferred the question, a Hearer abducts a set of strongest consistent, exhaustive, and pairwise inconsistent potential answers. The final outcome of this abductive phase of deliberation contains those potential answers that are the options between which one has decided to restrict one's choice. It is exactly as fine-grained and as coarse-grained as one finds it useful. Perhaps no general rules for forming a partition can be given. In a similar way, no general rules can perhaps be given for what demands of information an agent should have, or with what degree of caution he should reject hypotheses.

---

[2] For an empirical study of the example see [2], 334.

As we interact with agents, we take for granted at any moment that they have undertaken a number of attitudinal commitments. None of these may be justified in any particular way, but we have to start from somewhere, and all of these presumptions may be revised as we witness various events. Among these are events of language use: thus we have now again arrived at the dynamic semantics picture.

It seems like a natural model for "meaning", if such a concept is wanted, to let the meaning of an utterance in conversation consist in the set-difference of the hearer's partition of potential answers before and after the utterance has taken place. In this way we read off the meaning of a sentence from the inductive inferences (eliminations of options) that an agent performs. The more options are eliminated, the more significant (informative) the input might be said to have been.

3 The Idea of a Shared Language

In philosophical semantics and much of the linguistic one the focus in studying language has been on an external, public and by its essence *social* activity. In naturalistic attempts to study language, by contrast, the social and communicative aspect of language has been ignored (for motivation see [1]); the study of language is the study of a specific generative faculty of the mind, taking the form of an internal mechanism that produces linguistic expressions in the sense of structural descriptions consisting of complexes of phonetic, semantic, and syntactic properties.

Grammatical competence, together with performance systems implementing communicative intentions, enters into human action. But shared linguistic knowledge is no precondition for communication, beyond perhaps what is given by initial genetic endowment. More or less differences in the present state of Mary's and Joe's generative linguistic faculty, together with more or less differences in what they believe, may produce more or less differences in the way they talk. When communicating with each other they will have to work out these differences in a rough and ready way, relative to specific communicative purposes at hand.

Normativity, as generally in the attribution of attitudes, enters here. Propositional attitudes that we ascribe to agents guide us in interpreting their speech. If we take an utterance to express a belief that conflicts with what beliefs we find reasonable to attribute to a speaker, we withdraw the interpretation and assign a different meaning. If we find a speaker referring, for all it seems to us, to his girlfriend by the expression

(5) My wife is happy tonight

we may (i) withdraw our working theory that someone using the phrase *my wife* needs to attribute to anyone, or presupposing anyone to have the property, of being his wife; or (ii) we try the theory that the speaker exploits patterns of language use to induce a belief in his hearers that he knows not to be correct. It is practical reasoning that will decide, and which explicates the phenomenon, if it is one, that an expression like *my wife* "generates a presupposition". It is not the fact that an expression has, by itself, the property of generating a presupposition that explicates why hearers attribute attitudes to speakers.

If this is right, that the attitude decides about the meaning, not the meaning about the attitude, meaning is normative to the extent that attitudes are. It is a matter of the subjective assessment of an agent in the course of his inquiry. Subjective meaning is objectified in the assumption that it is external and shared language that we must study. But far from being a precondition for communication, it is an assumption that is *suspended* whenever the normative assessment of a speaker's actions leads an agent to the conclusion that he uses language in a slightly different way than he himself would.

Now a general normative feature of language use seems to be that an utterance act is attempted to be understood as being in *accordance* with various attitudinal commitments, rather than manifesting a *change* in those commitments. A language user may form an intention to communicate. Being committed to carrying out a communicative act s/he selects a sentence about whose usability he has certain opinions. But his eventual act does not *change* the commitments that he has. The change of commitment occurs at the point where an agent decides, following a deliberation, to use a certain form of expression in a certain way. The actual performance implements a decision but is not one.

Thus an utterance does not change any contextual attitudinal commitments of the speaker. But it does not induce a change in those of the hearer either. It may have an *influence* in a deliberation of the hearer that ends with the verdict that a new commitment is to be undertaken given that some particular utterance act was observed. But it will not induce it, and not be the reason for it.

We may conclude from this that if dynamic semanticists mean anything like a change of attitude, or commitment, by talking about context change, neither an utterance event nor the linguistic meaning of the sentence used is to be modelled as a change in the attitudes that an agent forms.

3.1 Contextual Expressions and Perspectives

The case against a public and shared language can be made quite independently of naturalistic commitments. A phenomenon widely studied under the headings of "nonce sense" or "transfer of meaning" (cf. [2], [8]) is a case in point.[3] For example, an expression like

(6) Alice did the lawn.

can mean an indefinite number of things (such as Alice mowed the lawn, raked, fertilized, or crossed it). What is intended depends on what one believes about the speaker and about Alice. Equally for expressions like

(7) Our mechanical typing machine got married.

(8) Christensen Miloseviced his way to a peace agreement.

(9) Mallory did a Milosevic.

---

[3] I am grateful to one of the referees of this paper for bringing Clark's and Nunberg's work to my attention.

Each of these can be perfectly meaningfully used, and can mean any number of things. (9) e.g. can mean that Mallory posed with a face like Milosevic, that he got a haircut like Milosevic, or whatever else.

Language is used in endless innovative ways, and there do not appear to be systematic rules for doing such innovations. "Contextual expressions" as exemplified in the previous examples are ubiquitous. Clark's conclusion seems plausible: standard parsers that are designed to *select* the most plausible among a number of lexically encoded senses that an expression may have would break down too often. None of the senses needed above are listed in any lexicon. Since Clark's "nonce sense" sentences do not have any "sentence meanings", his diagnosis is much in accordance with what I said above about *decisions* that a hearer makes about what a speaker *must have* rationally meant by an expression on an occasion of his use of it.

Finally it is worth recalling Chomsky's observation that reference is relative to "interests and concerns" (cf. [1]). Expressions, Chomsky argues, offer *perspectives* for looking at the world. Consider Chomsky's sentence

(10) London is so unhappy, ugly, and polluted that it should be destroyed and rebuilt 100 miles away.

where the same city name allows us to look at an object with an eye on its suffering population, its buildings, the not too high air above it, and with and without its location.

In present terms, interests and concerns are subjective value parameters one sets in one's inquiry. We could systematize principles for doing so in a decision theory that would take into account what the beliefs, values, and goals are that people have when they use words, thereby going much beyond what non-normative naturalistic inquiry can be concerned with. In particular, it would not allow us to distinguish matters of "semantic content" from matters of value.

4 The Shared Language Assumption Raises its Head

I have argued that if we model attitudes as commitments that agents undertake, it is not natural to model events of language use as context (commitment) changing devices. Equally, that it is not sentences that determine the contents of attitudes of speakers who them. Consider now the following statement from [10], often made in the dynamic semantics literature and there regarded as a truism:

How an assertion affects the context will depend on its content.

While the talk here is, as commonly, about assertion, I have not been talking about assertion but about attitudes that speakers undertake. These are normatively and intensionally specified; their content is nothing over and above their role in rational decision-making and reasoning. If we speak about overt acts like assertion, linguistically irrelevant (e.g. social) factors will enter, such as appropriateness conditions that are difficult to pin down and relations of a political kind. The category of assertion is vague. In the way suggested we may avoid it.

Secondly, it seems that while a context change will possibly depend in some indirect way on the utterance event that has taken place, what cannot be true is that the context change is determined by the sentence's linguistic meaning (content). Even even if sentences *did* come with fixed meanings, or expressed, by themselves or in context, "propositions", a hearer's grasp of them would be no reason why he should expand his present set of epistemic commitments to include the proposition. There may be no special incentive to do so and much incentive against doing so.

Interpreters may construct and take their departure from a passing commitment as to what expressions mean. But when particular such passing commitments require suspension, everything is open: no language is assumed to be shared, and the determination of content is matter of (normative) pragmatics. This general objection applied in different ways to both Stalnaker's semantics-cum-pragmatics program as well as to the dynamic semantics program.

4.1 Stalnaker

Recall Stalnaker's two-tiered theory of context changes. The first arises in virtue of the "manifestly observable event" ([11], 8) that a "statement was made". But together with it and "standing assumptions" that are part of the prior context we can "infer, (...) not only that the speaker uttered certain sounds, but also that she uttered an English sentence, and that she is saying something to us" (ibid.,8-9). Further assumptions (cooperativity, competence), Stalnaker goes on to assume, makes inferable from observational data, in fact, that we have a token *of an English sentence type whose meaning and the presuppositions of its utterance we know*. For example, when Phoebe asserts

(11) I can't come to the meeting – I have to pick up my cat at the veterinarian,

the first context change that takes place according to Stalnaker is that we now presuppose that Phoebe owns a cat, and that this is now a shared presupposition. From our assumption that she is cooperative, competent, and only willing to make "appropriate" speech acts (ibid.,9) (which in this case require that she uses the phrase *my cat* only if one owns a cat), we infer:

(i) that she means to presuppose that she owns a cat,
(ii) that "it is presupposed that presuppositions are shared information"
(iii) that she "presupposes that the addressee will be willing to suppose this".

So assuming we are willing, we now believe as a result of the first kind of context change, that Phoebe owns a cat and that this is shared information, available in the discourse context for future reference.

Stalnaker declares that this "derivation" (ibid., 10) of a presupposition doesn't commit him to the view that all of these are inferences we do or should draw. What we may note is that (i) *if* we draw them, they are non-monotonic or inductive; (ii) after it is clear what sounds were uttered, none of the inferences, because they are inductive ones, *needs* to be drawn (there being no commitments to the drawing of *inductive* inferences).

Thus at the point where we have got a Stalnaker-proposition (an absolute, non-contextual item of information, a set of possible worlds) and a presupposition associated with it, massive inferencing has already taken place. When it comes to Stalnaker's second kind of context change – where a proposed proposition is accepted or rejected -, what we have in effect is a product of this second kind of context change (a belief change, an either routine or deliberate expansion) already. The proposition that we attach to a sentence as well as its presupposition is a product of inductive reasoning. This is evident even given the assumptions Stalnaker makes in his example. It becomes abundantly clear if the shared language assumption fails, or the inductively inferred cooperativity and competence assumptions are given up.[4]

Stalnaker might think that how a context changes is in part merely a matter of the knowledge of language, while the pragmatics comes in only in cases like the one mentioned in the above quote. But can we make a categorical distinction between what is analytically given in a speech act, and what is inferred from it pragmatically (synthetically)? (Perhaps the distinction might be defended on epistemological lines: relative to a given set of attitudinal commitments, certain "analytic" connections might be marked as strongly entrenched, hence as epistemologically privileged since resisting revision.)

4.2 The Idea of a Discourse Semantics (DRT)

Now dynamic semantics equally assumes what Stalnaker does, namely that the *expression* "my cat" in

(12) I have to pick up my cat

"presupposes that the speaker has a cat". But even if an interpreter were certain of this, it would be of little help for his determination of what exactly is presupposed. Does one only have a cat if one owns it? Need the cat be alive? Can it be his wife? Is the phrase *my cat* used referentially rather than attributively, so that nothing in fact is presupposed, since no commitment has been undertaken? None of these pieces of information is determined by linguistic form, although a hearer will generally be able to work it out on the basis of practical and normative considerations.

Language by itself doesn't police the way we use it, and our use of it does not commit us. Expressions do not have presuppositions, because they do not make them. Whatever may be inductively inferred by an agent from a use of the expression *my cat*, there is nothing to the *expression* that makes it follow from a use of it that its user has a cat, even if it were clear what this exactly means. This is so in the same trivial way as it doesn't *follow* from my sincerely asserting, *I am bald*, that I am bald, or that I believe or presuppose that I am bald.

So while Stalnaker assumes that sentences come with their meanings and presuppositions, dynamic semantics assumes much the same thing. The difference is that these meanings and presuppositions together are held to constitute a "change in

---

[4] It is surprising that a discourse is rated "defective" if such assumptions fail (cf. ibid.,10). - Due to the defectiveness, Stalnaker argues, some *repair* is required. We may conclude from this that even for Stalnaker, in the *general* case how a context changes in the first sense *is* a matter of pragmatics and reasoning, hence is itself a context change in the second sense.

context". In one format currently discussed within Discourse Representation Theory (DRT), for example, the semantic value for a sentence[5] is defined to be a function

$$f: C \to C,$$

where C is a contextually given body of information relating variables and heir values at a moment of discourse, or a set of presuppositions against which a new utterance is interpreted. Semantically speaking, C is a set of possible worlds, but this set is "presented" in terms of a syntactic *discourse representation structure* (DRS). It is something like a formula of predicate logic which is made sensitive to the way a hearer cognitively represent a certain amount of truth conditional information. DRSs, in a slightly different format, are at the same time, used as representations of the contents of the *beliefs* and other attitudes that a hearer forms in response to a discourse. We should note that semantic interpretation and attitude formation are blended then, although in a different way than proposed above.

What is meant by this ubiquitous category of a "discourse"?[6] On the present approach, a "discourse" is a temporally extended scattered set of noises that are emitted by agents who interact strategically with each other on the basis of what attitudes they attribute to each other. On the approach defended in this paper these explain – normatively rather than naturalistically - why the agents put their grammatical competence to use in the way they do. Principles of rationality allow us to study discourses thus understood, and to do so in partially illuminating ways: to some extent we will be able to understand, for example, why an agent uses an interrogative with a certain grammatical structure at a certain point, and why another agent reacts to it by using a certain declarative. In short, we will have a model for understanding why a discourse progresses in the way it does.[7]

This is not the perspective on discourse adopted in primarily descriptive dynamic semantic frameworks like DRT. A discourse is looked at as a syntactic structure S in which sentences and sets of sentences (discourse segments) are distinguished. If it comes to the interpretation of the i'th sentence S_i, a mechanical device called the *construction algorithm* operates on the syntactic analysis of the sentence and adds its phrasal constituents to the syntactic representation K_{i-1} of the discourse up to the sentence S_{i-1}. The result is a syntactic representation K_i.

But can a syntactic structure be a *context for interpretation*, in the way a number of incurred attitudinal commitments can be, relative to which propositions (truth conditions) and preferences are fixed? It *is* assumed that such a syntactic structure determines a non-contextual semantic content. However, the way in which model-theoretic interpretations are assigned to DR structures is a trivial matter; it throws no

---

[5] This is here a well-determined *external object* that comes with a (truth-conditional) meaning, not an intensionally specified *theoretical entity* in the sense of the Chomskyan structural descriptions mentioned above.

[6] Textbook presentations of DRT ([5]) have mainly focussed on the semantic description of monologues, but the approach is clearly intended to extend to multi-speaker communicative exchanges (see [6]).

[7] Given the literally boundless complexity of the structure of games of conversation and common inquiry, one may well be sceptical as to prospects for predicting their outcomes or evolvement. There does not seem a limited set of rules for the game of conversation enabling us to make predictions. (Even if there were rules, the game may be too complex to make predictions, as is the case in chess).

light on the efforts of hearers to come to reasoned decisions as to the right interpretations, as well as the right strategies for expanding their present state of epistemic commitment (if DRT is used for the representation of attitudinal states). The motor for the dynamics of discourse is our deliberations and decisions about how to change our minds. It seems oddly depicted in the picture of a hearer in a certain epistemic state who witnesses a language use event, picks up a context change potential, applies it to his epistemic state, and gets a new epistemic state out of it. What the potential of a sentence to change my context is will obviously depend on contextual factors such as what my demands of information are, or my values, and probabilities. Information about these judgements might be added to the DRSs. But it is not clear what it means to say that an agent's judgements (about value, probability, etc.) are "internally represented", since it is not clear in what sense a normative decision theoretic epistemology can be regarded as a naturalistic psychological theory. Moreover, the semantic *interpretation* of this syntactic structure is truth theoretic, which would deprive items that do not have truth conditions, such as judgements of value, of a content.

If the update mechanism were to be upgraded by adding certain non-monotonic conversational rules to it, it will have to be argued that there is a (definite and limited) number of such norms; and whether they really can be regarded as linguistic ones rather than merely following from more general considerations in the theory of rational action.

5 A Note on Intuitionistic Type Theory (ITT)

In this final section I will make some remarks on one particular semantic framework that might be regarded as a dynamic one, and has been proposed as such in (Ranta [9]).[8] An important feature however that makes ITT different from other dynamic semantics frameworks and interesting with respect to the present meaning-theoretic proposal is its emphasis on acts rather than objects. It makes the category of a *judgement* central, making *propositions* the *objects* of such judgements. The making of judgements, qua acts, may be *justified*, while of propositions one cannot say that they are justified or "withdrawn". Thus

A is true

is a (potentially justifiable) judgement, in which **A** figures as the proposition whose truth is claimed. Other forms of judgement are considered, like judgements in which propositions are judged to be equal (**A=B:prop**), or in which **A** is judged to be a proposition (**A:prop**). To emphasize now some features with respect to the present approach, the latter form of judgement is interesting since I have claimed that proposition is an open concept. It cannot be determined beforehand what the propositions are; in particular, it is not language that determines this, and the way to arrive at propositions does not depart from language. It is thus useful to have an explicit form of expression formalizing judgements to the effect that something figures as a proposition. We should note in ITT the notion of proposition itself is

---

[8] Other than in standard ITT, assertion and judgement are here strictly separated issues, assertions being overt linguistic acts, while judgements are cognitive ones.

contextual in the sense that something may be a proposition in one context but not in another.

Secondly, ITT allows an epistemic interpretation in the sense that it does not take a world of referents for granted. Rather, according to the propositions-as-types principle adopted in ITT, every proposition is defined to determine a separate domain (a type or category), for whose elements separate identity criteria are given. Such types may depend on each other, in the sense that for example one of them can only be inhabited if the other is.

Thirdly, truth is not defined to be a relation in ITT. Nor could we do so on the present approach. The above judgement **A is true** is not a piece of meaningless formal-language syntax, for which a semantic interpretation must be specified. In the language of ITT every symbol comes together with a meaning explanation. In the case at hand, the meaning is that the type A is inhabited or has an instance, **a**. This judgement is written **a:A**, and **a** is whatever the ground is in terms of which an agent justifies the judgement **A is true** (or "expands" with A, as I called it above). It would not make sense to ask what the truth conditions or semantic interpretation of this judgement are: it *tells* us what the truth of A consists in, by giving an instance.

Fourthly, attitudes are no relations (holding of agents and propositions) in ITT. The forming of a belief is modelled as the making of a judgment that a proposition (a potential belief) is a true belief. Thus belief is not a propositional function defined over agents and propositions, returning a proposition when applied to such a pair of arguments. It is true that one may make a remark

(13) John believes that he is bald

and regard it as true. But John's *judgement* that the proposition that he is bald is true is not true or false.

Finally, inference is not a relation either (see [12]). In the way *consequence*

$$\Gamma \Rightarrow A$$

is defined in ITT, it *is* a relation: when applied to a sequence of antecedents Γ and a consequent A, it is assumed to either hold or not. But it is a different matter if we make a *judgement* that the above consequence *holds*, that is, judge that A is true provided all of the antecedents A_i in Γ are true. A judgement is made evident or justified in terms of drawing an inference, which is an act performed by an agent, hence an epistemic matter. Thus inference is not a relation (propositional function).

A consequence *holds* if any proof for the antecedents, if one were found, could be transformed into a proof for the consequent. Functions accomplishing this are *hypothetical proofs*; they are proofs of consequences. Consequences may of course hold without us ever coming to know that a function with that property exists. If we were to model the content of a presuppositional state of an agent as a consequence set in the sense of section 2.2, a commitment to such a consequence is a commitment that certain functions exist.

If we find proofs of the antecedent propositions $A_1,..., A_k$ of a consequence, we can instantiate the variable proofs for them that we have assumed in reasoning suppositionally from those antecedents. That is, we perform substitutions $a_1/x_1, ..., a_k/x_k$ which take the form of equality judgements

$$x_i = a_i : A_i, \text{ etc..}$$

These mean, e.g., that a_i and x_i are equal elements of the type A_i. If we are able to reach the consequent A as the conclusion of an *inference*, the proof of the consequent proposition A is a function that, for any proof-objects of the propositions in the assumptions in Γ that may be given, returns proofs of A. It is thus a function of the function type $(\text{type}(A_i),...\text{type}(A_k))\text{type}(A)$.

I have argued elsewhere ([4]) that all of this can be part of a coherent meaning-theoretic proposal. If however it is to be extended to a systematic theory of language use, on the lines of this paper, many more judgemental forms will have to be added. This may be an interesting program for the future.[9]

References

1. Chomsky, N.: Explaining Language Use. In: Philosophical Topics Vol. 20,1 (1992).
2. Clark, H.: Arenas of Language Use. Chicago (1992).
3. Grice, P.: Logic and Conversation. In: Cole, P., Morgan, J.L. (eds.): Syntax and Semantics, vol. 3: Speech Acts. New York (1975).
4. Hinzen, W.: Anti-Realist Semantics, forthcoming (1999).
5. Kamp, H. and Reyle, U.: From Discourse to Logic, Kluwer (1993).
6. Kamp, H.: A Model for shared Reference and speaker-transcendent Anaphora in Discourse, Handout for a Talk given at Rutgers University, February 1999.
7. Levi, I.: For the Sake of the Argument, Ramsey Test Conditionals, Inductive Inference, and Nonmonotonic Reasoning. CUP (1996).
8. Nunberg, G.: Tranfers of Meaning. In: J.of Semantics (1995,1).
9. Ranta, A.: Type-Theoretic Grammar. Oxford: Clarendon (1994).
10. Stalnaker, R.: Assertion. In: Cole, P. (ed.), Syntax and Semantics, vol. 9: Pragmatics. New York: Academic Press (1978).
11. Stalnaker, R., On the Representation of Context, JoLLI 7 (1998), 3-19.
12. Sundholm, G., Inference versus Consequence. In: LOGICA Yearbook, Czech Acad. Sc., Prague.
13. Zeevat, H., Scha, R.: Integrating Pragmatics into Update Semantics. In:Ortony, A., Slack, Stock,O. (eds.), Communication from an Artificial Intelligence Perspective, Springer-Verlag (1992) 17-34.

---

[9] This work was supported by a research grant from the Swiss National Foundation of Science, which is gratefully acknowledged.

Dynamics and Automaticity of Context:
A Cognitive Modeling Approach

Boicho Kokinov

Institute of Mathematics and Informatics, Bulgarian Academy of Sciences
Bl.8, Acad. G. Bonchev Str., Sofia 1113, BULGARIA
Central and East European Center for Cognitive Science, New Bulgarian University
21 Montevideo Str., Sofia 1635, BULGARIA
e-mail: kokinov@cogs.nbu.acad.bg

Abstract. AI and psychological approaches to context are contrasted and the dynamic and automatic nature of the continuous context change in human cognition is emphasized. A dynamic theory of context is presented which defines context as the dynamic state of human mind. It describes the interaction between memory, perception, and reasoning in forming context as well as how they are influenced by context. A general cognitive architecture, DUAL, is presented that implements the mechanisms of context formation and accounts for the context-sensitivity of human cognition. A model of human problem solving, AMBR, has been built upon the DUAL architecture and the simulation experiments performed with it produce data that are coherent with experimental data on human problem solving.

1. AI Approaches to Modeling Context: The Box Metaphor

Two world tour travelers who flew in a balloon landed in a small village and they wanted to know where they arrived. One of them asked the first person who came by:
"Could you, please, tell us where have we landed?".
"On the earth." the stranger replied and went further.
"This one must be a mathematician" commented the second traveler.
"How do you know that?" asked the first one.
"Well, he gave an absolutely correct and useless answer!"

AI systems need to give more useful answers than the mathematician[1] in the anecdote, therefore they have to provide not only correct but also relevant solutions to the problems in a specific context. Thus after leaving the toy worlds AI researchers faced

---

[1] Having my first degree in mathematics this joke applies to me as well.

the need to deal with the problem of context.[2] There are numerous reasons why context is important for an intelligent system and among them are the following:

- *AI systems need to provide correct solutions.* The problem here is that a particular system is designed for use in a typical context and therefore many assumptions behind the facts and rules in the domain are not explicated. Thus if context changes these facts and rules become no more valid and the system produces an incorrect response [13, 31]. One possible solution is to explicate all assumptions and always check whether these assumptions hold in a particular situation before using the corresponding facts or rules, however, this is not possible since the number of such assumptions is infinite. Another solution proposed by McCarthy is to keep the assumptions implicit, but to relate each fact or rule to a specific context where these assumptions hold [32], i.e. instead of stating that a particular proposition p is universally true, to state that it is true in a specific context c.

- *AI systems need to provide relevant solutions.* This means that they should not generate solutions which could work in principle (or in another possible world), but such that work here and now. Contexts might be useful for solving this problem by relating each operator or rule to a specific context allowing it to be applied only in this context.

- *AI systems need successful natural language communication.* The problem is that the meaning of words and phrases changes from one context to another.

- *AI systems need to act and communicate at the right level of granularity or right level of description.* Imagine a commentary of a soccer game which goes like this: "The ball flies with a speed of 62.3 km/h in a direction which is 36.4 degrees to the north of the side line. The ball hits the solid plane of the boot of Asparuhov under an angle of 47 degrees and gets an acceleration of 15 m/s^2 ...". This commentary is correct and to some extent relevant, but is made at an inadequate level of description. Contexts might be associated with a specific level of description of a domain.

- *AI systems need to act in an efficient way.* If the system has extensive knowledge it is inappropriate to search the entire knowledge base every time a fact or rule is needed – this would make it highly inefficient. Thus contexts have been used to play the role of smaller domains where the search is restricted.

AI researchers introduced the concept of context in order to make their systems more flexible and at the same time more efficient [25]. While context information was initially included in the domain rules making them more and more specific and complex [10], later on AI moved towards explicit representation of context. In most cases the "box metaphor" is used, i.e. context is considered as a box. "Each box has its own laws and draws a sort of boundary between what is *in* and what is *out*" [13]. The boxes are labeled and the reasoning system should always keep track of the box it is in. Boxes can be embedded in other boxes. Thus McCarthy [32] uses the labels of

---

[2] Even in the block world context-sensitive behavior can be demonstrated: by changing the goals of the intelligent system different reactions to the same external stimulation will be obtained. However, context is restricted to the goals of the system in this case.

the boxes as logical constants and designed a logical calculus that requires the box we are in to be always specified. There are special rules for entering and leaving a box. Giunchiglia and his colleagues [5, 12, 13] introduce another approach where the box is described by a separate logical theory (separate language, axioms, rules of inference) and again there are bridge rules which make it possible to travel from one box to another. Turner [42] uses a frame-like representation of the boxes and provides mechanisms for recognizing the context we should be using in a particular moment; for example, certain events trigger demons that change the box. Abu-Hakima and Brezillon [1] use a vector of variable-values which characterizes the box. Öztürk and Aamodt [34] represent a set of context features in each episode in a case-based reasoning model and describe how each particular type of task selects relevant episodes based on the prespecified relevant features.

In summary the AI approach to contextual reasoning may be characterized as navigation between and within the context-boxes (Figure 1). Crucial issues are how to represent the individual boxes, how to recognize that we have to change the box and how to choose a new box. In most cases the boxes are predefined, e.g. the logical theory or the frame representation describing the box should be defined in advance by the user or programmer. The issue of how to construct a new context on the fly is not addressed. The main issue being addressed is when and how the reasoner decides to change the context – either because the goal has been changed or because an external event has happened which should trigger a new context.

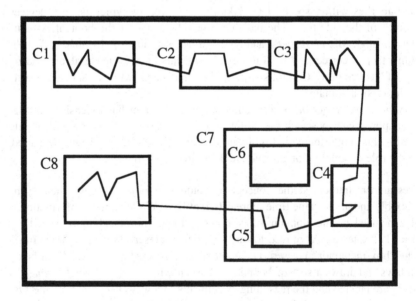

Fig. 1. Contextual reasoning as navigation between and within context-boxes (spaces). All boxes are labeled and can be referred to.

2. Psychological Approaches to Studying Context: Dynamics and Automaticity of Context Change

When psychologists study context effects they do not even think of changing the goals or beliefs of the subject, or the task or instruction to see whether a different perspective imposed on the subject would influence human reasoning. All this seems so obvious that nobody has studied it experimentally. Psychologist went further studying much more subtle influences – those that occur automatically but have no obvious explanation at the knowledge level – the level of human goals and beliefs.

Analyzing the automaticity of cognitive processes Bargh [3] has defined four different and more or less independent aspects that have to be studied: intentionality, controllability, awareness, and efficiency. *Intentionality* is related to the presence or lack of control on the start-up of the process by the individual. While problem solving is typically an intentional process since it starts when we decide to do so, categorization and evaluation are typically unintentional ones since these processes occur automatically when a stimulus is noticed and do not require a deliberate goal or intention. *Controllability* is related to the ability of the individual to stop a cognitive process once started or at least to override its influence if so desired. Examples of uncontrollable cognitive processes would be some strong visual illusions which occur even if one knows they are illusions. *Efficiency* refers to the extent to which the cognitive process requires attentional resources, i.e. its results would depend on the amount of attention paid to it. With respect to *awareness* a cognitive process may be automatic at several different levels. A person may not be aware of the presence of the stimulus event and still be influenced by it as in subliminal perception. A person may be aware of the stimulus but not be aware of the way it has been interpreted. Finally, a person may be aware of the interpretation of the stimulus but not aware of the way it influences his or her further behavior.

The results obtained in numerous experiments have shown that context effects can be produced without subjects' intention and awareness. For example, having cookies in the waiting room may influence subjects to produce a higher number of positively colored life experiences than in a controlled group [15]; a brief incidental touch by a waitress when returning change increases the size of the tip she receives [6]; even subliminal presentation (as short as 5 ms) of facial expressions can have an effect on a following target stimulus evaluation [33].

Psychologists have shown context effects on virtually all cognitive processes. Thus, for example, context effects on perception have been demonstrated by Gestalt psychologists in various forms: different interpretations of ambiguous figures; visual illusions depending on the background elements or on the presence of other stimuli. In language comprehension context effects can be exemplified by lexical, syntax, semantic, inference, thematic and other types of context effects [41]. In memory studies various effects of context have been demonstrated – context-dependence of recall and even recognition, memory illusions in false recognition, context-based interference, priming effects, etc. [7, 27]. In problem solving various forms of context effects have been shown: functional fixedness [9, 30], set effects [29], lack of transfer from previous problem solving experience [11], priming effects [17, 38], effects of incidental elements of the environment [26, 30]. In decision-making various context effects have been shown: framing effects – the effects of alternative descriptions, e.g. percentage dead or saved; effects of alternative methods of elicitation; and effects of added alternatives [39]. Barsalou [4] demonstrated context effects on concept characterization.

Two concrete examples of context effects on problem solving will be discussed. Kokinov [17] demonstrated that when the target problem was preceded by different priming problems subjects may solve it in different ways. Since the solution of the priming problem was known to the subjects in advance the only effect that its presentation had on the subjects was making certain concepts, facts, or rules more accessible. This turned out to be crucial for the problem solving process that followed. Moreover, the dynamics of the process has been studied and the results show that this priming effect decreases exponentially with the course of time and disappears within less than 20 minutes. Kokinov and his colleagues [24, 26] have demonstrated that a picture that is incidentally on the same page as the target problem can also influence the way the problem is being solved. Moreover, when prompted to use the picture subjects were less successful in solving the target problem than in the control condition, while when they seemingly ignored the picture they were still influenced by it and had a better performance than in the controlled condition.

The conclusion from this short review of the psychological studies of context effects is that context has often an unconscious and unintended influence on people's behavior and that this happens continuously and is triggered by all sorts of incidental elements of the environment but also by the previous memory states. On the other hand, this influence has its own internal dynamics and decreases and disappears in a short period of time. It seems very important that the previous memory state produces context effects since this maintains the continuity of the cognitive processes and prevents human thought from continuously running in leaps. It also ensures efficiency since it restricts the set of all possible interpretations, inferences, searches, etc. to the set of relevant ones. On the other hand, context effects produced by the perceptual processes are also important since they ensure that the cognitive system will be flexible and adaptive to changes in the environment.

The effects described in this section cannot be explained by postulating pre-existing and static contexts (boxes) and intentional decisions to switch between these contexts taken by the individuals. These effects require context to be considered as a continuously changing (evolving) state of the cognitive system which is not completely under its control. The fact that changes in context can take place automatically and without subject's intention and awareness is very important. If changes in context were taking place only under conscious human control, this would have raised a number of issues. For example, reasoning about contexts must also be context-sensitive and we would run into an endless meta-meta-meta-... explanation. This mechanism would also be very ineffective since the space of possible contexts is unlimited and the limited reasoning resources would have to be distributed among all these levels of reasoning about contexts.

3. Dynamic Theory of Context: A Cognitive Modeling Approach

Kokinov [21] introduced the following operational definition of context which is in accordance with the above psychological studies. *Context is the set of all entities that influence human (or system's) behavior on a particular occasion, i.e. the set of all elements that produce context effects.*

Although in most psychological experiments the manipulated elements are part of the physical or social environment within which the subject's behavior is tested [7, 8, 37], these elements cannot directly influence human behavior unless perceived and corresponding internal representations built. Thus in this paper *the term context refers to a set of internal or mental representations and operations* rather than a set of environmental elements. In other words *context refers to the current 'state of the mind' of the cognitive system* rather than the state of the universe. Similar views are shared by a number of researchers in AI, psychology, linguistics, and philosophy [13, 16, 28, 40]. Others consider context as the state of the universe or the environment.

Various mental representations or operations can have different degrees of influence on a cognitive process. This is determined by the degree to which they participate in or are used by the cognitive process: from not being used at all to being central for the processing. Thus, usually, the goal is much more important for the problem solving process than the representation of an incidental object in the problem solver's environment, but the latter can still play a role in processing as shown in the previous section. That is why if we define context as the set of important or relevant mental representations/operations (the ones that pay a role in processing) it cannot be considered as a set with clear-cut boundaries. It would be better to consider it as a fuzzy set with graded membership corresponding to the graded importance or relevance of the elements. How this graded relevance is computed is discussed later on.

The mental representations involved in the current context are being formed by the interaction between at least three processes: *perception* of the environment that builds new representations and activates old ones; *accessing and reconstructing memory* traces that reactivates or builds representations of old experiences; and *reasoning* that constructs representations of generated goals, inferred facts, induced rules, etc. It is also assumed that context in turn influences perception, memory, and reasoning processes (Figure 2).

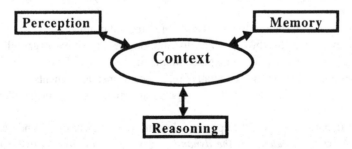

Fig. 2. Interaction of processes forming context and being influenced by it.

The representations built by the reasoning mechanism (e.g. goals, subgoals, and facts established by the inferential mechanism) form what we call *reasoning induced context*. Representations built by the perceptual mechanisms form what we call *perception induced context*. Finally, representations built by the memory processes form what we call *memory induced context*.

The interaction between reasoning, perception, and memory allows for a more efficient processing. Thus from all possible inferences that the reasoning mechanisms can construct only those which are somehow related to the representations produced by the perceptual and memory mechanisms should be actually constructed. Likewise, only those memory elements should be retrieved which are related to the currently reasoned and perceived elements. Finally, perception-built representations which are supported by related memory and reasoned elements should be stronger. All this would be possible only if the three processes are continuously running in parallel and interacting with each other. This would require a highly parallel cognitive architecture.

One way to describe how context influences cognitive processes is to assume that it assigns priorities to all mental representations and operations in a way that facilitates the usage of the more relevant elements and discourages the usage of the less relevant ones. How could the system know the relevance of a particular element prior to even trying to use it? Efficient processing requires that the system uses some relevance measure which will be cheap and will be based on its past experience. The measure that the dynamic theory of context uses is called *associative relevance*. It is defined by the *degree of connectivity* of the element in question with all other elements of the current context. The judgment of the degree of connectivity reflects the frequency of joint usage in past experience. Associative relevance is by definition graded because it is clear that all elements are somehow related to each other, so it is the degree of connectivity that matters. It is also important that this measure is a cheap one, i.e. its computation does not require a lot of resources, otherwise it would be pointless to use it as a heuristics. It is also important that relevance is computed relatively independently of the reasoning process itself, automatically (without intention and awareness) and continuously in parallel to the reasoning process itself. In this way the relevance computation can guide the reasoning porcess in one or another direction. On the other hand the reasoning process should also influence the computation of relevance, e.g. if a new goal is formed the relevance should change automatically.

Thus summarizing the main principles underlying the dynamic theory of context we can state that:

- context refers to the state of the mind and not to the environment;
- context corresponds to the specific distribution of priorities over all mental representations and operations in a given moment;
- priorities are measured by the associative relevance of mental elements;
- associative relevance is graded and is computed automatically and in parallel to the reasoning process;
- context is dynamic and the set of priority elements has no clear-cut boundaries.

Thus, *context is considered as the dynamic fuzzy set of all associatively relevant memory elements (mental representations or operations) at a particular instant of time.*

4. Context-Sensitive Cognitive Architecture DUAL

The cognitive archtecture DUAL[3] is one specific implementation of the Dynamic Theory of Context. It provides general structures and mechanisms for building context-sensitive models of cognitive processes [19, 20, 22, 36]. The DUAL approach rests on emergent and dynamic computations and representations. Context-sensitivity is explained in terms of dynamic re-organization of the cognitive system which continuously adapts to the changing situation. This approach allows for higher flexibility and efficiency compared to a system based on fixed computations and representations [25].

A system built on the DUAL cognitive architecture consists of a large number of relatively simple micro-agents whose collective behavior produces the global behavior of the system. Each micro-agent is a simple and specialized computational device which represents only a small piece of declarative and procedural knowledge. Thus the global computations in DUAL emerge from the local interactions between the agents and the representations in DUAL are distributed or decentralized over a set of agents.

Each micro-agent is a hybrid (symbolic/connectionist) processing device. Its symbolic component takes part in the emergent global symbolic computation processes and in the emergent representations, while its connectionist component takes part in a emergent global process of spreading activation which computes the associative relevance of the knowledge represented by its symbolic component. The speed at which its symbolic component is running depends on the activation level computed by its connectionist component [18, 19, 20, 36]. In this way the mental operation performed by the symbolic processor of the agent has a dynamically assigned priority. The current context-sensitive representation of a concept or episode emerges from the distribution of activation over the set of agents that represent various aspects of it.

The population of all micro-agents forms the Long-Term Memory of a DUAL system. The agents are connected into a network reflecting the typical patterns of interaction between them, each agent communicating directly with its local neighbors only. However, the agents can establish new links dynamically and thus change (temporary) the topology of the network. The agents that are active at a particular instant of time form the Working Memory (WM) of the system. Some of them are permanent and are part of the LTM. Others are temporary — constructed recently by other agents and belonging to the WM only. The latter usually disappear after a certain period of time but some can become permanent and join the LTM.

Knowledge is represented in DUAL by the symbolic components of the agents. The frame-like symbolic structures used for representation are dynamic and distributed over a coalition of agents. The slots are part of the same agent but the corresponding fillers are represented by other agents. The relations to the fillers are represented by links between the agents each link having a semantic interpretation (like co-reference, is-a, instance-of, etc.). The actual representation used in a particular moment will

---

[3] An extended description of DUAL, including the source code in LISP, is available on-line at http://www.andrew.cmu.edu/~apetrov/dual.

depend on the activation levels of all agents in the coalition and thus it will depend on the context. Episodes are represented in an even more decentralized way since there is no single agent with a list of pointers to all the aspects of the episode. The aspects of the episode which will be retrieved or constructed completely depends on the context.

Context is represented in DUAL by the distribution of activation over all micro-agents in the system, i.e. by the state of the WM of the system at a particular instant of time. This representation fulfills all the principles of the dynamic theory of context as outlined in the previous section:

- the state of the WM is in fact a complete description of the "state of the mind" of a cognitive system;
- the activation level determines the speed of processing and therefore assigns the priorities;
- the activation level of the WM elements corresponds to the calculated associative relevance of the corresponding piece of knowledge since this activation level reflects their connectivity with all other WM elements;
- the degree of membership to the WM is graded since it is measured by the activation levels which are real numbers in the segment $[0,1)$;
- the activation level is computed automatically, continuously and in parallel to all symbolic processes, including the reasoning process;
- the WM is dynamic as the set of its elements and the degrees of their membership change continuously.

In summary, context has a dynamic and distributed representation in DUAL: the distribution of activation over the set of all memory elements (the set of all agents). In other words the context is reflected by the specific group of agents performing the computations and representing various aspects of the situation in that moment. In this way the system re-organizes itself and adapts to the particular situation.

Thus context is implicitly represented by the distribution of activation over the set of all memory elements. Each pattern of activation represents a specific context. This does not exclude having additional explicit meta-context representations. The mental state of the cognitive system can be self-observed and part of it (which is consciously accessible) can be explicitly represented in a local structure and referred to on a later occasion. However, this is always a partial representation of the actual mental state.

The particular state of WM is computed by a connectionist mechanism of spreading activation which emerges from the local computations performed by the connectionists components of all agents. These computations are performed continuously and in parallel to all the symbolic processing done by the symbolic components of the agents. All the links in the network are used for spreading activation. This includes both the semantic and the associative links between the agents.

There are two agents which are considered as permanent sources of activation: the GOAL agent and the INPUT agent. They continuously emit activation and pass it over to their neighbors connected by weighted links to them. The agents directly related to the GOAL agent represent the particular goals that the system is currently pursuing and are called goal agents. On the other hand, the agents directly related to the *INPUT* agent represent objects (or their properties and relations) currently being perceived by the system and are called *input* agents.

The particular state of WM reached on a particular occasion and computed by the above mechanism depends on the particular list of *goal* and *input* agents as well as on the initial state of WM which is the distribution of activation computed in the previous context. It is important to stress that there is a decay process which decreases the activation of each individual node (agent) with time, however, its decay rate is relatively slow which enables the previous state to influence the new one.

Context is changed continuously by the connectionist mechanism in parallel to the reasoning process emerging from the symbolic computations. Thus context changes can influence the reasoning process. The changes in the context are not a result of the reasoning process although the reasoning process can influence the context changes by manipulating the *goal* agents.

The dynamics of the connectionist computation produces continuous changes in the context. However, more radical changes occur as a result of changes in the lists of *goal* and the *input* agents, i.e. in the sources of activation. This is performed by the processes of reasoning and perception, respectively. Both the reasoning and the perception processes are emergent from the collective behavior of many agents.

Perception plays a crucial role in context changes. Most of the well known context effects in psychology are about how the changes in the outside world (the environment) influence human behavior, i.e. about the influence of perception induced context. This is modeled in the following way. The perception process produces temporary agents corresponding to elements of the environment and connects them to the *INPUT* agent. Currently DUAL has quite simple perceptual abilities. The system receives both a formal description of the problem and its textual description as input and the formal description becomes a *goal* agent while the system produces *input* nodes for each word in the textual description. In this way the representations of the words (which are different from the representations of the concepts) form the perception induced context and the effects of different wordings on the problem solving can be modeled. The perception of objects from the environment is simulated by directly implanting an *input* agent in WM. Currently the architecture is being extended in order to equip it with more elaborate perceptual abilities. It should be able to construct the internal representation of the problem by itself starting from an image of the scene: in our case a text-processing situation. For this reason the architecture is extended with a visual buffer.

Goal agents are the other source of changes. These agents are produced and linked to the *GOAL* agent by the reasoning process or are old *goal* agents which are currently activated. This is the way in which the reasoning process can influence the process of changing the context.

DUAL is a specific version of a Society of Mind architecture and in that respect is similar to CopyCat and TableTop architectures developed by Hofstadter and his group [14]. Anderson's ACT-* architecture [2] is also related, but is much more centralized and goal-driven.

5. Context-Sensitive Problem Solving with AMBR

A computer model of human problem solving, AMBR[4], has been developed which simulates deductive and analogical reasoning and demonstrates some of the context effects shown in psychological experiments [18, 23]. Problem solving in AMBR is an emergent process. It emerges from the collective performance of many agents most of which are domain specific such as *water* agent, *heating* agent, *tea-pot* agent, etc.

The general idea of context-sensitivity of problem solving in AMBR is the following. Contexts may differ in their perceived and/or their memorized parts. The perception induced context is established by activating from outside some agents corresponding to words in the problem description as well as some agents corresponding to objects in the environment (e.g. stone) simulating their perception. The memory induced context is established by the initial distribution of activation as a residue of a previously solved problem. These different activation patterns result in different sets of agents contributing to the problem solving process as well as different distribution of their performance speeds. As a result different bases for analogy are found or different constraint satisfaction networks are built up and different correspondences between the same base and target are established. In other words in one particular context the system fails to solve the problem, in another one its solves it successfully, and in a third one it solves it in a different way.

The simulation results have replicated the experimental data about the dynamics of the memory induced context influence on problem solving demonstrating the same pattern of decreasing priming effect [18]. Moreover, these simulation results have predicted the influence of the perception induced context on the specific way the problem is being solved [18] and these predictions have been confirmed in successive psychological experiments [24, 26]. Recently new predictions have been made about the existence of mapping influence on retrieval and order effects [35] which have yet to be psychologically tested.

6. Conclusions

A dynamic theory of context has been proposed which considers context as the set of all entities that influence human behavior on a particular occasion. As a consequence context is thought of as the dynamic fuzzy set of all associatively relevant memory elements (mental representations or mental operations) at a particular instant of time.

In the cognitive architecture DUAL the memory elements are called agents and they have variable availability determined by their activation level. Problem solving is modeled by an emergent computation produced by the collective behavior of the agents (the AMBR model). Context influences problem solving by changing the availability of the agents. In this way different sets of agents take part in the computation in

---

[4] An extended description of AMBR, including its source code in LISP, is available on-line at: http://www.andrew.cmu.edu/~apetrov/dual/ambr

different contexts. They run at different speed depending on their estimated relevance. It is clear that these mechanisms produce different outcomes in different situations even if the goals of the system are fixed. Moreover, context changes dynamically because of the inherent dynamics both of the memory induced context (decreasing its influence with the course of time) and of the perception induced context (continuously changing the perceived elements of the environment).

The simulation experiments on priming and context effects performed with DUAL and AMBR have replicated successfully psychological data and have predicted results which later on have been confirmed experimentally.

References

1. Abu-Hakima, S., Brezillon, P.: Principles for Application of Context in Diagnostic Problem Solving. In: Brezillon, P. Abu-Hakima, S. (eds.) Working Notes of the IJCAI'95 Workshop on Modelling Context in Knowledge Representation and Reasoning. IBP, LAFORIA 95/11 (1995)
2. Anderson, J.: The Architecture of Cognition. Harvard Univ. Press, Cambridge, MA (1983)
3. Bargh, J.: The Four Horsemen of Automaticity: Awareness, Intention, Efficiency. and Control in Social Cognition. In: Wyer, R. & Srull, Th. (eds.) Handbook of Social Cognition. vol. 1: Basic Processes. 2nd Edition, Erlbaum, Hillsdale, NJ (1994)
4. Barsalou, L. Flexibility, Structure, and Linguistic Vagary in Concepts: Manifestations of a Compositional System of Perceptual Symbols. In: Collins, A., Gathercole, S., Conway, M., & Morris, P. (eds.) Theories of Memory. Erlbaum, Hillsdale, NJ (1993)
5. Bouquet, P., Cimatti, C.: Formalizing Local Reasoning Using Contexts. In: Brezillon, P. Abu-Hakima, S. (eds.) Working Notes of the IJCAI'95 Workshop on Modelling Context in Knowledge Representation and Reasoning. IBP, LAFORIA 95/11. (1995)
6. Crusko, A., Wetzel, C.: The Midas Touch: The Effects of Interpersonal Touch on Restaurant Tipping. Personality and Social Psychology Bulletin, 10 (1984) 512-517
7. Davies, G. & Thomson, D.: Memory in Context: Context in Memory. John Wiley, Chichester (1988)
8. Davies, G. & Thomson, D.: Context in Context. In: Davies, G. & Thomson, D. (eds.) Memory in Context: Context in Memory. John Wiley, Chichester (1988)
9. Dunker, K.: On Problem Solving. Psychological Monographs, 58:5 (1945)
10. Fikes, R., Nilsson, N,: STRIPS: A New Approach to the Application of Theorem Proving to Problem Solving. Artificial Intelligence, 2 (1971) 189-208
11. Gick, M. & Holyoak, K.: Analogical Problem Solving. Cognitive Psychology, 12 (1980) 306-355
12. Giunchiglia, F.: Contextual Reasoning. In: Epistemologia - Special Issue on I Linguaggi e le Machine, 16 (1993) 345-364
13. Giunchiglia, F. & Bouquet, P.: Introduction to Contextual Reasoning. In: Kokinov. B. (ed.) Perspectives on Cognitive Science, vol. 3, NBU Press, Sofia (1997)
14. Hofstadter, D.: Fluid Concepts and Creative Analogies. Basic Books, NY (1995)
15. Isen, A., Shalker, T., Clark, M., Karp, L.: Affect, Accessibility of Material in Memory, and Behavior: A Cognitive Loop? Journal of Personality and Social Psychology, 36 (1978) 1-12.

16. Kintsch, W.: The Role of Knowledge in Discourse Comprehension: A Construction-Integration Model. Psychological Review, 95(2) (1988) 163-182
17. Kokinov, B.: Associative Memory-Based Reasoning: Some Experimental Results. In: Proceedings of the 12th Annual Conference of the Cognitive Science Society, Erlbaum, Hillsdale, NJ (1990)
18. Kokinov, B.: A Hybrid Model of Reasoning by Analogy. Chapter 5. in: K. Holyoak & J. Barnden (eds.) Analogical Connections, Advances in Connectionist and Neural Computation Theory, vol.2, Ablex Publ. Corp., Norwood, NJ (1994)
19. Kokinov, B.: The DUAL Cognitive Architecture: A Hybrid Multi-Agent Approach. In: A. Cohn (ed.) Proceedings of ECAI'94. John Wiley & Sons, Ltd., London (1994)
20. Kokinov, B.: The Context-Sensitive Cognitive Architecture DUAL. In: Proceedings of the 16th Annual Conference of the Cognitive Science Society. Erlbaum, Hillsdale, NJ (1994)
21. Kokinov, B.: A Dynamic Approach to Context Modeling. In: Brezillon, P. Abu-Hakima, S. (eds.) Working Notes of the IJCAI'95 Workshop on Modelling Context in Knowledge Representation and Reasoning. IBP, LAFORIA 95/11 (1995)
22. Kokinov, B.: Micro-Level Hybridization in the Cognitive Architecture DUAL. In: R. Sun & F. Alexander (eds.) Connectionist-Symbolic Integration: From Unified to Hybrid Architectures, Lawrence Erlbaum Associates, Hilsdale, NJ (1997)
23. Kokinov, B.: Analogy is like Cognition: Dynamic, Emergent, and Context-Sensitive. In: Holyoak, K., Gentner, D., Kokinov, B. (eds.) – Advances in Analogy Research: Integration of Theory and Data from the Cognitive, Computational, and Neural Sciences. NBU Press, Sofia (1998)
24. Kokinov, B., Hadjiilieva, K., & Yoveva, M.: Explicit vs. Implicit Hint: Which One is More Useful? In: Kokinov. B. (ed.) Perspectives on Cognitive Science, vol. 3, NBU Press, Sofia (1997)
25. Kokinov, B., Nikolov, V., Petrov, A.: Dynamics of Emergent Computation in DUAL. In: Ramsay, A.. (eds.) Artificial Intelligence: Methodology, Systems, Applications. IOS Press, Amsterdam (1996)
26. Kokinov, B., Yoveva, M.: Context Effects on Problem Solving. In: Proceedings of the 18th Annual Conference of the Cognitive Science Society. Erlbaum, Hillsdale, NJ (1996)
27. Levandowsky, S., Kirsner, K., & Bainbridge, V.: Context Effects in Implicit Memory: A Sense-Specific Account. In: Lewandowsky, S., Dunn, J., & Kirsner, K. (eds.) Implicit Memory: Theoretical Issues. Erlbaum, Hillsdale, NJ (1989)
28. Lockhart, R.: Conceptual Specificity in Thinking and Remembering. In: Davies, G. & Thomson, D. (eds.) Memory in Context: Context in Memory. John Wiley, Chichester (1988)
29. Luchins, A.: Mechanization in Problem Solving: The Effect of Einstellung. Psychological Monographs, 54:6 (1942)
30. Maier, N.: Reasoning in Humans II: The Solution of a Problem and it Appearance in Consciousness. Journal of Comparative Psychology, 12 (1931) 181-194.
31. McCarthy, J.: Generality in Artificial Intelligence. Communications of the ACM, 30 (1987) 1030-1035
32. McCarthy, J.: Notes on Formalizing Context. In: Proceedings of the 13th IJCAI, AAAI Press (1993) 555-560
33. Murphy, S., Zajonc, R.: Affect, Cognition, and Awareness: Affective Priming with Optimal and Suboptimal Stimulus Exposures. Journal of Personality and Social Psychology, 64 (1993) 723-739

34. Öztürk, P., Aamodt, A.: A Context Model for Knowledge-Intensive Case-Based Reasoning. Int. J. Human-Computer Studies, 48 (1998) 331-355.
35. Petrov, A., Kokinov, B.: Mapping and Access in Analogy-Making: Independent or Interactive? A Simulation Experiment with AMBR. In: Holyoak, K., Gentner, D., Kokinov, B. (eds.) Advances in Analogy Research: Integration of Theory and Data from the Cognitive, Computational, and Neural Sciences. NBU Press, Sofia (1998)
36. Petrov, A., Kokinov, B.: Processing Symbols at Variable Speed in DUAL: Connectionist Activation as Power Supply. In: Proceedings of the 17th IJCAI, AAAI Press (1999)
37. Roediger, H. & Srinivas, K.: Specificity of Operations in Perceptual Priming. In: Graf, P. & Masson, M. (eds.) Implicit Memory: New Directions in Cognition, Development, and Neuropsychology. Erlbaum, Hillsdale (1993)
38. Schunn, C. & Dunbar, K. Priming, Analogy, and Awareness in Complex Reasoning. Memory and Cognition, 24 (1996) 271-284
39. Shafir, E., Simonson, I. & Tversky, A.: Reason-Based Choice. Cognition, 49 (1993) 11-36
40. Sperber, D. & Wislon, D.: Relevance. Communication and Cognition. Harvard University Press, Cambridge, MA (1986)
41. Tiberghien, G.: Language Context and Context Language. In: Davies, G. & Thomson, D. (eds.) Memory in Context: Context in Memory. John Wiley, Chichester (1988)
42. Turner, R. Context-Mediated Behavior for Intelligent Agents. Int. J. Human-Computer Studies, 48 (1998) 307-330

A Mental Space Account for Speaker's Empathy: Japanese Profiling Identity vs. English Shading Identity[†]

Soichi Kozai
University of Hawai'i

Abstract. Integrating Mental Space notions and transitivity elements, this paper discusses the phenomena of profiling a speaker's identity in Japanese with reference to shading a speaker's identity in English. There are three kinds of empathy prominent predicates in Japanese: giving/receiving verbs, psychological adjectivals, and *cognitive* verbs. These predicates require syntactic constraints with respect to empathy conditions, and these constraints have a strong correlation with transitivity. Employing a Mental Space framework (Fauconnier 1994, 1997) and ideas from this theory, I account for the phenomena as a manifestation of a single phenomenon. The key notions used in this study are *viewpoint, empathy, blending*, and *transitivity*.

1 Introduction

In this study I will present a unified account of empathy phenomena for Japanese predicates with comparisons to counterparts in English. *Empathy* is a notion that indexes a speaker's identification with a particular participant in a described event (Kuno 1987:203-206). This is analogous to a camera angle for shooting a picture. For example, when the speaker takes the viewpoint of an agent of a transitive verb, the profiled agent is marked for nominative case, however, when the speaker takes a patient's viewpoint, the shaded agent is marked for oblique case. Goldberg (1995:57), using Fisher's notion of *profiling* (1991), defines a participant whose viewpoint a speaker takes as *profiled* and a participant whose viewpoint a speaker does not take as *shaded*.

Just as the participants of referents in descriptions can be profiled or shaded, a speaker's identity can also be profiled or shaded. These profilings or shadings of a speaker's identity are syntactically constrained for particular sets of predicates in Japanese, whereas they are not for the counterparts of those predicates in English. First consider the example sentences of the psychological predicate[1] *atui* 'hot' below:

† I am indebted to Professors Roderick Jacobs, John Haig and Haruko Cook for comments and suggestions on earlier versions of this paper. The errors remaining are mine. I also would like to thank my friends who have supported me for this particular study: You-guang Ding, M.D., Given Tokunaga, Rev., Hirokuni Masuda, Ph.D., and Liane Louie, Ph.D.

1 Predicates that express the internal state of an animate entity, such as emotion, sensation, and cognition, are called psychological predicates. Those predicates of emotion and sensation in

(1) a. *I am hot.*

　　a'. *Boku wa atui.*　　　　　　a". * *Boku wa atu-gatte-iru.*
　　　　　I　T　hot/Prs　　　　　　　　I　T　hot-GARing-STA/Prs

　　b. *Taro is hot.*

　　b'. * *Taro wa atui.*　　　　　　b". *Taro wa atu-gatte-iru.*
　　　　　　T　hot/Prs　　　　　　　　　　T　hot-GARing-STA/Prs

In English, except for subject-verb agreement, the *person* of a grammatical subject does not impose on a speaker any syntactic constraint on the description of sensations, as in (a) and (b). On the other hand, there are some syntactic constraints on such descriptions in Japanese, as shown in (a', a", b', b"). For descriptions of a non-first person's psychological state, suffixation with the descriptive morpheme -*gar*- and the stative morpheme -*iru* are required because there is a conflict in identity between the speaker and the referent of the grammatical subject; these suffixations do not occur with the first person grammatical subject because there should not be an identity separation for the same person. Such suffixations, thus, indicate the reference point for the descriptions, i.e., the speaker, if the grammatical subject is other than a first person. Hence the linguistic variation highlights the speaker's identity in terms of empathy. However, there is no such constraint in English. Even when a third person's psychological state is described, the speaker's identity is not overtly profiled by linguistic devices like those used in Japanese.[2]

There are three kinds of empathy-prominent predicates in Japanese: giving/receiving verbs[3], psychological adjectivals, and cognitive verbs. The giving/receiving verbs are *yaru* 'give1', *kureru* 'give2', and *morau* 'receive'. Examples of psychological predicates are: *atui* 'hot', *kanasii* 'lonely', and -*tai* 'want to'. Cognitive verbs are *omou* 'think', *sinziru* 'believe', *utagau* 'doubt', etc. All of these predicates require syntactic constraints for their descriptions with respect to empathy conditions: whether the speaker's identity is harmonious or conflicting with the identity of a lexically empathy-marked participant, for giving/receiving verbs, or a grammatical subject, for psychological and cognitive predicates. The constraints on

---

[2] English are either verbs, *like, enjoy, feel hot/cold*, etc., or adjectivals, *be fond of, be delighted to, hot, cold*, etc. while those of cognition are verbs, *think, believe, know*, etc. (Jacobs 1995). In Japanese, however, predicates of emotion and psychical sensation are only adjectivals while those of cognition are verbs. In this paper, these adjectival predicates are labeled *psychological predicates* in contrast to the *cognitive verbs*. Of the psychological predicates, there are three kinds: *emotion* such as *uresii* 'glad', *sabisii* 'lonely'; *sensation* such as *atui* 'hot', *samui* 'cold'; and *wanting* as -*tai* 'want to' and *hosii* 'want'.

But, of course, since the referent of a grammatical subject takes the third person form, here it is *Taro*, rather than the first person forms, the speaker's identity is realized in some sense. Although this is also true in Japanese, Japanese has more elaborated systems to index the speaker's identity if there is any empathy conflict in such descriptions.

[3] There are three levels of speech register for the giving/receiving verbs – casual, plain, and honorific. However only casual forms are used in this paper for the sake of convenience.

the three kinds of predicates can be seen as the manifestation of a single phenomenon. However, some analyses covered only the giving/receiving verbs, some only psychological predicates, and others both psychological and *cognitive* predicates. Kuno (1987) and others used the notion of empathy or social group membership[4] to account for giving/receiving verbs; Kuroda (1973), Aoki (1986), and others used the notion of subjectivity to account for psychological predicates; and Iwasaki (1993) used the notion of perspective for both psychological predicates and cognitive verbs.

I present here a unified account of speaker's empathy for these predicates within the framework of Mental Space theory (Fauconnier 1994, 1997). This theory develops the key notions for this study: *Blending* (Fauconnier 1994, 1997, Coulson 1996, Kozai 1999c, e) and *three types of Viewpoint* (Kozai 1999a, b). I will show how speakers in Japanese are required to profile their presence in descriptions of events or states using empathy-prominent predicates whereas speakers in English tend to shade themselves.

First, we consider giving/receiving verbs.

2 Giving/Receiving Verbs

Mental Space theory views language as a system of prompts. These prompts lead to the building and interrelating of semantic spaces or domains, using minimal lexical and grammatical structures. This theory posits a Viewpoint space, from which other spaces are accessed and structured. When describing an event or a state, the speaker must take a particular stance for that description. The speaker's stance is, thus, the Viewpoint space.

Kozai (1999a) has proposed three types of Viewpoint to account for empathy phenomena with the giving/receiving verbs. These are Empathy viewpoint, Agentive viewpoint, and Subjective viewpoint.[5] Empathy viewpoint expresses the speaker's identification with a particular participant in an event - the speaker describes the event from this identified participant's perspective. When an in-group member appears in a description, s/he can only be the giver for *yaru* 'give1' and the recipient for *kureru* 'give2' and *morau* 'receive'. Thus forms of a first person or an in-group member have to be placed in these empathy-marked positions. When the distribution of in-group members conforms to the empathy restrictions, there is no conflict in

---

[4] The social group membership is called in/out(*uti/soto*)-group membership which is determined on the basis of speaker's relationship with a conversational partner and/or with referents of described events or states. Those interlocutors or referents who socially form a group with the speaker, i.e. an in-group, are in-group members and those who do not are out-group members. For example, when a speaker is talking to a friend about his/her family member, the speaker must take the family member as the in-group member while the friend is the out-group member. When the speaker is talking about him/herself, the first person alone forms the in-group. This membership changes depending on time, place, and occasion of utterances.

[5] The Agentive and the Subjective viewpoints are discussed in more detail in a later section.

empathy regarding the speaker and the empathy-marked participant. See the examples below in which *titi* 'father' can only be placed according to the empathy constraints for these verbs.

(2) a. *Titi   wa Taro ni hon o   yatta/*kureta.*
         father T   D book A gave1/gave2
         '(My) father gave Taro a book.'

     b. *Taro wa titi   ni hon o   *yatta/kureta.*
         T father D book A gave1/gave2
         'Taro gave (my) father a book.'

     c. <u>*Titi   wa Taro ni/*Taro wa titi   ni*</u>   *hon o moratta.*
         Father T   from   T father from book A received
   '(My) father received a book from Taro./*Taro received a book from (my) father.'

The empathy locus with each verb is schematized in Table 1 below:

Table 1. Empathy locus

'give1' *yaru*	Giver (nominative NP)
'give2' *kureru*	Recipient (dative NP)
'receive' *morau*	Recipient (nominative NP)

When these empathy conditions are met, i.e., the empathy condition between the speaker and the empathy-marked participant is harmonious, the speaker's identity itself is *shaded* while the participant's identity is *profiled*.

But there are apparent violations of these conditions. The giving/receiving verbs occur in certain exceptional empathy-marking constructions in which the Empathy viewpoint shifts to the other participant in a special context - a context presenting a double viewpoint, such as an indirect speech construction in which the *described* speaker's viewpoint is embedded within the *describing* speaker's presentation. Constructions with empathy shift are products of an empathy conflict between the speaker and the hearer or a discourse participant. Consider the following examples:

(3) a. *Titi   ni sore o yatta to   hito   ni iu-na!*
         Father D that A gave1 Qut person to say-Neg/Imp
         'Don't tell others that (you) gave it to (my) father!'

     b. *Titi   ga sore o kureta to   hito   ni iu-na!*
         Father N that A gave2 Qut person to say-Neg/Imp
         'Don't tell others that (my) father gave it (to you)!'

     c. *Titi   ni   sore o moratta to   hito   ni iu-na!*
         father from that A received Qut person to say-Neg/Imp
         'Don't tell others that (you) received it from (my) father!'

In (3a), the in-group member for the third person form, *titi*, is the recipient rather than the giver for *yaru*, which is a violation of the empathy assignment constraint. The same is true for the sentences with *kureru* and *morau* (3b, c). The in-group member, *titi*, appears in non-empathy positions with all three verbs. These exceptional empathy constructions are cases of empathy conflicts. Although a speaker should profile this in-group member, the third person forms of *titi* are shaded and the understood second person forms of the out-group member are profiled by being-located in empathy-marked positions. Unlike the previous examples for the psychological predicate as in (1), the apparently conflicting empathy between the speaker and participants is not marked by suffixation, but rather by the positioning of in-group members in non-empathy slots (refer to Table 1 above), despite the positioning constraints described.

What is happening in these exceptional empathy-marking constructions is that the speaker is expressing two viewpoints: one is the in-group member's and the other is the out-group member's which is exceptionally empathy-marked. These apparently conflicting viewpoints are blended into one.

Blending has been described as an integration of partial structures from two separate space domains into a single structure with emergent properties in the third domain (Fauconnier 1997). Computer viruses are one example of conceptual blending. Coulson (1996:69-70) describes an integrated computer virus schema such that viruses in the source domain of health are projected into the blended space and harmful computer programs in the target domain of computers are picked out as counterparts to the viruses, and this integration of two schemata allows us to map elements from both source and target domains into the blended space. The present study employs this blending notion and applies it specifically to the Empathy viewpoint.

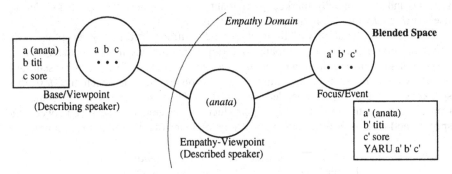

Fig. 1.

Such viewpoint blending can occur in particular contexts with which two viewpoints are associated, such as the indirect speech construction in which both viewpoints of the *describing* speaker and the *described* speaker are involved. See Figure 1 above for the indirect speech example (3a). The Base space here serves as the Viewpoint space for the *describing* speaker. If the speaker is not directly involved in the event, it represents the viewpoint of an in-group member participant. It is thus father's viewpoint with the example (3a). From this space, the Empathy-Viewpoint space of the exceptionally empathy-marked participant is set up, because this participant is profiled in the construction. From these two Viewpoint spaces a third, blended space, is created for the description of an event. This Empathy-Viewpoint space and any others which are relative to it form an Empathy Domain.

English has no such restrictions for the transfer of an object, e.g., between the first person and the third person. In the examples below, *Taro* could be described in either direction (*I* to *Taro* or *Taro* to *me*) with both *give* and *receive*:

(4) a. *I gave Taro a book.*   a'. *Taro gave me a book.*

  b. *I received a book from Taro.* b'. *Taro received a book from me.*

Speakers in English can take the viewpoint of the agent without any empathy restrictions in terms of group membership. With respect to empathy, speakers' identities are typically shaded and the referents of grammatical subjects are typically profiled.

Note however that English constructions contrast with Japanese in other ways regarding donatory verbs. The alternation between double-object constructions and constructions with *to* provides for a different semantic content. For some speakers, the double direct-objects constructions imply that ownership of the object has been transferred completely while those with *to*-marked indirect-objects imply that the ownership is temporarily transferred (Personal communication with R. Jacobs).

Before we move on to the analysis of empathy conflict in constructions with psychological predicates, we must consider the relationship between transitivity and viewpoint, one which turns out to be crucial in our analysis.

3 Transitivity and Three Types of Viewpoints

Kozai (1999b, d) has presented a correlation between the distributions of the three types of Viewpoint with giving/receiving verb constructions (see Table 2.) and the transitivity of these constructions.

Table 2. Distribution of the three Viewpoints

'give1'	**Emp/Subj/Agt**		
	Boku ga	Taro ni	yaru
'give2'	**Agt**	**Emp**	
	Taro ga	boku ni	kureru
'receive'	**Emp/Subj/Agt**	**Agt**	
	Boku ga	Taro ni	morau

(Emp: Empathy, Subj: the Subjective, Agt: the Agentive)

As noted earlier, Empathy viewpoint represents the speaker's identification with a particular participant in an event. The Agentive viewpoint represents an instigator of the event (there are two agents with *morau* (Shibatani 1979)), while the Subjective viewpoint expresses an internal state attributed to the referent of the grammatical subject. These three Viewpoints present elements central to the determination of transitivity. Empathy viewpoint indexes the profiling/shading of an agent, the

Subjective viewpoint the volitionality of an agent, and the Agentive viewpoint the controllability of an action by the agent.

The three viewpoints are concentrated in a nominative NP with *yaru* and, i.e., the agent is [+profiled], [+volitional], and [+control][6], and, thus, *yaru* has all the elements for transitivity. A nominative NP with *morau* also possesses the same viewpoint distribution, but the controllability of this agent is extremely low because, conceptually, it is a *passive* agent (the recipient) and besides there is an *active* agent (the giver) in the same clause and because a *by*-agent lacks strong transitivity features by itself, as in the passive construction, - it has no effect on the transitivity of the clause. The transitivity of *yaru* is, thus, higher than that of *morau*. The degree of transitivity of clauses with the giving/receiving verbs is in the order of *yaru*, *kureru*, and *morau*.

The Empathy viewpoint has little to do with transitivity. Thus, although the subject of a *kureru* clause is the Agent while the indirect object gets the Empathy viewpoint, the transitivity is as unaffected as for a *yaru* construction in which the subject is not only the agent but the locus of empathy. Agentivity is the key to the degree of transitivity. This is especially true if we consider *morau* 'receive'. The strength of agentivity is an important issue here since *morau* has two agents - the subject (the receiver) is a *passive* agent while the oblique NP (the giver) is an *active* agent. The agentivity is thus split between two participants and is thus less concentrated, i.e., weaker than for *kureru* and *yaru*. (For more detail discussion see Kozai 1999a).

Kozai (1999b) has found that the degree of transitivity for these inversely corresponds to the acceptability of constructions with empathy violations. In (3) we saw that all the exceptional empathy-marking constructions were acceptable because the context - indirect discourse - involved complete control of the *described* speaker's viewpoint by the *describing* speaker. But there are other double viewpoint contexts in which one viewpoint does not have control over the other. For example, in the context of shared knowledge, the speaker cannot control entirely the hearer's viewpoint. Since the viewpoints of the speaker and the hearer agree on the information being conveyed, the status of these two viewpoints is equal. Thus, in this context, one viewpoint is not embedded into the other. Instead, the viewpoints of both participants are projected on to the shared information described. Consider the examples below:

(5) a   * *Boku ni yatta   seetaa   o anna ni yogosita.*
          I D gave1 sweater A like-that dirtied
          'How dare (you) get the sweater that (you) gave me dirty like that.'

     b.   ??*Boku ga kureta seetaa o anna ni yogosita.*

---

[6]
Volitionality and controllability are treated as separate elements to determine transitivity in my works. For example, a sentence with *kureru* 'give2' can take an imperative form, i.e., [+control], but cannot take a volitional form, i.e., [-volition]. Consider sentences below:

(i)   *Okane o kure!*   (ii)   * *Okane o kure-yoo!*
       money A give2/IMP   money A give2-VOL
       'Give (me) money!'   'Let's give (someone) money!'

I D gave2 sweater A like-that dirtied
'How dare (you) get the sweater that I gave (you) dirty like that.'

c.   *Boku ni moratta   seetaa   o anna ni   yogosita.*
         I from received sweater A like-that dirtied
         'How dare (you) get the sweater (you) received from me dirty like that.'

All these constructions violate empathy restrictions, but there is a differential scale of acceptability in the order of *morau*, *kureru*, and *yaru*, one which correlates with relative degree of weakness in transitivity. The higher the transitivity, the more restricted the Viewpoint distribution, so that empathy shift is difficult in a clause which is higher in transitivity, and it is easier in a clause lower in transitivity. For each construction with giving/receiving verbs, the acceptability of empathy shifts and the degree of transitivity are correlated.

4 Psychological Predicates

Kuroda (1973) and many others (e.g., Aoki 1986, Uehara 1998) have described the grammaticality of sentences with Japanese psychological predicates on the basis of the *person* of the grammatical subject such that we need, at least, one evidential marker for the description of a non-first person as a grammatical subject. Since a speaker cannot know exactly the internal state of other psychological entities, such an evidential marker is, hence, used when there is a conflict in empathy between the speaker and a grammatical subject. These evidential markers are the descriptive -*gar*-, the factive *no*, the hearsay *soo*, and some others, as in the examples below, which partially repeat some in (1):

(6)   a.   *Boku wa atui.*
              I   T   hot/Prs
              ' I am hot.'

      b.   * *Taro wa atui.*
              T   hot/Prs
              'Taro is hot.'

      b'.   *Taro wa atu-gatte-iru.*
              T   hot-GARing-STA/Prs

      b".   *Taro wa atui no/soo da.*
              T   hot/Prs FCT/HS Cp/Prs
              'It is true that Taro is hot./I hear that Taro is hot.'

      b"'.   *Taro wa atu-gatte-iru*   *no/soo da.*
              T   hot-GARing-STA/Prs FCT/HS Cp/Prs

Although Kuroda and others are correct in claiming that evidential markers enable the speaker to describe a third person's internal state, we can also formulate another generalization, using the notion of empathy conflict. When a non-first person's internal state is to be described, the predicate must be stativized; it has to be lower in transitivity. All adjectivals are predicates in Japanese and any adjectival is a stative. However, as in (6b'), such an adjectival predicate needs to be doubly stativized with the stativizer -*iru* when used to describe other entities' internal states. Yet, if other evidential markers are used, such as in (6b"), the adjectival does not need to be stativized. But, we have to note that among many evidentials only -*gar*- does not present any commitment of the speaker towards the description. It simply helps the speaker to express his/her observation on psychological state of other epistemic entities. This morpheme -*gar*- can be used with any other evidentials, e.g., (6b'"). However, just as mentioned, this evidential is not a committal to, but an indirect marker of a psychological state. This evidential is, thus, not necessary when a psychological predicate is used with another evidential which presents a certain degree of the speaker's commitment to the described information. Thus when a psychological predicate is used with a committal evidential marker without -*gar*- plus –*iru* for a non-first person experiencer, we can see such a construction as omitting the stativized form. This omission is also economically motivated. All committal evidential markers are either adjectivals or nouns. If it is a nominal, a copula *da* follows. So, all evidentials are statives as well as psychological predicates. However, the only noncommittal evidential -*gar*- is a verbal so that it needs to be stativized. Hence, to eliminate the need to restore stativity, the omission of -*gar*- occurs.

Mental Space theory can treat these conflicting empathy situations as follows: for (6a), the experiencer *boku* is introduced in a Base space which also functions as the Viewpoint space. From this space is built a Focus/Event space in which the propositional content is expressed. With a first person subject, the experiencer is also the perceiver who describes the event. The empathy of the experiencer and the perceiver are thus one and the same. See Figure 2.

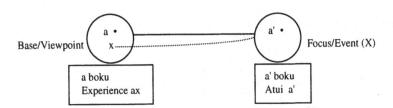

Fig. 2.

On the other hand, there are two distinct epistemic entities involved for a psychological sentence with a second or third person subject such as in (6b', b"). One is the speaker who perceives the event and the other is the subject who experiences the event. In the Base space, a speaker and a participant are introduced, which is also the Viewpoint space for the speaker to perceive the event. From this space, the other Viewpoint space for the participant is built to experience the event. These two Viewpoint spaces collaborate in building a third, blended space. Thus constructions with non-first person subjects require an additional space. (See Figure 3 below.) This is a representation of the empathy conflict and the speaker's identity is profiled linguistically marked by stativization.

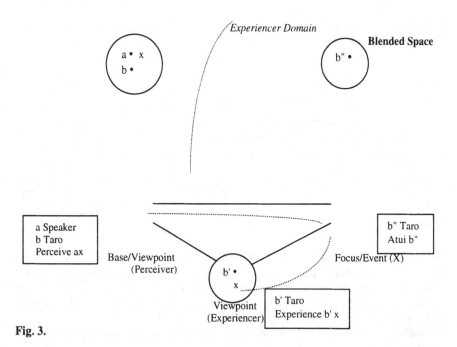

Fig. 3.

Iwasaki (1993) points out that clauses having sensation predicates without the morpheme *-gar-* are in the speaker's own perspective; with *-gar-*, the perspective is elsewhere. Following Iwasaki's distinction as to speaker's perspective, Uehara (1998:285) argues that the perspective factor is responsible for the syntactic constraints on these psychological predicate sentences.

Stativization can also occur with a first person grammatical subject. When the speaker is recalling what has happened or stipulating what will happen, the stativized psychological form is used:

(7) a. *Ano natu boku wa totemo atu-gatte-ita.*
         that summer I T very hot-GARing-STA/Pst
         'I was so hot that summer.'

     b. *Koko ga Hawai nara boku wa totemo atu-gatte-iru.*
         here N Hawaii if I T very hot-GARing-STA/Pst
         'If this is Hawaii, I am very hot.'

In these cases, the speaker is observing himself at a different point in time from the *now* of the utterance. So, he is objectifying himself. There is a conflict in empathy within the speaker - between the present speaker, and the past, the future or the hypothetical speaker. Also, note that, as we can see from the English translations, there are no explicit linguistic signs observed to index an empathy conflict within a single speaker in English. Thus the identity of speakers in English is always shaded, i.e., no empathy conflict, whereas speakers in Japanese can profile themselves even when talking about themselves. This English speakers' shading of identities, e.g., English translations of examples (6b, b'), can be schematized as in Figure 4 below:

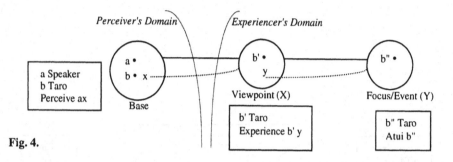

Fig. 4.

Although there are two distinct epistemic entities involved in psychological sentences, here the Base space only functions as a Viewpoint space for the speaker to introduce the experiencer. From this space in turn is built a Focus/Event space in which the non-first person's psychological state is expressed. Thus, unlike Japanese counterparts, a single Viewpoint space builds the Focus/Event space.

Finally, we will consider one other class of empathy-prominent predicates, the cognitive verbs.

5 Cognitive Verbs

Not only the knowledge of sensations but also the knowledge of cognitive states of other animate entities cannot be attributed to a speaker.

(8)   a.   *Boku wa soo omou.*
             I T so think/Prs
          'I think so.'

    a'.   * *Boku wa soo omotte-iru.*
             I   T so thinking-STA/Prs

    b.   * *Taro wa soo omou.*
               T so think/Prs
          'Taro thinks so.'

    b'.   *Taro wa soo omotte-iru.*
               T so thinking-STA/Prs

Iwasaki (1993:22-28) pointing out this phenomenon, explains the stativization of verbs of cognition by noting that when predicates denoting the internal state of animate entities are stativized, i.e., lower in transitivity, the information is presented as less accessible for the speaker. Since cognitive predicates are verbs, they do not need -gar- to be stativized, e.g., *omou* 'think' in (8b').

Thus, except for the suffixation of -gar-, all other facts observed with psychological predicates in the previous section apply to these verbs of cognition. When there is an empathy conflict, as with non-first person grammatical subjects, the speaker has to profile his/her identity by stativization of the predicate, as in (8b'), whereas such profiling of the speaker's identity is prohibited with first person subjects, as in (8a'). So as with psychological predicates such as (7a, b), when the speaker objectifies him/herself, stativized forms of the cognitive verbs are used with first person subjects. However, unlike psychological predicates, cognitive verbs may be stativized to describe the speaker of *now*, as in (9), when the speaker takes less commitment for what s/he cognizes (Personal communication with J. Haig). Because cognitive activities are controllable by the cognizer whereas psychological states are not controlled by the experiencer, the cline of commitment for what s/he feels cannot be allowed at the time of the utterance.

(9)   *Sukunakute-mo boku wa soo omou/omotte-iru.*

        little-even   I   T   so   think/thinking-STA/Prs
        'At least, I think so.'

Mental Space theory analysis of the cognitive verbs is essentially the same as for the psychological predicates. Where there is no empathy conflict, the cognizer is introduced in the Base/Viewpoint space and a Focus/Event space is built for the propositional content. With a first person subject, the cognizer and the perceiver are the same entity and no empathy conflict occurs; the speaker does not need to use stativization to profile his/her identity. (See Figure 5 below for the example (8 a).)

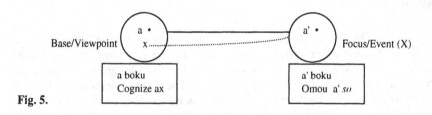

Fig. 5.

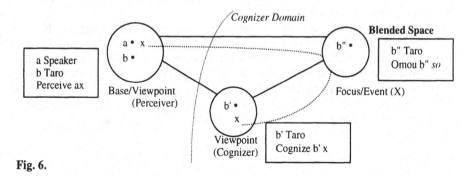

Fig. 6.

But the cognizer and the perceiver are distinct epistemic entities for second or third person subjects. One is the speaker who perceives the event and the other is the subject who cognizes the state. Thus another space is needed to profile the perceiver's identity prior to creating the Viewpoint space of the cognizer. (See Figure 6 for the example (8 b').)

On the other hand, the speaker's conflicting identity is, again, not profiled in English as we saw in the examples for psychological predicates in (6). The Focus/Event space is only created from the Viewpoint space of a cognizer, which is built from the Base space that is also the Viewpoint space for the perceiver. See Figure 7 for English translation of (8b):

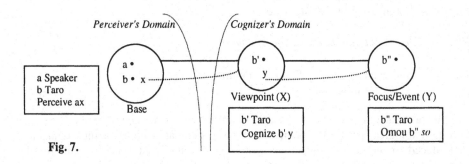

Fig. 7.

6 Summary

There are three kinds of empathy prominent predicates in Japanese in which the speaker's identity must be profiled if there is a conflict in empathy. This is achieved either by shifting the appropriate participant to a non-designated location for empathy-marking or by stativization of predicates. Where the subjects are first person forms, stativization is not allowed because there is no empathy conflict between the speaker and the referent of the subject. If the speaker objectifies him/herself, the profiling of a speaker's identity is possible. There are, however, no such constraints in English regarding speaker's identity.

We have accounted, in a unified way, for such conflicting identities between speakers and empathy-marked participants. When there is a conflict, an additional Viewpoint space is created, and the two Viewpoint spaces merge into a blended space. We have also found that transitivity and the profiling of a speaker's identity are strongly related: empathy violations in clauses of low transitivity are more acceptable than those in clauses of high transitivity. Psychological predicates and cognitive verbs are stativized when there is a conflict in empathy of the clause.

References

1. Aoki Haruo: Evidentials in Japanese. In: Chafe, W. and J. Nichols (eds.): Evidentiality: The Linguistic Coding of Epistemology. Ablex, Norwood, NJ (1986) 223-238
2. Coulson, Seana: Menendez Brothers Virus: Blended Spaces and Internet Humor. In: A. E. Goldberg (ed.): Conceptual Structure, Discourse and Language. CSLI Publications, Stanford, CA (1996) 67-81
3. Fauconnier, Gilles: Mental Spaces. Cambridge University Press, Cambridge New York (1994)
4. ___: Mappings in Thought and Language. Cambridge University Press, Cambridge New York (1997)
5. Fauconnier, Gilles. and M. Turner: Blending as a Central Process of Grammar. In: A. E. Goldberg (ed.): Conceptual Structure, Discourse and Language. CSLI Publications, Stanford, CA (1996) 113-130
6. Goldberg, E. Adele: A Construction Grammar Approach to Argument Structure. University of Chicago Press, Chicago (1995)
7. Hopper, J. Paul. and S. A. Thompson: Transitivity in Grammar and Discourse. Language (1980) 56(2):251-299
8. Iwasaki, Shoichi: Subjectivity in Grammar and Discourse. John Benjamins, Philadelphia (1993)
9. Jackendoff, Ray: Believing and Intending: Two Sides of the Same Coin. Linguistic Inquiry (1985) 16(3):445-460
10. Jacobs, Roderick: English Syntax: A Grammar for English Language Professionals Oxford University Press, Oxford New York (1995)
11. Kozai, Soichi: Three Types of Viewpoint - Empathy, Subjective, and Agentive: A Case Study from Japanese Giving and Receiving Verbs. In: Proceedings of Deseret Language and Linguistic Society Symposium 1999. Brigham Young University, Utah (1999a)
12. ___: Transitivity and Viewpoint in Japanese Giving and Receiving Verbs. In: Proceedings of Second Annual High Desert Student Conference in Linguistics. University of New Mexico, New Mexico (1999b)
13. ___: Blended Viewpoints: A Mental Space Analysis of Japanese Predicates. Paper Presented at Sixth International Cognitive Linguistic Conference. Stockholm University, Stockholm, Sweden (1999c)
14. ___: Viewpoint and Speech Attitude (Arrogance or Modesty) in Japanese: An Integrated Approach of Mental Space and Transitivity. In: Proceedings of The Fourth Conference of The Japanese Association of Sociolinguistic Sciences. Japan Women's University, Tokyo, Japan (1999d)
15. ___: Viewpoint Blending: A Mental Space Analysis of Japanese Donatory Verbs. In: Proceedings o The Second International Conference on Cognitive Science and The 16th Annual Meeting of the Japanese Cognitive Science Society. Waseda University, Tokyo, Japan (1999e)
16. Kuno, Susumu: Functional Syntax. University of Chicago Press, Chicago New York (1987)
17. Kuno, Susumu. and E. Kaburaki: Empathy and Syntax. Linguistic Inquiry (1977) 8(4):627-672
18. Kuroda, S.-Y.: Where Epistemology, Style, and Grammar Meet: A Case Study from Japanese. In: Anderson, S. R. and P. Kiparsky (eds.): A Festschrift for Morris Halle. Holt, Rinehart & Winston, New York (1973) 377-391
19. Lyons, John: Semantics. Vol. 2. Cambridge University Press, Cambridge New York (1977)
20. Shibatani, Masayoshi: Where Analogical Patterning Fails. Papers in Japanese Linguistics (1979) 6:287-307
21. Uehara, Satoshi: Pronoun Drop and Perspective in Japanese. Japanese/Korean Linguistics (1998) 7:275-289
22. Wetzel, J. Patricia: In-Group/Out-Group Deixis: Situational Variation in the Verbs of Giving and Receiving in Japanese. In: Forgas, J. (ed.): Language and Social Situations. Springer-Verlag, Berlin Heidelberg New York (1985) 141-157

On the Role of Context in Relevance-Based Accessibility Ranking of Candidate Referents[1]

Tomoko Matsui

International Christian University
Division of Languages
3-10-2 Osawa
Mitaka, Tokyo, 181 JAPAN
matsui@icu.ac.jp

Abstract. It is now a standard view that candidate referents are ranked according to their accessibility, based on either or both of the discourse structure and organisation of general knowledge. Various models of reference resolution based on such a view, including centering theory, have been ardently pursued and tested empirically, and the ones which are computationally workable have been given preferences in the past. In this paper, I propose an alternative view on accessibility ranking based on the consideration of relevance. Although it has not been tested computational• • , certain advantages over existing discourse-based approaches are demonstrated. It is suggested that one possible start to test the present approach computationally is to focus on the use of discourse connectives which constrain contextual assumptions by directing the way an utterance is likely to achieve relevance.

1 Introduction

Successful reference resolution involves the task of choosing the intended referent among several possible candidates. There are two fundamental assumptions generally shared about this task: (a) that such candidate referents are ranked according to their accessibility (or salience); (b) that the highest ranked should be the one chosen by the hearer. So far, two claims have been made as to how to determine accessibility ranking. The first and the currently most pursued is the idea that it is determined by sentence/discourse structure (Erku & Gundel 1987; Fretheim & Gundel 1996; Gernsbacher & Hargreaves 1988; Grosz et al. 1995; Sidner 1983a, b; Walker et al. 1998). The second, which is quite independent from, but also compatible with, the first, is the view that knowledge structure affects such a ranking, particularly by determining the accessibility of contextual assumptions (Fincher-Kiefer 1993; Kintch 1998; Magliano et al. 1993; McKoon & Ratcliff 1992; Sanford & Garrod 1981; Singer 1993).

---

[1] This is a revised version of the paper presented at the workshop of the Relation of Discourse/Dialogue Structure and Reference, ACL '99. I would like to thank the participants of the workshop for their invaluable comments. I would also like to thank the anonymous referees for their encouragements and helpful suggestions on an earlier version of this paper. All remaining inadequacies are mine.

In this paper, I would like to propose a third alternative, based on the hypothesis put forward by Sperber & Wilson that human communication is relevance-oriented (Sperber & Wilson 1986/1995). This particular view of communication predicts (a) that the overall interpretation of an utterance ultimately chosen by the hearer is the optimally relevant one (as defined below), and (b) the reference is resolved automatically as a by-product of pursuit of such an interpretation (Matsui 1993, 1995, 1998; Wilson 1992; Wilson & Matsui 1998). In this approach, the overall accessibility of candidate referents is determined both by accessibility based on linguistic/textual structure, and accessibility based on knowledge organisation. Both factors are seen to contribute to overall effort to process an utterance. Moreover, the current approach is crucially different from existing accounts in that it claims that the choice based on overall accessibility ranking still needs to be scrutinised in terms of whether the overall interpretation is likely to achieve adequate cognitive effects. Thus, in this approach, it is predicted that the accessibility ranking of candidate referents can still be altered as a result of the pursuit of cognitive effects.

In what follows, I will illustrate how the present approach differs from other existing account, and how it might complement their shortcomings, by comparing it with centering theory (Grosz et al. 1995; Walker et al. 1998), a prototypical example of discourse-based approaches to reference resolution. In particular, I will focus on the examples of Japanese zero pronoun resolution (Walker et al. 1994), for which the necessary heuristics have been well worked out. At present, however, unlike centering-based approaches to reference resolution, a relevance-based alternative has not been tested as a workable computational system. I will conclude the paper with a suggestion based on empirical data that, in order to test the validity of the reference-based approach computationally, the use of discourse connectives which constrain accessible contextual assumptions for utterance interpretation in advance might prove to be a practically achievable and at the same time effective way.

2 Comparison Between Two Approaches
2.1 Discourse-Based Accessibility Ranking: Centering Theory

The structure of discourse can be characterised by the notion of coherence (Hobbs 1978, 1985; Hovy 1990). One of the goals of centering theory is to sort out the various mechanisms used to maintain discourse coherence, and the use of various referring expressions is regarded as one such mechanism. Among the various hypotheses put forward by centering theory, what concerns us most is the following: that 'each utterance [except the initial utterance] in a coherent discourse segment contains a single semantic entity - the backward-looking center [or Cb] - that provides a link to the previous utterance, and an ordered set of entities - the forward-looking centers [or Cf] - that offer potential links to the next utterance'(Gordon et al. 1993:311). There are two rules to provide constraints on choosing centers, which are shown in (1):

(1)   Rule 1: If any element of Cf (Un) is realised by a pronoun in Un+1
             then the Cb (Un+1) must be realised by a pronoun also.

> Rule 2: Sequences of continuation are preferred over sequences of retaining; and sequences of retaining are to be preferred over sequences of shifting.

The first rule states that the most highly ranked element of the forward-looking center of a previous utterance is the backward-looking center of the current utterance, and must be realised by a pronoun if any element of the Cf of the previous utterance is realised by a pronoun in the current utterance. The following example from Gordon et al. (1993), shown here in (2), illustrates this rule:

(2)   [1]   Susan gave Betsy a pet hamster.
              Cf={Susan, Betsy, hamster 1}
       [2]   She reminded her such hamsters were quite shy.
              Cb=Susan; Cf={Susan, Betsy, hamsters}
       [3]   She asked Betsy whether she liked the gift.
              Cb=Susan; Cf={Susan, Betsy, gift=hamser 1}
       [3']   Susan asked her whether she liked the gift.

Here, the first utterance has no Cb because it is the initial sentence of a discourse. Its Cf includes the referents of 'Susan' and 'Betsy' and the semantic interpretation of 'a hamster', ranked in that order. The second utterance has Susan as the Cb and a Cf with Susan as its most highly ranked element. The third utterance preserves the Cb and prominent Cf from the previous utterance, therefore it pronominalises the Cb successfully. By contrast, utterance [3'], in which Susan is realised by a name and Betsy is realised by a pronoun, leads to stylistic infelicity. According to Gordon et al., this is due to violation of Rule 1 mentioned above.

The ranking of forward-looking centers is generally based on the discourse salience of each candidate entity. According to Grosz et al. (1995), although an ultimate criteria for deciding the ranking has not been worked out yet, there is evidence to support the idea that grammatical role such as SUBJECT, OBJECT, etc., can affect the Cf ranking. Thus, I will simply assume here the following preference in ranking forward-looking center shown in (3), as suggested by Grosz et al. (ibid.):

(3)   SUBJECT>OBJECT>OTHERS

The highest ranked member of the set of forward-looking centers is called the 'preferred center', or 'Cp'. As mentioned above, Cp is regarded as the most likely candidate for Cb in the following utterance.

Another important claim made by centering theory is that discourse segments are more coherent if they share the same Cb. On the basis of this idea, different degrees of coherence are proposed. For example, Walker et al. adopt the following 4 types of transition between discourse segments, each corresponding to different degree of coherence, using the notion of Cb and Cp; namely, 'continue', 'retain', 'smooth-shift' and 'rough-shift'. These are shown in (4). When two utterances, say Ui-1 and U share the same Cb, and the same entity is also the highest-ranked Cf, i.e. Cp, in Ui-1, the transition from Ui-1 to Ui is called 'continue'. When Ui-1 and Ui share the same Cb, but the same entity is not the highest-ranked Cf in Ui, the transition is called 'retain'. When Ui-1 and Ui do not share the same Cb, there are two possibilities: if Cb in Ui is the same as Cp in Ui, the transition is 'smooth-shift'; if Cb in Ui is not the same as Cp in Ui, it is 'rough-shift'. It is claimed that when the hearer has to choose one from several possible interpretations, the one based on the most coherent transition should be chosen. The 4 transition states are ordered in the following way according to their preference:

(4)   CONTINUE>RETAIN>SMOOTH-SHIFT>ROUGH-SHIFT

The second of the two rules is about the ordered preference of these transition states, although there were only 3 types of transition states in the original formulation by Grosz et al. (1983, 1995), namely, CONTINUE, RETAIN and SHIFT.

2.2 Some Problems with the Centering-Based Approach: The Case of Japanese Zero Pronoun Resolution

Now I would like to discuss some problems with the centering approach, using Walker et al.'s analysis of the Japanese zero pronoun. Needless to say, it has great advantages, such as relative ease of computational implementation. Moreover, I agree that accessibility of discourse entities plays an important role in reference assignment, and their forward center ranking is an adequate enough approximation of accessibility of discourse entities in different grammatical categories in Japanese. However, as I mentioned before, there are cases whose interpretation process cannot possibly be explained by the accessibility factor alone. Accounts of reference assignment which are largely based on accessibility of discourse entities tend to exhibit their weaknesses when they face cases which require some pragmatic inferences, and Walker et al. is not an exception here. I will illustrate two problems they need to solve below.

Walker et al. (1994) propose the following ranking order of forward-looking center to deal with Japanese:

(5)   (Grammatical or Zero) TOPIC > EMPATHY > SUBJECT >
         OBJECT2 > OBJECT> OTHERS

As you can see, they add two new grammatical roles, namely, topic and empathy, to the list of factors affecting pronoun resolution. Since the notion of topic will become important in the discussion which follows, I will briefly describe the Japanese topic marker below. For empathy-loaded verbs, please refer to Kuno 1987 and Kuno & Kaburaki 1977.

In Japanese, both in written and spoken discourse, NPs which can be recovered from context are often omitted. The omitted NPs are often called 'zero pronouns'. It is widely agreed that missing NPs in Japanese behave like pronouns in other languages such as English. Japanese zero pronouns should be distinguished from missing NPs in 'pro-drop' languages such as Italian, since in 'pro-drop' languages, information to recover missing NPs is morphologically encoded elsewhere in the sentence, e.g. in the form of verb inflection, whereas Japanese lacks such an overt encoding.

There are several postpositional particles in Japanese. The one we are interested in here is 'wa', which is often called a 'topic marker'. As the name suggests, 'wa' is typically used to construct a grammatical topic of a sentence, which is characterised as an entity whose existence is presupposed. The function of 'wa' might become clearer when it is compared with another particle 'ga', which marks a NP in the subject position, which typically conveys new information. Compare (6a) and (6b):

(6)   a. *John ga hana o katta.*
         SUB flowers ACC bought
         'John bought flowers.'
        b. *John wa hana o katta.*
         TOP flowers ACC bought
      'John bought flowers.'

(6a) and (6b) share the same propositional content. However, only (6a) is acceptable as an answer to the question such as 'Who bought flowers?' while only (6b) is acceptable as an answer to the question such as 'What did John buy?'. There are various suggestions about how to characterise functions of the two particles (see e.g. Shibatani 1990; Tanaka 1991), and although it is an interesting question on its own, it shouldn't concern us here. This is because Walker et al. are only interested in the surface form of 'NP+wa', which is automatically given the highest accessibility ranking in their framework.

One of the most important claims by Walker et al. is that a topic NP is more likely to be realised as a zero pronoun in the subsequent discourse than any other NPs due to its highest degree of accessibility. Moreover, in Walker et al.'s framework, topic NP is given two further advantages: they suggest (a) that a NP marked by 'wa' becomes the backward-looking center even at the onset of the discourse; and (b) that once topic NP is realised as the backward-looking center, as long as it continues to be realised as a zero pronoun in subsequent discourse, it could continue to be the backward-looking center. The second advantage given to the topic NP is called 'zero topic assignment', which is defined as in (7):

(7)   Zero Topic Assignment (ZTA) (optional)
        When a zero in Ui+1 represents an entity that was Cb (Ui), and when no other CONTINUE transition is available, that zero may be interpreted as the ZERO TOPIC of Ui+1

Walker et al. demonstrate that their framework, including an optional rule of zero topic assignment, can successfully explain the preference in the interpretation of the last sentence in (8):

(8)   [1]   *Hanako wa siken o oete, kyooshitu ni modorimashita.*
                TOP exam ACC finish classroom to returned
                'Hanako returned to the classroom, finishing her exams'
                Cb=Hanako; Cf={Hanako, exam}

[2]   0 *hon o rokka ni shimaimashita.*
          book ACC locker in took-away
          '(She) put her books in the locker'
          Cb=Hanako; Cf={Hanako, book} [CONTINUE]

[3]   *itsumo no yooni Michiko ga* 0 *mondai no tokikata o*
          always like   SUB questions solve-way ACC
          setumeishimashita.
          explained
          'Michiko, as usual, explained (to her) how to answer questions.'
          Cb=Hanako;
          Cf1={Hanako, Michiko ...} ZTA [CONTINUE]
          Cf2={Michiko, Hanako, ...}   [RETAIN]

[4]   0 0 *ohiru ni sasoimashita*
          lunch to invited
          '(She) invited (her) to lunch'
          Cb1= Hanako;
          Cf1={Hanako, lunch, Michiko} [CONTINUE]from [3]-Cf1
          Cb2=Michiko
          Cf2={Michiko, lunch, Hanako} [S-SHIFT]from [3]-Cf2

According to the questionnaire carried out by Walker et al., the preferred interpretation of [4] is that Hanako invited Michiko to lunch. As you can see, in fact, there are two possible ways of ranking forward-looking center in [3], and two possible ways of deciding both the backward-looking center and the ranking of forward-looking center in [4]. In their analysis of (8), the preference in the interpretation in [4] is explained by zero topic assignment in [3] and preference on 'continue' transition in [4].

2.2.1 Multiple topics

One of the most obvious shortcomings of Walker et al.'s approach is that it cannot handle situations where there is more than one topic in a sentence. In their framework, in order to identify zero pronouns, the backward-looking center has to be identified first. The backward-looking center, in turn, is determined by the way forward-looking centers are ranked. Therefore, the most powerful mechanism in their framework is the forward-looking center ranking shown in (18) above. However, notice that it is only useful if there is no more than one entity in each category in a sentence.

    Let us concentrate on the category of topic here. In Walker et al.'s framework, the topic marker 'wa' is given a special status: the topic marker 'wa' is so powerful that the topic NP becomes the most highly ranked forward-looking center even at the onset of a discourse; in addition, once a topic NP is realised as the backward-looking center, as long as it continues to be realised as zero pronoun in subsequent discourse, it could continue to be the backward-looking center. This status of the topic NP rightly allows the possibility of multiple topics as in (9), which is very often seen in Japanese discourse:

(9)   [1]   *Mary to Jane wa shinyuu da*
                and TOP best friends are
                'Mary and Jane are each other's best friend.'

        [2]   *Senshuu no Doyoubi, Mary wa kaze o hiite nete-ita*
                last week GEN Saturday TOP cold ACC had lying-was
                'Last Saturday, Mary had a cold and was lying on the bed.'

        [3]   *Itsumo no youni, Jane wa ohiru goro denwa shita.*
                always GEN as   TOP noon around telephone did
                'As always, Jane phoned (Mary) around noon.

        [4]   0 0 *eiga ni sasou tsumori datta.*
                    film to invite planning to was
                    '(She) was planning to invite (her) to a film.'

However, cases of multiple topics case a serious problem to Walker et al. Here, the preferred interpretation of [4] is that Jane was planning to invite Mary to a film. Walker et al. might explain this preference by saying that this is because 'Jane' is the backward-looking center in [4]. According to their framework, however, the alternative interpretation, namely, that Mary was planning to invite Jane to a film, is equally accessible, since 'Mary' could continue to be the backward-looking center in [4]. The problem is that in their current framework, Walker et al. do not provide any mechanism to choose one interpretation and discard the other.

There is another problem concerning multiplicity of entities with equal degree of accessibility. In Japanese, post positional particles such as 'wa' and 'ga' shouldn't be used more than once in a sentence. Thus, you wouldn't come across sentences with two overtly marked topics or subjects. However, it is possible to have more than one NP with more or less equal salience in one sentence, for example, when two nouns, the first being a modifier and the second being the head noun, form a NP. A noun modifier is followed by a particle 'no', the Genitive Case particle. Some examples of NPs which contain noun modifiers are shown in (10):

(10)   a. *Mary no tomodachi*
            GEN friend
        'Mary's friend'
        b. *Niwa   no ki*
           garden GEN tree
        'A tree in the garden'
        c. *Tegami no henji*
           letter GEN reply
        'A reply to the letter'

Here, the first noun in each NP is the modifier. The most typical relation exhibited between two nouns combined by the particle 'no' is the 'possessive' relation, as in (10a). However, the use of 'no' is by no means restricted to that relation, as illustrated in (10b) and (10c). Now consider (11), which include a NP with this structure:

(11)   (A memo written by a man, and addressed to his wife)
        [1]   *Kooto no botan ga   toreta.*

coat GEN button SUB came off
'One of the buttons of (my) coat has come off'

[2]   0 0 *sagashi-temo,*   0 *mitsukaranakatta.*
      search-although   was not found
      '(I) tried to find (it), but failed.'

[3]   *Kyou jyuu ni 0 0 0 sagashite tsukete-hoshii.*
      today within at   find   fix -want
      '(I) want (you) to find and fix (it) today.

[4]   *Ashita 0 0 hitsuyou da.*
      tomorrow need
      'Tomorrow, (I) will need (it)'

Here, in [1], 'one of the buttons of my coat' is introduced as the subject of the sentence. What is important here is that the NP introduces two conceptual entities, namely, a 'coat' and a 'button', which are equally accessible. The question is whether Walker et al.'s framework can handle cases like (11). For [2], the preferred interpretation is that the speaker wants his wife to find and fix the button today. Walker et al.'s system would successfully predict that the button is the backward-center for [2] and [3]. However, for [4], the preferred interpretation is that the speaker will need his coat tomorrow, rather than the button. I do not see how Walker et al. can explain this. The point I would like to make here is that there are many cases in Japanese discourse where there is more than one roughly equally salient discourse entity in a sentence which subsequently become equally strong candidate referents for zero pronouns, and some mechanism of choosing the right one is needed.

2.2.2 Ordered preference of transition states

Now I would like to move on to a different kind of problem, which concerns their ordered preference of transition states shown in (4). Walker et al., as well as centering theorists in general, assume that when there is more than one possible overall interpretation available, the one which exhibits 'continue' transition is preferred. This is based on the assumption that maximally coherent segments are those that require less processing effort and the hearer will prefer an interpretation which requires less processing effort. However, it is not difficult to think of examples which go against their assumption. For example, look at (12):

(12)   [1]   *John wa joushi ni atama ga agaranai.*
                TOP boss with head SUB hold-not
                'John cannot hold up his head before his boss (i.e. John
                cannot help feeling ashamed of himself in front of his boss).
    [2]   *Itsumo 0 kaisha ni 0 saki ni kuru.*
                always office to   earlier come
                '(He) always comes to the office earlier (than him).'
                a. (John) always comes to the office earlier (than his boss).
                b. (John's boss) always comes to the office than (John).

Here, the preferred interpretation for [2] is definitely [2b]. However, Walker et al. predict that [2a] should be preferred. Obviously, their mechanism based on the accessibility of transition states makes wrong predictions. In the next section, I will consider why this is the case.

2.3 Relevance Theory

Sperber & Wilson's relevance theory (Sperber & Wilson 1986/95) inherits the Gricean assumption that the hearer's goal of verbal understanding is to find an interpretation intended by the speaker. However, it differs from Gricean approach in two crucial points: it does not take the view that we have to follow maxims, nor the view that we have to be co-operative, to achieve successful communication. Sperber & Wilson claim that what makes communication achievable at all is a fundamental mechanism built in our cognitive system, namely, the pursuit of relevance. This is expressed as the First, or Cognitive, Principle of Relevance:

(13)   *Cognitive Principle of Relevance*
         Human Cognition tends to be geared to the maximisation of relevance.

The notion of relevance is defined in terms cognitive effects, i.e. some changes in the belief system, and processing effort to obtain such effects:

(14)   *Relevance*
         a. The greater the cognitive effects, the greater the relevance;
         b. The smaller the effort needed to achieve those effects, the greater the relevance.

Cognitive effects result from the interaction of new and old (or contextual) information in one of the following three ways: (a) combining with an existing assumption to yield contextual implications; (b) strengthening an existing assumption; (c) contradicting and eliminating an existing assumption. Processing effort is the mental effort needed to parse the utterance, decide what proposition and propositional attitude it was intended to express, access an appropriate context, and work out the contextual effects of the utterance in the context. When an utterance has more than one possible interpretation, the hearer should look for the one which satisfies the following conditions of optimal relevance:

(15)   *Optimal relevance*
         An utterance is optimally relevant to the hearer iff:
         a. it is relevant enough to be worth the hearer's processing effort;
         b. it is the most relevant one compatible with the speaker's abilities and preferences.

The Second, or Communicative Principle of Relevance, governs this search process:

(16)   *Communicative Principle of Relevance*

Every utterance communicates a presumption of its own optimal relevance.

The pursuit of optimally relevant interpretation suggests a pattern of comprehension procedure the hearer should follow, which can be spelled out as (17):

(17)   *Relevance-theoretic comprehension procedure*
        a. consider cognitive effects in their order of accessibility (i.e. follow a path of least effort);
        b. stop when the expected level of relevance is achieved.

2.4 Discussion: A Relevance-Theoretic Solution to Walker et al.'s Problems

Now let me illustrate how this comprehension procedure should work for Japanese zero pronoun resolution illustrated in (11) and (12). In Matsui (1995, 1998, also Wilson and Matsui 1998), I have developed the idea proposed by Wilson (1992) that in addition to the factor of accessibility of candidate referents, there is another important factor which affects the hearer's choice of referent, namely, accessibility of contextual assumptions. Accessibility of contextual assumptions becomes particularly crucial when there is more than one roughly equally accessible candidate referent, and it is the factor which is vital to solve problems with Walker et al.. In fact, the importance of contextual assumptions in reference resolution had been recognised before and various proposals were made as to how to retrieve the right context: some appeal to situationally partitioned knowledge (e.g. Sanford & Garrod 1981) and others are motivated by textual coherence (e.g. Hobbs 1978; Asher & Lascarides 1993). The account pursued here is different from any existing accounts in that it claims that the selection of contextual assumptions is ordered in terms of *both their accessibility and likeliness to contribute towards the cognitive effects of the utterance*. In other words, in relevance theory, it is assumed that these candidate referents are tested in parallel, with the one which gives quickest access to a context in which the utterance as a whole yields an acceptable overall interpretation being selected.

As a working hypothesis, let us assume that certain contextual assumptions are accessed by the hearer after the immediately preceding utterance is processed, during and after the current utterance is being processed. I have no specific claim here concerning what triggers the retrieval or the construction of certain contextual assumptions, and can go along with existing suggestions (e.g. it can be triggered by lexical information, or/and by situational knowledge). As the second working hypothesis, I would like to suggest that after having understood an utterance, the hearer tends to have, if not always, fairly accurate expectation as to what kind of cognitive effects he would like to obtain from the next utterance. Relevance theory predicts that when an utterance creates in the hearer an expectation for a specific cognitive effect to be achieved by the next utterance, other things being equal, the hearer is more likely to spend his processing effort to find an interpretation which can achieve such cognitive effect when interpreting the utterance. As a consequence, the candidate referent which is not the highest in the general accessibility ranking can become the most accessible to the hearer if the referent is expected to contribute to the interpretation he is looking for. In other words, relevance theory predicts the alteration of accessibility ranking of the candidate referents as a result of the pursuit of certain cognitive effects.

Consider example (11) in the context discussed above. In (11), the utterance in [3] is a request to the wife to find and fix the missing button of the speaker's coat before tomorrow. Generally, if someone asks you to do something by certain time, there should be a good reason for such a time limit, since the time limit in turn may create certain priority. Thus, it should be reasonable to assume that after hearing the utterance in [3], the question such as 'why do I have to do it today?' or 'can't it wait a little while?' occurred in the hearer's mind. If so, the utterance in [4] can readily be interpreted as the reason why he made such a request: he wants to wear the coat on the following day. The referent is assigned automatically during the process of finding expected the cognitive effects. Of course, what he needs is the coat with the button fixed, and this interpretation is only possible with the overall interpretation in which the 'coat', rather than the 'button', is the referent of the zero pronoun.

The interpretation of (12) might be explained like this. After processing the first utterance, certain assumptions might become moderately accessible (but not necessarily at the conscious level) to the hearer: e.g. various assumptions about John and his boss, and more general assumptions about 'being ashamed of', e.g. that one must feel unhappy about such situation, or that one must have specific reasons for such feeling, etc. In this way, *contextual assumptions might contribute to form the hearer's anticipation about the way subsequent utterances achieve relevance.* When the hearer interprets the second utterance in (12), further assumptions related to the event described, such as that 'workers are encouraged to come to work early', or 'bosses like their workers to arrive before them' etc., might become highly accessible. Such assumptions contribute to the hearer's search for the way the utterance could achieve cognitive effects. At the final stage of the interpretation process, the hearer finds the only way in which the second utterance in (12) might be intended to achieve relevance in a context created by the first - namely, as an explanation for why John cannot help feeling ashamed of himself in front of his boss - and the zero-pronouns are resolved automatically in the process.

Furthermore, notice that as a consequence of using the notion of accessibility of contextual assumptions, an ad hoc system such as the ordered preference in transition states in Walker et al.'s account becomes automatically unnecessary. For example, our framework could easily accommodate cases such as (12), where the referent of a zero pronoun in the current discourse is not the same as that of a zero pronoun in the preceding discourse, as well as cases where the most accessible candidate referent indeed coincides with the referent chosen on the basis of the preferred overall interpretation. Recall that the ordered transition states is created on the basis of the assumption that the hearer prefers an interpretation which exhibits 'continue' relation, because such an interpretation requires less processing effort. I suggest that this assumption is ultimately wrong for the following reason: *the preferred interpretation by the hearer is the one which provides enough cognitive effects worth his processing effort, rather than the one which merely requires less processing effort.* Walker et al. would predict that the preferred interpretation for the second sentence in (12) is that 'John always comes to his office earlier than his boss.' The question we have to ask here is: how could this interpretation possibly achieve relevance? I cannot easily see how. Relevance theory predicts that such interpretation will never be considered when there is an alternative interpretation accessible which achieves relevance, even if the latter might require more processing effort. Notice here that the relevance theory shares the view that the intended interpretation should be the most accessible one for the hearer. However, in the framework of relevance theory, *it is accessibility of contextual assumptions, together with the accessibility of contextual referents, that determines the overall accessibility of an interpretation.* In this way, the fact that the preferred interpretation of the second sentence in (12) is more accessible overall for most of us, than the alternative interpretation, is adequately explained in this framework.

3. A Way Forward: Use of Discourse Connectives

Needless to say, an expectation of specific cognitive effects cannot be generated in everyone by every utterance. However, for a speaker, such expectation is something to be better manipulated than ignored in order to make communication successful. As demonstrated in the study of bridging reference in Matsui (1995), discourse connectives such as 'however', 'nevertheless' and 'you see' play a role to create exactly such an expectation. One of the questionnaires used in Matsui (ibid.) which was designed to test the preference for one of the alternative candidate referents includes the pairs of examples (18) to (20):

(18a) I prefer Italy to England. I hate the pasta there.
(18b) I prefer Italy to England. *However*, I hate the pasta there.

(19a) Sara left Australia for England. She loves the sandy beaches.
(19b) Sara left Australia for England. *Nevertheless*, she loves the sandy beaches.

(20a) Kevin moved from New Zealand to England. He hates the sheep.
(20b) Kevin moved from New Zealand to England. *You see*, he hates the sheep.

24 subjects, first year linguistics students at UCL, were asked read short passages such as the examples above and answer questions which ask which of the two candidates is the intended referent. The results for (18) to (20) are as follows:

(18a) Italy   20%   England 80%
(18b) Italy   100%   England   0%

(19a) Australia 20%   England 80%
(19b) Australia 80%   England 20%

(20a) New Zealand 60% England 40%
(20b) New Zealand 100% England   0%

The results for (18) might be explained as follows: after hearing the first sentence in (18a) and (18b), the question such as 'why the speaker prefers Italy' is likely to have been occurred to the hearer; the information communicated by the second sentence cannot be the reason why she prefers Italy, but can, after some thought, be the reason why she dislikes England; hence the hearer of (18a) chose 'England' as the place where the speaker hates the pasta; on the other hand, 'however' in (18b) plays a role to alter the hearer's expectation: now the hearer expects to hear something which will contradict the information conveyed by the first utterance; the interpretation that the speaker hates the pasta in Italy, although she prefers the country to England, fits the expectation. 'The sandy beaches' in (19a) was interpreted by the majority as being in England presumably because subjects interpreted the second part as either the reason of Sara's moving or the consequence of such moving. In (19b), however, 'nevertheless' seems to have blocked such interpretations. In (20a), the subjects' choice of referent was split: it suggests that the interpretation in which the second part explains the event described by the first is equally accessible as the interpretation in which the second part describes the consequence of the event described by the first. In (20b), by contrast, with 'you see' at the beginning of the second part, only the explanation-interpretation becomes accessible. In a relevance-theoretic framework, discourse connectives are seen as facilitating the pursuit of optimal relevance by imposing constraints, in advance, on the type of contextual effects the hearer should look for (Blakemore 1987, 1992). For example, 'however' and 'nevertheless' introduce an utterance which is intended to achieve relevance by contradicting and eliminating existing assumptions. On the other hand, 'you see' introduces an utterance which achieves its congnitive effects by strengthening existing assumptions. I would like to suggest that in order to facilitate a computational model of reference assignment's ability to account for the use of context when the content of the utterance itself does not provide any bias towards specific congnitive effects, ultimately, the model needs to incorporate ways to manipulate the hearer's expectations (such as the discourse connectives) which inevitably affect the accessibility of contextual assumptions.

References

1. Asher, N. & Lascarides, A.: Lexical Disambiguation in a Discourse Context. In: Journal of Semantics 12. (1993) 69-108.
2. Blakemore, D.: Semantic Constraints on Relevance. Blackwell, Oxford (1987)
3. Blakemore, D.: Understanding Utterances. Blackwell, Oxford (1992)
4. Erku, F. & Gundel, J.: Indirect anaphors. In: J. Verschueren and M. Bertuccelli-Papi (eds): The Pragmatic Perspective. Benjamins, Amsterdam (1987) 533-546
5. Fincher-Kiefer, R.: The Role of Predictive Inferences in Situational Model Construction. In: Discourse Processes 16. (1993) 99-124
6. Fretheim, T & Gundel, J.: Reference and Referent Accessibililty. Benjamins, Amsterdam (1996)
7. Gernbacher, M. & Hargreaves, D.: Accessing Sentence Participants: The Advantage of First Mention. In: Journal of Memory and Language 28. (1988) 735-755
8. Gordon, P., Grosz, B. & Gilliom, L.: Pronouns, Names, and the Centering of Attention in Discourse. In: Cognitive Science 17. (1993) 311-347.

9. Grosz, B., Joshi, A. & Weinstein, S.: Centering: A Framework for Modeling the Local Coherence of Discourse. In: Computational Linguistics 21(2). (1995) 203-224.
10. Hobbs, J.: Resolving Pronoun References. In: Lingua 44. (1978) 311-338.
11. Hobbs. J.: On the Coherence and Structure of Discourse. Report No. CSLI-85-37. CSLI, Standford University (1985)
12. Kintch, W.: The Role of Knowledge in Discourse Comprehension: A Construction-Integration Model. In: Psychological Review 85. (1988) 363-394
13. Magliano, J., Baggett, W. , Johnson, B. & Graesser, A.: The Time Course of Generating Causal Antecedent and Causal Consequence Inferences. In: Discourse Processes 16. (1993) 35-53
14. Matsui, T.: Bridging Reference and the Notions of Topic/Focus. In: Lingua 90. (1993) 49-68.
15. Matsui, T.: Bridging and Relevance. University College London, PhD thesis. (1995)
16. Matsui, T.: Pragmatic Criteria for Reference Assignment: A Relevance-Theoretic Account of the Acceptability of Bridging. In: Pragmatics and Cognition 6(1/2). (1998) 47-97.
18. McKoon, G. & Ratcliff, R.: Inference During Reading. In: Psychological Review 99 (3). (1992) 440-466.
19. Sanford, A. & Garrod, S.:Understanding Written Language: Explorations in Comprehension Beyond Sentence. Wiley, Chichester. (1981)
20. Sidner, C.: Focusing and Discourse. In: Discourse Processes 6. (1983a) 107-130.
21. Sidner, C.: Focusing in the Comprehension of Definite Anaphora. In: M. Brady & R. Berwick (eds): Computational Models of Dicsourse. MIT Press, Cambridge, MA. (1983b)
22. Singer, M.: Causal Bridging Inferences: Validating Consistent and Inconsistent sequences. In: Canadian Journal of Experimental Psychology 47. (1993) 340-359.
23. Sperber, D. & Wilson, D.: Relevance: Communication and Cognition. Blackwell, Oxford. (1986/1995)
24. Walker, M.A., Iida, M. & Cotes, S.: Japanese Discourse and the Process of Centering. In: Computational Linguistics 20(2). (1994) 193-232.
25. Walker, M. A., Joshi, A.K. & Prince, E.F.: Centering Theory in Discourse. Clarendon Press, Oxford. (1998)
26. Wilson, D.: Reference and relevance. In: UCL Working Papers in Linguistics 4. 1992. 167-191.
27. Wilson, D. & Matsui, T.: Recent Approaches to Bridging: Truth, Coherence and Relevance. In: UCL Working Papers in Linguistics 10. (1998) 173-200.

Contextual Inference in Computational Semantics

Christof Monz

Institute for Logic, Language and Computation (ILLC)
University of Amsterdam, Plantage Muidergracht 24,
1018 TV Amsterdam, The Netherlands
E-mail: christof@wins.uva.nl,
Phone: +31 20 525 6095, Fax: +31 20 525 5101

Abstract. In this paper, an application of automated theorem proving techniques to computational semantics is considered. In order to compute the presuppositions of a natural language discourse, several inference tasks arise. Instead of treating these inferences independently of each other, we show how integrating techniques from formal approaches to context into deduction can help to compute presuppositions more efficiently. Contexts are represented as Discourse Representation Structures and the way they are nested is made explicit. In addition, a tableau calculus is present which keeps track of contextual information, and thereby allows to avoid carrying out redundant inference steps as it happens in approaches that neglect explicit nesting of contexts.

1 Introduction

The notion of presupposition has a long tradition in natural language semantics; from early philosophical approaches (e.g., [17]) to recent computational approaches (e.g., [15]). Almost all accounts of presupposition rely on contextual information in order to compute the presuppositions of a natural language expression. The role that context plays hereby can be seen best by considering an example.

(1) a. Hank likes his wife.
    b. Every man who has a wife likes his wife.

The noun phrase *his wife* behaves as a presupposition trigger which requires that the context in which (1.a) has been uttered provides information allowing to conclude that Hank is married. Compare this to (1.b) where the presupposition trigger *his wife* occurs in the scope of *every* and the restrictor is *man who has a wife*. It is not necessary that the context in which (1.b) is uttered contains the fact that the referent of *his* is married, because this information is provided by the relative clause modifying *man*, where we tacitly assume that the possessive pronoun *his* refers to *a man*. One can say that the relative clause is a local context augmenting the global context in which the whole sentence occurs.

Presupposition triggers are resolved against their local context. If this context provides the presupposed information, then we say that the presupposition does not project. If, on the other hand, the local context does not provide the presupposed information, it does project.

How do we decide whether the context already provides the information expressed by the presupposition trigger? There are basically two ways: [8] states that a presupposition π is contained by its context CON if CON logically entails π, i.e., if $CON \models \pi$. The second way, as it has been proposed by [19], is to consider presuppositions as anaphoric expressions that have to be resolved against their context. Whereas Karttunen's approach is easy to grasp, we explain van der Sandt's approach in some more detail in the following section. His approach is especially worth considering because, up to now, it seems to be the best approach according to the range of phenomena that can be correctly predicted.

The main goal of this paper is to show how the actual computation of presupposition projection can be improved by combining context and automated deduction. For more general information on context and its use in linguistics the reader is refereed for instance to [16].

One of the few implemented NLP systems which actually compute presupposition projections in natural language discourses is DORIS, cf. [3]. We will have a closer look at DORIS later on, and see how formal theories of context, e.g., [1, 2], can help devising more efficient and elegant deduction methods for computing presuppositions.

This paper can be regarded as a follow-up of [14], where some of the techniques we are using here have been introduced and applied to a simpler definition of context. Now, we apply some of these techniques to a more complex notion of context employing Discourse Representation Theory (DRT, cf. [9]), on which van der Sandt's theory of presupposition projection is based.

The rest of this paper is organized as follows. Section 2 briefly explains van der Sandt's theory of presupposition projection, and shows how it is implemented in the DORIS system. Section 3 introduces a way of extracting the inference problems that arise during the computation of presuppositions and how these problems can be expressed in a fashion that considers the way context is nested within a discourse. In addition, we present a tableau calculus that can be applied to expressions representing contextual information explicitly. Finally, some conclusions and prospects for future work are provided in Section 4.

2 Presupposition in DRT

This section provides some background on van der Sandt's approach on treating presuppositions as anaphora. After having introduced the basic data structures, van der Sandt's algorithm for presupposition projection is explained. The second subsection shows how this is realized in the DORIS system and to which extent theorem proving is employed.

2.1 Representing Presuppositions as Anaphora

Before we embark on van der Sandt's theory, the concept of an *anaphor* is briefly explained. An anaphor, or anaphoric expression, refers back to something that has been mentioned before. Simple examples are the pronouns *he*, *she*, and *it*. They refer to a (fe)male person, or thing mentioned before, without imposing any further constraints on it. Definite noun phrases containing a possessive pronoun, such as *his wife*, impose more constraints. Here, we are looking for a particular woman mentioned before, who also has to be the wife of a male person who has been mentioned before, too. Obviously, contextual information is necessary to determine the meaning (reference) of an anaphoric expression, and this is also the reason for the strong similarity of presuppositions and anaphora.

Next, we see how anaphoricity is expressed within DRT. DRT is well-suited for explaining anaphora resolution, because it is a dynamic semantics, mainly devised for representing the meaning of discourses, and describing the way contextual information flows through a discourse. The basic data structures of DRT are Discourse Representation Structures (DRSs) which hold the semantic content of sentences as a pair $\langle U, C \rangle$, in which U is a set of variables (or referents) and C is a set of conditions upon them.

Definition 1 (Discourse Representation Structure). *If U is a set of referents, and C is a set of conditions, then $\langle U, C \rangle$ is a DRS. Let K_1, K_2 be DRSs, then K is a condition, if it is of the following form:*
$K ::= P(x_1 \ldots x_n) \mid \neg K_1 \mid K_1 \Rightarrow K_2 \mid K_1 \vee K_2 \mid \alpha : K_1$
where $x_1 \ldots x_n$ are discourse referents and U_1' is a subset of the discourse referents of K_1.

Alternatively, we will sometimes write DRSs as $[x_1 \ldots x_m | c_1 \ldots c_n]$ because it is less space consuming.

Another important notion within DRT is the accessibility relation which can hold between two DRSs.

Definition 2 (Accessibility). *A DRS K_1 is accessible from a DRS K_2 within a DRS K_0 if K_2 occurs within a condition of K_1 or one of the following holds:*
$K_1 = K_2$, $K_1 \Rightarrow K_2 \in C_0$
Note, that accessibility is transitive, i.e., if K_1 is accessible from K_2 and K_2 is accessible from K_3, then K_1 is also accessible from K_3.

Due to the limitation of space, we cannot provide any further details on DRT, but the reader is referred to [9] for a comprehensive introduction to DRT.

In [19] presupposition triggers are expressed by α-DRSs.[1] Consider the sentences in (2) and their respective DRSs in (3).

(2) a. Every man likes his wife.
    b. Every man who has a wife likes his wife.

---

[1] [19] does not call them α-DRSs, but here, I follow [6], a very slight modification of van der Sandt's theory, which can be implemented more straightforwardly.

(3)

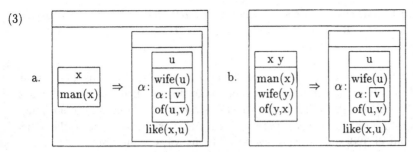

In (3.a), one variable x (or referent) is introduced by the antecedent of the conditional of the DRS. In addition, there is a free variable u to which an α-DRS is attached. This α-DRS contains three conditions. The first condition says that the person u is referring to has to be a wife. $\alpha : \boxed{v}$ is again an anaphor which is referring to somebody in the context, i.e., the accessible DRSs. Finally, both persons have to be in the of-relation.

The α-DRS in (3.b) is exactly the same as in (3.a), but they occur in different contexts. To see whether an α-DRS can be resolved, one has to check whether the DRS that results from substituting the variable which is the argument of the α-operator by an accessible variable is a sub-DRS of the DRS representing the context. The sub-DRS relation is defined as follows:

Definition 3 (Sub-DRS). K_1 *is an immediate sub-DRS of* $K_0 = \langle U_0, C_0 \rangle$, *if* $K_1 = K_0$ *or a* $c \in C_0$ *is of the form:*
$\neg K_i$, $K_i \Rightarrow K_j$, $K_i \vee K_j$, *or* $\alpha : K_i$
where either $i = 1$ *or* $j = 1$.
The sub-DRS relation is the transitive and reflexive closure of the immediate sub-DRS relation; i.e., if K_1 *is an immediate sub-DRS of* K_2, *then* K_1 *is a sub-DRS of* K_2, *and, if* K_1 *is a sub-DRS of* K_2 *and* K_2 *is a sub-DRS of* K_3, *then* K_1 *is a sub-DRS of* K_3.

In the sequel, a context is represented by a DRS. To see whether a DRS K_1 occurring in a DRS K_0 is entailed by its context, we need an algorithmic way to determine the context of K_1 with respect to K_0.

Definition 4 (Context-DRS). *Given a DRS* $K_0 = \langle U_0, C_0 \rangle$ *and a sub-DRS* K_1 *of* K_0, *the context-DRS of* K_1 *with respect to* K_0 *can be computed recursively:*

$\mathsf{con}(K_1, K_0) = \langle U_0, C_0 \backslash \{c\} \rangle \oplus \mathsf{con}(K_1, c)$ *if* K_1 *occurs in* c, $c \in C_0$
$\mathsf{con}(K_1, K_0) = \langle \emptyset, \emptyset \rangle$ *if* $K_1 = K_0$
$\mathsf{con}(K_1, c) \quad = K_2 \oplus \mathsf{con}(K_1, K)$ *if* c *is of the form:*
$\qquad\qquad\qquad K_2 \Rightarrow K_3$, *where* K_1 *is a sub-DRS of* K_3
$\mathsf{con}(K_1, c) \quad = \mathsf{con}(K_1, K_3)$ *if* c *is of the form:*
$\qquad\qquad\qquad K_3 \Rightarrow K_2, K_3 \vee K_2, K_2 \vee K_3, \neg K_3$ *or* $\alpha : K_3$
$\qquad\qquad\qquad$ *where* K_1 *is a sub-DRS of* K_3

In Definition 4 we use the merging function $\oplus$ (cf. [21]) which allows the information expressed by two DRSs to be merged into one DRS.

Definition 5 (Merging DRSs). *Given two DRSs* $K_1 = \langle U_1, C_1 \rangle$ *and* $K_2 = \langle U_2, C_2 \rangle$, *the merge* $K_1 \oplus K_2$ *is simply defined as* $\langle U_1 \cup U_2, C_1 \cup C_2 \rangle$, *the union of the universes and conditions.*

Definition 5 assumes that the universes of the DRS are distinct. This means that in general variables are supposed to be introduced only once; i.e., the DRS are *pure*, cf. [10]. Although Definition 5 introduces the most simple way of merging, it does not impose any severe restrictions on the expressiveness of the DRS language; but cf. [20] for an overview on different ways of merging.

The resolution tasks of (3.a) and (3.b) are as follows. In (3.a), the only variable that is accessible from v is x, and we see immediately that wife(x) does not occur in the context-DRS of the α-DRS. Hence, the α-DRS in (3.a) cannot be resolved; i.e., the presupposition projects. In (3.b) on the other hand, substituting v by y allows to wife(y) because it occurs already in the context. Now, substituting u by x allows to solve the whole resolution task as of(y,x) as also part of the context. After resolution, the α-DRSs are simply deleted. Because the resolution task in (3.b) can be solved, the presupposition does not project.

In [19], presupposition projection is considered as an instance of accommodation, cf. [11]. Accommodation is a strategy to repair the context in a way such that it allows to conclude the presupposed material. In DRT, repairing the context amounts to adding the presupposed material (the α-DRS) to the context. As contexts are represented as DRSs which have themselves internal structure, it is possible to insert an α-DRS in several positions in the context. In general, three kinds of accommodation can be distinguished. Considering (3.a), they result in (4).

(4) a. **global accommodation**   b. **intermediate accommodation**   c. **local accommodation**

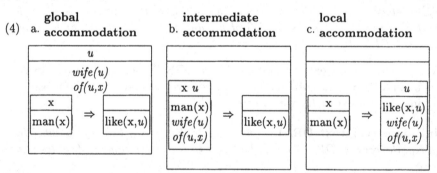

In (4), the accommodated material is typeset in *italics*. Global accommodation adds the presupposed material to the outer-most DRS that is part of the context. Intermediate accommodation adds the α-DRS to some DRS that is a proper sub-DRS of the context, but not the DRS in which the α-DRS occurs as a condition. Local accommodation simply adds the content of the α-DRS to the DRS where the α-DRS occurs as a condition.

According to [19], it is only possible to accommodate an α-DRS if it contains conditions upon the presupposed variable. Therefore, it is possible to accommodate u and the relevant conditions, but it is not possible to accommodate v, because $\alpha:\boxed{v}$ does not contain any further restrictions on v. $\alpha:\boxed{v}$ can only be resolved against the context. In (4), $\alpha:\boxed{v}$ is resolved to x, the only accessible variable, and v is substituted by x in (4.a)–(4.c).

Deciding which of the different ways of accommodation are correct underlies certain criteria. First of all, accommodation cannot lead to free occurrences of a variable. This constraint is violated by (4.a), where x occurs free in $of(u,x)$. In addition, accommodation should preserve local consistency and local informativity, see [4].

Definition 6 (Local Informativity). *No sub-DRS is redundant. If K' is a sub-DRS of K, then K is locally informative if $\mathsf{con}(K', K) \not\models K'$.*

Definition 7 (Local Consistency). *No sub-DRS is inconsistent. If K' is a sub-DRS of K, then K is locally consistent if $\mathsf{con}(K', K) \oplus K' \not\models \bot$; i.e., if $\mathsf{con}(K', K) \oplus K'$ is satisfiable.*

How the accommodations violating one of those constraints are filtered out in a computational way will be considered in the next subsection.

2.2 Implementing Anaphora Resolution

The DORIS system (Discourse Oriented Representation Inference System), cf. [3], parses a natural language discourse and generates the corresponding DRS representing its semantic content. This also involves a treatment of presuppositions. Given a sequence of sentences, a DRS possibly containing α-DRSs (unresolved presuppositions) is constructed. Then, a generate-and-test procedure returns all DRSs where the presupposed material is either resolved or accommodated and which do not violate the constraints mentioned above.

For instance, if K_0 represents a discourse and a sub-DRS K_2 of K_0 contains an α-DRS $\alpha : K_3$ as a condition, then after resolving all simple α-DRSs of the form $\alpha:\boxed{x}$ to some accessible variable in $\mathsf{con}(K_3, K_0)$, three possible ways of accommodation are generally possible. In general, local informativity means that the local context of the accommodation site merged with the accommodation site itself do not entail the accommodated DRS. Analogously, local consistency holds if the merge of the local context of the accommodation site and the accommodation site itself and the accommodated DRS is consistent. Global accommodation generates a DRS where K_3 is added to K_0; i.e., $K_0 \oplus K_3$ is generated. To see whether this obeys local informativity, we have to check whether $\mathsf{con}(K_0, K_0) \oplus K_0 \not\models K_3$ holds. Similarly, being locally consistent means that $\mathsf{con}(K_0, K_0) \oplus K_0 \oplus K_3$ has to be satisfiable. Intermediate accommodation adds K_3 to a sub-DRS K_1 of K_0, which is accessible from K_3 and $K_1 \neq K_0$ and $K_1 \neq K_2$. Again, if $K_1 \oplus K_3$ is locally informative and consistent, it has to hold that $\mathsf{con}(K_1, K_0) \oplus K_1 \not\models K_3$, and $\mathsf{con}(K_1, K_0) \oplus K_1 \oplus K_3$ has to be satisfiable. Finally, if K_3 is locally accommodated, then it has to be the case that $\mathsf{con}(K_2, K_0) \oplus K_2 \not\models K_3$ holds (locally informative) and that $\mathsf{con}(K_2, K_0) \oplus K_2 \oplus K_3$ is satisfiable (locally consistent). Summing up, we present the six inference tasks that are connected to the different ways of accommodation in Table 1.

	informativity	consistency
global	$con(K_0, K_0) \oplus K_0 \not\vdash K_3$	$con(K_0, K_0) \oplus K_0 \oplus K_3$ is satisfiable
interm.	$con(K_1, K_0) \oplus K_1 \not\vdash K_3$	$con(K_1, K_0) \oplus K_1 \oplus K_3$ is satisfiable
local	$con(K_2, K_0) \oplus K_2 \not\vdash K_3$	$con(K_2, K_0) \oplus K_2 \oplus K_3$ is satisfiable

Table 1. Inference tasks for computing informativity and consistency

Local informativity and consistency can be decided by having run a theorem prover on the different inference tasks.[2] In the sequel, we will focus on local informativity, and the way how it can be computed more efficiently.

Consider example (5.a) and its DRS (5.b).

(5) a. Hank is married. Every man likes his wife.

b.

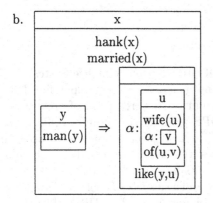

Any straightforward approach to computing the possible accommodation sites has to face five inference tasks, see Table 2, where $\vdash^?$ is an inference task.

If the α-DRS is globally accommodated, only one inference task arises as resolving v to y is ruled out because it violates the free-variable condition. Intermediate and local accommodation have to consider two cases, respectively: one in which v is resolved to x, (ii) and (iv), and the other where v is resolved to y, as in (iii) and (v). DORIS computes the five inference tasks (i)–(v) independently of each other. In this example, the proving method will filter out (i), (iii), and (v), because these are the valid inferences, and thereby they violate local informativity. and (ii) and (iv) remain as possible accommodations sites, since the α-DRSs do not follow from their respective contexts; i.e., they pass the local informativity check.

What is striking about Table 2, is that the DRSs share a lot of information. For instance, the information stemming from the first sentence in (5), namely

---

[2] Another and maybe better way of solving the problem of satisfiability is to apply a model generator to the satisfiability task, cf. [3].

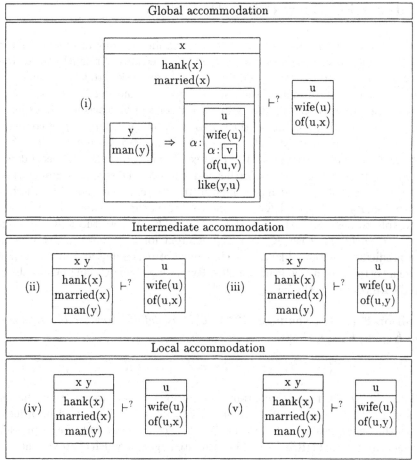

Table 2. The inference tasks of (5)

$\langle\{x\}, \{hank(x), married(x)\}\rangle$ occurs in the premise DRS of all five inferences. Therefore, the corresponding deduction rules are applied five times to exactly the same formulas. As far as (5) is concerned, this does not appear to be too dramatic, because this redundancy concerns only the introduction of x and two conditions. On the other hand, in general, the presupposition trigger *his wife* in (5) can occur in a much larger context, containing not only one sentence expressing that Hank is married, but arbitrarily many sentences. In this case, the corresponding DRS representing that context would be much more complex, and consequently the redundancy of treating that context five times would have a much bigger impact on the performance of the computation of the possible accommodation sites: it would slow down significantly.

3 Integrating Context into Deduction

In the previous section, we have seen that a significant amount of redundancy arises if possible accommodation sites are computed in a straightforward way. This is mainly due to the fact the different inference tasks are treated independently of each other, although they share some information. It is possible to overcome the problem of redundancy by taking context into account. In order to do this, we need a richer language that enables us to express nesting of contexts. Here, we use the in-predicate, cf. [1, 2], which takes two arguments. The first argument is a DRS representing the contextual addition, and the second is a conjunction of DRSs and maybe further in-formulas. The second argument represents the consequence that has to hold in the context represented by the first argument. $in(K_1, \varphi)$ is true if $K_1 \vdash \varphi$.[3] Since φ itself can contain an in-predicate, we are able to nest contexts. E.g., $in(K_1, \varphi \wedge in(K_2, \psi))$ is true if $K_1 \vdash \varphi$ and $K_1 \oplus K_2 \vdash \psi$. In this case, K_2 is a local context for ψ. A language containing the in-predicate functions like a meta-language of reasoning, and in the sequel, we give a corresponding tableau calculus. Extending the DRS language with the in predicate results in the language $\mathcal{L}^{con}$.

Definition 8 (The Language $\mathcal{L}^{con}$). $\mathcal{L}^{con}$ *is defined recursively as follows, where K_1 and K_2 are DRSs:*

$$\varphi ::= P(x_1 \ldots x_n) \mid \neg K_1 \mid K_1 \Rightarrow K_2 \mid K_1 \vee K_2 \mid in(K_1, \varphi)$$

Note, that $\mathcal{L}^{con}$ does not contain α-conditions, as we assume that the formulas of $\mathcal{L}^{con}$ represent possible accommodations. $\mathcal{L}^{con}$ is not used in order to express the semantics of a natural language discourse, but only for expressing which accommodated DRSs have to be evaluated against which context. The purpose of $\mathcal{L}^{con}$ is to express these local informativity problems in a non-redundant fashion. In $\mathcal{L}^{con}$ it is now possible to express the five inference tasks in (2) by a single formula:

(6) $in([x|hank(x), married(x)], [u|wife(u), of(u, x)]$
$$\wedge in([y|man(y)], [u|wife(u), of(u, x)]$$
$$\vee [u|wife(u), of(u, y)]))$$

The first in-predicate describes the global context as it was relevant for deciding (i) in Table 2. The nested in-predicate augments the global context for deciding whether intermediate and local accommodation are locally informative. In this example, it is not necessary to distinguish between the informativity of intermediate and local accommodation because the DRS which is the local accommodation site does not add any further information to the DRS functioning as the intermediate accommodation site; cf. (ii)–(iv), where the context-DRS remains the same. The disjunction represents the two ways in which the pronouns for intermediate and local accommodation can be resolved; i.e., (ii,iv) vs. (iii,v).

---

[3] We slightly diverge from [1, 2] where the argument positions of in are interchanged.

Before a tableau calculus for $\mathcal{L}^{con}$ is presented, it is necessary to show how the inference tasks arising by a DRS K containing α-DRSs can be extracted from K and re-stated in $\mathcal{L}^{con}$ in a compact way. We define a function τ from DRSs to $\mathcal{L}^{con}$. The function τ is defined in Table 3. As the definition is rather complex and we have only limited space, we just try to sketch its rationale. τ is recursively applied to a DRS, and it takes two additional parameters: a DRS K representing the current relevant context, and a set A of variables consisting of all accessible variables. It is necessary to keep track of the accessible variables as we have to resolve α-DRSs of the form $\alpha\!:\!\boxed{x}$, and substitute x by an accessible variable. During the first application of τ to a DRS, the parameter K is set to $\top$, i.e., the empty or true DRS, and $A = \emptyset$, as no variables have been introduced so far.

$$[U|C]^{\tau,K,A} = \begin{cases} \mathrm{in}(K, (\bigwedge_{i=1}^{n} \alpha\!:\!K_i^{\tau,\top,A\cup U}) \wedge \langle C, \emptyset\rangle^{\tau,[U|],A\cup U}) & \text{if } K \neq \top \\ (\bigwedge_{i=1}^{n} \alpha\!:\!K_i^{\tau,\top,A\cup U}) \wedge \langle C, \emptyset\rangle^{\tau,[U|],A\cup U} & \text{if } K = \top \end{cases}$$

$$\langle C \cup \{c\}, C_\alpha\rangle^{\tau,K,A} = \begin{cases} \langle C, C_\alpha\rangle^{\tau,K\oplus[|c],A} & \text{if } c \text{ does not contain an } \alpha\text{-DRS} \\ \langle C, C_\alpha \cup \{c\}\rangle^{\tau,K,A} & \text{if } c \text{ contains an } \alpha\text{-DRS} \end{cases}$$

$$\langle \emptyset, \{c_1,\ldots,c_n\}\rangle^{\tau,K,A} = \begin{cases} \mathrm{in}(K, \bigwedge_{i=1}^{n} c_i^{\tau,\top,A}) & \text{if } K \neq \top \\ \bigwedge_{i=1}^{n} c_i^{\tau,\top,A} & \text{if } K = \top \end{cases}$$

$$\alpha\!:\![U|C]^{\tau,K,A} = \begin{cases} \mathrm{in}(K, \bigvee_{i=1}^{n} [U|C_i]^{\tau,\top,A}) & \text{if } K \neq \top \\ \bigvee_{i=1}^{n} [U|C_i]^{\tau,\top,A} & \text{if } K = \top \end{cases}$$

where $C_1,\ldots,C_n$ are like C but all variables x that occur in an α-DRS of the form $\alpha\!:\!\boxed{x}$ are substitued in C by a variable occurring in A; i.e., the universe of the context. In addition, all α-DRSs of the form $\alpha\!:\!\boxed{x}$ are deleted in $C_1,\ldots,C_n$

$$(\neg[U|C])^{\tau,K,A} = \begin{cases} \mathrm{in}(K, (\bigwedge_{i=1}^{n} \alpha\!:\!K_i^{\tau,\top,A\cup U}) \wedge \langle C, \emptyset\rangle^{\tau,[U|],A\cup U}) & \text{if } K \neq \top \\ (\bigwedge_{i=1}^{n} \alpha\!:\!K_i^{\tau,\top,A\cup U}) \wedge \langle C, \emptyset\rangle^{\tau,[U|],A\cup U} & \text{if } K = \top \end{cases}$$

$$([U_1|C_1] \Rightarrow K_2)^{\tau,K,A} = [U_1|C_1]^{\tau,K,A} \wedge K_2^{\tau,K\oplus[U_1|C_1],A\cup U_1}$$

$$(K_1 \vee K_2)^{\tau,K,A} = K_1^{\tau,K,A} \wedge K_1^{\tau,K,A}$$

Table 3. Extracting informativity tasks from DRSs

The rules in Table 3 are subdivided into three sets of rules. First, if we encounter a DRS which has α-DRSs as sub-DRSs, then all the α-DRSs are added as conditions of the subordinating DRS. If it is the global DRS, this amounts to global accommodation. The resulting DRS is embedded in an in-predicate if the context is not trivial; i.e., the context-DRS does not equal $\top$. Otherwise, the resulting DRS is not embedded in the in-predicate.

The second set of rules sorts conditions which contain α-DRSs and those which do not. All conditions which do not contain α-DRSs are simply added to the context. Later, the α-DRSs will be evaluated against this context.

The last set of rules mirrors how contextual information is threaded through conditions. For instance, the antecedent of an implication is accessible from the succedent, therefore, the antecedent is added to the context parameter of the succedent. Note, that the rules in Table 3 also take care of the free variable constraint, as α-DRSs of the form $\alpha : \boxed{x}$ are only resolved against the respective contexts of their accommodation sites.

The main advantage of this transformation is that DRS conditions that are used to prove local informativity have to be considered only once. For instance, in (6), it is not necessary to mention again the conditions that are part of the global DRS for checking local informativity of both ways of local accommodation (i.e., whether v is resolved to x or y). In (6), both local accommodation problems are embedded in the global context. Therefore, we can apply the appropriate tableau expansion rule to the in-predicate.

The most important rule of our tableau calculus $\mathcal{T}^{con}$ is the rule $(- : \mathsf{in})$. Before we introduce the other rules, it is helpful to have a closer look at $(- : \mathsf{in})$, in order to understand the way context is represented in $\mathcal{T}^{con}$.

$$\frac{(i, \sigma, -) : \mathsf{in}(K, \varphi)}{\substack{(j, \sigma \cup \{i\}, +) : K \\ (j, \sigma \cup \{i\}, -) : \varphi}} \;(-:\mathsf{in})$$

To keep track of the contextual information, labels are attached to the nodes of the tableau. A label has two arguments. Its first argument i is a natural number ($i \in \mathbb{N}$), which is the identifier of the context. I.e., if two nodes have the same number as the first argument of their labels, then they belong to the same context. The second argument σ is a set of natural numbers. This set contains the identifiers of the contexts that are accessible. We say that a context K_1 is accessible from a formula ψ, if there is a formula of the form $\mathsf{in}(K_1, \varphi)$ and ψ is a subformula of φ. For instance, considering the formula $\mathsf{in}(K_1, \varphi \wedge \mathsf{in}(K_2, \psi))$, K_1 is accessible from φ and $\mathsf{in}(K_2, \psi)$. Also K_2 is accessible from ψ. Since accessibility is transitive, it holds that K_1 is accessible from ψ; but K_2 is not accessible from φ because φ is not embedded in K_2 by an in-predicate.

The $(- : \mathsf{in})$-rule is similar to the upwards direction (entering a context) of the (CS)-rule in [5]:

$$\frac{\vdash_{\bar{\kappa} * \kappa_1} \varphi}{\vdash_{\bar{\kappa}} \mathsf{ist}(\kappa_1, \varphi)} \;(\mathrm{CS})$$

$\bar{\kappa}$ represents a sequence of contexts and the upwards direction of the rule says that if it is true in the context $\bar{\kappa}$ that φ holds in the extension with κ_1, then φ holds in the context $\bar{\kappa} * \kappa_1$ itself. Comparing (CS) to $(- : \mathsf{in})$, we can say that $\bar{\kappa}$ corresponds to $\sigma \cup \{i\}$ and j, the identifier of the context extension with K and not φ, corresponds to κ_1.

Table 4 gives the complete set of tableau rules. The rules for the usual boolean connectives and quantifiers are omitted, but cf. [7] for a comprehensive introduction to tableau methods.

$$\frac{(i,\sigma,+):\mathrm{in}(K,\varphi)}{(j,\sigma\cup\{i\},-):K\,|\,(j,\sigma\cup\{i\},+):\varphi}\,(+\!:\mathrm{in})$$

$$\frac{(i,\sigma,-):\mathrm{in}(K,\varphi)}{\begin{array}{c}(j,\sigma\cup\{i\},+):K\\(j,\sigma\cup\{i\},-):\varphi\end{array}}\,(-\!:\mathrm{in})$$

$$\frac{(i,\sigma,+):[x_1\ldots x_n|C]}{(i,\sigma,+):[x_1\ldots x_{n-1}|C[x/f(X_1\ldots X_n)]]}\,(+\!:\mathrm{U})$$

$$\frac{(i,\sigma,-):[x_1\ldots x_n|C]}{(i,\sigma,-):[x_1\ldots x_{n-1}|C[x/X]]}\,(-\!:\mathrm{U})$$

$$\frac{(i,\sigma,+):[|\{c\}\cup C]}{\begin{array}{c}(i,\sigma,+):[|C]\\(i,\sigma,+):c\end{array}}\,(+\!:\mathrm{C})$$

$$\frac{(i,\sigma,-):[|\{c\}\cup C]}{(i,\sigma,-):[|C]\,|\,(i,\sigma,-):c}\,(-\!:\mathrm{C})$$

$$\frac{(i,\sigma,+):\neg K}{(i,\sigma,-):K}\,(+\!:\neg K)$$

$$\frac{(i,\sigma,-):\neg K}{(i,\sigma,+):K}\,(-\!:\neg K)$$

$$\frac{(i,\sigma,+):[x_1\ldots x_n|C_1]\Rightarrow K_2}{(i,\sigma,+):[x_1..x_{n-1}|C_1[x_n/X]]}\,(+\!:\Rightarrow_\forall)$$

$$\frac{(i,\sigma,-):[x_1\ldots x_n|C_1]\Rightarrow K_2}{(i,\sigma,+):[x_1..x_{n-1}|C_1[x_n/f(X_1..X_m)]]}\,(-\!:\Rightarrow_\forall)$$

$$\frac{(i,\sigma,+):[|C_1]\Rightarrow K_2}{(i,\sigma,-):[|C_1]\,|\,(i,\sigma,+):K_2}\,(+\!:\Rightarrow)$$

$$\frac{(i,\sigma,-):[|C_1]\Rightarrow K_2}{\begin{array}{c}(i,\sigma,+):[|C_1]\\(i,\sigma,-):K_2\end{array}}\,(+\!:\Rightarrow)$$

$$\frac{(i,\sigma,+):K_1\vee K_2}{(i,\sigma,+):K_1\,|\,(i,\sigma,+):K_2}\,(+\!:\vee)$$

$$\frac{(i,\sigma,-):K_1\vee K_2}{\begin{array}{c}(i,\sigma,-):K_1\\(i,\sigma,-):K_2\end{array}}\,(-\!:\vee)$$

Table 4. The tableau rules of $\mathcal{T}^{con}$

The contextual information carried by the labels becomes important when we want to define the closure conditions of a branch.

Definition 9 (Closure of a Branch). *A branch of a tableau tree is closed if it contains two nodes of the form $(i,\sigma,+):R(t_1\ldots t_n)$ and $(j,\sigma',-):R(t'_1\ldots t'_n)$ such that*
(a) t_m and t'_m are unifiable $(1\le m\le n)$, and
(b) (i) $i=j$ or (ii) $i\in\sigma'$ or (iii) $j\in\sigma$

(a) is the standard condition on branch closure. (b) considers three cases. If $i=j$, then both literals belong to the same context. If $i\in\sigma'$, then φ belongs to an extension of j. The case where $j\in\sigma$ is analogous to the previous one.

4 Conclusions and Future Work

Computing the presuppositions of a natural language discourse is an important task for a natural language processing system. Employing a language like $\mathcal{L}^{con}$ allows for a non-redundant way of stating inference problems that arise in the computation of presuppositions. To this end, we presented a way of extracting local informativity tasks from DRSs and re-stated them in $\mathcal{L}^{con}$. In addition, a tableau calculus $\mathcal{T}^{con}$ has been presented, allowing to compute informativity problems more efficiently than approaches neglecting context.

Our future work will focus on combining theorem proving and presupposition projection. I.e., whether a presupposition projects or not is only computed if this is necessary in order to derive a certain conclusion. This work is along the lines of [12, 13], but it has to deal with more complex data structures representing the context, namely DRSs. In order to to so we have to consider computing local consistency, too; but we think that this can be efficiently accomplished similar to the way local informativity was computed in this paper.

Acknowledgments. The author was supported by the Physical Sciences Council with financial support from the Netherlands Organization for Scientific Research (NWO), project 612-13-001.

References

1. G. Attardi and M. Simi. Building proofs in context. In *Proceedings of Meta '94*, LNCS 883, pages 410–424. Springer, 1994.
2. G. Attardi and M. Simi. Proofs in context. In J. Doyle and P. Torasso, editors, *Principles of Knowledge Representation and Reasoning: Proceedings of the 4th International Conference*. Morgan Kaufmann, 1994.
3. P. Blackburn, J. Bos, M. Kohlhase, and H. de Nivelle. Inference and computational semantics. In H. Bunt and E. Thijsse, editors, *3rd International Workshop on Computational Semantics (IWCS-3)*, pages 5–21. Tilburg University, 1999.
4. D. Beaver. Presupposition. In van Benthem and ter Meulen [18], pages 939–1008.
5. S. Buvač and I.A. Mason. Propositional logic of context. In R. Fikes and W. Lehnert, editors, *Proceedings of the 11th National Conference on Artificial Intelligence*, pages 412–419, Menlo Park, CA, 1993. AAAI Press.
6. J. Bos. Presupposition and VP-ellipsis. In *15th International Conference on Computational Linguistics (COLING '94)*, Kyoto, Japan, 1994.
7. M. Fitting. *First-Order Logic and Automated Theorem Proving*. Springer-Verlag New York, 2nd edition, 1996.
8. L. Karttunen. Presupposition and linguistic context. *Theoretical Linguistics*, 1(1):181–194, 1974.
9. H. Kamp and U. Reyle. *From Discourse to Logic*. Kluwer Academic Publishers, 1993.
10. H. Kamp and U. Reyle. A calculus for first order Discourse Representation Structures. *Journal of Logic, Language and Information*, 5(3–4):297–348, 1996.
11. D. Lewis. Scorekeeping in a language game. *Journal of Philosophical Logic*, 8:339–359, 1979.

12. C. Monz and M. de Rijke. A resolution calculus for dynamic semantics. In J. Dix, L. Fariñas del Cerro, and U. Fuhrbach, editors, *Logics in Artificial Intelligence (JELIA '98)*, LNAI 1489, pages 184–198. Springer, 1998.
13. C. Monz and M. de Rijke. A tableau calculus for pronoun resolution. In N.V. Murray, editor, *Automated Reasoning with Analytic Tableaux and Related Methods (TABLEAUX '99)*, LNAI 1617, pages 247–262. Springer, 1999.
14. C. Monz. Computing presuppositions by contextual reasoning. In P. Brézillon, R. Turner, J-C. Pomerol, and E. Turner, editors, *Proceedings of the AAAI-99 Workshop on Reasoning in Context for AI Applications*, 1999.
15. P. Piwek and E. Krahmer. Presuppositions in context: Constructing bridges. In P. Brézilon and M. Cavalcanti, editors, *Formal and Linguistic Aspects of Context.* Kluwer Academic Publishers, 1999.
16. R. Stalnaker. On the representation of context. *Journal of Logic, Language and Information*, 7(1):3–19, 1998. Special issue on Context in Linguistics and Artificial Intelligence.
17. P. Strawson. Referring. *Mind*, 59:320–344, 1950.
18. J. van Benthem and A. ter Meulen, editors. *Handbook of Logic and Linguistics.* Elsevier Science Press, 1997.
19. R. van der Sandt. Presupposition projection as anaphora resolution. *Journal of Semantics*, 9:333–377, 1992.
20. J. van Eijck and H. Kamp. Representing discourse in context. In van Benthem and ter Meulen [18], pages 179–237.
21. H. Zeevat. A compositional approach to Discourse Representation Theory. *Linguistics and Philosophy*, 12:95–131, 1989.

Contexts and Views in Object-Oriented Languages

Renate Motschnig-Pitrik

Department of Applied Computer Science and Information Systems, University of Vienna
Rathausstrasse 19/4, 1010 Vienna, Austria
motschnig@ifs.univie.ac.at

Abstract. The object-oriented paradigm views systems as being composed of objects that model real-world entities. Objects sharing the same properties and responsibilities are categorized under one class. However, object oriented languages, in general, lack means that allow objects to be grouped on extrinsic grounds, such as concerning some specific topic of interest, being relevant to a particular user group, or being dependent on changes made to other objects. Also, object-oriented (OO) languages do not allow objects of the same class to exhibit relativized structure and behavior, for example in order to meet specific user needs.

View mechanisms developed for OO databases address the above issues, although, as will be argued, to a limited degree only. Therefore, this paper proposes a context mechanism for OO languages that extends the functionality of views. It will be shown in which way the context mechanism can deal with issues such as relativized structure and behavior of objects, relativized method execution, content-based authorization, and propagation of changes across contexts.

1 Introduction

Advanced systems that are used by several users and applications accommodate the demands of their users more effectively, if they can be organized in the form of possibly overlapping fragments, called contexts. The latter allow objects to be viewed from different perspectives and processed separately, with well-defined effects on surrounding contexts. For example, software designers may want to partition a software system under development into components they work on individually, to be merged once their respective tasks are done. Likewise, an information system might have its database split into several views so that particular groups of users have only access to information relevant to their work. Also, a ticket reservation system used for cinemas might be adopted for a theatre such that both systems share common data.

Contexts as means for partitioning and filtering information have gained recognition in- and outside of computer science. In architecture, for instance, different views such as bird's eye-, front-, side-, and various perspective views are indispensable tools of every architect for decomposing complexity in the course of modeling a building. Note that the individual views can be interpreted as contexts for drawing entities or objects visible from these views and intentionally neglecting others. Further note, that these objects, e.g. a door, window, or wall, look different depending on the view or, in our terms, context selected. Also, not all objects are visible in each view.

Within computer science, mechanisms for partitioning and coping with a fragmented software artifact have appeared in different forms, including (database) views, multidatabases, versions, workspaces, (knowledge base) partitions and contexts, (programming language) modules, packages, scopes, (hypertext) perspectives, (requirements engineering) viewpoints, etc. A detailed feature-by-feature comparison of such mechanisms appears in [1] and has served as the starting point for the design of a generic framework for information base partitions, called *contexts* [2] that generalize the notions mentioned above [3]. Since all these notions provide means to reduce the complexity of a system by emphasizing some aspects while ignoring others, they realize a form of abstraction referred to as *viewpoint abstraction* [1]. This abstraction significantly differs from classical mechanisms involving abstraction: Whereas the latter are based on intrinsic properties of entities such as similarity or inclusion [4], [5], [6], the viewpoint abstraction organizes objects on extrinsic grounds, making the decision into which context an object shall be placed dependent on the way the object is going to be used.

Due to the fact that object-orientation is a unifying paradigm that applies the same concepts to analysis, design, programming, databases, and knowledge representation, we find it particularly suitable to specialize the generic context framework for use with object-oriented (OO) languages. In this context, we use the term *OO language* as a generalization of terms such as OO programming-, modeling-, design-, knowledge representation-, data manipulation-, and data definition language. Thus, in this paper, we adopt the generic context framework for use in an object-oriented environment. The resulting object-oriented context mechanism has been strongly influenced by our research into view concepts for OO databases (OODB's [7]). We will argue that the marriage between contexts and views results in a particularly powerful mechanism, in particular, when keeping with the object-oriented paradigm. Further contributions of this paper are to:

- Introduce the notion of a context into OO languages and compare its functionality and features with (OODB) views;
- Illustrate the benefits of extending OO languages by a context mechanism, in particular:
- relativized naming and context-dependent structure and behavior of objects,
- provision of flexible mechanisms for authorization and change propagation;

In general, we envisage the primary use of contexts as a means to provide a flexible and powerful decomposition- and customization mechanism for OO applications. The next section introduces the notion of a context by presenting an example. In Section three we discuss the strengths and limitations of OODB views. Section four then discusses contexts in more detail. The final Section gives a feature comparison of views and contexts, argues in which ways the two mechanisms complement each other to result in a powerful realization of the viewpoint abstraction, surveys related work, and points to further research.

2 Requirements on an OO Context Mechanism

Before introducing contexts more formally, we advise the reader to think about a context as an encapsulated, interconnected fragments, containing of a set of classes, objects, and predicates regarding authorization and change propagation. The example we use to explain contexts deals with a fragment of an OO enterprise information system. Assume, it includes one context that encapsulates all objects relevant for the sales department, a second context representing all objects of interest to the R&D department, and a third context containing all objects relevant for accounting. Typically, the third context encompasses the personnel of all departments, but associates them with different state- and behavior information than, say, the context of the R&D department. Also, the individual contexts typically are associated with different access rights. For example, accountants are allowed to access all units in the accounting context but are restricted, for example, just to read certain information from the individual department's contexts.

In an OO model that is fragmented into contexts, typically, multiple object versions that contain different, possibly overlapping subsets of the state and/or behavior of an object coexist and thereby provide alternative descriptions of that object, relative to individual contexts. In accordance with [1], we refer to the data structure modeling an object relative to a context as a *perspective object*, or short *perspective*. A perspective is exactly like an object except that a perspective's state and/or behavior is determined by considering its context. In the enterprise information system example introduced above, assume that there exists an employee with name 'tom' (compare Fig. 1). In the 'SalesDepartment' context , 'tom' may be characterized by an object having the attributes: 'socialInsuranceNo', 'name', 'projects', and 'regions', whereas in the 'Accounting' context, this same employee may be described by the attributes: 'socialInsuranceNo', 'name', 'dateOfBirth', and 'salary'. Thus, the employee 'tom' gives rise to two perspectives: one visible in the 'SalesDepartment' context, the other in the 'Accounting' context. Note that 'tom' typically is not visible in the 'R&Ddepartment' context, although the class 'Employee' should be visible there in a customized version.

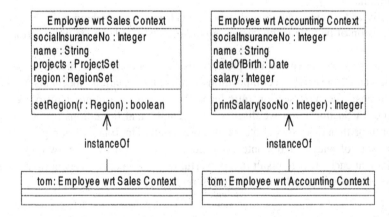

Fig. 1. Example of different perspectives of one class included in different contexts using the UML [8]

Complementary to the task of mapping conceptual entities into perspectives according to standpoints or situations, it often appears useful to represent the situations themselves within the model. This is specifically the case if several conceptual entities are to be viewed from the same situation (e.g. accounting, in the example above). The latter then can be interpreted as a special object that encloses the conceptual entities viewed. In accordance with [9], we refer to an object that denotes a situation in a model as a *context*. Thus, a context is a meaningful slice of the model or, in a special case, represents the universal context, such as the whole enterprise. Unlike contexts in [9], however, we associate contexts with further features, such as relativized naming, authorization, and channels for change propagation. Contexts being objects in their own right, they can be classified, associated with properties, enclosed in contexts, and dealt with like ordinary objects.

In [1] we argued that any context mechanism gains much power if, first, contexts are *first-class citizens* in a notation (e.g. objects in an OO notation) and, second, both aspects of the viewpoint abstraction, in our terminology *contexts* and *perspectives* are considered. The latter issue appears analogous to the phenomenon that objects gain much of their power from being associated with classes. The major difference between the class-instance and the context-perspective relationship, however, is that classes group instances based on equality of properties, whereas contexts group perspectives based on situation-dependent, extrinsic grounds.

3 Views

This section is aimed to summarize the notion of an OODB view, in order to prepare for the comparison and subsequent "marriage" of views and contexts. While current commercial OODB's do not (yet) support views, the latter constitute a thoroughly investigated and pragmatically indispensable concept of relational systems. A *view* in the relational data model is defined as a virtual relation being derived by a query on one or more base relations. Views, like base relations, consist of sets of tuples, whereby all information contained in a view is *derived* from base relations or other views. A (flat) collection of views is referred to as a *view schema*. View schemas in the realm of relational databases have become popular for providing a number of useful features, most importantly, *logical data independence*. This means that view schemas can be defined such that they reflect information that is restructured to optimally support the needs of individual user groups. Also, these schemas can be associated with access rights allowing for content-based authorization.

One goal of view concepts is to provide as much analogous functionality of base- and view schemas as possible. This is because the user of a view schema should be able to work with the latter in much the same way as with the base schema. In this respect, however, relational views are deficient in so far, as, in general, views may not be updated [10]. Informally, this is because the tracing of view updates back to updates of base relations is ambiguous except for views that contain the key of their single underlying base relation.

In the OO approach, view schemas can be designed such as to be more powerful than their relational cousins, although the support of view mechanisms in OODB is a lot more complex. This can be explained by the larger expressive power of OO databases and by the organization of objects in class hierarchies, rather then in flat relations. In particular, OODB view concepts are feasible that exhibit the following features:

Updateable views. If an OO view is derived by an object preserving query, i.e. a query that does not generate new objects, this view can be updated such that the update can be propagated to base objects in a unique way. It has been shown, that object preserving queries are sufficiently powerful in practice to accomplish the vast majority of view derivations [11].

Capacity augmenting views. In analogy to relational algebra, an OO algebra can be designed to specify views in the object model. This algebra can be defined such as to allow views to carry information derived from the base schema or other views--the classical case--as well as original, non-derived information. As a concrete example consider the OO algebra as proposed in [12] and extended in [11]. In a nutshell, this algebra encompasses the usual set-based operators for *union*, *difference*, and *intersection*, yielding, respectively, the views whose type is the lowest common supertype of the input types, a subset of its first argument with the same type, and the greatest common subtype of the input types. Further, the algebra provides the *select*, *hide* and *refine* operators. The *select* operator returns a subset of the input set of objects satisfying a given predicate with the type of the resulting set being unchanged. The *hide* operator is used to blend out certain properties of a type and hence results in a type that is a supertype of the input type. Finally, the *refine* operator yields a result that is a subtype of the input type since it allows properties (attributes or operations) to be added to input-type definition. These properties can either be derived or original, in other words, capacity-augmenting.

Automated view classification. This means automated support for placing a view into the view schema, in order to avoid inconsistencies caused by manual insertion.

Assuring the closure property. The closure property of a view schema with respect to the property decomposition- or the is-a hierarchy means that every property function or is-a link emanating from a class in the view schema is defined in the view schema. In the case that a view schema is not closed, the minimal set of classes to be added to it shall automatically be suggested. The good news regarding these features is that algorithms addressing them already exist [12], [13]. While closure can be checked in linear time, view classification is more sophisticated: Due to the fact that the classification problem is not decidable in general, the proposed algorithm is sound but incomplete. However, experiments have shown that, practically, the incompleteness does not cause problems, since the respective algorithm proposes a correct, although not optimal solution in the worst case.

In order to illustrate OO view mechanisms and subsequently allow the reader to compare them with contexts, we first give an example of the view construction process in MultiView, one of the most advanced OODB view systems. For this purpose consider a simple base schema, such as the one specified on the left-hand-side of Fig. 2. Our goal is to derive a view such as to accommodate for the fact that every full-time employee shall be given a permit to park his/her car on the newly acquired parking place at the company's campus.

First, individual view classes need to be specified. This can be achieved by formulating expressions in object algebra. For example, the class FullTimeEmployee is derived from Employee via the expression:

FullTimeEmployee' := select from Employee where status = fullTime .

This expression yields the desired subset of the class Employee. Then, all full-time employees need to be associated with the new attribute 'parkingPermitNo' via the expression:

FullTimeEmployee := refine (parkingPermitNo: Integer) for FullTimeEmployee' .

Analogously, further view classes could be defined. The next step is to select all classes, base as well as view, to be included in the target view schema. For example, let us select the classes Person, Employee, and FullTimeEmployee. The MultiView system then is capable of constructing a view schema that is consistent with the base schema with respect to isa-links and, futhermore, is closed. Should the latter not be the case, the algorithm ensuring the closure property in Multiview yields the minimal set of classes to be added to the view schema in order to make it closed. In our example, the class Company needs to be added.

Reflecting on the example, the primary advantage of using views rather that integrating new classes into the base schema is that unforeseen changes can easily be accommodated and all existing applications can run on their unmodified, original schema. Only new applications run on the view schema that is customized to exactly fit their purpose. Nevertheless, the view concept is limited in a number of respects. For example, the propagation channels for updates are 'hardwired' to be directed from the base schema to all view schemas and from every view schema to the base schema. Also, authorization models based on OO views have not (yet) been discussed in the literature. In the next section we present an OO context mechanism that incorporates some useful features not addressed by views.

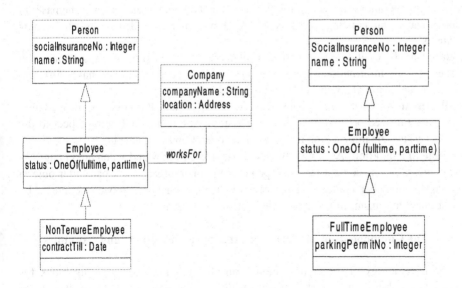

Fig. 2. A base schema and an OO, capacity-augmenting, non-closed view

4. An Object-Oriented Context Model: Scope, Definitions, and Operations

4.1 Scope of the Context Framework

The object model underlying this work corresponds to core object model features generally agreed upon in the literature (for example: encapsulation, polymorphism, full- and multiple inheritance, etc.) [14], [8]. For simplicity, we introduce the term property function $p \in P$, where P is an infinite set of property functions. Each $p \in P$ can be either a value from a simple enumeration type, an object instance from some class, an arbitrarily complex function, or an object method. Each $p \in P$ has a name and a signature. Let t be the set of all types. Each $t \in T$ is associated with a set of property functions. A Class is defined such that is has a unique name, is associated with a type and with a set of objects--its instances. The type associated with a class corresponds to a common interface for all instance of the class. Note that classes are special objects and that we distinguish between the terms type and class.

One fundamental principle guiding the design of the framework was to make only minimal assumptions on the underlying object model, notably that an object space consists of a set of uniquely identified objects being associated with property functions via 'their' class. We further assume that objects are part of an object base being operated upon by transactions that are triggered by users. The main contribution of the context model rests with the features chosen to be addressed by the context mechanism, namely:

Partitioning and encapsulation. What facilities are provided for defining fragments of an information base? What is the basic structure of a context? Are contexts "special" members, or can they be dealt with as ordinary objects?

Construction. What operations are provided for constructing contexts? How are they related to operations provided for constructing OO views and view schemas? In which ways can existing contexts be combined and extended to result in new contexts?

Relativism. In what sense do contexts relativize the execution of transactions with respect to an information base? Can the same conceptual entity have different structure, behavior, and names across contexts?

Authorization. What mechanisms are offered to protect the contents of a context from unauthorized operations? How can visibility be relativized with respect to the user accessing the information base and to the operation being executed?

Change propagation. Assuming that contexts overlap, how and when are changes to the contents of one context (e.g. an update of the internal state of a particular object) propagated to other contexts? How can propagation channels between contexts be constrained to transmitting only selected categories of change?

4.2 The Components of the OO Context Model: Definitions and Examples

In the terminology of the context model, an object is the basic building block for object bases. Let Objects be the set of all possible objects. Likewise, we define Predicates to be the set of Boolean expressions transferable to Horn-clause form, used as components of context definitions, while Users is the set of potential users who may access an information base. `Transactions` is the set of all possible atomic operations on contexts. Each transaction is executed with respect to (`wrt`) a context, assuming it has proper authorization. Finally, `Contexts` is the set of all possible contexts.

Contexts are instances of the class 'Context'. They are special objects representing the decomposition of an object base. The class 'Context' includes (amongst others) the following property functions.

```
CLASS Context
contents: OidSet
  {associates the context with a set of unique object identifiers, oid's}
lexicon: OidReferentnamePairSet
  {associates each oid of the context's contents with a name for the entity referred to}
authorP: AuthorizationPredicate
  {associates the context with an authorization predicate, based on users and
  transactions}
propagateFrom, PropagateTo: PropagationPredicate
  {associates each context with a set of change propagation links, based on the partner
  context(s), users, and transactions}
ownwers: OwnerSet
```

Note that objects provide an object-base-wide unique identification of their referent conceptual entities as well as a context dependent name and representation of their referents in terms of perspective objects. In some more detail, an objects's oid uniquely determines the object's referent such that within one object base no two conceptual entities are referred to by the same oid. Although only a single perspective of some object may be visible within one context at one point in time, nested contexts may contain further perspectives of that unit. Also, information on a conceptual entity need not necessarily be captured in any 'base context', but rather may be scattered across contexts, as long as the correspondence between each perspective and the conceptual entity it represents is maintained.

To illustrate the lexicon, consider, for example `lexicon(accounting, oid1)` which evaluates to the referent of oid1, say 'tom' (compare Fig. 1) with respect to the accounting context. Note that perspective objects modeling the same conceptual entity may have different names with respect to different contexts and, conversely, the same name may refer to different oid's in different contexts.

Authorization. Each context is associated with a predicate which determines whether user u is authorized to execute transaction t within that context. In brief, the authorization model proposed for contexts shares most essential features with the models presented in [15] and [16]. This applies in particular to its content-based nature, the reliance on implication hierarchies for authorization domains (in particular for users and objects), and the fact that authorization is expressed in the form of predicates. The approach taken here, however, differs from current models in two major respects. Firstly, we chose to specify authorizations for domains of transactions rather than for system-defined operations. In fact, providing transaction-based authorization can be designed to generalize operation- or access-type-based provision of authorization (compare also [17]). This is in so far as system-defined operations, such as those provided by some query language, can be considered to be executed as transactions and hence be integrated into the hierarchy of transaction domains.

The second major distinguishing feature inherent to our approach is the fact that authorization is associated with contexts as units of authorization. This allows one to achieve a flexible grain-size of authorization objects such that authorizations can be defined not only on three levels--such as database, class, and instance in other object-oriented models--but for any meaningful constellation of objects encapsulated within a context. As an example, consider a context, call it workEnvironment, that contains the classes Employee, Employer, Student, Enterprise, and University. If a user being assigned the role of ExpertUser should be authorized to create instances of these classes, it would suffice to associate the following authorization predicate with the context workEnvironment:

```
authorP(u,t) = ExpertUser(u) ∧ Create(t)
```

In authorization models not providing contexts as authorization objects, a predicate like the one above has to be specified for each of the four classes in order to achieve analogous authorization.

Change propagation. The functions propagateFrom and propagateTo select for each context c and context-user-transaction triple (c, u, t) a predicate which determines the incoming/outgoing change propagation links and associated constraints. The need for change propagation, in general, arises in all applications where contexts have a non-empty intersection and want to communicate over 'shared' objects, or want to keep objects in their intersection consistent, thus realizing a common interface.

Propagation of changes between two contexts is determined by mutual consent of the contexts involved as well as their respective authorization rules. In particular, change propagation between two contexts, say from 'sales' to 'accounting', is declared through two complementary predicates:

```
propagateFrom(c, u, t) = sales(c)
```

{appears in 'accounting' that declares to receive all changes from 'sales'}

```
propagateTo(c, u, t) = accounting(c)
```

{appears in 'sales' that declares to propagate all changes to 'accounting' }.

Given the above declarations, we say that there exists a propagation channel or link from 'sales' to 'accounting'. Note that in the above declarations, no constraints regarding changes affected by specific users and/or transactions are specified. In order to allow one to define more precisely what changes are to be propagated or received on propagation channels, propagateFrom and propagateTo functions depend on two further arguments: users and transactions. These serve to define filters for the changes to be propagated from or received in (exported/imported to) a particular context. Given that only UpdateEmployee transactions executed by Manager users shall be propagated from 'sales' to 'accounting', the propagateTo declaration in 'sales' would have the form:

```
propagateTo(c, u, t) = (accounting(c) ∧ Manager(u) ∧
UpdateEmployee(t));
```

One of the strengths of our proposal is that it separates the encapsulation of objects in a context, from change propagation to/from that context.

Owners. Each context is assigned one or more owners. By default, a context's owner is the user who initiated the creation of the context and who is authorized to perform any operation or transaction on his/her context.

4.3 Primitive Operations on Contexts

There are three sets of primitive operations on contexts. The first set encompasses all operations that allow one to observe and modify the contents, lexicon, authorization predicate, change propagation specification, and ownerset of a context. All these operations support contexts to be treated as encapsulated, abstract data types. They are defined in more detail in [3].

Secondly, since OO views can be considered as special cases of contexts, all operations provided by OO view mechanisms are also applicable for contexts. Thus, there are operations for deriving perspective objects (called virtual- or view objects in OODBs) from existing ones, potentially refining them by new, original information. These operations are based on an object algebra (see e.g. [12]) and have been summarized in Section 3.

The third set contains high-level operations that allow one to construct contexts from sets of object classes or in terms of existing contexts. It is assumed that each newly created context is added to the contents of the context with respect to which the current transaction is executed. For example, the operation

```
newContext(classSet,tupleSet,authorP(u,t),
            propagateFrom(c,u,t),propagateTo(c,u,t))
```

creates a new context containing all the classes of 'classSet', having lexicon 'tupleSet', authorization predicate 'authorization(u,t)', and change propagation predicates 'propagateFrom(c,u,t), propagateTo(c,u,t)'. The new context is added to the contents of the context with respect to which the current transaction is executing.

A further particularly powerful category of operations are set-based operations, such as the union, difference and product of contexts. Note, however, that all these operations potentially lead to conflicts in all cases where different perspectives of the same object are to be included into one context. This is because each context may contain at most one perspective of an object. Different to our original proposal [2], we suggest that such conflicts be resolved with the intervention of the user. For example, if two contexts to be united contain different perspectives of the same conceptual entity (identified by the same oid), the user has to decide which perspective shall be included in the target context. Alternatively, a masking operation, which behaves much like set difference, could be used.

4.4 Transactions

Transactions define meaningful operations for the whole object base. They are defined in terms of primitive operations and compositional constructs such as sequencing, conditional, iteration. Transactions are always executed with respect to a particular context. However, they may contain subtransactions that access and/or effect change in different contexts. The context with respect to which a transaction execution is carried out is referred to as its execution context. An execution context provides, through its lexicon, the symbol table used by a transaction execution. As with other modern database transaction models, our transaction model incorporates features of advanced transaction models such as those discussed in [18].

5 Comparison, Discussion, and Further Research

5.1   Comparing Contexts with Views in Object-Oriented Databases

Database views constitute a well-known technique for providing users with customized, external schemas as well as for integrating databases. Contexts share with object preserving approaches to OO views (for example, [19], [12]) the advantage of not having to cope with the view update problem [10]. As discussed in [19], this is because objects in OO notations have an identity independent of their associated values. Thus, if the view definition language preserves object identity, view updates can unambiguously be traced back to their parent objects.

The context mechanism departs in major ways from comparable mechanisms found in databases: Firstly, our proposal eliminates the assumption that an object base is defined in terms of a single, global schema. In our framework partial, overlapping, and even possibly contradictory schemas may co-exist within a single object base.

Secondly, the authorization model adopted for contexts follows other discretionary, content-based models, such as [16] in that it allows one to express authorizations in terms of authorization predicates. Like other advanced discretionary models (for example [15], [16]) our model is based on hierarchies of user roles (authorization subjects) as well as authorization objects. However, two distinguishing features of our model are the flexible grain size of authorization objects, namely contexts, and the reliance on transaction hierarchies rather than on hierarchies of (primitive) operation types [17].

Third, a flexible model of change propagation is offered. This model extends the classical conception of change propagation, which is oriented from base classes to views in so far, as in our model any direction, or none at all, of propagating changes between a parent and a derived context is supported. Also, propagations may be constrained to changes performed by selected users and/or transactions.

Finally, powerful operations for context creation and extension are provided in addition to the capability of defining a context as the result of a query.

5.2   Related Work, Conclusion, and Further Research

In order to improve the organization and management of information, this paper proposes a mechanism for decomposing systems built by utilizing object-oriented technology into possibly overlapping fragments, called contexts

As indicated at numerous places in this paper, several articles in the literature relate to our proposal. Database views have been traditionally used to present partial, but consistent, viewpoints of the contents of a database to different user groups. More recently, such mechanisms have been adopted for object-oriented databases (compare, e.g. [19], [22], [20], [12], [21]) and, in particular, for providing views on multi-database systems [22]. Commercial software engineering tools such as SUN NSE [23] provide basic support for workspaces but offer only a limited change notification mechanism such that our proposal for a change propagation mechanism significantly extends change propagation facilities found in other workspace models. Since the early days of AI, contexts have found uses in problem solving ([24]), in knowledge representation, as representational devices for partitioning a knowledge base ([25],

[26]) and in multi-agent planning, as ways of representing agent viewpoints [27]. In addition, [28] proposes comparable notions in order to represent topicality. [29] and [30] employ contexts for reasoning, but the focus of their work is (logic-based) knowledge bases and the relativization of inferences, rather than transaction executions.

The main contribution of our work rests with the provision of a viewpoint abstraction mechanism that deals with both aspects, namely contexts as well as perspectives in an object-oriented environment. The support of these two aspects has been identified as an essential requirement on any powerful viewpoint mechanism as a result of [1]. While this paper discussed the integration of the context framework into the world of object-orientation at a conceptual level, further work is directed towards implementing a prototype of the framework using component technologies, in particular JavaBeans.

One feature of the context mechanism we found quite restrictive on certain occasions is the fact that within one context only one perspective of some object is visible at one point in time. This restriction has an analogy in the single classification mechanism (i.e. every object is direct instance-of exactly one class) of commercial OO languages [31]. Although workarounds for this limitation have been implemented e.g. in the form of object-slicing [32], the most "natural" solution would be to allow for multiple classification in OOL (as it is the case, for example, in Telos [33]).

In general, we illustrated in which ways contexts have the potential to provide a flexible customization mechanism for OO applications, in particular, if combined with OO view technology. The reader should appreciate that only minimal assumptions on the underlying object model have been made such that the results are applicable to a wide range of OO applications, ranging from OO analysis to OO programming and databases. Further, this paper addressed the individual features chosen for the context mechanism, namely: Relativized naming, object properties, and transaction executions; authorization; and change propagation.

A related research direction we follow is the application of the context mechanism to accompany view-directed requirements engineering [34]. In this approach, specification fragments are encapsulated as contexts within an OO repository system. Considering that particular application, the fact that contexts may contain partial, relativized, and potentially inconsistent information on objects has proved most supportive. A prototype system that implements a selection of the features mentioned above is described in [35].

Further research needs to address the efficient implementation of contexts considering the results from research on the maintenance of materialized, OO views [13]. While an in-depth theory on relativized, context-based naming in information bases that could be adapted to enrich our proposal has already been developed [36], we also propose to conduct further research on guidelines for context construction in various application areas such as OO development. In general, this work showed the feasibility of a unifying notion and accompanying support mechanisms for partitioning and focus of attention mechanisms which can be found in many areas of computer science. In our view, the numerous areas of related and further research can be seen as an indication of the high significance of the ubiquitous notion of context. Its relevance rises with the increase of information that needs to be focused, filtered, and reorganized on extrinsic grounds in order to be most useful.

Acknowledgements: Sincere thanks to John Mylopoulos for his tight cooperation on shaping the concept of a context and for several insightful discussions.

References

1 Motschnig-Pitrik R.: "An Integrating View on the Viewing Abstraction: Contexts and Perspectives in Software Development, AI, and Databases";.*Journal of Systems Integration*, 5 (1) Kluwer (April 1995) 23-60

2 Mylopoulos J., Motschnig-Pitrik R.: "Partitioning Information Bases with Contexts"; Proc. of the 3rd International Conf. on Cooperative Information Systems, Vienna (May 1995)

3 Motschnig-Pitrik R., Mylopoulos J.: "Semantics, Features, and Applications of the Viewpoint Abstraction", Proc. of CAiSE'96, 8th Internat. Conference on Advanced Information Systems Engineering, Lecture Notes in Computer Science Vol. 1080, Springer Verlag, Berlin Heidelberg New York (1996) 514-539

4 Winston M.,E., Chaffin R., Herrmann D.: " A taxanomy of part-whole relations", *Cognitive Science*, 11 (1987) 417-444

5 Storey V.,C.: "Understanding Semantic Relationships"; *Very Large Database Journal* 2(4), (October 1993) 455-488

6 Motschnig-Pitrik R.: "Analyzing the Notions of Attributes, Aggregates, Parts, and Members in Data/Knowledge Modeling", *Journal of Systems and Software* 33(2) (May 1996) 113-122

7 Motschnig-Pitrik R.: "Requirements and Comparison of View Mechanisms for Object-Oriented Databases"; *Information Systems* 21(3) (1996) 229-252

8 Rumbaugh J., Jacobson I., Booch G.: The Unified Modeling Language Reference Manual; Addison-Wesley (1999)

9 Schneider, P., F.: "Contexts in PSN"; Proc. of the AI-CSCSI-SCEIO Conference, Victoria, B.C., Canada (May 1980) 71-78

10 Gottlob G., Paolini P., Zicari R.: "Properties and Update Semantics of Consistent Views"; *ACM TODS* 13(4) (December 1988) 486 - 521

11 Ra Y-G., Rundensteiner E., A.: "A Transparent Schema-Evolution System Based on Object-Oriented View Technology"; *IEEE TKDE*, 9(4) (July/August 1997) 600-624

12 Rundensteiner E.: "MultiView: A Methodology for Supporting Multiple Views in Object-Oriented Databases"; Proc. of the 18th Int. Conference on Very Large Databases (VLDB), Vancouver (1992) 187-198

13 Kuno H., A., Rundensteiner E., A.: "Incremental Maintenance of Materialized Object-Oriented Views in MultiView: Strategies and Performance Evaluation"; *IEEE TKDE* 10(5) (September/October 1998) 768-791

14 Beeri, C.: "New Data Models and Languages - the Challenge"; Proc. of PODS 92 (1992)

15 Rabitti F., Bertino E., Kim W., Woelk D.: " A Model of Authorization for Next-Generation Database Systems", *ACM TODS* 16 (1) (March 1991) 88-131

16 Bertino E., Weigand H.. " An approach to authorization modeling in object-oriented database systems"; *Data & Knowledge Engineering* 12 (1) (February 1994) 1-29

17 Constantopoulos P., Tzitzikas Y.: "Context-Driven Information Base Update"; Proc. of CAiSE'96, 8th Internat. Conference on Advanced Information Systems Engineering, Springer LNCS 1080 (June 1996) 319-344

18 ElMagarmid A. K. (ed.): "Database Transaction Models for Advanced Applications"; Morgan Kaufmann, San Mateo, CA (1993)

19 Scholl M., H., Laasch C., Tresch M.: "Updateable Views in Object Oriented Databases"; Proc. of the 2nd Conf on DOOD, Munich (Dec. 1991)

20 Bertino E.: "A View Mechanism for Object-Oriented Databases"; EDBT 92'; Vienna, April 1992, Lecture Notes in Computer Science Vol. 580, Springer Verlag, Berlin Heidelberg New York (1992) 136-151

21 dos Santos C. S., Abiteboul S., Delobel C.: "Virtual schemas and bases"; in Jarke, Bubenko, Jeffery (ed.), Advances in Database Technology - EDBT '94, 81-94, Springer Verlag (1994) 81-94

22 Scholl M. H., Schek H.-J., Tresch: "Object-algebra and views for multi-objectbases"; in Oezsu, Dayal, Valduriez (ed.), Distributed Object Management, Morgan Kaufmann (1993) 352-373

23 SUN Microsystems. "Introduction to the NSE.SUN Part No. 800-2362-1300, March 1988.

24 Hewitt C.: "Procedural Embedding of Knowledge in PLANNER"; Proc. of the 2nd IJCAI (September 1971) 167-182

25 Hendrix, G.: "Expanding the Utility of Semantic Networks Through Partitioning"; Advanced Papers of the IJCAI'75 (1975) 115-121

26 Attardi, G. and Simi, M., "Completenes and Consistency of OMEGA, A Logic for Knowledge Representation", Proc. of the IJCAI'91 Vancouver (1991)

27 Cohen, P. and Levesque, H., "Intention is Choice with Commitment", *Artificial Intelligence* 42(3) (1990)

28 Schubert L., GoebelR., Cercone N.: "The Structure and Organization of a Semantic Net for Comprehension and Inference"; in Findler N. (ed.): Associative Networks; Representation and Use of Knowledge by Computers, Academic Press (1979)

29 McCarthy J., Buvac S.: "Formalizing Contexts"; Technical Report, STAN-CS-TN-94-13, Stanford University (1994)

30 Demolombe R., Jones A.: " On sentences of the kind sentence 'p' is about topic 't': some steps toward a formal, logical analysis"; in: Logic, Language and Reasoning. Essays in Honor of Dov. Gabbay, Ohlbach H-J, Reyle U., editors, Kluwer Academic Press (1996)

31 Motschnig-Pitrik R., Mylopoulos, J., "Classes and Instances"; *Int. Journal on Intelligent and Cooperative Information Systems* 1(1) (1992) 61-92

32 Martin J., Odell J.:"Object-Oriented Analysis and Design"; Prentice Hall (1992)

33 Mylopoulos, J., Borgida, A., Jarke, M. and Koubarakis, M., "Telos: Representing Knowledge About Information Systems", *ACM Transactions on Information Systems*, 8(4) (Oct. 1990)

34 Motschnig-Pitrik R., Nissen H., Jarke M.: "View-Directed Requirements Engineering: A Framework and Metamodel"; in Proc. of SEKE'97, Intl. Conference on Software Engineering and Knowledge Engineering, Madrid, Spain (June 1997)

35 Nissen H.: "Spezifizierung und Resolution von multiplen Perspektiven in der Konzeptuellen Modellierung"; Dissertation, Institut für Informatik, RWTH-Aachen, Germany (1996)

36 Theodorakis M., Constantopoulos P.: "Context-Based Naming in Information Bases"; *International Journal of Cooperative Information Systems*, 6(3&4) (1997) 269-292

Objective and Cognitive Context*

Carlo Penco

Department of Philosophy - University of Genoa (Italy)
Via Balbi, 4 – 16126 Genova (Italy)
penco@unige.it

Abstract. In what follows I consider the apparent contrast between two kinds of theories of context: a theory of objective context - exemplified in the works of Kaplan and Lewis - and a theory of subjective context -exemplified in the works of McCarthy and Giunchiglia. I consider then some difficulties for the objective theory. I don't give any formalization; instead I give some theoretical points about the problem. A possible result could be the abandon of the double indexing for a development a multi-context theory (I give an example of a case). However other results could be possible and a challenge is posed to solve problems using the best results from each tradition of research.

1 Two Concepts of Contexts

Contexts are not things we find in Nature; there are so many different ways of using the term "context" (in philosophy, linguistics, psychology, theory of communication, problem solving, cognitive science, artificial intelligence) that it would be better to speak of a "family-resemblance" concept. Since Dummett we speak of the "context principle" in Frege and Wittgenstein; we speak of "context of utterance" in pragmatics; we speak of "context sensitive" grammars in linguistics, and we speak also of "linguistic context" and "non linguistic context". Studying the many attempts to have a better grasp of what kind of concept a context is, it is easy to find a strong counterposition between an objective and a subjective view of context[1]. Two paradigmatic positions representing these alternative views are the model theoretical tradition and the artificial intelligence tradition. Both traditions give formal settings to treat contexts; here I will restrict myself to conceptual analysis. On one hand I will focus - for its clarity - on the original theory presented by David Kaplan, even if the model

---

* The main ideas of this paper have been discussed in a talk at Pittsburgh Center for the Philosophy of Science during 1998; I wish to thank Horacio Arló Costa, Paolo Bouquet, Michael Green, Marcello Frixione and some unknown referees for their very useful comments

[1] In giving this counterposition I strongly rely on [7], who speak of the contrast between "pragmatic" and "cognitive" contexts, and on [3], who speak of the contrast between metaphysical and cognitive context

theoretical tradition encloses many further developments[2]. On the other hand I will use some basic concepts shared by multi-context theories in A.I., relying on the recent literature stemming from McCarty's original ideas on formalizing contexts. The two different conceptions can be summarized as follows:

(a) context is a set of features of the world, we can express as: ⟨time, place, speaker,...⟩

(b) context is a set of assumptions on the world, we can express as: ⟨language, axioms, rules⟩

In "Afterthoughts" [11] Kaplan speaks explicitly of the "metaphysical" point of view in describing contexts, while in "Notes on formalizing contexts" Mc-Carthy uses a notion of context which leads towards the idea of "microtheory" (Guha) or towards the idea of a subjective point of view on the world (Giunchiglia)[3]. Given these differences I will distinguish the contexts thus:

— context as an objective, metaphysical state of affair, and
— context as a subjective,cognitive representation of the world.

However, in making this distinction we are presupposing already a basic choice. Given two different names we think as we had two radically different concepts. But in what sense are these two concepts different? We might be in a situation similar to the concept of probability, where - with Carnap - it was possible to distinguish $probability_1$ and $probability_2$ (subjective and objective probability) as two different concepts linked by the common obedience to Kolmogoroff's axioms. In this case we should have two concepts strictly correlated, for which it is possible to have a unique formal framework but different interpretation and therefore, also from an historical point of view, different theories. We have two different interpretations of what a context is: features of the world or representations of features of the world; we might call the two different interpretation:

— "objective" or "metaphysical" (ontological) theory of context, and
— "subjective" or "cognitive" (epistemic) theory of context.

---

[2] Many works in model theoretic semantics and dynamic semantics (e.g. Stalnaker, Kamp, Heim, Asher) could exemplify different solutions to the problem of context. The varieties of the literature compels me to choose a single trend to make the discussion reasonable

[3] Let us see some relevant quotation.

On (a): "context is a package of whatever parameters are needed to determine the referent ... of the directly referential expressions"; "each parameter has an interpretation as a natural feature of a certain region of the world" [10].

On (b) "context is a group of assertions closed (under entailment) about which something can be said" [17]; context is "a theory of the world which encodes an individual's perspective about it" [6]

However we are in a different situation than the one characterizing the concept of probability after Kolmogoroff's axioms. As far as the concepts of context are concerned, we have different formal standards and axiomatisations. Therefore our main questions are:

– Shall we be content to have two different concepts and two different theories?

– Is it possible to look for some higher theoretical and formal setting on which to place the two concepts of context?

1.1 Terminology and the naïf theory of contexts

Some warning on terminology are needed. [20] speaks of three different levels of context: pre-semantic, semantic and post-semantic context. The pre-semantic context is simply what we need to give a syntactic evaluation to a linguistic expression, whose ambiguity depend on the surrounding occasion of utterance (listening to the sentence "I saw her duck under the table" we need some information to decide whether "duck" is a noun or a verb or whether "her" is an indexical or a possessive pronoun: e.g. the person in question may have lost her pet or she may seek security in an earthquake). Semantic context is what we need after having determined which syntactic structures and meaning are being used. Indexicals are the typical case: if we know that "her" is an indexical and not a possessive pronoun, we still need contextual information (speaker, audience, time, location) to decide which individual is the referent of the indexical. Post-semantic context is whas is taken for granted in the linguistic interchange of a community. Although this three-partition is promising, I prefer to stress the differences of semantic content on one hand and pre and post semantic context on the other hand. Pre and post semantic context can be viewed as different levels of cognition on the situation, while semantic context is normally presented as the objective features of reality we must rely upon. My problem is the following: how can we give a central role to the objective feature of reality in our theory? Can we speak of the objective context as the reality *as it is*?

I speak of "objective" or "metaphysical" context using Kaplan's terminology. I do not choose a particular metaphysics; I simply mean that context, as intended by Kaplan, represents the objective state of affairs, independently of our access to it (this is the "metaphysical" aspect). When I say "subjective" or "cognitive" context I don't mean to speak of an individual's set of beliefs, but of an individual set of beliefs. The set of beliefs may also belong to a community, or it may be a set of information stored for some purpose and accessible to many.

At first sight the relation between the two contexts is apparent and may be presented in a naïf conception: cognitive context gives the beliefs on objective context. Any time I have a belief I have a belief about what I judge to be an objective context; however I may get it wrong. If I am in Rome and I believe I am in Paris, I believe it true something false. There is nothing wrong with this conception about the relations between objective and subjective context. However, in this conception, some problems remain unanswered. We might be unable in principle to know what the objective context is. Different standards of measurement or standards of precision may be in conflict and may make it impossible to determine in a unique way what we have to take as objective context. Besides we might be unable to know where and when something happened or some utterance has been produced; think of situations where people may rely only on memory and testimony.

Somebody could reject the identification of "objective" and "metaphysical" context, suggesting that metaphysical context is a sort of trans-cognitive and absolute phenomenon, while objective context is what is taken as objective depending on some standard of individuation and on some perspective or point of view. Making this step means, to me, plugging the objective context inside the cognitive one: the one which decides which standards are to be used or the one which is the most powerful. If objective is only what is taken as objective under a point of view, we have no clue to what objective reality could be, we fall into a simple relativism. On the other hand, a realistic theory which relies on the basic assumption of a description of the objective features of reality without further contraints runs the risk to come to troubles and to be blind in front of many problems. The initial contrast between objective and cognitive is a good move for understanding what correct and incorrect assertion is, and what we mean by true and false belief. After that move, we need some more sophistication. This is the main intuition behind this paper.

1.2 Reduction of theories, not of concepts

The distinction between objective and cognitive context seems to be a natural and well grounded one insofar it reproduces a general distinction we normally make between representation and what is represented. However, notwithstanding the intuitive distinction between the two above mentioned theories of context, the line of demarcation is not so easy to pose. In his classical paper on General Semantics Lewis [14] thought it useful to put many parameters in the index, enclosing the background knowledge of the speaker. As soon as [15] accepted Kaplan's theory of double indexing (an index for possible words and an index for contexts), he held to his strategy to put inside the index for contexts relevant subjective information, as the speakers' beliefs or background knowledge, plugging in the "objective" context a subjective content. Contexts however are rich in features, while indexes are poor and cannot exhaust contexts; therefore the features of an index must be chosen according to some criterion. What I want to point out here is the following: a concept born to represent the objective features of the world seems to have a natural tendency to become subjective (even if somebody might say that the background knowledge or the speaker's beliefs still belong to the objective world). On the other hand the subjective context has to deal with objective states of affair, and also with the reference of "I" and "you" when uttered in some specific situation - and with the objective reference of any element of the cognitive context. If context is intended as a set of assertions, certainly these assertions will be - or would like to be - about something objective; therefore it is natural to think that they should give a representation not only of subjective points of view, but also of what is represented by them. If we cannot "reduce" the concept of objective features of the world to the concept of representation of them, we still have the problem of the possible reduction of the correlated theories. We have two theories and we have to check which of the two has more expressive power, which is better suited to help us in understanding the working of our language and of our relations with the world.

We might embed the theory of cognitive context inside the model-theoretical framework, using the most recent development of model theoretic semantics[4]. We might try the alternative strategy of reducing theories of objective context to a theory of cognitive context (e.g. via reduction of modal logic to multi context theory)[5]. I lack the logical ability to pursue either of these strategies. Therefore I will give just some intuitive and sketchy doubts and hints towards the possibility of this reduction at the level of conceptual frameworks. In fact, besides the development of formalism, we need conceptual clarification. And if we do not attain clarification at a conceptual level, our formalisms might not help us to reach a unifying theoretical framework.

2 Problems about a Theory of Objective Context

We may distinguish two basic aspects in Kaplan's theory: (a) the distinction between content and character, which is absolutely helpful in distinguishing the evaluation of indexicals in different worlds; (b) the distinction between context of utterance and circumstance (possible world plus time). I am inclined to accept a development of the first distinction, while casting some doubt on the viability of the second. Certainly in Kaplan the two ideas are strongly dependent one another, being the distinction of character and content defined in term of context (character being defined as a function from context to contents). However the content-character distinction can be considered as a general distinction concerning different levels of meaning, which could be developed and generalized in many different ways. It can be viewed, for instance, as an heir of Carnap's attempts to give more fine grained distinctions in meaning than just intension can give (think of intensional structure). Or it could be developed in an inferential framework: if meaning is defined in inferential terms, we might define the difference between character and content through the different kinds of inferences which are available or permitted to the speaker or the hearer. Take the cases of [19] on the use of "I" and "he" when the content of the two indexicals is the same ("he is attacked by a bear", "I am attacked by a bear" ...); we may distinguish the inferences available from the point of view of somebody not knowing

---

[4] There are many possibilities from preferential logics to the logics of explicit and implicit belief (Levesque or Fagin and Halpern). A recent attempt by Thomason [22] preserves the framework of modal logic, trying to restore the information about the different aspects of belief in an agent (e.g.the antecedents of a belief). The solution is "to replace a single unanalysed belief modality with a family of modalitites corresponding to different sources of information" (p.59)

[5] Attempts have been made by Giunchiglia, Serafini, and Frixione [9], Giunchiglia and Serafini [8]. An intermediate approach is the "syntactic" approach by Konolige [12], with a modal logic where the belief operator is interpreted on a set of sentences.

the identity of "I" and "he", and the inferences available to somebody who acknowledges the identity. These two points of view can be considered two different cognitive contexts, two theories with some relation of accessibility. Leaving aside the first basic aspect, let us focus on Kaplan's basic distinction of (metaphysical) context and circumstance. This distinction can be considered as an attempt to devise a contrast between conceptual elements and non conceptual ones inside a proposition. The conceptual elements are expressed by predicates and definite descriptions and are evaluated at every circumstance; the non conceptual element, the causal or contextual one, is expressed by indexicals. Indexicals are the linguistic items which connect us directly to the external world. Therefore we need a special account for extracting information from indexicals: information on indexicals such as "I" or "now" has to be derived directly from the (physical) context of utterance. We need therefore to plug in our formalism a new index, referring to the physical features of the world, such as time and location of utterance or speaker, and so on.

2.1 Doubts on direct reference

However what is it the direct connection to the world which is supposedly given by the use of indexicals? The direct connection to the world is given by the use of symbols for referring; therefore any use of any symbols for referring gives a connection with the world. The logic of Demonstrative should become a logic of demonstration, of the use of linguistic items for demontrative purposes. However, as Robert Brandom [4] has variously shown, there are doubts about the foundation of "connection with the world" in the demonstration and use of tokens; any use of linguistic items as demonstration has a reason to occur in language only because it is possible to embed the linguistic item in an anaphoric chain, as anaphoric initiator. There is no use of demonstration without anaphora; but with anaphora we build a conceptual link around our terms and use them always inside a kind of theory (right or wrong) about what is happening.

2.2 "Physical" parameters are always given inside cognitive contexts

The conclusion given before can be said in other terminology: an evaluation of the Logic of Demonstratives gives the referent of the indexical (of "now" for instance) depending on the information about the time, and on the accessibility of this information. We represent the actual and possible worlds always inside a cognitive context, inside a point of view. An objective indefeasible metaphysical point of view is not expressible by us (may be it is not expressible at all); a formal system will represent the point of view of the kind of information and rules embedded in the system. Every system cannot but represent a point of view among others; therefore it belongs to a cognitive context (let us say the context of the semantic of classical modal logic).

Any point of view purports to represent objective reality, but no point of view can be taken to be "the" representation of the objective reality. Even the most abstract levels of representation of objective reality gives different and possibly contrasting representations: a fragment of classical logic represents a different point of view from a fragment of intuitionistic logic. Considering the more concrete level of indexicals: when a system evaluates a demonstrative such as "you" or "I" at a time and location of utterance, it is always bound to be criticized and my evaluation can be rejected as mistaken (for instance: depending on the accessibility of time and location; see later par.3) . Any theory or system of representation (be it an individual, a logical system, a society) is always a defeasable representation of reality. It would be desirable to express this feature (defeasability) inside our formalism.

2.3   Doubts on double indexing

The idea of double indexing means that we need an index for referring to possible worlds, where different conceptual possibilities arise, and an index for referring to physical features of the actual world at which to evaluate indexicals or demonstratives.

Does the above criticism imply that we ought to abandon double indexing? This sounds unfair to this wonderful novelty in logic, but we might always check whether some other trick can do the job. Actually it is not question of tricks, but of theory: we need an overall view of the working of our language and of our (formal and not formal) representations of the world. Every representation purports to represent the objective state of affair; however no representation can be absolutely certain and undefeasible beyond any doubt; therefore we may only give cognitive or "marked" representations of the world. My suggestion is that we could obtain the same richness of double indexing with a a special operation of selection amongst cognitive contexts. Objective contexts are given by some of the many possible descriptions of the world; they are always given - explicitly or implicitly - inside a cognitive context. The selected context performs the role of objective context for us if we use it as such. But we have to be always ready to revise it in the face of new contrasting information.

3   What a Metaphysical Theory of Context Cannot Do

A theory is better than another if it can solve the problems solved by the previous one and also has some advantages. I list hereafter some cases which can be considered - at least - a challenge to be posed to both kinds of theory. Some of these cases are discussed in the literature; some can be solved in one version or another of both paradigms. Given the limitation of time and location, I will expand only the last example, and I will give only a few hints on the other cases, beginning with a general restriction on the problem of a logic of contextual reasoning.

- *conditions on a logic of contextual reasoning*

"I am here now": Kaplan says that the sentence is true in all contexts, depending on speaker, place and time of production. Giunchiglia and Bouquet

[7] claim that two further conditions must be fulfilled: (a) we must *know* that the meaning of the sentence depends on speaker, place and time; (b) the value of these parameters (speaker, place and time) must be *represented* as a part of the cognitive state of such an individual. These two condition seem to be a general requirement that all logics of contextual reasoning should possess.

- *built in sortals in demonstratives*

"This (book) is boring": Kaplan says that demonstratives need an act of demontration; in many cases however the use of "this" and "that" depends on cognitive context, on a built-in sortal which helps to individuate the intended object. The point has been stressed by Bonomi [2]: "If you say *this book is boring* you are likely to use no demonstration, since the situation in which the utterance takes place is (usually) definite enough to specify what the relevant book is. ...[A]ny demonstration is potentially ambiguous without an associated sortal term".

- *cases of different inferences permitted by different indexicals*

"He is pouring sugar" and "I am pouring sugar": the two sentences, uttered referring to the same individual, permit different practical inferences, while the Logic of Demonstratives can only give the relevant evaluation of the indexicals; this case has been present by Perry some times ago [19], to show the cognitive relevance of the indexicals, which seems to go beyond the simple mastery of the linguistic rule, and have some influence on the relation between belief and behavior.

- *possibility of false utterances with indexicals*

"Now I am here": this is the preferred sentence used by Kaplan to give a case of an utterance true in all context, and not necessary. There are at least two cases which put a doubt on that. Think of an utterance of the sentence said to somebody who believes (and I know she does) I am elsewhere. First of all what I say is an intentional lie, and a lie is supposed to tell a falsehood. It might be said that what I say is strictly true; however, from a conversational point of view, we should take into account not only the speaker, but also the audience. Besides it has pointed out the case of the truth of an occurrence of "I am not here (now)" (e.g. written on a post-it on a door), which falsifies the idea that "I am here now" should be true in all contexts.

- *vagueness and dependence on cognitive context of the meaning of indexicals*

"I am here" may mean many different things. Certainly location is objective and it can be defined more and more precisely; however the kind of precision is given by the cognitive context (I am in Italy, in Trento, in this room, on this chair); and other kinds of use of "here" seem to go beyond this problem of definition of the physical space (I am reading this passage on the text; I am with you; "now I an not here" said in front of a video representing the place where you are at the moment);

- *cases where the partition of the world does not mean a physical partition*

"All dogs are sleeping", referring to our dogs put here and there, while other dogs are barking; we have the double problem of quantifying on a subset of dogs (belonging to our domain) and locating dogs which are not in a same location. On this second problem, it is always possible that "the criteria of partition of the world is not space-time organized ... how is it possible to divide the world in portions without thinking of a cognitive intervention of an agent, who "cuts" reality following his aims, interests, beliefs ... ?."[3]; the problem has been posed by Bonomi [1] and can find different treatments in the literature. See also [21].

 • *ambiguities between speaker's reference and semantic reference.*

I have chosen to give some space to this last case because of its large use in the literature. I have preferred to examine a single example at large than to give some, but not enough space, to the other examples. In the following I will restrict myself to this single example.

4 The Kind Husband

Before trying to give a reduction of an objective theory of context to a cognitive theory of context we might try a possible integration of the two different perspective. I take a philosophical example from Kripke's distinction of speaker's reference and semantic reference. [13] debates the problems which arise from the possibility to use a literally wrong description of somebody to refer to him; take the following example invented by Kneale and discussed by Donnellan and Kripke:

John says: "her husband is kind to her"

The person referred to by John is not the husband, but John uses this description with the intention to refer to the person which is in the scene. Actually we could say that this case is a case of demonstration, where the definite description, even if it were false, is used as a proxy for an indexical; or we could use the term forming operator "..., who is F", in this case "he, who is her husband". Instead of saying just "he", the speaker says something more specific with the intention to help the audience to pick up the right person (and with the wrong presupposition that, being kind, the person is a husband) . The objective, metaphysical context is a set of parameters where we might put: (speaker, time, audience, person which is object of the demonstration). This set of parameters picks up the only person who is the speaker's referent, notwithstanding his wrong belief about the status of the person to whom he referred. The alliance between the two theories here would help: a metaphysical theory of context gives the existence of a unique individual referred to in the objective context, individual which is the same in all possible worlds; cognitive context explains the misunderstandings which arise in misplacing some description in the actual demonstration. There are however some problems which are not answered in a theory of the metaphysical context, dealing with identity and identification. The metaphysical context postulates the existence of a unique object referred to by the demonstrative; the individual referred by "he, who is her husband" must be the same in all possible worlds. On the one hand the metaphysical theory cannot be used to decide how to reidentify the same individual in all the worlds. On the other hand a logic of demonstratives should be able to pick up and re-identify the unique individual referred to. But how? We need the "how" if we want to explain the possibility of misunderstanding. We need to express the set of assumptions which represents information shared in the relevant community; e.g. we may rely on some data-base which contains information about the marital status of all the persons belonging to the community and check the name of the lady's husband; then we may compare this name with the name of the referred person and verify whether they match or not. If they match, speaker's reference and semantic reference coincide; if they do not, speaker's reference and semantic reference are to be distinguished. However this seems to be an empirical matter of no interest for a general theory of context.

The point is that we may doubt whether this kind of problems is really only an empirical matter. Keeping this kind of problems in mind we may search a general explanation of the working of language and reasoning using only a theory of cognitive context, whether the work done with the interplay between metaphysical and cognitive theories of context can be given using only a cognitive theory of context. Having the concept of a representation of reality from some point of view, we apparently have the concept of a represented thing; however we do not start from a list of parameters giving the "real" and "objective" elements of reality, but we start with different points of view about what is real or not, and reach the idea of objectivity at the end of the interplay among cognitive contexts.

Let us see how the interplay among contexts brings about a view on objectivity. I will not use any of the different formalisations of multi-context theories, but I will give an intuitive formulation which can be coherent with most of them. I assume that each context shares the same inference rules and has the minimum information required for interpreting the sentence " her husband is kind to her".

Context c_0 (beliefs of the reporter)

(0) s believes that a (=the person referred to as b's husband) is kind to b

Context c_1 (beliefs of speaker s)

$$(1)\ a\ \text{is kind to}\ b$$
$$(2)\ a = \text{husband of}\ b$$

Context c_2 (typically shared knowledge)

$$(3)\ c = \text{husband of}\ b$$
$$\text{therefore:}$$
$$(4)\ a \neq \text{husband of}\ b$$

Context c_1 and context c_2 have contrasting information. How to choose between one or the other? How to define the correct identities? We need some relation between contexts, a relation of reliability (*more-reliable-than*), which helps us to decide which context gives the right representation of the reality:

Context c_3 (competent obs)
in c_2: (1) a is kind to b; (4) a $\neq$ husband of b
in c_1: (1) a is kind to b; (3) a = husband of b
c_2 more reliable than c_1
discard (2), keep (3) and (1)
revise c_1
assert: (4) and (1)

This may also help us to verify some implicit assumption in the discussion of the example. The supposition that the relevant person is the lover and not the husband is the one we (or Kripke, Donnellan and Kneale) make. However we may be making a mistake. The relevant person could have been really the husband. Who knows? We need not only justification but also possibility of doubt. We must be ready to accept the introduction of other points of view which would enable us to discard the objectivity we have reached with some difficulty. We may be informed that "he" is the husband in disguise, pretending to be the lover. Given the right "testimony" a new context may arise with this new piece of information with evidence for it to decide for the reliability of what is expressed in context c_1 (even if based on chance and not on knowledge; e.g. on the person revealing with highly reliable means this identity). We need in this case another context c_4 which could verify the validity of the conclusion in c_3 and eventually accept of reject it.

5 Conclusion

This sketchy presentation is intended just to give an idea of how we may always make our cognitive context explicit; the objective context is, most of the times, the context we *recognize* as objective. We know both that there is some objective reality and that we might get it wrong. To describe an objective context as such, independent of a cognitive one, is therefore a risky enterprise. Any attempt to define it in an absolute way is misleading, because it takes a description - given always inside some theory or cognitive context - as an objective unrevisable description. Objectivity is always a result of our interactions, not a datum: in any situation of dialog among many agents we may elaborate an outer context which has some mastery of each of the other contexts; all terms and predicates can be lifted into the outer context which serves as a paradigm of de-contextualisation. But the de-contextualization is always relative (a point stressed by McCarthy). We cannot assume that we have reached the definitive representation of the structure of the reality; there is no ultimate outer context, but it is always possible to transcend the context in which we are. This gives rise to the possibility of an infinite regress, but it seems that this infinite regress is harmless, and represents our condition of being limited humans. To stop the regress we simply choose to *use* a cognitive context as provisional outermost context. But there is no outermost context.

This picture contrasts with the idea of a metaphysical context, which gives the "real" features of the reality. The general suggestion is that a multicontext theory might perform what a logic of demontratives performs; we may abandon the idea of expressing metaphysical context, relying only on relative decontextualizations. That may appear an idealistic step, but it does not follow. Speaking of relativity of contexts is just a reminder of the fact that the world is given to us only inside a net of views. We cannot speak of things in the world but ¿from some perspective, some point of view - more or less reliable.

This idea has been suggested in different ways inside the A.I. community, where the term "view" is often used: Konolidge speaks of views as syntactic devices; Barwise and Perry speak of situations as the reference of a speaker's utterance representing an incomplete model of the world; Levesque speaks of incomplete models as representation of the way an agent sees the world. Recently Giunchiglia and Bouquet have suggested a contrast between (a) giving a set of parameters as real features of the world (place, time, speaker...) and (b)giving a view of the world. The basic idea is that formal models "do not formalise (a portion) of the world, but rather a view of some portion of the world", and "each view is thought of as an agent-centered representation of some domain" [7]. A view is the only way we have to speak of the world and gives the content of our empirical observations[6]. Shall we still be allowed to speak of objective context? Are we falling into the naïf idea we have expressed at the beginning of the paper? The naïf idea is that the objective context is always objective relative to some point of view. We have said that this idea runs the risk of relativism, and of abandoning any common criterion of objectivity. Maybe we will not find an ultimate common criterion; however we cannot be content with a simple relativization to points of view. On one hand we have to recognize that the objective features of the world are always given to us inside some view. On the other hand we have the right to make comparisons, when necessary, and make decisions on which is the best approximation to objectivity and truth (think of the relation "more reliable than"). As limited agents we cannot reach truth *per se* or objectivity *per se*. As agents in a community we have the right and the duty to fight for achieving them. For that purpose, the most important thing we need is a study of the relations among contexts, in order to represent the complex web of views. The real novelty of the logic of contextual reasoning in A.I. is the analysis of the different kinds of rules which regulate the relations among cognitive contexts (lifting rules, bridge rules, depending on which formalization

---

[6] From a general philosophical perspective this solution - as the authors point out in a footnote - seems to represent a Kantian approach to epistemology. Kantian approaches have been widely discussed in recent literature, e.g., by Bonomi, by McDowell and Brandom. Bonomi has been the first to give an attempt to distinguish and make it possible an interaction between possible worlds and cognitive contexts, inside a Kantian framework. McDowell insists on the radical connection between language aquisition and our perceptual links to the world: we perceive objects we see as humans when we enter a conceptual community thought (language) learning.

we choose). This line of work seems to be the most promising way to face the problem of dealing with our representation of objectivity and truth in a world where we have always limited knowledge.

The analysis of rules among contexts may also fill a gaps in Brandom's analysis of the way the idea of objectivity is reached. Brandom claims that objectivity is what towards which we converge, when we recognize that we have different views; when we recognize the concepts of right and wrong, we are building the idea of something objective, which goes beyond our limited resources. However this idea comes at the end of a long journey in our linguistic and social interchange. The argument is this: all of us have different perspectives; we share just the idea that there is a difference between what is objectively correct and what is taken to be so. Therefore, we do not share conceptual contents, but the structure of our treating them as correct or not. What is shared is "the structure, not the content." However it is really difficult to see what "structure" could mean, unless we mean the structure of our abilities to make comparison between contexts and to shift from one context to another. Through these comparisons we make decisions about what is to be taken as objective, with the acknowledgement of the defeasability of our decisions.

Saying that the context is normally *rich*, McCarthy suggests that we can never exhaust the features of the context; the point has already been made by Lewis, even if the technical answer was different. Probably we need a careful research to integrate the best of the model theoretical paradigm and of the A.I. paradigm of contextual reasoning. I hope to have given some reason to push toward this direction.

References

1. A. Bonomi. *Eventi mentali*. Il Saggiatore, 1983.
2. A. Bonomi. Indices and Contexts of Discourse. *Lingua e Stile*, 33, 1998.
3. P. Bouquet. *Contesti e ragionamento contestuale. Il ruolo del contesto in una teoria della rappresentazione della conoscenza*. Pantograph, Genova (Italy), 1998.
4. R. Brandom. *Making it Explicit*. Harward University Press, Cambridge (MA), 1994.
5. M. Frixione. *Logica, significato e Intelligenza Artificiale*. FrancoAngeli, 1994.
6. F. Giunchiglia. Contextual reasoning. *Epistemologia, special issue on I Linguaggi e le Macchine*, XVI:345–364, 1993. Short version in Proceedings IJCAI'93 Workshop on Using Knowledge in its Context, Chambery, France, 1993, pp. 39–49. Also IRST-Technical Report 9211-20, IRST, Trento, Italy.
7. F. Giunchiglia and P. Bouquet. Introduction to contextual reasoning. An Artificial Intelligence perspective. In B. Kokinov, editor, *Perspectives on Cognitive Science*, volume 3, pages 138–159. NBU Press, Sofia, 1997. Lecture Notes of a course on "Contextual Reasoning" of the European Summer School on Cognitive Science, Sofia, 1996.
8. F. Giunchiglia and L. Serafini. Multilanguage hierarchical logics (or: how we can do without modal logics). *Artificial Intelligence*, 65:29–70, 1994. Also IRST-Technical Report 9110-07, IRST, Trento, Italy.

9. F. Giunchiglia, L. Serafini, E. Giunchiglia, and M. Frixione. Non-Omniscient Belief as Context-Based Reasoning. In *Proc. of the 13th International Joint Conference on Artificial Intelligence*, pages 548–554, Chambery, France, 1993. Also IRST-Technical Report 9206-03, IRST, Trento, Italy.

10. D. Kaplan. On the Logic of Demonstratives. *Journal of Philosophical Logic*, 8:81–98, 1978.

11. D. Kaplan. Afterthoughts. In *Themes from Kaplan*. Oxford University Press, Oxford, 1989.

12. K. Konolige. *A deduction model of belief.* Pitman, London, 1986.

13. S. Kripke. Speaker's referent and semantic referent. In French, Uehling, and Wettstein, editors, *Studies in the Philosophy of Language*. University of Minnesota Press, 1977.

14. D. Lewis. General Semantics. *Synthese*, 22:18–67, 1970. Reprinted in [16].

15. D. Lewis. Index, Context, and Content. In S. Kranger and S. Ohman, editors, *Philosophy and Grammar*, pages 79–100. D. Reidel Publishing Company, 1980.

16. D. Lewis. *Philosophical papers.* Oxford University Press, 1983.

17. J. McCarthy. Notes on Formalizing Context. In *Proc. of the 13th International Joint Conference on Artificial Intelligence*, pages 555–560, Chambery, France, 1993.

18. J. McCarthy and S. Buvač. Formalizing Context (Expanded Notes). In A. Aliseda, R.J. van Glabbeek, and D. Westerståhl, editors, *Computing Natural Language*, volume 81 of *CSLI Lecture Notes*, pages 13–50. Center for the Study of Language and Information, Stanford University, 1998.

19. J. Perry. The Problem of the Essential Indexical. *Nous*, 13:3–21, 1979.

20. J. Perry. Indexicals and Demonstratives. In R. Hale and C. Wright, editors, *Companion to the Philosophy of Language*. Blackwell, Oxford, 1997.

21. F. Récanati. Domains of discourse. *Linguistics and Philosophy*, 19:445–475, 1996.

22. R.H. Thomason. Intra-agent modality and nonmonotonic epistemic logic. In I. Gilboa, editor, *Theoretical Aspects of Rationality and Knowledge*. Morgan Kaufmann, 1998.

Dynamics between Contextual Knowledge and Proceduralized Context

J.-Ch. Pomerol and P. Brezillon

LIP6, Case 169, University Paris 6, 4 place Jussieu, 75252 Paris Cedex 05, France
E-mail: {Patrick.Brezillon, Jean-Charles.Pomerol}@lip6.fr

Abstract. In this paper, we use our experience as Intelligent Assistant System designers to clarify some notions about context and to study the question of context sharing. In the framework of the control of a subway line, the context plays a crucial role especially for incident solving. The analysis of the operators' behavior during incident solving shows that context takes three different forms, namely external, contextual knowledge and proceduralized context. Moreover, the paper discusses the dynamics of the exchanges between these three kinds of context.

1 Introduction

Many authors have raised the issue of context use within interactive systems [2], [16]. On the one hand, the cognitive aspect preponderates in most studies where people have gathered cognitive data about process control [2], [15]. On the other hand, our contribution does not rely on a cognitive background as in the preceding references but on our experience of system developers. In this perspective, especially based on a recent implemented system for the interactive control of a subway line, we propose some ideas on the role of context in interactive systems, and we focus on the problem of context sharing [6].

The SART project (French acronym for support system for traffic control) aims at developing an intelligent decision support system to help the operators who control a subway line to react to incidents that occur on the line. SART has to accomplish several functions such as acquiring knowledge from operators; simulating train traffic on the line, possibly with incidents; changing the model of the line on operator's request for helping the operator to test alternative issues; proposing alternatives for an incident solving; training a new operator not familiar with a given line; etc. All these functions are highly context-dependent. A presentation of SART can be found in [7].

This paper is organized as follows. In Section 2, we present our approach of context. Firstly, we give in brief some elements of the literature. Secondly, we present our view on three kinds of context. Thirdly, we illustrate the three kinds of context with examples drawn from the SART application. Section 3 discusses the dynamics between these three kinds of context, considering first the context sharing and, second, the dynamics of the decision making process.

2 Various Considerations on Context

2.1 The Context in the Literature

There is already an abundant literature on context. Brézillon [3] showed that context has played an important role in a number of domains for a long time, especially for activities such as foreseeing context changes, explaining unanticipated events and facilitating their handling, and helping to focus attention. Turner [27] developed these ideas of context-sensitive reasoning in the framework of underwater vehicles. In this work, context is mainly considered as a way for representing counter-factual or hypothetical situations, for circumscribing the effects of some actions to particular situations and for directing the focus of attention of an agent to the salient features of a situation. Thus, the context facilitates the reasoning by mobilizing underlying and relevant knowledge. Contextual knowledge is represented as a set of contextual schemas (c-schemas). In a given context, the system retrieves the most appropriate c-schemas and merges them to support the "reasoner," a module which helps the system to behave appropriately.

Brézillon and Abu-Hakima [4] showed that context has different meanings depending on the background. On the one hand, the cognitive viewpoint is that context is used to model interaction and situations, and as such it is dynamic and evolves continuously. This *a posteriori* view implies that context can be elicited only during task handling or problem solving. On the other hand, engineers try to represent context and consider it as a raw material for problem solving. They think that context has an *a priori* existence and can be represented. Adopting an *a priori* view, although we do not try to represent context as such, we will define context as the set of all the knowledge that could be evoked by a human being facing a situation, assuming that he has an unlimited time to think about it.

Moreover, context possesses a time dimension that raises some problems in modeling. Some have suggested that context is related to the interactions among agents, as opposed to context as a fixed concept relative to a particular problem or application domain [18]. In communication, the context is considered as the history of all that occurred over a period of time, the overall state of knowledge of the participating agents at a given moment, and the small set of things they are expecting at that particular moment. Thus, context appears as a shared knowledge space. One important point underlined by Mittal and Paris [21] is that communication, including explanations, and context interact with each other: the context of the situation triggers some actions, and this, in turn, modifies the context of the situation.

In a knowledge engineering setting, Grant [12] argued that the term "context" has some features in common with scripts (Schank & Riesbeck, 1989), frames or schemata as developed in human cognition. The context here is a candidate for something that is stored in long-term memory, and recalled as a whole, as a viable unit of a task appropriate to some step in a decision making.

2.2 Contextual Knowledge and Proceduralized Context

It is difficult to define the concept of context without considering the people involved in a situation. This is due, at a first glance, to the fact that the context involves knowledge that is not explicit. The "explicitness" depends on the persons, different from one person to another. Some common knowledge is implicit but well-known, for example the fact that it is easier to organize emergency operations in a station than in a tunnel.

We define *contextual knowledge* as all the knowledge which is relevant for one person in a given situated decision problem and which can be mobilized to understand this problem and explain the choice of a given action. Contextual knowledge is evoked by situations and events, and loosely tied to a task or a goal. Although the contextual knowledge exists in theory, it is actually implicit and latent, and is not usable unless a goal (or an intention) emerges. Figure 1 shows that contextual knowledge is a part of the "context", the rest of the context, which is not relevant to the situation, is called *external knowledge*.

When an event occurs, the attention of the actor is focused on it and a large part of the contextual knowledge will be proceduralized. We call the proceduralized part of the contextual knowledge, at a given step of a decision making, the *proceduralized context*. The proceduralized context is invoked, structured and situated according to a given focus. Giunchiglia [11] proposed a similar view by pointing out that context makes the reasoning local. This is a more or less "compiled" knowledge which can be elicited by the usual techniques of knowledge acquisition. The representation of the proceduralized context is either evoked from the underlying contextual knowledge or built during the proceduralization process.

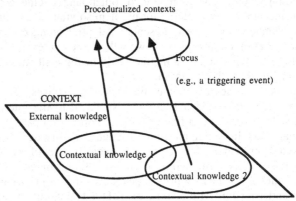

Figure 1: Different types of context

At a given step of a decision making, one has: proceduralized context which is the knowledge commonly known by the actors of the problem and directly (but often tacitly) used for the problem solving; contextual knowledge which is the knowledge not explicitly used but influencing the problem solving; and external knowledge which is the knowledge having nothing to do with the current decision making step, but known by many actors of the problem.

There are some similar views in the literature. For example, Anderson's theory [1] assume that knowledge is first acquired in a declarative form which encodes the basic facts and examples found in the instructions (our contextual knowledge). Once acquired, this knowledge is used by general problem-solving rules to create rules specific to a given context (our proceduralized context). Turner [28] considers descriptive and prescriptive knowledge that are close from our contextual knowledge and proceduralized context respectively. The descriptive knowledge is the information about what the context is, and prescriptive knowledge is the information about how to behave in the context. In Turner's work, all the contexts are represented by contextual schemas (c-schemas), and the c-schema representing the current context is a combination of c-schemas more elementary. In some sense, the set of all the c-schemas represents the explicit part of the contextual knowledge, while the current c-schema may be considered as a part of the proceduralized context. Nevertheless, the set of all the c-schemas is already structured before use.

There is another parallel with the *global-context* and *local-context* in [9]. *Global-context* (the contextual knowledge here) indicates the current topic under discussion. It contains the place in the dialogue history where this topic begun. *Local-context* (the proceduralized context here) points to the most recent utterance. As regards Schank's theory, assuming that context is the set of all the possible stories, the case corresponds approximately to our proceduralized context while contextual knowledge is the set of paradigmatic cases.

Note also that in our work "contextual" is not opposed to "linear" reasoning as in [2]; see also [15] for a criticism of "linear" models of diagnosis. As Pomerol [23] stated, the analysis of decision systems which separate diagnosis from anticipations is just an engineer's simplification and not a cognitive model, however many observations about what is called "decision bias" in decision theory may be due to the wrong intertwining of diagnosis, anticipation and preferences. It is also noteworthy that during the transformation of contextual knowledge into proceduralized context, some interpretations and rationalizations occur; this is reminiscent of the transformation of data into facts in the sense of Hoc and Amalberti [15]. Note also that our views about context are not inspired by a holistic point of view as opposed to a decomposition of the actions and reasoning (see [16] for a holistic argumentation).

2.3 Context Representations in SART

In the SART application, the context is the sum of all the knowledge, which is known by the operators, regarding the controlling task at large. Contextual knowledge constitutes the context of the incident solving (and a part of the operator's decision making framework). It is composed of all what the operator can learn in the control room, namely:

- from his colleagues who watch the operator and intervene from time to time by a question or a recall to the operator,
- information from outside (from the place of the incident and from outside the subway area), and
- by watching the visual monitoring and control panel, which is visible by all operators in the control room and acts as a kind of shared memory, if not a blackboard.

In Figure 2, taken up from [7], one can see the different types of contextual elements which are limited to the resolution of the incident "Sick traveler in a train." (Incidents are represented by ovals and actions by rectangular boxes as "Answer Alarm signal".) As contextual knowledge pieces are organized in layers, as onion skins, we coined the term *onion metaphor* [7]. The onion metaphor stresses the fact that all the facts are not at the same distance of the triggering fact (here « Stop at the next station »).

How are layers of contextual knowledge used by the operators in a diagnosis process? Contextual knowledge is always evoked by an event, such as a signal of power cutoff on a section of the subway line. Then, the operator reminds pieces of contextual knowledge such as type of day (e.g., working day), the period of the day (e.g., afternoon), the traffic state (e.g., rush hours), the section load (e.g., very busy). This allows the operator to have a clear picture of the context in which the incident occurs. Indeed the operator's reminding is made at two levels, namely a local level (the incident solving itself) and a global level (for ensuring as much as possible a normal exploitation of the rest of the line).

Consider the partial reasoning resulting in the action "Stop at the next station" in Figure 2. This reasoning stems from some chunks of implicit knowledge which are imposed on the driver because they correspond to mandatory procedures or instructions. In fact, at RATP (the French metro company), most of the incidents have been well-known for a long time (object on the track, lack of power supply, suicide, etc.). Thus, the company has established procedures for incident solving on the basis of their experience. We discuss in more details this point in a companion paper [22].

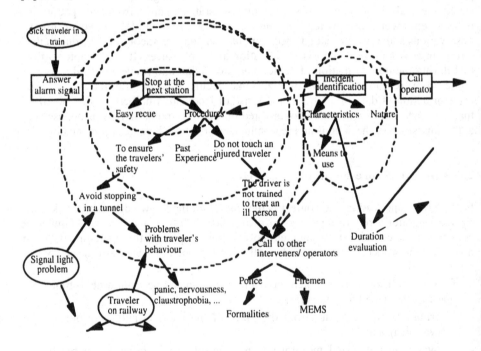

Figure 2: Context-based representation of the incident "Sick traveler in a train"

However, each operator develops his own practice to solve complex incidents, and one observes almost as many practices as operators for a given procedure because each operator tailors the procedure in order to take into account the current proceduralized context, which is particular and specific. More generally, in many working processes human beings can be observed to develop genuine procedures to reach the efficiency that decision makers intended when designing the task. Some parts of this practice are not coded [13]. Such know-how is generally built up case by case and is complemented by "makeshift repairs" (or non-written rules) that allow the operational agents to reach the required efficiency. This is a way of getting the result whatever the path followed. The validation of unwritten rules is linked more to the result than to the procedure to reach it. De Terssac [25] spoke of logic of efficiency. Let us give an example of the link which are weaved either by the operators or the procedures to build the proceduralized context.

Consider the problem raised by "Sick traveler on a train" (Figure 2). The change from the step "Answer the alarm signal" to "Stop at the next station" was surprising to us (as knowledge engineers). The triggering of the alarm signal implied for many years an immediate stop of the train, even in a tunnel because an alarm signal needed immediate attention. To explain the skipping of the action "Answer the alarm signal," the operator said that, based on company experience, they have decided to stop only at the next station for several reasons (see Figure 2). Some reasons are easy to understand (*e.g.*, rescue is easier in a station than in a tunnel). Other reasons needed additional knowledge (*e.g.*, drivers follow procedures because a traveler may be sensible to claustrophobia in a tunnel). Once we were able to gather all these reasons into a coherent proceduralized context, we understood the change. Note that other reasons are left implicit (*e.g.*, if the stop will last a long time in a station, other travelers may leave the train to go by bus, reducing the number of travelers waiting on the platform).

These pieces of knowledge, which are not necessarily expressed, result in more or less proceduralized actions that are compiled as the proceduralized context. Very often many pieces of proceduralized context are structured together in a comprehensive knowledge about actions. Moreover, there is no procedure for solving complex incidents, but a set of procedures for solving parts of the incident. For example, when a train cannot move in a tunnel, there are procedures for evacuating travelers at the nearest station, for clearing the damaged train by another train, etc. Some procedures are sequential, but others may be accomplish in any order. For example, when a train must push a damaged train, both trains must be empty but the order in which travelers of the two trains are evacuated is not important and mainly depends on the context. What is important is that the two actions must be accomplished. As a consequence, there are many strategies for solving an incident: Cases that are similar in one context may be totally dissimilar in others as already quoted by [29].

3 The Dynamics Between Different Types of Context and Context Sharing

Hoc and Amalberti [15] noted that the dynamics of the process is very important in diagnosis as well as control of complex systems. We think that it is not only important to understand the dynamics of planning and action but also the dynamics of knowledge management. This is a twofold phenomenon that consists of focusing on some stimuli and, on moving contextual information from back-stage to front-stage. Interaction between agents appears to be a privileged way for moving contextual knowledge to the proceduralized context.

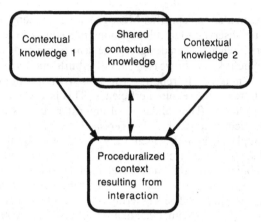

Figure 3: A representation of the interaction context

3.1 A Context Sharing

Figure 3 represents how the proceduralized context is built from contextual knowledge during interaction between two agents. The interaction context contains proceduralized pieces of knowledge in the focus of attention of the two agents. These pieces of knowledge are extracted from the contextual knowledge of each agent; they are jointly structured by the two agents and result in a shared knowledge. Generally, the first utterance of an agent gives a rule such as "Stop at the next station" if the alarm signal is triggered. Then, on the request of the second agent, the first agent may add some pieces of knowledge related to his first utterance. If this knowledge chunk belongs to the common part of the contextual knowledge of the agents, the pieces are integrated into a mutually acceptable knowledge structure, and the knowledge structure then is moved to the shared proceduralized context. Thus, the proceduralized context contains all the pieces of knowledge that have been discussed and accepted (at least made compatible as quoted by Karsenty and Brézillon [17] by all the agents. These pieces of proceduralized context become then a part of the shared contextual knowledge of each agent, even if they do not remain within the focus of the proceduralized context. Later, this proceduralized context may be recalled, as any piece of contextual knowledge, to be integrated in a new proceduralized context. Thus, the more an operator is experimented, the more the operator possesses ready to use structured knowledge. Note that the process is particularly important because whereas the operator makes alone his decision, colleagues present in the control room very often intervene in this process either by reminding an information or questioning the operator. As such, this is a collective problem solving process.

3.2 Dynamics of the Decision Making Process and Contextual Exchanges

Let us illustrate now the transformation of contextual knowledge into proceduralized context. In a normal situation, the control operator faces the following concern:

F0:   the "normal" focus of attention is to see that schedules and intervals between trains are respected

This task F0 can be regarded as routine and does not require special attention. Nevertheless, contextual knowledge about control is involved. In this task, the word 'normal' has different meanings according to the context; let us look at some possible contexts.

CO: the normal context associated with F0 involves:
   k1:   type of day (*e.g.*, working day, Saturday, Sunday, Holidays),
   k2:   period of the day (morning, afternoon, evening),
   k3:   traffic state (rush hours, off-peak hours),
   k4:   the section load (very busy, few people),

All these pieces of knowledge are some of the elements defining the contextual knowledge describing the environment of the problem with which the following pieces of knowledge are associated:

   k5:   the interval between trains according to the situation,
   k6:   the stopping time in stations, etc.

It is noteworthy that k5 and k6 are the only pieces of knowledge which are proceduralized in any cases, even when there is no incident. This means that, according to the contextual knowledge, they have a well defined value resulting from the company instructions, called procedures. However, the values of k5 and k6 are not explicitly linked to ki ($1 \leq i \leq 4$). This is not necessary during normal operations.

This example shows that contextual knowledge is therefore quite large and not focused. Many "normal" contexts are contained in this contextual knowledge. Assume now that an incident occurs on the subway line; the pieces of knowledge k1 to k4 are (or should be) immediately invoked. This results in k5 and k6 being invoked too and more importantly, the links between k5-k6 and k1-k4 are instantiated. Thus, now all the ki ($1 \leq i \leq 6$) become a part of the proceduralized context in which the incident occurs; contextual knowledge appears as back-stage knowledge, whereas the proceduralized context is in the front-stage in the spotlights (see Figure 1). When an incident occurs, k1 to k4, which are normally not proceduralized, move from contextual knowledge to the proceduralized context. It is noteworthy that, as far as engineering is concerned, only the proceduralized context matters, but contextual knowledge is necessary because this is the raw material from which proceduralized context is made. In a sense, the proceduralized context is the contextual knowledge activated and structured to make diagnoses or decisions.

Once the first pieces of contextual knowledge are mobilized, some other pieces of contextual knowledge, such as the position of the incident on the line, also enter the focus of attention and are proceduralized. The proceduralized context may also evolve to integrate some knowledge that, up to now, has neither been proceduralized nor is contextual (*i.e.* external knowledge) such as maintenance activity on the line, the number of trains on the line, the available help in the control room or the experience of the train driver. Thus, the diagnosis context evolves jointly and continuously with the reasoning process. This shows that the importance of the proceduralized context depends on the situation. The more complex the situation is, the more impoortant the proceduralized context is.

Operators solve an incident by choosing a scenario, which is a sequence of actions conditional on possible events. The choice of a scenario greatly relies on contextual knowledge. One operator said us: "When an incident is announced, I first look at the context in which the incident occurs." The reason is that the operators want to have a clear idea of future events; the purpose of this look-ahead reasoning [23] is to reduce, as far as possible, the uncertainty in the scenario. The problem for the operators is that many scenarios are similar at the beginning and then diverge according to the context. Thus, a scenario is a sequence of actions intertwined with events that do not depend on the decision makers but that result in a limitation of their actions. For instance:

<u>Focus of attention</u>:   Removal of a damaged train from the line.

<u>Contextual information</u>:   Level of activity on the line.

<u>Action</u>:   Lead the damaged train:

                               - to the terminal if the line activity is low

                               - to the nearest secondary line if line activity is high.

As many of the contextual elements may intervene in several scenarios (*e.g.*, traffic activity, position of the next train), the operators prefer to take them into account as soon as possible to get a general picture of the best path to choose. At this step, contextual knowledge is proceduralized and in the meantime operators postpone actions and gather together elementary actions the sequences of actions into macro-actions. The main objective is to eliminate event nodes and to use contextual information for the choice of the actions.

In a previous paper [5], we introduce the word "macro-actions" to describe a sequence of actions without intertwined events. This grouping of elementary actions plays an important role in operators' behavior. Roughly speaking, the idea of the operators by grouping actions in a macro-action and postponing the decisionas far as possible is twofold. Firstly, the operators try to replace uncertainty about events by the identification of the current context. Secondly, by using macro-actions, they try to facilitate the mapping between context and action, each macro-action being supposed to be adapted to one or several contexts. The role of the contexts is then more or less similar to the states of nature [23]. In our framework, we can think of macro-actions as a way to proceduralize contextual knowledge and to introduce modularity in the diagnosis process by managing different modules accomplishing the same function in different ways according to the context [5]. However, action postponement is not always possible, and it is preferable to look for pruning the decision tree in some situations [8]. Another interest of macro-actions is that they realize a kind of compilation of several actions (elementary actions or previous macro-actions) originated from experience. In this compilation, a part of the knowledge about each action becomes implicit in the proceduralized context. This is close to Edmondson & Meech's view [10] on context as a process of contextualization. However, for explaining a macro-action (and thus the whole reasoning involved in), an operator needs to decompile the macro-action for retrieving the rationales. Such an operation is not always easy, especially when experience comes from previous generation of operators.

Conclusion

In this paper, we introduced three types of context by refering to the SART application for the subway control, we mainly focused on the decision making process during incident solving. We considered three parts in context, namely external knowledge, contextual knowledge and proceduralized context. External knowledge is the part of context that has nothing to do with the incident solving at a given step of the incident solving. Contextual knowledge is knowledge that does not intervene directly in the decision making process but constrains it. Proceduralized knowledge is a part of contextual knowledge that is structured to be explicitely used in the reasoning at a given step of the decision making.

Another result that we discussed in the paper is the dynamics among these three parts of context when the decision making progresses from one step to the following one. Some pieces of the proceduralized context leave the interaction context to become shared contextual knowledge. Other pieces of contextual knowledge (and possibly from the external knowledge) enter the proceduralized context. These two aspects, static description of context and the dynamics of context are modeled in our application at the level of the domain knowledge and included in the reasoning for incident solving.

We definitely believe that one cannot apprehend contextual issues in a static framework and that expliciting and sharing of contextual knowledge is key process for addressing and understanding context problem.

Acknowledgments:

The SART project enters an agreement between two universities, the University Paris 6 (France) and the Federal University of Rio de Janeiro (FURJ, Brazil), a contract between the University Paris 6 the company of the subway in Paris (RATP), and another contract between the FURJ and Metrô that manages the subway in Rio de Janeiro. Grants are provided by RATP and COFECUB in France and CAPES in Brazil. We also thank J.-M. Sieur at RATP, and C. Gentile, L. Pasquier, I. Saker and M. Secron, Ph.D. students working in the SART project.

References

1. Anderson, J. R. (1993). Rules of the Mind. Hillsdale, NJ: Erlbaum
2. Bainbridge, L. (1997) The change in concepts needed to account for human behavior in complex dynamic tasks. *IEEE transactions on Systems, Man and Cybernetics*, 27, 3, 351-359.
3. Brézillon, P. (1999). Context in human-machine problem solving: A survey. *Knowledge Engineering Review*, 14(1): 1-37.
4. Brézillon, P. & Abu-Hakima, S. (1995). Using Knowledge in its context: Report on the IJCAI-93 Workshop. *AI Magazine, 16*, 1, 87-91.
5. Brézillon, P. & Pomerol, J.-Ch. (1998) Using contextual information in decision making. In: Chapman & Hall. Widmeyer G., Berkeley D., Brezillon P. & Rajkovic V. Eds.: Context-Sensitive Decision Support Systems, pp. 158-173.
6. Brézillon, P. & Pomerol, J.-Ch. (1999) Contextual knowledge sharing and cooperation in intelligent assistant systems. Le Travail Humain (to appear).
7. Brézillon, P., Gentile, C., Saker, I., & Secron, M. (1997). *SART: A system for supporting operators with contextual knowledge.* Paper presented at the *International and Interdisciplinary Conference on Modeling and Using Context (CONTEXT-97).* Rio de Janeiro, Brasil, Feb.
8. Brézillon , P., Pomerol, J.-Ch., & Saker, I. (1998). Contextual and contextualized knowledge and application in subway control. *International Journal of Human-Computer Studies*, 98, 357-373.
9. Carenini, G. & Moore, J.D. (1993). Generating explanations in context. International Workshop on Intelligent User Interfaces, Orlando, Florida.
10. Edmondson, W.H., & Meech, J.F. (1993), A model of context for human-computer interaction. Paper presented at the IJCAI-93 Workshop on Using Knowledge in its Context (Report 93/13) LAFORIA, Université Paris 6, 31-38.
11. Giunchiglia, F. (1995). Contextual reasoning. Proceedings of the IJCAI-93 Workshop on Using Knowledge in its Context, Research report 93/13, LAFORIA, pp. 39-48.
12. Grant, A.S. (1992). *Mental models and everyday activities.* Paper presented at the 2nd *Interdisciplinary Workshop on Mental Models*, Cambridge, UK, March, 94-102.
13. Hatchuel, A. & Weil, B. (1992). *L'expert et le système.* Paris: Economica.
14. Henninger, S. (1992). *The knowledge acquisition trap.* Paper presented at the *IEEE Workshop on Applying Artificial Intelligence to Software Problems: Assessing Promises and Pitfalls (CAIA-92).* Monterey, Canada, March.
15. Hoc, J.M., & Amalberti, R. (1995). Diagnosis : Some theoretical questions raised by applied research. *Current Psychology of Cognition*, 14, 1, 73-101.
16. Hollnagel, E. (Ed.). (1993). *Human Reliability Analysis, Context and Control.* London: Academic Press.
17. Karsenty, L., & Brézillon, P. (1995) Cooperative problem solving and explanation. Expert Systems With Applications, **8**(4): 445-462.
18. Maskery, H., & Meads, J. (1992). Context: In the eyes of users and in computer systems. *SIGCHI Bulletin*, 24, 2, 12-21.
19. McCarthy, J. (1993). *Notes on formalizing context.* Paper presented at the *13th IJCAI*, Vol. 1, pp. 555-560.
20. Millot, P., & Hoc, J.M. (1997). *Human-Machine Cooperation: Metaphor or possible reality.* Paper presented at *the European Conference on Cognitive Sciences (ECCS 97),* Manchester U.K.
21. Mittal, V.O., & Paris, C.L. (1995). Use of context in explanations systems. *International Journal of Expert Systems with Applications*, 8, 4, 491-504.
22. Pasquier, L., Brézillon, P., & Pomerol, J.-Ch. (1999). Context and decision grpahs in incident management on a subway line. Proceeding of the 2nd International and

Interdisciplinary Conference on Modeling and Using Context, CONTEXT-99, Trento, Italy, September (submitted).

23. Pomerol, J.-Ch. (1997). Artificial Intelligence and Human Decision Making. *European Journal of Operational Research, 99*, 3-25.

24. Schank, R.C., & Riesbeck, C.K. (Eds.). (1989). *Inside case-based reasoning*. Lawrence Erlbaum Associates, chap. 1-2.

25. de Terssac, G. (1992). *Autonomie dans le travail*. Série Sociologie d'Aujourd'hui, Paris: Presses Universitaires de France.

26. de Terssac, G. & Chabot, C. (1990). Réferentiel opératif commun et fiabilité. In J. Leplat and G. de Terssac (Eds.), *Les facteurs humains de la fiabilité*, Toulouse: Octarès, 110-139.

27. Turner, R.M. (1998). Context-mediated behavior for intelligent agent. International Journal of Human-Computer Studies, Special issue on Using Context in Applications, vol. 48, no. 3, pp. 307--330.

28. Turner, R.M. (1999). Context-mediated behavior: An approach to explicitly representing contexts and contextual knowledge for AI Applications. Working Notes of the AAAI-99 Workshop on Modeling and Using Context in AI Applications, AAAI Technical Report (to appear).

29. Tversky, A. (1977) . Features of similarity, Psychological Review 84(4): 327--352.

30. van den Bosch, R.J. (1994). Context and cognition in schizophrenia. In: Boer, J.A. den, Westenberg, H.G.M. and Praag, H.M. van (Eds.) Advances in the neurobiology of schizophrenia. Chichester, Wiley, 1994

A Context-Based Audiovisual Representation Model for Audiovisual Information Systems*

Yannick Prié[1,2], Alain Mille[2], and Jean-Marie Pinon[1]

[1] LISI 502, 20 av. Albert Einstein, INSA Lyon,
F-69621 Villeurbanne Cedex, France
Yannick.Prie@insa-lyon.fr
pinon@if.insa-lyon.fr
[2] LISA, CPE-LYON, 43, Bd. du 11 novembre 1918,
F-69616 Villeurbanne Cedex, France
am@cpe.fr

Abstract. In this paper we present a contextual representation model of audiovisual (AV) documents for AV information systems. In the first part, we study AV medium, and show that AV intra-document context is always related to a user task seen as a general description task. We then present the AI-Strata model for AV description: audiovisual units (pieces of AV documents) are annotated with annotation elements described in a knowledge base. The annotation elements are connected at the document level. The whole system being considered as a single graph, we define a context of one element as end points of graph-paths starting with this element. In order to control contextual paths, we define the notion of potential graphs as graph-patterns instantiated in the general graph. Finally, we show how these graphs are used in the main task of AV information system: navigation, indexing and retrieval.

1 Introduction

With the huge growth of data storage capacity and computing power, multimedia documents have become a reality (*e.g.* web pages, CD-ROMs). Among them, audiovisual (AV) documents, *i.e.*, documents composed of several sequential streams using a single temporal line (TV, video, radio...), can now be captured, edited, stored, and seen/heard in a digital form. These changes will surely induce on the long term changes in the media themselves, but on the short term, considering the increase in networking capabilities, many issues related to digital libraries have to be met, both for institutions (public libraries, audiovisual repositories) and companies (TV Channels), but also, and in an increasing way, for private users. Hence, the design of *audiovisual information systems* (AVIS) becomes an important research area.

* This work is partially supported by France Télécom (through CNET/CCETT), research contract N° 96 ME 17.

AVIS should allow users to *describe* and *index* audiovisual documents, in order to be able to manage them easily. Thus description schemes are needed[1], first for AV documents retrieval from the AVIS, that can then be played, second for the re-use and the manipulation of these documents (for instance an excerpt of a movie can be reused on a TV report). The overall design of audiovisual information systems is also crucial, and should benefit from results obtained in the study of textual and hypertextual information systems, mainly about the relations between the system and its users. For instance the user should be able to explore at his own pace the system, mainly using *navigation* (which has become a standard); the system should also help the user in his task, trying to reformulate his queries (relevance feedback), using a model of the task the user is performing, and even learning from his actions and results. In other words, the user and the system have to *collaborate* to reach a solution that matches the user's needs in various contexts.

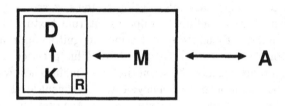

Fig. 1. A framework for identifying different views of context

Information systems, more and more heavily based on knowledge, gain from being studied along "contextual points of view", *i.e.*, considering how context, or contexts can be defined among the different parts of such a system. Used for a long time, *context* has been studied for itself only a few years ago[2]. In [4], Brézillon et al., though they admit that in fact this notion has multiple appearances — depending mainly on the ongoing task needing it — have made an attempt to retain its main characteristics. Indeed context is "something surrounding an item and giving meaning to it"; and it "cannot be considered out of its use". Moreover, "there are different types of contexts with respect to what we consider, and in which domain we are", and "all these contexts are interdependent". Restricting their purpose to information seeking systems in [5], Brézillon et al. propose an adaptation of a Newell and Simon model as a framework for the consideration of different views of the context. In figure 1, we refine this model into a documentary information processing system, with the repository R composed of two

---

[1] Several normalization comities like MPEG7 [10], or the EBU/SMPTE task force (see `http://www.ebu.ch/pmc_es_tf.html`) are currently working on these issues.

[2] Of course the word "context" is also often used is a very general way, for instance in their scheme for information retrieval, [13] name after context the content-theme of the searched document, which mainly reduce context to document genre *e.g.*, a cooking recipe.

interacting parts: a set of documents D and a knowledge base K (for instance metadata on the documents, thesauri, knowledge about the search task, *etc.*) A is an agent (human or machine) interacting with the system, and M is the set of "mechanisms" allowing access to R.

Depending on the research area considered, it is possible to associate several definitions of the context to elements or relations between elements of this framework, as in [5]. For instance the *interaction context* (somewhat related to pragmatics and discourse analysis) is at the level of the double arrow. The *knowledge-representation context* (linked with the reasoning context in AI and logics) lies at the K level and deals with internal inferences implying a symbolic notation of context. The *organizational context*, which contains the enunciation context in which the user is, takes place around A. Moreover, if we consider the documents as texts, the *internal linguistic context* [7] is located inside the documents in D. Of course, it is possible to define other contexts that rely on other simpler contexts.

Getting back to documentary information systems, it seems to us that the main dichotomy in context definition opposes internal textual/linguistics approach of the documents themselves, and a more cognitive approach using the document-user point of view, and the *situation* of his practice. In this rough scheme, the AI approach wanders between these two main poles, with the useful constraint of symbolic computing efficiency: at the document level, computerized knowledge helps enlighting the documents, while at the user level, it deals with the task (*i.e.*, the machine representation of the task) performed by the user.

In the first part of this article we will study audiovisual medium modelling, and show how intra-document context is always related to user tasks. In the second part, we will present AI-Strata, a generic model for representing AV documents, designed for tackling up intra-document context. Inter-document context, and context knowledge on AV documents are also supported, all these contexts being also related to tasks. We will then present our very pragmatic definition of context, and methods designed to use it. We will finally show how these methods are used in main audiovisual information system user tasks.

2 Modelling Audiovisual Documents in a Context-oriented Way

2.1 Audiovisual Medium and Modelling

An audiovisual document is composed of a superposition of streams that can be *aural* (music, voices) and/or *visual* (video, texts). The streams are both *sequential* (like text) and *temporal* (a speed rate is imposed). In the case of video stream, the 24 to 30 images per sec. frequency and the retinal persistence creates the *illusion of reality* (objects seem to live on the screen, and thus look more vivid than in still images). Above this first level of frame sequentiality, we can consider a second level, built on shot[3] sequences: *montage* of shots into sequences allows to make sense across shot cuts, just like sequences of sentences make sense into a text. Finally, superposing different streams of different modalities allows to benefit from the global effect of their union: for instance music can link totally different images using an audio metaphor, sound can reinforce the visual effects of a fight, *etc.*

Because of the proper nature of the AV media, which is mainly *non-textual*, its contents have to be reformulated in a semiotic form in order to facilitate their manipulation as symbols in a computer. In the modelization of digital sequential documents for computer representation, *annotation* is the fundamental process, which attaches an annotation (a description) to a piece of the document, each piece being delimited by two limits. For temporal media, these limits are obviously two instants in the AV stream. To characterize annotation of AV data according to that scheme, we proposed in [12] several criteria. *Time granularity* is the first; it deals with with the level of abstraction and the regularity of the cutting-up of documents into AV pieces: document level, shot or scene level with full decomposition, or video pieces as simple *strata*. The *kind of data* used to annotate the pieces is the second criterion: from the low-level features automatically extracted from the stream (color histograms, textures) to higher conceptual level characteristics like shots, keywords, or texts, everything is possible. The third criterion is the *degree of complexity* of the organization of characteristics into annotations: simple or atomic when a term or a numerical feature is attached to a piece, it can reach higher complexity like attributed structures or even semantic networks. According to these criteria, there exist many ways to describe, at different levels, with different complexities, AV material pieces that are cut following different granularity schemes. Our last and fourth criterion for annotation characterization is the structuration of pieces of the different pieces of a document, and is strongly related with granularity choices. There are two main approaches for the structuration of AV documents: *segmentation* and *stratification*.

Segmenting an AV document consists in cutting it up into *pre-defined* pieces which will be annotated later. An arborescent structural organization is also set-up to express a document structure [11] (see figure 2, left). On the contrary, the *stratification* approach [1] (see figure 2, right) means that the annotator freely defines *strata* (pieces) when needed. An *a posteriori* useful cutting-up can be derived from strata intersection. The essential difference between these two approaches lies in the definition of the temporally situated and annotated pieces of documents. In one case the cutting-up exists *before* an annotation that can be considered as *second* while in the other case it is *dynamically* created by the annotation process, annotation and cutting being tightly linked.

---

[3] Visual shots: stream of n contiguous frames continuously recorded by a single camera; extended to aural shots: n seconds of an audio stream, with an internal semantic coherence.

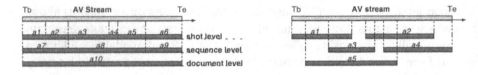

Fig. 2. Segmentation and stratification approach, the annotations are the a_i

2.2 Contextual Necessities

Our liminary remarks show that the *intra-document context* plays a very important role in an audiovisual document. At the montage level for instance, it has been proved a long time ago that a shot doesn't convey the same meaning when seen alone, or nearby another shot[4]. At the superposition level, sound can also totally modify the meaning of an image.

We can at least define two different types of contexts in an audiovisual document: the *temporal* context is linked with the temporality of the medium (for instance in the stratification approach the annotations of two strata that temporally overlap can be mutually influenced); the *semantic* context deals with the others contextual relations. In the semantic context comes first the *structural* context, dealing with the structure of the document. Indeed, a document is generally composed of sequences, themselves composed of shots: this hierarchy allows mutual influences between annotations from different structural units (for instance a sequence is enriched by the annotations of its shots [6], or a shot inherits the annotations of the document to which it belongs [15]). More generally, any co-reference meaningful context between any parts of a document is possible and belongs to the semantic context (for instance "each time this little character appears on the screen, I can hear that funny tune, and here the tune is used alone, thus represents the character").

If the temporal context — related to the fact that the audiovisual superposed streams are temporal — is shared in every usage of audiovisual material (*i.e.*, based on visualisation), *semantic context is related to the circumstances of the contextualization by the spectator*. As a consequence, in the more specific case of an AVIS, contextualization is related to the different tasks of the users.

Moreover, performing these tasks always entails the description of pieces of audiovisual documents. As the description of AV material is nothing but the elicitation of symbolic annotations and their placement in contexts where they are meaningful, "inserting in context" is the basic operation of any describing task, such as:

– Indexing : each symbolic annotation chosen for the representation an elicited object in the AV document is "explained" by its context.

---

[4] In 1920 years, a soviet director, Kuleshov, made the following experiment: he showed to an audience a shot of a man expressing no feelings, preceded by 1- a shot of a burial, 2- a shot of a child playing, 3- a shot of a soup plate. For the audience, the man was first sad, then happy, and at last, hungry.

- Searching : a searched item is described by a set of annotations together with their meaningful contexts.
- Navigating : surfing through the AV document, from one piece to another following meaningful links defined by the context where they make sense.
- Analysing : starting from a given studied, finding pieces of the video that are reachable in such a context.

As a conclusion, we claim that there is a clear link between task oriented contexts and intra-document contexts, as becoming aware of a contextual relation in an AV document is done in a description process. In next part we propose a description model of AV document able to operate with these contexts, but also with inter-documents context, and knowledge context in information systems.

3 The Annotations-Interconnected Strata Model

In this part we describe our model for the description of AV documents (for a more detailed presentation, see [12]). In our model, we privilege the stratification scheme for the following reasons: first, it is obviously more adequate to the representation of the dynamic aspects of AV material ; second, we consider strata and atomicity of the annotation as primordial, before any *a priori* segmentation (moreover, stratification approach is more general than segmentation: shots are just strata described as shots).

Objects of interest, analysis dimensions. We call *object of interest* any object (in the general sense of the term) that can be spotted when watching/listening to an AV stream. Objects of interest can refer to any kind of characteristic, at any level of abstraction; there are as many of them as there exists analyses of the stream. We group these analyses into *analysis dimensions* that allow to spot the same kinds of objects. For instance an analysis dimension can be related to shots, faces, people, moves, or President Clinton detection.

Audiovisual units, annotation elements. As soon as an object of interest is detected, it defines a temporally extended *audiovisual unit* (AVU) representing a stratum (the name of the stream and two temporal limits[5]), and at least one *annotation element* (AE) as a term, symbolic expression of its meaning. The annotation element annotates (is in relation R_a with) the audiovisual unit it has defined (we stay in the stratification approach). For instance, spotting a shot leads to define an AVU annotated by the AE $\langle Shot \rangle$, spotting for instance a well-known face leads to the creation of another AVU annotated by $\langle Mandela \rangle$, and so on for any object of interest: $\langle Zoom \rangle$, $\langle Round\_shape \rangle$, $\langle Sad \rangle$... A second description level is provided by *AE attributes*, for instance the numerical value of the histogram for $\langle Color\_histo \rangle$, a text as a speech excerpt for $\langle Script \rangle$ or a representative image for $\langle Shot \rangle$ (see figure 3).

---

[5] An important fact is that we do not represent temporal knowledge except in the audiovisual units: we consider that the use of this knowledge will proceed from the link between annotations and strata.

Elementary relations. To complete the primitive annotation that defines an AVU, it is possible to add as many AEs as necessary. The first way to do so is to add AE with the same temporal range, for example adding to an AVU defined by ⟨*Document*⟩ an AE regarding its ⟨*Author*⟩. The second and the most important way is derivated from the *structuration* of the annotation: in order to express more complex information than simply symbol-terms with a temporal extension, we allow *relations* between them. For instance, to express that "this shot has Mandela as video focus", we define relations between annotations elements *in the way* we already annotated. As on the example figure 3, we can use a third AE ⟨*VideoFocus*⟩ that acts as a relation term and then connect them with two elementary relations R_e. This method can be used to express any relation between any annotations elements as "this character is doing this action", and even between AEs in different AV stream, for "this shot is reused in that document". The model of the *Annotations Interconnected Strata* (AI-Strata) is named because of those relations.

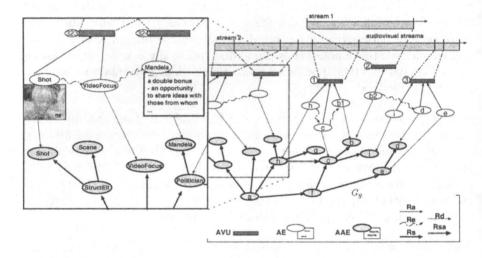

Fig. 3. General overview of AI-STRATA

Abstract annotation elements. In the same way as representation units and indexes, annotation elements and their relations are the operating substra that supports every access to AV material (thanks to AVU). The annotation process leading to this graph is done by a user who can be a professional (an archivist) or anyone. In order to facilitate and monitor further access, it is necessary to consider AE as terms issued from a controlled vocabulary in a knowledge base. An AE is then issued from an *abstract annotation element* (AAE), it is in *decontextualization relation*[6] R_d with it. The knowledge base is in fact a network

---

[6] This name comes from an analogy with linguistics.

of AAE with classical thesaurus relations (hierarchical: specialisation relation R_s and others, like see-also link R_{sa}), to which is added information regarding possible attributes of AE, or privileged relations. It acts as a shareable ontology, which is also necessary for reusing knowledge, serving as means for integrating problem solving, domain-representation and knowledge-acquisition modules (cf. [14]). Analysis dimensions are sets of abstract annotation elements.

4 Context in AI-Strata

4.1 Definition of context and contextualization in AI-Strata

As seen before, the basic elements of AI-Strata are the audiovisual units, the annotation elements, the abstract annotations elements and the relations between them. An AI-Strata system can then be considered as a unique oriented attributed *graph* G_g. This graph being connected, we can consider for any pair of elements $(x, y) \in G_g$ at least one *path* allowing to place x into relation with y. One can say that y belongs to the context of x (for instance on figure 3, the EA d belongs to the context of the AVU 2 considering a path containing b2).

We define the notion of *context* of an element x of G_g as any element $y \in G_g$ that can be placed into relation with it through a path in G_g. This definition is strict, general and well defined: a context is always a context of something that is known, in the knowledge-based system represented by the graph.

The process of *contextualization* consists first in the choice of one element of the graph as a beginning node for paths in the graph, and then in the search for the extremitates of these paths. For instance, if we consider an audiovisual unit as a beginning node (representing a Mandela shot in raw AV material), we can look for other audiovisual units contextually related to it (*e.g.*, representing all the documents where this shot has been re-used), as belonging to its audiovisual context when performing an analysing task. In the navigation task, we could search for annotation elements endpoints, and navigate towards them. Considering an abstract annotation element as beginning node, in a searching task we could look for audiovisual units in its context (*i.e.* AVU that are annotated with it). We will analyse these tasks in a more detailed way later.

4.2 AI-Strata methods for Manipulating Contexts

As we have seen, the context of any element of the system graph is potentially composed of the whole graph. This state of fact is indeed normal (after all, it is possible to find a semantic relation between any two concepts), but not very useful. So we need to gain *control* over the context, *i.e.*, over contextual paths in the graph. Keeping this in mind, we define two closely related types of graphs. A *fully attributed graph* is an oriented attributed graph with vertices (resp. edges) name attributes taking their values in a vocabulary V_V (resp. V_E). For instance, in our system graph G_g, the vertices take their values in $V_V = T \times E$, with T the types of nodes (here AVU, AE and AAE), and L the labels (for instance *Shot* or

Mandela for AEs, and 324 for AVUs); while V_E contains the possible relations between elements $(R_e, R_a, R_s \ldots)$. In a very similar way, a *partially attributed graph* is an oriented attributed graph defined under the same constraints as a fully one, with the exception that the vertices and edges names can also take a special value $*$. These pattern graphs are also called *potential graphs*. The name attribute value $*$ acts as a "wildcard" when the process attempts to *instantiate* a partially attributed graph g_p into a fully attributed one g_f. The instantiation of g_p into g_f consists in finding a partial subgraph g_s from g_f such as there exist an application between g_p and g_s that preserves the structure of the graph (syntactical constraint) and the name of the vertices and edges provided that $*$ acts as any other attribute value (semantic constraint)[7]. On figure 4, g_p is a potential graph, g_{i1}, g_{i2} and g_{i3} are the three instances of g_p in the fully attributed graph G_g of figure 3.

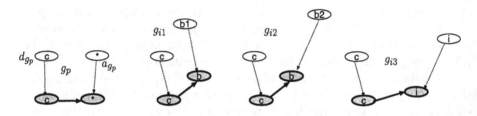

Fig. 4. Partially attributed graph and its instances

The potential graphs are characterized by some of their vertices, they can be named, manipulated, joined, *etc.*. As a first example of a potential graph, let us consider *designation graphs*. Designation graphs designate abstract annotation elements in the knowledge base; they are composed uniquely of AAE, and are characterized by one node. For instance, on figure 5, g_{p1} is instantiated into two subgraphs of G_g, the designation nodes in the instances designate the AAE $\langle Scene \rangle$ and $\langle Shot \rangle$.

Potential contextual relations express contextual paths. They are characterized by a source node and a final node. The skeleton of the graph (in grey on g_{p2} figure 5) expresses the path the graph designates, whereas other branches bear information about some intermediate nodes of the path (this could be related to the simple context notion of [8]).

For instance g_{p2} designate a contextual path between an annotation element and another one, with two intermediate AEs and one AAE. The branch ensures that the AAE needs to be a specialization of the AAE c. Using this potential

---

[7] Finding a subgraph isomorphism is a very difficult problem in the general case, and we put reasonable restrictions on our potential graphs: in a valid potential graph, at least one unambiguous association of the isomorphism must be known. For instance a AAE is known (it is unique by definition), or a AVU or a AE is precisely defined. The resulting trivial associations act as initialization for a propagation algorithm (multi-propagation if there are several initialization associations).

graph means *applying* it to an AE element of the graph in order to find the context of that element corresponding to the designated contextual path. For instance, if we apply g_{p2} to the annotation element c from figure 3 by the attribution to the beginning node of g_{p2} of a c value instead of *, we will find no instance of g'_{p1} in G_g; on the contrary, by applying it to h, we will find one instance of g''_{p2}, and the AE b2 designated by the end node will belong to the context of h across g_{p2}.

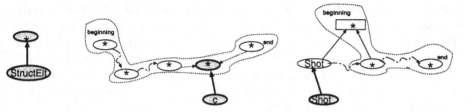

Fig. 5. Examples of potential graphs

Another important example of a potential contextual relation deals with the context of audiovisual units, *i.e.*, when the beginning node of the potential path is an AVU. For instance, the graph g_{p3} expresses a path dealing with the context of an AVU that is a ⟨*Shot*⟩. Applied to the AVU 323, it allows us to get back the EA ⟨*Mandela*⟩ as belonging to the context of the AVU. We should also note that potential graphs can be manipulated and joined; for instance we could build a potential graph g_{p4} by linking the beginning node of g_{p3} and the end node of g_{p2}, thus describing a new contextual path. These manipulations allow to create contexts from others contexts.

4.3 Exploiting an AI-STRATA based AVIS : managing contexts according to different tasks

As seen earlier, *navigation* has become a mandatory feature of any information system. We consider navigating as going from one element of the graph to another, using any path. In AI-Strata, navigating means then simply applying a contextual potential graph to the current element, and selecting among the end nodes results which one is to be explored. We should note that this type of navigation is a generalisation of the standard one: the contextual path of navigation is controlled at any level, it is not just a selection of a predefined link. Navigation can occur at any level of the graph:

– inside the knowledge base as exploration of the annotation vocabulary and knowledge. The context of any concept in the knowledge base is an indication of its meaning (for instance abstraction and difference relationships with siblings in the hierarchy). These contexts are also indices about the knowledge base creation task;

- inside the document base, as intra- or inter-stream navigation. Intra-stream navigation is related to internal contexts, while inter-stream navigation can be related to hypertext jumping and "intertextuality" study;
- from the documents to the knowledge base, for instance for a better understanding of a term that is explained with its concept relations as in [9].
- from the knowledge base to documents, for instance for explaining a concept with its use in a real case.

Indexing uses *contextual annotation* in a large manner, because any audiovisual unit is considered as annotated with the annotation elements it is directly in relation with (local context) but also with annotation elements that are in other contexts. For instance, in figure 3, the AVU 323 is directly annotated with ⟨*Shot*⟩, but also, and to the extend controlled by potential graphs, by ⟨*Mandela*⟩ or even ⟨*StructElt*⟩. This means that the semantic content of an AVU depends on the context around it that we consider. This context (*i.e.*, potential graphs) depends of course on the will of the user.

Searching or *querying* audiovisual units in AI-Strata can take several forms. In a *precise* query, the user describes the AVU u he is looking for by designing a potential graph with a *virtual* AVU (with a $*$ name attribute), in relation with AEs, which have in turn relations, and so on. Answers to the query are then the u AVUs from the instantiations of the graph in G_g. For instance, g_{p3} itself can be considered as a query, whose answer is the AVU 323. In a general AI-Strata query, the user just describes which annotations elements should annotate the AVU he is looking for, and from what context (expressed as contextual potential graph) these annotations should come. The system then transforms the query into potential graphs, instantiate them, and gives back the results.

The queries we have just evoked only interfer with at the first level of description, *i.e.*, the surface knowledge of annotation given by AE name values. But other queries have to do with the deeper knowledge represented in other AE attributes, like image features, or texts. In such cases the instantiation process has to take into account not only binary name similarity, but also other ones, adapted to other attributes. The important point here is that AI-Strata, because it provides a way to represent any audiovisual characteristic at the same description level, allows to mix many searches in a natural way, using potential graphs. For instance, a potential graph mixing surface knowledge (a shot must be annotated by a politician) and deeper knowledge (face recognition knowledge) can help to reduce the search space — the context — in a tremendous way for the application of expensive feature similarity computations (for instance the face recognition will only be used for shot annotated by politicians). It is also a possibility to consider the context of an AVU as a pre-annotation that monitors image-processing methods, as in [3]. For instance, if a document is already annotated as ⟨*TVNews*⟩, the presence of this AE in the close context of the AVU to be studied could trigger a better image processing method than the general one.

Finally, some words about the notion of *valences*, which are possibilities of relation for annotation elements, represented as contextual potential graphs, and stored as attributes of abstract annotation elements. Valences are useful for annotation and are used when an abstract annotation element is used to annotate, as annotation element, an audiovisual unit. If there is a valence, the system looks for instantiation of the potential graph in order to detect in the context of the new AE if there is another AE that could be placed into elementary relation with it. For instance, when using the AAE ⟨Mandela⟩ as a character to annotate an AV with the AE ⟨Mandela⟩, one could use its valence attribute to detect if in the context, there were no ⟨Action⟩-related AE, able to express the fact that ⟨Mandela⟩ is doing this action (for instance ⟨ToDance⟩). These steps are illustrated in figure 6: (1) Instantiation of the potential graph in the valence attribute, here representing a simple co-occurence context in an AVU. (2) An instance of the potential graph designate with its endpoint the AE ⟨ToDance⟩ in the context of the AE ⟨Mandela⟩. (3) An elementary relation is set up between ⟨Mandela⟩ and ⟨ToDance⟩.

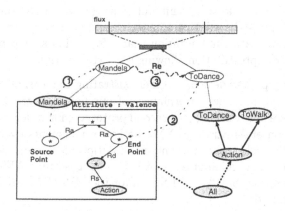

Fig. 6. Example of a valence of the AAE ⟨Mandela⟩

Valences, as part of the knowledge base, are useful for learning possibilities of relations from local and idiosyncratic relations and contexts. A context that has been set up by a user can eventually be generalized in a valence, and a valence that is much used for the annotation could entail the creation of a concept relation in the Knowledge Base.

5 Concluding discussion

In this article, we have presented an original approach for the modelization of audiovisual documents in a context oriented way. As computer representation means eliciting symbolic annotations, and as any AVIS-related task entails describing AV document pieces and putting them in context, we have shown that a context-suited representation model was needed. The Annotation-Interconnected

Strata approach allows to take into account both temporal (related to the fundamental temporality of audiovisual streams) and semantic contexts (related to the task the user is performing). The annotation graph is considered as a whole, and we have given a strict definition of a context of a graph element. Apart from this simple modeling of context, we have presented the potential graphs as patterns enabling to control contexts, and how these graphs (hence the contexts they represent) are used in the main description tasks of an audiovisual information system. Contextualization hence appears related to a description task, which is itself related to potential graphs. Such an approach and modelling of context is original in the multimedia document research area.

The AI-Strata approach represents an original approach in the multimedia representation field, indeed it subsumes segmentation, does not make any assertion about the document structure and allows to represent any different characteristics at the same description level. Having been designed with context in mind, many tasks of an AI-Strata based AVIS can be thought of as annotation elements description tasks in meaningful contexts. Moreover, since our notion of the context is graph-based, this approach could be extended to any other information systems, with the limitation that information should be represented with graph-based representation allowing contextualization.

A first prototype was developped, demonstrating the feasability of the ideas we have presented, and the performances of our potential graph instanciation algorithm. We are now working on a second prototype, for which we are studying the representation of AI-Strata in XML-designed documents (works like [2] are precursors in that field), and how the instantiation algorithms can be adapted to the XML world. In collaboration with France Télécom CNET, we are also working on a proposal based on AI-Strata for the MPEG-7 audiovisual content description standard.

On a more theoretical side, the ability of the model to tackle up any sequential media, like texts, could open fruitful uses in textual information system, and linguistics fields. We intend to deepen the study of the relations between internal linguistic contexts, and internal document context (in the reformulation approach for modelling, elementary relations between instances of annotations provide linearity to terms). Indeed, the semantic content associated with each annotation element depends on the position of the abstract annotation element which it is extracted from in the knowledge base (in the conceptual world), but also from its position in the annotation network. We should also remark that audiovisual units, as semiotic units of any temporal length (from one image to the length of the stream), can represent both local and global contexts for other audiovisual units, depending on the chosen contexts. This illustrates the fact that global meaning determines local meaning, while local meaning in turn has an influence on global meaning, in a very natural way.

Finally, it appears that an interdisciplinary research becomes more and more necessary for the design of representation models for future information systems; as document models should now be constructed in cooperation with humanities scientists (linguists, semioticians), while sufficiently general computerized models can in turn help scientists from these fields to design and test new hypotheses.

References

1. T. G. Aguierre Smith and G. Davenport. The stratification system, a design environment for random access video. In *Proc. Network and Operating System Support for Digital Audio and Video - 3th International Workshop*, La Jolla, 1992.
2. G. Auffret, J. Carrive, O. Chevet, T. Dechilly, R. Ronfard, and B. Bachimont. Audiovisual-based hypermedia authoring: using structured representations for efficient access to AV documents. In *ACM Hypertext'99*, Darmstadt, Germany, Feb. 1999.
3. F. Brémond and M. Thonnat. Issues in representing context illustrated by scene interpretation applications. In *Proc. of the first Int. and Interdisciplinary Conf. on Modeling and Using Context*, Rio de Janeiro, 1997.
4. P. Brézillon and M. Cavalcanti. Modeling and using context: Report on the first international and interdisciplinary conference context-97. *The Knowledge Engineering Review*, 12(4):1-10, 1997.
5. P. Brézillon and I. Saker. Modeling context in information seeking. In *International Conference on Information needs, Seeking and Use in Different Contexts, ISIC'98*, Sheffield,UK, 1998.
6. T.-S. Chua and L.-Q. Ruan. A video retrieval and sequencing system. *ACM Transactions on Information Systems*, 13(4):372-407, October 1995.
7. J.P. Desclés, E. Cartier, A. Jackiewicz, and J.L. Minel. Textual processing and contextual exploration method. In *Proc. of the first Int. and Interdisciplinary Conf. on Modeling and Using Context*, Rio de Janeiro, 1997.
8. B. Edmonds. A simple-minded network model with context-like objects. In *European Conference on Cognitive Science (ECCS'97)*, Manchester, 1997.
9. J. Nanard and M. Nanard. Adding macroscopic semantics to anchors in knowledge-based hypertext. *Int. J. Human-Computer Studies*, 43:363-382, 1995.
10. F. Pereira. Mpeg-7 : A standard for content-based audiovisual description. In *2nd Int. Conf. on Visual Information Systems*, pages 1-4, San Diego, Dec. 1997.
11. D. Ponceleon, S. Srinivasan, A. Amir, and D. Petkovic. Key to effective video retrieval: Effective cataloging and browsing. In *ACM Multimedia 98 Proc.*, Sept. 1998.
12. Y. Prié, A. Mille, and J.-M. Pinon. Ai-strata: A user-centered model for content-based description and retrieval of audiovisual sequences. In Springer Verlag, editor, *First Int. Advanced Multimedia Content Processing Conf.*, number 1554 in LNCS, pages 143-152, Osaka, Nov. 1998.
13. S.W. Smoliar and L.D. Wilcox. Indexing the content of multimedia documents. In *2nd Int. Conf. on Visual Information Systems*, pages 53-60, San Diego, Dec. 1997.
14. E. Walther, H. Eriksson, and M.A. Musen. Plug and play: Construction of task specific expert-system shells using sharable context ontologies. In *Proc. of the AAAI workshop on Knowledge Representation Aspects of Knowledge Acquisition*, San Jose, 1992.
15. R. Weiss, A. Duda, and D.K. Gifford. Composition and search with a video algebra. *IEEE Multimedia*, 2(1):12-25, 1995.

Putting Similarity Assessments into Context: Matching Functions with the User's Intended Operations[*]

M. Andrea Rodríguez and Max J. Egenhofer

National Center for Geographic Information and Analysis
and
Department of Spatial Information Science and Engineering
University of Maine
Orono, ME 04469-5711, USA
(207) 581-2188
{andrea,max}@spatial.maine.edu

Abstract. This paper presents a practical application of context for the evaluation of semantic similarity. The work is based on a new model for the assessment of semantic similarity among entity classes that satisfies cognitive properties of similarity and integrates contextual information. The semantic similarity model represents entity classes by their semantic relations (is-a and part-whole) and their distinguishing features (parts, functions, and attributes). Context describes the domain of an application that is determined by the user's intended operations. Contextual information is specified by a set of tuples over operations associated with their respective entity-class arguments. Based on the contextual information, a partial word-sense disambiguation can be achieved and the relevance of distinguishing features for the similarity assessment is calculated in terms of the features' contribution to the characterization of the application domain.

1 Introduction

Similarity is a judgment process that requires two "things" to be decomposed into aspects or elements in which they are the same and aspects in which they are different. These types of judgments are typically intuitive, subjective, and part of the everyday life such that they usually display no strict mathematical models [1]. In information systems similarity assessment is part of several processes, such as information retrieval [2-4] and data integration [5, 6]. Similarity assessment is

---

[*] This work was partially supported by the National Imagery and Mapping Agency under grant number NMA202-97-1-1023. Max Egenhofer's research is further funded by grants from the National Science Foundation under NSF grant numbers IRI-9613646, SBR-9600465, BDI-9723873, and ISS-9970123; the National Institute of Environmental Health Sciences, NIH, under grant number 1RO1 ES09816-01; the Air Force Research Laboratory under grant number F30602-95-1-0042; Bangor Hydro-Electric Co.; and by a Massive Digital Data Systems contract sponsored by the Advanced Research and Development Committee of the Community Management Staff.

particularly important for applications in which no precise definitions underlie the matter of discourse. In such domains, data stored in a database represent particular views of reality and users' queries express only an approximation of what users want to retrieve, which is likely an inexact match to any stored data.

This paper explores the use and effect of context over a model of semantic similarity among entity classes, the matching-distance model [7]. Like feature-based models [1, 8, 9], the matching-distance model defines a similarity function in terms of common and different features of entities (i.e., descriptors and attributes). The matching-distance model, however, defines asymmetric evaluations of semantic similarity that are a product of the weighted contribution of the similarity among different types of distinguishing features (parts, functions, and attributes). The model makes use of a hierarchical structure constructed with is-a and part-whole relations to determine the level of abstraction of entity classes and the model's asymmetric factors.

The matching-distance model has a strong basis in linguistics. Since entity classes are identified by words, this model takes into account two linguistic concepts—synonymy and polysemy—that characterize the mapping between words and meanings [10]. Polysemy arises when a word has more than one meaning (i.e., multiple *senses*). Synonymy corresponds to the case when two different words have the same meaning. In linguistics terms, the model represents entity classes as nouns, which are organized into sets of synonyms. Thus, this model allows not only the definition of synonyms, but also the identification of polysemous words.

Context becomes important for similarity assessment, because it affects the determination of the relevant features [1, 8, 9]. Although a feature-based approach is sensible to the way people assess similarity, it may be argued that the extent to which a concept possesses or is associated with a feature may be a matter of a degree. Consequently, a specific feature can be more important to the meaning of an entity class than to another. Furthermore, since the matching-distance model allows polysemous words to occur, context helps to distinguish among entity classes identified by the same word (polysemous word).

The remainder of this paper is structured as follows: Section 2 describes the main characteristics of the matching-distance model. Section 3 presents the definition and role of contextual information for the similarity assessment. An example illustrates the use context in Section 4. Section 5 discusses the results found when introducing contextual information into the matching-distance model. Conclusions and future work are presented in Section 6.

2 The Matching-Distance Model

Focusing on the spatial domain, Rodríguez et al. [7] defined the matching-distance model for the evaluation of semantic similarity among entity classes. For this work entity classes denote concepts in the real world, rather than entities modeled in a database. These concepts in the real world are cognitive representations that people use to recognize and categorize objects or events [11]. In this sense, this work has a top-down approach by starting from the semantics of entities in the real world instead of the semantics of data stored in a database [12].

The matching-distance model complements the feature-based approach by using semantic relations to organize concepts and a semantic-distance function [13] to determinate the degree of generalization of entity classes. The degree of generalization reflects the prototypical characteristics of entity class definitions, such that more general concepts are located in the top level of the hierarchical structure. Two semantic relations are considered for the entity class definitions: is-a [14] and part-whole [15]. In addition to these semantic relations, the matching-distance model describes entity classes by their distinguishing features. The model differentiates distinguishing features by classifying them into parts, functions, and attributes. Parts are structural elements of a class, such as roof and floor of a building. Function features are intended to represent what is done to or with instances of a class. For example, the function of a college is to educate. Attributes correspond to additional characteristics of a class, such as name, color, and owner. Since the matching-distance model deals with concepts instead of specific real-world objects, the model matches type of attributes rather than attributes values. The classification of distinguishing features attempts to facilitate the implementation of the entity class representation as well as to enable the separated manipulation of each type of distinguishing features. The matching-distance model groups synonyms that identify the same entity class. While these synonym sets are considered equivalent for the similarity evaluation, each of the entity classes associated with a polysemous word is handled as an independent definition.

The global similarity function $S(c_1,c_2)$ is a weighted sum of the similarity values for parts, functions, and attributes (Equation 1), where ω_p, ω_f, and ω_a are the weights of the similarity values for parts, functions, and attributes, respectively. These weights define the relative importance of parts, functions, and attributes that may vary among different contexts. The weights all together must add up to 1.

$$S(c_1,c_2)=\omega_p \cdot S_p(c_1,c_2)+\omega_f \cdot S_f(c_1,c_2)+\omega_a \cdot S_a(c_1,c_2) \qquad (1)$$

Similarity assessment for each type of distinguishing features (i.e., parts, functions, and attributes) is given by Equation 2a-b. In $S_t(c_1, c_2)$, c_1 and c_2 are two entity classes, t symbolizes the type of features, C_1 and C_2 are the respective sets of features of type t for c_1 and c_2, $\#()$ is the cardinality of a set, $\cap$ is the set intersection, and $-$ is the set difference.

$$S_t(c_1,c_2) = \frac{\#(C_1 \cap C_2)}{\delta(c_1,c_2)} \qquad \text{with} \qquad (2a)$$

$$\delta(c_1,c_2)=\#(C_1 \cap C_2)+\alpha(c_1,c_2)\cdot\#(C_1 - C_2)+(1-\alpha(c_1,c_2))\cdot\#(C_2 - C_1) \qquad (2b)$$

The function $\alpha()$ is determined as a function of the distance between the entity classes (c_1 and c_2) and the immediate superclass that subsumes both classes. Here a superclass denotes an entity class that is either *parent* or *whole* of an entity class. The function $\alpha()$ provides asymmetric values for entity classes that belong to different levels of generalization in a hierarchical structure. For instance, the similarity between a museum and a building is greater than the similarity between a building and a museum. The assumption behind the determination of α is that the concept used as a reference (the second argument) should be more relevant in the evaluation [8, 16]. In the study of semantic categories, Rosch [17] supported the view that categories are naturally formed and defined in terms of focal points or prototypes. She hypothesized that (1) in sentences such as "a is essentially b," the focal stimuli (i.e., prototypes) appear in the second position, and (2) the perceived distance from the prototype to the variant is greater than the perceived distance from the variant to the prototype. By combining the value of α and the fact that classes inherit features from their superclasses, the non-common features between a class and its superclass become more significant when the class is used as a second argument in the evaluation of similarity.

3   Context Specification

Context is an important aspect for such diverse areas as natural language processing (NLP), knowledge-based problem solving, database systems, and information retrieval [18-22]. Despite this recognition, the meaning of context in information systems is usually left to the user's interpretation and its role may vary among different domains [23]. For NLP, context has a sense-disambiguation function [18] so that otherwise ambiguous statements become meaningful and precise. Studies in NLP analyze the meaning of words within either a topical context or a local context of a corpus [24]. Knowledge representation involves statements and axioms that hold in certain contexts; therefore, context determines the truth or falsity of a statement as well as its meaning [19]. For knowledge-based problem solving, context is usually defined as the situation or circumstances that surround a reasoning process [20, 25, 26]. Recent studies on data semantics and interoperability have stressed the importance of context to describe data content. In this domain, context is the knowledge needed to reason about another system [27], the intentional descriptions of database objects [21], and the extent of validity for an ontology [28]. For information retrieval, context provides a framework for well-defined queries and consequently, it improves the matching process between a user's query and the data stored in a database [22].

Following the ideas of Naive Physics [29] and Naive Geography [30], it is possible to derive a common sense definition of entity classes such that entity classes are described by their essential properties. From this, we could then expect to obtain a good approximation of the similarity assessment among entity classes by considering these essential properties as equally important. We argue, however, that similarity assessment is used in an information system with a purpose in mind and, therefore, some features may be more important than others. Psychologists and cognitive scientists were the first to point out the importance of context for the determination of the relevant features in a similarity assessment [1, 8]. These studies have suggested that the relevance of features is associated with how *diagnostic* the feature is for a particular set of objects under consideration. The diagnosticity of features refers to how significant a feature is for classifying objects into subclasses [1]. Since a classification process produces groups of entities that share some features, the criteria for classifying a set of entities can be found by looking at these common features.

Our work makes use of this notion of diagnosticity and defines weighted values for the similarity among parts, function, and attributes (ω_p, ω_f, and ω_a of Equation 1) by analyzing the frequency with which distinguishing features characterize entity classes of the domain of discourse. High frequency is then translated into a high relevance. We support our approach by arguing that entities associated with a domain of discourse share some features that make them subject to interest for this domain. This way of determining the relevance of distinguishing features is in agreement with the observation that people tend to give more attention to similar than to distinctive features in the evaluation of similarity [1].

Our approach to the determination of the relevance of distinguishing features is built upon the determination of a domain of discourse. By the domain of discourse we mean the set of entity classes that are subjects of interest for an application. Since a domain of discourse may change among applications, the relevance of distinguishing features changes as well. We describe this situation as the *context dependence* of the similarity assessment, which is given by the user's intended operations. People assess the meaning of a word within the context they can use it [31], which is congruent with the notion of use-based semantics [32]. The user's intended operations may be abstract, high-level intentions (e.g., "analyze" or "compare") or detailed plans (e.g., "purchase a house"). From a linguistics point of view, the user's intended operations are associated with verbs that denote actions. Verbs alone, however, may not be enough to completely describe operations, since they can change the operations' meaning depending on the kinds of noun arguments with which they co-occur [33]. For example, different senses of the verb *play* are *play a role*, *play the flute*, and *play a game*. Hence, verbs together with their noun arguments describe the underlying goal for the use of the similarity assessment.

We specify contextual information (C) as a set of tuples over operations (op_i) associated with their respective noun arguments (e_j) (Equation 3). The nouns correspond to entity classes in the matching-distance model, while the operations refer to verbs that are associated as methods with those classes. In this specification an entity-class argument may be empty if no further explanation is needed to describe the intended operation. Since the context specification uses operations and entity classes, the knowledge base used by the entity class representation of the matching-distance model can be extended to represent the components of the context specification.

$$C = \left\langle \left(op_1, \{e_1, \ldots, e_i\}\right), \ldots, \left(op_j, \{e_k, \ldots, e_l\}\right) \right\rangle \qquad (3)$$

For example, if a user wants to analyze some on-line datasets with the purpose of purchasing a cottage, she would describe her intention by C = <(purchase, {cottage})>. By using the hierarchical structure of the knowledge base, the operations' arguments can be expressed at different levels of generalization. For example, a user may be looking for sports facilities and in such a case, she can specify C = <(search, {sports facility})> or C = <(search, {athletic field, bowl park, tennis court, sports arena, stadium}>. Another user's intention can be described by using operations without arguments, such as C = <(play, {})>. In this case, the operation *play* corresponds to a common function that characterizes the entity classes the user is looking for.

When contextual information is specified, not only relevance of distinguishing features can be determined, but also word-sense ambiguities may be solved. Since the domain of the application is usually a subset of the entire knowledge base, the contextual specification decreases the number of entity classes that possess the same name (i.e., polysemy). Unfortunately, this approach has the same disadvantage of the use of topical context for word-sense disambiguation [34], since it may not distinguish polysemous terms that are semantically similar and belong to the same domain of discourse.

The semantic relations among entity classes provide a flexible way to describe context since the specification of one entity class can be used to obtained other entity classes that are semantically related. We follow a top-down approach in a hierarchical structure to retrieve all entity classes that belong to the application domain. This approach consists of selecting

(1) entity classes whose functions correspond to the intended user's operations,

(2) entity classes that are parameters of the operations in the context specification, and

(3) entity classes derived from a recursive search of parts and children of the entity classes found in (1) and (2).

Once entity classes of the application's domain are obtained, the diagnosticity of a type of feature t (P_t) is calculated as the sum of the frequency with which each distinguishing feature of the type t characterizes an entity class in a domain of discourse (Equation 4). In P_t, o_i is the number of occurrence of the feature i in the entity class definitions, n is the number of entity classes, and l is the number of features in a domain of discourse.

$$P_t = \sum_{i=1}^{l} \frac{o_i}{n} \qquad (4)$$

The final weights ω_p, ω_f, and ω_a in Equation 1 are functions of the probability of a type of feature with respect to the probability of the other two types of features (Equations 5a-c).

$$\omega_p = \frac{P_p}{(P_p + P_f + P_a)} \qquad (5a)$$

$$\omega_f = \frac{P_f}{(P_p + P_f + P_a)} \qquad (5b)$$

$$\omega_a = \frac{P_a}{(P_p + P_f + P_a)} \qquad (5c)$$

A special case is when the maximum variability occurs, i.e., each distinguishing feature characterizes only one entity class. In such a case, P_p, P_f, and P_a are zero and the model assigns equal importance to parts, functions, and attributes. The same weights are also obtained when either an application domain has only one entity class or entity classes share all features. When there are no common features among the entity classes, the similarity values are zero, regardless the assignment of weights. Likewise, when features are shared by all entity classes, the similarity values are 1.0, independently of the assignment of weights.

4 Using Contextual Information with the Matching-Distance Model

To illustrate the integration of context into the matching-distance model, we analyze different scenarios for the similarity assessment. A prototype of the matching-distance model has been implemented in C++ and a knowledge base with around 60 entity class definitions was derived from the combination of WordNet [36] and the Spatial Data Transfer Standard [37]. Based on this knowledge base, four scenarios for the similarity assessment were selected:

(1) Context-0: All distinguishing features are equally important, since context has not been considered in the similarity assessment.
(2) Context-1: The user's intention is to retrieve recreational facilities. Figure 1 shows how the user describes her intention with the operation described by the synonym set {*recreate, play*} without arguments.

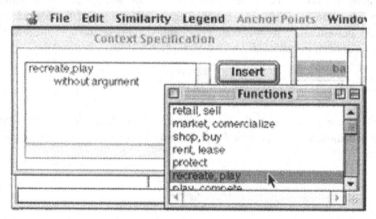

Fig.1. Context-1: Context specification with an operation without argument.

(3) Context-2: The user's intention is to compare downtowns. The user describes her intention with the operation *compare* and the argument *downtown* (Figure 2).
(4) Context-3: A user is searching for specific types of buildings and building complexes. This scenario is described by the operation *search* with specific entity classes (i.e., low level in the hierarchical structure) as the operation's argument (Figure 3).

As a result of the different context scenarios, different weights are generated for the similarity of parts, functions, and attributes. Except for the first scenario (Context-0), the other three scenarios define weights as a function of the variability of features within the application domain. The second scenario (Context-1) defines an application domain with entity classes that contain *play* as a function (*stadium, sports arena, athletic field*, and *park*). The third scenario (Context-2) results in a domain application with the entity class *downtown* and all entity classes that are semantically related to *downtown* by is-a or part-of relations (e.g., *artifact, construction, facility*, and *travelway*). The last scenario defines a small application domain that contains only the specific entity classes listed in the context specification (i.e., *apartment building, office building, shopping center*). Figure 4 shows the context specification window (for Context-1), and the window with the weights for each type of distinguishing features.

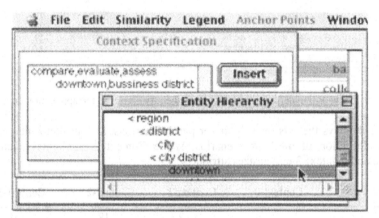

Fig.2. Context-2: Context specification with an operation and a general entity class (top level in the hierarchy) as an argument.

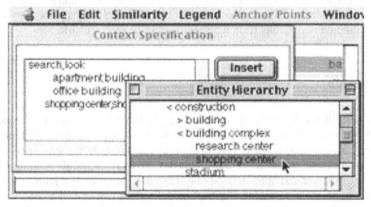

Fig.3. Context-3: Context specification with an operation and specific entity classes (low level in the hierarchy) as arguments.

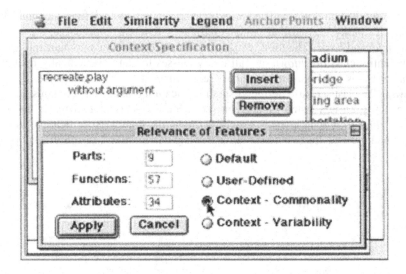

Fig.4. Partial view of the hierarchy with highlighted entity classes in the application domain.

Table 1 displays the sets of weights for parts, functions, and attributes that result from the definition of the four scenarios. While Context-1 highlights functions, Context-2 and Context-3 emphasizes attributes.

Weights	Context-0	Context-1	Context-2	Context-3
Parts (ω_p)	33	9	19	31
Functions (ω_f)	33	57	16	7
Attributes (ω_a)	33	34	55	62

Table 1. Weights (%) for different specification of context.

Table 2 presents results of the similarity evaluation between a *stadium* and a subset of the entire knowledge base. Some of these entity classes may not be part of the application domain that results from the specification of each scenario.

5 Discussion

Examples with different context specifications show that context has an influence on the determination of the relative importance of distinguishing features and, therefore, the similarity assessment. Context specification affects not only the similarity values, but also the relative location of entity classes in a ranking of similarity. The significance of the context specification may vary depending on the knowledge base used for the similarity assessment. Entity class definitions can embed a context, since only the relevant distinguishing features for a particular application may have been listed. Therefore, context specification becomes more useful when a large and

Similarity (Stadium, X)

X	Context-0	Context-1	Context-2	Context-3
Sports arena	0.76 (2)	0.89 (1)	0.79 (1)	0.73 (1)
Athletic field	0.64 (3)	0.89 (2)	0.77 (2)	0.66 (3)
Theater	0.51 (4)	0.49 (5)	0.67 (4)	0.66 (4)
Park (ballpark)	0.78 (1)	0.86 (3)	0.72 (3)	0.69 (2)
Park (green)	0.41 (5)	0.59 (4)	0.46 (6)	0.38 (6)
Museum	0.38 (6)	0.29 (6)	0.56 (5)	0.58 (5)

Table 2. Example of semantic similarity values for each of the four scenarios. Numbers in parenthesis refer to the similarity rank (1: best match, 6: worst match).

general-purpose knowledge base exists and a very detailed or specific application domain is desired.

The domain of an application reflects the underlying hierarchical structure of the knowledge base. For example, a context specification with operation's arguments that are entity classes located at the upper level of the hierarchy (e.g., Context-2) leads to an application domain that contains a large number of entity classes (67% of our global knowledge base). Since the top levels of the hierarchy are usually less detailed (i.e., less distinguishing features are described), what matters for the variability of distinguishing features is the number of entity classes in the application domain that belong to the more detailed levels.

We performed an informal test with 21 human subjects, asking them to rank five entity types (sports arena, athletic field, park, theater, and museum) with respect to a *stadium* under the four different contexts. If we consider that people may have used the sense of park that refers to a green or commons, people's answers correlate with the ranks of the similarity among entities for Context-0, confirming the best three matches and the least similar entity (Table 3).

Similarity (Stadium, X)

X	Most similar	Second most similar	Third most similar	Least similar
Sports arena	16	3		1
Athletic field	4	13	2	
Theater		4	12	1
Museum			2	9
Park			5	4

Table 3. Human subjects' answers for similarity assessment with Context-0 (in number of people).

A similarly good match was obtained for Context-2. For Context-3, subjects agreed with the top and bottom ranks, but disagreed about the ranks of the second and third most similar cases. The responses for this context showed much more variation in the judgments and, therefore, small differences—often a single vote—influenced the rankings. One possible explanation for these less focused assessments may be that

Context-3 led to a similarity assessment was done over entity classes that are outside of the application domain.

For Context-1 (play) there was a clear tendency to make the functional characteristics of the entity class a relevant factor for the similarity evaluation. Although our model also emphasizes functional characteristics and the three most similar entity classes are the same as the three most similar entities given in people answers, the ranking among these three entity classes differs (Table 4). Note, however, that the similarity values for *sports arena*, *athletic field*, and *ballpark* have insignificant differences and that people's judgments of the three most similar entities disagree.

Similarity (Stadium, X)

X	Most similar	Second most similar	Third most similar	Least similar
Sports arena	4	4	12	
Athletic field	8	12	1	
Theater				4
Museum				13
Park	9	5	7	

Table 4. Human subjects' answers for similarity assessment with Context-1 (in number of people).

The main difference between the model and people's judgment is with the ranking of *park*. One possible explanation is that these differences are due to the ambiguity of the term *park*. People seem to consider the sense of park that is more similar to the entity class against which it is compared (i.e., park as a *ballpark*), which is consistent with the idea of using context for word-sense disambiguation [18].

6   Conclusions and Future Work

Context has an important effect on the determination of semantically similar entity classes. Two entity classes may be more closely related to each other in one context than in another, since the importance of their distinguishing features varies with the context. In this paper we developed an approach to integrate context into a model for the assessment of semantic similarity among entity classes. This approach emphasizes the semantics derived from the use of entity classes and defines contextual information as the set of a user's intended operations. A preliminary human-subject test over a set of four context scenarios showed that that model determined in three out of four cases the best match from a list of five terms, as well as the least similar term.

As future work, we will test and calibrate the matching-distance model by performing a formal human-subject test. Like entity classes, operations can be also semantically interrelated [38]. Thus, a further study should explore semantic relations among verbs to allow for a flexible and more accurate definition of entity classes that belong to the domain of the application.

A different approach to the determination of the relevance of distinguishing features is to analyze the degree of informativeness of a feature. Following the standard argument of information theory [35], the information content of a feature is defined as being inversely proportional to the probability of occurrence of this feature. While the degree of informativeness highlights variability, this work emphasizes commonality. A combination of both approaches (i.e., variability and commonality) account for cases when the similarity evaluation is done exclusively among the entity classes within the domain of discourse. In such a case, what characterizes the application domain becomes less relevant for distinguishing entity classes within the domain.

Although we have focused on the use of context for similarity assessment, the specification of the user's intended operations may play an important role for a wider range of processes in information systems. Instead of the user's intended operations, operations associated with the data modeled in a database have been suggested for solving problems of interoperability [32]. A description of the user's intended operation can create a bridge between user's expectation and information retrieved from individual or multiple databases.

Acknowledgments

Discussions with Werner Kuhn, Bob Rugg, and Gio Wiederhold helped with the development of the similarity model and the context specifications.

References

1. Tversky, A., 1977, Features of Similarity. *Psychological Review* 84(4): 327-352.
2. Voorhees, E., 1998, Using WordNet for Text Retrieval, in: C. Fellbaum (editor), *WordNet: An Electronic Lexical Database*, pp. 285-303, The MIT Press: Cambridge, MA.
3. Ginsberg, A., 1993. A Unified Approach to Automatic Indexing and Information Retrieval. *IEEE Expert* 8(5): 46-56.
4. Lee, J., M. Kim, and Y. Lee, 1993, Information Retrieval Based on Conceptual Distance in IS-A Hierarchies. *Journal of Documentation* 49(2): 188-207.
5. Bishr, Y., *Semantic Aspects of Interoperable GIS*. 1997, Wageningen Agricultural University and ITC, The Netherlands.
6. Bouguettaya, A., B. Benatallah, and A. Elmagarmid, Interconnecting Heterogeneous Information Systems. 1998, in: A. Elmagarmid (editor), *Advances in Database Systems*, Kluwer: Norwell, MA.
7. Rodríguez, A., M. Egenhofer, and R. Rugg, 1999, Assessing Semantic Similarity Among Geospatial Entity Class Definitions, in: A. Vckovski, K. Brassel, and H.-J. Schek, (editors), *Interoperating Geographic Information Systems INTEROP99, Zurich, Switzerland*, Lecture Notes in Computer Science 1580, pp. 189-202, Springer-Verlag: Berlin.
8. Krumhansl, C., 1978, Concerning the Applicability of Geometric Models to Similarity Data: The Interrelationship Between Similarity and Spatial Density. *Psychological Review* 85(5): 445-463.
9. Goldstone, R., D. Medin, and J. Halberstadt, 1997, Similarity in Context. *Memory and Cognition* 25(2): 237-255.

10. Miller, G., R. Reckwith, C. Fellbaum, D. Gross, and K. Miller, 1990, Introduction to WordNet: An On-Line Lexical Database. *International Journal of Lexicography* 3(4): 235-244.

11. Dahlgren, K., 1988, *Naive Semantics for Natural Language Understanding*, Kluwer: Norwell, MA.

12. Sheth, A., Data Semantics: What, Where, and How?, 1979, in: R. Meersman and L. Mark (editors), *Database Application Semantics,* Chapman and Hall.

13. Collins, A. and M. Quillian, 1969, Retrieval Time From Semantic Memory. *Journal of Verbal Learning and Verbal Behavior* 8: 240-247.

14. Smith, J. and D. Smith, 1977, Database Abstractions: Aggregation and Generalization. *ACM Transactions of Database Systems* 2(2): 105-133.

15. Winston, M., R. Chaffin, and D. Herramann, 1987, A Taxonomy of Part-Whole Relations. *Cognitive Science* 11: 417-444.

16. Rosch, E. and C. Mervis, 1995, Family Resemblances: Studies in the Internal Structure of Categories. *Cognitive Psychology*, 7: 573-603.

17. Rosch, E., 1973, On the Internal Structure of Perceptual and Semantic Categories, in: T. Moore (editor), *Cognitive Development and the Acquisition of Language,* Academic Press: New York.

18. Leech, G., 1981, *Semantics: The Study of Meaning.* Penguin: Harmondsworth, UK.

19. McCarthy, J., 1987, Generality in Artificial Intelligence. *Communications of the ACM* 30(12): 1030-1035.

20. Aïmeur, E. and C. Frasson. 1995, Eliciting the Learning Context in Co-Operative Tutoring Systems. in: *Workshop on Modelling Context in Knowledge Representation and Reasoning.* Institute Blaise Pascal: Paris, France.

21. Kashyap, V. and A. Sheth, 1996, Schematic and Semantic Similarities between Database Objects: A Context-based Approach. *Very Large Database Journal* 5(4): 276-304.

22. Hearst, M., 1994, *Context and Structure in Automated Full-Text Information Access.* Computer Science Division, University of California at Berkeley.

23. Akman, V. and M. Surav, 1996, Steps Toward Formalizing Context. *AI Magazine* 17(3): 55-72.

24. Leacock, C. and M. Chodorow, 1998, Combining Local Context and WordNet Similarity for Word Sense Identification, in: C. Fellbaum (editor) *WordNet: An Electronic Lexical Database.* pp. 265-283, The MIT Press: Cambridge, MA.

25. Turner, R., 1998, Context-Mediated Behavior for Intelligent Agents. *International Journal of Human-Computer Studies* 48: 307-330.

26. Dojat, M. and F. Pachet. 1995, Three Compatible Mechanisms for Representing Medical Context Implicitly. in: *Workshop on Modelling Context in Knowledge Representation and Reasoning,* Institute Blaise Pascal: Paris, France.

27. Ouksel, A. and C. Naiman, 1994, Coordinating Context Building in Heterogeneous Information Systems. *Journal of Intelligent Information Systems* 3(1): 151-183.

28. Wiederhold, G. and J. Jannink. (in press), Composing Diverse Ontologies. in: *8th Working Conference on Database Semantics (DS-8).* Rotorua, New Zealand, IFIP/Kluwer/Chapman & Hall.

29. Hayes, P., 1990, Naive Physics I: Ontology for Liquids, in: D. Weld and J. de Kleer (Editors) *Reading in Qualitative Reasoning about Physical Systems,* pp. 484-502, Morgan Kaufmann Publishers: San Mateo, CA.

30. Egenhofer, M. and D. Mark, 1995, *Naive Geography.* in: A. Frank and W. Kuhn (editors) *Spatial Information Theory International Conference COSIT'95.* Semmering, Austria, Lecture Notes in Computer Science 988, pp. 1-15, Berlin: Springer-Verlag.

31. Miller, G. and W. Charles, 1991, Contextual Correlates of Semantic Similarity. *Language and Cognitive Processes* 6(1): 1-28.

32. Kuhn, W. 1994, Defining Semantics for Spatial Data Transfers. in: T. Waugh and R. Healey (editors), *Sixth International Symposium on Spatial Data Handling,* pp. 973-987, Edinburgh, Scotland: International Geographical Union.

33. Fellbaum, C., 1990, English Verbs as a Semantic Net. *International Journal of Lexocography* 3(4): 270-301.
34. Gale, W., K. Church, and D. Yarowsky, 1992, A Method for Disambiguating Word Senses in a Large Corpus, *Computers and Humanities* 26(5/6): 415-450.
35. Ross, S., 1976, *A First Course in Probability*, Macmillan, New York.
36. Miller, G., 1990, Nouns in WordNet: A Lexical Inheritance System. *International Journal of Lexicography* 3(4): 245-264.
37. USGS, *View of the Spatial Data Transfer Standard (SDTS) Document*. 1998, available at http://mcmcweb.er.usgs.gov/sdts/standard.html. Last Modification: Friday, 12-Jun-98.
38. Fellbaum, C., 1998, A Semantic Network of English Verbs, in: C. Fellbaum (editor) *WordNet: An Electronic Lexical Database,* pp. 69-104, The MIT Press: Cambridge, MA.

Presupposition, Implicature and Context in Text Understanding

Marina Sbisà

Department of Philosophy, University of Trieste
via dell'Università 7, 34123 Trieste, Italy
Sbisama@univ.trieste.it

Abstract. This paper examines the roles which presupposition and implicature play with respect to what is asserted by a text and to its context, as a part of the process of text understanding. This process involves constructing and updating the representation of the context. Assertion, implicature and presupposition can be described as three different ways in which changes in the representation of the context are induced. On the basis of such a description, it is claimed that, contrary to most of the literature on the subject (in which presupposition and implicature seem not to be allowed to coexist without being identified with each other), there are reasons for considering presupposition and implicature as two distinct phenomenona.

1. Two perspectives on text understanding

It is by now widely recognized that discourse understanding involves more than the understanding of what is explicitly said. In order to understand discourse, or as (I shall say here) in order to understand a text, we must understand more than what is encoded in the text itself, and draw inferences. This broader comprehension, which is closely connected with contextual knowledge, is often described as the comprehension of what is presupposed and/or implicated by the text.

There are two main ways in which we can conceive of the role of this broader comprehension (which I will call comprehension of the implicitly conveyed meaning) with respect to the overall understanding of the text.

(i) Sometimes it may seem that the understanding of what a text presupposes or implicates, as well as the contextual knowledge involved in such understanding, are necessary conditions for a full comprehension of the text. If we do not know the circumstances in which a text has been written, or if an utterance is reported to us without any information about the circumstances in which and the goals for which it has been uttered, we may not be able to make sense of it. If we do not share the speaker's pragmatic presuppositions (the assumptions he or she takes for granted in speaking) (Stalnaker [18], [19]), we might misunderstand him or her. As to

---

[1] Thanks to Christopher Gauker and to an anonymous referee for comments on earlier drafts.

conversational implicatures, they depend on the assumption that the speaker is observing the Cooperative Principle (Grice [7]: p. 26) and therefore, in order to infer them, the hearer should already know whether, in the circumstances of the ongoing verbal exchange, the Cooperative Principle holds. According to relevance theory (Sperber and Wilson [17]), another pragmatic theory concerned with discourse understanding, in understanding a text we have to take into account the contextual premises which make the speaker's contribution relevant. In all these ways, knowledge of, or at least beliefs about, what may in one word be called "the context" are represented as necessary to the comprehension of the text. This might lead us to conclude that we can, and must, acquire knowledge of or beliefs about the context prior to, and independently of, our understanding of a text.

(ii) Suppose, however, that we find ourselves in a situation in which we have little independent access to the context, as it happens in reading, in certain phone calls, or in those cases of face to face interaction in which we know little about our interlocutor and his or her possible aims. Should we despair of making sense of the text we are faced with? In such cases, it might be convenient to exploit all the details of the text in order to project as much of its context as we can. After all, many presuppositions have linguistic markers or triggers, and this enables receivers to detect them even in absence of text-independent information. As to implicatures, it could be claimed that the speaker's observance of the Cooperative Principle must not be known in advance, but can be assumed in absence of evidence contrary to it, so as to allow for the working out of as many implicatures as possible. Finally, relevance theory admits of the possibility of inferring missing contextual premises, when the assumptions which are already available to the hearer do not make the speaker's contribution relevant. In this perspective, context (or more precisely, the representation of context which is associated with the understanding of the text) is not something which has to be given independently of the text, but something constructed in the very process of text understanding.

Although I do not want to deny that perspective (i) has its merits, here I am going to adopt perspective (ii), because I would like to outline a description of the text-context relationship which optimizes the chances of text understanding even in unfavorable conditions.

In this framework, I would like to claim that presupposition and implicature play different roles with respect to text understanding and that therefore they should be considered as distinct phenomena. This runs contrary to most of the literature on the subject: presupposition and implicature belong, as it were, to two different conceptual frameworks and authors who use one of these notions do not use the other, so that only one of them does all of the work. Those authors who mention both notions have (since Karttunen and Peters [10]) identified presupposition with one kind of implicature, conventional implicature. I would like to claim that presupposition is different from both conversational and conventional implicature as to the role it plays with respect to what is asserted by a text and to its context.

2. On text and context

I choose here to use the word "text", following the semiotic (Hjelmslevian in particular) rather than the philosophical tradition, in a sense akin to the one recently specified by M. Stubbs with reference to the practice of discourse analysis: "By text, I mean an instance of language in use, either spoken or written: a piece of language behaviour (…)" ([23]: p. 4). This definition of "text" leaves it open which size a text should have: a text (the relevant piece of language behaviour) could well coincide with the utterance of one sentence, but might also consist of the utterance of more or, for that matter, less than one. The utterance of a syntactically complete and isolated sentence is therefore one case falling under the more general idea of the production of a text. As to the problem of text delimitation, it should be remarked that, whenever what is focused upon as a text is in turn a part of a larger episode of language behaviour, we can (i) include relevant parts of this larger episode into the text focused upon, thus changing the delimitation of what is under consideration or (ii) consider the larger episode of language behaviour in which our text is embedded as a part of the context. Choice (i) turns linguistic context into text, while choice (ii) considers linguistic context as a part of the context.

As to context, I believe that insofar as we are concerned with its capacity of being that against which a text is evaluated (as to appropriateness and/or truth), it must be conceived of as "objective" or mind-transcendent (Gauker [5]). It is only with respect to something external to speakers and independent of what is focused upon as the presently considered text, that it makes sense to evaluate, or attempt to evaluate, that text as a piece of linguistic behaviour. I will here conceive of objective contexts in an intuitive way, namely, as consisting of the set of facts which have to be taken into consideration by the participants if a given verbal exchange is to achieve its goals. One problem with this view it that evaluation may (or perhaps must) remain provisional, or defeasible. But this trouble is shared by all of our knowledge, which aims at objectivity, but is nevertheless persistingly defeasible.

Here, however, we will not be concerned with the function of context in text evaluation, but in text comprehension. In particular, in conformity to perspective (ii) outlined above, I want to specify the ways in which the information contained in a text can tell or show us something about its context. So we will be concerned with that representation of the context, relative to a given text, which can be worked out on the basis of that text in the process of understanding it. This representation of the context is, of course, directed at the objective context, but should not be confounded with it, since it has to be worked out by the participants, while the objective context transcends their cognitive processes.

3. The dynamic relation between text and context

A text entertains a dynamic relation with its context. During text production, the addition of new speech acts to those already performed can be described as having context-changing effects (Gazdar [6]), so that the context at time 2 is different from the context at time 1 as regards the addition or elimination of some contents. On the notion of text I am using here, a text T1 is correspondingly changed into a text T2 as soon as new parts are added to it. The updating of the context is always relative to a new delimitation of the text, so that one-to-one correspondence between texts and contexts is preserved.

However, the distinction (outlined above) between the objective context and the representation of it has to be taken into account.

It might be thought that the objective context, being independent of the text, cannot be changed by it. In fact, nonverbal actions, bearing on the circumstances relevant to the goal of the exchange within which the text is produced, change the objective context, but they do not belong to the text either. However, it has to be conceded that the very occurrence of linguistic behaviour changes the context, providing part of the context for subsequent text production. Moreover, it can be claimed that a text performs a context-changing action if the speech acts it contains have effects consisting of the bringing about of intersubjectively recognizable states of affairs (such as new obligations or rights or their cancelation). I have elsewhere called such effects "changes in the conventional context" (and following Gazdar [6], I have defined illocutionary acts in their terms: [14], [15]), where the "conventional context" may be construed as a specialized part of the objective context (insofar as we believe that human conventions too have their own kind of objectivity).

Although the consideration of the ways in which the objective context is affected by changes can be an important issue, here we will be concerned with the changes which are produced in the representation of the context as a part of the process of text understanding. We will be concerned with (some) changes in the objective context only insofar as these play a role in inducing changes in the representation of the context. I shall try to describe three main ways in which the latter kind of change can be achieved: assertion, implicature, and presupposition. The proposed description will enable me to claim that presupposition cannot be identified with implicature.

4. Assertion

I consider assertion as bringing about the addition of its content to the representation of the context. This view is partly inspired by the one proposed by Stalnaker [20] [21]. But Stalnaker considers the context as a set of assumptions which the speaker takes as shared, while I am here drawing a distinction between the objective context and the representation of it. The representation of context associated with text understanding does not necessarily consist of assumptions actually made by the speaker, nor of assumptions which the speaker takes as shared by the participants. I view it, basically, as the information about the objective context which the text enables, and entitles, its receivers to work out.

After a certain assertion has been made, both the speaker who has made it and is committed to its truth, and the hearer (unless he or she decides to challenge the speaker's assertion) take the content of the assertion to be part of the representation of the context. It is the speaker who has the responsibility for this addition to the representation of the context and the sanction to which the speaker is liable if the resulting representation of the context later turns out to be inadequate is that he or she will be deemed to have said something false. However, it is in part also the hearer's responsibility to accept the addition of the content of the assertion to the representation of the context. In fact, the hearer might well choose to challenge the speaker's assertion. We could envisage the assertion as a proposal on the part of the speaker to add a certain content to the representation of the context, a proposal which the hearer might refuse, but which, if not refused, is effective by default (as has been claimed, albeit in a framework different from mine, by Perrault [13]).

It should be noted that assertion, if it is considered as an illocutionary act (at least on my understanding of what an illocutionary act is), should involve a change in the objective context too, and more precisely, in what I have called above "the conventional context". The speaker's commitment resulting from assertion can be considered as the attribution of a new obligation to the speaker, since the speaker is then obliged not to contradict him or herself and to give evidence or reasons if his or her assertion is challenged. This obligation can be considered as a fact and, insofar as it is relevant to the goals of the conversation, it belongs to the objective context. Since no conventional change is unilateral (obligations assigned to one partner are usually countered by rights assigned the other, and vice versa) it could be claimed that the hearer is modified in his or her turn by the acquisition of a right, which can be construed as the right to make the same assertion him or herself, or as the right to claim second-hand knowledge. These conventional changes justify the changes in the representation of the context associated with text understanding, but should not be identified with or reduced to them. The former changes can be described as changes in the set of modal predicates ("can", "ought to") to be attributed to the participants, while the latter consist of the addition of new content to the representation of the context.

A trouble about assertion regards its relationship to "what is said" by a text. We are in need both of a notion of assertion and of a notion of "what is said": we need the former in order to describe one kind of change in the representation of context, and the latter in order to contrast it with all the aspects of the overall meaning of a text which are understood by inference. Following Bach [1], I shall assume that these are two separate notions, and that what is asserted (or, in general, what the content of a speech act amounts to) may draw on inferences from what is said.

5. Implicature

The notion of implicature, proposed by Grice in 1967 ([7]: pp. 22-40), is well known. In order to characterize the way in which implicatures contribute to changes in the representation of the context, I will recall some of their salient features.

Implicatures are invited inferences in which the inferred proposition bears no truth functional relationship to any utterance contained in the text: when "p" implicates that q, the falsity of q has no consequence on the truth value of p. So, for example,

(1) Mary is pretty, but intelligent.

conveys by implicature that Mary, being pretty, is not likely to be intelligent, but is not false nor wholly unacceptable if this is false, since the truth functional conjunction of "Mary is pretty" and "Mary is intelligent" can well be true. Likewise:

(2) Jane has two children

(as issued in the framework of a cooperative conversation about how many children certain people have) conveys by implicature that Jane has no more than two children; but is not false if this is false, since, if she has four children, it is still true that she has two.

There are two main ways in which such inferences arise: (a) they can be invited by the fact that a certain word is used, which (because of linguistic conventions) has the function of inviting that inference (as is the case in (1) above, containing "but": a "conventional" implicature); or (b) they can be required in order to make viable an interpretation of the speaker's linguistic behaviour as conforming to the Cooperative Principle. So in the case of example (2) (a "conversational" implicature), the implicature arises from the assumption that the speaker is conforming to the Cooperative Principle and, more specifically, is giving as much information as is required by the goals of the conversation.

In case (a), Grice has suggested that the inferences which arise are connected with the performance of "non central" speech acts, namely, further specifications of the central speech acts of asserting, asking, commanding ([7]: pp.121-22, p.362). In this vein, "but" may be taken as indicating an objection, or "therefore" an explanation. This view of conventional implicatures contrasts, however, with the idea also expressed by Grice that they might derive from conventionalizations of generalized conversational implicatures ([7]: p.39): reference to speech act notions does not seem to be necessary in this case. I believe that the connection of certain words conventionally suggesting implicatures with non central speech acts is a puzzling fact, the role of which has still to be thoroughly explained, but I will not tackle this issue here. I shall distinguish conventional from conversational implicature only on the basis of the fact that the former is invited by the use of certain words.

In case (b), in which the Cooperative Principle is involved, the inferences can be drawn on the basis of what is said (the words uttered, considered as the starting point for all the inferences which can be drawn from the text) or on the basis of what is asserted (which may already involve inferences). In the former case, they contribute to the content of the assertion which is actually made; in the latter case, they associate with the assertion an additional content, which is conveyed together with the assertion but not as a part of its content. So, since the words used in

(3) You are the cream in my coffee ·

(said to a human being) would give rise to a patently false assertion, if this utterance is to be interpreted as giving a cooperative contribution to the conversation, the asserted content must be somewhat different, although related ("You are my pride and joy") (Grice [7]: p. 34). And in the following exchange

(4) A: Where's Bill?
    B: There's a yellow VW outside Sue's house

B's contribution is a relevant answer to A's question only insofar as it licenses the inference that if Bill has a yellow VW, he may be in Sue's house (Levinson [11]: p. 102).

I have couched my examples as inferences from the utterance of a sentence "p" to its implicature that q. This choice does not reflect one feature of implicature, that is, the fact that in the Gricean framework, what the hearer infers is primarily not the proposition that q, but the proposition that the speaker thinks that q. This is especially true for conversational implicatures, since the requirement for interpreting the speaker as conforming to the Cooperative Principle, on which they depend, is not that q holds, but that the speaker thinks that q. Here, however, we are concerned with text understanding, particularly with the ways in which a text enables its receivers to update their representation of the context. Implicature is relevant for us only insofar as, whether with or without the mediation of the proposition that the speaker thinks that q, it licenses inferences about facts in the objective context. Facts about what the speaker thinks are not necessarily relevant to the goals of an exchange and therefore are not always to be taken into consideration in the representation of the context. I take it that in examples like those I have quoted, the relevant inference which is licensed is about facts in the objective context and, therefore, is not generally about what the speaker thinks.

Thus, implicatures are contributions or additions to the content of the speech act performed by the text unit. Their contribution to the update of the representation of the context is, so to say, on a par with that given by assertions (cfr. Thomason [24]: pp. 351-52). They convey information which either contributes to the information conveyed by assertions, or supplements it. In the former case, the changes in the representation of the context associated with the text can be explained in the same way as for assertion. In the latter case, the speaker is not committed to the truth of the implicated content so strictly as to the truth of the content of an assertion (as is clear from the fact that, when what is implicated is false, the speaker is not responsible for saying something false). Correspondingly, the implicature counts merely as a suggestion, which makes a certain update of the representation of the context available to the participants.

6. Presupposition

Semantic presupposition was introduced as a relationship between an assertion and a proposition whose truth is a necessary condition for the assertion to have a truth value (Frege [4], Strawson [22]). This account was meant to capture the ordinary intuition that when the presupposition of an assertion is false, the question whether the assertion is true or false doesn't arise. But the account had also some flaws. It required abandoning standard two-valued logic in favour of a three-valued one. Besides, one of its claims is highly questionable: according to semantic presupposition theorists, if the utterance of an affirmative sentence has a presupposition, the same presupposition is shared by the corresponding negative sentence, so that, for example:

(5a) John has stopped smoking
(5b) John has not stopped smoking

both presuppose

(6) John used to smoke.

To this, it can be objected that if John never used to smoke, an utterance of the negative sentence can well be considered as true:

(7) John has not stopped smoking (in fact he never used to smoke).

The relationship of the presupposition to the utterance of the positive sentence appears not to be identical to its relationship to the utterance of the negative sentence, since in the latter case the presupposition is cancelable.

Since the '70s, a pragmatic conception of presupposition has been preferred to the semantic one. According to this conception, presuppositions are the assumptions shared by speaker and hearer, which form the background of their ongoing discourse (Stalnaker [18], [19]). Some if not all of these shared background assumptions have linguistic markers (or triggers). An utterance can be said to presuppose a proposition when it contains a linguistic element which functions as a presupposition trigger, and is therefore appropriate only if the associated presupposition is among the interlocutors' shared assumptions. A problem for this approach is raised by the informative use of presuppositions. Often utterances which contain presupposition triggers are issued without assuming that the hearer already shares their presupposition or even knowing that he or she does not share it. In these cases, contrary to the theory's predictions, no inappropriateness is felt, but the hearer "accommodates" the presupposition by adding it to his or her own background assumptions (Karttunen [9], Lewis [12]). To describe this phenomenon in the framework of the pragmatic conception of presupposition is undoubtedly difficult and none of the answers which have been proposed (in terms of the speaker pretending to presuppose something: Stalnaker [19], or in terms of the hearer being prepared to add the presupposition to the context without objection: Soames [16]) are fully satisfactory. In fact, a speaker would more successfully pretend to take something for granted by non mentioning it at all; and a hearer might well find an informative presupposition objectionable, without therefore considering the utterance which conveys it as inappropriate (Gauker [5]).

The picture of presupposition I would like to outline aims at recapturing the original intuition that when the proposition presupposed by the utterance of a sentence does not hold, that utterance is in some way out of order. In the perspective adopted here (see §1), we are not interested in background assumptions which have no textual manifestation, but only in those presuppositions which are linguistically triggered. I propose to consider those presuppositions not as shared assumptions, but as assumptions which ought to be shared. If we admit, as we have done above, that conversations are governed by objective contexts (the content of which is selected by the goals of the conversation), and that only sentences whose presuppositions are satisfied by the objective context are appropriately assertible, it follows that a hearer, by deeming that a presupposition which is triggered by a text is not satisfied by the context, is considering the speaker not merely as being factually wrong, but as violating a normative requirement. Such a judgement on the speaker's linguistic behaviour would lead to a communicative breakdown. In fact, this is what happens when, faced with an assertion whose presupposition does not hold, we feel we do not know how to reply. Given the general tendency to avoid communicative breakdowns, in all the cases in which there is some possibility left that the objective context does satisfy the presupposition, the hearer's default tendency will be to assume that it is so, namely, that the presupposition is in fact satisfied.

What is the function of presuppositions, so conceived, with respect to the representation of context? Presupposed propositions have to be included into the representation of the context associated with a given text just because some utterance belonging to the text is in order only if the presupposition is satisfied by the objective context. Irrespective of whether the presupposed propositions are old or new information for the hearer, and more generally, irrespective of whether they initially belong to the speaker's representation of the context, to the hearer's, to both, or to neither, they must find a place in the representation of the context which is worked out in the process of text understanding. Thus the addition of the content of an assertion to the representation of the context is accompanied by the obligation to add to the representation of the context those presuppositions of it which happen not to be yet there. This obligation, which is not to be confounded with the speaker's commitment relative to an overt assertion, concerns both speaker and hearer and protects the presupposed proposition from challenges, giving rise to the characteristic feeling that the presupposed proposition is, or is to be, "taken for granted".

The function of linguistic presupposition triggers is to indicate that speaker and hearer ought to take the presupposed content for granted. To say that a text has a certain presupposition means, therefore, that it conveys something as having to be taken for granted.

7. The distinction between presupposition and implicature

Pragmatic presupposition and implicature have often been considered as one and the same phenomenon. Within the framework outlined above, I will now put forward some remarks which give reasons for rejecting this claim.

7.1. Interactions with asserted contents

We have described the function of implicatures with respect to the changes in the representation of the context as either that of contributing to the change brought about by an assertion, or that of making a supplement to it available. The function of presuppositions seems to be quite different. They do not contribute to the content of assertions, as do implicatures such as that exemplified by (3), nor suggest supplementary information, as do implicatures such as those exemplified by (1), (2) and (4), but set requirements for the acceptability of utterances, the satisfaction of which depends on the objective context. This difference is confirmed by the following observations.

We have said that the propositions presupposed by an utterance have to belong to the representation of the context and are therefore added to it when they are not yet there. Now, of course it is possible that they are already there, because they have just been asserted, and in this case the presupposition does not bring about any update. Nevertheless, the utterance which contains the presupposition trigger can still be said to carry the presupposition. So, in the following dialogue:

(8) A: Billie likes ice cream
    B: Susie likes ice cream too

B's utterance can be said to presuppose that someone other than Susie likes ice cream, since its appropriateness requires this presupposition to be satisfied by the objective context. The presupposition of B's utterance has no business updating the representation of the context, because it has already been said by A that Billie likes ice cream; but B's utterance is appropriate just because of this. If we wanted to interpret "too" as conventionally implicating, rather than presupposing, that someone other than Susie likes ice cream, we would have no explanation for its use by B, since it is clear that no suggestion is made to supplement the content of the assertion in any way (cfr. Thomason [24]: p. 361).

In fact, the utterance of a sentence like

(9) Jane has not four children, nor three; she has two children.

just lacks the implicature that Jane has no more than two children. There is no need to draw such an inference, and moreover, there would be no point in supplementing what is asserted by associating the implicature with it, since the same content has already been explicitly asserted. Likewise, the utterance of a sentence containing a word which invites a conventional implicature, such as

(1) Mary is pretty, but intelligent

does not sound completely natural if a content corresponding to its conventional implicature has just been explicitly stated. Consider:

(10a) Being pretty, Mary is not likely to be intelligent. She is pretty, but intelligent.

The "but" here seems at least misplaced. In fact, the following sequence of utterances makes by far more sense:

(10b) Being pretty, Mary is not likely to be intelligent. But she is both pretty and intelligent.

Here, however, the conventional implicature conveyed by "but" has changed, amounting now roughly to

(11) The fact that Mary is both pretty and intelligent runs contrary to the assumption that, being pretty, she is not likely to be intelligent.

A related phenomenon which can be observed is the following. There are cases in which the content of a presupposition is linguistically formulated in the very utterance which triggers the presupposition (for example, in a subordinate clause). This happens regularly with factive verbs:

(12) John realized that he was in debt

contains, as a subordinate clause, the sentence "he was in debt", corresponding to the presupposed proposition that John was in debt. Thus, the presupposed content is at hand and no inference is needed in order to grasp it. Also in the cases of it-clefts and of definite descriptions, practically all of the linguistic material needed for making the presupposition explicit is at hand in the sentence which triggers the presupposition. But this does not make presupposition pointless: its point is not to invite additional inferences, but to convey that a certain content has to be taken for granted. In contrast, implicatures involve inference: conversational implicatures depend on a heuristic strategy relying on the Cooperative Principle, and conventional implicatures license inferences on the basis of the use of certain words, but in neither case the content of the implicature is linguistically encoded to such an extent, to make inference unnecessary. This would eliminate the implicature itself.

7.2. Implicatures and background assumptions

Another consideration which might lead to identify implicature and presupposition is that sometimes at least, implicatures seem to coincide with background assumptions of the speaker. Thus in

(13) A: Are you going to invite John to your party?
    B: No. I'm inviting nice people

it might be said that B's comment is understood as relevant only on the background of B's assumption that John is not nice. This assumption might therefore be considered as being "presupposed" by B's reply to A.

Now, it is indeed very likely that B is taking for granted that John is not nice. But does this contingent fact about B suffice to make his or her assumption a presupposition in the sense we have outlined above? Does the appropriateness of B's utterance require the satisfaction of the presupposition that John is not nice by the objective context? Is "I'm inviting nice people" in any sense not appropriately assertible if this requirement is not met? It does not seem to be so. There is no normative requirement to be met in order to make the utterance appropriate, and therefore no normative requirement for the representation of the context to contain the proposition that John is not nice. In contrast, it is obviously necessary for a hearer to take B's reply to be relevant, if he or she aims at a full understanding of its point, and this assumption of relevance is enough to suggest the conversational implicature that John is not nice as an integration of the explicitly conveyed information. The representation of the context will be updated by adding not only the information explicitly conveyed by B's utterance, but also the content of the conversational implicature.

The content of an implicature, on our view, can happen to be "shared knowledge" because of previous experiences and interactions shared by the participants. This does not make the implicature useless, as would do the explicit assertion of its content within the same text. There is still some inferential work to be done, which will establish a relationship between the text and a certain content which happens to be a shared piece of knowledge, and remind the participants of it. But this does not suffice to turn the implicature into a presupposition.

7.3. Negative sentences and presupposition cancellation

The claim that presupposition really is implicature has sometimes been raised with particular respect to the presuppositions of negative sentences. It has been claimed that the relationship between the utterance of a negative sentence and its alleged presupposition is in fact an implicature, while the relationship between the utterance of a positive sentence and its presupposition can be reduced to entailment (Chierchia and Mc Connell-Ginet [2]). This claim is based on the fact, noted above, that

(6) John used to smoke

seems to be a cancelable presupposition of

(5b) John has not stopped smoking

while in connection with

(5a) John has stopped smoking

it does not seem to be deniable without contradiction. Moreover, from the negation of (6):

(14) John never used to smoke

(5b) seems to follow, just as it should be the case if the relationship between (5a) and (6) were one of entailment.

Now, I do not think it is necessary to resort to implicature in order to explain the cancelability of (6) as a presupposition of (5b). Presupposition cancellation can be viewed as one aspect of the same process which, by default, leads to presupposition accommodation (Heim [8]: p. 401). In our terms: the representation of the context has to be internally consistent; two propositions contradicting each other should not be both added to it; if an utterance triggering a certain presupposition is introduced in a text at a point at which previous assertions have already added to the representation of the context some content contradictory with that presupposition, the obligation to include the presupposition in the representation of the context is suspended. So, when (5b) is introduced as a consequence of (14), it cannot carry the presupposition that John used to smoke and the appearance of entailment reversal is created. Such an explanation of presupposition cancellation is quite compatible with the fact that (5b), considered in isolation, has an intuitive relationship with (6), while nothing similar occurs in standard cases of entailment, and permits to describe this relationship as a presupposition triggered (in default conditions) by the verb "to stop", that is, in the same terms in which the relationship between (5a) and (6) can also be described. It does not seem justified, therefore (at least, it is not economical), to consider the presuppositions of the utterance of a positive sentence and of its corresponding negative sentence as instances of two different relationships, one of which an implicature.

8. Concluding remarks

Concluding then, there are reasons for considering presupposition as a phenomenon distinct from implicature. Presuppositions play a specific role in the ways in which we project the representation of context from our acquaintance with a text. Presuppositions convey that a certain content has to belong to the representation of the context, irrespective of whether it does already belong to it or not and of whether inferences going beyond the rearrangement of linguistic material contained in the text are needed. The ways in which implicatures contribute to the representation of context are undoubtedly different: they aim at bringing about updates of the representation of the context, either by contributing to the content of assertions, or by suggesting supplementary information, and typically require inferences going beyond the linguistic material contained in the text. The fact that in some cases what is inferred may belong to the participants' shared knowledge is not enough to make the implicature a presupposition. Moreover, resort to implicatures in order to explain the cancelable presuppositions carried by the utterance of a negative sentence, appears to be an unnecessary complication.

Research on text understanding has the task to specify the strategies which enable the receiver to recover implicitly conveyed information and which may be used to justify such a recovery, distinguishing it from the working out of mere psychological associations not warranted by the text. These strategies are clearly connected with the ways in which implicit information is conveyed, namely, the ways in which it contributes to the representation of context. If, as I have tried to show, presupposition and implicature contribute to the update of the representation of context in different ways, for the aims of research on text understanding it will be useful to distinguish them from each other. Therefore, the development a conceptual framework in which presupposition and implicature coexist, receiving separate, complementary definitions, turns out to be highly desirable.

References

1. Bach, K.: Conversational impliciture. Mind and Language 9 (1994) 124-162
2. Chierchia, G., Mc Connell-Ginet, S.: Meaning and Grammar. MIT Press., Cambridge, Mass. (1990)
3. Davis, S. (ed.): Pragmatics. A reader. Oxford University Press, Oxford (1991)
4. Frege, G.: Sinn und Bedeutung. Zeitschrift fuer Philosophie und philosophische Kritik, 100 (1892) 25-50. English transl. in: Philosophical Writings of Gottlob Frege, ed. by P. Geach and M. Black. 3rd edn. Blackwell, Oxford (1980)
5. Gauker, C.: What is a context of utterance? Philosophical Studies 91 (1998) 149-172
6. Gazdar, G.: Speech act assignment. In: Joshi, A.K., Webber, B.L., Sag, I.A. (eds.): Elements of Discourse Understanding. Cambridge University Press, Cambridge (1981) 64-83
7. Grice, P.: Studies in the Way of Words. Harvard University Press, Cambridge, Mass. (1989)
8. Heim, I.: On the projection problem for presuppositions. In Flickinger, D. et al. (eds.): Proceedings of the Second West Coast Conference on Formal Linguistics. Stanford University Press, Stanford, Ca (1988). Repr. in [3] (1991) 397-405
9. Karttunen, L.: Presupposition and linguistic context. Theoretical Linguistics 1 (1974) 181-194. Repr. in [3] 406-415
10. Karttunen, L., Peters, S.: Conventional implicature. In Oh, Ch.-K., Dinneen, D. (eds.): Syntax and Semantics 11: Presupposition. Academic Press, New York (1979) 1-56
11. Levinson, S.C.: Pragmatics. Cambridge University Press, Cambridge (1983)
12. Lewis, D.: Scorekeeping in a language game. Journal of Philosophical Language 8 (1979) 333-359. Repr. in [3] 416-427
13. Perrault, C.R.: An application of default logic to speech act theory. In Cohen, Ph. R., Morgan, J., Pollack, M.E. (eds.): Intentions in Communication. MIT Press, Cambridge, Mass. (1990) 161-185
14. Sbisà, M.: Speech acts and context change. In Ballmer, T., Wildgen, W. (eds.): Process linguistics. Niemeyer, Tubingen (1987) 252-79
15. Sbisà, M.: Linguaggio, ragione, interazione. Il Mulino, Bologna (1989)
16. Soames, S.: How presuppositions are inherited. A solution to the projection problem. Linguistic Inquiry 13 (1982) 483-545. Repr. in [3] 428-70
17. Sperber, D. , Wilson, D.: Relevance. Blackwell, Oxford (1986)

18. Stalnaker, R.: Presuppositions. Journal of Philosophical Logic 2 (1973) 447-457
19. Stalnaker, R.: Pragmatic presupposition. In Munitz, M., Unger, P. (eds.): Semantics and philosophy. New York University Press, New York (1974) 197-214. Repr. in [3] 471-81
20. Stalnaker, R.: Assertion. In Cole, P. (ed.): Syntax and Semantics 9: Pragmatics. Academic Press, New York (1978) 315-22. Repr. in [3] 278-89
21. Stalnaker, R.: On the representation of context. Journal of Logic, Language and Information 7 (1998) 3-19
22. Strawson, P.F.: On referring. Mind 59 (1950) 320-44. Repr. in Strawson, P.F.: Logico-Linguistic Papers. Methuen, London (1971)
23. Stubbs, M.: Text and corpus analysis. Blackwell, Oxford (1996)
24. Thomason, R.H.: Accommodation, meaning and implicature: interdisciplinary foundations for pragmatics. In Cohen, Ph. R., Morgan, J., Pollack, M.E. (eds.): Intentions in Communication. MIT Press, Cambridge, Mass. (1990) 325-365

The Formal Structure of Ecological Contexts

Barry Smith[1] and Achille C. Varzi[2]

[1] Department of Philosophy, SUNY Buffalo, NY 14260, USA
phismith@acsu.buffalo.edu
[2] Department of Philosophy, Columbia University, New York, NY 10027, USA
achille.varzi@columbia.edu

Abstract. This paper presents the outline of a formal ontology of contexts. More specifically, it deals with the ontology of ecological contexts (niches, habitats, environments, ambients) and of the relations between organisms, niches, and the spatial regions they occupy. The first part sets out the basic conceptual background. The second part outlines a semi-formal theory which builds upon notions and principles of mereology, topology, and the theory of spatial location.

1 Introduction

The ecological literature distinguishes between two ways of conceiving a "niche" (habitat, ecotope, biotope, microlandscape) [22, 39]. On the one hand, there is the traditional *functional* conception of a niche as the role or position enjoyed by an organism or population within an ecological community. As C. Elton [14] famously put it, "When an ecologist says 'there goes a badger' he should include in his thoughts some definite idea of the animal's place in the community to which it belongs, just as if he had said 'there goes the vicar'." The world of niches might, in this sense, be viewed as a giant evolutionary hotel, some of whose rooms are occupied (by organisms which have evolved to fill them), some of whose rooms are for a variety of reasons unoccupied but can become occupied in the future. On the other hand, there is the *environmental* conception advanced by G. E. Hutchinson [19] and R. Lewontin [21]. On this second conception, a niche is thought of as the hypervolume defined by the limiting values of all environmental variables relevant to the survival of a given species. A niche is not a mere location, but a location in space that is defined additionally by a specific constellation of ecological parameters such as degree of slope, exposure to sunlight, soil fertility, foliage density, and so on. It is, we might say, an *ecological context*. The purpose of this paper is to outline a formal theory of this notion.

Our account expands on the theory put forward in [30], which builds upon certain fundamental notions and principles of mereology, topology, and the theory of spatial location. We focus on niche *tokens*, which is to say on the environmental niche determined by a given organism or population of organisms in a given place, and we aim to be more explicit than is customary in the ecological literature as concerns the ontological marks of these entities. Thus, while our theory will be illustrated above all by means of simple ecological and biological examples, it should be understood as being applicable in principle to a wide range of different domains. The concept of niche and its cognates are indeed already employed ubiquitously in many disciplines, from sociology [15] and economics [23] to organization science [3]. Yet the underlying principles have thus far been investigated not at all from the formal point of view. This is in part because the mereotopological tools needed for such an investigation have been developed only recently. But it is in part also a consequence of the fact that formal ontologists have tended to shun holistic structures, preferring to conceive reality in terms of what can be simulated via (normally set-theoretic) constructions from out of postulated atoms or *Urelemente*. Our account, in contrast, is resolutely holistic: it proceeds from the idea that there are structured wholes, including the medium of space, which come before the parts that these wholes contain and that can be distinguished on various levels within them.

2   General Background

Our theory has two main progenitors. One is the Aristotelian theory of place, as sketched in the *Physics* [29]. Each body, in Aristotle's view, has a place, and the place *contains* the body—it relates to its body in something like the way the interior boundary of an urn relates to the liquid contained within it. Thus, a place exactly *surrounds* the body in such a way that the body is separate from but yet in perfect contact with its surrounding place, the latter being therefore marked by a certain sort of interior cavity or hole. An ecological context, in our sense, is like the place of the relevant organism or population, in Aristotle's sense.

The second progenitor is the account of settings elaborated in great detail by the ecological psychologist Roger Barker [1, 2, 25]. Consider, on the one hand, the recurrent settings that serve as the environments for the everyday activities of persons and groups of persons. Examples are: John's swimming pool, your favorite table in the cafeteria, the 7:50am train to Verona. Each of these settings is marked by certain stable arrays of physical objects and physical infrastructure (by 'surface layouts', in Gibson's [16] terms). But each recurrent setting is associated, on the other hand, with certain stable patterns of behavior on the part of the persons involved. Physical-behavioral units are the conjunct of these two aspects. They are built out of both physical and behavioral parts. As Barker [1] puts it, they "are common phenomenal entities, and they are natural units in no way imposed by an investigator." Each physical-behavioral unit has thus two sorts of components: people behaving in certain ways (lecturing, listening, eating) and non-psychological objects with which behavior is transacted (walls, chairs, electricity, etc.). Each unit is marked by the opposition between an organized internal (foreground) pattern from a wider external (background) pattern [20]. And each is circumjacent to its components: the former surrounds (encloses, encompasses) the latter—the pupils and equipment are *in* the class; the swimmers are *in* the swimming pool. All of these are features that are shared by ecological contexts, as we understand them here. Moreover, ecological contexts, like physical-behavioral units, may be nested together in hierarchies. There are typically many units of each lower-level kind within a given locality, and these are typically embedded within larger units, as a game is embedded within a match. The same goes for ecological contexts.

It is somewhat remarkable that similar characterizations may be found in quite different domains of application. For instance, the notion of a mobile ambient employed in the theory of network security is close in spirit—ontologically—to that of a physical-behavioral unit. Cardelli and Gordon [4] characterize an ambient as "a bounded place where computation happens", with a boundary around it. Examples include: a web page (bounded by a file), a virtual address space (bounded by an addressing range), a Unix file system (bounded within a physical volume), a laptop (bounded by its case and data ports). "If we want to move computations easily we must be able to determine what should move; a boundary determines what is inside and what is outside an ambient." [id.]

Related ideas may be found also in the anthropological literature on territoriality, a phenomenon that arises whenever there obtains a type of relation between an individual or group and a structured area or volume of space which is of such a sort that the individual or group will seek to *defend* the latter against invasion by other conspecific individuals or groups [24]. (Compare also the related psychological phenomenon of 'personal space' [17].) Anthropologists have shown that, in the case of both human and non-human animal species, a nested hierarchy of types of site must be distinguished around any given individual or group. The force of territoriality then diminishes with increase in group size and spatial area. In the first place there are territories in the narrow sense, the characteristically tiny areas in relation to which the occupying individual or group demands exclusive use. This central area is then extended to comprehend various attached regions, for example watering holes, where desirable resources are available on a routine basis. Finally we have the *home range*, that larger surrounding area within which the group spends almost all of its time [33]. Again, we find here the idea that niches (territories, settings) form a nested hierarchy around an individual or group occupying a privileged locus at its center.

Let us, then, summarize the ontological marks of niches, understood as genuine ecological contexts. (i) A niche is not simply a location in space; rather, it is a location in space that is constrained and marked by certain functional properties (of temperature, foliage density, federal jurisdiction, etc.). (ii) A niche occupies a physical-temporal locale within which is a certain privileged locus—a hole—into which the relevant organism fits exactly. (iii) A niche is a connected whole with a more or less determinate outer boundary: there are things that fall clearly within it, and other things that fall clearly outside it. (iv) A niche may have parts that are also niches, and a niche may similarly be a proper part of larger, circumcluding niches. (v) A niche may overlap spatially with other niches (of different organisms) with which it does not share common parts. As we said, these ontological marks correspond to the environmental notion of niche—the concrete (token) ecological context that is actually occupied by a given organism or group of organisms on a given occasion. We may nonetheless assume that functional niches, too, to the extent that they are realized at all, are realized in (or as) some concrete environmental niches or habitats of the sort considered here.

3 The Formal Theory

We shall now lay out the formal principles underlying this characterization. As in [30], we shall initially suppose that all tenants are *compact*, in the sense that they have no interior cavities. Later we shall see how the account can be extended to the case of tenants with one or more cavities. Note that our principles are to be given a tensed reading: we are concerned here with the panoply of niche-tenant relations *at a given time*.

The first axiom fixes the basic spatial relationships between niches and their tenants. Formally, a niche is a certain type of neighborhood—a perforated or deleted neighborhood of its tenant. Thus, we require that a niche should not overlap but rather surround its tenant:

A1   *If x is a niche for y, then x surrounds y.*

This implies that a niche is disjoint from its tenant, not only in the mereological sense of not sharing any part with the niche, but also in the purely spatial sense of not sharing any common location. This is important, because we must in the present context draw a clear distinction between those mereological (part-whole) relations that apply to a given set of spatial entities and those that apply to the spatial regions those entities occupy [7, 35]. It is a characteristic property of physical objects that they may not be in the same place at the same time. But this principle does not hold when entities of other kinds are countenanced. For instance, we want to say that the region where a niche is located may be occupied by objects that are not a part of the niche. The niche around the sleeping bear may be full of flies, but it need not be the case that the flies themselves are a part thereof. Moreover, the tokened environmental niches which form the center of our theory are bounded not just spatially, and not just via physical material (the walls of the cave), but also via thresholds in quality-continua (for instance, temperature). Distinct niches, therefore, may occupy the same or overlapping spatial regions, and different organisms, or organisms of different types, may be able to find niches within the same spatial region without its thereby being implied that they share a niche. A niche for the fly on the bear's nose is not a part of the niche for the bear (or at least: we need not assume that it is), though it overlaps spatially therewith.

As a second axiom, we require that a niche be in contact with its tenant (that nothing can squeeze in between them, as it were):

A2   *If x is a niche for y, then x is connected to every tangential part of y.*

A tangential part is, of course, a part that is connected to the spatial complement of the relevant entity. And the relevant notion of contact is to be understood along the lines of classical topological connection: two entities are connected if they share at least a boundary. More precisely, there must be a common boundary which is part of one or the other, though not necessarily of both [5, 27]. This notion if connection is not unproblematic [28, 37], and there are ways of characterizing a relation of topological connection which do not rely on the boundary concept at all [10, 11]. Here, however, we shall content ourselves with this ordinary account. In particular, we shall assume that two discrete entities can be in contact only if one of them is open (i.e., if it does not include its boundary) where the other is closed (in the sense that it includes its boundary as a proper part). Thus, if John and Mary are topologically closed, then genuine contact between them is impossible if contact is understood in terms of topological connection. Due to the density of space, the surfaces of two distinct physical bodies cannot be in contact topologically, though they may of course be so close to each other that they appear to be in contact to the naked eye. (This is in agreement with ordinary topology, and also with standard physics, but see [26, 31] for more details on the underlying issues.)

Note indeed that A1 implies that a niche is always *externally* connected to its tenant: they are connected, but they do not overlap. Since nothing is externally connected to itself, it follows immediately that the niche-tenant relation is irreflexive. Moreover, note that A2 depends crucially on our supposition concerning the compactness of all tenants. The presence of an inner cavity would split the tangential parts of the tenant into two classes, but A2 is only meant to apply to those tangential parts that face outwards, as it were. We shall come back to this point in the next section.

Our third axiom constrains the topology of niches by ruling out the possibility that they be spatially scattered:

A3   *If x is a niche for y, then x is self-connected (i.e., in one piece).*

Again, the relevant notion here is to be understood in classical topological terms: x is self-connected if and only if any two parts that make up x are connected to each other [5]. Thus, every niche must enjoy a certain natural completeness or rounded-offness. Note that we do not assume a corresponding principle concerning the topological structure of a tenant. In agreement with standard ecological treatments, a tenant may be a single organism or a population of separate organisms. There is, for instance, a natural niche surrounding John and Mary as they enjoy a romantic candle-light dinner. For another example, avatars (a shoal of fish in a lake, a herd of buffalo) are causally integrated and more or less reproductively isolated subpopulations of conspecifics, and their identity conditions typically involve reference to a relevant ecological context [12, 13]. Avatars play an important role in evolutionary theory in light of the fact that it is avatars, and not whole species, that are the most plausible candidate subjects of selective pressures at the group level.

A constraint on the topology of tenants comes from our fourth axiom, which rules out the possibility of "open" tenants:

A4   *If x is a niche for y, then y is closed (i.e., its parts include its boundaries).*

This is motivated by our ecological interpretation of the niche-tenant relationship: a tenant is an organism or a population of organisms, so its boundaries are its surfaces (the outer layers of the organism's skins) which face out toward the niche. We take it that every topologically closed entity has an interior (has divisible bulk). It follows, therefore, that no niche can be a mere boundary. Since niches are externally in contact with their tenants (A2), a niche must always be open in the region in which it makes contact with its tenant (for, as we have seen, where two entities are externally connected, one must be open and the other closed). Indeed, if niches were mere boundaries, they would be parts of their tenants by A4, and this would contradict A1.

An immediate corollary is that the tenant of a niche cannot itself be a niche, which in turn implies that the niche-tenant relationship is not only irreflexive but fully *asymmetric*. More generally, it follows that niches cannot themselves be niched. This does not exclude an organism from being such as to constitute a niche or natural setting for another entity, for example a micro-organism inside a human body. What it does rule out is that the hosting organism might serve this hosting function by itself. To see what is at issue here, note that, if every organism is topologically closed and every niche open (in the relevant contact area), then it follows that a micro-organism lodged inside your body as a niched entity is not topologically connected to your body: there must be some distance between them, however small. The niche for the micro-organism is thus not your body itself (which is closed), nor a proper part thereof, but rather an entity including also the area immediately surrounding the micro-organism and separating the latter from you. (Clearly, this presupposes that your body has inner cavities, and therefore that it is not compact in the sense that we are here assuming to hold of all tenants. But this assumption will eventually be relaxed in the sequel.)

Our next axiom imposes on niches and their occupants a common constraint of topological regularity:

A5   *If x is a niche for y, then x and y are both regular.*

An open entity x is said to be regular, topologically, if it coincides with the interior of its own closure, i.e., of the entity obtained from x itself by adding its boundary; and a closed entity y is said to be regular if it coincides with the closure of its own interior, i.e., of the entity obtained from y by removing its boundary. Thus, a regular object is, roughly speaking, an object which does not possess outgrowing boundary spikes, does not lack a single interior point, does not consist of two or more voluminous parts connected by interiorless filaments, and so on. The point of this axiom, then, is to exclude from the orbit of our theory niches and tenants with strange topologies, for example space-filling curves, deleted Tychonoff corkscrews, and other monsters. There are, to be sure, organisms that have a quasi-fractal structure (sponges, mosses) and niches whose porosity is important to their ecological role. The hole-part structure of such entities is enormously complex; they are nonetheless, like all entities falling within the province of biological science, regular in the sense at issue here.

Our last axiom says that niches are *exclusive* environmental contexts: they cannot be shared by distinct entities (though distinct entities may have overlapping niches, both in the mereological and in the spatial sense of 'overlap').

A6   *If x is a niche for y and also for z, then y and z are identical.*

Consider the inside of an ant's nest. This is, no doubt, an ecological niche for a clutch of eggs when they are laid (a disconnected tenant). But is it not also a niche for each separate egg? To see why this is not so, consider that the surrounding environment of each individual egg includes, or is determined by, the boundaries of its neighbors. The surface layout of the collective niche is quite different from the surface layout of the niche for each egg taken individually. Similar considerations apply in relation to a pair of twin fetuses inside a mother's womb. Each fetus helps to determine the niche for its neighbor. The womb as a whole serves as niche for the twinned pair.

4 Remarks and Refinements

The elementary apparatus defined by A1–A6 identifies what we regard as the basic (synchronic) theory of niches, understood as ecological contexts. A few comments are in order, at this point.

First, note that our axioms suggest that for every niche there is a tenant (as is clear from the use of a relational predicate, 'x is a niche for y'), but not that every organism or population is always in a niche. A diver crossing the boundary between water and air is arguably not in a niche but rather moving *from* one niche to another. The issues raised by cases such as this, however, are part and parcel of the general problem of motion and change, which goes beyond the limits of the purely synchronic framework presented here.

Second, our axioms do not guarantee that niches are closed under the basic mereological operations of fusion and product. If an object has two niches, their fusion need not be a niche, for it might lack the sort of homogeneity by which niches are typically characterized. Likewise, if an object has two niches, their intersection need not be a niche. Consider a group of cows in the middle of a large field with a water tank at each of the two extremities A and B. The whole field is a niche for the cows, as is the middle plus A and the middle plus B. But the intersection of the latter is not a niche, since the cows need water. This asymmetry of behavior with regard to mereological operations is one respect in which the concept of niche deviates from the purely topological concept of neighborhood. But there are many other properties of neighborhoods whose analogues for niches have an uncertain status. For instance, should we assume that every two niches of the same tenant have a common part? That every niche for a given tenant has a proper part which is itself a niche for that tenant? That every niche has a *compact* part which is itself a niche for the same tenant (a niche with no internal holes except those occupied by the tenant)?

Third, note that our axioms do not imply that niches are dissective: a niche for an entity y may have proper parts that are not niches for y, even if those proper parts fully surround y. Thus, for instance, no non-regular proper part of a niche ever qualifies as a niche. Our axioms do not imply, either, that niches may be arbitrarily large. Thus, in particular, the mereological complement of an organism (the result of imagining the organism as having been deleted from the remainder of the universe) need not be a niche, according to the axioms here listed. (The axioms do not however rule this out. Indeed, a straightforward consistency proof for A1–A6 can be obtained precisely by taking 'x is a niche for y' to hold only if x is the complement of y.) There is in fact a problem of vagueness here. For what can be said about the *outer* boundaries of niches? In some cases the surface layout of the surrounding physical environment provides an upper limit to the niche extension (the worm in its wormhole, the scholar in her cell). In other cases, however (the fish in the ocean, the bird in the sky), no such physical limit may be provided: the outer boundary of the relevant niche is then in some sense vague, though we leave it open here whether this vagueness is onto-logical [34] or merely conceptual [18]. (This alternative is not peculiar to the vague-ness of niches and arises in connection with most entities countenanced by ordinary discourse: what are the boundaries of a cloud? of a hurricane? of a mountain?)

Let us, finally, consider the question of the *inner* boundaries of ecological con-texts—the boundaries that niches share with their tenants. As we have already pointed out, our axioms assume that tenants involve no internal cavities. However, this as-sumption is for complex organisms too strong. Thus if niches are to be self-connected (by A3) and tenants closed (by A4), this means that for complex organisms A2 will in general fall short of capturing the relevant sense in which a niche and its tenant are connected: the boundary around a tenant's inner cavity cannot be connected to an exte-rior niche. Difficulties arise even in cases where the tenant has a connected boundary. Topologically, all animals are doughnut-shaped; yet it hardly seems reasonable to suppose that every niche of John would snake through his digestive tract (though we may naturally suppose that the finger through Mary's wedding ring is part of the ring's niche). To resolve these issues, we therefore need to amend axiom A2. Let the *compact closure* of an object be the entity that results (intuitively) when we take the object together with those parts of its complement that lie on its inside and through its perforations—the mereological sum of the object together with all its holes [36]. It can be verified that the compact closure of a closed, regular object is always closed and regular. Accordingly, we may reformulate A2 as follows:

A2'. *If x is a niche for y, then x is connected to every tangential part of the compact closure of y.*

There is, to be sure, a further complication here. Typically a hole in an organism is a genuine hole, analogous to the hole inside a wedding ring. But there seem to be cases where the putative hole is, in virtue of the intimate causal interconnection of processes on either side of its boundary, analogous to an organ within the interior of the organism in question. And there are also some mixed cases, perhaps of the sort illustrated by the womb conceived abstractly as dilation in the uterine tract. If we allow for such possibilities, then A1 must be amended too, to allow for the possibil-ity of spatial—though not mereological—overlap between a niche and its tenant. (The solution to this problem may well be a question of granularity: when viewed from the microscopic level, it seems, more holes become visible within the organism, and thus also more possibilities for the hosting of interior tenants.)

5   Open Issues

There are many issues left open by the theory of niches *qua* ecological contexts pre-sented above.

One family of issues arises out of the fact, already mentioned above, that A1–A6 provide only a synchronic account: we would still need to introduce the important factors of dynamics and change, and above all to address the issue of the identity of niches and niched objects over time. We also need to address issues relating to the movement and interaction of organisms within and between their respective niches. We need to find a place for the special types of causal integrity that characterize niches and niched entities, and for the special types of niche assembly-structure that arise for example when groups of individuals collaborate. And we need to consider the question of how the niches for given objects are determined by the properties of their surroundings. What determines the shape and size of a niche? How do animal niches in this respect relate to those of organisms of other types, for example corals or crustaceans?

A second important family of problems relates to the question of the status of niches when tenants are absent. As we have seen, the use of a relational predicate, 'x is a niche for y' suggests that every niche has a tenant. But are niches *essentially* dependent entities, as Lewontin [21] would have it? Are they merely generically dependent on their tenants in the same sense in which a hole is dependent on its material host, or a boundary on the voluminous body that it bounds? Do we need to distinguish different types of niche, some of which will survive the temporary or permanent departure or replacement of their tenants?

Further questions concern the patterns of interaction between different niches, or between niches of different sorts. What is the relation between my niche and your niche when you occupy a position within my niche and I within yours? What is the relation between my niche and yours when we are in conflict, for example when we compete for occupation of a given territory, or when you are predator and I am prey, or when we interact symbiotically? What, finally, is the biologically very important relation between the individual or *token* niche or habitat of a single organism or population of organisms and the niche-*type* of the corresponding species?

Some of these questions arise specifically with reference to the ecological notion of niche on which we have focused in the foregoing. But some have a more general status, and concern the notion of an ecological context at large, including its ramifications into other domains such as economics, anthropology, evolutionary biology, or even the theory of network security (see again [4]). The formal theory outlined in the above will, we hope, provide at least a starting point for providing answers to these questions.

Appendix: Formal Matters

In [30] the niche-tenant relation is axiomatized as a first-order theory on the basis of a simple apparatus built around three primitive relations: the mereological relation $P(x, y)$ ("x is part of y"); the topological relation $B(x, y)$ ("x is a boundary for y"); and the locative relation $L(x, y)$ ("x is located exactly at y"). (See [9] for a study of the axiomatic principles governing these relations.) As it turns out, this is sufficient to axiomatize a fourth primitive, $N(x, y)$, corresponding to the relation "x is a niche for y", in a way that conforms to principles A1–A6 above. However, the formalization of our A1 in terms of the three basic primitives gives rise to some problems. A better account can be given if we allow ourselves another basic primitive, $H(x, y)$, to be understood as expressing the relation "x is a hole in y". Using this primitive (axioma-

tized as in [6]), it is easy to define the notion of an interior hole, or cavity, and consequently the notion of one object (a niche) surrounding another (a tenant):

D1 $IH(x,y) =_{df} H(x,y) \land \forall z(B(z,y) \to B(z,x))$ interior hole
D2 $S(x,y) =_{df} \exists z \exists u \exists w(IH(z,x) \land L(z,u) \land L(y,w) \land P(w,u))$.   surrounding

Accordingly, we can formalize A1 as follows:

A1* $N(x,y) \to S(x,y)$.

As for A2, we need the auxiliary notions of *connection* and *tangential parthood*, whose
ordinary characterization is as follows:

D3 $C(x,y) =_{df} O(x,y) \lor \exists z(P(z,x) \land B(z,y) \lor P(z,y) \land B(z,x))$ connection
D4 $TP(x,y) =_{df} P(x,y) \land \exists z(C(x,z) \land \neg O(z,y))$.   tangential part

A2 can then be formalized as

A2* $N(x,y) \to \forall z(TP(z,y) \to C(z,x))$.

The more general version, A2', can be formalized in a similar fashion, using the operator of compact closure k as defined in [30]:

A2'* $N(x,y) \to \forall z(TP(z,y) \to C(x,k(z)))$.

Alternatively, we can rely on a stricter notion of surrounding:

D5 $ES(x,y) =_{df} \exists z \exists u(IH(z,x) \land L(z,u) \land L(y,u))$.   exact surrounding

Then A1* and A2'* can be fused into a single axiom:

A1'* $N(x,y) \to ES(x,k(y))$.

The formalization of the remaining axioms A3–A6 then proceeds exactly as in [30]
(see axioms A17–A21 therein).

Acknowledgments

Support of the National Science Foundation through award BCS-9975557 from the
Geography and Regional Science program is gratefully acknowledged.

References

1. Barker, R. G., 1968, *Ecological Psychology. Concepts and Methods for Studying the Environment of Human Behavior*, Stanford: Stanford University Press.
2. Barker, R. G., and Associates, 1978, *Habitats, Environments, and Human Behavior*, San Francisco: Jossey-Bass Publishers.
3. Bruggeman, J. P., 1996, *Formalizing Organizational Ecology. Logical and Mathematical Investigations in Organization Theory*, Dissertation, Center for Computer Science in Organization and Managenemt, University of Amsterdam.

4. Cardelli, L., and Gordon, A. D., 1998, 'Mobile Ambients', in M. Nivat (ed.), *Foundations of Software Science and Computational Structures. Proceedings of the First International Conference*, Berlin and Heidelberg: Springer-Verlag, pp. 140-155.
5. Cartwright, R., 1975, 'Scattered Objects', in K. Lehrer (ed.), *Analysis and Metaphysics*, Dordrecht: Reidel, pp. 153-171.
6. Casati, R., and Varzi, A. C., 1994, *Holes and Other Superficialities*, Cambridge, MA, and London: MIT Press (Bradford Books).
7. Casati, R., and Varzi, A. C., 1996, 'The Structure of Spatial Location', *Philosophical Studies* 82, 205-239.
8. Casati, R., and Varzi, A. C., 1997, 'Spatial Entities', in O. Stock (ed.), *Spatial and Temporal Reasoning*, Dordrecht, Boston, and London: Kluwer Academic Publishers, pp. 73-96.
9. Casati, R., and Varzi, A. C., 1999, *Parts and Places: The Structures of Spatial Representation*, Cambridge, MA, and London: MIT Press (Bradford Books).
10. Cohn, A. G., and Varzi, A. C., 1998, 'Connection Relations in Mereotopology', in H. Prade (ed.), *Proceedings of the 13th European Conference on Artificial Intelligence*, Chichester: John Wiley & Sons, pp. 150-154.
11. Cohn, A. G., and Varzi, A. C., 1999, 'Modes of Connection', in C. Freksa (ed.), *Spatial Information Theory. Proceedings of the Fourth International Conference*, Berlin and Heidelberg: Springer-Verlag, in press.
12. Damuth, J., 1985, 'Selection among "Species": A Formulation in Terms of Natural Functional Units', *Evolution* 39, 1132-1146.
13. Eldredge, N., 1989, *Macroevolutionary Dynamics: Species, Niches, and Adaptive Peaks*, New York: McGraw-Hill.
14. Elton, C., 1927, *Animal Ecology*, New York: Macmillan.
15. Freeman, J., and Hannan, M. T., 1983, 'Niche Width and the Dynamics of Organizational Populations', *American Journal of Sociology* 88, 1116-1145.
16. Gibson, J. J., 1979, *The Ecological Approach to Visual Perception*, Boston: Houghton-Mifflin.
17. Hall, E. T., 1966, *The Hidden Dimension*, Garden City: Doubleday.
18. Heller, M., 1996, 'Against Metaphysical Vagueness', *Philosophical Perspectives* 10, 177-186.
19. Hutchinson, G. E., 1978, *An Introduction to Population Ecology*, New Haven: Yale University Press.
20. Johansson, I., 1998, 'Pattern as an Ontological Category', in N. Guarino (ed.), *Formal Ontology in Information Systems*, Amsterdam: IOS Press, pp. 86-94.
21. Lewontin, R., 1979, 'Sociobiology as an Adaptationist Program', *Behavioral Science* 24, 5-14.
22. Looijen, R. C., 1995, 'On the Distinction Between Habitat and Niche, and Some Implications for Species' Differentiation', in T. A. F. Kuipers and A. R. Mackor (eds.), *Cognitive Patterns in Science and Common Sense*, Amsterdam and Atlanta: Rodopi, pp. 87-108.
23. Milne, G. R., 1990, *An Ecological Niche Theory Approach to the Assessment of Brand Competition in Fragmented Markets*, Dissertation, School of Business Administration, University of North Carolina at Chapel Hill.
24. Sack, R. D., 1986, *Human Territoriality. Its Theory and History*, Cambridge: Cambridge University Press.
25. Schoggen, P., 1989, *Behavior Settings. A Revision and Extension of Roger G. Barker's Ecological Psychology*, Stanford: Stanford University Press.
26. Smith, B., 1995, 'On Drawing Lines on a Map', in A. U. Frank and W. Kuhn (eds.), *Spatial Information Theory. A Theoretical Basis for GIS*, Berlin and Heidelberg: Springer-Verlag, pp. 475-84.
27. Smith, B., 1996, 'Mereotopology: A Theory of Parts and Boundaries', *Data and Knowledge Engineering* 20, 1996, 287-304.

28. Smith, B., 1997, 'Boundaries: An Essay in Mereotopology', in L. H. Hahn (ed.), *The Philosophy of Roderick Chisholm* (Library of Living Philosophers), Chicago and La Salle, IL: Open Court, pp. 534–61.
29. Smith, B., 1999, 'Objects and Their Environments: From Aristotle to Ecological Psychology', in A. Frank (ed.), *The Life and Motion of Socioeconomic Units*, London: Taylor and Francis, in press.
30. Smith, B., and Varzi, A. C., 1999a, 'The Niche', *Noûs* 33, 198–222.
31. Smith, B., and Varzi, A. C., 1999b, 'Fiat and Bona Fide Boundaries', *Philosophy and Phenomenological Research*, in press.
32. Sterelny, K., and Griffiths, P., 1999, *Sex and Death: An Introduction to the Philosophy of Biology*, Chicago: University of Chicago Press.
33. Taylor, R. B., 1988, *Human Territorial Functioning. An Empirical, Evolutionary Perspective on Individual and Small Group Territorial Cognitions, Behaviors and Consequences*, Cambridge: Cambridge University Press.
34. Tye, M., 1990, 'Vague Objects', *Mind* 99, 535–557.
35. Varzi, A. C., 1996a, 'Parts, Wholes, and Part-Whole Relations: The Prospects of Mereotopology,' *Data and Knowledge Engineering* 20, 259–86.
36. Varzi, A. C., 1996b, 'Reasoning about Space: The Hole Story', *Logic and Logical Philosophy* 4, 3–39.
37. Varzi, A. C., 1997, 'Boundaries, Continuity, and Contact', *Noûs* 31, 26–58.
38. Varzi, A. C., 1998, 'Basic Problems of Mereotopology', in N. Guarino (ed.), *Formal Ontology in Information Systems*, Amsterdam: IOS Press, pp. 29–38.
39. Whittaker, R. H., and Lewin, S. A. (eds.), 1975, *Niche Theory and Applications* (Benchmark Papers in Ecology 3), Stroudsburg, PA: Dowden, Hutchinson, and Ross.

Type Theoretic Foundations for Context, Part 1: Contexts as Complex Type-Theoretic Objects

Richmond H. Thomason[1]

Computer Science Department,
University of Michigan,
Ann Arbor, MI 48109-2110, USA
rich@thomason.org

Abstract. This paper presents Contextual Intensional Logic, a type-theoretic logic intended as a general foundation for reasoning about context. I motivate and illustrate the logical framework, and conclude by indicating extensions that may be desirable.

1 Introduction

In several previous works, [15, 16], I proposed and explored (very briefly), the idea of fitting the logic into a version of type theory that is designed to deal with the phenomena that are discussed in the literature of context. This paper will improve, refine and extend these type-thoretic ideas.

There are a number of logical advantages to type theory.

(1) The underlying logical architecture, which goes back to [4], is beautifully simple and has been thoroughly investigated by logicians.
(2) The framework of types provides a rich, highly structured ontology that is potentially useful in formalization.
(3) The theory is a straightforward extension of Richard Montague's Intensional Logic, [11, 6, 1], which has been the dominant formalism for the logical interpretation of natural language. Using it provides direct connections to an extensive body of work in natural language semantics. So the type theoretic approach can facilitate linguistic applications of the theory of context.
(4) The use of types provides conceptual clarity.

In this paper, I will introduce and explain the basic ideas of the formalism, using these to illustrate and support point (4), above. I will also discuss some ways in which the formalism can (and should) be extended.

2 Brief Introduction to Intensional Logic

Any version of type theory will involve not only a domain of individuals, with variables ranging over this domain, but domains corresponding to higher-order types: sets of individuals, sets of sets of individuals, etc. Formalizations of type theory based on [4] use functional abstraction to organize these domains; in general, where D_1 and D_2 are domains of the type theory, the set $D_2^{D_1}$ of functions from D_1 to D_2 is also a domain of the theory.

This leads to the following recursive definition of types, in which there are primitive types for individuals and truth values, and all other types are functional.

(2.1) e is a type.
(2.2) t is a type.
(2.3) If σ and τ are types, so is $\langle \sigma, \tau \rangle$.

Here, e is the type of individuals (entities), t is the type of truth-values, and $\langle \sigma, \tau \rangle$ stands for the type of functions from objects of type σ to objects of type τ.

The language of type theory has an infinite set of variables of each type.[1] The language has only three primitive syntactic constructions.

Identity: If α and β are expressions of type τ, so is $\alpha = \beta$.

Functional application: If ζ is an expression of type $\langle \sigma, \tau \rangle$ and α is an expression of type σ, then $\zeta(\alpha)$ is an expression of type τ.

Lambda abstraction: If ζ is an expression of type τ, then $\lambda x_\sigma \zeta$ is an expression of type $\langle \sigma, \tau \rangle$.

With these resources, the full set of boolean operations can be defined, as well as universal and existential quantification over domains of any type. The model theory of the logic is straightforward; arbitrary domains are assigned to primitive types, the domain of $\langle \sigma, \tau \rangle$ is the set of functions from the domain of type σ to the domain of type τ; $=$ is interpreted as identity, () is interpreted as functional application, λ is interpreted as functional abstraction. See [6] for details on these matters.

A number of ontological policies come along with this approach to types: sets are represented by the corresponding characteristic functions (i.e., a set of objects of type τ is represented as a function of type $\langle \tau, t \rangle$), and n-place functions from types $\langle \sigma_1, \sigma_2, \ldots, \sigma_n \rangle$ to type τ are represented as a nested type $\langle \sigma_1, \langle \sigma_2, \ldots \langle \sigma_n, \tau \rangle \ldots \rangle \rangle$ made up of 1-place functions. According to these policies, for instance, a set of 2-place relations between individuals and sets of individuals would have type $\langle \langle e \rangle, \langle \langle e, t \rangle, t \rangle \rangle$. An object of this type would be a function that inputs a first-order object and outputs a function that inputs a set of first-order objects (which itself is a function from first-order objects to truth-values) and outputs a truth-value.

---

[1] In writing formulas of intensional logic, I will label the first occurrence of a variable with its type unless the type is e, in which case the label may be omitted. Later occurrences will not be marked for type; no confusion can arise, as long as all independent uses of bound variables involve distinct variables.

This formalism uses truth values to represent sentences. Obviously, a domain containing only two values will be unable to represent sentence meanings adequately, an inadequacy that is reflected in the inability of the logic to deal with *propositional attitudes* such as belief. Montague's intensional logic remedies this problem by introducing a third primitive type w, the type of possible worlds. This makes available a type τ-Prop $= \langle w, t \rangle$ of propositions.

Treating propositions as sets of possible worlds is, of course, problematic. (See, for instance, [12, 7].) But it is an approach that has been pursued with some success in philosophical logic, computer science, economics, and natural language semantics. It is certainly possible to generalize the possible worlds approach to intensionality to obtain a less restrictive account of propositions. But it seems to me that such generalizations are premature. Without constraints, hyperintensional theories are uninformative. Appropriate constraints seem to require better general models of the reasoning agent than we have at present. Until such models are developed, it seems better to me to use the possible worlds formalisms, which in any case have many features that would need to be preserved in any more general approach.

Richard Montague showed not only that the framework of intensional logic provides not only a type for propositions, but that many other higher-order types are ontologically natural and useful in the interpretation of natural language semantics. I will now explain why this framework also provides an appropriate starting point for categorizing contexts.

3 Contexts as Modalities

The integration of knowledge sources seems at present to be the origin of the most detailed and illuminating examples of the ways in which the theory can be used.[2] If we look at a context as a knowledge source, the most simple way to model a context in the ontology of type theory would be to identify a context with the set of propositions that it delivers. This would locate contexts in the type $\langle \langle w, t \rangle, t \rangle$: this is the type that I assigned to contexts in [16].

This type-theoretic account of contexts would suffice for applications in which an agent (which is not itself a context) is simultaneously accessing information from many contexts. Each context would then deliver its set of propositions to the collecting agent. But if we want to allow *contexts* to access information from other contexts, we need an enriched representation of contexts.

The problem is this. The type $\langle \langle w, t \rangle, t \rangle$ makes contexts have propositions as inputs. This intensionality of contexts is mandated by the desired applications: we certainly do not want a context to support *every* true sentence if it supports *any* true sentence. Since the output of a context c is only a truth value, although we can access a proposition p that holds in c there will be no way to construct from c and p the proposition that says that p holds in c. Therefore, we can't pass the output of applying a context to a proposition to another context.

---

[2] See, especially, the example in [10, Section 6].

To solve this problem, we need to assign contexts a type with an enriched output. Iteration of contexts can be managed in several ways within intensional logic; the following formalization corresponds directly to multi-agent epistemic logics, of the sort discussed in [5], in which epistemic agents a are associated with a binary relation R_a over worlds.

This standard relational semantics for modal operators specifies that $\Box_a A$ is true in w if and only if A is true in all worlds w' such that wR_aw'. The idea can be captured in Intensional Logic by (i) locating contexts in the type $\tau_1\text{-Mod} = \langle\langle w,t\rangle, \langle w,t\rangle\rangle = \langle\tau\text{-Prop}, \tau\text{-Prop}\rangle$, (ii) introducing a function Rel of type $\langle\tau_1\text{-Mod}, \langle w,w\rangle\rangle$ that associates a relation over worlds with each contexts, and (iii) adding the following axiom, which guaratees that the behavior of the context is determined according to the standard satisfaction condition for modalities.

$$(3.1) \quad \forall x_{\tau_1\text{-Mod}}\forall p_{\tau\text{-Prop}}\forall y_w[x(p) \leftrightarrow \forall z_w[Rel(y,z) \rightarrow p(z)]]$$

Within this framework we can provide a definition of McCarthy's *ist* relation, reconstructed here as a relation between contexts and the *propositions* (not the sentences) that hold in these contexts.

$$(3.2) \quad ist_1 = \lambda x_{\tau_1\text{-Mod}}\lambda y_{\tau\text{-Prop}}\lambda z_w\forall z'_w[x(z) \rightarrow y(z')]$$

This definition gives *ist* the type $\langle\tau_1\text{-Mod}, \langle\tau\text{-Prop}, \tau\text{-Prop}\rangle\rangle$ which inputs a modality and a proposition, and outputs a proposition.

This approach to context has several shortcomings, some of them substantive and some of them a matter of public relations. I will address the second of these first, leaving the substantive issues for the remaining sections.

If we treat contexts as modal operators, it is hard to see what is new about the logic of context. Modal logic is a well developed area of logic that has received a great deal of attention over the last forty years. Regarding contextual logic as a branch of modal logic seems to leave relatively little work for us to do.

While it is true that this conservative approach may rule out a more logically creative program, it still leaves room for some innovations, because (as I will argue in the next section), the logic of context can't in fact be identified with modal logic. But treating it as a generalization which preserves the main features of modal logic has many advantages. First, it enables us to import results and applications from modal logic. It is in fact, very useful to regard contexts as simple epistemic agents, agents which know information about other agents and can communicate with other, similar agents. This enables us to import ideas concerning protocol design and knowledge-based programming into the logic of context.[3] We may also be able to import the techniques that have been developed for modal theorem proving. (See [14].)

---

[3] See [5] for discussion of these matters, and for further references.

4 Contextual Intensional Logic

There is a serious limitation to this approach to context; it will not deal with cases in which the meanings of terms can differ from context to context. The computational literature has regarded variation in meaning as an essential application of the logic of context. Modal logic can't represent the reasoning that deals with ambiguous expressions. Take the simplest case: two "personal assistant" databases with two users, a and b. Both databases record information about their users, using an internal constant @USER to refer to their users. To merge this information coherently, we have to assign different propositions to expressions like

(4.1) BIRTHDATE(@USER, $\langle 4, 4, 1969 \rangle$).

But modal logic has no natural way to represent the reasoning that produces these different assignments.[4]

Translating ideas from Kaplan [9] into the type-theoretic framework proposed above, I want to address this problem by introducing a fourth primitive type: the type i of indices. Kaplan thinks of indices as contextual interpretations of "indexical expressions" such as 'I', 'here', and 'now'.

I want to extend this notion, by thinking of an index as a simultaneous disambiguation of the relevant *contextualizations*: the lexical indexicalities and ambiguities that can arise in an application. If the only contextualizations arise from 'I' and 'here', we could identify an index with a pair consisting of a person and a place. If the only contextualizations arise in the ambiguity of ten lexical items that we have identified as each having two possible meanings, then we will need indices corresponding to the 2^{10} possible disambiguations. Introduce a primitive type i for indices. I will call the extension of Intensional Logic that is obtained by adding the primitive type i *Contextual Intensional Logic* (CIL).

Following Kaplan, I want to think of the evaluation of contextualized expressions as taking place in two phases: (1) a disambiguation phase, where the expression is assigned an intension and (2) an evaluation phase, where the intension is evaluated in a world. Thus, to interpret an expression like

(4.2) 'I'm over 21 years old'

we first need to identify the speaker, s; this yields the proposition that is true in a world if and only if s is over 21 years old in that world. We can think of this as the two-stage evaluation of an abstract representation of the sentence's meaning called its *character*, a representation which captures the potentiality of a sentence meaning to yield different propositions in different "contexts" by treating the character as a function from indices to propositions. In general, the

---

[4] We could, of course, formalize the reasoning as syntactic, i.e. we could treat it as reasoning about expressions. I will not explore this alternative here; despite its apparent naturalness, it is much less satisfactory in the long run, I believe, than the intensional approach that I assume here. The main formal problem that a syntactic approach raises, of course, is that it reintroduces the semantic paradoxes.

character is first evaluated at an index to yield a *content*, which then may be evaluated in a world to produce an extension. In CIL, it is natural to assign sentences a character of type τ-Char-Prop $= \langle i, \tau$-Prop$\rangle$; this type will input an index and output a proposition.

Now, a context of the sort envisaged by McCarthy will perform two different functions: it will serve as a source of disambiguation and as a local knowledge source. From the standpoint of CIL, the first of these functions is represented by an index, or object of type i; the second, as before, is represented by a modality, or object of type τ_2-Mod. Therefore, a context is a pair consisting of an index and a modality. This yields no very natural type for such contexts in CIL, which provides no clean encoding for ordered pairs of objects of different type. However, if we use one of the (unnatural) encodings in CIL of the cross product $\sigma \times \tau$ of σ with τ, or (better) if we add a cross-product operation to the underlying type definition, we can situate *indexical contexts* in the type

$$\tau_2\text{-Con} = i \times \tau_1\text{-Con}.$$

But we can avoid the need to provide a type for indexical contexts by making indices and modalities separate inputs to *ist*. If we want this *ist* to iterate, it should output a propositional character. Then *ist* will have the type $\langle i, \langle \tau_2$-Mod, $\langle \tau$-Char-Prop, τ-Char-Prop$\rangle\rangle\rangle$.

These ideas are contrary in spirit to remarks in which McCarthy suggests that contexts should be formally treated as primitives. I take these remarks to mean that, although in applications we can axiomatize general knowledge about contexts, it is pointless to attempt to define contexts. Actually, I agree with McCarthy that relatively little of the work that needs to be done to explicate contexts can be done with definitions. But I do think it is enlightening and helpful to separate contexts into two components, one of them (the index) dealing with indexicality and ambiguity, while the other (the modality) deals with knowledge.

Before giving a definition of *ist* in CIL, it will be helpful to present an example. There are two personal databases, DB(Ann) and DB(Bob); both databases have a first-person pronoun, as well as constants referring to Ann and to Bob. DB(Ann) is Ann's database, and in it, 'I' refers to Ann. DB(Bob) is Bob's database, and in it, 'I' refers to Bob. Indices, then, can be identified with people. Assume that each world contains information about meetings, in the form of a set of triples whose whose first and second members are people, and whose third member is a time. They also contain information about databases, in the form of a set of quadruples whose first member is a database, whose second and third members are people, and whose fourth member is a time.

Ann's database induces a relation between worlds that holds between w and w' if and only if the following hold in w', where 'I' refers to Ann:

(ADB.1) MEET(I, Charlie, 9)
(ADB.2) MEET(I, Bob, 10)
(ADB.3) MEET(DB(Ann), I, Charlie, 9)
(ADB.4) MEET(DB(Ann), I, Bob, 9)
(ADB.5) $\Box \forall u, x, y, z[\text{MEET}(\text{DB}(u), x, y, z) \rightarrow \text{MEET}(\text{DB}(u), y, x, z)]$

(ADB.6) $\Box\forall x, y, z[\text{MEET}(\text{DB}(x), x, y, z) \to \text{MEET}(\text{DB}(y), x, y, z)]$

Bob's database induces a relation between worlds that holds between w and w' if and only if the following hold in w', where 'I' refers to Bob:

(BDB.1) $\text{MEET}(\text{I}, \text{Ann}, 10)$

(BDB.2) $\text{MEET}(\text{I}, \text{Charlie}, 11)$

(BDB.1) $\text{MEET}(\text{DB}(\text{Bob}), \text{I}, \text{Ann}, 10)$

(BDB.2) $\text{MEET}(\text{DB}(\text{Bob}), \text{I}, \text{Charlie}, 11)$

(BDB.3) $\Box\forall u, x, y, z[\text{MEET}(\text{DB}(u), x, y, z) \to \text{MEET}(y, x, z)]$

(BDB.4) $\Box\forall x, y, z[\text{MEET}(\text{DB}(x), x, y, z) \to \text{MEET}(\text{DB}(y), x, y, z)]$

The first and second conditions represent data; the third entry represents general knowledge about meetings. The fourth entry represents knowledge about knowledge of meetings; it ensures that, for instance, it is necessary (and hence, is known by all the databases) that if Ann's database knows that Ann is to meet with Bob at 9, then Bob's database knows that Ann is to meet with Bob at 9. In this case, we can show informally that

$$ist(\text{Ann}, \text{DB}(\text{Ann}), ist(\text{Bob}, \text{DB}(\text{Bob}) Ch(\text{MEET}(\text{I}, \text{Ann}, 10))),$$

where $Ch(\text{MEET}(\text{I}, \text{Ann}, 10))$ is the character that holds at an index a and world w if and only if $\text{MEET}(a, \text{Ann}, 10)$ holds in w. The argument goes as follows.

(i) Ann's database knows that Ann's database knows that Ann has a meeting at 10 with Bob.

(ii) So Ann's database knows that Ann's database knows that Bob has a meeting at 10 with Ann.

(iii) So Ann's database knows that Bob's database knows that Bob has a meeting at 10 with Ann.

(iv) The character expressed by 'I have a meeting at 10 with Ann' expresses in Bob's database the proposition that, according to (8.3), Ann's database knows that Bob's database knows.

(v) So there is a character expressing in Bob's database the same proposition that is expressed in Ann's database by the character 'Bob has a meeting at 10 with me', and Ann's database knows that Bob's database knows this proposition.

(vi) Restating (v),
$$ist(\text{Ann}, \text{DB}(\text{Ann}), ist(\text{Bob}, \text{DB}(\text{Bob}), Ch(\text{MEET}(\text{I}, \text{Ann}, 10))))$$

This leads to the following definition of ist in CIL.

(4.3) $ist = \lambda u_i \lambda x_{\tau_2\text{-Mod}} \lambda y_{\tau\text{-Char-Prop}} \lambda v_i \lambda z_w \exists y'_{\tau\text{-Char-Prop}}[y'(u) = y(v) \wedge \forall z'_w[x(z)(z') \to y'(u)(z')]]$

Recall that in this example, we are identifying indices with people; and we can represent each of the two databases with an appropriate modality. Let $\text{MDB}(\text{Ann})$ and $\text{MDB}(\text{Bob})$ be the modaliites corresponding to Ann's and Bob's databases; also recall that these modalities are functions from propositions to propositions. Then $ist($Ann, $\mathrm{DB}($Bob$)$, $\mathrm{MEET}($Bob, I, 10$))$, for instance, says that the proposition expressed by 'Bob has a meeting with me at 10' true according to Ann's interpretation of 'I' in Bob's database.

For example, it follows from this definition that

$$(4.4) \quad ist(\text{Ann}, \mathrm{DB}(\text{Ann}), ist(\text{Bob}, \mathrm{DB}(\text{Bob}), \mathrm{MEET}(\text{I}, \text{Ann}, 10)))$$

returns a propositional character that expresses (at any index) a proposition that holds in w if and only if there is a propositional character cp that expresses for Ann a proposition that is the same as the one expressed for Bob by $Ch(\mathrm{MEET}(\text{I}, \text{Ann}, 10))$, and this proposition is known in w by $\mathrm{DB}(\text{Ann})$.

In the version of the theory presented here, where all functions are total functions and quantifiers are unrestricted, it will be trivially true for any proposition and any index that there is a character expressing the proposition at this index. Therefore, (4.3) is equivalent to the following simplified definition.

$$(4.5) \quad ist \; = \; \lambda u_i \lambda x_{\tau_2\text{-Mod}} \lambda y_{\tau\text{-Char-Prop}} \lambda v_i \lambda z_w \forall z'_w [x(z)(z') \; \to \; y(v)(z')]$$

Since the variable u does not appear on the right side of this equation, it follows that $ist(\iota, \mu, \xi)$ will be a constant character, one whose value is the same for all values of x. Although ist statements may vary from context to context, this variation can only be due to what the context knows about other contexts—it cannot be due to how the context disambiguates characters.

In a partial version of CIL, (4.3) would not be equivalent to (4.5), so that indices could play a significant role in iterations of ist. The equivalence would fail in cases where there are propositions expressible at one index that are not expressible than the other. In cases where all indices are equally expressive, however, the index-independence of ist is not implausible. At any rate, I have been unable to construct a plausible case of index-dependence of ist where all indices are equally expressive and knowledge of other contexts is not a factor.

5 Conclusion

There are several dimensions in which the logical framework that I have presented needs to be generalized in order to obtain adequate coverage:

(5.1) The logic needs to be made partial, to account for expressions which simply lack a value in some contexts.

(5.2) The logic needs dynamic operators of the sort described in McCarthy's papers; e.g., an operator which chooses a context and *enters* it.

(5.3) To account for default lifting rules, we need a nonmonotonic logic of context.

We have a general sense of what is involved in making a total logic partial, in making a static logic dynamic, and in making a monotonic logic nonmonotonic. For these reasons, I have adopted the strategy of concentrating on how to formulate an appropriate base logic to which these extensions can be made.

There are a number of approaches to the formalization of partial logics; indeed, the main problem with the logic of partiality, it seems to me, is that there are so many alternatives, and it is hard to select between them. Three-valued logic has been used in connection with the logic of context; see [3]. However, a four-valued logic is more symmetrical, and plausible arguments, starting with [2], have been given for its computational usefulness. Most important for the project at hand, [13] provides an extended study of how to modify Intensional Logic using this approach to partiality. It is relatively straightforward to adopt Muskens' work to CIL.

There is, however, a much more ambitious application of partiality, according to which indices are regarded not as full, but as partial disambiguations of expressions. This program, which would require a more radical rethinking of the theory, may be needed to deal with applications of context to natural language interpretation, though perhaps it is unnecessary in cases in which indices correspond to carefully constructed knowledge sources. See, for instance, [17] for information on partial disambiguation.

For dynamics, I favor an approach along the lines of [8]. This involves relativizing satisfaction not to just one index, but to a pair of indices, an input index and an output index. The resulting logic would be dynamic with respect only to indices, not to modalities. A more general dynamic contextual logic could be devised, but I'm not sure whether we really need such a logic.

As for nonmonotonicity, it is relatively straightforward to add a theory of circumscription to Intensional Logic, and to its extension to CIL. (Circumscription is usually formulated in second-order extensional logic, but the generalization to intensional logic of arbitrary order is straightforward.)

None of these logical developments is entirely trivial, and in fact there is material here for many years of work. I hope to report on developments in these directions in future work.

References

1. C.A. Anderson. General intensional logic. In Dov Gabbay and Franz Guenther, (eds.), *Handbook of Philosophical Logic, Volume II: Extensions of Classical Logic*, pp. 355-385. D. Reidel Publishing Co., Dordrecht, 1984.
2. N.D. Belnap. A useful four-valued logic. In J.M. Dunn and G. Epstein, (eds.), *Modern Uses of Multiple-Valued Logic*. D. reidel Publishing Co., Dordrecht, 1977.
3. S. Buvac and I. Mason. Propositional logic of context. In R. Fikes and W. Lehnert, (eds.), Proceedings of the *11th National Conference on Artificial Intelligence*, pp. 412-419, Menlo Park, California, 1993. American Association for Artificial Intelligence, AAAI Press.
4. A. Church. A formulation of the simple theory of types. *Journal of Symbolic Logic*, 5:56-68, 1940.

5. R. Fagin, J.Y. Halpern, Y. Moses, and M.Y. Vardi. *Reasoning About Knowledge*. The MIT Press, Cambridge, Massachusetts, 1995.
6. D. Gallin. *Intensional and Higher-Order Logic*. North-Holland Publishing Company, Amsterdam, 1975.
7. F. Giunchiglia, L. Serafini, E. Giunchiglia, and M. Frixione. Non omniscient belief as context-based reasoning. In R. Bajcsy, (ed.), Proceedings of the *13th International Joint Conference on Artificial Intelligence*, pp. 548-554, San Mateo, California, 1993. Morgan Kaufmann.
8. J. Groenendijk and M. Stokhof. Dynamic predicate logic. *Linguistics and Philosophy*, 14:39-100, 1991.
9. D. Kaplan. On the logic of demonstratives. *Journal of Philosophical Logic*, 8:81-98, 1978.
10. J. McCarthy and S. Buvac. Formalizing context (expanded notes). Available from http://www-formal.stanford.edu/buvac, 1995.
11. R. Montague. Pragmatics and intensional logic. *Synthèse*, 22:68-94, 1970. Reprinted in *Formal Philosophy*, by R. Montague, Yale University Press, New Haven, CT, 1974, pp. 119-147.
12. Y. Moses. Resource-bounded knowledge. In M.Y. Vardi, (ed.), *Theoretical Aspects of Reasoning About Knowledge: Proceedings of the Second Conference on Theoretical Aspects of Reasoning About Knowledge*, pp. 261-276, San Francisco, 1988. Morgan Kaufmann.
13. R. Muskens. *Meaning and Partiality*. Cambridge University Press, Cambridge, England, 1996.
14. M. Stone. *Modality in Dialogue: Planning, Pragmatics and Computation*. Ph.d. dissertation, Computer Science Department, University of Pennsylvania, Philadelphia, Pennsylvania, 1998.
15. R.H. Thomason. Type theoretic foundations for context. In S. Buvac and L. Iwanska, (eds.), Working Papers of the AAAI Fall Symposium on Context in Knowledge Representation and Natural Language, pp. 173-175, Menlo Park, California, 1997. American Association for Artificial Intelligence, American Association for Artificial Intelligence.
16. R.H. Thomason. Representing and reasoning with context. In Jacques Calmet and Jan Plaza, (eds.), *Proceedings of the International Conference on Artificial Intelligence and Symbolic Computation* (AISC'98), Plattsburgh, New York, pp. 29-41, Berlin, 1998. Springer-Verlag.
17. K. van Deemter and S. Peters, (eds.). *Semantic Ambiguity and Underspecification*. Cambridge University Press, Cambridge, England, 1996.

Violation Contexts and Deontic Independence

Leendert van der Torre

Department of Artificial Intelligence, Vrije Universiteit
De Boelelaan 1081a, 1081 HV Amsterdam, the Netherlands
torre@cs.vu.nl
http://www.cs.vu.nl/~torre

Abstract. In this paper we discuss the role of context and independence in normative reasoning. First, deontic operators – obligations, prohibitions, permissions – referring to the ideal context may conflict with operators referring to a violation (or contrary-to-duty) context. Second, deontic independence is a powerful concept to derive deontic operators from such operators of other violation contexts. These two concepts are used to determine how to proceed once a norm has been violated, a key issue of deontic logic applications in computer science. We also show how violation contexts and deontic independence can be used to give a new analysis of several notorious paradoxes of deontic logic.

1 Introduction

Deontic logic is a modal logic in which Op is read as 'p ought to be (done),' Fp as 'p is forbidden to be (done)' and Pp as 'p is permitted to be (done).' Deontic logic has traditionally been used by philosophers to analyze the structure of the normative use of language. In the eighties deontic logic had a revival, when it was discovered by computer scientists that this logic can be used for the formal specification and verification of a wide variety of topics in computer science (for an overview and further references see [42]). For example, deontic logic can be used to formally specify soft constraints in planning and scheduling problems as norms. The advantage is that norm violations do not create an inconsistency in the formal specification, in contrast to violations of hard constraints. Recently new interest in deontic logic has arisen, because in the multi agent system discipline *social* norms and laws are used to improve coordination and cooperation [10, 37], in qualitative decision theory norms are used to represent the agent's goals [22, 7, 17], and in computer security norms are used to analyze and specify security issues for electronic commerce [12].

In this paper we study the violability of norms, and in particular how to proceed once a norm has been violated. Clearly this issue is of great practical relevance, because in most applications norms are violated frequently. In the fine print of a contract it is therefore usually stipulated what has to be done if a term in the contract is violated. For example, if the delivery time is over due the responsible agent might be obliged to pay the extra transport and warehousing costs that result from the delay. If the violation is not too serious, or was not intended by the violating party, the contracting parties usually do not want to consider this as a breach of contracts, but simply as a disruption in the execution of the contract that has to be repaired.

The crucial problem of violability is that a violation changes the context of normative reasoning. New obligations may arise as a result of the violation, and old obligations may no longer be in force. Consequently, obligations are context-dependent. The so-called *violation context* of an obligation distinguishes between ideal and varying sub-ideal contexts to formalize contrary-to-duty (hereafter: CTD) reasoning as it occurs in Forrester's and Chisholm's notorious deontic paradoxes [9, 13, 23, 24, 36]. In these paradoxes obligations referring to the ideal context conflict with obligations referring to the sub-ideal context. If the violation context is left implicit, then the paradoxes result in a counterintuitive inconsistency. This type of context should be distinguished from epistemic or world-based contexts, as is explained later in detail, because it refers to an implicit set of norms called the *normative system*. In this paper we are interested in the relation between violation contexts and independence. They can be used to analyze the following example of Prakken and Sergot [24], that motivates much of their study in contextual deontic reasoning.

Example 1 (Cottage housing). Consider the following sentences.

(1) There must be no dog.
(2) If there is a dog, then there must be a sign.
(3) There must be no sign.

Prakken and Sergot argue that (2) and (3) are inconsistent, because the CTD obligation (2) regulating the violation of (1) does not respect the primary obligation (3). CTD obligations are intended to regulate norm violation, but they cannot just ignore all other norms. In the absence of prioritisation we may conclude that on the one hand there must be a sign if there is a dog, but on the other hand there must not. They continue to consider the following variant.[1]

(1a) There must be no dog.
(2a) If there is a dog, it must be a poodle.
(3a) There must be no poodle.

The first two sentences are a version of Forrester's gentle murderer [13] ('Smith should not murder Jones,' but 'if he murders him, then he should do it gently'), because poodles are dogs. Intuitively (1a) and (2a) should therefore be consistent. Moreover, Prakken and Sergot suggest that (2a) and (3a) are inconsistent in precisely the same way that (2) and (3) are. (2a) regulates the violation of (1a)

---

[1] Since Forrester's paradox is better analyzed when different types of killing are replaced by different colors [14], Prakken and Sergot also consider the following alphabetic variant: (1b) The door must be painted red; (2b) If the door is not painted red, it must be left unpainted; (3b) The door must not be left unpainted. Again they want to say that (1b)-(3b) are inconsistent, even though (1b)-(2b) are consistent, and (1b) implies (3b).

but it does not respect another primary obligation, (3a). The new feature of the poodle example, of course, is that (3a) is implied by (1a). At first sight, it seems that we have to abandon consequential closure, because this is the only way to make (1a)-(3a) logically stronger than (1a)-(2a) (such that we can add constraints that make only the latter set inconsistent). However, if a normgiver forbids having dogs he surely also implicitly forbids having any particular kind of dog. Consequential closure should not be disregarded when determining what is obligatory.

Prakken and Sergot conclude that 'the difference between what appears consistent and what appears inconsistent seems to depend critically on what is stated explicitly.' Moreover, they sketch the development of an entailment relation $\Gamma \models A$ in which designated *explicit obligations* in premises Γ will be given special status.

In this paper we argue that the crucial distinction between (1a)-(2a) and (1a)-(3a) is an implicit independence assumption. In this paper we show that the three obligations are inconsistent only if the independence assumption is added. Prakken and Sergot's conclusion simply means that the explicit manner of representation suggests that (3a) depends on (1a) if it is derived from (1a), whereas it is independent of (1a) when it is given explicitly.

This paper is organized as follows. In Section 2 we discuss the relation between deontic and contextual reasoning and we introduce a simple contextual deontic logic. In Section 3 we discuss deontic independence and we analyze the cottage housing regulations. Finally in Section 4 we show how independence assumptions can be derived from the explicit manner of representation, which also shows the distinction between deontic independence and world-based factual independence.

2 Violation Contexts

Deontic reasoning is context dependent in different though related ways.

The norm context of a descriptive obligation (a normative proposition) refers to a set of prescriptive obligations (the norms or the normative system) [39]. This reflects the distinction, much debated in the philosophical literature, between descriptive obligations, that have a truth value, and prescriptive obligations, that do not [1, 41, 18, 39, 35, 38, 37]. The norm context is explicitly represented in labeled deontic logic [31, 18, 32], see also [19, 30]. A descriptive obligation $\bigcirc \alpha_L$ contains a label L that represents the norm context in which the obligation for α is derived, and it thus explains *why* the obligation is derived.

The violation context of a descriptive obligation refers to a set of violations of prescriptive obligations, where the violation of a norm 'α should be (done) if β is (done)' is $\neg \alpha \wedge \beta$, i.e. the negation of the material implication $\neg(\beta \to \alpha)$. It distinguishes between ideal and varying sub-ideal contexts. Obligations that refer to the ideal context are called ideal (or primary) obligations, and obligations that refer to the sub-ideal context are called contrary-to-duty (or secondary) obligations.

The reasoning context of an obligation refers to the circumstances which are considered. Within a reasoning context some fact or action may be optimal and therefore obligatory, whereas it is not ideal in the most general reasoning context. In other words, an obligation may refer to a sub-ideal context if the reasoning context excludes the ideal context. The reasoning context may extend the actual evidence in order to reason about hypothetical violations. Two reasoning contexts in temporal deontic reasoning are the context of deliberation and the context of justification, used by Thomason [28] to distinguish a (deliberative) ought that implies 'practical-temporal can' from a (judgmental) ought that does not imply 'practical-temporal can.'

The following example illustrates the distinction between the different kinds of contexts.

Example 2 (Cottage housing, continued). Consider only the first two obligations, i.e. 'there must be no dog ' and 'if there is a dog, it must be a poodle,' together with the fact that there is a pitbull. There are three violation contexts: the ideal context there is no dog, the sub-ideal context there is a dog and the sub-sub-ideal context there is a dog that is not a poodle. There is an obligation *'there must be no dog'* referring to the ideal context, and there is an obligation *'there must be a poodle'* referring to the sub-ideal context. Obviously, both obligations are violated by the pitbull. Selling the dog as well as exchanging it for a poodle are improvements of the present state of affairs. However, in the general reasoning context its owner should sell it; only in the reasoning context in which it is not sold she should exchange it. Whether the dog must be sold or exchanged depends on the context referred to, because different reasoning contexts make different violation contexts optimal.

The two derived obligations *'there must be no dog'* and *'there must be a poodle'* are contradictory. In a logic that does not distinguish between contexts, like so-called Standard Deontic Logic,[2] the facts together with the two sentences of the regulations are inconsistent. Two extensions of Standard Deontic Logic, developed to analyze contrary-to-duty reasoning, introduce either temporal references or an explicit context. In the first approach the context is implicitly represented by facts that refer to the same moment in time as the obligatory fact, and the condition refers to an earlier moment in time. To formalize the regulations without introducing the background knowledge that poodles and pitbulls are dogs, Prakken and Sergot represent the poodle by $p \wedge d$ and the pitbull by $i \wedge d$, where d stands for dog.

Explicit time. We write $\beta \Rightarrow \bigcirc\alpha$ for 'if β then $\bigcirc\alpha$,' where $\Rightarrow$ is a suitably defined conditional. If the reasoning context is the ideal context then dogs

---

[2] Standard Deontic Logic is a normal modal system that is closed under the inference rules modus ponens $\frac{p, p \to q}{q}$ and necessitation $\frac{\vdash p}{\vdash \bigcirc p}$ and contains the propositional tautologies and the axioms $K : \bigcirc(\alpha \to \beta) \to (\bigcirc\alpha \to \bigcirc\beta)$ and $D : \neg(\bigcirc\alpha \wedge \bigcirc\neg\alpha)$.

are forbidden ($\bigcirc \neg d_t$) and if the reasoning context is the sub-ideal context then there must be a poodle ($d_t \Rightarrow \bigcirc(p_t \wedge d_t)$). These obligations hold regardless of the actual evidence. If there is a pitbull then we still have $i_{t-1} \wedge d_{t-1} \Rightarrow \bigcirc \neg d_t$ and $i_{t-1} \wedge d_{t-1} \wedge d_t \Rightarrow \bigcirc(p_t \wedge d_t)$.

Condition-context. We write $\bigcirc_\gamma(\alpha|\beta)$ for 'α ought to be (done) if β is (done) in the context γ,' and we represent the reasoning context γ by a propositional sentence. Again, if the reasoning context is the ideal context then dogs are forbidden ($\bigcirc \neg d$) and if the reasoning context is the sub-ideal context then there must be a poodle $\bigcirc_d(p \wedge d)$. Moreover, if there is a pitbull then the obligations are both still in force $\bigcirc(\neg d|i \wedge d)$ and $\bigcirc_d(p \wedge d|i \wedge d)$. Contextual obligations can formalize hypothetical reasoning, because the latter two obligations can be read as 'I have a pitbull and I should sell it, but if I will not sell it (hypothesis) then I should at least exchange it for a poodle.'

In this paper we are interested in the second type of logic. We use the phrase 'contextual deontic logic' (hereafter: CDL) to refer to the logic that contains formulas of the type $\bigcirc_\gamma(\alpha|\beta)$, $F_\gamma(\alpha|\beta)$ and $P_\gamma(\alpha|\beta)$. If we have $\bigcirc\alpha$ without $\bigcirc(\alpha|\beta)$, then we say that β represents exceptional circumstances in which the obligation for α is defeated. A priori there is an obligation for α, but de facto there is not. Conversely, if we have $\bigcirc\alpha$ without $\bigcirc_\beta\alpha$ then it does *not* mean that the obligation for α is defeated by exceptional circumstances β. It means that if we assume β then we refer to another violation context that no longer prefers α.

We keep the semantics as simple as possible. The dynamic preference semantics proposed below generalizes Hansson's preference semantics [15], that is also used by Boutilier [7] in his qualitative decision theory. The basic idea is that, when evaluating the truth condition of the obligation for α, the condition β determines the relevant preference ordering, and the context γ determines the relevant part of the preference ordering. Now, the obligation for α is true if α is true in the preferred states of this sub-ordering.

Definition 1 (CDL). *Let $M = \langle W, \leq_\alpha, V \rangle$ with W a set of worlds, $\leq_\alpha$ a set (for each propositional formula) of transitive, reflexive and totally connected accessibility relations, and V the valuation function. We have $M \models \bigcirc_\gamma(\alpha|\beta)$ iff there exists a γ world w such that for all worlds $w' \leq_\beta w$ we have $M, w' \models \gamma \to \alpha$ (all preferred γ worlds of the β ordering satisfy α). Prohibition and (weak) permission are defined by $F_\gamma(\alpha|\beta) =_{def} \bigcirc_\gamma(\neg\alpha|\beta)$ and $P_\gamma(\alpha|\beta) =_{def} \neg \bigcirc_\gamma (\neg\alpha|\beta)$. We write $\bigcirc_\gamma\alpha$ for $\bigcirc_\gamma(\alpha|\top)$, $\bigcirc(\alpha|\beta)$ for $\bigcirc_\top(\alpha|\beta)$, $\bigcirc\alpha$ for $\bigcirc_\top(\alpha|\top)$. Similarly for F and P.*

In the semantics the violation contexts are represented implicitly by the preference relation $\leq$. It could be represented more explicitly in several different ways. For example, we can explicitly represent the violations of the violation contexts, or we can explicitly represent the equivalence classes of the relation $\{(w, w') \mid w \leq w' \text{ and } w' \leq w\}$ by a set of constants, like e.g. Åqvist's optimality classes [2]. Moreover, we can explicitly represent the norm context or the prescriptive obligations in the semantics, and deduce the preference relation, violation contexts or optimality classes from them. Since in this paper we are interested in deontic independence we keep our semantics as simple as possible and we do not further consider this kind of semantic extensions.

In contextual deontic logic we cannot represent the problematic conditions that occur later than the consequents, as the obligation in Chisholm's notorious paradox 'if the man goes to the assistance, then he should tell them before that he will come' [9]. We thus 'solve' the backwards version of the paradox by restricting the language, see [34] for a discussion. The following example adapted from Pearl [22] further illustrates the dynamic preference semantics.

Example 3 (Switch [22]). We will test the assertability of the following dialogue:

> Robot 1: It is too dark here.
> Robot 2: Then you ought to push the switch up.
> Robot 1: The switch is already up.
> Robot 2: Then you ought to push the switch down.

The challenge would be to explain the reversal of the "ought" statement in response to the new observation "The switch is already up." A CDL model can, in contrast to a single preference ordering of static preference semantics, represent that after it is known that the switch is up but still it is dark, the preference is reversed.

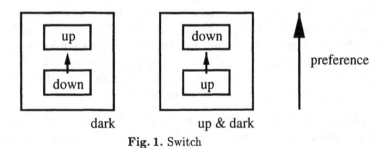

Fig. 1. Switch

CDL does not impose any restrictions on the condition. Such restrictions can be added depending on the application of the logic. For example, for reasoning by cases one could add the following disjunction rule.

$$O_\gamma(\alpha|\beta_1) \wedge O_\gamma(\alpha|\beta_2) \to O_\gamma(\alpha|\beta_1 \vee \beta_2)$$

3 Deontic Independence

In this paper we are interested in the relation between contextual deontic reasoning and independence, and in this section we consider explicitly given independence assumptions. Qualitative independence has been studied to deal with the irrelevance problem of default reasoning: 'red birds fly' $r \wedge b \Rightarrow f$ can be derived from 'birds fly' $b \Rightarrow f$ if red 'r' is independent of flying 'f' [11]. In contextual deontic reasoning there are two types of qualitative independence which can be used to deal with irrelevance problems. *Factual independence* is independence with respect to the condition, and *deontic independence* is independence with respect to the context. Thus, β' is factually independent with respect to the obligation for α if β in the context γ if and only if we have

$$FI : O_\gamma(\alpha|\beta) \leftrightarrow O_\gamma(\alpha|\beta \wedge \beta')$$

Following [11], we call $O_\gamma(\alpha \mid \beta)$ the *a priori* obligation, and $O_\gamma(\alpha \mid \beta \wedge \beta')$ the *de facto* obligation, and we discriminate between nine different situations (a priori and de facto α is either obliged, forbidden, or it and its negation are both permitted). The following continuation of Example 2 shows that factual independence plays a similar role in defeasible deontic reasoning as independence in default reasoning.

Example 4 (Cottage housing, continued). The CDL prohibition 'dogs are forbidden' Fd is factually independent of the existence of a pitbull, and from this independence relation we can derive the prohibition 'if there is a pitbull, then dogs are forbidden' $F(d|i \wedge d)$. Moreover, the obligation is factually dependent on the needs of a blind owner, from which we can derive the permission '*if the owner is blind, then it is permitted that there is a dog*' $P(d|b)$.

It is well-known that we have to distinguish between decision variables and parameters or events (controllable and uncontrollable variables), because it does not make sense to oblige someone to see to it that a parameter has a desirable value [7, 29, 17]. In the example we take blindness as a parameter, because we do not want to be able to infer that it is obligatory or forbidden that the owner is blind.

Moreover, γ' is deontically independent with respect to the obligation for α if β in the context γ if and only if we have[3]

$$DI : O_\gamma(\alpha|\beta) \leftrightarrow O_{\gamma \wedge \gamma'}(\alpha|\beta)$$

Factual and deontic independence are very powerful concepts. We can derive obligations from obligations and permissions from permissions in case of independence, and we can derive obligations from permissions and permissions from obligations in case of dependence. The following example illustrates how deontic independence can be used to analyze the Cottage Housing Regulations in Example 1.

Example 5 (Cottage housing, continued). Consider the two sets of CDL formulas $S_1 = \{Fd, O_d(p \wedge d)\}$ and $S_2 = \{Fd, O_d(p \wedge d), F(p \wedge d)\}$. Without the independence relations, the two sets are equivalent. A typical CDL model consists of three equivalence classes (of $\{(w, w') \mid w \leq w' \text{ and } w' \leq w\}$), in order

---

[3] Prakken and Sergot [23] call the formula $O_{A \wedge B}C \rightarrow O_A C$ up, and the formula $O_A C \rightarrow O_{A \wedge B}C$ is called down.

of preference the $\neg d$ worlds, the $p \wedge d$ worlds and the $\neg p \wedge d$ worlds. However, in S_1 the prohibition of poodles deontically depends on dog, whereas they are deontically independent in S_2. Hence, S_2 also contains the following formula, and S_1 its negation.

$$DI : F(p \wedge d) \leftrightarrow F_d(p \wedge d)$$

With the deontic dependence and independence assumption we have respectively $S_1 \models P_d(p \wedge d)$ and $S_2 \models F_d(p \wedge d)$. The latter obligation is inconsistent with $O_d(p \wedge d)$, and S_2 is therefore inconsistent. We thus explained Prakken and Sergot's problem in Example 1. Moreover, the deontic independence relation is suggested by the explicit manner of representation, because $F(p \wedge d)$ is deontically independent of d only if it is given explicitly (in S_2).

Deontic independence can also be used to analyze the Reykjavik Scenario [5, 29]. The example is taken from a discussion by Makinson [18]. The explicit obligations are that neither Reagan nor Gorbatchov should be told the secret, if Reagan is told the secret then Gorbatchov should be told, and if Gorbatchov is told then Reagan should be told. Intuitively, under the condition that Gorbatchov is told, we would like to be able to conclude that Reagan should be told, without also deriving its negation. On the other hand, if the first item is broken down into two parts, saying separately that Reagan should not be told and that Gorbatchov should not be told, so that there are four explicit obligations, then the conclusion seems intuitively more ambiguous, depending on whether promulgations are prioritized according to, say, specificity of their antecedents. In the absence of prioritisation we seem authorized to conclude both that Reagan should be told and that he should not; with prioritisation, only the former.

Example 6 (Reykjavik Scenario). Consider the two sets of CDL formulas $S_1 = \{O(\neg r \wedge \neg g), O_r g, O_g r\}$ and $S_2 = \{O(\neg r) \wedge O(\neg g), O_r g, O_g r\}$. Without independence relations S_1 and S_2 are logically equivalent, and a typical CDL model consists of three equivalence classes, containing in order of preference the $\neg r \wedge \neg g$ worlds, the $r \wedge g$ worlds and the $r \leftrightarrow \neg g$ worlds. Moreover, let in S_1 the obligation $O \neg r$ be deontically dependent on $\neg g$, and let them in S_2 be independent (as suggested by the explicit manner of representation). That is, S_2 additionally contains the following formula, and S_1 its negation.

$$DI : O \neg r \leftrightarrow O_g \neg r$$

With the additional formulas we have $S_1 \models P_g \neg r$ and $S_2 \models O_g \neg r$. The set S_2 is inconsistent, because the premise $O_g r$ and the derived $O_g \neg r$ are contradictory. Only with the independence assumption the sets are inconsistent.

Summarizing, an obligation is deontically independent if it refers to the same violation context, and factually independent if it is not overridden. Deontic independence and factual independence are thus quite different. One aspect of this difference is that different types of independence relations can be inferred from the explicit representation, as discussed in the following section.

4 Manner of Representation

Independence relations can either be given explicitly, or inferred from the explicit manner of presentation of the obligations. In this section we discuss the second option. For simplicity we assume that the premise set only contains contextual obligations, i.e. no disjunctions, negations, permissions, prohibitions or facts. We study the explicitly represented premises in combination with derived obligations, i.e. deontic operators without independence assumptions.

We start to propose a formal approach to study the explicit manner of representation. It is based on the introduction of an additional deontic operator $①_\gamma(\alpha|\beta)$, to be read as '$O_\gamma(\alpha|\beta)$ is explicitly represented,' i.e. we have $O_\gamma(\alpha|\beta)$ as well as independence relations suggested by the fact that it is explicitly represented. Note that this approach is quite different from the explicit obligations suggested by Prakken and Sergot, because in their approach logical properties of explicit operators are not studied. Proof-theoretically, the formal approach leads to a two-phase proof theory [27]. We therefore replace the operator O by the more suggestive $②$.

Definition 2 (The two phase approach). *Premises are phase-1 operators like $①_\gamma(\alpha \mid \beta)$, conclusions are phase-2 operators like $②_\gamma(\alpha \mid \beta)$, and the two phases are related via the axiom $①_\gamma(\alpha|\beta) \to ②_\gamma(\alpha|\beta)$.*

We first discuss deontic independence and then factual independence. The following independency notion says that a premise is deontically independent of any fact, unless it violates 'ought implies can.'

Definition 3 (Deontic Independence). *If $O_\gamma(\alpha \mid \beta)$ is a premise, then we have that it is deontically independent of γ' iff $\alpha \wedge \gamma \wedge \gamma'$ is consistent.*

In other words, if we define $M \models \Diamond(\alpha)$ as 'M contains an α world,' and $Indep(②_\gamma(\alpha|\beta), \gamma')$ as '$②_\gamma(\alpha|\beta)$ is deontically independent of γ',' then we have:

$$M \models ①_\gamma(\alpha|\beta) \Leftrightarrow M \models ②_\gamma(\alpha|\beta) \text{ and } \forall(\gamma') : \Diamond(\alpha \wedge \gamma \wedge \gamma') \to Indep(②_\gamma(\alpha|\beta), \gamma')$$

This definition can be simplified to the following one.

$$M \models ①_\gamma(\alpha|\beta) \Leftrightarrow \forall(\gamma') : \Diamond(\alpha \wedge \gamma \wedge \gamma') \to M \models ②_{\gamma \wedge \gamma'}(\alpha|\beta)$$

Several properties of this new operator are that it does not have weakening of the consequent, but it has strengthening of the context and a kind of cut rule.

$$\models ①_\gamma(\alpha|\beta) \wedge \Diamond(\alpha \wedge \gamma \wedge \gamma') \to ①_{\gamma \wedge \gamma'}(\alpha|\beta)$$

$$\models ①_\gamma(\alpha|\beta) \wedge ①_{\gamma \wedge \alpha}(\alpha'|\beta) \wedge \Diamond(\alpha \wedge \alpha' \wedge \gamma) \to ①_\gamma(\alpha \wedge \alpha'|\beta)$$

The following example illustrates why we cannot use a similar strong independence notion for factual independence, well-known from dyadic deontic logic [40, 33].

Example 7 (Window [40]). The diamond 'the window should be closed if it rains' ①$(c \mid r)$ and 'the window should be open if the sun shines' ①$(\neg c \mid s)$ should not derive the contradictory ②$(c \mid r \wedge s)$ and ②$(\neg c \mid r \wedge s)$.

Obviously, the factual independence relations implied by the explicit representation are much weaker than the deontic independence relations due to possible conflicts. As a consequence of these conflicts, in more specific circumstances there are only *prima facie* obligations [25, 3, 21, 35]. For example, there are only prima facie obligations to close and to open the window when it rains and the sun shines. In this paper we can only sketch the logic of prima facie obligations. The crucial distinction is that the connected ordering is replaced by a possibly non-connected ordering. There is a prima facie obligation for α if there is an equivalence class of preferred worlds that satisfies α.

Definition 4 (CDL with prima facie). *Let $M = \langle W, \leq_\alpha, V \rangle$ with $\leq_\alpha$ a set (for each propositional formula) of transitive, reflexive but possibly not totally connected accessibility relations. We have $M \models O_\gamma(\alpha \mid \beta)$ iff for all γ worlds w there is a γ world $w' \leq_\beta w$ such that for all worlds $w'' \leq_\beta w'$ we have $M, w'' \models \gamma \rightarrow \alpha$ (the preferred γ worlds of the β ordering satisfy α). We have $M \models O_\gamma^{pf}(\alpha \mid \beta)$ iff there exists a γ world w such that for all worlds $w' \leq_\beta w$ we have $M, w' \models \gamma \rightarrow \alpha$ (all worlds of an equivalence class of preferred γ worlds of the β ordering satisfy α). The obligation $O_\gamma(\alpha \mid \beta)$ weakly factually depends on β' iff we have*

$$O_\gamma^{pf}(\alpha \mid \beta) \leftrightarrow O_\gamma^{pf}(\alpha \mid \beta \wedge \beta')$$

Definition 5 (Factual Independence). *If $O_\gamma(\alpha \mid \beta)$ is a premise, then we have that it is weakly factual independent of β' iff $\alpha \wedge \beta \wedge \beta'$ is consistent.*

Additional machinery has to be introduced in the logic to formalize conflict resolution mechanisms based on the non-monotonic overriding of obligations.

5 Further Research

In this paper we argued that deontic reasoning should be considered as context-dependent reasoning, and we showed how independence assumptions can be used in this perspective. There are many ways to continue this line of research.

First, the preference-based semantics has to be weakened to invalidate the counterintuitive axioms characteristic of the preference-based approach, such as for example:

$$O_\gamma \alpha \leftrightarrow O_\gamma(\alpha \wedge \gamma)$$

A counterintuitive consequence of this theorem is that two independent obligations ①p and ①q derive not only ②$_{\neg(p \wedge q)}p$ and ②$_{\neg(p \wedge q)}q$ but also the contradictory ②$_{\neg(p \wedge q)}(p \wedge \neg q)$ and ②$_{\neg(p \wedge q)}(\neg p \wedge q)$ [33]. This illustrates that the strong independence assumption is usually too strong for the preference-based contextual obligations discussed in this paper. For example, in [19, 30] a logic has been proposed that does not have the counterintuitive axioms but that still validates the intuitive derivation of 'if a then $\bigcirc y$' from 'if a then $\bigcirc x$' and 'if $a \wedge x$ then $\bigcirc y$.'

Second, the here developed concepts can be used to analyze and classify other recently proposed deontic logics. For example, we already mentioned that Åqvist's optimality classes [2] can be interpreted as contextual parameters. Moreover, Jones and Pörn's bimodal logic [16] and more recent proposals of Carmo and Jones [8] are also based on different degrees of ideality and the idea of some facts being settled (like our context of reasoning).

Third, the repair approach to conditional knowledge bases [6] has been proposed as an alternative to independence assumptions. The main idea is to take advantage of the main features of nonmonotonic inference with respect to rule addition. Contrary to classical logic, it is legitimate to expect that undesirable conclusions can be blocked by adding new rules (and thus not only by deleting them). Moreover, it is also conjectured that reasoning on basis of a ranking is expressive and flexible enough to capture any 'reasonable' expected behavior of a normative base. It is an open problem whether this repair approach can be used to formalize contrary-to-duty reasoning too.

Fourth, the relation between the notion of context introduced in this paper and the recent ideas of formalizing context in the AI literature (such as for example McCarthy's formalism based on an ist-operator) has to be considered. Moreover, the relation between deontic dependence and dependence in other areas has to be investigated. Gärdenfors studied independence inspired by the axiom of probability theory that for disjoint sets A and B we have that the probability of $A \cup B$ is the sum of the probabilities of A and B, i.e. $Pr(A \cup B) = Pr(A) + Pr(B)$ if $A \cap B = \emptyset$. Moreover, independence relations between sets of variables is an important concept to reduce complexity in probability and utility functions in respectively Bayesian networks (reasoning about uncertainty and default reasoning, and in epistemic reasoning) and decision-theoretic planning (reasoning about goals and desires), such that for example for independent x and y we have $p(x, y) = p(x)p(y)$ and $u(x, y) = u(x) + u(y)$. In normative reasoning, such independence relations between variables could be used for example to derive for independent p and q the permission $P(p \wedge q)$ from Pp and Pq.

Fifth, a technical problem for future research is the interference between factual and deontic independence. We have $\bigcirc \alpha$ without $\bigcirc(\alpha \mid \beta)$ if β expresses exceptional circumstances, and we have $\bigcirc \alpha$ without $\bigcirc_\gamma \alpha$ if γ expresses a violation. The obligation is factually dependent if it is overridden, and deontically dependent if it is violated. The two different types of independence are related to different types of defeasibility, that have been observed in [29, 31, 32]. Another topic for further research is the relation between contextual deontic reasoning and defeasible [36] and temporal reasoning [28].

Sixth, a practical problem for future research is how the user can efficiently state independence relations.

One way is to derive independence relations from the explicit representation. Another one is the graphical representation of independence by independence networks [4].

6 Conclusion

An important question for deontic logic applications is how to proceed once a norm has been violated. In this paper we studied violation contexts and deontic independence in contextual deontic logic. We showed how factual and deontic independence can be used to deal with different types of irrelevance problems in deontic logic. In contrast to the use of a relevant implication [20], and relevant deontic logic [26], the use of independence relations enables the derivation of deontic operators from such operators of other violation contexts. It is therefore a powerful tool to deal with contrary-to-duty reasoning.

References

1. C.E. Alchourrón and Bulygin. The expressive conception of norms. In R. Hilpinen, editor, *New Studies in Deontic Logic: Norms, Actions and the Foundations of Ethics*, pages 95–124. D. Reidel, 1981.
2. L. Åqvist. Systematic frame constants in defeasible deontic logic. In D. Nute, editor, *Defeasible Deontic Logic*, pages 59–77. Kluwer, 1997.
3. N. Asher and D. Bonevac. Prima facie obligation. *Studia Logica*, 57:19–45, 1996.
4. F. Bacchus and A.J. Grove. Utility independence in a qualitative decision theory. In *Proceedings of KR'96*, pages 542–552, 1996.
5. M. Belzer. A logic of deliberation. In *Proceedings of the AAAI'86*, pages 38–43, 1986.
6. S. Benferhat, D. Dubois, and H. Prade. Practical handling of exception-tainted rules and independence information in possibilistic logic. *Applied Intelligence*, 9:101–127, 1998.
7. C. Boutilier. Toward a logic for qualitative decision theory. In *Proceedings of the KR'94*, pages 75–86, 1994.
8. J. Carmo and A.J.I. Jones. A new approach to contrary-to-duty obligations. In D. Nute, editor, *Defeasible Deontic Logic*, pages 317–344. Kluwer, 1997.
9. R.M. Chisholm. Contrary-to-duty imperatives and deontic logic. *Analysis*, 24:33–36, 1963.
10. R. Conte and R. Falcone. ICMAS'96: Norms, obligations, and conventions. *AI Magazine*, 18,4:145–147, 1997.
11. D. Dubois, L. Farinas del Cerro, A. Herzig, and H. Prade. Qualitative relevance and independence: a roadmap. In *Proceedings of the IJCAI'97*, pages 62–67, 1997.
12. B.S. Firozabadi and L.W.N. van der Torre. Towards a formal analysis of control systems. In *Proceedings of the ECAI'98*, pages 317–318, 1998.
13. J.W. Forrester. Gentle murder, or the adverbial Samaritan. *Journal of Philosophy*, 81:193–197, 1984.
14. L. Goble. Murder most gentle: the paradox deepens. *Philosophical Studies*, 64:217–227, 1991.
15. B. Hansson. An analysis of some deontic logics. In R. Hilpinen, editor, *Deontic Logic: Introductory and Systematic Readings*, pages 121–147. D. Reidel Publishing Company, Dordrecht, Holland, 1971.
16. A.J.I. Jones and I. Pörn. Ideality, sub-ideality and deontic logic. *Synthese*, 65:275–290, 1985.
17. J. Lang. Conditional desires and utilities - an alternative approach to qualitative decision theory. In *Proceedings of the ECAI'96*, pages 318–322, 1996.

18. D. Makinson. On a fundamental problem of deontic logic. In P. McNamara and H. Prakken, editors, *Norms, Logics and Information Systems. New Studies on Deontic Logic and Computer Science*, pages 29–54. IOS Press, 1999.
19. D. Makinson and L. van der Torre. *The logic of reusable propositional output*. 1999. Submitted.
20. L.T. McCarty. Modalities over actions: 1. model theory. In *Proceedings of the KR'94*, pages 437–448, 1994.
21. M. Morreau. *Prima Facie* and seeming duties. *Studia Logica*, 57:47–71, 1996.
22. J. Pearl. From conditional oughts to qualitative decision theory. In *Proceedings of the UAI'93*, pages 12–20, 1993.
23. H. Prakken and M.J. Sergot. Contrary-to-duty obligations. *Studia Logica*, 57:91–115, 1996.
24. H. Prakken and M.J. Sergot. Dyadic deontic logic and contrary-to-duty obligations. In D. Nute, editor, *Defeasible Deontic Logic*, pages 223–262. Kluwer, 1997.
25. D. Ross. *The Right and the Good*. Oxford University Press, 1930.
26. W. Stelzner. Relevant deontic logic. *Journal of Philosophical Logic*, 21:193–216, 1992.
27. Y. Tan and L. van der Torre. How to combine ordering and minimizing in a deontic logic based on preferences. In *Deontic Logic, Agency and Normative Systems. Proceedings of the ΔEON'96*, Workshops in Computing, pages 216–232. Springer, 1996.
28. R. Thomason. Deontic logic as founded on tense logic. In R. Hilpinen, editor, *New Studies in Deontic Logic: Norms, Actions and the Foundations of Ethics*, pages 165–176. D. Reidel, 1981.
29. L. van der Torre. Violated obligations in a defeasible deontic logic. In *Proceedings of the ECAI'94*, pages 371–375, 1994.
30. L. van der Torre. The logic of reusable propositional output with the fulfilment constraint. In *Labelled Deduction*, Applied Logic Series. Kluwer, 1999.
31. L. van der Torre and Y. Tan. Cancelling and overshadowing: two types of defeasibility in defeasible deontic logic. In *Proceedings of the IJCAI'95*, pages 1525–1532, 1995.
32. L. van der Torre and Y. Tan. The many faces of defeasibility in defeasible deontic logic. In D. Nute, editor, *Defeasible Deontic Logic*, pages 79–121. Kluwer, 1997.
33. L. van der Torre and Y. Tan. Prohairetic Deontic Logic (PDL). In *Logics in Artificial Intelligence*, LNAI 1489, pages 77–91. Springer, 1998.
34. L. van der Torre and Y. Tan. The temporal analysis of Chisholm's paradox. In *Proceedings of the AAAI'98*, pages 650–655, 1998.
35. L. van der Torre and Y. Tan. An update semantics for prima facie obligations. In *Proceedings of the Thirteenth European Conference on Artificial Intelligence (ECAI'98)*, pages 38–42, 1998.
36. L. van der Torre and Y. Tan. Contextual deontic logic: violation contexts and factual defeasibility. In M. Cavalcanti, editor, *Formal Aspects in Context*, Applied Logic Series. Kluwer, 1999.
37. L. van der Torre and Y. Tan. Rights, duties and commitments between agents. In *Proceedings of the IJCAI'99*, 1999.
38. L. van der Torre and Y. Tan. An update semantics for defeasible obligations. In *Proceedings of the UAI'99*, 1999.
39. L. van der Torre and Y. Tan. An update semantics for deontic reasoning. In P. McNamara and H. Prakken, editors, *Norms, Logics and Information Systems. New Studies on Deontic Logic and Computer Science*, pages 73–90. IOS Press, 1999.

40. G.H. von Wright. A new system of deontic logic. In R. Hilpinen, editor, *Deontic Logic: Introductory and Systematic Readings*, pages 105–120. D. Reidel Publishing Company, Dordrecht, Holland, 1971.

41. G.H. von Wright. Deontic logic: as I see it. In P. McNamara and H. Prakken, editors, *Norms, Logics and Information Systems. New Studies on Deontic Logic and Computer Science*, pages 15–25. IOS Press, 1999.

42. R.J. Wieringa and J.-J.Ch. Meyer. Applications of deontic logic in computer science: A concise overview. In J.-J. Meyer and R. Wieringa, editors, *Deontic Logic in Computer Science*, pages 17–40. John Wiley & Sons, Chichester, England, 1993.

A Model of Explicit Context Representation and Use for Intelligent Agents*

Roy M. Turner

Department of Computer Science, University of Maine, Orono, ME 04469 USA
rmt@umcs.maine.edu

Abstract. Explicit representation of context and contextual knowledge is critical to intelligent agents. In this paper, we discuss our view of context and context-sensitive reasoning, based on several years of work on representing and using contextual knowledge. We describe our approach to context-sensitive reasoning, called *context-mediated behavior* (CMB), and discuss our experience related to reasoning in context in AI programs and our ongoing and future work in the area.

The context in which an intelligent agent operates profoundly affects how it behaves. This is both intuitive and has been supported by psychological and sociological studies (see discussion in [1]). This should be true for artificial agents as well. Indeed, it is difficult to imagine a definition of "appropriate behavior" that does not make reference to the context in which the behavior takes place.

Of course, AI programs have always taken their context into account to some extent. Usually, however, this has been done in an ad hoc way, without the designer paying explicit attention to context-sensitive reasoning, and without the programs having any explicit representation of their context or any clear sense of or access to their own contextual knowledge (cf. [2]). For example, AI planners (e.g., [3, 4]) create plans that must work in a particular task context, yet they do not represent the context as an object in its own right, nor do they explicitly identify the contextual aspects of planning knowledge. Observable features of the current situation constitute the program's view of its context, and its contextual knowledge is distributed in its operator preconditions and inference rules and, implicitly, in the assumptions encoded in the program itself.[2] Similar implicit context representation occurs in rule-based systems, neural networks, and other AI programs.

The result is that these AI programs are unable to capitalize on knowing what context they are in and how to behave in that context. They cannot do situation

---

* This material is based upon work supported by the National Science Foundation under Grant Nos. BES–9696044 and IIS–9613646 and under contracts N0001–14–96–1–5009 and N0001–14–98–1–0648 from the U.S. Office of Naval Research. The content of the information does not necessarily reflect the position or the policy of the Government, and no official endorsement should be inferred.

[2] Some planners do include meta-rules [5], but even here, only rudimentary attention is paid to representing the context as an object in its own right.

assessment, since they have no clear notion of what the space of possible situations might be, nor which classes of situations might have implications for how they are to behave. The programs are without the ability to truly reason about what contexts they are in and how they should behave while in them. Behavior is conditioned by aspects of the current context, but not by the context as a whole. A program cannot conclude, based on its current knowledge of the world, "I am in context X", and then behave appropriately until the context changes. Instead, it must waste effort constantly deciding if its behavior is appropriate for the situation, for example by checking rule antecedents, goals/preconditions of operators, etc. Neither can a program easily learn important information about how to behave in a context, since it has no clear idea of what it means to *be* in that context. Further, it is difficult to acquire and maintain knowledge about how to behave in a context, since such knowledge will be distributed across many other pieces of knowledge (e.g., rules). This can lead to problems maintaining the consistency of the knowledge base.

For over ten years, we have investigated ways to explicitly represent contexts and contextual knowledge and to use those representations to control an agent's behavior. This work has taken place in the domains of medical diagnosis and intelligent agent (autonomous underwater vehicle) control. Currently, our research group is also examining context representation and use in multiagent systems and multi-modal interfaces. The approach developed, *context-mediated behavior* (CMB) [1], has strong ties to work in diagnosis, situation assessment, and case-based reasoning; indeed, we argue that identifying the current context *is* situation assessment, and that the process itself is a kind of diagnosis.

In this paper, we will first discuss context and our model of how context representations and contextual knowledge can be effectively used by intelligent agents. We next describe CMB, then discuss its development and use in two AI programs and our plans for its use in two other domains. Some conclusions and directions for future work are then presented.

1 Context Assessment

As has been pointed out repeatedly over the last several years at workshops, at conferences, and in on-line discussions focusing on context, the word "context" does not yet have a technical meaning that all researchers can agree with or even understand (e.g., [6]). Consequently, we need first to define what we mean by context in this paper, as well as provide some related definitions.

Definition 1. In this paper, we use the term *world state* to mean the state of the agent's world at some particular time: i.e., all features of the world, including all objects in existence, their properties and internal states, and relationships between them.

Definition 2. We define a *situation* to mean the portion of the world state that affects the agent in a significant way. The *perceived situation* is a set of features (which may or may not correspond to features in the real situation) that the agent believes belong to its current situation.

We realize that this appeals to the reader's intuition rather than being a formal or even a very exact definition. By this definition, the current situation includes all and only those features of the world that an omniscient viewer would realize affect the agent. So, for example, we would normally rule out the position of a satellite in its orbit as being part of the situation for, say, an autonomous underwater vehicle (AUV) on an oceanography mission, but would include that in the situation should the AUV's mission require it to communicate using that satellite.

The agent's knowledge about a particular situation is more than the sum of the features that are observable, even in principle, by an agent. An agent brings to a situation expectations about features it has not yet seen as well as predictions about future situations. It brings knowledge it has about the results of actions it took in previous, similar situations. It brings to bear knowledge of how it should act in the situation so that its behavior is appropriate. It has knowledge of how the situation is similar to and different from other situations.

An agent thus knows about *classes* of similar situations that share features and implications for how it should behave. We call such classes of situations *contexts*.

Definition 3. A *context* is a distinguished (e.g., named) collection of possible world features that has predictive worth to the agent.

A context corresponds to a range of world states and situations. By "predictive worth", we mean that recognizing that the current situation is an instance of a known context is useful in helping the agent understand its situation and behave appropriately. Once an agent knows it is in a particular context—that is, that the current situation is an exemplar the context—then it immediately and relatively effortlessly knows a great deal about the situation, simply based on its *a priori* knowledge about the context. It can predict unseen features of the situation and how the situation may change over time. It knows what constitutes appropriate behavior in the situation.

Consider medicine. Doctors (and medical AI programs) do not as an end in itself perform diagnosis to identify what disease is present. There is no reason in principle that treatment could not be prescribed and predictions made about the patient's future health (prognosis) based solely on reasoning about the signs and symptoms, without recourse to explicitly identifying the disease(s). After all, the disease is not a real thing, in the sense of something present in the world that one can point to. It is just a name for a particular constellation of signs, symptoms, pathophysiological states, presence or absence of etiological agents (e.g., bacteria), and so forth. But the concept of "disease" provides the medical reasoner with several benefits. It clusters *predictive* knowledge about commonly-occurring and/or important recurring patterns in the world (i.e., the disease). Recognizing the presence of the disease allows the diagnostician to make rapid, accurate predications about the prognosis for the patient. More important, it allows appropriate treatments to be associated with the pattern; when the disease is detected, knowledge about the treatments immediately comes to mind. By explicitly recognizing the existence of these recurring patterns, the diagnostician can reason about them and compare them to one another. Thus the diagnostician can engage in differential diagnosis, using predictions from one disease to gather evidence to differentiate it from other candidate diseases [7]. Having explicit names for such patterns also allows doctors to communicate easily with others about the disease.

Diseases are just one kind of context.[3] There are a myriad of others, recurring patterns in the welter of the features of the world that an agent should recognize because they have predictive worth. For example, an autonomous underwater vehicle (AUV) should recognize such contexts as being in a harbor, operating under sea ice, and having low power. By understanding that these are important classes of situations, the agent gains the same advantages as does the diagnostician from knowledge about diseases. The context can serve to organize the agent's knowledge about predictions that can be made and behavior that is appropriate in the situation. Further, if the contexts are explicitly represented, they can allow the agent to do differential diagnosis to determine which among several possible contexts it is actually in. And explicitly representing contexts allows the agent to communicate with others about those contexts.

A major task facing an intelligent agent is *situation assessment* (e.g., [8]): given the features of the current situation it can see and its other beliefs about the situation, what context does this correspond to? We believe that situation assessment, which we could also think of as *context assessment*, is a process of diagnosis.

In medical diagnosis, the history of the patient, signs and symptoms, and other features of the diagnostic situation all are used to diagnose the presence of a disease (or set of diseases). This is an abductive process that has been approached in a number of ways in AI (e.g., [9, 7]). One very effective approach was encoded in INTERNIST [7]. In this approach, findings *evoke*, or bring to mind, candidate disease hypotheses. For example, an abnormal chest x-ray might evoke lung cancer, tuberculosis, and possibly other diseases. That is not the end of the story, however; the diagnostician needs to assess how well each hypothesis fits the current situation. When two or more disease hypotheses conflict, the diagnostician also needs to determine which of them (if any) is indeed present in the patient. This can be done by *differential diagnosis*, the process of using predictions made by the hypotheses to differentiate between them.

We see this as a good model of context assessment, as well. Features of the perceived situation should evoke one or more contexts that are candidate assessments of the situation. Where the fit is sufficiently good, and where there are no competing contexts, then the process is complete. For example, when walking into a church on Sunday morning, with people sitting in the pews and a minister in the pulpit, the evoked context is "at a church service". Very few

---

[3] More precisely, the presence of a particular disease in a patient is a kind of context.

other contexts fit this situation. Immediately the person knows a wealth of things about the situation he or she has not observed, including predictions about the kinds of things the minister will or will not say, that there will be hymns sung, and so forth. He or she also immediately knows how to behave and how not to behave. Sitting down quietly and paying attention is appropriate; turning cartwheels down the aisles is not. This addresses Oztürk's [10] identification of two major functions of context, relevancy and efficiency. Contextual knowledge associated with a context is the knowledge that is relevant to the situations that context describes. The association of the knowledge with the contexts addresses efficiency by allowing knowledge appropriate for behaving in the context to be evoked along with the context.

Sometimes, however, there will be competing hypotheses about what the context is, just as there are often competing disease hypotheses in diagnosis. For example, suppose a person walks into a room at a university in which he or she often studies. There are a few people sitting around in a circle, with one person standing addressing them. Several contexts might be evoked in this situation, including: a class is going on; a meeting of a club is in progress; and a group of friends are talking. The person needs to differentiate between these competing contexts if he or she is to know whether it is appropriate to stay and study or to leave unobtrusively. Predictions based on knowledge about each context can help in this differential diagnostic process. For example, the person might look to see if the people sitting are taking notes, or if the person addressing them looks like a professor, etc. This all would happen quickly, but nonetheless, something very much like it would happen.

Contexts have the property of composability. Just as a patient can be suffering from several diseases simultaneously, the current situation can be characterized simultaneously by several contexts. In our example above, in addition to the contexts evoked by seeing the people listening to the speaker, being in the room itself forms a context, as does the fact that the person is (say) hungry, that he or she has work to do, etc. Each of these contexts or contextual aspects [11] carries with it predictions about the world (e.g., "this room is generally quiet") and suggestions for behavior (e.g., "find a place to work"). All of the contexts that fit the current situation can be composed, or merged, to give rise to the complete context assessment. For example, suppose an AUV is on a search mission, has low power, and there is a hurricane overhead. Knowledge about each of these contexts could be combined to yield a description of the current, perhaps novel, context that could then help the AUV behave appropriately.

Figure 1 summarizes our view of how an agent does context assessment and uses contextual knowledge. The agent's perceived situation is the product of its perceptions (including communication from other agents), its beliefs, and the process of abstraction and interpretation (e.g., recognizing that a computer is present from seeing its keyboard and display). Candidate contexts are evoked based on features of the perceived situation. A process of differential diagnosis then determines which of these contexts are the most appropriate characterizations of the current situation. The combination of these contexts gives a complete

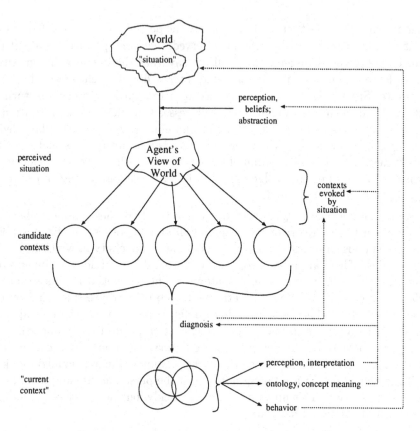

Fig. 1. Overall process of determining the context.

description of the current situation. Knowledge about these contexts can then provide predictions useful for further interpreting sensory input and for behaving appropriately in the situation.

In the figure, there are lines leading from the current context representation back to processes that are instrumental in determining what the context is. These lines are meant to indicate that to some extent, the process of context assessment includes circularities. The current context affects what is perceived to be the current situation, which contexts are evoked by the perceived situation, and even the diagnosis of the (next) context.

2 Context-Mediated Behavior

We have developed an approach to context-sensitive reasoning based on the model discussed above. This work was begun over ten years ago in the domain of medical diagnosis [12, 13] and is currently continuing in the domain of controlling autonomous intelligent agents [14, 13, 15, 1], such as autonomous underwater vehicles. We have just begun extending the work to the domain of multi-modal interfaces [11] and to multiagent systems, in particular autonomous oceanographic sampling networks [16].

We call our approach *context-mediated behavior* (CMB) [1] because it is based on the idea that all behavior depends upon, or is mediated by, context. The key ideas in CMB are: contexts should be explicitly represented; contextual knowledge should be associated with context representations; and contextual knowledge should guide all facets of an agent's behavior.

In this section, we describe CMB. We first discuss the knowledge structures that represent contexts, *contextual schemas*, and then how those schemas are used. In the next section, we discuss CMB in relation to several AI systems.

2.1 Contextual Schemas

In our approach, contexts are represented by *contextual schemas* (c-schemas). C-schemas are frame-like knowledge structures that are descendents of Schank's *memory organization packets* (MOPs) [17]. They are organized in a content-addressable conceptual memory similar to the CYRUS [18] program.

C-schemas contain both *descriptive* and *prescriptive* knowledge about the contexts they represent. The descriptive knowledge consists of:

- Features of the situation that must be present (or not present) in order for it to be considered an instance of the context. This allows the agent to "diagnose" the current situation as an instance of a context it knows about.
- Features of the situation, perhaps yet unseen, that are expected in this context. This allows the agent to make predictions about things it is likely to see that may affect problem solving (e.g., to allow it to recognize anticipated events). It also allows the agent to disambiguate sensory input based on contextual, top-down predictions.
- Context-specific ontology/meaning of particular concepts. Concepts often have different meanings in different contexts; contextual knowledge provides this information to the agent. For example, changes in the meaning of fuzzy linguistic values can be handled by storing context-specific membership functions for the values in c-schemas [19]. Similarly, neural networks could be made to recognize different things in different contexts by storing context-specific weights in c-schemas.

Prescriptive knowledge, that is, information about how to behave in the context, is also stored in c-schemas. This includes information about:

- handling unanticipated events: how to detect them, how to diagnose their meaning in the context, their context-specific importance, and how to appropriately handle them;
- focusing attention: which goals should/should not be worked on and how important particular goals are in the context;
- goal-directed behavior: knowledge about how to achieve goals appropriately in the situation;

- non-goal-directed behavior: knowledge governing the expression of behavior that is not directly related to goals, such as turning off obstacle avoidance when an AUV is in the context of docking, etc; and
- new goals that should be pursued because the agent is in the context.

2.2 Context Assessment in CMB

In CMB, a *context manager* module is responsible for context assessment and ensuring that contextual knowledge is distributed to other modules as needed. In the Orca AUV mission controller, the context manager is being implemented as ECHO (Embedded Context-Handling Object) [1].

To do context assessment, the context manager first retrieves the appropriate c-schemas from a schema memory based on features observed in the current situation. This corresponds to the perceived situation evoking candidate contexts in the model above. It then uses information from these c-schemas to do differential diagnosis. The process proposed for differential diagnosis in CMB is that developed by Miller and colleagues and Feltovich for medical differential diagnosis [7, 20]. C-schemas are grouped into logical competitor sets, each of which defines a diagnostic problem to be solved. How strongly the c-schema is evoked by the situation affects its rating. Predictions from a c-schema that are satisfied in the perceived situation increase the confidence that the c-schema fits the situation; violated predictions decrease the confidence. Comparisons between the c-schemas drive the focus of diagnosis.

The product of the diagnostic process is a set of c-schemas, each of which represent a context that describes the situation. These are then merged by the context manager to create a complete picture of the context, called the *context object*. Knowledge from this representation is then used to affect all aspects of the agent's behavior.

The context manager parcels out information from the context object to the rest of the agent. In ECHO, the current plan is to implement this as follows. The agent's other modules register their interests with the context manager, much as agents register with facilitators in multiagent systems based on KQML (knowledge query and manipulation language) [21]. When the a new context has been diagnosed, ECHO will either tell the interested modules that there is a new context or send them the information they requested, depending on how they registered.

The context manager constantly monitors the situation to determine if the context has changed. If so, then a new context object is created. One way that it can notice a changed context is when new c-schemas are evoked based on new features in the situation. It can also explicitly examine the current situation from time to time to decide if it is still adequately described by the context object.

This process is similar to case-based reasoning (CBR) in many respects. Indeed, the process is part of an overall approach called *schema-based reasoning* [13] that grew out of and is a generalization of CBR. Differences from CBR include the use of generalized rather than particular cases and using diagnostic reasoning to select the (general) cases to use.

3   CMB in Intelligent Agents

CMB was partially implemented in a medical diagnostic reasoner, and a full version is currently being implemented in the Orca AUV controller. In addition, we have plans to test the approach in other applications, as discussed here.

MEDIC. MEDIC [12, 13] was a schema-based diagnostic reasoner whose domain was pulmonary infections. It grew out of both work in case-based reasoning and reactive planning. It was an *adaptive, schema-based reasoner*, using generalized cases to control its reasoning and capable of changing the way it behaved based on techniques from reactive planning [22] research.

Contextual information is very important in medical diagnosis. The meaning of a sign (objective finding) or symptom (subjective) depends on context; for example, a persistent cough in a young, generally healthy person should make the diagnostician think of something different than when observed in a chronic smoker or an inner city dweller with HIV (e.g., respiratory infection, cancer, and tuberculosis, respectively).

In MEDIC, the contexts we were interested in had to do with patient presentation. These were early on called *diagnostic MOPs*, then later the name was changed to "contextual schemas" as it became clear that they were an instance of a larger, more generally-useful class of knowledge structures. Each c-schema represented a picture of the current diagnostic session centered around the patient presentation. For example, MEDIC had c-schemas for "consultation", "cardiopulmonary consultation", and "cardiopulmonary consultation in which the patient is an alcoholic". Contextual schemas in MEDIC were monolithic structures representing the entire problem solving context; the best c-schema returned by memory was used as the context object (though not referred to by that name). In a superficial way, MEDIC's c-schemas were similar to earlier work on prototypes in diagnosis by Aikins [23].

Other contexts are important in medicine that MEDIC did not examine. For example, diseases themselves, or rather their presence, define contexts; indeed, the ultimate goal of a purely diagnostic program is to determine the current context to the level of what disease (or set of diseases) is present in the patient. Disease contexts can provide additional information that is very important, such as the prognosis and suggestions for treatment.

MEDIC ignored an important feature of contexts in general, and in medicine in particular: the evolution of contexts over time. For instance, a context defined by patient P having disease D has many "sub-contexts" corresponding to the evolution of the disease, possibly in response to treatment. This fluid nature of contexts is very difficult to capture in AI knowledge structures. MEDIC was concerned with diagnosing "snapshots" of a patient, similar to the clinicopathological conference (CPC) exercises that doctors engage in, or to diagnosis on an outpatient basis. Consequently, tracking the patient through time was not necessary.

There was, however, some evolution of contexts during a session with MEDIC. As the program's understanding of the case grew as findings were presented and questions answered, different c-schemas would match the situation. Usually, the new c-schemas were specializations of the old, allowing fine-tuning of MEDIC's behavior, but sometimes the c-schema would correspond to a different context altogether, which would change the hypotheses MEDIC was considering.

Orca. The CMB process as described above is being implemented in Orca, an intelligent mission controller for oceanographic AUVs [14, 13, 15, 1]. In particular, the ECHO context manager will overcome some of the limitations of MEDIC's approach. It will diagnose c-schemas and merge them into a coherent picture of the overall context. A variety of context types is being considered, for example having to do with the vehicle, the environment, and the mission. Orca will have c-schemas, for example, that represent the contexts "has low power", "on a search mission", "in a harbor", "in Bar Harbor", and so on. Some work has also begun on handling the changing character of the situation while within a context; for example, the physical properties of the environment change as an AUV transits a harbor, but throughout it makes sense to consider the AUV in the context of "in a harbor".

We will not further describe ECHO here, as it is adequately described by the preceding section and elsewhere [1]. However, it is instructive to see how a context manager such as ECHO is integrated into an agent. Figure 2 shows the internal structure of the Orca program. As can be seen, ECHO watches the current situation, attempting to detect when the context changes. It detects this in part when new c-schemas are retrievable from the long-term memory based on the changing situation's features. When this happens, it reassesses the context and possibly forms a new context object. Information from the object is then made available to Orca's other modules. Knowledge about event handling is sent to Event Handler. This includes information useful for detecting events as well as diagnosing their cause, assessing their importance, and responding to them. Knowledge about goals is sent to the Agenda Manager. This module uses the knowledge of goal importance and appropriateness to manage Orca's focus of attention. Knowledge about appropriate ways to achieve goals is sent to Schema Applier. This knowledge is in the form of suggestions of procedural schemas (p-schemas) that are likely to be useful for the goals in the current context. (P-schemas are packets of procedural knowledge that can represent plans, scripts, or rules.) Knowledge about the context-dependent meaning of concepts, as well as predictions about unseen features of the world, are available to all modules.

CoDA. We are beginning to look at the role and use of contextual knowledge in multiagent systems. Our initial domain is the control of an autonomous oceanographic sampling network (AOSN) [24], and our project is CoDA (Cooperative Distributed AOSN controller) [16].

We are just beginning to look at context in this setting. Some of the issues that come to mind are how to use context to help select organizational structures, to select communication modes and channels, and to recognize and respond to opportunities to reorganize the system.

Other interesting issues to be explored include the notion of shared context between the agents and how the agents can agree on what the context is. We believe that explicit context representation is critical in this case, since agents must

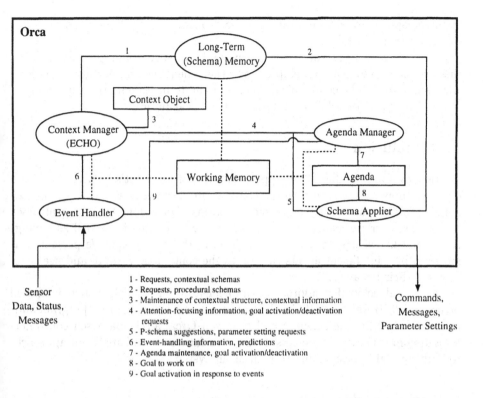

Fig. 2. Internal structure of Orca. After Turner [1998].

be able to agree on the context they are in. While it will not be necessary (or perhaps even possible in the general case) for the agents to have identical representations of contexts, explicit context representation will allow them to reason about their own contexts as well as others', and to communicate about contexts, in order to come to an agreement about what the current shared context is.

We believe CMB can be extended to the multiagent case, and we plan to explore this in the near future.

Multi-modal interfaces. We have also begun to examine the role of context in multi-modal (natural language and graphics) interfaces to geographical information systems. This work is describe elsewhere [11, 25]. Briefly, we have identified several kinds of contexts (or components of the context) active in this application: the natural language discourse context; the graphics context, including a graphical equivalent to discourse context; the task context; the context defined by the kind of user and the particular user; a context defined by the location(s) being discussed; the temporal context of what is being discussed (e.g., "a building used to be here" versus "there is a building here now"); the context of where the system is being used; and a context defined by explicitly-identified symbol–object mappings. We call each of these kinds of contexts *contextual aspects*, since they describe aspects of the context present in each session. Two of these aspects are similar to four of the "context-space" dimensions recently discussed by Lenat [2].

We are investigating the use of contextual knowledge from representations of these aspects to understand ellipsis and other phenomena important to understanding multi-modal communication. We intend to investigate the applicability of CMB to a multi-modal GIS interface in the near future.

4 Conclusion

Context profoundly affects the appropriateness of an agent's behavior. Consequently, an agent needs to take the context into account when deciding how to behave. In this paper, we have argued that this is best done by the agent having an explicit representation of contexts it may find itself in as well as having contextual knowledge about how to behave in those contexts. We presented a model of how intelligent agents can assess the context they are in and use that to guide their behavior.

We have developed an approach to implementing this model, context-mediated behavior. CMB was partially implemented in a medical diagnostic program and is now being fully implemented and tested in Orca, a schema-based controller for autonomous intelligent agents. In the near future, we will apply our approach to multi-modal interfaces and to multiagent systems.

5 Acknowledgements

The author would like to thank Elise Turner and other members of the University of Maine Cooperative Distributed Problem Solving Research Group as well as Patrick Brézillon for many helpful discussions.

References

1. R. M. Turner. Context-mediated behavior for intelligent agents. *International Journal of Human–Computer Studies*, 48(3):307–330, March 1998.
2. D. Lenat. The dimensions of context-space. Published on-line at URL http://www.cyc.com/context-space.rtf, accessed March 28, 1999., 1998.
3. R. E. Fikes and N. J. Nilsson. STRIPS: A new approach to the application of theorem proving to problem solving. *Artificial Intelligence*, 2:189–208, 1971.
4. D. E. Wilkins. Domain-independent planning: Representation and plan generation. *Artificial Intelligence*, 22(3), 1984.
5. R. Davis and B. G. Buchanan. Meta-level knowledge. In B. G. Buchanan and E. H. Shortliffe, editors, *Rule-Based Expert Systems: The MYCIN Experiments of the Stanford Heuristic Programming Project*. Addison–Wesley Publishing Company, Reading, Massachusetts, 1984.
6. P. Brézillon, C. Gentile, I. Saker, and M. Secron. SART: A system for supporting operators with contextual knowledge. In *Proceedings of the 1997 International and Interdisciplinary Conference on Modeling and Using Context (CONTEXT-97)*, pages 209–222, 1997.

7. R. A. Miller, H. E. Pople, Jr., and J. D. Myers. INTERNIST–1, an experimental computer-based diagnostic consultant for general internal medicine. *New England Journal of Medicine*, 307:468–476, 1982.

8. D. F. Noble. Schema-based knowledge elicitation for planning and situation assessment aids. *IEEE Transactions on Systems, Man, and Cybernetics*, 19(3):473–482, May/June 1989.

9. E. H. Shortliffe. *Computer-based Medical Consultations: MYCIN*. Elsevier, New York, 1976.

10. P. Öztürk and A. Aamodt. Towards a model of context for case-based diagnostic problem solving. In *Proceedings of the 1997 International and Interdisciplinary Conference on Modeling and Using Context (CONTEXT-97)*, 1997.

11. E. H. Turner, R. M. Turner, J. Phelps, C. Grunden, M. Neale, and J. Mailman. Aspects of context for understanding multi-modal communication. In *Proceedings of the 1999 International and Interdisciplinary Conference on Modeling and Using Context (CONTEXT-99)*, Trento, Italy, 1999.

12. R. M. Turner. When reactive planning is not enough: Using contextual schemas to react appropriately to environmental change. In *Proceedings of the Eleventh Annual Conference of the Cognitive Science Society*, pages 940–947, Detroit, MI, 1989.

13. R. M. Turner. *Adaptive Reasoning for Real-World Problems: A Schema-Based Approach*. Lawrence Erlbaum Associates, Hillsdale, NJ, 1994.

14. R. M. Turner and R. A. G. Stevenson. ORCA: An adaptive, context-sensitive reasoner for controlling AUVs. In *Proceedings of the 7th International Symposium on Unmanned Untethered Submersible Technology (UUST '91)*, pages 423–432, 1991.

15. R. M. Turner. Intelligent control of autonomous underwater vehicles: The Orca project. In *Proceedings of the 1995 IEEE International Conference on Systems, Man, and Cybernetics*. Vancouver, Canada, 1995.

16. R. M. Turner and E. H. Turner. Organization and reorganization of autonomous oceanographic sampling networks. In *Proceedings of the 1998 IEEE International Conference on Robotics and Automation (ICRA'98)*, pages 2060–2067, Leuven, Belgium, May 1998.

17. R. C. Schank. *Dynamic Memory*. Cambridge University Press, New York, 1982.

18. J. L. Kolodner. *Retrieval and Organizational Strategies in Conceptual Memory*. Lawrence Erlbaum Associates, Hillsdale, New Jersey, 1984.

19. R. M. Turner. Determining the context-dependent meaning of fuzzy subsets. In *Proceedings of the 1997 International and Interdisciplinary Conference on Modeling and Using Context (CONTEXT-97)*, Rio de Janeiro, 1997.

20. P. J. Feltovich, P. E. Johnson, J. A. Moller, and D. B. Swanson. LCS: The role and development of medical knowledge and diagnostic expertise. In W. J. Clancey and E. H. Shortliffe, editors, *Readings in Medical Artificial Intelligence*, pages 275–319. Addison–Wesley Publishing Company, Reading, Massachusetts, 1984.

21. R. Patil, R. Fikes, P. Patel-Schneider, D. McKay, T. Finin, T. Gruber, and R. Neches. The DARPA Knowledge Sharing Effort: Progress report. In *Proceedings of the Third International Conference on Principles of Knowledge Representation and Reasoning*, 1992.

22. M. P. Georgeff and A. L. Lansky. Reactive reasoning and planning: An experiment with a mobile robot. In *Proceedings of the Sixth National Conference on Artificial Intelligence*, pages 677–682, Seattle, Washington, 1987.

23. J. S. Aikins. *Prototypes and Production Rules: A Knowledge Representation for Computer Consultations*. PhD thesis, Stanford University, 1980.

24. T. Curtin, J. Bellingham, J. Catipovic, and D. Webb. Autonomous oceanographic sampling networks. *Oceanography*, 6(3), 1993.

25. E. H. Turner, R. M. Turner, C. Grunden, J. Mailman, M. Neale, and J. Phelps. The need for context in multi-modal interfaces. In *Workshop Notes for the 1999 AAAI Workshop on Reasoning in Context for AI Applications*, AAAI Technical Report (ISBN 1-57735-098-7), pages 91–95, Orlando, FL, July 1999. AAAI Press.

Context-Scanning Strategy in Temporal Reasoning

Nikolai Vazov

Sofia University, Dept. of Russian Studies

email: niki@slav.uni-sofia.bg

http://www.slav.uni-sofia.bg/pages/ruspages/niki/niki.html

Abstract. This paper presents a method for temporal reasoning based on context-scanning rules. The method uses exclusively linguistic markers (tensed forms, temporal and non-temporal adverbials, interjections, particular syntactic structures) which allow to carry out temporal reasoning centred on the act of utterance. Due to the information extracted from the analysed texts, the method is capable to identify aspecto-temporal values in isolated utterances but also temporal structures of larger text units. The aspecto-temporal information receives formal representation in combinatory logic which allows its machine processing.

1 Introduction

Different aspects of temporal reasoning have been in the focus of a large number of works on linguistics (Benveniste 1962; Mourelatos 1978; Hornstein 1993; Verkuyl 1993; Bartsch 1995), logic (Bestougeff, 1989; ter Meulen, 1995; Reichenbach, 1947 (second edition 1966); Kamp, 1988; Dowty, 1986), artificial intelligence (Desclés 1990; Allen 1991) and natural language processing (Yip 1985; Bennett, Herlick et al. 1990; Berri, Maire-Reppert et al. 1991; Zablit 1991; Desclés 1994; Gagnon & Lapalme 1995). This paper is an attempt to put together the results of different approaches and to formulate a method for temporal reasoning using context-scanning rules. The method considers the situations as products of utterances. Hence, unlike other approaches whose goal is to fix the *time of realisation* of the events on the temporal axis, the discussed method identifies *their relevance* to the time of utterance. It manipulates linguistic units denoting the relevance of the situations (to the speaker) rather than units encoding the time of occurrence of these situations. In order to "compute" the relevance of situations, the method operates rules which scan the texts under analysis and retrieve the information necessary for understanding the temporal organisation of their situations.The first section of this paper presents the information processed by the temporal reasoning. It also postulates the principles of organisation and interaction of this information. The second section discusses the development of the context-scanning rules. A major issue in this section is the determination of their scope of operation. The scope is the minimal text unit in which the rules obtain maximal searching results. The third section considers the possible ways to formalise the procedure of temporal reasoning in order to allow for its machine processing.

2 Aspecto-Temporal Values and Temporal Structures of Texts: Central Notions in Temporal Reasoning

2.1 Aspecto-temporal Values of Situations

The relevance of situations with regard to the time of utterance is rendered by their aspecto-temporal (AT) values. The AT value is a central notion in this approach and contains four semantic components:

1) it bears information on the internal structure of situations (durative, punctual, etc.);

2) it fixes the position of the situations with regard to the speaker's position (past, future, etc.);

3) it fixes the relative position of each situation with regard to the other situations in the text;

4) it locates the time period where the speaker considers the situations as relevant.

According to their internal structure, situations can take one of the three aspectual values: *processes*, *events* or *states*. Once the position of the situations has been fixed with regard to the speaker's position (T_0), their aspectual values become aspecto-temporal. The latter are represented by topological intervals on the temporal axis of the speaker (Desclés 1980; Desclés 1991).

Processes express ongoing situations with a beginning (initial break), but without an explicitly specified end (final break). They are represented by semi-open intervals, closed to the left and open to the right. The predication defined as a process holds over the whole interval except for its right bound. Example 1 represents a process which takes place before the time of utterance and receives the value of *past process*.

$$-----------[///////[---[T_0----- \qquad (1)$$

I *was driving* in the right lane when his car crashed into mine.

Events describe situations perceived as an indivisible whole, containing initial and final break. They are represented by closed intervals, the predication holding over the whole interval, bounds included. The event in example 2 precedes the time of utterance and receives the value of *past event*.

$$-----------[///////]---[T_0----- \qquad (2)$$

Mary drank up the beer.

States denote situations with no explicitly marked beginning and end. They are represented by open intervals where the value of the predication is identical at every point of the interval. The state in example 3 is assigned the value of *past state* because the interval of the state is anterior to the time of utterance.

$$-----------]///////[---[T_0-------- \qquad (3)$$

The car *was standing* across the road when we came up to it.

The interval representation allows to describe the four semantic components of the AT values. 1) Different configurations of bounds denote the internal structure of the situations. 2) The position of the interval on the temporal axis fixes the position of the situation with regard to the speaker's position (T_0). 3) The relative positions of the bounds of two (or more) intervals account for the relative positions of the situations. 4) The interior and the closure of the intervals (the slashed zones) represent the time periods where the speaker considers the situations as relevant. In the rest of this paper the slashed zones shall be referred to as *validation intervals*.

In the examples above, the intervals of realisation of the situations overlapped with their validation intervals. This configuration means that the speaker considers the situation as relevant over the period where it took place. However, languages allow the speakers to distinguish between the period of occurrence and the period of relevance of a situation:

Peter has already opened the door (≈ The door is open now)   (4)

In example 4, the speaker does not refer explicitly to the moment when Peter opened the door but emphasises the fact that at the time of the utterance the door is open. Situations with different intervals of validation and realisation are expressed by a configuration of two conjunct topological intervals: a closed interval denoting the event and an open interval denoting the state which results from this event. These situations receive the value *resulting state*.

$$------------[-------]//////////[T_0--------$$ (5)

Example 4 and configuration 5 represent a present state (the open interval extending to T_0) resulting from a past event (the closed interval). This state accounts for the natural inference that, at the time of utterance, the door is open.

2.2 Temporal Structures

In order to carry out temporal reasoning it is necessary to take into account the values of all the situations in a given text. The set of all AT values of the situations forms the *temporal structure* of the text[1]. Diverse configurations of AT values and the relative positions of the validation intervals of situations determine the variety of possible temporal structures. The present approach considers two basic types of temporal structures: *homogeneous* and *heterogeneous*.

The homogeneous structures require that the entire set of validation intervals should be located within the same zone of temporal axis of the speaker. A zone of temporal axis is any of the three time periods which are situated before, during or after the utterance time[2]. An example of such a structure is the following text[3]:

After years of despair and loneliness, I *got* in touch (1) with Hanussen. He   (6)
showed (2) me the exact place where I could find my daughter. I *went* (3) there and
I *met* (4) my Sylvia, indeed. (5) We *came back* together from Rome the same
evening.

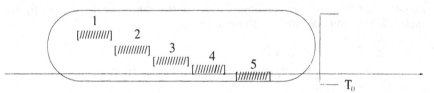

Fig. 1. Homogeneous structure preceding the time of utterance

---

[1] Temporal structures are built exclusively out of the values of the main clauses. Figure 1 shows a series of ordered events represented by closed intervals...

[2] Hypothetical situations (*They would come*) are located in a separate zone, called *temporal axis of hypothetical situations*.

[3] The research presented in this paper was carried out on French. In order to avoid double (original + translation) examples, their English version only will be given in this section.

Heterogeneous structures do not impose any restrictions on the position of the validation intervals of their constitutive AT values. Consequently, these values can be located in any zone of the temporal axis of the speaker and even on axes different from the axis or real situations (for example, on the axis of hypothetical situations):

(1) The Société des Bourses françaises, MONEP, MATIF and Deutsche Börse (7) *signed* a letter of intention whose goal is to extend the cooperation between the French and the German financial markets. (2) This letter *would develop* double grounds for negotiations, concerning physical markets, on one hand, and derived products, on the other. (3) However, the French-German cooperation *remains* liable to one condition : the adoption by the German Stock market of the new system of quoted values of the Paris Stock market. (4) Furthermore, MATIF *plans* to modify the status of its members and to found its own administrative council. (5) Creation of special licences for negotiation *is* also *envisaged*. (6) The project *is about* to be handed over to experts soon.

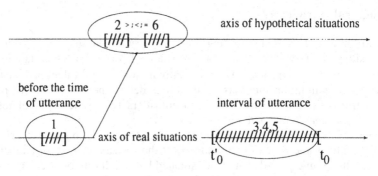

Fig. 2. Heterogeneous structures

Homogeneous structures can be further subdivided into dynamic and static (Vazov, 1996). Dynamic structures contain at least one pair of disjoint closed validation intervals (see Figure 1). Disjoint closed intervals denote events ordered in time (situation$_n$ < situation$_{n+1}$). This ordering is typical for narrative texts where the event organisation accounts for the building of the plot and, consequently, for the dynamic character of their temporal structure (see example 6).

Homogeneous dynamic structure if:

$$\exists i_i \, \exists i_j \, [(i_i, i_j \in I_{closed}) \wedge ((i_i < i_j) \vee (i_j < i_i))]$$
where
$$i_i, i_j \text{ are validation intervals}$$

The validation intervals which constitute static structures, can be either open, or semi-open. Unlike dynamic structures, the static ones incorporate all the validation intervals of the situations in the text into one *common interval*. The common interval is the biggest open interval within the intersection of all validation intervals.

Homogeneous static structure if:

$$\exists j \, \forall i \, [(j \in I_{open}) \wedge (i \in I_{open \text{ or semi-open}})$$
$$\wedge$$
$$((j = (i_i \cap i_j \cap \ldots i_n)) \wedge \neg \exists j_i \, (j_i \supset j))]$$

where

i_i, i_j... i_n are validation intervals

j is the common interval

This characteristic of the static structures prevents them from expressing ordered events. Usually, texts with static structures represent descriptions of objects where all situations (object features) are considered as relevant over the same time period (common interval):

(1) Your skin *is* delicate, soft, and sensitive. (2) In order to meet the different (8) needs of your skin POND's *has developed* a full treatment which adapts to all major types of skin. (3) The products *have been* dermatologically *tested* to optimally reduce irritation risks. (4) From cleansing to regular skin care, each POND's product *contains* important nutrition elements, hydrants and skin protectors

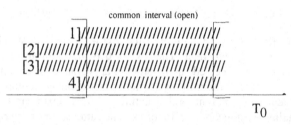

common interval (open)

Fig. 3. Static structure

However, the static structures do not imply that their constituent situations should be necessarily static. Some static structures may contain dynamic situations as well. The texts with such structures represent the scene (the set of all situations) as a snapshot where all the situations are relevant at the same time. Thus, the utterances 1 & 2 in example 9 denote static situations (state + resulting state) whereas the utterances 3 & 4 express dynamic situations (ongoing process + ongoing process). All four utterances are validated over the same common interval which overlaps with the utterance time:

(1) Riccardo Muti *is* the musical director of La Scala in Milan and of the (9) Philadelphia Orchestra - functions which he fulfilled at the Musical May in Florence (1969-80) and at the London Philharmonic orchestra (1972-82).(2) He *has conducted* in all major European Opera theatres, performing a repertoire including Mozart and the most eminent Italian composers. (3) He often *conducts* Berlin and Vienna Philharmonic orchestras in his capacity of invited conductor. (4) Riccardo Muti also regularly *appears* at the Salzburg festival. (Le Monde CD-ROM)

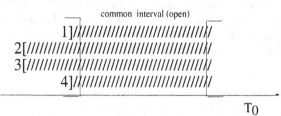

common interval (open)

Fig. 4. Static structure integrating dinamic situations

2.3 Organisation of AT Values within the Temporal Structures

AT values of situations are encoded in the utterances by various linguistic means: grammatical tenses, adverbials, specific interjections. Hence, the organisation of the temporal structures can be represented as a stack of values assigned incrementally to each (next) utterance in the text. The AT value of the first utterance is the starting point of the temporal structure. The value of the second utterance is then added to the value of the first one to form the temporal structure of the first two utterances, for example,

$$value_{utter1} + value_{utter2} = temporal\ structure_{utter1 + utter2}$$

The values of the situations in the following utterances are integrated into the already created temporal structure:

$$temporal\ structure_{utter1 + utter2} + value_{utter3} = temporal\ structure_{utter1 + utter2 + utter3}$$

The formation of the temporal structure of the text is carried out step by step until all the values become integrated in it. The text in 6 is an example of such a structure where the AT values are processed "in the order of appearance" of the utterances.

However, there is a large number of texts whose heterogeneous temporal structures are not built incrementally. The temporal structures of these texts can be interrupted by insertion of smaller homogeneous structures. The latter are configurations of values assigned to a sequence of utterances inserted in the body of the entire text.

> (1) I have always considered my job as being strictly related to the (10) communication. (2) In the Collède de France all doors are open. (3) *And I said that I accepted to write for large audience. (4) Then I engaged myself in a project for culture television.* (5) I believe that France should have its TV cultural channel. (Le Monde CD-ROM)

The temporal structure of example 10 will have the following configuration:

$$\left(\begin{array}{c} (temporal\ structure_{utter1 + utter2}) + (temporal\ structure_{utter3 + utter4}) \\ temporal\ structure\ ((utter_1 + utter_2)(utter_3 + utter_4)) \\ + \\ value\ utter_5 \end{array}\right)$$

The values of utterances 1 & 2 create a homogeneous static temporal structure (*resulting state + state*). Yet, the values of utterances 3 & 4 form a new structure, namely a homogeneous dynamic one (*event + event*). The interaction of the two homogeneous structures brings about a heterogeneous structure completed by the value of utterance 5. The latter does not modify the structure set by the first four utterances.

2.4 Interdependence between AT Values and Temporal Structures

The linguistic means *in* the utterances sometimes prove to be insufficient to assign a unique AT value to the situations expressed by these utterances. These situations usually receive more than one value, and remain undetermined until some additional markers allow to clear up the ambiguity. As a rule, these markers are situated in other, not necessarily neighbouring, utterances of the same text. In example 11

Dominique est partie pour Londres. Quelques jours plus tard elle est revenue   (11)
Dominique has left / left for London. Ten days later she came back.

the first utterance receives two AT values: *past event (Dominique left to London)* or *resulting state (Dominique has left to London)*. To remove this ambiguity it is necessary to identify the AT value of the second utterance (*A couple of days later she came back*) which will then serve as a marker for the value of the first one. Due to the adverbial *quelques jours plus tard (a couple of days later)* which is a past event marker, the second utterance receives the value of a *past event* and eventually determines the selection of the same value for the first utterance.

It should be pointed out that the linguistic markers which operate at the utterance level (for example, *a couple of days later*) are different from those which determine the AT values in other utterances. The former are represented by grammatical paradigms or lexical units and they determine the values of the situations only in the utterances where they occur. The latter are *values-markers* which do not directly determine the values of the other utterances. Instead, they interact with the ambiguous values and form temporal structures (stacks of values). It is within these temporal structures that the ambiguity is cleared up and the relevant AT values are filtered out. The procedure of disambiguation becomes possible due to two characteristics of the temporal structures:

1. Temporal structures integrate the AT values of all the situations expressed by the utterances in the text. Yet, the type of temporal structure (homogeneous vs. heterogeneous, for instance) can be determined by some, and not necessarily all, constituent values.

Thus, the configuration [ambiguous value *present state* vs. *past event* + unambiguous value *past event*] (example 11) points to a homogeneous dynamic temporal structure *past event* + *past event* and rules out the structure *present state* + *past event*[4].

2. The internal organisation of temporal structures acts as a background pattern for different configurations of values. This pattern allows for some configurations of values and rules out other configurations.

The values in example 11 potentially form two temporal structures: 1) *past event* $_{utter1}$ + *past event* $_{utter2}$, or 2) *resulting state* $_{utter1}$ + *past event* $_{utter2}$. However, in the absence of markers of resulting state in the first utterance, only the first configuration of values is compatible with the existing patterns of values, namely, with the homogeneous dynamic temporal structure.

The above discussion has shown that the temporal reasoning cannot be regarded as a strictly incremental procedure. It requires the identification of a certain number of unambiguous values which allow to recognise the temporal structure of the entire text. In turn, the identified temporal structure authorises the relevant configurations of AT values and removes the indetermination in the ambiguous values. Hence, the identification of a temporal structure of a text shall be considered as an intermediate rather than the final step of the temporal reasoning.

---

[4] The structure *present state* + *past event* is possible only if the first utterance contains a linguistic marker of a *present state*. Yet, if such a marker were detected during the analysis of the first utterance, it wouldn't have received an ambiguous value.

3 Context-scanning Strategy for Identification of AT Values and Temporal Structures

3.1 General Principles of the Context-scanning Strategy

The context-scanning strategy (Maire-Reppert 1990; Berri, Maire-Reppert et al. 1991; Oh 1991; Desclés and Jouis 1993; Jouis 1994) is based on the hypothesis that a considerable number of semantic representations are configurations integrating pieces of local interacting information. Their interaction is supported by a set of mechanisms which incrementally build the entire semantic representation by putting together all the pieces of local information. The latter are encoded in the lexical and grammatical semantics as well as in some contextual phenomena. Hence, the semantic representations are not necessarily determined by global knowledge like, for example, world knowledge.

The context-scanning strategy has a two-step organisation. The first step identifies the pieces of local information and studies their role in the semantic configurations where they occur. This role is then represented by production rules of the following form:

if A then B

Actually, these rules are expressions in propositional logic ($A \Rightarrow B$) in which A is the premise (a marker of local information) and B is the conclusion (a semantic value obtained in the presence of the marker).

The second step is the application of the context-scanning procedure. Using a complete set of production rules, the strategy launches a search engine whose goal is to detect local information markers in a given linguistic context (for example, simple sentence, complex sentence or paragraph). If such markers are identified in the context, the semantic values become automatically assigned to the linguistic forms. Thus, the assignment procedure boils down to a logical deduction:

$$\frac{A \Rightarrow B, A}{B}$$

An example of a real context-scanning rule for identification of *past event* value is given below:

Rule 1: *(past event)*
　　IF a morpheme of the grammatical tense *passé composé* has been detected in the clause C
　　AND IF an element of the list *temporal adverbials indicating past events* has been detected in the clause C,
　　THEN the situation in the utterance is assigned the value *past event*

3.2. Context-scanning Strategy in Temporal Reasoning

Every context-scanning strategy shall provide a solution to three problems: 1) it shall give a detailed description of the phenomenon to be analysed (as a rule, each strategy shall process one phenomenon at most); 2) it shall draw up a list of all linguistic markers relevant for making a decision; 3) it shall define the scope of the operation of the context-scanning rules.

The phenomenon discussed in this paper is the AT values of situations. Hence, the entire set of context-scanning rules will be focused on markers which allow to assign an AT value to the situations expressed in the utterances.

All markers are divided into *triggering markers* and *contextual markers*. The triggering markers are the central and obligatory markers in the analysed semantic representation. They set off the research for contextual markers which eventually complement or modify the representation created by the triggering markers. The triggering markers in this approach are the paradigms of finite (conjugated) verb forms. Once detected, these forms will start the search for contextual (additional) markers like temporal adverbials, specific interjections, expressions and syntactic structures as well as other AT values in the other utterances.

To reduce the total number of rules, the contextual markers with identical function are organised in lists. For example, all temporal adverbials which induce the past event value constitute the list of temporal adverbials indicating past event: yesterday, last {night, minute, year}, etc. Thus, a single rule with a reference to this list will account for all the utterances containing such temporal adverbials (see rule 1).

The most difficult issue in the development of a context-scanning strategy is the scope of operation of its rules. This approach subdivides the potential scope into three hierarchically organised contexts: a) simple sentence level; b) complex (compound & subordinate) sentence level and c) paragraph level[5] (Vazov 1998). If the context-scanning rules cannot detect a marker at the first (simple sentence) level, they expand the scope and resume the search at the next (complex sentence) level. If the latter fails to provide relevant information for the analysed AT value, then the search restarts at the paragraph level. Figure 5 shows the hierarchy of the contexts and the incremental application of the context-scanning rules. If the precise value cannot be assigned at the utterance level, then the strategy looks for markers in the complex sentence which contains the utterance. If the complex sentence does provide a relevant marker, usually a value-marker, the goal is achieved and the research stops. Otherwise, the research is resumed at paragraph level where the value-marker can be the value of a neighbouring simple or complex sentence. If the initial utterance is not a part of a complex sentence, the second level is skipped and the research is resumed directly at paragraph level.

The first level rules operate exclusively on linguistic markers: finite (conjugated) verb forms, adverbials and interjections. The rules at the second level operate on value-markers. Yet, some of the rules in compound sentences (of the form S_1 and S_2) look for particular syntactic structures. For example, a set of rules detects if the grammatical subjects and direct objects in both utterances of the compound sentence are identical or different. This information proves to be crucial for the identification of their AT values. The identity of subjects and objects in the constituent clauses of a compound sentence *usually* implies that the same entity (agent or object) appears in a temporally ordered sequence of situations. This configuration of situations rules out the possibility to consider the situations as simultaneously relevant and therefore each simple clause is assigned the value of past event in a dynamic homogeneous structure (S - subject, Ø - empty subject, O - object):

The Hindu rioters$_{<S1>}$ *have taken / took* the three Muslims$_{<O1>}$ out of their cars,   (12)
Ø$_{<S1>}$ *have stabbed / stabbed* them$_{<O1>}$ and Ø$_{<S1>}$ *have burned / burned* them$_{<O1>}$
(Le Monde CD-ROM)

---

[5]   By paragraph we shall understand the text included between two paragraph marks. If the paragraph contains one single sentence, the context-scanning strategy will launch the rules for simple or complex sentence, respectively.

paragraph

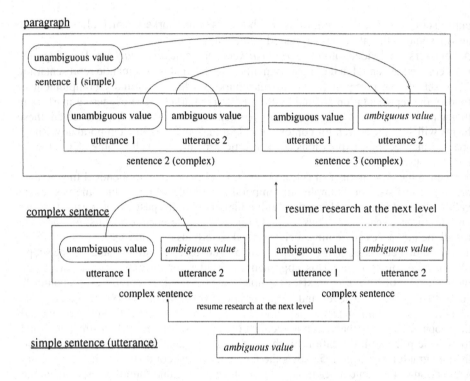

Fig. 5. The architecture of the context-scanning strategy

The goal of the rules operating on the third level[6] is to identify the temporal structure of the entire text. The rules are organised in a systemic network whose systems (choice points) lead to the selection of a precise temporal structure. Thus, all temporal structures can be seen as paths in the network representing various sets of options. Each option is a result of the operation of a context-scanning rule which detects the presence or the absence of different markers. Figure 6 (example 13) shows a piece of this network which allows to identify the temporal structure of texts containing forms of passé composé in French. The marked path reads: if the text contains only past tensed forms; if it only contains forms of *passé composé*; if the AT values of the utterances in the text are *state* or *ambiguous* (resulting state or past event), then the text has homogeneous static structure. This information allows to assign the value of *resulting state* to all ambiguous forms in the text.

> Nine booby-trapped cars, each stuffed up with 100 to 200 kg of dynamite, the   (13)
> evidence of their attacking capacity, *have been disactivated* in the capital of
> Antioqia. Seventy policemen *have been killed* in the city since Tyson's death -
> one of the accomplices of the godfather. Tyson *has been given up* by a colleague
> of his. Since his execution, the number of anonymous denunciations *has
> doubled.*(Le Monde CD-ROM)

---

6   So far, the set of rules covers the texts containing tensed forms of passé composé.

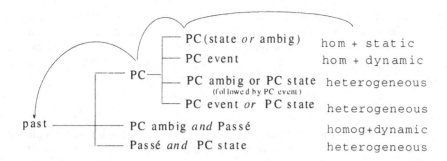

Fig. 6. The path of the multiple options points specifying the AT value in example 13

4 Formal Representations of AT Values and Temporal Structures

4.1 Formal Representations of AT Values

AT values of the situations are considered as complex aspecto-temporal operators which apply to their operands - atemporal and non-aspectualised predicative relations - in order to obtain temporal and aspectualised predicative relations (utterances). Complex operators combine several simple operators. Each of these simple operators conveys an important piece of aspecto-temporal information (Desclés 1994). Let's take as an example the utterance *Peter is writing a book.* It can be represented by the following expression in combinatorial logic (Curry & Feys 1968; Desclés 1990; Ginisti 1997): $\mathbf{X}$(write a_book Peter). $\mathbf{X}$ stands for the complex aspecto-temporal operator and (write a_book Peter) for the atemporal and non-aspectualised predicative relation $(P_2T^2T^1)$. (P_2) represents the binary predicate write and (T^2) and (T^1) its second and first argument, respectively, a_book and Peter.

The context-scanning rules assign to the situation in the above utterance the AT value of an ongoing process. This value is represented by a semi-open interval J^1 and expressed by the aspectual operator $ONG\text{-}PROC_J{}^1$. The latter operates on the atemporal and non-aspectualised predicative relation $(P_2T^2T^1)$ and transforms it into an atemporal but already aspectualised predicative relation $ONG\text{-}PROC_J{}^1$ $(P_2T^2T^1)$.

The position of all utterances is located with regard to the act of utterance represented by the predicative relation $SAY(\dots)S^0$. The binary predicate SAY stands for the enunciation activity, the symbol S^0 stands for the speaker and the missing element in brackets refers to the predicative relation expressed by the utterance. Like any other predicative relation which extends in time, the utterance act is also aspectualised. It receives the value of an ongoing process (semi-open interval J^0) as it represents an activity which has a beginning but no explicit end. Hence, the aspectualised predicative relation of the utterance act is rendered by the expression $ONG\text{-}PROC_J{}^0$ $(SAY(\dots)S^0)$ where the operator $ONG\text{-}PROC_J{}^0$ applies to $SAY(\dots)S^0$.

The aspectualised predicate relation $ONG\text{-}PROC_J{}^1(P_2T^2T^1)$ takes the position of the missing element and fits into the expression corresponding to the utterance act:

$$ONG\text{-}PROC_J{}^0(SAY(ONG\text{-}PROC_J{}^1 (P_2T^2T^1))S^0) \tag{14}$$

In order to complete the construction of the aspecto-temporal operator it is necessary to add the information about the intervals of the utterance act and the situation in the utterance. The present tense form detected by the context-scanning rules indicates that the right bounds (δ) of the intervals coincide: $([\delta(_J{}^1) = \delta(_J{}^0)])$. This information is integrated in the expression constructed so far by the simple operator &:

$$\&(\text{ONG-PROC}_J{}^0(\text{SAY}(\text{ONG-PROC}_J{}^1(P_2T^2T^1))S^0))([\delta(_J{}^1) = \delta(_J{}^0)]) \qquad (15)$$

By application of different combinators (complex operators) in combinatorial logic the above expression undergoes a procedure of integration (Desclés 1994, Vazov 1998). The output of this procedure is one single aspecto-temporal operator PRES-PROGR which operates over its sole operand, the predicative relation $(P_2T^2T^1)$:

$$\text{PRES-PROGR}\ (P_2T^2T^1) \qquad (16)$$

4.2 Formal Representation of Temporal Structures

Like AT values, temporal structures can also be represented as complex operators. The structures which do not contain inserted temporal structures are built incrementally (example 6). At the first step of construction, the value of the first utterance (V_1) applies as an operator to its operand (V_2), the value of the second one, to obtain a new operator (V_1V_2). This operator is in fact the temporal structure of the first two utterances. Then (V_1V_2) applies to the next operand (V_3) to obtain a new operator (($V_1V_2)V_3$) corresponding to the structure of the first three utterances. The values of all the utterances are organised in one complex operator (($V_1V_2)...V_{n-1})V_n$. This operator applies to the value of the last utterance (V_n) to produce the temporal structure of the entire text. Figure 7a shows the organisation of the values in a temporal structure containing 5 utterances and built incrementally. (*) stands for the operation of application.

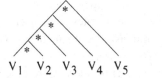
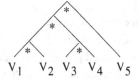

Fig. 7a. Temporal structure of example 6   **Fig. 7b.** Temporal structure of example 10

Temporal structures with inserted homogeneous dynamic structures organise the values in two complex operators, one for each temporal structure (example 10). The first two utterances form the operator (V_1V_2) and the third and the fourth one - the operator (V_3V_4). Then the operator (V_1V_2) applies to the operator (V_3V_4) to obtain the complex operator (($V_1V_2)(V_3V_4)$) whose sole operand is the value V_5. This configuration is shown on Figure 7b. The order of application of values is controlled by some combinator **X**. The latter encodes a programme which transforms the linear order of values, i.e. their order in the text, into a logical expression of operators and operands. This expression is the formal representation of the temporal structure of the text.
The values in the temporal structure on Figure 7a will be organised by the combinator

of identity **I** which postulates that each value operates on the next one, in order of their appearance: $IV_1V_2V_3V_4V_5 \rightarrow ((((V_1V_2)V_3)V_4)V_5)$.

In turn, the values on Figure 7b will be organised by the combinator **BB**. **B** is a binary complex operator. It composes two simple operators XY and postulates the order of their application - first, Y applies to the operand Z and then X applies to the obtained result: $BXYZ \rightarrow X(YZ)$ (Desclés 1990). The programme of the combinator **BB** allows to compose two sets of values. The first occurrence of **B** composes values which build the initial temporal structure, namely V_1V_2. The second occurrence composes the values which form the inserted temporal structure - V_3V_4. Eventually, the two pairs of values form a complex operator which applies to value V_5. The programme of transformations introduced by **BB** is shown in example 17:

$$BBV_1V_2V_3V_4V_5 \rightarrow B(V_1V_2)V_3V_4V_5 \rightarrow ((V_1V_2)(V_3V_4))V_5 \tag{17}$$

In order to represent temporal structures with a larger number of values, each occurrence of the combinator **B** can be raised to the power of n. Raised to the power of 2, **B** shall apply its programme twice: once to the initial linear order of values, and then to the result of the first transformation. For example, the combinator B^2B applied to $V_1V_2V_3V_4V_5V_6$ will produce the following expression: $B^2BV_1V_2V_3V_4V_5V_6 \rightarrow BB(V_1V_2)V_3V_4V_5V_6 \rightarrow B(V_1V_2V_3)V_4V_5V_6 \rightarrow ((V_1V_2V_3)(V_4V_5))V_6$. This expression will stand for an initial temporal structure containing three, instead of two, values (cf. Figure 7b and examples 10 & 17). Similarly, if the second occurrence of **B** is raised to the power of 2, the applicative expression will represent a structure with an inserted structure containing three values: $BB^2V_1V_2V_3V_4V_5V_6 \rightarrow B^2(V_1V_2)V_3V_4V_5V_6 \rightarrow B(V_1V_2)(V_3V_4)V_5V_6 \rightarrow ((V_1V_2)(V_3V_4V_5))V_6$.

The combinator of the temporal structures with inserted homogeneous dynamic structures can be defined as follows[7]:

$$B^{n-1}B^{m-(n+1)} \; V_1 \ldots\ldots V_nV_{n+1}\ldots\ldots V_mV_{m+1}\ldots\ldots \tag{18}$$

The use of applicative expressions with combinators proves to be well adapted for the formal representation of temporal structures. This is due to the fact that the temporal structures are determined by the interaction of various sets of operators and operands (aspecto-temporal values). The programmes encoded by the combinators allow to dynamically modify the order of applications which is crucial for the construction of the final temporal structure of texts.

5 Conclusion

This paper presented a method for temporal reasoning based on context-scanning rules. The method uses exclusively linguistic markers (finite verb forms, temporal and non-temporal adverbials, interjections, particular syntactic structures) which allow to carry out temporal reasoning centred on the act of utterance. Due to the information extracted

---

[7] It should be pointed out that the power raising in the algebra of combinators and in the algebra of real numbers are not identical. Thus, $4^2 4^2 = 4^{2+2}$, but $B^2 B^2 \neq B^{2+2}$. Consequently, the combinator $B^{n-1}B^{m-(n+1)}$ is not equivalent to $B^{n-1+m-n-1}$, or B^{m-2}, which determines the concatenation of the combinator of the entire temporal structure of texts with inserted structures.

from the analysed texts, the method is capable not only to interpret the aspecto-temporal values in isolated utterances but also to identify temporal structures of larger text units. The representation of the aspecto-temporal information by expressions in combinatory logic allows its machine processing. The method has already been implemented by members of LaLIC group at the Université Paris IV - Sorbonne. So far the computer programme is capable to assign AT values to isolated sentences containing finite verb forms of passé composé and imparfait in French. It is a module of a larger project on information retrieval.

References

1. Allen, J.: Temporal Reasoning and Planning. The Morgan Kaufmann Series in Representation & Reasoning. Y. Overton. San Mateo, CA, Morgan Kaufmann Publishers, Inc. (1991)
2. Bartsch, R.: Situations, Tense and Aspect (Dynamic Discourse Ontology and the Semantic Flexibility of Temporal System in German and English). Berlin-New York, Mouton de Gruyter (1995)
3. Bennett,W., Herlick,T., Hoyt,K., Liro,J., Santisteban,A.: Toward a Computational Model of Aspect and Verb Semantics. Linguistics Research Centre, University of Texas (1990)
4. Benveniste, É.: Problèmes de linguistique générale. Paris, Éditions Gallimard (1962)
5. Berri, J., Maire-Reppert, D., Oh, H. (eds.): Traitement informatique de la catégorie aspecto-temporelle. In: T.A.Informations . N°1 (1991) 77-90
6. Bestougeff, H., Ligozat, G.: Outils logiques pour le traitement du temps: de la linguistique à l'intelligence artificielle. Paris, Masson (1989)
7. Church, A.: The Calculi of Lambda-conversion, Princeton (1941)
8. Curry, H. B., Feys,R.: Combinatory Logic (1st edn. 1958), North-Holland Publishing Company (1968)
9. Desclés, J. P., Jouis, C.: Logiciels d'exploration contextuelle pour l'analyse sémantique de textes, Compte rendu de fin d'étude d'une recherche financée par le Ministère de la Recherche et de l'Espace. N°3, Centre d'analyse et mathématiques sociales, Paris (1993)
10. Desclés, J.-P.: Construction formelle de la catégorie grammaticale de l'aspect (essai). In: J. David, Martin, R. (eds.): Notion d'aspect. Paris, Klincksieck (1980) 198-237
11. Desclés, J.-P.: Langages applicatifs, langues naturelles et cognition. Hermès, Paris (1990)
12. Desclés, J.-P.: Archétypes cognitifs et types de procès. In: Travaux de Linguistique et de Philologie, N°XXIX, Paris, Klincksieck (1991) 171-195
13. Desclés, J.-P.: Calculs et raisonnements aspecto-temporels. In: Raisonnement et calcul. Université de Neuchâtel., Suisse, 63 (1994) 51-90
14. Dowty, D.: The effects of Aspectual Class on the Temporal Structure of Discourse: Semantics or Pragmatics? In: Linguistics and Philosophy, 9 (1986) 37-61
15. Gagnon, M.: Expression de la localisation temporelle dans un générateur de texte . Thèse de doctorat. Université de Montréal (1993)
16. Gagnon, M., Lapalme, G.: Prétexte: A Generator for the Expression of Temporal Information. Internal report, Institut de Recherche en Informatique de Toulouse - Université de Montréal (1995)
17. Ginisti, J.-P.: La logique combinatoire. Presses Universitaires de France, Paris (1997)
18. Hornstein, N.: As Time Goes By. Cambridge, Mass, A Bradford Book, The MIT Press (1993)
19. Jouis, C.: Contextual Approach: SEEK, a Linguistic and Computational Tool for Use in Knowledge Acquisition. In: Proceedings of First European Conference "Cognitive Science in Industry", Luxembourg (1994)
20. Maire-Reppert, D.:L'imparfait de l'indicatif en vue d'un traitement informatique du français: étude théorique et méthode de description avec ses conséquences didactiques dans l'enseignement des langues. Thèse de doctorat. Université de Paris IV - Sorbonne (1990)
21. Mourelatos, A. P. D.: Events, Processes and States. In: Linguistics and Philosophy: 2 (1978) 415-434
22. Oh, H.-G.: Les temps de l'indicatif du français en vue d'un traitement informatique: passé composé . Thèse de doctorat. CNRS - École des hautes études et sciences sociales - Université Paris IV - Sorbonne (1991)
23. Vazov, N.: Temporal Ambiguity in French (The Case of Passé Composé). In: Proceedings of Computer Science and Natural Language Processing, Dublin City University, Dublin (1996)
24. Vazov, N.: Identification des valeurs aspecto-temporelles de situations en vue de traitement automatique - Le cas de passé composé. Thèse de doctorat. Institut des sciences humaines appliquées - CAMS - Université Paris IV - Sorbonne (1998)
25. Verkuyl, H.: A Theory of Aspectuality. The Interaction between Temporal and Atemporal Structure. Cambridge University Press (1993)
26. Yip, K.: Tense, Aspect and the Cognitive Representation of Time. In: Proceedings of IJCAI-85 (1985)
27. Zablit, P.: Construction de l'interprétation temporelle en langue naturelle: un système fondé sur les graphes conceptuels . Thèse de doctorat. Université Paris-Sud, Orsay (1991)

The Role of Context in the Analysis and Design of Agent Programs

Wayne Wobcke

Intelligent Systems Research Group
BT Laboratories, MLB 1/PP 12
Martlesham Heath, Ipswich Suffolk IP5 3RE
United Kingdom

Abstract. We discuss the notion of context as applied to the verification of agent programs, and in particular, to the verification of agent programs based on the PRS agent architecture, Georgeff and Lansky [6]. Agent programs are an interesting domain for theories of context for the following reasons: (i) the context of an agent program has both internal (mental state) and external (embedding in the world) aspects, (ii) a logical theory of agent program verification using context-based reasoning must therefore address both syntactic and semantic issues, and (iii) the context of execution of an agent program is dynamic since agents are situated in a dynamically changing environment. We then consider the development of PRS agent programs from the designer's perspective, and present a logical system of context-based reasoning that enables PRS programs to be proven correct. The methodology involves the program designer constructing contexts for the various procedures used by the agent, so the variety of contexts relevant to the PRS agent is fixed in advance by the programmer and is highly constrained by the PRS agent architecture. The study of context in agent programs thus raises a wide range of general questions that may be considered in the more controlled settings of particular agent architectures and execution environments.

1 Introduction

In this paper, we discuss the notion of context as applied to the verification of agent programs, and in particular, to the verification of agent programs based on the PRS agent architecture, Georgeff and Lansky [6]. PRS and its successor dMARS are two of the most widely used architectures for building agent systems, and have been used in air traffic management, business process management and air combat modelling, Georgeff and Rao [7]. PRS is a type of *rational* agent architecture, by which is meant that it is based on taking seriously the notion of intention, e.g. as expounded by Bratman [3]. Agent programs are an interesting domain for theories of context for the following reasons: (i) the context of an agent program has both internal (mental state) and external (embedding in the world) aspects, (ii) a logical theory of agent program verification using context-based reasoning must therefore address both syntactic and semantic issues, and (iii) the context of execution of an agent program is dynamic since agents are situated in a dynamically changing environment. Compared to studies of context in, for example, natural language understanding, the analysis of agent programs requires addressing a similarly wide range of issues, but in a limited, although still potentially highly complex, setting. As a result, we believe that fundamental questions about the role that contextual reasoning plays in cognitive architectures may be illuminated by studying agent architectures.

A second, and perhaps as important, motivation of this work is to consider agent programs for the PRS architecture from the perspective of the program designer. We shall propose a logical system that uses context-based reasoning that enables, under some simplifying assumptions, PRS agent programs to be proven correct. The methodology involves the program designer *constructing* various contexts with respect to which different subprograms work correctly (each PRS procedure comes with a 'context', a formula which must be true in any state in which the procedure is executing). Thus in a very real sense, the variety of contexts encountered by a PRS agent is determined in advance by the programmer. In constructing these contexts, the program designer must pay attention to both internal and external aspects of context: internal in that the operation of the agent program is dependent on the beliefs, desires and intentions of the system, and external in that the execution is embedded in the real world. The view of context arising from this work is then that the context of an agent program is an interdependent combination of internal (representational) aspects and external (execution) aspects arising out of the interaction of an agent with its environment, the nature of which is highly constrained by the agent architecture. Thus we believe architectural considerations assume an importance that has perhaps not always been recognized in earlier research.

In outline, our approach is based on viewing PRS as a simplified operating system capable of concurrently running a series of plans, each of which at any time is in a state of partial execution. The system uses a simplified interrupt mechanism which enables it, using information about goal priorities, to "recover" from various contingencies that arise during program execution so that blocked plans can be resumed and eventually completed. The designer must reason both *within* contexts to verify subprograms, and *between* contexts to verify whole agent programs. Our formalism extends a logic for reasoning about explicit contexts initially developed in Wobcke [20] with additional inference rules specifically for reasoning about PRS programs. The semantics of our earlier formalism was based on situation semantics, Barwise and Perry [1]; the semantics of PRS programs is based on dynamic logic, and thus programs are construed as state transition functions (but where in Computer Science, the states are internal machine states, our states are external world states).

The organization of the paper is as follows. In section 2, we discuss general issues in the formalization of context that further motivate this line of research. In section 3, we review the PRS architecture, and in section 4, present a simple method for constructing PRS agent programs. We give a formalism for reasoning about PRS program construction based on our methodology in section 5, and illustrate the use of the formalism with a simple correctness proof.

2   Context: Logical Considerations

The study of agent programs requires a wide range of general issues to be addressed: in this section, we discuss related work bearing on logical considerations (syntax and semantics of logical formalisms), and what we call architectural considerations (highlighting the role of agent architecture in more general questions of context-based reasoning).

Perhaps the starting point for logical theories of context is possible worlds semantics, in which the truth conditions for natural language sentences are relative to possible worlds. Various authors construe possible worlds in different ways, e.g. work on formal semantics typically makes no particular assumption about possible worlds except that they play a pragmatic role in the development of a semantic theory (a similar position to that taken by Stalnaker [18]), whereas Kripke [10] and Lewis [13] argue that possible worlds are real entities, metaphysical 'ways the world might have been'.

Barwise and Perry [1] questioned the role of such unanalysed constructs in developing a 'real' (as opposed to formal) semantic theory for language, and proposed the use of situations (parts of the world) as the basis of an alternative theory, in part based on Dretske's theory of information flow [4]. In particular, they advocated a relational theory of meaning in which sentence meaning was relative to context. The context of an utterance was further decomposed into the discourse situation (speaker beliefs) and resource situation (external world).

Concordant with, but predating, possible worlds semantics is modal logic. Concerning situation semantics, various logical formalisms have been proposed, but most related work borrows from partial logic, e.g. Blamey [2]. In Wobcke [20], we developed a logic of explicit contexts containing formulae of the form $c : \phi$ in which c denotes a situation and ϕ a fact or event. The semantics was based on supervaluations, a method originally developed by van Fraassen [19] for dealing with truth value gaps that preserves all the axioms of standard propositional calculus (so a formula such as $\phi \vee \neg\phi$ is a tautology). A supervaluation is essentially a set of interpretations, so in our approach, a situation was modelled as a set of propositional models.

McCarthy [14] also presented a logic for reasoning with explicit contexts. Compared to our work, this approach focuses more on inter-contextual reasoning: in Wobcke [20, 21], we treated nested contexts using conditional sentences, following Lewis [12]. Similar logical formalisms have been used in the CYC project, Lenat and Guha [11], and by Giunchiglia and Serafini [8]. However, a major drawback of these approaches is the lack of any formal, or even intuitive, semantics for contexts. The point here is the familiar one that, although syntactic formalisms can be studied in isolation, the use of logic in a particular AI application (or in the study of the relationship between language and the world) is as much driven by modelling considerations of a semantic nature as by intuitions about formal rules. In particular, in the case of logics of context, unless it is made clear what context symbols represent, there is no guarantee that any particular formal theory applies in any particular problem domain. This is nowhere more so than with agent programs, in which the context is an execution state of an agent program which has an external (real world) aspect and an internal (mental state) aspect. With a logical system for reasoning about agent programs, the two aspects must mesh or else the formalism does not accurately describe the agent's behaviour.

This is the methodology informing our earlier work and which is also adopted here; however, where in the earlier work a context symbol denotes a situation modelled as a set of possible models, in the present work a context symbol denotes a set of world states forming the execution context of a PRS program (representing the given context formula of the PRS procedure). Reasoning about PRS programs is reasoning about the execution of procedures in context, for which we use dynamic logic, and about the interactions between the execution contexts of different procedures, for which we use our general framework for context-based reasoning augmented with specific inference rules.

For PRS agent programs, context has both an internal and external aspect. The external aspect refers to the world states in which the program is executing. The internal aspect refers to the beliefs, desires and intentions of the agent, which influence the decisions made by the interpreter, mainly concerning which action to execute and how to update the internal state. Properties of the architecture determine when decisions are made and the range of options available to the agent; thus architectural considerations are central in theorizing about agent program verification. Another way of looking at the two aspects of context is that the external context provides the background against which actions executed by the agent to fulfil its intentions are performed, c.f. Searle [17], while the internal context determines how, when and which intentions are fulfilled.

3 PRS Agent Programs

PRS (*Procedural Reasoning System*) was initially described in Georgeff and Lansky [6]. Basically, PRS agent programs (as I will call them) are collections of plans, officially called Knowledge Areas (KAs). These plans are essentially the same as standard plans in the Artificial Intelligence literature, in that they have a *precondition* (a condition under which the plan can be executed), an *effect* (a condition which successful execution of the plan will achieve), and a *body* (a collection of subactions which when successfully executed will achieve the effect). The body of a plan is very similar to a standard computer program, except that there can be subgoals of the form *achieve g*, meaning that the system should achieve the goal *g* in whichever way is convenient: these are the analogues of procedure calls. In addition, PRS plans have a *context* (a condition that must be true when each action in the plan is initiated), a *trigger* (a condition that indicates when the interpreter should consider the plan for execution), a *termination condition* (a condition indicating when the plan should be dropped), and a *priority* (a number indicating how important the plan's goal is to achieve). The trigger is important in dynamic settings: when there are a number of ways of achieving a particular goal, the trigger helps the interpreter to find the "best" way of achieving the goal, given the current execution context. Note that due to unforeseen changes in the world, the execution context of a goal cannot always be predicted at planning time. The priority of each plan enables the system to determine which plan to pursue given limited resources (usually a plan with the highest priority is chosen for execution). Thus the use of triggers embodies a kind of "forward-directed" reactive reasoning, whereas goal reduction embodies a kind of "backward-directed" goal-driven reasoning. It is this combination of techniques which gives PRS its power.

The original definition of PRS allowed for meta-KAs, or plans that are used to determine which other plans to execute. But in practice, these meta-plans have not been widely used, and so Rao and Georgeff [16] defined the simplified PRS interpreter shown in Figure 1. In the following abstract interpreter, the system state consists of a set of beliefs B, goals G and intentions I. Each intention is, in effect, a partially executed program which has been interrupted due to a higher priority goal being pursued. Each cycle of the interpreter runs as follows. The process begins with the collection of external events recorded in an event queue, each of which may trigger pre-existing plans. Simple deliberation determines which plan is chosen for execution (usually a plan with the highest priority). The first action in this plan is then executed. After obtaining new external events, the set of system plans is updated. First, those plans which have completed execution are discarded from the set I, then the system drops those plans which are determined to be impossible as a result of changes to the world or lack of resources.

```
PRS Interpreter:
    initialize-state();
    do
        options := option-generator(event-queue, B, G, I);
        selected-options := deliberate(options, B, G, I);
        update-intentions(selected-options, I);
        execute(I);
        get-new-external-events();
        drop-successful-attitudes(B, G, I);
        drop-impossible-attitudes(B, G, I)
    until quit
```

Fig. 1. PRS Interpreter

We assume the above version of PRS in this paper. Moreover, we make the following further simplifying assumptions.

- Deliberation always chooses the highest priority intention for execution.
- The priority of any subgoal of a plan is at least that of the original plan.

This means that we can effectively view PRS as a kind of operating system executing a number of interruptible processes, each process corresponding to one high level intention. Each process consists of a list of partially executed plans suspended at a call to achieve some subgoal, ordered according to the priority of the subgoals (higher level subgoals having lower priority). An interrupt occurs when an external event means that the current plan can no longer be executed. The interrupt is handled successfully when it triggers a plan that enables the system to "recover" from the change in the world to a point where the original plan can be resumed. Provided the programmer has defined sufficient contingency plans, i.e. at least one for each possible context in which each possible contingency can occur, the system should be able to recover and successfully achieve any assigned goal. Note the recursion inherent in this definition in that there can be contingencies to contingencies, i.e. contingencies that arise while a contingency plan is being executed.

4 PRS Program Construction

Our treatment of correctness relies on a particular approach to the construction of PRS programs which we present in this section, then formalize in section 5. Consider designing a plan to achieve a particular goal g. We give the following intuitive picture as to how this might be done, taking for now the simple case in which it is assumed that there are no calls to subgoals and no contingencies that arise during execution. Recall that each plan has an associated context, a condition that must be true throughout the plan's execution. It seems natural to start by determining a collection of possible initial states S, then proceed by dividing this set into subsets of states S_i such that for each subset S_i, it is possible to define a single plan P_i that can achieve g without leaving the states in S_i (except possibly at the end of the plan, when g itself is true). The subsets S_i need not be disjoint, but their union should equal S. The next task is to define formulae c_i that characterize the S_i, meaning that each c_i is true of all the states in S_i but not true of any state not in S_i (because P_i does not work in these states)—this is not necessarily straightforward! The correctness of the plan P_i can be expressed as the dynamic logic formula $c_i \Rightarrow [P_i]g$, and proven so using standard techniques. Furthermore, the formula $c_1 \vee \cdots \vee c_n$ (assuming there are a finite number of contexts $1, \cdots, n$) characterizes the set of initial states S, and the assumption that S contains all the possible initial states is expressed by the formula $\Box(c_1 \vee \cdots \vee c_n)$. From this and the correctness of the individual plans, it follows that $([P_1]g \vee \cdots \vee [P_n]g)$.

Now consider designing plans to respond to "procedure calls", i.e. to satisfy subgoals of the form *achieve g* occurring in a plan P. The plan will have a context c that characterizes a set of states S: each state in S is one in which P achieves its goal, assuming that all the calls to *achieve g* succeed. Note first that, not only should the procedure achieve g, but it should also maintain the context c. Thus the context of the subprogram should entail c. Now we may proceed as above, decomposing S into subsets S_i, characterizing those subsets by context formulae c_i, and defining plans P_i with contexts c_i that achieve g. The priorities of each subplan P_i should be at least that of P. It is apparent that by repeating this process for calls to achieve subgoals within subprograms, the programmer defines a hierarchy of contexts by continually partitioning the original set of states S. For each subprogram P_i with set of states S_i and context c_i of a plan P with set of states S and context c, we have that $S_i \subseteq S$ and $c_i \vdash c$. That is, the hierarchy forms a partial order on sets of states with the ordering inherited from set inclusion. Note that, as above, from a collection of formulae $c_i \Rightarrow [P_i]g$ for $i = 1, \cdots, n$, it follows that $c \Rightarrow ([P_1]g \vee \cdots \vee [P_n]g)$, where $c \equiv c_1 \vee \cdots \vee c_n$.

The next stage is to consider the contingencies that can arise while executing a plan P. The purpose of the contingency plans is, whenever possible, to restore the context of the original plan c (or if this is impossible, to cause the original plan to be dropped by achieving $\neg c$). However, it is not necessary that *each* contingency plan achieve c: below, we give a simple example where executing a *sequence* of contingency plans restores c. Moreover, a contingency plan need not directly achieve c; rather it can block the original plan from being executed until c is true. This is also illustrated in the example below. Even so, it seems natural to start with a set of states S that defines when the contingency occurs, and to divide this set into subsets for each of which a contingency plan can be defined. The priority of any contingency plan must be greater than that of the original plan to ensure that the contingency plan is chosen by the interpreter for execution in preference to the original plan. Any subgoals in the contingency plan can be handled as described above. Now by repeating this process, i.e. by defining contingencies to handle contingencies, the programmer also defines a hierarchy of contexts, but in contrast to that defined for subprograms, this is a hierarchy of exceptions. That is, if P_i is a contingency plan with set of states S_i and context c_i, for a plan P with set of states S and context c, then there is no necessary relationship between S_i and S, nor between c_i and c. The whole design process stops when there are no remaining contingencies to consider.

For example, consider designing a simplified program for an aircraft to take off. Assume the basic takeoff plan can be defined, and succeeds provided the runway is free. That is, the condition $\neg runway\_free$ is a contingency. Two plans are defined to deal with this contingency, differing in their context of application. In one, the plane is on the runway and must be diverted; in the other, the plane is not on the runway and simply waits. Note the subtleties in even this program: the *divert* plan does not restore the original context *runway_free*, but changes the context to $\neg on\_runway$ so that the *wait* plan is invoked. Also, the *wait* plan may be repeatedly invoked until its trigger is false; when this is the case, the context of the *takeoff* plan is true, so this plan can be resumed. It only remains to assign priorities to the plans such that the contingency plans have higher priority than the *takeoff* plan (this can be done in any way convenient, so just let the priority of *takeoff* be 10 and the priority of *divert* and *wait* be 20).

The final program is shown in Figure 2. Boxes indicate contexts and an arrow from one context to another indicates that the first handles a contingency that can arise while the second is executing.

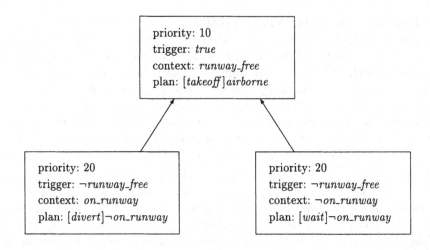

Fig. 2. Takeoff Program

5 Correctness of Agent Programs

We now present a formalism that can be used to reason about PRS programs constructed as in section 4. The essence of the formalism is the combination of dynamic logic and context-based reasoning, Wobcke [20, 21]. The technical formalism is related to labelled deductive systems, Gabbay [5], in which each formula is assigned a label, signifying a context in which the formula is true. For a formula representing the correctness of a plan, the label can be identified with the possible execution contexts of the plan, and hence the label also indirectly represents a set of assumptions under which the plan can be proven correct.

More precisely, we define a formal language LPDL (*Labelled Propositional Dynamic Logic*), whose atomic formulae are of the form $l : A$ where l is drawn from a given set of *labels* and A is a formula of propositional dynamic logic. In this section, we first review dynamic logic and present our approach to context-based reasoning, then define rules for reasoning about PRS agent plans, which are illustrated using the aircraft takeoff plan.

5.1 Formal Semantics

In propositional dynamic logic, Pratt [15], program execution is modelled using state transition functions. But whereas in Computer Science the states are internal machine states, in AI the states are external world states, and where in Computer Science the programs are guaranteed to succeed (if they terminate), in AI actions are not guaranteed to be successful. Moreover, in Computer Science the internal machine states change only as the result of the program's execution, whereas in AI there may be unforeseen changes to the world that are not the result of any action of the agent.

The formal language we use is a propositional dynamic logic, consisting of a set of formulae defined as follows, see Goldblatt [9]. First, program terms are built from atomic action symbols and the connectives ; (sequencing), ∪ (non-deterministic alternation), * (iteration) and ? (test). Formulae are built from a set of atomic proposition symbols that can be combined in the usual way with the connectives ¬, ∧, ∨ and ⇒, and modal operators $[\pi]$ for each program term π. Here $[\pi]A$ is intended to indicate that A is true in all possible states that result from the successful execution of π. Note that the standard programming constructs can be defined in terms of these primitives as follows.

$$\textbf{if } A \textbf{ then } \alpha \textbf{ else } \beta \equiv (A?; \alpha) \cup (\neg A?; \beta)$$
$$\textbf{while } A \textbf{ do } \alpha \equiv (A?; \alpha)^*; \neg A?$$

The semantics of dynamic logic is based on binary state transition relations. More precisely, an interpretation M consists of a modal frame F and a valuation on atomic proposition symbols V. The frame F consists of a nonempty set of states S together with a binary relation R_π on S for each program term π. The valuation V is a mapping from the set of atomic proposition symbols to the power set of S.

Satisfaction at a state s in an interpretation M is defined as follows.

$M \models_s A$ iff $s \in V(A)$ for A an atomic formula
$M \models_s \neg A$ iff $M \not\models_s A$
$M \models_s A \wedge B$ iff $M \models_s A$ and $M \models_s B$
$M \models_s A \vee B$ iff $M \models_s A$ or $M \models_s B$
$M \models_s A \Rightarrow B$ iff $M \not\models_s A$ or $M \models_s B$
$M \models_s [\pi]A$ iff for all t such that $R_\pi(s, t)$, $M \models_t A$

Finally, there are a number of constraints on the R_π to ensure that each reflects the operational semantics of the program construction operations.

$R_{\alpha;\beta} = R_\alpha \circ R_\beta = \{(s, t) : \exists u (R_\alpha(s, u) \text{ and } R_\beta(u, t))\}$
$R_{\alpha \cup \beta} = R_\alpha \cup R_\beta$
$R_{\alpha^*} = R_\alpha^*$ (the transitive closure of R_α)
$R_{A?} = \{(s, s) : M \models_s A\}$

It can be shown, Goldblatt [9], that the following axiom schemata and rule are sound and complete with respect to the above semantics (that includes the constraints on the R_π).

$[\alpha; \beta]A \Leftrightarrow [\alpha][\beta]A$
$[\alpha \cup \beta]A \Leftrightarrow ([\alpha]A \wedge [\beta]A)$
$[\alpha^*]A \Rightarrow (A \wedge [\alpha][\alpha^*]A)$
$[\alpha^*](A \Rightarrow [\alpha]A) \Rightarrow (A \Rightarrow [\alpha^*]A)$
$[A?]B \Leftrightarrow (A \Rightarrow B)$
$[\alpha](A \Rightarrow B) \Rightarrow ([\alpha]A \Rightarrow [\alpha]B)$
If $\vdash A$ infer $[\alpha]A$

We now define a formal language **LPDL** (*Labelled Propositional Dynamic Logic*) for use in context-based reasoning. The atomic formulae of **LPDL** are of the form $l : A$, where l is drawn from a given set of *labels* and A is a formula of propositional dynamic logic. These atomic formulae can be combined using the propositional connectives ¬, ∧, ∨ and ⇒. An **LPDL** interpretation I is an assignment of a dynamic logic interpretation M_l to each label l. Satisfaction of **LPDL** formulae is defined as follows.

$$I \models l : A \text{ iff } M_l \models A \text{ for } A \text{ an atomic LPDL formula}$$
$$I \models \neg A \text{ iff } I \not\models A$$
$$I \models A \wedge B \text{ iff } I \models A \text{ and } I \models B$$
$$I \models A \vee B \text{ iff } I \models A \text{ or } I \models B$$
$$I \models A \Rightarrow B \text{ iff } I \not\models A \text{ or } I \models B$$

It is straightforward to axiomatize LPDL, given an axiomatization of dynamic logic. LPDL contains all instances of propositional calculus axioms and modus ponens obtained by replacing an atomic proposition symbol by an LPDL formula, and the following axiom schemes in which l stands for any possible label.

$$l : A \text{ for } A \text{ an axiom of propositional dynamic logic}$$
$$l : (A \Rightarrow B) \Rightarrow (l : A \Rightarrow l : B)$$
$$l : A \Rightarrow \neg(l : \neg A)$$
$$l : A \Rightarrow l : \Box A$$

5.2 Reasoning About Correctness

The reasoning behind the process of designing PRS programs described in section 4 is essentially one of combining context-based reasoning for reasoning between contexts with dynamic logic for reasoning within contexts. For a given PRS program, there are numerous contexts that need to be considered. First, each plan is associated with a labelled context that corresponds to its execution context, as illustrated for the takeoff plan in Figure 2. Second, each contingency is itself associated with a labelled context corresponding to the execution contexts of the set of plans that may be invoked to deal with the contingency. Finally, each priority level is associated with a labelled context corresponding to the execution contexts of the set of plans of that priority—these are plans that can possibly compete with each other for selection by the interpreter for execution.

A proof of correctness of a PRS program proceeds in stages, mirroring the design process. First, standard techniques are used to show correctness of plans and subprograms that execute in a single context. These proofs are all on the assumption that execution never leaves the assigned context, except possibly at the end of the plan when the goal is achieved. Next, reasoning between contexts is used to infer that all contingencies that arise during the execution of any plan can be successfully met. Any such proof of correctness is therefore reliant on the programmer's having identified the range of possible contingencies to any plan. Finally, conclusions about lower level plans are "lifted" to higher level contexts, and the process repeated until the top level plans are reached. We present three rules corresponding to these types of inference. The soundness of these inference rules follows from properties of the PRS interpreter. We take it that they are intuitively correct, although future work would be to formalize the interpreter shown in Figure 1 to a degree where this could be verified formally.

A proof begins with assumptions about the lowest level plans in the hierarchy, and proceeds inductively according to the structure of the context hierarchy, as indicated in the plan in Figure 2. The required assumptions all mean that there are no exceptions arising at the lowest level (highest priority) plans, and all have the following form.

$$c : \Box((context \lor goal) \land \neg termination)$$

We need *context* $\lor$ *goal* rather than just *context* because of the technical complication that the final state in the plan's execution may not satisfy the context formula (it satisfies the goal formula). We envisage, therefore, that the proof of correctness for the plan involves verifying that the goal formula is false after execution of each subaction in the plan, except possibly at the final state.

The Contingency Rule is used to infer that all contingency plans achieve some goal g. Here Achieves(g) (used informally to mean something like *eventually*) is a special formula intended to indicate that the agent has a plan or plans that achieve g, and knows in which context to execute which plan. Here $l_1, \cdots l_n$ are any finite number of context labels.

$$\frac{l_1 : t \Rightarrow [\alpha_1]g, \cdots, l_n : t \Rightarrow [\alpha_n]g}{l_1 \cup \cdots \cup l_n : t \Rightarrow \text{Achieves}(g)} \quad (Contingency \ Rule)$$

The onus is on the programmer, when applying this rule, to ensure that $l_1, \cdots l_n$ denote *all* the contexts that correspond to a plan dealing with the given contingency. Typically these plans are all at the same level of priority.

The Priority Rule is used to infer that out of all plans that have a given priority (the same priority as a contingency plan), the agent can achieve some goal. This rule is needed to ensure that the interpreter is still able to choose the correct plan(s) for execution when it must choose from a larger set of plans. The rule is as follows, assuming that $l_1, \cdots, l_n$ are all the plans that have priority p, and that p is also a new context label. It is intended that t denote a trigger for a contingency, and g the goal achieved by the contingency plans.

$$\frac{l_1 : t \Rightarrow \text{Achieves}(g), \cdots, l_n : t \Rightarrow \text{Achieves}(g)}{p : t \Rightarrow \text{Achieves}(g)} \quad (Priority \ Rule)$$

The Lifting Rule connects contingency plans to the higher level plans from which their contingency derives. We use the rule to infer that in the higher level context the contingency can be handled correctly. The statement of the rule assumes that the priority of the plan in context c is less than p. Again, t denotes a trigger and g the goal achieved by the contingency plans.

$$\frac{p : t \Rightarrow \text{Achieves}(g)}{c : \Box(t \Rightarrow g)} \quad (Lifting \ Rule)$$

Intuitively, while the trigger t is true and the goal g is not true, the agent's execution is in context p, hence all states in c satisfy the negation of $t \land \neg g$, i.e. $t \Rightarrow g$.

To illustrate the use of these rules in reasoning about PRS programs, consider the aircraft takeoff plan from Figure 2. We first assign labels (arbitrarily) to the execution contexts of the plans; let c correspond to *takeoff*, c_1 to *divert* and c_2 to *wait*. The reasoning starts at the leaves of the tree, where it is assumed there are no contingencies that arise during the context of executing these plans. In this example, the assumptions that are needed are as follows.

$$c_1 : \Box(on\_runway \lor \neg on\_runway) \tag{1}$$

$$c_2 : \Box(\neg on\_runway \lor \neg on\_runway) \tag{2}$$

Assumption (1) is trivially true: it implies that there is no logical need for an exception to the *divert* plan. Intuitively this is because whenever such an exception could arise, the goal would already be true. However this does not preclude the possibility of plan failure for other reasons, and this could mean that further contingency plans are required. Assumption (2) is nontrivial: it states that when executing the *wait* plan, it is assumed that the plane is not on the runway. This would be false if it were possible for some event to cause the plane to become on the runway whilst waiting: this also could be reason for another contingency plan (perhaps the *divert* plan could be reused, although this would have to be verified).

By constructing the proof, we aim to verify the following formula, which represents the assumption under which the *takeoff* plan should be proven correct.

$$c : \Box(runway\_free \lor airborne) \tag{3}$$

Forming the basis of the proof, we assume that the following formulae representing the correctness of the individual plans relative to their execution contexts can be proven using dynamic logic using the above assumptions. Each formula says that whenever the plan is initiated in a state in which its context is true, the plan achieves its goal.

$$c : \Box(runway\_free \Rightarrow [takeoff]airborne) \tag{4}$$

$$c_1 : \Box(on\_runway \Rightarrow [divert]\neg on\_runway) \tag{5}$$

$$c_2 : \Box(\neg on\_runway \Rightarrow [wait]\neg on\_runway) \tag{6}$$

As an aside, the following formulae can also be proven using standard dynamic logic.

$$c_1 : \neg on\_runway \Rightarrow [wait^*]\neg on\_runway \tag{7}$$

$$c_2 : on\_runway \Rightarrow [divert; wait^*]\neg on\_runway \tag{8}$$

These formulae indicate that both $[wait^*]$ and $[divert; wait^*]$ are possible plans in their respective these contexts, but note that it does not follow that these are the *only* plans that can be executed in these contexts.

Now we need to start reasoning about contexts. Let $c_1 \cup c_2$ denote the context corresponding to the contingency $\neg runway\_free$. In the present example, the Contingency Rule enables the inference of the following formula from (5) and (6), which means that in every context associated with the contingency $\neg runway\_free$, the condition $\neg on\_runway$ is achieved.

$$c_1 \cup c_2 : \neg runway\_free \Rightarrow \mathsf{Achieves}(\neg on\_runway) \tag{9}$$

The Priority Rule is now used to infer the following formula, which means that the set of plans at priority 20 handle the contingency $\neg runway\_free$ correctly (recall that the contingency plans both have priority 20).

$$20 : \neg runway\_free \Rightarrow \mathsf{Achieves}(\neg on\_runway) \tag{10}$$

Finally, the Lifting Rule is used to prove the following formula, meaning that while the plane is attempting to take off, it is not on the runway unless the runway is free. This represents a "safety" condition that it is desirable to verify in this example.

$$c : \Box(\neg runway\_free \Rightarrow \neg on\_runway) \tag{11}$$

This means that the following formula holds at every state in context c, and so is a candidate for the context of the *takeoff* plan.

$$on\_runway \Rightarrow runway\_free \tag{12}$$

But (12) does not entail the plan's current context $runway\_free$. However, it is apparent that (12) more correctly represents the plan's context—in the sense that if it does not represent the context, there is no guarantee the plan will work (with the current plan, it is assumed, but not required, that the plane is always on the runway). It should therefore be possible to prove (4) using this weaker context assumption. Alternatively, the condition $\neg on\_runway$ could be added as a termination condition for the *takeoff* plan, so that (12) together with the negation of this condition imply the current context. In either case, the proof of correctness for the modified plan is now complete.

6 Conclusion

Agent programs provide an interesting domain for theories of context for the following reasons: (i) the context of an agent program has both internal (mental state) and external (embedding in the world) aspects, (ii) a logical theory of agent program verification using context-based reasoning must therefore address both syntactic and semantic issues, and (iii) the context of execution of an agent program is dynamic since agents are situated in a dynamically changing environment. Architectural constraints are important in defining the allowable contexts of interaction between an agent and the world, and consequently for reasoning about the correctness of agent programs. We have developed a formal method for verifying PRS programs based on reasoning within contexts (using dynamic logic) for verifying individual procedures, and reasoning between contexts (using special inference rules) for verifying whole agent programs. The principal advantage of using context-based reasoning is that this provides a way for the designer of a system to manage the complexity involved in developing agent programs. More precisely, the designer is able to concentrate on a subset (hierarchically ordered) of the possible execution contexts, rather than having to consider all possible worlds (or equivalently, all possible sets of beliefs, goals and intentions). Thus the task of reasoning about correctness is significantly simplified.

References

1. Barwise, J. & Perry, J. (1983) *Situations and Attitudes*. MIT Press, Cambridge, MA.
2. Blamey, S. (1986) 'Partial Logic.' in Gabbay, D.M. & Guenthner, F. (Eds) *Handbook of Philosophical Logic. Volume 3*. Reidel, Dordrecht.
3. Bratman, M.E. (1987) *Intention, Plans and Practical Reason*. Harvard University Press, Cambridge, MA.
4. Dretske, F.I. (1981) *Knowledge and the Flow of Information*. Blackwell, Oxford.
5. Gabbay, D.M. (1996) *Labelled Deductive Systems. Volume 1*. Oxford University Press, Oxford.
6. Georgeff, M.P. & Lansky, A.L. (1987) 'Reactive Reasoning and Planning.' *Proceedings of the Sixth National Conference on Artificial Intelligence (AAAI-87)*, 677–682.
7. Georgeff, M.P. & Rao, A.S. (1998) 'Rational Software Agents: From Theory to Practice.' in Jennings, N.R. & Wooldridge, M.J. (Eds) *Agent Technology*. Springer-Verlag, Berlin.
8. Giunchiglia, F. & Serafini, L. (1994) 'Multilanguage Hierarchical Logics (or: How we can do without modal logics).' *Artificial Intelligence*, **65**, 29–70.
9. Goldblatt, R. (1992) *Logics of Time and Computation. Second Edition*. Center for the Study of Language and Information, Stanford, CA.
10. Kripke, S.A. (1972) 'Naming and Necessity.' in Davidson, D. & Harman, G. (Eds) *Semantics for Natural Language*. Reidel, Dordrecht.
11. Lenat, D.B. & Guha, R.V. (1991) *Building Large Knowledge-Based Systems*. Addison-Wesley, Reading, MA.
12. Lewis, D.K. (1973) *Counterfactuals*. Blackwell, Oxford.
13. Lewis, D.K. (1986) *On the Plurality of Worlds*. Blackwell, Oxford.
14. McCarthy, J.M. (1993) 'Notes on Formalizing Context.' *Proceedings of the Thirteenth International Joint Conference on Artificial Intelligence*, 81–98.
15. Pratt, V.R. (1976) 'Semantical Considerations on Floyd-Hoare Logic.' *Proceedings of the Seventeenth IEEE Symposium on Foundations of Computer Science*, 109–121.
16. Rao, A.S. & Georgeff, M.P. (1992) 'An Abstract Architecture for Rational Agents.' *Proceedings of the Third International Conference on Principles of Knowledge Representation and Reasoning*, 439–449.
17. Searle, J.R. (1983) *Intentionality*. Cambridge University Press, Cambridge.
18. Stalnaker, R.C. (1984) *Inquiry*. MIT Press, Cambridge, MA.
19. van Fraassen, B.C. (1966) 'Singular Terms, Truth-value Gaps, and Free Logic.' *Journal of Philosophy*, **63**, 481–495.
20. Wobcke, W.R. (1988) *A Logical Approach to Schema-Based Inference*. Ph.D. Thesis, Department of Computer Science, University of Essex.
21. Wobcke, W.R. (1989) 'A Schema-Based Approach to Understanding Subjunctive Conditionals.' *Proceedings of the Eleventh International Joint Conference on Artificial Intelligence*, 1461–1466.

Context and Supercontext

R. A. Young

Philosophy Department, University of Dundee, Scotland
r.a.young@dundee.ac.uk

Abstract. Think of a context as expressed in a language which an agent, at some time, is learning to apply by some finite means to some aspect of the world. Think of that aspect as one amongst indefinitely many others. Think of the language as having a model or set of models whose domain consists of components of that aspect. Thus the language has a set of local models, see Giunchiglia and Ghidini[3]. The context may be defined in terms of that set of local models. Think of a possibility (as opposed to a possible world) as something that is partial, as argued by Humberstone [6]. In contrast, many philosophers discuss semantics as if (in principle) there is some complete language of fundamental (base) description for the world and its associated set of scientifically possible worlds. The complete language for describing the base might be identified with the language of a final theory of physics. This papers offers a critique of the view that there is even in principle a final theory of physics. The argument is based on a proof in algorithmic information theory by Chaitin [1, 2]. The paper sketches a view, based on possibilities and local models semantics, of how to think of semantics in a world in which there is not, even in principle, a complete language of base description. It sketches an ontology for this world. If there is a supercontext, then it will not itself be a context. This is because it will not be completely describable using a finitely intelligible language. Each aspect of it will be describable in this way, but it itself will be ineffable.

1 Introduction

One standard meaning of the term context in philosophy of language is the situation in which a linguistic act occurs, as recognised in Hale and Wright [5][p.657]. Indexicals and demonstratives as they are used in speech acts, reference and the illocutionary force of speech acts may all be understood as being dependent on context in this sense. The place and time is understood as being at some index in a possible world (the actual world is understood to be one amongst other possible worlds). Each possible world is understood to be completely determinate. It has a complete fundamental description in some metalanguage. This is a standard meaning in philosophy of language, but analytic philosophy of language and analytic philosophy of mind are closely related. Therefore this view is standard in philosophy of mind as well. Thus, mental content may be understood to be dependent on context. In contrast, we may think of the context as something that is available to the agent. What agents can use in communication is what is available to them. What is relevant to the mental content of an agent is what is available to it. Complete descriptions of universes are not available to agents. What is available to each agent is somewhat different from what is available to other agents. We can think of 'availability' in different ways. Here are some ways in which information is available to the agent:

1. Actual sensory or memory states,
2. States available through sensing,
3. States available through some finite sequence of movement together with 2,
4. States available through some finite sequence of actions on the environment together with 2,
5. States available through a finite set of external instruments,
6. States available through adopting a finite set of different procedures and or axioms for reasoning,
7. States available through some finite communication in the agent's language,
8. States available through learning a finite set of different languages with finite vocabularies and finitely specifiable (recursively axiomatisable) grammars.

In philosophy there is a long standing conception that, if a thought is about some reality, then it must be possible for the thought to obtain without the reality. That is to say, it must be possible for there to be a mistake. If there is to be separation between an agent's context and what it thinks it to be, then we need to think of the information about a context as being available through some selection of 2 to 8 and not just through 1.

A context is expressed in a language. At least, this is so on both the afore-mentioned accounts of context. On the standard view, context is expressible in a metalanguage. Equally, if we think of the context as something available to the agent, then it must be expressible in some form of representation available to the agent. If the agent is capable of making mistakes in thought about the context, then the agent must be capable of representing the context in some way in which it might be but is not. The context belongs to an agent at some time and place. The language describes a partial aspect of the world that is available to the agent. The agent has a theory of that aspect.

Why should we think that the language will only describe a partial aspect? The beginnings of an answer is as follows. An agent, human or computational, has finite resources to deploy at any one time. Of course, finite resources can be used to describe an infinity. However, finite resources can only be used to determine all the properties of an infinity when there is a recursively axiomatisable theory of those properties and it can be coded into the available resources. The agent may have a theory of how the world might be beyond what it can sense and what it can deduce. It may be part of the agent's context that certain properties are determined ad infinitum in the space that surrounds it. However, within that space there may be much detail that escapes the agent. The agent may know what is possible in the space that surrounds it and yet not know how things are. In one case, we might think, this will be simply because the agent does not have a theory from which to deduce all the detail. In a second case, we might think it is computationally intractable to learn a theory of all the detail. In a third case we might think the theory is simply too large for the agent. In a fourth case it will be because it cannot conceivably know all the detail. This will be because there is no recursively axiomatisable theory of the contents of the surrounding space. I will argue that empirical reality is of this fourth kind.

We might think that the agent could at least have a language capable of describing everything in the surrounding space. It might not be able to list all the true facts that obtain, yet it could have sentences to be true or false of them. However, the language that an agent can deploy at any one time will have a finite vocabulary. If the agent had a different primitive vocabulary, then it might have been possible for it to say different things and to discover them to be true about the world. The general idea is that, if we think of a context as being available to an agent, then the availability in any particular case will be through finite deployment of finite resources. Beyond the context which is determined by whatever finite limits are specified, the suggestion is that there will be further contexts to be explored. An important theoretical question is why we should think that there are always such contexts. Perhaps, an agent's finite deployment of its finite resources could exhaust the space around it? Perhaps, it could at least discover all the relevant vocabulary for describing the space around it? Before we attempt to answer these questions, let us delineate a theoretical framework in which to place them.

One account of context that provides for transcendence of a given context is that of McCarthy in 'Notes on Formalising Context' [7] in its section on 'Transcending Contexts'. It provides for formal reiteration of truths from a given outermost context in a new outermost context. Thus if p is true in a context c0, then it is possible to derive a proposition ist(c0,p) which is true in a context c-1, and so we can derive truths in new contexts ad infinitum. However, if one simply reiterated truths, then the creation of a new context would be a trivial and pointless exercise. Therefore, McCarthy proposes that the new context can differ because assumptions are dropped. In that case the exercise is non-trivial, but, if that were all that transcending a context involved, then iteration of the technique would lead to new outer contexts with fewer and fewer assumptions. An ultimate aim of McCarthy's work on context is [op.cit.]:

> ... to make AI systems which are never permanently stuck with the concepts they use at a given time because they can always *transcend* the context they are in - if they are smart enough or are told how to do so. To this end, formulas ist(c,p) are always considered as themselves asserted within a context, i.e. we have something like ist(c',ist(c,p)). The regress is infinite, but we will show that it is harmless.

If transcendence of context is to lead to understanding of the concepts of an interlocutor by being 'told' how to apply novel concepts, then this cannot always be done by dropping assumptions. On some occasions new assumptions may be necessary. A way of conceiving of this is that an outer context is identified for one's own context and then the context of the other is treated as a specialisation of a shared outer context. Also, if one is 'smart enough' to create new concepts for oneself, then new assumptions may be necessary and so may the shift to an outer context which is then specialised anew. However, it is not obvious that in all cases the new context is best treated as a parallel context which shares an outer context with the original context. Perhaps in some circumstances, a new context is best interpreted as itself the outer context of one's original context. Suppose that the language expressing the new context can specify the referents and truth-conditions of the old context, but not vice versa. In that case, the new context can be treated as the outer context of the old context. Thus there are very important questions about relationships between different contexts and about the means by which novel contexts may be articulated. There are questions about the logic to be used, and also about extra-logical means of concept learning. McCarthy does not give us a full formal account of the logic to be used, although it is to be non-monotonic. He leaves concept-learning as a future goal for A.I.

A contrast between McCarthy's position and that of the present paper is that McCarthy envisages contexts as having a certain richness. Thus he says [op.cit.]:

> Some contexts will be *rich* objects, like situations in situation calculus.
> For example, the context associated with a conversation; we cannot list
> all the common assumptions of the participants. Thus we don't purport
> to describe such contexts completely; we only say something about them.

Instead, I will assume that the fundamental common assumptions of a finite set of participants in a conversation are finitely listable. Whether any participant is able to list them on a given occasion is, of course, a quite different matter. These assumptions are listable using a finite set of finitely specifiable languages. These languages have semantic interpretations or models which constitute contexts. These models are aspects of the world. The world itself is rich, but any one language will only be about a restricted aspect of it.

The present paper is not meant to provide an account at the detailed level of inference rules or learning procedures. Instead, it is devoted to the question of whether systems, artificial or organic, could eventually discover a context that could be treated as the outermost context. Formally, it might be possible to transcend it, but not by developing novel concepts that are both fundamental and empirical. All other contexts would then be understood in terms of this outermost context. If we think of the standard view in philosophy, where there is a metalanguage for describing the set of possible worlds, then this language could be treated as expressing the outermost context. The semantics of other languages would be given using this language. Other contexts would be understood as specialisations of this fundamental context. An important question here is whether we could ever discover a finitely expressible outermost context. If we could, then the standard philosophical account of context, in terms of a given metalanguage, would coincide with an account of context as what is available to the agent. To put it another way, could there be a recursively axiomatisable theory of such a context? Could there be one language, with a finite vocabulary for describing that context? I shall argue that there cannot be.

I address this question by asking whether a final, recursively axiomatisable, theory of physics could enable us to describe the set of physically possible worlds completely and thereby to have an outermost context. To be sure, beyond that theory, we could drop assumptions in order to consider logically possible worlds, as opposed to physically possible worlds. However,if there were a final theory of physics,then it would provide an outermost context for empirical purposes. The language of this context would provide a metalanguage in which to articulate a semantics for all other languages usable to describe our empirical world. It would identify the intensions of physical predicates and of other empirical predicates. The move to logically possible worlds would simply be transcendance by dropping assumptions. In order to provide a theoretical framework for my argument against a final theory of physics, or outermost context, I will first question whether a semantics of possible worlds should be treated as fundamental.

2 Possibilities and Contexts

Possible worlds can be thought of as points in logical space, as opposed to regions. That is to say, they are fully determinate with every dimension completely determined. In contrast, the line of thought that we are exploring is that beyond every description of a world there might be a further more extensive description of it. From our point of view, each description would be made using a language with a finite primitive vocabulary. Beyond any one such vocabulary, there might be a further one. The thought that possible worlds are points in logical space led Humberstone [6] to ask whether they can be treated like instants in the theory of time. A metaphysician of time can propose that intervals are fundamental, not instants of time. Instants of time are to be treated as the limit of a sequence of subdivided intervals. To demonstrate the feasibility of this metaphysics of time it is necessary to express it in a semantics for temporal logic. When Humberstone raised his question about possibilities he had already developed an interval-based semantics for temporal logic. He set out to extend his semantics to the logic of possibilities. He wanted [op.cit. pp.317-8]'to show how to do model theory for the familiar systems of modal logic without appealing to collections of possible worlds'.

For his purposes, a model is a quadruple $< W, \geq, R, V >$. W is a non-empty set of entities he calls possibilities. He uses 'X'&'Y' as variables over these (he uses upper case letters to contrast with the use of lower case for possible worlds). R and $\geq$ are binary relations on these entities. V is a partial function from pairs of possibilities and propositional variables to truth-values. R is a relation akin to the accessibility relation of modal logic. It is $\geq$ that is the interestingly different relation. Intuitively, '$X \geq Y$' stands for X being a refinement of Y. The relation $\geq$ gives us a weak partial ordering that fulfils the following two conditions [p. 318]:

Persistence: For any propositional variable π and any $X, Y \in W$, if $V(\pi, X)$ is defined and $Y \geq X$, then $V(\pi, Y) = V(\pi, X)$.
Refinability: For any π and any $X, Y \in W$, if $V(\pi, X)$ is undefined, then there exist Y and Z in W such that $Y \geq X$ with $V(\pi, Y) = T$ and $Z \geq X$ with $V(\pi, Z) = F$

The idea of Persistence is that further determination of a possibility should not reverse truth values. The idea of Refinability is that reduction of indeterminacy is possible by either determining something to be true or false. Humberstone emphasises [op.cit. p. 318] that Refinability does 'not require that any element of W should have a refinement in which the value of every propositional variable is defined'. In his semantics, Humberstone gives a truth definition and introduces modal operators, but we will not pursue all the detail here.

In order to have an intuitive grasp of what he means by a refinement, it may help to consider examples he gives of 'modal indeterminacy and vagueness' [op.cit. p.317]. An example of vagueness is:

Harriet crossed the equator in the *late afternoon* of January 1, 1980 (my italics),

whereas an example of modal indeterminacy is simply:

Harriet crossed the equator on January 1, 1980.

The reason why this second sentence is said to be modally indeterminate is that if it is used to express a possibility by prefacing it with 'it could have been the case that', then it is incomplete. Thus Humberstone points out that it leaves open such things as the exact time of the crossing, the colour of Harriet's scarf and the details of what was going on in Tokyo at the time of the crossing. A critic of Humberstone's line of thought might think that it must be possible to give a complete description of at least some possibilities. Thus, it might be thought Harriet need not have a scarf and there might not be a Tokyo. Therefore, the line of thought goes, it ought to be possible in a metalanguage to specify everything relating to a possibility and to make the general claim that nothing else is true of it. Moreover the critic might argue that amongst the completely determinate possibilities will be the possibility that constitutes the actual world. Thus, one might think that, if one had the true physical theory of the world, then one would be able to describe the actual world and to state that one's description was complete. In section three of the paper I shall argue that, on standard assumptions, including possible worlds, the assumption that there is a complete theory of the empirical world, even a complete theory of physics, leads to paradox. I shall argue that the best way to resolve the paradox is to drop the assumption that there can be a complete theory. Thus, on my view it is worth paying serious attention to Humberstone's semantics.

However, one can reasonably ask of what it is a semantics. This is especially true if one holds that any context available to an agent is something that is partial, because agents employ finite means, for example languages with finite vocabularies. In that case, Humberstone's vistas of indefinite refinements will not be necessary for any one language. One can take the view that an agent may begin with one context, but that it can envisage discovering that there is another agent with a language whose truth conditions cannot be stated using the language for describing the initial context. Thus, the agent can come to have a different context. In that context a further context can be discovered and so on.

We can envisage that the language for each of these contexts has a local models semantics as proposed by Giunchiglia and Ghidini [3]. We can also envisage that the sequence of contexts fulfils a compatibility constraint [op.cit.]. Therefore we can think that Humberstone provides us with a semantics for sequences of languages developed as the agent explores different contexts. In order to express this semantics in a language we will need to describe a sequence of languages and their local models. The local models will not be directly expressible in any one language, but only indirectly by employing the languages in the sequence. In any one language, compatibility constraints for other languages will be expressible, but truth conditions will not be expressible for all other languages. Perhaps, the overall account of the logic can combine Humberstone's approach with the multicontext approach of Giunchiglia and Ghidini [op.cit.], but see also Giunchiglia and Serafini [4].

One feature of Humberstone's semantics is that negation is defined as follows [op.cit. p.320]:

$$X \models \tilde{\ }\alpha \text{ iff for all } Y \geq X, Y \not\models \alpha$$

Note that on the proposed interpretation of Humberstone, the universal quantifier in this definition (and corresponding quantifiers in his Persistence and Refinability conditions), need to be interpreted as remarks about whether there will ever be reason to accept sentences that are incompatible with $\tilde{\ }\alpha$ as the sequence of languages expressing novel contexts is developed. In that case the proposal is not to quantify directly over the domains described by these languages, but to quantify over sentences that we may have reason to accept. Humberstone's idea is that the truth of a negation records something determinate, not just failure of the negated formula to be true. Consider Wright's concept of superassertibility [8][p. 44 foll.], which is given as one account of the truth predicate. If there is a proposition P that an agent would have reason to assert if it had gained enough information and that it would never have reason to retract no matter how much information it gained, then P is superassertible in Wright's sense. The definition of superassertibility does not presuppose that there is any complete state of information. It may be thought that negation is to be understood in terms of superassertibility.

The modal operator '$\Box$' ('it is necessarily the case that') is interpreted as follows [op.cit. p.323]

$$< W, \geq, R, V > X \models \Box\alpha \text{ iff for all } Y \in W \text{ such that } RXY, < W, \geq, R, V > Y \models \alpha$$

Constraints are imposed on R in order to guarantee its persistence and refinability [op.cit. p.324].

We are thinking in terms of learning to apply languages to aspects of the world. Is it true that learning about the world could go on without end? In particular, could we continue to learn new improved concepts of the world forever? To put it another way, is it the case that our understanding of the world is invariably partial? I do not mean simply that we might be able to go on learning new facts to add to a list, but that we might be able to go on making theoretical and conceptual improvements for ever. This would alter the nature of what we counted as facts to be listed. Note that these questions are simultaneously questions about the potential of the world as an object of thought and questions about the potential of thinkers to have cognition about the world. Theorists of context, in the sense in which I am using the term, postulate that a context is partial and subject to improvement. If we make the assumption that our concepts can always be improved upon, then, so long as there is more than one of us, each thinker needs to recognize that another thinker might already have improved on its concepts, as I argue elsewhere [9, 10]. Note that our assumptions about this matter affect the relationship between thinkers, at least at the limit.

3   Why Contexts are Partial

In the first section of this paper, I asked whether there could be a final outermost context for agents interacting with the empirical world. The language expressing this context would be a metalanguage for all other languages that described the empirical world. In posing this question I asked whether we could continue to learn new and improved concepts of the world forever. By world, I meant the contingent, empirical universe. Note that if I had posed my question about the formal, or mathematical universe, then there would be a ready answer. Even if we take elementary number theory then it is provable that we cannot have one finitely specifiable (recursively axiomatisable) theory from which we can deduce all truths about the properties of those numbers. On the other hand, what one theory cannot prove, another can. Thus, our mathematical concepts (procedures for deciding mathematical truths) are subject to indefinite improvement. I am going to argue that this is also true of the empirical world. Indeed, the two issues are connected. As we explore the world of numbers, we identify new mathematical concepts. Those mathematical concepts may be applicable in constructing theories about the empirical world. Note that the classical position in mathematics is that we are exploring infinities. Infinities are necessary if mathematical concepts are to be capable of indefinite improvement. A question about the empirical world is whether there are comparable infinities to explore in it.

Is it true that learning about the world could go on without end? In particular, could we continue to learn new improved concepts of the world forever? These are questions about our potential relations with things in the world, not just about our actual relations. It might be that, if only one of our research teams could get money out of a funding council, then its experiments would show that fundamental physical theory needs revision. Questions about whether our concepts of the empirical world could be improved, are questions about the nature of physical things and our learning capacity, not questions about the limits of funding. How does this connect with arguments about infinity? Suppose that the physical universe is deterministic and has a beginning in time. In that case the decision of the funding council could only have been different, if the initial conditions of the universe were different. In considering the nature of the physical world, it is relevant to consider the experiments that could have been done if only the funding council had provided the money. It follows that it is also relevant to consider different initial conditions for the universe. When I consider the nature of physical things, I am going consider what we might have discovered about them if the initial conditions of the universe had been a little bigger or a little bigger or ... The view for which I am arguing is that the empirical world needs to understood as having potentialities not just its actually measurable properties.

In contrast with the position of the present paper, many philosophers discuss semantics as if there is some complete language of description for the world and its associated set of scientifically possible worlds. Or, at least, there is some complete language of fundamental or base description - e.g. a language for describing micro physical properties (higher-order properties, e.g. macro-physical, functional and semantic, are dependent - 'supervene' - on these base properties). There are various definitions of the supervenience relation. The idea is that one property may realise another property without being identical with it. Thus, computational states are realised in hardware, but the same computational state might be realised in different hardware on different occasions. If one only has descriptions of the base, then one cannot deduce from that complete descriptions of all aspects of the world, for one cannot deduce descriptions of all the higher-order properties as I argue elsewhere [11]. However, in the present paper I will concern myself with the language of base description, as opposed to languages for describing higher order properties. The standard conception is that one can use this language of base description as the metalanguage in which to express the semantics of other languages for describing the world. If we think of this in terms of contexts, then the language of base description would express the outermost context for deploying concepts of the empirical world. An agent would arrive at this context if it increased its knowledge of the physics of the empirical world to the maximum. The language of base description, expressing an outermost empirical context, would be used to identify the essential properties of empirical objects. Further contexts could, it is true, be expressed by dropping assumptions and thinking about logical possibility. However, logical possibilities may be understood in terms of a purely formal semantics.

Does the science, physics, determine a complete language of base description? It might, if it determined a final theory of physics. We would be committed to an ontology by treating that theory as true. We would be committed to an ontology including possible worlds. The rest of this paper consists of a critique of the idea that there could ever be a final recursively axiomatisable theory of physics, and brief final consideration of what kind of theory of physics and metaphysics there can be. There is a variety of reasons for thinking that there can be no final theory of physics determined by human science:

1. There is no clear limit to the variety of kinds of evidence that might be available(measuring machines, sensory systems).
2. There is a potentially infinite stream of evidence.

3. Not all relevant evidence could be obtained even in infinite time.
4. Any evidence obtained might be misleading.
5. There is no clear agreement on criteria for theory selection.

I agree with these reasons for thinking that human science is not capable of determining a final theory, but I want to explore another reason:

6. There is no finite limit to relevant theorising in physics.

Is (6) independent of the other reasons? In order to explore this question let us assume, in addition to the assumption that there is a final theory of physics:

a. no matter how (finitely) big the universe is it could have been bigger
b. (classically) an entire ordering of properties that it is feasible to measure, defined in terms of some finite set of measuring instruments with each measurement digital rather than analogue, can be given for the actual universe, or
c. (quantum mechanically) an entire tree of branching measurables can be given starting from the initial conditions of the actual universe
   (i) with branches corresponding to actions of measurement
   (ii) and with leaves corresponding to alternative measurable properties,
d. that the final theory is the theory that affords the most concise combination for the actual universe of
   (i) descriptions of initial conditions (these need not be measurable and are distinct from the theory itself) and
   (ii) descriptions of the theory itself (i.e. the set of universal laws),
e. that allows us to deduce a description of any finite section of the ordering of measurables.

The measure of conciseness is space to code the descriptions of the theory and its associated initial conditions (together with a standard inference engine) on a standard machine. Or rather, let us refine this further. Call a theory, than which there is no more concise theory, an elegant theory. Since there might be more than one equally elegant theory let us adopt the view that:

> if there is more than one elegant theory that fits the evidence, then let the language determined by physics describe a multiple-aspect world.

In that case, our proposed criterion is for a final set of theories. A theory will be one of the final set of theories if it is an elegant theory in the above sense. Is there a justification for choosing elegance (in the foregoing sense) as a criterion for selecting theories to be included in the final set of theories? A justification is that theory construction in science can be seen as an exercise in information compression. Take the entire ordering of measurables, we can expect this to be infinite, even if we consider fundamental properties as measured by a finite set of measuring instruments. Nevertheless, in theory construction, we seek to identify a finite (recursively axiomatisable) theory of this ordering. In selecting theories, there may be other criteria than that they compress information, but, at least, this is one requirement. In the absence of cogent arguments for other criteria, we can concentrate on elegance. In passing, note that if anyone argues that there are a multiplicity of other criteria for selecting theories, for example what happens to be convenient or useful to each agent, then they implicitly concede that there can be no final theory of physics. Thus, they concede what I am arguing for, even if they concede it for different reasons.

Elegance, as a criterion of theory selection, produces the following anomaly. In identifying the anomaly, I will describe it in terms of possible worlds. This is appropriate, because my argument is a critique of the standard philosophical view, which is formulated in terms of possible worlds. Suppose the actual world is w_1 and its ordering of measurables is M_{w_1} which has one elegant theory $T_{M_{w_1}}$. The theory $T_{M_{w_1}}$ determines a set of possible worlds in which it is true. Consider a world in that set, w_n, it has an ordering of measurable properties M_{w_n}, M_{w_n} in turn determines a set of elegant theories, suppose it contains just $T_{M_{w_n}}$. The anomaly is that it is not necessarily the case that $T_{M_{w_n}}$ is identical with $T_{M_{w_1}}$

It is important to realise that the two theories can have different implications for measurable properties. $T_{M_{w_n}}$ might imply that another world, w_r, is not possible whereas $T_{M_{w_1}}$ implies it is, or vice versa. What causes the anomaly or paradox? It is caused by the criterion of conciseness that was chosen earlier, where I said:

> the final theory is the theory that affords the most concise combination
> for the actual universe of
> i. descriptions of initial conditions (these need not be measurable and
>   are distinct from the theory itself) and
> ii. descriptions of the theory itself (i.e. the set of universal laws),
> that allows us to deduce a description of any finite section of the ordering
> of measurables

Clearly, as the descriptions of initial conditions vary from world to world, the descriptions of laws that make for concision can also vary. If we consider theories computationally there is a sharp proof, due to Chaitin, in algorithmic information theory, about elegance [2][1][p.142, p.198]. Consider an elegant program of a given size. It is, ex hypothesi, the most concise program (on a canonical machine) for generating its output. Chaitin proves that one cannot use a program of a given size to prove the elegance of a program that is significantly larger. The proof is via consideration of a Berry-type paradox - if there were a proof from the smaller program that the larger program were elegant, then (smaller program + inference engine) would be a program for generating the output of the 'significantly' larger program but, if 'significantly' means by an increment of size greater than the inference engine, then the larger program cannot be elegant. Of course, some larger programs must actually be elegant. Otherwise, contrary to the theory of computing, the number of functionally equivalent programs would be finite. A version of the proof applies to sets of axioms. A set of laws of physics, together with a set of initial conditions, is a set of axioms. Thus, there is no proof that because a theory for our world is elegant, the theory will be elegant for larger worlds in the set of worlds that it itself determines. Other theories will be elegant for some of these larger worlds.

There is a case for thinking that if we take two worlds w_1 and w_2,

- the initial conditions of w_2 are bigger than the initial conditions of w_1
- the elegant theories of the two worlds are different from each other
- the elegant theory of each world explains the other world

then the theory to be preferred is the theory of w_2, even if w_1 is the actual world. The case is that, if w_1 and w_2, were models of fragments of our actual world, we would prefer a physical theory that could handle bigger cases elegantly and therefore prefer the elegant theory of w_2. If we generalise this preference, then we ought to prefer the elegant theory of w_2, even if w_1 is the actual world. Note that one could consider elegance as a property of theories, in abstraction from initial conditions. But the abstract property of being the most elegant theory for generating the abstract output of a given theory of physics cannot be our criterion of theory selection. It would beg the question in favour of some one theory or other.

Let us consider how I apply Chaitin's proof in a little more detail. The argument depends upon the following assumptions in addition to those given above. First, the final theory of physics is to be a computational physics. Second, we can express any set of axioms for scientific explanation, including axioms about initial conditions in a physical world, in some canonical programming language. Third, inference from any of these sets of axioms can be implemented using a standard set of rules of inference. Given these assumptions, we can apply Chaitin's result in algorithmic information theory to a system of scientific explanation. Let me explain what this result is. Call a program 'elegant' if no smaller program has the same output. Chaitin proves that, however big an axiom set, there is always a limit to the size of program that it can prove to be elegant. From this it follows that there is also a limit to the size of axiom set that it can prove to be elegant. Consider adding extra axioms to a given science. We soon come to a point at which we cannot prove from the old science that the new science, with its extra axioms, is elegant. Consider any finitely specifiable (recursively axiomatisable) set of deductive axioms and rules of logic. It is provable that there is a limit to the size of program that it can prove to be elegant. This limit is the sum of the size of the axiom set as it is expressed in program code for a machine (standardly a Turing machine), together with a constant. The constant is a function of the total size of a theorem prover and search program which searches the space of proofs from that axiom set. The search program begins with the smallest proofs constructible using that axiom set, together with a system of deductive rules. It searches them in some canonical order. Then it considers the next largest proof size and so on. Consider a search program S, which includes an axiom set A, and a standard set of rules of inference. S is designed to search for a program P, whose elegance is provable from A using the standard rules. When S finds P, S is to write out, as its own output, the output of the elegant program P, and then halt. It is provable that any program P that S proves to be elegant *cannot be bigger than S itself*. This is because S is designed to output just exactly what

P outputs. Thus, if P were bigger than S, then it couldn't be elegant! S would be a more concise program than P itself, for generating the output of P. Thus the limit of program size that is provably elegant from a set of axioms A is the size of A itself + a constant c. The constant c is the size of the code necessary to implement the search algorithm, including the theorem prover and its standard rules of inference. This is the limit of program size that is provably elegant from A, but it also establishes a limit for the size of the set of axioms that is provably elegant from A. This limit is at most the size of S itself. The size of any theorem prover and search program, implementing a search for proofs from a set of axioms, cannot be less than 0. Hence, an elegant set of axioms that is provably elegant from A can be no bigger than the biggest program that is provably elegant from A.

This proof of Chaitin's has application to physics in the following way. Suppose we identify the simplest system of initial conditions and laws to generate the sequence of events in the actual world. The system of laws will identify other possible worlds. Suppose we consider a possible world with a set of initial conditions larger than our own. It will not follow that just because our system of laws provides the simplest account of our actual world that it provides the simplest account of a larger possible world. Adding axioms about initial conditions is just another way of adding axioms. Therefore, if the inhabitants of this larger possible world selected the theory giving the simplest system of causes sufficient to generate their world, then they would choose a different system of causes from the ones we would select in our world. This result seems anomalous. It provides a reason for refusing to treat a theory, which is simplest for any one world, as the ultimate theory of physics.

4 Metaphysics and Supercontext

At first sight, these considerations not only call into question the notion of a canonical theory of physics, and an outermost context for empirical inquiry, but they also call into question the notion of a scientifically determined canonical metaphysics of physical properties. However we do not have to abandon the conception of a general metaphysics. First, we can concede that there is no complete explanatory theory of the world to be identified. Second, we can adopt the metaphysics of physical properties that we take to be superassertible -see above and Wright 1992 [8][p.44 foll.]. On this account, we presume that physical properties exist of which the following is true. They will continue to be recognised no matter how many additional axioms we add to our current physics. They will continue to be recognised no matter how large the possible worlds we consider (or rather we should say no matter how large the possibilities we consider, if we adopt Humberstone's framework). The account allows us to preserve simplicity as a means of theory selection that can be used at any given stage of our theoretical development. It allows us to acknowledge that there is no one final recursively axiomatisable scientific theory. Can there be a general theory of physics on this view? It has been argued that the physical world cannot be completely described.

It has not been argued that every law of physics is ephemeral. All that has been argued is that there can be no final recursively axiomatisable theory. The account that has been given is perfectly consistent with superassertible ceteris paribus laws in physics.

On this view, what account can we give of possible worlds? Perhaps, we should abandon talk of possible worlds as opposed to possibilities, a view which Humberstone discusses [6][p.315]. Alternatively, if we drop one of our earlier assumptions and recognise that there is no one canonical finite set of measuring instruments, then we can attempt to identify each world with an infinite set of sets of token measurable properties, together with theoretical properties that are superassertible. However, no one language can be used to specify all possible measuring instruments and theories. Instead, perhaps we need to think of an infinity of languages for which the following is true. First, they are languages whose truth conditions we can learn to recognise either directly ourselves or indirectly through the judgements of others. Second, these languages introduce new measuring instruments and theories. Does this mean that there is a supercontext? One can say so, if one wants. However, the supercontext will not itself be a context. This is because it will not be completely describable using a finitely intelligible language. Aspects of it will be describable in this way. We will be able indefinitely to learn new aspects of it. It itself will be ineffable.

References

1. G.J. Chaitin. *Algorithmic Information Theory.* Cambridge University Press, 1997.
2. G.J. Chaitin. *The Limits of Mathematics*, chapter Elegant Lisp Programs. 1997.
3. F. Giuinchiglia and C. Chidini. Local models semantics, or contextual reasoning = locality + compatibility. In *Proceedings of the Sixth International Conference on Principles of Knowledge Representation and Reasoning*, 1998.
4. F. Giunchiglia and L. Serafini. Multilanguage hierarchical logic (or: how we can do without modal logics). *Artificial Intelligence*, 65, 1994.
5. B. Hale and C.G Wright, editors. *A Companion to the Philosophy of Language.* Blackwell, 1997.
6. I.L. Humberstone. From worlds to possibilities. *Journal of Philosophical Logic*, 1981.
7. J McCarthy. Notes on formalizing context. In *Proceedings of the Thirteenth International Joint Conference on Artificial Intelligence*, 1993.
8. C.G. Wright. *Truth and Objectivity.* Harvard University Press, 1992.
9. R.A. Young. The mentality of robots. *Proceedings of the Aristotelian Society*, Supp., 1994.
10. R.A. Young. Embodied agents as interactive agents. In *AAAI Fall Symposium on Embodiment*, 1996.
11. R.A. Young. Incompleteness and emergence. *British Journal for the Philosophy of Science*, forthcoming.

The Role of Context in Interpreting Perceived Events as Actions

Elisabetta Zibetti [1], Elizabeth Hamilton[1], Charles Tijus[1]

[1]Laboratoire CNRS UPRES - A - 7021 Cognition & Activités Finalisées
Université de Paris VIII, 2, rue de la Liberté,
93526 Saint-Denis Cedex 02 France
Elisabetta.Zibetti@univ-paris8
Elizabeth.Hamilton@univ-paris8
Tijus@univ-paris8

Abstract. In this paper we discuss the role of context in interpreting and understanding perceived events as actions carried out by other people. The context is defined both as temporal (relations between events) and as being comprised of the state of the situation as cognitively processed (object properties) at any given time. We begin by presenting this overlooked field through previous work and perceived action models in psychology and in artificial intelligence. We will argue that the principal mechanism involved in perceiving action is categorisation of the objects in the environment (environmental context) and of the temporal relations between events (temporal context). The mechanisms involved in this process are modelled using the Dynamic Allocation of Meaning Model (C.A.D.S.). This model proposes an explanation of the manner in which temporal information and the perceived properties of a situation interact.

1 Introduction

For many years it was considered that context had no more than a "modulating" role in the processing of information. It was thought that once perceptual information was assembled, knowledge of context could intervene to favour certain interpretations over others through association. This position was dominant in the fields of language understanding but also in the field of visual perception [7]. Our position is that stimulus and context are processed simultaneously.

2 Perceived Action

The same succession of events can lead to very different interpretations or perceptions in terms of action. This is true to such an extent that it has become a central theme in mystery and detective novels. For example, Hitchcock bases a scene in one of his films on whether the person seen leaving the scene of a crime is "fleeing" or "running for help". Thus, the attribution of meaning to an event is not solely determined by the

Cartesian coordinates of movement but also by the properties attributed to the objects in motion, the relation of the different properties these objects have to each other (*environmental context*) and the succession of events and their relations to each other (*temporal context*) and to the objects. In our view, context has a remarkable incidence on the manner in which events are processed, interpreted and understood in terms of action.

3 What is known about perceived action

Much research in psychology has examined the conceptual organization and understanding of action in written texts, action and learning (learning by doing, the "hands-on" approach), as well as planning and understanding in on-line task situations. However, research on the actual perception of action as it occurs is rare.

In social psychology, studies in perceiving the actions and intentions of other people began before mid-century [4]. In general psychology, Michotte (1963) was the first to take an interest in the regularities of the perception of movement and causality. In the 1970s, Newtson and his colleagues [10], [11], [12], [13] examined the perceptual units of ongoing behaviour and determined that these were discrete. More recently, Heft (1996) has produced work on the organization of temporally structured visual information as perceived by moving agents. Zacks and Tversky (1997) have examined the nature of the often remarked hierarchical structure of perceived action. Thommen (1991) has shown that even very young children attempt to establish coherency in perception by adjusting perceived goals to what they know about objects. And finally, Gergely, Nadasdy, Csibra, & Biro (1995); Csibra, Gergely, Biro, & Koos (in press) and Premack (1990, 1995), have shown that as early as 12 months-old, young children construct interpretations based on rational expectations.

Of late, the remarkable development of models in artificial intelligence has led to a mushrooming of studies in the artificial perception of visual motion. Though this work provides approaches to perceived action on a number of levels (e.g. [1], [19]), it remains, in our opinion, unconcerned with psychological relevance. One of these recent models is Intille and Bobick's (1998) probabilistic model. Temporal context is represented by graphs in which the primitives are "agent-based belief networks that can recognize agent goal by probabilistic integration of visual evidence," (p.80). Like most AI models, Intille and Bobick's focuses on attributing goals to agents in order to recognize and determine the type of action being executed. However, nothing is said about how agent and patient roles are determined to begin with.

Thibadeau's (1986) model also uses probability and belief networks. Yet it represents an attempt to integrate psychologically pertinent aspects derived from Miller and Johnson-Laird's (1976) "componential" theory: action primitives are grouped and combined with notions of intentionality, manner, direction, agent and so forth to form complex action. This model takes the transformations (from one state to another) rather than the nature of actions into account. Thibadeau believed that action could be perceived directly and did not consider the fact that changing the objects in the situation could change interpretation of the action. However, if perception of the objects in a situation is secondary, how is it that identical primitives can be combined into different perceived actions?

We believe that the perception of objects can not be dissociated from the perception of actions. Our work is along the lines of research in psychology showing the importance of categorization in understanding the kind of situations human beings are confronted with every day, not only in recognizing objects but also in much more complex activities such as planning and problem solving. As far as we know, ours is the first research in perceived action to attribute the central role to categorization. Our position is that this activity, which is the very basis of our knowledge about the world, is not only strongly implicated in the perception of events and their interpretation in terms of action, but it is the principal mechanism that can explain contextual effects in perceived action.

4 What is perceived action?

Actions can not be perceived directly. They are possible interpretations of an event and as such, they are cognitive. The information an observer picks up is composed of events and the context in which they take place. This information is integrated with knowledge about the world in order to construct interpretation.

Imagine the event illustrated in figure 1: two animals travelling one behind the other in a field.

Fig. 1. two animals moving across a field

The movement of the two animals is likely to be interpreted according to available contextual information. What we have called the "environmental" context of this movement might be, for example, that the animal in front is a cat and the animal behind it, a dog. In such case, the action perceived will most likely be "a dog is chasing a cat" or perhaps, "a cat is running away from a dog". But if the first animal is a dog and the second, a puppy, identical movement through space will probably not be interpreted in terms of chasing or fleeing but in terms of guiding and following. However, if the observer happens to know the particular cat and dog in question and knows, for example, that they grew up together and often play together, the interpretation will most likely change. Likewise, knowing that the particular puppy is aggressive could also have an impact on perception.

The understanding that comes out of processing information is not an understanding of the *event* per se (i.e. "the dog moved horizontally to the right and the cat moved horizontally to the right", and so on) but an understanding in terms of *action* with agents purposefully doing things with and to other things or beings, for particular reasons in a particular context, (i.e. "the dog is chasing the cat" or "the puppy is following the dog" or "the cat and dog are playing"). The cognitive components attributed to the movement guide the observer in making specific ("chasing") rather than general ("moving") interpretations.

In the above examples, the cognitive components attributed to the event are based on stable knowledge about dogs and cats in general or about specific dogs and cats: this is the object-based, environmental component of context. The other important aspect of context is temporal. When the dynamic information events contain is processed, it is processed in a specific order that is coherent with causal representation based on the attribution of intentions and goals to agents. In contrast to the *environmental context*, the elements of the *temporal context* are never co-present at any given time. These elements are knowledge about previous states of the event (the past and immediate past) and projections into the future, i.e. anticipating what is going to happen.

5 Environmental context and perceived action

We propose formalising the environmental context as an organized description of the properties of the objects that are present. In order to do so, the properties and the links between them need to be defined and operationalised. Let's take the example of seeing someone in a supermarket whose hands are on the handle of a shopping cart. Both person and cart are moving in the same direction. You understand that the person is "pushing the cart" and even that he or she "is shopping" despite the fact that all that can be seen are two objects in contact moving in the same direction in an environment. General knowledge about the world tells us that shopping carts are not (or are not yet) self-propelled but that they can easily be moved (they have wheels) by pushing. This knowledge can be represented as a series of object-based cognitive properties (cart: has wheels, can be pushed; person: can push) attached to stable categories (the category of things with wheels, the category of persons). These properties can be attributed to the objects perceived through categorization. If the event in question takes place in a supermarket (rather than on the street where many people also push shopping carts) then the person pushing will probably be categorized either as a client or as someone who works in the supermarket. The supermarket, like the cart and the person, makes certain categories and not others available. If the person is categorized as a "client" then he or she will be perceived as "shopping". However, if he or she is categorized as an "employee" (i.e. because of the property "is in uniform"), then the movement may be perceived as "stocking the shelves".

What this example illustrates is that the properties of the objects in the situation are of two kinds: those that are directly available to the senses and those that are attributed through categorization, the first determining the latter.

5.1 Object, Property and Action

Many studies of categorization have shown that the perceptual properties of objects are what activate the process of constructing a mental representation of the object. It is also known that the mental representation of an object depends to a large extent on its relational properties, i.e. the properties it has in relation to the other objects in the context (bigger than, sharper than, etc.).

The immediately perceptible physical properties of objects provide access to the functional properties of the same objects through categorization (what it can do, what can be done with it). Functional properties are thus closely related to action concepts and we believe that actions are properties attributed to objects. For example, that perceiving something as "flying" can provide the object with the prerequisite properties for the action such as "is aerodynamic". Functional properties and actions attributed to objects are also relational properties (can do y to x). This is related to the fact that as Kintsch (1974), Norman et Rumelhart (1975), observe, verbs are interpreted in conjunction with their nominal arguments. Likewise, in understanding a dynamic situation, objects and actions exercise mutual interpretative constraints on each other.

If these observations are correct, then the verbs used to describe perceived action should vary as a function of environmental context. Altering the visual characteristics of objects alters the functional and action properties that are inferred: pressing the keys of a piano may be perceived as "playing music" whereas pressing the keys of a typewriter may be perceived as "writing".

5.2 Object's Reciprocal Relationships

We examined the role of object properties in perceived action by comparing interpretations provided by participants for identical movements in three different environmental contexts [26], [26]. In these experiments, context was manipulated by altering the physical properties of the three moving geometric figures in Heider and Simmel's (1944) famous animated film. The three figures are a large yellow triangle (Y), a small blue triangle (B) and a small pink circle (P). A fourth figure is a large rectangle, often perceived as a "house", with a mobile segment that can open and close like a door (figure 2). We describe the animation in the anthropomorphic terms participants often use for the sake of clarity:

> The large triangle approaches the house, opens the door,
> enters and then closes the door. The small blue triangle
> and the small pink circle appear on the screen, circle the
> house and stop by the door. Y comes out of the house and
> moves towards the couple. Y and B knock each other
> around while P enters the house. Y wins the fight, joins P
> in the house and appears to chase P around the house. B
> moves in the direction of the door, opens it and P comes
> out. They close the door. Y appears to be attempting to get
> out of the house but can not open the door. Meanwhile B
> and P circle the house and touch several times. Y opens
> the door, comes out, and chases B and P around the
> outside of the house. The couple leave the screen and Y
> breaks the walls of the house.

The principal advantage of this material is its simplicity: the contextual parameters are easy to control. We designed two variations of the animation. In the *inverse* condition, the shapes and sizes of the objects were all inversed. We thus obtained a small yellow circle (Y), a big blue circle (B) and a big pink triangle (P). In the *equal* condition, the objects were all big triangles varying only in colour. The movements remained unchanged (figure 2).

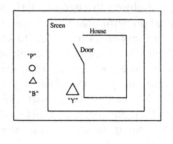

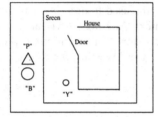 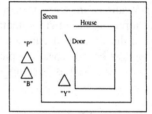

Fig. 2. At top, the material for Heider and Simmel's animation. From left to right, the two experimental conditions in which environmental context was modified

When the properties of the objects in the animation were altered, the interpretations given by participants varied considerably. The attribution of agent and patient roles varied as a function of experimental condition. Different verbs were also used to describe the movements and both of these factors led to describing very different scenarios. Like Heider and Simmel's subjects, the participants in our experiments usually described the original animation as a fight between two men (Y and B) over a woman (P). In contrast, in the *inverse* condition, participants often perceived a story about a child (Y) coming home from school to greet its parents or a story about two older children who refuse to play with a younger one (Y, sometimes described as a "pest") and then run off together. In the *equal* condition, the three figures are seen as playing together or engaging in some common activity such as visiting a house. The terms by which the figures were designated ("the bad guy", "the child", etc.) had a direct impact on the verbs that were used to describe the figures' actions ("attacking", "kissing", etc.). Thus we were able to observe that altering the environmental context can radically change perceptions of identical movements and events.

6 Temporal Context and Perceived Action

We have established that object properties have an effect on perceived action. The function is reversible: the action perceived has an effect on the properties attributed. In the reverse function, temporal context is important. The causes and consequences attributed to a first event constrain and enrich the perception of ulterior events. The more temporal information is available, the richer is interpretation of events in terms of action, and the richer and more specific is the perceived action, the more specific are the properties attributed to the objects involved in that action.

Temporal context consists of the perceived actions previous to a given on-line event and of the expectations as to future actions that have been generated. Generally speaking, it can be said that observing and understanding a situation means integrating successive events into a coherent whole, because when a series of events is not perceived as a succession of actions with causal links it gives rise to a series of change of state descriptions (x moved right, moved left, etc.).

Evaluating the manner in which an observer represents changing events calls for taking the succession into account (event B occurs after event A and before event C) in order to generate both inter-event relations of causality and the attribution of goals to agents, the goals being possible action outcomes. The causal relations and possible outcomes are inferences observers continue to make the entire time a representation is being constructed. In this way, events are perceived as being produced by agents and undergone by patient objects.

6.2 Causal Links and Goal Attribution

The attribution of agency to an object involves linking one object's movement to changes of state or movement in another. In order for this link to become effective, there are a number of prerequisites. Let's take an example from Heider and Simmel's animation: a figure moving toward the "door" of a "house" may be perceived by an observer as having the goal of entering it. To the extent that it is perceived as having an intention, the figure is perceived as the agent of the action which is "entering". In order for the attribution of agency relative to this action to become effective, the figure must not only continue to move in the direction of the door but also to open it and to cross the threshold. At this point, the attributed goal becomes effective and the causal links are backwards generating: it moved toward the door *because* it wanted to open it *because* it wanted to enter the house. The door is in this case a patient object: it was opened by the figure wanting to enter the house, it did not open of its own accord.

7 The Interaction between Environmental and Temporal Context

We propose a computer model that integrates these two aspects of context. The model represents an attempt to account for the interaction of the mechanisms underlying perceived action. It is designed to infer the implicit components of perceived actions from the immediate perceptual properties of objects and events. It establishes the coherence of an episode by structuring events into temporal units of meaning and rationalising actions.

7.1 C.A.D.S., Modelling Perceived Action Through Categorial Ascription

The results of the experiments reported above stress the importance of both stable and incidental knowledge about objects. With C.A.D.S. (the Dynamic Allocation of Meaning Model, [18], [22], [23]) an evolving situation is modelled as a sequential process in which categories are created and modified as objects appear and disappear. These *ad hoc* categories activate superordinate categories and their properties. Interpreting a situation thus consists of ascribing an object and its properties (including action) to the most specific (subordinate) of categories to which it might be attributed.

7.2 How C.A.D.S. works

Let's suppose the following situation as the stimulus. On a computer screen is a rectangle containing a triangle. The first category to which these objects may be attributed is the category of inanimate objects (general), and more specifically, that of geometric figures. When the triangle begins to move, it will be re-ascribed: it becomes a self-propelled object with intentional movements (a cartoon figure or animate). This categorial ascription has an impact on the other figures, the rectangle becomes an enclosed space (such as a house) in which an animate figure is moving. The screen is also recategorized, it is perceived as the sort of space in which the house or other enclosed structure might stand, it is a place. If the triangle moves towards a side of the rectangle and simultaneously a segment of the side opens, then the constraints furnished by the categorization that has already occurred make the line segment a "door" and, retrospectively, the movement of the figure in the direction of the door, an intentional "going toward the door to open it". At this point, further intentions can be attributed to the triangle. These are expectations of what is going to happen based on what has preceded. The triangle "is leaving the house" or "is going out for a walk." In this way, the perception of objects and actions is integrated into a single evolving representation which becomes richer as events unfold (figure 3). C.A.D.S. is operated by STONE, a programme that automatically constructs hierarchies of object categories (S. Poitrenaud, Laboratoire CNRS Cognition et Activités finalisées, Université de Paris 8).

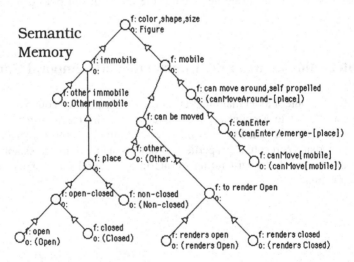

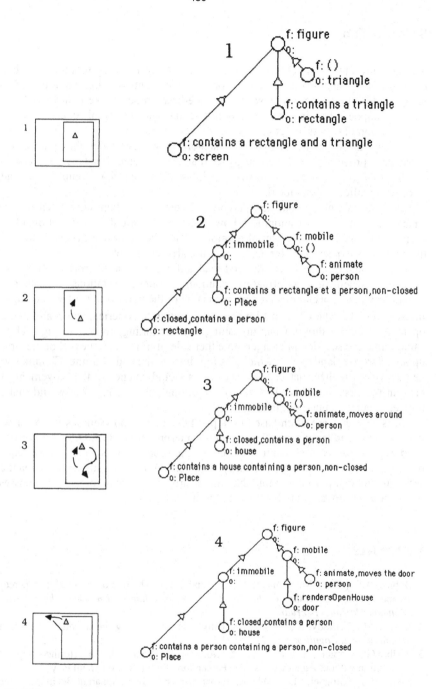

Fig. 3. Modelling perceived action with C.A.D.S. Network A describes a portion of knowledge contained in semantic memory. The nodes of the network represent categories of objects (o) defined by properties which include action. The arcs represent categorial implication. Networks 1, 2, 3, and 4 describe the process of categorial ascription of the figures in the animation (left of networks) by integrating information furnished as the animation unfolds

8 Conclusions

We have presented C.A.D.S., a model for attributing meaning to situations through the process of categorization. Such a process represents an alternative to activating ready made action schemas as well as to rule-based models. We believe C.A.D.S. is better equipped for integrating environmental and temporal contexts into the interpretation of events as actions.

Through the elasticity of dynamic categorisation, our model shows how context determines processing and the categories that are activated. For C.A.D.S., context is much more than a series of *a posteriori* considerations that complete and adjust information already assembled.

In situations where events are perceived in terms of action, contextual data often enables the observer to anticipate how events will unfold as a function of goals attributed to agents and the causal relations established between events. Nonetheless, the observer's expectations for action may not always be met.

It often happens that we are obliged to abandon the initial interpretation of a series of events when new information contradicts our expectations. Recategorizing situations when expectations are not met is one of the mainsprings of visual gags. For instance, in a Charlie Chaplin film about emigration to America, an ocean liner scene opens with a close shot of Chaplin leaning over the railing, his convulsing back to the camera like the sea-sick passengers to either side of him. In the next shot, he straitens up and, surprise, lands a fish which is struggling on the end of a line. Chaplin's visual genius was to realize that because spectators would categorize the movement of his back in the first shot as an instance of "vomiting", the second shot would make the trapped spectators burst out in laughter.

Jokes and gags are often based on a pivotal action or polysemous word for which the context suddenly specifies a new interpretation. C.A.D.S. has produced encouraging results in simulating the comprehension of jokes as situations requiring recategorization [22]. We are presently using C.A.D.S. to investigate the semantics of action in an attempt to determine the kind of properties that an object must possess in order for a certain action to be attributed to it.

References

1. Bobick, A.F. (1997). Mouvement, Activity, and action: The role of knowledge in perception of motion. In *Proceedings of the Royal Society Workshop on Knowledge-based Vision in Man and Machine, February.*
2. Gergely, G.,Nadasdy, Z.,Csibra,G., & Biro S. (1995). Taking the intentional stance at 12 months of age. *Cognition, 56 (2),* 165-193.
3. Csibra,G., Gergely, G., Biro S., & Koos,O. & Brockbank, M. (forthcoming). Goal Attribution without Agency Cues: The Perception of' Pure Reason' in infancy.
4. Heider, F., & Simmel, M., (1944). An Experimental Study of Apparent Behavior. *American Journal of Psychology, 57,* 243-259.
5. Intille, S. S., & Bobick, A.F. (1998). Representation and Visual Recognition of Complex, Multi-agent Actions using Beliefs Networks. In *Proceedings of the IEEE Computer Society Workshop: The Interpretation of Visual Motion, CVPR'98, Santa Barbara, CA, June 22.* 73-80
6. Kintch, W. (1974). *The Representation of Meaning in Memory.* Hillsdale, NJ: Erlbaum.
7. Medin, D. L. (1975). A theory of contxt in discrimination learning. In G. Bower (Ed.) *The psychology of learning and motivation* (Vol.9). New York:Accademic Press.

8. Michotte, A.E. (1963). *The Perception of Causality* (E. Miles & T. R. Miles, Trans). New York: Basic Books.

9. Miller, G. A., & Johnson-Laird, P. N. (1976). *Language and Perception*. Cambridge, MA: Harvard Univ. Press.

10. Newtson, D. (1973). Attribution and the Unit of Perception of Ongoing Behavior. *Journal of Personality and Social Psychology, 28,* 28-38.

11. Newtson, D., & Engquist, G (1976). The Perceptual Organisation of Ongoing Behavior. *Journal of Experimental Social Psychology, 12,* 436-450.

12. Newtson, D., Engquist, G., & Bois, J. (1977). The Objective Basis of Behavior Units. *Personality and Social Psychology, 35 (12),* 847,862.

13. Newtson, D., & Rinder, R (1979). Variation in Behavior Perception and Ability Attribution. *Journal of Personality and Social Psychology, 37,*1847-1858.

14. Norman, D. A., & Rumelhart, D. E. (1975). *Explorations in Cognition*. San Francisco: Freeman.

15. Poitrenaud, S. (1995). The Procope Semantic Network: an alternative to action grammars. *International Journal of Human-Computer Studies,42,* 31-69.

16. Premack, D., (1990). The infant's theory of self-propelled objects. *Cognition, 36 (2), 1-16.*

17. Premack, D., (1995). Cause/induced motion: Intention/spontaneous motion. in Changeux, J.P., Chavaillon, J.: *Origins of the human brain.* (Eds). Oxford: Clarendon Press. (pp.286-309).

18. Richard, J.F., & Tijus, C. A. (1998). Modelling the Affordances of Objects in Problem Solving. In A.C. Quelhas & F. Pereira (Ed.), *Cognition and Context*. Lisboa ISPA, 293-315.

19. Rosales, R. & Sclaroff, S. (1998). Improved Tracking of Multiple Humans with Trajectory Prediction and Occlusion Modeling. In *Proceeding of the IEEE Computer Society Workshop: The Interpretation of Visual Motion, CVPR'98, Santa Barbara, CA, June 22.* 73-80.

20. Thibadeau, R. (1986). Artificial Perception of Actions, *Cognitive Science, 10,*177-149.

21. Thommen, E. (1991). La genése de la perception de l'intentionnalité dans le mouvement apparent. *Archives de Psychologie, 59,* 195-223.

22. Tijus, C.A., & Moulin, F. (1997). L'assignation de signification étudiée à partir de textes d'histoires drôles. *L'année Psychologique, 97,* 33-75.

23. Tijus, C. A. & Poitrenaud, S. (1997). Modeliser l'Affordance des Objets. *Actes du 6ème colloque: Sciences Cognitives, Individus et Société,* p 57-65.

24. Zacks., J. and Tversky, B. (1997). What's happening? The Structure of Event Perception. In *Proceedings of the 19th Annual Meeting of the Cognitive Science Society, Stanford, CA..*

25. Zibetti, E., & Tijus, C. A. (1997). L'Effet des Propriétés d'Objet sur l'Interprétation de l'Action Perçue. In *Actes du Colloque des Journées Internationales d'Orsay sur les Sciences Cognitives, JIOSC 97.* Centre Scientifique d'Orsay. 1-2 december 1997. 197-202.

26. Zibetti, E., Hamilton, E. & Tijus, C.A. (en revision). The role of visual components in interpreting perceived actions.

Contexts, Domains, and Software

Alfs Berztiss[1,2]

[1] University of Pittsburgh, Pittsburgh PA 15260, USA
[2] SYSLAB, University of Stockholm, Sweden

Abstract. We survey some issues that relate to context dependence and context sensitivity in the development of software, particularly in relation to information systems by defining a range of context-related concepts. Domain models are identified as the appropriate framework for dealing with context-related issues.

The importance of context is being increasingly recognized in many areas of computing. The aim of this note is to arrive at a classification of contexts in a rather informal way, by defining a number of terms. We hope that this will further the discussion of what effect context has on the design of software systems, and on the relationship between contexts and domain modeling.

The interpretation of the word context shows considerable variety — indeed, the definition is itself context-sensitive. Linguists may see it as a psychological construct, a subset of a hearer's assumptions about the world that is used in interpreting an utterance [1]. To an organizational theorist context is a social environment in which actions are taken [2]. To a sociologist, context is provided by macrosocial forms, such as gender, national ethos, and economic maturity of a society [3]. An axiomatic approach is taken in [4].

As a first step toward a classification of contexts we take a dictionary definition of context: the parts of a written or spoken statement that precede and follow a specific word or passage, or a set of circumstances or facts that surround a particular event, situation, etc [5]. This two-way split suggests a partitioning of contexts into internal and external. The term *internal context* relates to cases in which the actions of a software system depend on internal factors. For example, computer systems contain clocks, and an operation may be triggered by such an internal clock. When the software actions depend on external factors, such as a temperature reading or a stock market quote, we shall use the term *external context*. In all cases the effects of the context can be expressed as rules, which we call context rules. A set of context rules relating to a particular setting of interest will be called a *contextual domain model* (CDM).

For uniformity we assume that all context rules of CDMs have the form "if c then q." An example: "If x is in the United States, then temperatures at x are measured in Fahrenheit." The c will be called a *context*; the q will be called an *effect*. Both c and q form populations that can be partitioned into classes that can be related to domains.

Not all software systems are context-dependent. To identify those that are, we partition computations into *procedural* and *transactional*. A procedural computation transforms inputs into outputs by means of some algorithm. An example is the computation of the cosine of an angle, and a characteristic of the cosine of angle x is that it is always and everywhere the same. To generalize, procedural computations are independent of context. Transactional computations are not: the result of a transactional computation depends on the state of the environment in which it is carried out. The distinction between procedural and transactional systems is not clear-cut: a predominantly transactional system often contains procedural components, e.g., an interest-computing procedure in a system that manages bank accounts.

We equate the *domain* in which a software system operates with a context for this system. To start off, let us establish a rationale for this interpretation. The environment or domain in which the word pen is used, a children's nursery, a cattleyard, a writers' workshop, or a bird watchers' excursion, lead to the interpretation of the word as a play area, a cattle enclosure, a writing implement, or a female swan. In terms of the if-then approach, we can state "If pen is located in a children's nursery, then it is likely to refer to an enclosed play area." The pen as play area becomes a working hypothesis, and the hypothesis remains in force unless additional evidence negates it.

The expression "If inventory level for item x is below c, then reorder y of x from z" is also a context-effect expression, but there is a taxonomic difference between its consequent and that of the children's nursery expression. In one case the consequent suggests a definition for a term, in the other it initiates an operation. Moreover, and this is a crucial difference, in the case of the pen there is context sensitivity in that a choice of interpretation exists, while there is no choice in the reordering situation. There is no obvious difference in the antecedents. Now consider the rule "If inventory level for pens is below c, then reorder y pens from z." If this expression is used in an office, then it is unlikely that pens will be interpreted as female swans. This enables us to distinguish between a *linguistic context* and a *nonlinguistic context.*

The defining characteristic of context sensitivity is choice. Of course, there is choice in all instances of the ordering of pens: the pens are either to be ordered or not ordered. The choice we have in mind has to be more complex than a simple yes/no decision. To emphasize this difference we shall talk of context sensitivity only when a choice is more complex than a yes/no decision. In all cases there is a context dependence: every transactional system that aims at influencing its environment has to be aware of the current state of the environment.

Whether a domain model provides an internal or external context depends on how it is used. If it is closely tied to a particular application, e.g., if it serves to allow greater sophistication in the use of a particular data base, or if it tells when pens are to be reordered, then it is internal. When the model requires, for example, information on the possibility of a strike at the factory supplying pens, then it becomes external because the c of our "if c then q" is then supplied in part by the external environment of the software system. The internal-external distinction does not much matter, except that an external domain is more likely to undergo change. The meaning of words changes slowly, and changes in a linguistic domain are therefore quite slow. On the other hand, business environments can change very rapidly.

What is an appropriate domain model depends on the purpose to which it is put. We have examined domain models for reuse in software development [6], conceptual modeling [7], and decision support systems [8]. In all these cases the domain models have to have a process orientation, and we call them *process domain models* (PDMs). Another type of domain model relates the concepts that pertain to a domain, and thus defines the static structure of the domain. This type of model will be called a *structural domain model* (SDM). What matters here is that the domain model is to represent contexts, and for a CDM the form "if c then q" appears the most suitable. Note that this form is used also by Brezillon and Pomerol in their work on context in decision making [9]; such forms have been used extensively in business models and knowledge-based systems.

We have considered two types of context change, *context evolution* and *context switch* [8]. An example of context evolution relates to a rental company that is taking note of changes in its environment and is now allowing rental reservations to be made not just by mail or telephone, but also electronically. The interactions between personnel, software system, and customers are different for the two existing reservation modes, and the addition of the third mode requires that a third interaction pattern be added to the domain model. Context switch relates to the migration of a software capability from one domain or subdomain to another. For example, although car rental and video rental are similar applications, there are differences.

We noted earlier that in a context-sensitive situation the rule "if c then q" expresses a choice. Actually we should limit the use of the simple form to cases in which there is just context dependence, i.e., where merely a yes/no decision is to be made. In the more complex cases we should put the rule in the form "if c_1 then q_1 else if c_2 then q_2 else if c_3 then q_3 ...". We call the c of the simple case a *trigger*; the c_i of the forms expressing choice are called *selectors*. Let us look at an example, the query "Was it cold on September 5?" The reference to a calendar and a determination of where the questioner is located allow the the system to sharpen the query to "What was the minimum temperature in Fahrenheit at Pittsburgh on September 5, 1999?" Here we have several rules with selectors: if reference made to cold use minimum temperature; if the calendar reference is incomplete, complete it to the closest relevant calendar reference before today; if the question originates in place x, relate the answer to this place; if x is in the United States, use Fahrenheit.

The effect of a context rule is a control action, the furnishing of information to a user, or a request for further inputs. Systems based on rules of these types are, respectively, control systems, information systems, and dialog systems. Of course, a system can be a hybrid. Control systems are in some respects the easiest to develop, in some respects the most difficult. They are easy because a context rule is defined by a domain expert, and the software developer merely implements the rule. But control systems are not just aggregates of independent rule-based actions. They implement processes, so that the appropriate model is a PDM rather than a CDM, and the construction of a PDM from individual context rules is a complex, intellectually demanding cooperative effort of domain experts and software engineers. We are not considering dialog systems here.

Information systems operate in a much broader context than control systems. The model of the environment of a control system, i.e., the model of the host system into which the control system is embedded, does not change; only values of the parameters of the model change, and the purpose of the control system is to keep these values within acceptable ranges. As regards information systems, the CDM may itself be changing — the context evolves. At its mildest, context evolution or context switch manifests itself merely in a different effect q when the context c is refined. For example, although normally temperatures in the United States are measured in Fahrenheit, in a hospital they may be expressed in Centigrade. This is a context effect.

We have introduced a large number of terms. To begin with, we partitioned contexts into linguistic and nonlinguistic, and internal and external. We saw that an action can be independent of context, can depend on context, or can be context-sensitive. We identified context with a particular type of domain model, the CDM. Two other domain models, PDM and SDM, were introduced as well. We noted that a domain model can change slowly or rapidly, and that a context change can be context evolution or context switch. The CDM was seen as being composed of context rules of the type "if c then q," where the c could be either a selector or a trigger. Turning to computing, we identified procedural and and transactional software, and the latter was partitioned into control, information, and dialog systems.

References

1. Sperber, D., Wilson, D.: Relevance — Communication and Cognition. Harvard University Press (1986).
2. Weick, K.E.: Sensemaking in Organizations. Sage Publications (1995).
3. Layder, D.: New Strategies in Social Research. Polity Press (1993).
4. Buvac ,S., Buvac, V., Mason, I.A.: Metamathematics of contexts. Fundamenta Informaticae 23 (1995) 263-301.
5. Webster's Encyclopedic Unabridged Dictionary of the English Language. Portland House (1989).
6. Berztiss, A.T.: Domains, patterns, reuse, and the software process. In: Domain Knowledge for Interactive System Design. Chapman & Hall (1996) 79-89.
7. In: Information Modelling and Knowledge Bases VIII. ISO Press (1997) 213-223.
8. Berztiss, A.T.: Domain models for flexible decision support systems. In: Context Sensitive Decision Support Systems. Chapman & Hall (1998) 216-226.
9. Brezillon, P., Pomerol, J.-Ch.: Using contextual information in decision making. In: Context Sensitive Decision Support Systems. Chapman & Hall (1998) 158-173.

Contextual Data and Domain Knowledge for Incorporation in Knowledge Discovery Systems

Alex G. Büchner[1], John G. Hughes[1] and David A. Bell[2]

[1] Northern Ireland Knowledge Engineering Laboratory, University of Ulster
[2] School of Information and Software Engineering, University of Ulster
Shore Road, Newtownabbey, BT37 0QB, UK
phone: +44 (0)1232 368394   fax: +44 (0)1232 366068
email: {ag.buchner, jg.hughes, da.bell}@ulst.ac.uk

Abstract. The concepts of contextual data and domain knowledge is proposed and incorporated in a generic knowledge discovery architecture. The outlined concepts are supported electronic commerce examples.

1 Introduction

Data and domain knowledge are the two most essential input ingredients for data mining applications. The former is either provided by operational databases or by their warehoused counterparts in form of materialised views, which can be reused for multiple model building exercises. The latter, in whatever form provided, has to be re-specified, or at least modified, depending in which context patterns are to be discovered. This limits the concept of domain knowledge, and thus, the objective of this paper is to propose the notion of contextual data and domain knowledge, which can be reused across multiple related knowledge discovery exercises.

The structure of this paper is as follows. First, the organisation of contexts is outlined, which includes a brief recapitulation of contextual data as well as contextual domain knowledge. Then, the concepts, which are based on previous work, are incorporated in a generic knowledge discovery framework.

2 Organisation of Contexts

A context represents behavioural aspects that are shared by attributes of the same ontology, which are organised hierarchically. The general idea is that every single attribute instance is being allotted an additional attribute context identifier in a multi-database scenario, where each attribute instance is represented by a semantic value [1]. The same concept is also applied to domain knowledge, which guarantees consistent handling of the two components.

2.1 Contextual Data

Contextual data is represented by semantic values, which consist of a type, a value and a context [2]. This approach is a generalisation of proposals, in which every attribute — but not each attribute instance — has a specific context allotted to it. In order to allow database operations function correctly, contextual comparison operations have been introduced, which are handled by a data context mediator. The mediator is an evaluation mechanism that takes two semantic values and returns their type- *and* context-specific order. A variety of constructs has been suggested in the literature, but to reconcile context heterogeneity for data mining input, functions (which encompass arithmetic expressions as well as rules) and tables are sufficient.

> context mediator $\leftarrow s_1, s_2$
> func <conversion_function> | table <collation>
> context mediator $\rightarrow \{-1, 0, 1\}$

Fig. 1. Data Context Mediator Structure

The data context mediator, which has been embedded in an object data model, supports atomic, abstract, as well as complex data types (see [2] for more details).

2.2 Contextual Domain Knowledge

Domain knowledge can be used for making patterns more visible, for constraining the search space, for finding more accurate knowledge, and for filtering out uninteresting patterns [3]. For the purpose of a contextual data mining environment, four types of domain expertise are supported: Taxonomies, which encompass bandings (ranges), concept hierarchies and network models, constraints (aka. attribute-relationship rules), previously discovered knowledge, and user preferences (see [3] for details). Each domain knowledge type is investigated from two different dimensions. The first is concerned with the degree of reality, where reality is represented in a spectrum from a physical world to a logical model world (Fig. 2.). The second is interested in the degree of reusability of the specified types of domain knowledge [3].

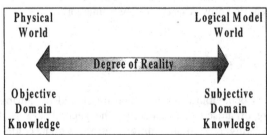

Fig. 2. Domain Knowledge Degrees of Reality

Objective domain knowledge consists of a set of quasi facts within the domain a data mining exercise is carried out. Although it can have a certain degree of context-dependency, it is almost always kept as holos and only exchanged in total for its contextual counterpart. *Subjective domain knowledge* has a higher degree of context-dependency than its objective counterpart. As a consequence, either entire domain knowledge entities or large parts thereof have to exist for multiple contexts. It is desirable to handle the entire range of domain knowledge degrees of reality using the same underlying techniques. Thus, contextual domain knowledge has been proposed, independent of its degree of reality. Basically, each piece of domain knowledge is allotted a context, which conforms to the handling of contextual data.

For example, contextual concept hierarchies are of high interest to data mining exercises. Because each node in a hierarchy is allotted a context identifier, it is possible to reuse a collection of nodes and their sub-trees. The marketing manager Europe (context c_m) might only be interested in the sub-hierarchy with all European countries, whereas the person responsible for introducing a product at educational level (c_e) would only be concerned about the according sub-trees (see Fig. 3.).

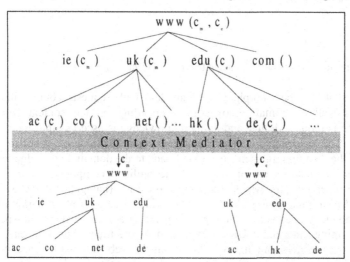

Fig. 3. Example Contextual Concept Hierarchy

Similar to contextual data, contextual domain knowledge has to be mediated. The purpose of the domain knowledge context mediator is to decide what expertise is to be included and what is to be excluded from a data mining task. This decision is based on the context the knowledge has been created in and the context it is to be applied to. These two sites are referred to as knowledge source s and receiver r. Owing to the fact that a user can only be in one context at a time, the mediator returns the pieces of expertise that have been allotted to the context in which the user is currently in. More formally, this can be expressed as following, where D is the set of domain knowledge.

---

context mediator $\leftarrow c_r$

$$D_r := \bigcup d_s \mid d_s \in D_s \wedge c_s(d_s) = c_r$$

context mediator $\rightarrow D_r$

Fig. 4. Domain Knowledge Context Mediator Structure

3 Contextual Data Mining Architecture

In order to deploy contextual data as well as contextual domain knowledge in data mining applications, a simplified knowledge discovery architecture has been created.

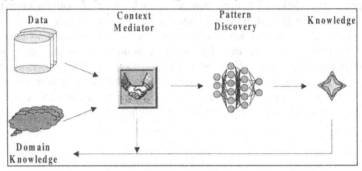

Fig. 5. Simplified Contextual Knowledge Discovery Architecture

The mediator is polymorph, i.e. it can deal with requests about multiple data sources as well as domain knowledge. Depending on the context from which information is requested, data and domain knowledge is used as input for knowledge discovery. The discovered patterns are then contextualised, i.e. labelled with the context of the data mining exercise, and fed back to the domain knowledge repository.

In order to illustrate the operation of the outlined components, consider an e-commerce example, in which sequential patterns (navigational behaviour) are discovered from internet log files. The types of log data as well as marketing-related domain knowledge depend on the type of operating e-tailer. Having site-specific log files (containing data about URLs, login and logoff times, http referrers, statuses, cookies, etc.), the marketing manager as well as the web administrator are looking for interesting patterns. The former has specified her expertise in form of region-based concept hierarchies and target-related age bandings. The latter has created a network topology of the retailer's web site. The thresholds are budget- and cache size-driven, respectively. The discovered sequences are most likely to be different, since they are goal- *and* context-driven. They are kept in the domain knowledge repository after they have been tagged with the current context and memorised for future usage.

References

1. Sciore, E., Siegel, M., Rosenthal, A.: Using Semantic Values to Facilitate Interoperability Among Heterogeneous Information Systems, ACM Transactions on Database Systems 19 Vol. 2 (1994) 254-290
2. Büchner, AG., Bell, DA., Hughes, JG.: A Contextualised Object Data Model based on Semantic Values, 11th Int Conf Parallel & Distributed Computing Systems (1998) 171-176
3. Anand, SS., Büchner, AG.: Decision Support using Data Mining, FT Pitman Publishers (1998)
4. Büchner, AG., Bell, DA., Hughes, JG.: Contextual Domain Knowledge for Incorporation in Data Mining Systems,. AAAI Workshop Reasoning in Context for AI Applications (1999)

The Differential (?) Processing of Literal and Nonliteral Speech Acts: A Psycholinguistic Approach

Maud Champagne[1], Jacques Virbel[2], and Jean-Luc Nespoulous[1]

[1] Laboratoire de Neuropsycholinguistique Jacques-Lordat
Maison de la Recherche, Université de Toulouse-Le Mirail, France
Champagn@univ-tlse2.fr
[2] Institut de Recherche en Informatique de Toulouse IRIT-CNRS
Université Paul Sabatier, France

Abstract. When we speak, we often use nonliteral utterances in which the meaning intended is different from the literal meaning. So, we must be able to differentiate what the speaker says from what he wants to say, using contextual information to understand the speaker's intention and to make assumptions, predictions and inferences.The aim of this study is to determine whether there exists a hierarchy of complexity between various nonliteral speech acts. In other words, does an indirect request, for instance, require more processing to be understood than an ironic statement ? Some evidence was found for the existence of a hierarchy of complexity. Results emphasizes the particular role of "conventionality" and confirm the idea that conversational rules are very strongly dependent upon context.

1 Introduction

In the "speech act" framework, as defined by Austin [1] and Searle [6], the comprehension of a nonliteral speech act requires at the same time (a) the processing of what is explicitly said, and (b) the capacity to go beyond this literal meaning to perceive the speaker's intention in the given context. In other words, the hearer must be able to grasp both the literal and the nonliteral meaning of the message, what the speaker says and what he intends to say. Therefore, he must use contextual information to make inferences, assuming, of course, that the speaker respects some conversational maxims (Grice [5]) in the pragmatic context within which statement is made.

Following · Searle, an indirect speech act occurs whenever the speaker wants to say what he says and something more, in other words, when he makes two distinct acts with only one statement (in this way, " it's cold here! " means " I assert it's cold here " and " close the window!"). From this definition and according to Grice's conversational principles, we defined four types of stimuli as follows :

- violations of the maxim of relation and violations of the maxim of quantity (L says p, and he wants to say exactly q)
- indirect requests (L says p, and he wants to say exactly p+q)
- ironic statements (L says p, and he wants to say exactly non p (in other words, he wants to say exactly the opposite of p in the context of utterance))

– direct speech acts (L says p, and he wants to say exactly p)

The aim of this study, among healthy subject, is to determine whether there exists a hierarchy of complexity between various nonliteral speech acts compared to literal speech acts. In other words, does an indirect request, for instance, require more processing to be understood than a ironic statement ?

In order to test such an hypothesis, we compare reading time measurements for different subtypes of stimuli belonging to each of the four above mentioned categories. Later on, our intention is to further assess the differential processing of literal and nonliteral speechs acts by testing right hemisphere brain damaged subjects, who have been shown to have problems in using context to understand nonliteral meanings (Brownell & al. [2]). The current study will thus be used as a reference to compare the results of healthy subjects and right brain damaged subjects.

2 Experiment

2.1 Method

40 young, right-handed students, all native French speakers, were tested individually. They had to read the randomized stimuli presented on a computer screen. Subjects had to read each story in two stages. They had to push on the space key to move from the first part of the text to the next. Then, they had to make a true-false judgement by using either the " V " (" Vrai ", " true ", in French) or the " F " (" Faux ", " false ", in French) key. Subjects had not the possibility to make any corrections afterwards.

Before starting the proper experiment, subjects were trained with ten stimuli, different from the ones to be used in the experiment. The task lasted about 30 minutes, with a pause of three minutes halfway across the test. The computer recorded both the latency of the reading/comprehension of the target sentence (Reading Time : RT) and the decision latency of the the judgement task (Decision Time : DT).

There were 112 stimuli distributed as follows : 56 nonliteral, or " implicit " speech acts , with : 14 violations of the maxim of relation (VMR), 14 violations of the maxim of quantity (VMQ), 14 indirect requests, 14 ironic statements, and 56 literal, or " explicit ", speech acts (corresponding to the literal counterparts of the 56 previous stimuli).

2.2 Results

Table 1 presents the reading/comprehension time (RT) of the target sentences and the decision time (DT) taken to judge the assertion. The Rts have been corrected in order to take sentence length (number of characters) into account.

About the reading/comprehension times for the target sentences, the analysis of variance reveals a significant effect of the implicit or explicit category on the Reading Time, $F(1,39) = 155.276$, $p<.0001$. Thus, subjects process more rapidly an explicit stimulus than an implicit stimulus. Anova shows that the various implicit categories RTs are significantly different, $F(3,39)=52.845$, $p<.0001$. A comparison (two by two)

of the implicit categories shows partial differences. Indeed, subjects process more quickly :
- the indirect requests than the VMQ (F(1,39)=1.06E2, p<.0001),
- the indirect requests than the ironic statements (F(1,39)=98.157,p<.0001),
- the indirect requests than the VMR (F(1,39)=74.915, p<.0001),
- the VMR than the VMQ (F(1,39)=18.231,p<.0001),
- the VMR than the ironic statements (F(1,39)=9.237,p<.0042).

However, there are no significant differences between violations of the maxim of quantity and ironic statements.

Our analysis indicates that there is a global significant effect of the implicit/explicit dichotomy across all subtypes of speech acts F(3,39)=28.854,p<.0001. More precisely, such a significant effect between implicit Vs. explicit stimuli holds for the VMR (F(1,39)=57.202,p<.0001), for the VMQ (F(1,39)=1.35E2,p<.0001) and for the ironic statements (F(1,39)=48.901,p<.0001). Nevertheless, there is no such effect for the indirect requests.

3 Discussion

Some results of the current experiment confirm our main prediction : the explicit stimuli are indeed easier to process than the implicit ones. This may appear to be quite normal since, with explicit stimuli, there is no need for contextual cues for a first-pass interpretation to be rejected. The speaker says p, and he means p. Therefore, the implicit stimuli would be more complex than the explicit ones because they require some contextually determined inferences to be computed.

Concerning the existence of a hierarchy of complexity, our results give only partial support to our hypothesis. Indeed, if indirect requests are understood more easily than the other nonliteral speech acts, and if the violations of the maxim of relation are understood more easily than the violations of the maxim of quantity and than the ironic statements, we cannot say anything about the differences between ironic statements and violations of the maxim of quantity.

Indirect requests appear be the easiest nonliteral speech acts to be processed. A possible explanation of this observation may lie in the fact that we only used conversational requests and several studies (Clark [3], Gibbs [4]) have shown the prominent role of conventionality in discourse processing. According to Gibbs, hearers would use the context to understand *directly* nonliteral utterances, without processing *first* the literal meaning of the sentence (this challenges Grice's and Searle's models).

Here again, the percentage of errors of ironic statements decreases as we go from the implicit to the explicit version. This fact most likely underlines the relative complexity of this category, a complexity that might also be explained by the lack of marked ironic intonation, for those sentences within our experiment ... and indeed intonation may be considered as a prominent contextual cue in oral ironic statements. Rts in such a case are markedly longer than in the other categories, and longer than in the implicit version. Such an observation is certainly in favour of Grice's explanation [5]. According to him, the hearer identifying, from the context, that the literal truth of the remarks contrasts with the known facts, but assuming that the speaker has said this for some reason reinterprets the utterance in order to make it consistent with the context, and then derives the intended meaning that is usually the opposite of what is said. Moreover, it does not challenge the echoic model of Sperber & Wilson (1986,1987), because, in many stimuli used in our experiment, the context indeed mentions what is uttered in an ironic way by the speaker.

These results go against Grice's conception [5]. According to him, the process used by the hearer to understand the intentional meaning is the same as the process proposed to interpret the indirect speech acts. As Searle [7] states, ironic statements, in particular, have to be distinguished from indirect speech acts. The whole of this experiment confirms the idea that conversational rules are very heavily context-dependent. It does seem that a hierarchy of complexity exists. Thus, when a speaker says p, it would be easier to understand that he wants to say p+q, then q (when there is a violation of the maxim of relation), then non p. The results of this experiment give us an idea of what a hierarchy might look like, but, as we have been seeing several times, some of the results must be indeed qualified.

Table 1. Reading Time (RT) and Decision Time (DT) (in ms.) for the implicit and explicit subcategories.

-	-	VMR	VMQ	Indirect request	Irony
Implicit	RT	45	48	38	47
	DT	2251	2429	2369	2274
	% of errors	(3,2%)	(9,3%)	(8,9%)	(4,5%)
Explicit	RT	37	39	38	42
	DT	2198	2259	2329	2294
	% of errors	(3,4%)	(3,9%)	(9,3%)	(1,4%)

References

1. Austin JL (1962) How to do things with words. Oxford Clarendon Press
2. Brownell HH & al. (1986) Inference deficits in right brain-damaged patients. Brain and Language 27: 310-321
3. Clark HH (1979) Responding to indirect speech acts. Cognitive psychology 11: 430-477
4. Gibbs RW (1982) A critical examination of the contribution of literal meaning to understanding nonliteral discourse. Text 2: 9-28
5. Grice HP (1975), Logic and Conversation. In Cole P and Morgan JL (eds). Syntax and Semantics vol 3 Speech Acts. Academic Press
6. Searle JR (1969) Speech Acts. Cambridge University Press
7. Searle JR (1979) Expression and meaning. Cambridge University Press
8. Vanderveken D (1988) Les actes de discours. Mardaga, Bruxelles

Open Theories and Abduction for Context and Accommodation

Henning Christiansen

Roskilde University, Computer Science Dept.,
P.O.Box 260, DK-4000 Roskilde, Denmark
E-mail: henning@ruc.dk

Abstract. A model is proposed for the representation of context by means of open logic theories parameterized by metavariables covered by constraints. The model is formalized and implemented using constraint logic and metalogic programming notions. Accommodation, understood as the process of extracting presuppositions embedded in a discourse or, in general, extracting the contents embedded in a stream of observations, fits naturally into this model as abduction. A possible worlds' semantics is given similar to a proposal given by Stalnaker.

1 Introduction

Context in linguistics and artificial intelligence usually refers to the amount of common knowledge shared among the participants in a discourse or to the knowledge currently held by an agent attending a discourse. As the discourse proceeds, more and more knowledge is gained which means that the context becomes more and more specific as the result of an accommodation process. This paper describes an abstract model and implementation of context and accommodation which can be seen as a formalization of Stalnaker's informal characterization summarized in [13], which inspired to this more systematic presentation based on earlier *ad hoc* experiments with simplified natural language analysis by means of abduction in a metalogic setting [4,5]. For a full version of this paper with more details, examples and comprehensive references, see [9].

2 The basic model

In order to model the dynamic evolution of context, i.e., accommodation, we consider *open logic theories* useful. A theory being open means, at the semantic level, that several interpretations (i.e., worlds in a Kripke-style semantics) are possible, namely all those that are compatible with the knowledge gained from the discourse so far, perhaps restricted within a set of "reasonable" interpretations (worlds). We distinguish between an *object language* in which theories about states of affairs can be formulated and a *metalanguage* in which properties about such theories are expressed. Some object sentences are *closed theories* and we assume a set of possible *worlds* and a *semantic function* w mapping each closed theory T into a world $w(T)$.[1] An entailment relation $w \models s$ is assumed with the intended meaning that object sentence s holds in w; for a set of worlds W we write $W \models s$ iff $w \models s$ for all $w \in W$. A *naming relation* is assumed, giving for each element o of the object language a metalevel term $\lceil o \rceil$ which serves as a name for o. An *open theory* arises when parts of the name for a theory are left out, indicating their positions by metavariables. Metavariables inside name terms are indicated by reverse brackets so, e.g., $\lceil p(Y) \leftarrow \lfloor B \rfloor \rceil$ is a scheme for names of object clauses whose head is $p(Y)$ and whose body is unknown, indicated by the metavariable B. A metalevel term which can be instantiated to the name of a theory is said to be of *theory type*.

A *context* is a pair $K = \langle T, C \rangle$ where T is a metalevel term of theory type and C a metalevel formula; T is called the *theory part* and C the *constraint part* of K. The intended meaning is that a given context captures all those possible worlds contained in the open theory represented by T, however, only those permitted by C. We make this precise by the following definition: The *context set* for a context $\langle T, C \rangle$ is the set of worlds $W(\langle T, C \rangle)$ defined as

$$W(\langle T, C \rangle) = \{ w(t) \mid \langle \lceil t \rceil, C' \rangle \text{ is a ground instance of } \langle T, C \rangle \text{ in which } C' \text{ is true} \}$$

Open theories fit well with accommodation understood as specialization and with abduction applied as the means for specialization; abduction means to reason backwards using rules already present in the context, as background knowledge or perhaps learned during the discourse, in order to identify contextual facts that can explain the observed actions (utterances, sensor signals, etc.). We assume a class *Action* of object formulas (typically facts) called *actions*; a sequence of actions is called a *discourse*. A *specialization* of a context $\langle T, C \rangle$ is a new context $\langle T, C \wedge S \rangle \sigma$ where σ is a metalevel substitution and S a metalevel formula. An *accommodation function* is a function

$$\text{accomodate} : \textit{Context} \times \textit{Action} \rightarrow \textit{Context}$$

where accommodate(K, A) is a specialization of K; *Context* refers to the set of all contexts. An accommodation function is extended for sequences of actions in the natural way, and if it reaches a context $\top$ with $W(\top) = \emptyset$, it is said to fail. Some nonmonotonic aspects can be accounted for by allowing accommodation functions to be nondeterministic in the sense that they may produce more than one resulting new context; this fits with the backtracking provided by an implementation in logic programming. We require that an accommodation function satisfies the property that, for all contexts K and actions A, $W(\text{accomodate}(K, A)) \models A$, a definition that includes abduction and induction as special cases. Accommodation starts from an *initial context* which may include "background knowledge"

---

[1] There are no open theories represented at the object level, openness is obtained by parameterization at the metalevel. We chose the closed-theory–single-world formulation in order to stress that the interesting degrees of freedom are expressed at the level of open theories. The framework can easily be extended for, say, disjunctive object theories, by having $w(t)$ to be a (finite) set of worlds.

as well as metaknowledge to guide the accommodation function corresponding to, e.g., integrity constraints in database update, "bias" in inductive logic programming, or the "abducibles" in abduction.

3 Representation in metalogic programming

This model can be embedded in the DEMO system [5, 8] which is a constraint-based metaprogramming systems built on top of Prolog. The object language is that of positive Horn clauses and we let $w(P)$ be the least Herbrand model of P for any such program. The most important metalevel predicates are two proof predicates demo($\lceil P \rceil, \lceil Q \rceil$) and fails($\lceil P \rceil, \lceil Q \rceil$) with the meaning that object query Q succeeds, resp. fails, in the object program P. The interesting property of this system is the *reversibility* of demo: It works correctly also when the program argument contains metavariables standing for unknown parts of the object program. In this case, the execution of demo may generate object programs which make the object query provable. The fails predicate works basically as a metalevel version of negation-as-failure that delays subcomputations for the "missing parts" of the object program, thus providing an incremental evaluation of integrity constraints [6].

We can sketch the implementation of accommodation by the following meta-level query which captures the accommodation of a single action.

$$\text{abd(A), fails}(\lceil CT \mathbin{\&} IC \mathbin{\&} \lfloor A \rfloor \rceil, \lceil \perp \rceil), \text{demo}(\lceil CT \mathbin{\&} \lfloor A \rfloor \rceil, \lceil Action \rceil)$$

The 'abd' predicate defines object programs consisting of abducible atoms, CT is the know part of the theory in the current context. Integrity constraints are specified by an object program IC defining the predicate $\perp$. The metavariable A is the "opening" in the current context which will be partly instantiated during the execution of this query as to reach a new context in which the observed *Action* can be explained. See [5, 7, 9] for examples.

4 Related work

Compared with earlier models of context, e.g., [1, 12] and successors, this is a simplification in the sense that the general mechanism of abduction only refers to rules appearing in a description of the current domain so that an additional and orthogonal layer of so-called lifting rules or specialized modal operators becomes unnecessary. The model proposed here can host many existing knowledge representation formalisms, e.g., conceptual structures [14], terminological logic [2], and various other apparata biased towards the syntax and semantics of natural language. The fact that the framework is embedded in logic programming provides a direct interface to syntax analysis methods of which numerous have been described in the literature.

The use of abduction for natural language analysis is not new, e.g., [10]; our contribution is mainly at the semantic level, giving a new formulation in a meta-logic setting which integrates abduction with open theories and possible worlds' semantics. Open logic theories have been studied in different shapes, e.g. [11, 15]. Our version differs from the mentioned by a more "fine-grained" parameterization obtained by metavariables that may stand in arbitrary positions in the expression naming the theory and controlled by arbitrary metalogic constraints.

Acknowledgment: This research is supported in part by the OntoQuery and DART projects funded by the Danish Research Councils.

References

1. Attardi, G., Simi, M., Metalanguage and reasoning across viewpoints. *Proc. ECAI94: Advances in Artificial Intelligence* O'Shea, T.O., (ed.), pp. 315–324. Elsevier Science Publishers, 1984.
2. Brachman, R.J., Levesques, H.J., Competence in knowledge representation. *Proceedings of the National Conference on Artificial Intelligence. Pittsburgh, PA, August 18–20, 1982*, Walz, D.L., AAAI Press pp. 189–192, 1982.
3. Buvač, S., Quantificational Logic of Context. *Proc. AAAI 96 & IAAI 96, Thirteenth National Conference on Artificial Intelligence and Eighth Innovative Applications of Artificial Intelligence Conference*, pp. 600–606, AAAI Press/MIT Press, 1996.
4. Christiansen, H., Why should grammars not adapt themselves to context and discourse? *4th International Pragmatics Conference, Kobe, Japan, July 23–30 1993*, (Abstract collection), International Pragmatics Association p. 23, 1993. (Extended abstract: http://www.dat.ruc.dk/~henning/IPRA93.ps).
5. Christiansen, H., Automated reasoning with a constraint-based metainterpreter, *Journal of Logic Programming*, vol. 37, pp. 213–253, 1998.
6. Christiansen, H., Lazy negation-as-failure for incremental integrity checking, *To appear*, 1999.
7. Christiansen, H., Abduction and induction combined in a metalogic framework. *Abductive and Inductive Reasoning: Essays on their Relation and Integration*, Flach. P., Kakas, A., (eds.), To appear, 1999.
8. Christiansen, H., Martinenghi, D., *The DemoII system.* Source code for implemented system, example files, and manuals available by World Wide Web, http://www.dat.ruc.dk/software/index.htm. Released 1998.
9. Christiansen, H., Open theories and abduction for context and accommodation. Full version of present paper. *To appear*, 1999 (currently available from http://www.dat.ruc.dk/~henning).
10. Hobbs, J.R., Stickel, M.E., Appelt D.E., and Martin, P., Interpretation as abduction. *Artificial Intelligence* 63, pp. 69-142, 1993.
11. Mancarella, P., Pedreschi, D., An algebra of logic programs. *Proc. Fifth International Conference and Symposium of Logic Programming*, pp. 1006–1023, MIT Press, 1988.
12. McCarthy, J., Generality in artificial intelligence. *Communications of the ACM*, vol. 30, pp. 1030–1035, 1987.
13. Stalnaker, R., On the representation of context. *Journal of Logic, Language, and Information*, vol. 7, pp. 3–19, 1998.
14. Sowa, J.F., *Conceptual Structures: Information Processing in Mind and Machine*, Addison-Wesley, 1984.
15. Verbaeten, S., Denecker, M., De Schreye, D., Compositionality of Normal Open Logic Programs, Logic Programming, Proceedings of the 1997 International Symposium, Maluszynski, J., (ed.), pp. 371–385, MIT Press, 1997.

Context as Fuzzy Degrees of Acceptability for Knowledge Base Integrity

John Debenham

University of Technology, Sydney,
School of Computing Sciences,
PO Box 123, NSW 2007, Australia
debenham@socs.uts.edu.au

Abstract. Knowledge base context is defined as a graduated region 'surrounding' a knowledge base expressed in terms of fuzzy measures of acceptability. The graduated regions of a knowledge base's context provide a formal basis for questioning knowledge integrity. The knowledge representation used is uniform in the sense that data, information and knowledge are all modelled as items. Items inherit the context of their components. Objects are item-building operators that are independent of such context.

1. Introduction

The terms 'data', 'information' and 'knowledge' are used here as follows. The *data* in an application are those things that can be represented as simple constants or variables. The *information* is those things that can be represented as tuples or relations. The *knowledge* is those things that can be represented either as programs in an imperative language or as rules in a declarative language. A unified knowledge representation for conceptual modelling is described in [1]. That representation is unified in the sense that no distinction is made between the knowledge, information and data throughout the design process. The approach reported in [1] is extended here to describe knowledge base context as a graduated region 'surrounding' a knowledge base. This is achieved by introducing fuzzy functions to measure varying degrees of acceptability. These fuzzy functions are generalisations of the knowledge constraints described in [2]. So here "a knowledge base's context" is the degree of acceptability of each possible instance of that knowledge base. Context [3] will, to some extent, determine the set of valid knowledge base instances. So to that extent the graduated region provides a view of knowledge base context.

An approach to specifying knowledge constraints is described in [2]. Those constraints are two-valued in the sense that either they are satisfied or they aren't. The *constraint domain* is the union of all knowledge base instances that satisfy a given set of knowledge constraints. The constraint domain can be visualised as an area within which the valid instances of a given knowledge base should reside, and outside which the integrity of instances should be questioned. The two-valued division of knowledge base instances by the constraint domain is too simple to be related to knowledge base context. But an *acceptability region* in which knowledge is "more acceptable" the "closer" it is to the constraint domain could make such a claim. Acceptability is defined in that sense here. *Context* is fuzzy degrees of acceptability for knowledge base integrity. A knowledge base's context is a graduated "comfort zone" into which the knowledge base may extend whilst raising questions of integrity at differing fuzzy degrees of confidence.

2. Items

Items are a formalism for describing the things in an application. Items have a uniform format no matter whether they represent data, information or knowledge things [1]. Items may be simplified with the application of a single rule [4]. The notion of an item is extended here to incorporate two powerful classes of acceptability measures. The key to this formalism is the way in which the "meaning" of an item, called its *semantics*, is specified.

The semantics of an item is a function that *recognises* the members of the "value set" of that item. The *value set* of an information item is the set of tuples that are associated with a relational implementation of that item. Knowledge items, including complex, recursive knowledge items, have *value sets* too [1]. The value set of an item will change in time, but the item's semantics should remain constant. For example, the item, *[part/sale-price, part/cost-price, part/type, type/mark-up]*, which represents the rule "the sale price of parts is the cost price marked up by a universal mark-up factor" has a value set consisting of a set of 8-tuples. Items incorporate two distinct classes of acceptability measures. Items are *either* represented informally as "i-schema" *or* formally as λ-calculus expressions. The i-schema notation is intended for practical use.

Formally, given a unique name A, an n-tuple $(m_1, m_2,..., m_n)$, $M = \Sigma_i \, m_i$, if:

- S_A is an M-argument expression of the form:

$$\lambda y_1^1 \cdots y_{m_1}^1 \cdots y_{m_n}^n \bullet [S_{A_1}(y_1^1 ,..,y_{m_1}^1) \wedge .. \wedge S_{A_n}(y_1^n,..,y_{m_n}^n) \wedge J(y_1^1 ,..,y_{m_1}^1,..,y_{m_n}^n)] \bullet$$

where $\{A_1,..., A_n\}$ is an ordered set of not necessarily distinct items, each item in this set is called a *component* of item A.

- V_A is an M-argument fuzzy expression of the form:

$$\lambda y_1^1 \cdots y_{m_1}^1 \cdots y_{m_n}^n \bullet [V_{A_1}(y_1^1 ,..,y_{m_1}^1) \wedge .. \wedge V_{A_n}(y_1^n,..,y_{m_n}^n) \wedge K(y_1^1 ,..,y_{m_1}^1,..,y_{m_n}^n)] \bullet$$

where $\{A_1,..., A_n\}$ are the components of item A, K is a fuzzy predicate and $\wedge$ is the standard "min" fuzzy conjunction.

- C_A is a fuzzy expression of the form:

$$[\, C_{A_1} \wedge C_{A_2} \wedge ... \wedge C_{A_n} \wedge (L)_A \,]$$

where $\wedge$ is the standard "min" fuzzy conjunction and L is a fuzzy expression constructed as a logical combination of:

- Card_A lies in some numerical range;
- $\text{Uni}(A_i)$ for some i, $1 \leq i \leq n$, and
- $\text{Can}(A_i, X)$ for some i, $1 \leq i \leq n$, where X is a non-empty subset of $\{A_1,..., A_n\} - \{A_i\}$;

subscripted with the name of the item A,

then the named triple $A[\,S_A,\,V_A,\,C_A]$ is an M-adic *item* with *item name* A, S_A is called the *item semantics* of A, V_A is called the *item value acceptability function* of A and C_A is called the *item set acceptability function* of A. "Uni(A_i)" is a fuzzy predicate whose truth value is "the proportion of the members of the value set of item A_i that also occur in the value set of item A". "Can(A_i, X)" is a fuzzy predicate whose truth value is "in the value set of item A the proportion of members of the value set of the set of items X that functionally determine members of the value set of item A_i,". "Card$_A$" means "the number of different values in the value set of item A". The subscripts identify the item's components to which that measure applies.

The *semantics* of an item is a function that recognises the members of that item's value set. The *value acceptability* measure of an item is a fuzzy estimate of the likelihood that a given tuple is *not* in the item's value set. The *set acceptability* measure of an item is a fuzzy estimate of the likelihood that the general structure of the item's value set is invalid. So an item's semantics specifies what should be in the value set, and the two acceptability measures are measures of invalidity of the value set of a knowledge base instance [5].

For example, an application could contain a spare-part thing that is represented by the item *part*. Suppose that the generally expected range for part numbers is [0, 2 000]. Then the value acceptability measure for the item *part* could be $\lambda x \bullet [f(x)] \bullet$ where:

$$f(x) = \begin{cases} 0 & if\ x < 0 \\ 1 & if\ 0 \le x \le 2\,000 \\ 2 - \dfrac{x}{2\,000} & if\ 2\,000 < x < 4\,000 \\ 0 & if\ x \ge 4\,000 \end{cases}$$

Card$_{part}$ is the number of *different* part-numbers. Suppose that the generally expected range for Card$_{part}$ is less than 100. Then the set acceptability measure, C_{part}, for the item *part* is a fuzzy predicate; it could be:

$$C_{part} = \begin{cases} 1 & if\ Card_{part} \le 100 \\ 2 - \dfrac{Card_{part}}{100} & if\ 100 < Card_{part} < 200 \\ 0 & if\ Card_{part} \ge 200 \end{cases}$$

In this way, value and set acceptability measures are developed for data items, and similarly for information and knowledge items.

3. Objects

An item is expressed in terms of its set of component items. So items inherit the properties of their component items including the context of those items. In particular this reference to an item's components prevents knowledge items from representing the essence of rules [6]. Objects [1] are item building operators that are defined independently of such a context.

Object names are written in bold italics. Suppose that the conceptual model already contains the item "*part*" which represents spare parts, and the item "*cost-price*" which represents cost prices; then the information "spare parts have a cost price" can be represented by "*part/cost-price*" which may be built by applying the "***costs***" object to *part* and *cost-price*:

part/cost-price = ***costs***(*part*, *cost-price*)

Suppose that the conceptual model already contains the item "*part/sale-price*" which represents the association between spare parts and their corresponding selling price, and the item "*mark-up*" which represents the data thing a universal mark-up factor. Then the rule "spare parts are marked up by a universal mark up factor" can be represented by *[part/sale-price, part/cost-price, mark-up]* which is built by applying the "***mark-up-rule***" object to the items "*part/sale-price*", "*part/cost-price*" and "*mark-up*":

[part/sale-price, part/cost-price, mark-up] =
    mark-up-rule(*part/sale-price*, *part/cost-price*, *mark-up*)

The conceptual model [7] contains items. A fundamental set of data items in the conceptual model is called the "basis". The remaining items in the conceptual model are built by applying object operators to the other items in the conceptual model. As for items, objects may either be represented informally as "o-schema" or formally as typed λ-calculus expressions.

References

1. Debenham, J.K. "*Knowledge Engineering*", Springer-Verlag, 1998.
2. Debenham, J.K. "Constraints for Knowledge Maintenance", in *proceedings AAAI Spring Symposium in Artificial Intelligence in Knowledge Management*, Stanford, California, March 1997.
3. McCarthy, J. "Notes on Formalizing Context" in *proceedings 13th International Joint Conference on Artificial Intelligence*, Chambery, France.
4. Debenham, J.K. "Representing Knowledge Normalisation", *in proceedings Tenth International Conference on Software Engineering and Knowledge Engineering SEKE'98*, San Francisco, US, June 1998 pp132—135.
5. Coenen F. and Bench-Capon, T. "Building Knowledge Based Systems for Maintainability", in *proceedings Third International Conference on Database and Expert Systems Applications DEXA'92*, Valencia, Spain, September, 1992, pp415-420.
6. Debenham, J.K. "Knowledge Simplification", in *proceedings 9th International Symposium on Methodologies for Intelligent Systems ISMIS'96*, Zakopane, Poland, June 1996.
7. Walker, A., Kowalski, R., Lenat, D., Soloway, E. and Stonebraker, M., "Knowledge Management", in (L. Kerschberg, Ed.), "*Proceedings from the Second International Conference on Expert Database Systems*", Benjamin Cummings, 1989.

Building Context with Intonation

Thorstein Fretheim and Wim A. van Dommelen

Linguistics, NTNU, N-7491 Trondheim, Norway
{thorstein.fretheim, wim.van.dommelen}@hf.ntnu.no

Abstract. In Sperber and Wilson's Relevance Theory (RT), the relevance of a given utterance in discourse is treated as given, while the context which the relevance of the utterance depends on is treated as a variable to be actively sought and selected by the hearer. This paper explores how the speaker's choice of intonation - in this case Norwegian intonation - can facilitate the hearer's inferential derivation of the contextual premises needed to obtain the intended contextual effects.

1 'Context' in Relevance Theory

There is a gap between knowing what a given sentence generated by the grammar of a given language means and understanding all that a speaker intends to communicate by uttering it on any given occasion. The hearer's understanding of what the speaker means to convey depends upon the extra-linguistic, or contextual, information available to him at the time of utterance. However, communication would not be possible if the hearer was unable to sort out and bring to bear in the comprehension process exactly those contextual assumptions which the speaker intends him to activate for the purpose, and to refrain from processing any accessible information that is irrelevant to the task of inferring what the speaker means to communicate. Utterance comprehension relies on utilization of two distinct and complementary kinds of cognitive process: on the one hand linguistic decoding of what the speaker has encoded, on the other hand inferential processing that involves use of the central thought processing system in human beings rather than their grammar.

Dan Sperber and Deirdre Wilson [3] have developed a cognitively based theory of ostensive human communication, according to which (a) human cognition is geared towards the maximisation of relevance, i.e. the achievement of as many contextual (cognitive) effects as possible for as little processing effort as possible, and (b) every utterance communicates a presumption of its own optimal relevance (called the principle of relevance). Contexts are selected in accordance with the principle of relevance, which implies that only the most accessible contextual assumptions compatible with the hearer's general encyclopedic knowledge will be considered. The source of those inferred assumptions could be the long-term memory of the hearer, or it could be the preceding discourse, but one rich source of contextual premises is the very linguistic stimulus whose contextual effects is being computed. RT assumes a basic distinction between two kinds of encoding of meaning. On the one hand there is *conceptual semantics*, whose domain is those linguistic forms whose encoded meaning contributes concepts to the propositional schema of an utterance; on the other hand there is *procedural semantics*, whose domain is those linguistic forms that contribute nothing to conceptual structure but which instead provide constraints on the way that the encoded conceptual structure should be manipulated in the inferential process of comprehension, thus facilitating access to the contextual effects intended by the speaker.

The meaning that can be inferentially derived from the intonation imposed on a given utterance is strictly procedural. In this short paper there is room for just one illustration of how intonation - here Norwegian intonation - can create context, thereby making the stimulus more relevant by facilitating the hearer's computation of its intended contextual effects.

2 Intonational constraining of the context selection task

Imagine that an utterance of the sentence in (1) appears in the middle of a Norwegian discourse.

(1) Barna   sover   vel   hvis   de   ikke   hører   på   radio.
    the-kids sleep   particle if   they   not   hear   on   radio
    'The kids are presumably sleeping if they aren't listening to the radio.'

Since it is hardly possible to listen to the radio while sleeping, the conditional clause in (1) is understood to state a necessary condition for the truth of the main clause proposition. But why does the speaker of (1) add the condition expressed by the conditional clause? As we have no access to the discourse preceding (1), the most accessible contextual assumption is that the conditional clause echoes the content of something already uttered by the hearer.

The lack of indication of a prosodic break between the clauses in (1) is meant to suggest that the main clause and the following conditional clause belong to the same intonational utterance (IU). However, an utterance of (1) would normally consist of not one but two intonational phrases (IPs), the immediate constituent of the IU. The Norwegian IP is delimited by a right-edge phrase accent realized as an F0 (fundamental frequency) peak. Figure 1 is an F0 tracing of an utterance of (1). The first rising F0 slope culminates in an IP-final peak, which lends prominence to the only item in that IP that carries a word accent, namely the low-pitched verb form *sover* ('sleep'). The

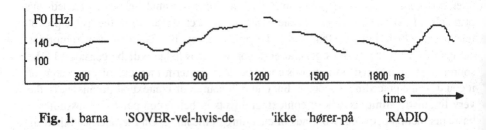

Fig. 1. barna   'SOVER-vel-hvis-de   'ikke 'hører-på   'RADIO

utterance-final peak similarly gives prominence to the last accented word in the second IP, the nominal *radio*. A Norwegian IU with two phrase-accentual peaks (two IPs), as in Figure 1, offers the hearer the procedural information that one of its IPs expresses new information, while the other IP provides the hearer with a contextual increment (cf Fretheim [1], [2]).

In the F0 tracing shown in Figure 2 there is one IU per syntactic clause, with a prosodic break between the clauses. This contour offers the procedural information that both peaks are to be associated with new information.

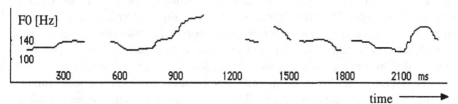

Fig. 2. barna 'SOVER-vel   hvis de 'ikke 'hører-på   'RADIO

While the conditional clause in Figure 1 is very likely to echo an utterance produced by the interlocutor, the one in Figure 2 sounds like an afterthought utterance suggesting lack of conviction that the main clause proposition is true. This conditional clause is not an echo of something uttered previously. It expresses one out of a gigantic number of conditions that have to be fulfilled in order for it to be true that the kids are sleeping. Why did the speaker choose to express exactly this contextual premiss? The most reasonable answer is that s/he expressed the negative proposition in the conditional clause because s/he suspected that its positive counterpart might be true. Observe that the function of the conditional clause as such is the same in Figure 2 as in Figure 1 but the intonation assigned to it in Figure 2 instructs the hearer to associate it with a piece of new information, as if it had been a declarative sentence used to assert the truth of the proposition expressed. While a conditional clause is not normally supposed to reveal the speaker's epistemic stance, an afterthought clause that forms a separate IU is easily inferred to add procedural information about the speaker's propositional attitude.

By adding the final sentence in (2) to the conditional construction in (1) it is possible to test our claim about the procedural meaning conveyed by the speaker's choice of either a double-peak IU as in Figure 1, or else two single-peak IUs as in Figure 2. The English translation (2i) is meant to capture the procedural meaning of the former intonation pattern, and (2ii) is meant to capture the procedural meaning of the latter intonation pattern (note the use of 'unless' in (2ii)).

(2) Barna sover vel, (--) hvis de ikke hører på radio. Dét er nok mest sannsynlig.
     the-kids sleep particle, if they not hear on radio. that is particle most likely
     i. 'The kids are presumably sleeping if they are not listening to the radio.'
     ii. 'The kids are presumably sleeping -- unless they are listening to the radio.'
       'That, in my opinion, is most likely what they are doing.'

The accented Norwegian pronominal *dét* in the follow-up statement in (2), corresponding to sentence-initial 'that' in the English translation, can refer to a state of affairs represented by the main clause proposition ('The kids are sleeping'), but could it also refer to a contrary state of affairs ('The kids are listening to the radio') implicitly activated by the kind of intonation illustrated in Figure 2? A pilot study, to be followed up by a large-scale test in the near future, indicated that while Norwegian hearers invariably select the main clause as the antecedent of the pronoun *dét* in (2) when the intonation is as shown in Figure 1, the intonation in Figure 2 causes a majority of informants to say that the final sentence means the kids are most likely listening to the radio. Thus the intonation shown in Figure 2 enables the hearer to expand the set of contextual premises needed to resolve the reference of the pronoun *dét* in (2) differently than if the intonation had been as in Figure 1. The antecedent of *dét* is not the proposition expressed by the negative conditional clause, however, but rather its positive contradictory counterpart, a proposition which the skeptical attitude made accessible by the use of a separate IU for the conditional clause causes the hearer to activate.

3   Conclusion

Context is not something given, it is something that the addressee of an utterance must actively select in his quest for the cognitive effects that make an utterance relevant. The speaker can assist the hearer in his inferential processing work by using a specific intonation which will constrain the search for those contextual premises that a satisfactory utterance interpretation guided by the principle of relevance must be based on. If an intonation contour were something that always had to be adjusted to an independently existing extra-linguistic context, then intonation would not be the important transmitter of procedural meaning that it is. What we have attempted to show is that a given intonation structure can help the hearer pick up a contextual assumption which the speaker intends him to activate and which could be completely inaccessible if a different intonation were used.

References

1. Fretheim, T.: The effect of intonation on a type of scalar implicature. Journal of Pragmatics 18 (1992) 1-30.
2. Fretheim, T.: Intonation: Pragmatics. In: Mey, J.L. (ed.): Concise Encyclopedia of Pragmatics. Elsevier, Amsterdam (1998) 404-7.
3. Sperber, D., Wilson, D.: Relevance: Communication and Cognition. Blackwell, London (1986/1995).

Parrot-Talk Requires Multiple Context Dimensions

Sabine Geldof

Vrije Universiteit Brussel
Artificial Intelligence Laboratory
Pleinlaan 2, B-1050 Brussels, Belgium
sabine@arti.vub.ac.be
http://arti.vub.ac.be

Abstract. The analysis of human-generated utterances reveals that not only the linguistic (i.e. discourse) context but also the physical context and the user profile of the hearer should be considered when aiming at 'natural' language generation (NLG) embedded in a real-life situation. We propose a framework that allows for annotating the propositional content of sentences to be generated along these three dimensions of context and illustrate this with concrete examples. The context of our research is the COMRIS project, where text is generated for output on a wearable device (parrot).

1 Introduction

Human language processing is characterised by a strong ability to adapt utterances to the context in which they occur. 'M. Walker will give a presentation later today in the same room as where the opening session was held. He is currently in the coffee room, just around the corner and he might be an interesting person for setting up a project on ubiquitous computing.' In this example the speaker knows about the current time, about the places where the hearer was or is and about the hearer's interest (in setting up a project). We argue that these different context dimensions should be integrated in the text generation process, especially for output on a wearable device.

In COMRIS [1] human agents in the physical world are supported by software agents in a virtual world. Every human agent can have several Personal Representative Agents (PRAs), each one pursuing one of her particular interests. For example in the conference center application PRAs explore the virtual world in search for information and interesting encounters with other PRAs who share the same interest. They try to push information to the user by competing for her attention [1] via the Personal Assistant Agent (PA) -a virtual representative of the user as a person. The propositional content of a winning PRA's message,

---

[1] COMRIS (Co-habited Mixed Reality Information Systems) is an EU funded project in the programme 'Intelligent Information Interfaces' see also http://arti.vub.ac.be/~comris

annotated with context information by the PA, is forwarded to the NLG module and then further to the user's wearable device, her parrot, for speech synthesis. Several components of the COMRIS infrastructure contribute to capturing context features.

2 Tri-dimensional Model of Context

2.1 Linguistic Context

In human conversations or text, what is said earlier influences the form of subsequent natural language output. This dimension of context has been the object of a lot of research in (computational) linguistics dealing with problems of coreference, anaphora etc. (see [2]). We encode the linguistic context of an object for a particular hearer as a numerical value denoting the distance (for the concept: a and for the instance: b) in number of messages from the last mention to the actual point in the discourse history: **lcv (a,b)** (see Table 1). These values are obtained by querying the discourse model (updated after text is generated), e.g.: look-up (P_ID 25, concept person, instance 26) => lcv(5,5) means that the very person with ID 26 was mentioned to hearer with ID 25 in the previous message; this situation will typically give rise to pronominalization in the next utterance, as in: John wrote a letter to Mary. *He* loves *her*.

2.2 Extra-linguistic Context

Utterance variations in function of the time and place in which the hearer finds herself (e.g. today, on this floor) also need to be considered. Apart from [3], these features have been studied less systematically. Table 1 gives an overview of how the different types of extra-linguistic context information are encoded and rendered, further illustrated with the following example:

```
:-pract (make-pract
    :-date (make-date    :-day 31    :-month 1    :-d_elcv 0)
    :-timing (make-timing    :-hour 10    :-minute 0)
    :-place (make-place    :-l_name "the coffee room" :-l_ID "9910"
                           :-l_elcv "around the corner"))
```

This input structure will cause the text generator to produce: '... today at 10 o'clock in the coffee room around the corner' and supposes that the hearer is actually only a corner away from the coffee room on January 31st.

Spatial context information is captured through beacons distributed over the conference location. Knowing in which room a user finds herself, we can infer information about her social context: is the user attending a talk, or in the coffee room, talking to someone? The temporal dimension is more easy to reason about, since the (computer) system is aware of time and standard time calculations are applicable. Like for linguistic context, these values are constantly evolving and need to be looked up or calculated at the moment they are needed.

Table 1. Overview of context annotation values in COMRIS

Linguistic context	lcv (a,	b)
Concept/ Instance (mentioned to user:..)	NUMeric focus on **Concept** 1: occurred 2/more messages ago 3: occurred 1 message ago 5: occurred in previous message	NUMeric focus on **Instance** 1: occurred 2/more messages ago 3: occurred 1 message ago 5: occurred in previous message
Extra-Linguistic context:	d_elcv (+/- n)	l_elcv ("string")
(user is in ..) time/ space social implicature: (user is..)	(date) 0: today (time) +1: in one hour (time) +.10: in 10 minutes s_elcv (n) 1..2: standing, wandering around 3: moving towards a goal 4: attending an event 5: talking to someone	(location) close-by, at the other side of the building, on the same floor, ...
Profile Value: user's interest	t_pv (n)	
..in a topic:	1..2: .. you might be interested in 3: .. you are interested in 5: .. your favourite topic	
	p_pv (pnumval n	{pqval "string"})
..in a person:	1..2: .. you might want to meet 3: .. you wanted to meet 5: .. you absolutely wanted to meet	for dicsussion, for introduction, for lobbying, for socializing, as an expert,...

2.3 User Profile

Humans also adapt the content and form of their utterances to their knowledge about the hearer. User-adaptivity has been focused on since early NLG systems, see e.g. [4]. More recent research in hypertext generation focuses on the dynamic aspects of a user model, as can be inferred from the user's browsing behaviour. See [5] and [6]. The COMRIS user profile is acquired explicitly from the user: at conference registration she is asked to specify her interest in a number of topics on a scale of 1-5. Similarly, she can indicate a number of persons (conference participants, speakers, etc.) whom she would not like to miss. The user profile is stored and made accessible in the information layer, the COMRIS component that manages all the information relative to the conference. Numeric values allow to decide whether or not an object is to be mentioned and to choose an expression denoting that degree of interest (see Table 1 for the details). Qualitative context annotations can be added to express the reason of interest in a person: (**p_pv (pnumval n) {(pqval "string")}**). Example:

```
:-person (make-person :-p_info (make-p_info
     :-p_fname "Bob"   :-p_lname "Fernandez "
     :-p_ID "7755"    :-p_sex 'm
     :-p_pv (make-p_pv    :-pnumval 5
                     :-p_qval " for socializing")
     :-lcv (make-lcv    :-concept 3   :-entity 1)))
```

This input structure will cause the text generator to produce: 'Bob Fernandez, whom you absolutely wanted to meet for socializing, ...'

3 Conclusion

As we move towards an area of 'ubiquitous computing', context information cannot be limited to discourse information anymore as in 'classical' NLG applications [7]. Just like in the HIPS project [8], we deal also with extra-linguistic and profile context, although our notion of virtual space is radically different. This paper focused on how to acquire context values of different dimensions and to encode them uniformally and demonstrates what is their effect on the generation of text. Our experiments so far validated our model as being appropriate for generating different sentences for one propositional content, according to explicit context annotations. The acquisition of context information remains a critical issue, comparable to challenges in knowledge acquisition. Global context parameters and parametrization techniques might be a complementary way towards more context-sensitive NLG. Further developments and refinements of our model will be steered by user evaluations in real context.

Acknowledgments This research is funded by the EC as part of the COMRIS project (LTR-25500). Our use of TG/2, a text generation tool developed at DFKI is subject to a research licence agreement. We are grateful to Walter Van de Velde and Stephan Busemann for suggestions and comments.

References

1. Van de Velde, W., Geldof, S., Schrooten, R.: Competition for attention. In: Singh, M.P., Rao, A.S., and Wooldridge, M.J., (eds.) Proc. of ATAL: 4th Int. Workshop on Agent Theories, Architectures and Languages, LNAI Vol. 1365. Springer-Verlag, Heidelberg (1998) 282-296.
2. Dale, R.: Generating referring expressions. MIT Press, Cambridge, MA (1992)
3. Maybury, M.: Topical, temporal and spatial constraints on linguistic realization. Computational Intelligence 7(4)(1991) 226-275
4. Paris, C.L.: Tailoring object descriptions to a user's level of expertise. Computational Linguistics, 14(3) (1988) 64-78
5. Milosavljevic, M., Tulloch, A. and Dale, R.: Text Generation in a Dynamic Hypertext Environment. In Proc. of the 19th Australasian Computer Science Conference, Melbourne, Australia (1996)
6. Geldof, S., Van de Velde, W.: Context-sensitive hypertext generation. In: Working notes of the AAAI'97 Spring Symposium Workshop on Natural Language Processing for the Web. Stanford University, CA (1997) 54-61
7. van Deemter, K.; Odijk, J.: Context modeling for language and speech generation. In Proc. of the first Int. and Interdisciplinary Conf. on Modeling and Using Context (Context-97). Universidade Federal do Rio de Janeiro, Brazil (1997) 75-88
8. Not, E., Petrelli, D., Stock, O., Strapparava, C. and Zancanaro, M.: Person-oriented guided visits in a physical museum. In: Proc. of the 4th Int. Conf. on Hypermedia and Interactivity in Museums (ICHIM97), Paris (1997)

Contextual Divorces:
Towards a Framework for Identifying Critical Context Issues in Collaborative-Argumentation System Design

Alain Giboin

INRIA, Acacia Project
Sophia-Antipolis, France
Alain.Giboin@sophia.inria.fr

Abstract. This paper provides some theoretical and empirical bases of a framework aimed at identifying critical context issues related to the design of collaborative-argumentation systems — especially systems supporting collective design rationale. The framework is intended to help developers anticipate, diagnose, and repair divorces from context which can impede system usability. The theoretical bases of the framework are the notion of *contextual divorces*, and a descriptive model of context, adapted from Kerbrat-Orecchioni (1990), which describes the context in terms of the main components of an interaction situation, e.g., scene, participants, spatial setting, tasks, etc. The empirical bases of the framework are the evidence provided by some studies evaluating the usability of design rationale systems.

1 Introduction

Computer-Supported Collaborative Argumentation (CSCA) is the domain of computer science and technology which is aimed at constructing systems for collaborative argumentation [3]. A growing category of CSCA systems are intended to support Design Rationale (DR), i.e. the production and understanding of "statements of reasoning underlying the design process that explain, derive, and justify design decisions" [7] (see also [2][4]).

Some CSCA-DR system developers observed that fundamental obstacles impede the systems to be really usable [4][7]. One of these obstacles is that the systems are "divorced from work contexts, so they can neither capture knowledge as it is articulated nor target retrieval to work states" [9]. From this observation, we can naturally conclude that to get really usable systems, developers need to avoid divorces from work context, and more generally all kinds of *contextual divorces*: by foreseeing them, or recognizing them when they occur, so that they can be overcome.

To identify the divorces properly, however, developers need to get some framework. In this paper, I provide some theoretical and empirical bases of such a framework, which I will call the *Contextual-Divorce Framework*.

2 Theoretical Bases of the Framework

The framework rests (a) on the notion of "contextual divorces," and (b) on a model of context related to collective activities. *The notion of "contextual divorce"* is an elaboration of the Fischer et al.'s notion of "divorces from work context." It refers to a separation of some constituent of the argumentation system (e.g., the argumentation notation or scheme, some argumentation functionality) from a contextual component in fact closely united to it (e.g., the design object, the task at hand, the designer); contextual divorces are said also to impede system usability.

The model of context, adapted from Kerbrat-Orecchioni [11], describes the context in terms of the main components of the social situation in which an interaction between participants occurs (see Table 1).

Table 1. The components of a social situation (Adapted from [11])

SITUATION	*SCENE*	*Setting*	Spatial setting Physical setting Social setting Temporal setting
		Purpose	Maxi-Purposes Tasks Mini-Purposes
	PARTICIPANTS	*Individual Features*	Biological and Physical Features Social Features Psychological Features
		Mutual Relationships	Degree of Mutual Knowledge Nature of the Social Link Nature of the Affective Link

This descriptive model decomposes the *situation* into constituents that play a major role in the processes of production and comprehension of (argumentative) discourses. At the top level are the *scene* and the *participants*; these two constituents in turn decompose into sub-constituents (*setting, purpose, individual features, and mutual relationships*), etc. The model allows to type contextual divorces, i.e. to define theoretical classes of divorces such as *divorces from participants, divorces from scene*, and so on.

3 Empirical Bases of the Framework

To search for evidence of contextual divorces, I analyzed a set of empirical studies evaluating the usability of DR systems (schemes and/or tools). In these studies, subjects were asked to produce or understand DR documents using some DR scheme and/or some related tool. For example, in the Karsenty's study [10], six experienced professional designers were asked to understand and to assess a past design from DR documents elaborated with the QOC scheme. All the studies reported the evaluations of systems in which design reasoning is viewed as arguments about issues. Precisely, the studies assessed three *DR schemes*: IBIS, PHI and QOC. These schemes (and their related methods) have been implemented in several issue-based hypertext *tools*. For example, IBIS has been implemented in gIBIS, or graphical IBIS [6], and PHI in JANUS-ARGUMENTATION [8] (see [3] for more information on DR schemes and tools).

To identify contextual divorces in the studies, I used the descriptive model of context reported in Table 1 as a starting grid.

Examples of Observed Contextual Divorces. One aim of DR is to help designers improve their own work [7]. *Divorces* of DR *from purpose* impede this improvement. Such divorces refer partially to what Fischer et al. [9] called "divorces from work contexts."

The typical divorce from work context mentioned by Fischer et al. is what can be called *Divorce from the main task.* Evaluating IBIS and PHI, these authors noticed that for argumentation to serve design, it must serve construction (e.g., drawing in architectural design). If argumentation is not integrated with construction, it loses relevance to the task at hand: "Without the ability to relate construction and argumentation to each other, it is impossible to discuss the solution. Without construction situations, design rationale cannot be contextualized."

Another aim of DR is to help designers, or stakeholders, communicate with past, present, and future designers, or stakeholders. All these actors may show different individual features, in particular psychological (e.g., perspectives, background) and social (e.g., status) features. These individual differences, if not taken into account, may block argumentative communication. In particular, it can make the later recovery and appropriate reuse of DR hard or impossible [5].

An example of a *Divorce from psychological features* is what can be called *Divorce from background design knowledge.* Evaluating the usability of QOC for a software design project involving "modellers" and designers reusing the DR space of a past design, Bellotti and MacLean [1] observed that modellers, who had not taken part in the past design, had considerable problems with the DR space because they lacked contextual information and disagreed with its structure. To the contrary, designers, who had taken part in the past design, found the space very easy to understand.

4 Further Work

We have now to establish the relevance and the usefulness of the Contextual-Divorce Framework. *The relevance of the framework* indeed depends on the relevance of the model of context which underlies it: the model must contain crucial contextual elements. The current model needs to be refined and fitted by taking account of other models of context or situation (see e.g. [12]), and of critical aspects identified in the usability studies.

The usefulness of the framework strongly depends on its operationality. For the framework to be really operational, it needs to be specified more; for example, we have to draw a map as complete as possible of the potential and observed divorces as well as of their related actual and possible "repairs." The procedure for using the framework has also to be explicited so that system developers can effectively anticipate, diagnose and repair divorces from context.

References

1. Bellotti, V. & MacLean, A. Integrating and communicating design perspectives with QOC design rationale. The Amodeus Project, ESPRIT Basic Research 7040, Working Paper # ID/WP29, 1994.
2. Buckingham Shum, S. Design Argumentation as Design Rationale. The Encyclopedia of Computer Science and Technology (Marcel Dekker Inc: NY), Vol. 35, Supp. 20, 95-128, 1996.
3. Buckingham Shum, S. Computer-Supported Collaborative Argumentation Resource Site, 1997 [http://kmi.open.ac.uk/~simonb/csca/]
4. Buckingham Shum, S. and Hammond, N. Argumentation-Based Design Rationale: What Use at What Cost? International Journal of Human-Computer Studies 40 (4), 603-652, 1994.
5. Buckingham Shum, S., MacLean, A. Bellotti, V. & Hammond, N.V. Graphical argumentation and design cognition. Human-Computer Interaction.12, pp. 267-300, 1997.
6. Conklin, J.E. & Begeman, M.L. gIBIS: A Hypertext Tool for Exploratory Policy Discussion, ACM Transactions on Office Information Systems, 6,303-331, 1988.
7. Fischer, G., Lemke, A.C., McCall, R. & Morch A.I. Making argumentation serve design. Human-Computer Interaction, 6, 393-419, 1991.
8. Fischer, G., McCall, R. & Morch A.I. Design environments for constructive and argumentative design Proceedings of the CHI'89 Conference on Human Factors in Computing Systems, New York, ACM Press, pp. 269-275, 1989.
9. Fischer, G., Ostwald, J. & Stahl, G. Conceptual Frameworks and Computational Support for Organizational Memories and Organizational Learning, Project Report, Department of Computer Science and Institute of Cognitive Science, University of Colorado at Boulder. 1997.
10. Karsenty, L. An empirical evaluation of design rationale documents. Proceedings of the CHI'96 Conference on Human Factors in Computing Systems, New York, ACM Press, 1996.
11. Kerbrat-Orecchioni. Les interactions verbales. Paris, Armand Colin, 1990.
12. van Dijk. T.A. Towards a theory of context and experience models in discourse processing. In H. van Oostendorp & S. Goldman (Eds.), The Construction of Mental Models during Reading. Hillsdale, NJ: Erlbaum, 1998.

The Role of Context in Pronominal Reference to Higher Order Entities in English and Norwegian

Jeanette K. Gundel[1,2], Kaja Borthen[1], Thorstein Fretheim[1]

[1]Linguistics, NTNU, N-7491 Trondheim, Norway
{jeanette.gundel, kaja.borthen, thorstein.fretheim} @hf.ntnu.no
[2]Linguistics, Univ. of Minnesota, Minneapolis, MN 55455, USA

Abstract. Production and understanding of different pronouns referring to higher order entities is sensitive to the distinction between entities assumed to be in focus for the addressee and those that are activated, but not in focus. Our study reveals that this distinction is influenced by the number of times an entity has been processed, regardless of whether such processing is triggered by overt linguistic or other contextual factors.

1 Introduction

Higher order entities such as events, facts, or propositions can be referenced with an unstressed personal pronoun, *it*, or a demonstrative, *that* or *this*, as shown in (1).

(1)   John won the race. I know that because I saw it happen. But it's still hard to believe it. (Fraurud [2]).

This paper reports on conditions determining the distribution and interpretation of *it* vs. *that* and their Norwegian counterparts when referring to higher order entities.

2 In Focus vs. Activated

Gundel, Hedberg, and Zacharski [4] (henceforth GHZ) propose that different determiners and pronominal forms conventionally signal that the referent of the expression has a certain cognitive (memory or attention) status for the addressee. These forms thus serve as processing cues which constrain possible interpretations of a nominal expression. GHZ propose six linguistically relevant cognitive statuses, which are implicationally related in the following 'givenness hierarchy':
in focus > activated > familiar > uniquely identifiable > referential > type identifiable.
According to GHZ, the personal pronoun *it* conventionally signals the status 'in focus, whereas the demonstrative pronouns *this* and *that* only require their referents to be activated, but not necessarily in focus. Activated entities are those which are

assumed to be in working memory. Entities in focus include that subset of activated entities which the addressee's attention is focused on at a given point in the discourse.

3 What Brings an Entity into Focus of Attention?

To the extent that syntax and prosody serve to highlight constituents whose referents the speaker wants to bring into focus, membership in the in-focus set is partially determined by linguistic form. For example, the subject of a matrix sentence is highly likely to bring an entity into focus, whereas this is not the case for elements in subordinate clauses and prepositional phrases (cf. the Centering algorithms in Grosz, Joshi and Weinstein [3]). Since concrete objects are normally introduced with a noun phrase, they can obtain the 'in focus' status after being mentioned only once. But a higher order entity such as a situation or fact is typically expressed by a whole sentence the first time it is introduced into the discourse. The first mention of such entities will therefore usually not correspond to expressions that have prominent syntactic functions in the sentence, and we would expect them to be activated, but not yet in focus after being mentioned only once. Reference to higher-order entities with it, which requires its referent to be in focus, thus typically requires more than one previous mention. Consider the examples in (2) and (3) (from Borthen et al [1]).

(2) There was a snake on my desk. It scared me.
(3) There was a snake on my desk. That scared me; it scared my office mate too.

In (2), the pronoun it is most naturally interpreted as referring to the snake, not to the situation of a snake being on the desk. But in (3), it is more easily interpreted as referring to the fact that there was a snake on the speaker's desk. Since this situation was referred to twice, once by the first sentence and once in the second, it is now in focus and can be referred to with it in the final clause of (3). Borthen et al show that implicit arguments can also raise the status of an entity from merely activated to in focus; overt mention is not required. In general, then, a situation introduced with a whole sentence will be brought into focus only after it has been mentioned again, either overtly or covertly, as illustrated by the unacceptability of it in (4b).

(4) a. I hear that linguists earn less than computer scientists, and that's terrible.
    b. ?? I hear that linguists earn less than computer scientists, and it's terrible.

But the pronoun it is sometimes acceptable when it refers to a situation that has been mentioned only once, as in (5).

(5) A: What do you think of the fact that linguists earn less than computer scientists?
    B: It's terrible!   B': That's terrible!

The difference between (4) and (5) may be due to the fact that some contexts are more potentially salience-promoting than others. A question in an interview situation can establish a topic and bring it into focus right away. Note also the subtle difference between (5B) and (5B'). By overtly signaling that the intended referent is in focus, *it* in (5B) makes accessible a context where the fact that linguists earn less than computer scientists is not news to the speaker. By contrast, the most accessible context for (5B') is one where this fact either contradicts earlier assumptions or is something the speaker hadn't thought much about. Consider also the example in (6).

(6) A: You have an appointment with the Minister of Defense at three o'clock.
    B: That's true.   B': #It's true.   B'': It's true, then.

If the mere utterance of a sentence does not bring the expressed state of affairs into focus, this would explain why (6)B' is unacceptable, assuming that *it* requires the referent to be in focus, whereas *that* merely requires activation. But then why is B'' acceptable? We believe the explanation is as follows. *Then* is an interpretive particle which conveys the meaning that the content of the sentence it is appended to is being attributed to the addressee, possibly because it follows by way of inference from something he just said. But since the proposition expressed by the sentence *then* is appended to in B'' simply repeats what A said (assuming that if someone asserts something they believe the content of the assertion to be true), the only way the utterance in B'' can yield contextual effects (in the relevance-theoretic sense of Sperber and Wilson [5]) is if B had been entertaining the proposition herself, and B knows that A is aware of this. Thus, the fact that B had an appointment with the Minister at 3 was not activated for the first time by A; rather, A's utterance brought into focus a fact that was already manifest to A and B beforehand, thereby licensing the use of *it* in B''. Note that this interpretation is made relevant by the presence of *then* only because simply attributing to A the belief that he believes what he just said to be true would not yield adequate contextual effects. When the predicate is something other than 'is true', the situation changes, as in (7).

(7) A. You have an appointment with the Minister of Defense at three o'clock.
    B: That's on my calendar. B': It's on my calendar. B'': It's on my calendar then.

In (7), both *that* and *it* are possible with or without the particle *then*. But whereas *that* in B' can refer to the appointment (the intended referent of an NP in A's utterance) or to the whole proposition that B has an appointment with the Minister at 3, *it* in both B' and B'' can only have the former interpretation. In this example, contrary to the one in (6), the particle *then* does not make accessible a context where the fact that B has an appointment has already been thought about and would thus be brought into focus the first time it was mentioned in A.

The Norwegian example in (8) also shows how contexts made accessible by various factors can trigger extra processing of an entity, thus bringing it into focus.

(8) i. Jeg ga Eva et skjerf. ii.Hun takket ikke. iii. Jeg hadde ikke ventet det.
    i. I gave Eva a scarf. ii. She thanked not. iii. I had not expected it/that.
        'I gave Eva a scarf. She didn't thank me.   I didn't expect it/that.'

(8iii) can be produced with or without stress on *det*, the difference corresponding roughly to English *that* and *it*, respectively. Stressed *det* is most naturally interpreted as referring to the situation activated by (ii) (She didn't thank me for the scarf); but unstressed *det* is not fully acceptable here, since there is no in focus state of affairs that it could refer to. It is indeterminate between an interpretation where the referent is 'NOT (she thanked me)' or 'she thanked me'. Sentence (iii) with an unstressed *det* is improved greatly, however, by an added utterance-final particle *altså* (here most appropriately translated as 'mind you'), as in (9).

(9) i. Jeg ga Eva en skjerf. ii. Hun takket ikke. iii. Jeg hadde ikke ventet det altså.

Like *then* in (6)-(7), *altså* is an interpretive particle; it encodes the information that the sentence it is appended to expresses the speaker's reaction to a thought she attributes to the addressee as a result of what she believes to be his inferential derivation of the contextual effects of the preceding utterance. The presence of *altså* in (9iii) indicates that the speaker assumed the addressee derived the implicature that she had expected Eva to thank her for the scarf. Thus, since the attributed thought 'speaker expected (Eva thanked the speaker)' is part of the assumed context for (9iii), the proposition 'Eva thanked the speaker' is covertly mentioned (hence processed) a second time; it is thereby brought into focus, licensing the unaccented *det*.

4   Conclusion

Reference resolution must take into account the cognitive statuses signaled by different forms. The status 'in focus' is influenced by the number of times an entity has been processed, and it can be partially determined by overt structural factors alone. But a full account of how an entity is brought into focus requires a general pragmatic theory of how context and meaning are constructed in language understanding.

References

1. Borthen, K., Fretheim, T., Gundel, J.K.: What Brings a Higher-order Entity Into Focus of Attention? In: Mitkov, R. , Boguraev, E. (eds.): Operational Factors in Practical, Robust Anaphora Resolution. Proceedings of a Workshop sponsored by the ACL, Universidad Nacional de Educación a Distancia, Madrid (1997) 88-93.
2. Fraurud, K.: Processing Noun Phrases in Natural Discourse. Ph.D. Thesis. Stockholm University, Dept. of Linguistics (1992)
3. Grosz, B. J., Joshi, A.K., Weinstein, S.: Towards a Computational Theory of discourse interpretation. Computational Linguistics 21/2 (1995) 203-25.
4. Gundel, J. K., Hedberg, N. Zacharski, R.: Cognitive Status and the Form of Referring Expressions in Discourse. Language 69 (1993) 274-307.
5. Sperber D., Wilson, D.: Relevance: Communication and Cognition. Blackwell, London (1986/95).

Connectionist Analysis and Creation of Context for Natural Language Understanding and Knowledge Management

Timo Honkela

Media Lab, University of Art and Design Helsinki,
Hämeentie 135 C, FIN-00560 Helsinki, Finland,
timo.honkela@mlab.uiah.fi,
WWW home page: http://www.mlab.uiah.fi/~timo/

Abstract. Context affects many aspects of the behavior. Natural language understanding is one of the prime examples. This paper summarizes how an artificial neural network, the self-organizing map, can be used in modeling contextuality in data analysis and natural language processing. Important aspects are adaptivity gained by using a learning system, autonomous nature of the processing based on unsupervised learning paradigm, and gradedness of the representation. Examples in the application areas of information retrieval and knowledge management are considered. For instance, the visualization of self-organizing maps provides meaningful context for documents.

1   Introduction

Levels of natural language interpretation span from phonology, morphology, syntax and semantics to pragmatics. In all those levels, relevant context is needed to find proper interpretation. An isolated spoken phoneme, written letter, or a word is inherently ambiguous. Contextual information is needed for disambiguation. The contextuality is easily neglected, being, nevertheless, a very commonplace phenomenon in natural language (see, e.g., [4]). Human perceptual processes use additional sources of knowledge to disambiguate the input. Anticipation influences the perception which is one of the key ideas of constructivism in cognitive psychology. The local ambiguities that formal rule-based systems detect often remain even unnoticed by human readers or listeners.

Computational methods such as rule-based formalisms and transformational grammars are suitable for the study of structural phenomena. The artificial neural network models seem to offer a promising methodology for dealing with contextual phenomena in natural language semantics and pragmatics. In the following, the self-organizing map is considered as a means for modeling contextual phenomena in data analysis and natural language interpretation.

2 Self-Organizing Map in Context Analysis

The basic self-organizing map (SOM) [9, 10] is a sheet-like neural-network array the nodes of which become specifically tuned to various input signal patterns or classes of patterns in an orderly fashion. The learning process is competitive and unsupervised. No teacher is needed to define the correct output for an input. The locations of the responses in the array tend to become ordered in the learning process [10].

While organizing numerical data, e.g., measurements of any kind, one relevant issue is whether the values come essentially from a similar source that is comparable with the other values under consideration. For instance, if the machinery of a factory is replaced by considerably different one, the comparison between the "old" and the "new" data in the process monitoring system is questionable. Similarly, medical measurements can be considered. If a set of people is studied, one can question whether all the persons are similar enough with respect to the phenomenon under consideration. The similarity or the lack of it can be considered to be a contextual phenomenon. In statistical terms, analysis of the hidden variables is needed. It may be necessary to divide the subjects or items into smaller coherent groups so that meaningful analysis results can be achieved. The SOM is very well suited for such an analysis: it both can form the clusters as well as visualize the relationships between the clusters as neighborhood relations on the map. The number of variables considered can be rather high. For instance, in a study of the socio-economic status of the countries in the world based on World Bank data, 39 variables were used [10].

It is important to discover patterns and hidden variables that are relevant only for a small portion of the whole set of individuals or cases. For instance, one small area of a map may indicate cases that correspond to 3 percent of the whole collection, and in which there are several hidden variables that strongly influence the variables under consideration. However, the variables relevant for the analysis of the 3 percent need not be relevant for the other 97 percent. Thus, it may be suggested that the data should be first organized using the SOM taking into account large number of potentially relevant variables in order to obtain an overall view on the cases [3].

3 Contextual Relations of Words

The self-organizing map can be used for contextual analysis of natural language expressions. In several studies, maps of words have been created [1, 5, 15]. The context of the words may simply consist of the immediate neighboring words (cotext). Single nodes of the SOM can be considered to serve as adaptive prototypes. Each prototype is involved in the adaptation process in which the neighbors influence each other and the map is gradually finding a form in which it can best represent the input. The areas on an organized map can be considered as implicit categories or classes that have emerged during the learning process. Typically, the overall organization of a map of words reflects syntactic classes. Local organization seems to follow semantic features. Often a node becomes labeled by several symbols that are synonyms, antonyms or otherwise belong to a closed class.

The importance of context becomes evident when ambiguity is considered: the interpretation of ambiguous expressions is based on their context. One possibility to handle ambiguity using the SOM is to teach small "context maps" so that the main SOM can process the contextual information into clusters [14]. Each model vector of the single-word maps corresponds to a particular "sense" of the word. The SOM is used to resolve ambiguity also in [16]. In [17] co-occurrence information is used to create lexical spaces. The dimensionality reduction is based on singular value decomposition. In computing the context vectors, the window size is, e.g., 1000 characters rather than a fixed number of words.

4 Context for Information Retrieval and Knowledge Management

In information retrieval it would be beneficial if the documents could be presented in context of similar documents rather than a collection of unordered query results. Metaphorically speaking, the fact that the near-misses of a query are not shown by any means in traditional information retrieval corresponds to a situation in which a sword is used in a dark room to pick up papers from the floor: one does not know what was left behind.

By virtue of the self-organizing map algorithm, documents can be mapped onto a two-dimensional grid so that related documents appear close to each other The visualized document map provides a general view of the document collection. To produce maps that display similarity relations between document contents a suitable statistical method must be devised for encoding the documents. In an early study, a small map of scientific documents was formed based on the word forms in their titles [13]. In the WEBSOM method similar documents become mapped close to each other on the map [2, 6, 7] [1]. The self-organized document map offers a general idea of the underlying document space. In the WWW implementation, the user may view any area of the map in detail by simply clicking the map image with the mouse. The WEBSOM browsing interface is implemented as a set of HTML documents that can be viewed using a graphical WWW browser [12]. Methods that enable computation of very large document maps have been developed [11]. In content-addressable search the user provides a query, a list of terms or a document. The nodes that best represent the query are then highlighted on the map display to facilitate the exploration of the map. The document map can be considered as a knowledge management tools that facilitates understanding the relationships of data. The SOM has been used in a similar manner in a large number of application areas for numerical data (see [8]).

---

[1] Demonstrations are available at $http://websom.hut.fi/websom/$

References

1. Honkela, T., Pulkki, V. and Kohonen, T. (1995). Contextual relations of words in Grimm tales analyzed by self-organizing map. *Proceedings of ICANN-95, International Conference on Artificial Neural Networks*, F. Fogelman-Soulié and P. Gallinari (eds), vol. 2, EC2 et Cie, Paris, pp. 3-7.
2. Honkela, T., Kaski, S., Lagus, K., and Kohonen, T. (1996). Newsgroup exploration with WEBSOM method and browsing interface. Technical Report A32, Helsinki University of Technology, Lab. of Computer and Information Science, Espoo, Finland.
3. Honkela, T. (1998). Kohonen's Self-Organizing Maps in Intelligent Systems Development. Proceedings of FODO'98, The 5th International Conference on Foundations of Data Organization, Kobe, Japan, pp. 13-19.
4. Hörmann, H. (1986). *Meaning and Context.* Plenum Press, New York.
5. Kaski, S., Honkela, T., Lagus, K., and Kohonen, T. (1996). Creating an order in digital libraries with self-organizing maps. In *Proceedings of WCNN-96, World Congress on Neural Networks*.
6. Kaski, S. (1997b). Data exploration using self-organizing maps. *Acta Polytechnica Scandinavica, Mathematics, Computing and Management in Engineering Series No. 82*. DTech Thesis, Helsinki University of Technology, Finland.
7. Kaski, S., Honkela, T., Lagus, K., and Kohonen, T. (1998). WEBSOM–self-organizing maps of document collections, Neurocomputing, vol. 21, pp. 101-117.
8. Kaski, S., Kangas, J., and Kohonen, T. (1998). Bibliography of Self-Organizing Map (SOM) Papers: 1981-1997. Neural Computing Surveys, 1: 102-350. Available also at http://www.icsi.berkeley.edu/~jagota/NCS/
9. Kohonen, T. (1982). Self-organizing formation of topologically correct feature maps. *Biological Cybernetics*, 43(1):59-69.
10. Kohonen, T. (1995). *Self-Organizing Maps.* Springer, Berlin, Heidelberg.
11. Kohonen, T., Kaski, S., Lagus, K., and Honkela, T. (1996b). Very large two-level SOM for the browsing of newsgroups. In von der Malsburg, von Seelen, Vorbrüggen, and Sendhoff, editors, *Proceedings of ICANN96, International Conference on Artificial Neural Networks, Bochum, Germany, July 16-19, 1996*, Lecture Notes in Computer Science, vol. 1112, pp. 269-274. Springer, Berlin.
12. Lagus, K., Honkela, T., Kaski, S., and Kohonen, T. (1996). Self-organizing maps of document collections: A new approach to interactive exploration. In Simoudis, E., Han, J., and Fayyad, U., editors, *Proceedings of the Second International Conference on Knowledge Discovery and Data Mining*, pp. 238-243. AAAI Press, Menlo Park, California.
13. Lin, X., Soergel, D., and Marchionini, G. (1991). A self-organizing semantic map for information retrieval. In *Proceedings of 14th. Ann. International ACM/SIGIR Conference on Research & Development in Information Retrieval*, pp. 262-269.
14. Pulkki, V. (1995). Data averaging inside categories with the self-organizing map. Report A27, Helsinki University of Technology, Laboratory of Computer and Information Science, Espoo, Finland.
15. Ritter, H. and Kohonen, T. (1989). Self-organizing semantic maps. *Biological Cybernetics*, 61(4):241-254.
16. Scholtes, J. C. (1992b). Resolving linguistic ambiguities with a neural data-oriented parsing (DOP) system. In Aleksander, I. and Taylor, J., editors, *Artificial Neural Networks, 2*, volume II, pp. 1347-1350, North-Holland, Amsterdam, Netherlands.
17. Schütze, H. (1992). Dimensions of meaning. In *Proceedings of Supercomputing*, pp. 787-796.

The Notion of Context in Organisational Memories

Roland Klemke

GMD – German National Research Center for Information Technology
Schloß Birlinghoven
D-53754 Sankt Augustin
Roland.Klemke@gmd.de

Abstract. Moving from implicitly modelling context to explicit context models allows to regard contextual information throughout the whole lifecycle. Explicit context models created at information production time (i.e. the context of the information producer) may be stored together with the information itself. The explicit retrieval context model may then be matched against the stored model, enhancing retrieval. We define our understanding of context, show how context models change the information flow within an OM, and present ideas on how to construct, represent, and use explicit context models.

1 Introduction

Context has been recognised by a wide range of researchers as being an important concept to consider when looking at the meaning of information. Psychologists perform memory tests to analyse the effect of context on the remembrance of words [6], Researchers from machine learning study the effects of context on the automatic learning of concepts with promising results [3], Organisational Research people use communication models to investigate the role of context in information product evaluation [4], and cognitive scientists stress the importance of context for expertise [5]. Some philosophers even deny that there is a context-independent meaning of concepts [2]. A quite diverse understanding of the nature of context exists in the scientific community. The introduction of explicit context modelling thus instantly raises one important question: *what is context*? Depending on the area of research very different definitions will be given: from a cognitive science perspective [6] context is operationalised as external context, *"i.e. the situation in which a word is seen (with another word) or the scene within which an object is embedded (with other objects, in coherent scenes)"* whereas from an intelligent agents approach [7] context is regarded as *"any identifiable configuration of environmental, mission-related, and agent-related features that has predictive power for behaviour"*.

The different focus of these definitions shows the dilemma which the designer of an OM system has to resolve: on the one hand, context is obviously the context of the current system user (a human being) and thus rather complex while on the other hand the OM system has to focus on those elements of context which are identifiable and relevant (mission-related) for the purpose of the OM system.

The goal of OMs is *to improve the competitiveness of organisations by improving the way in which they manage their knowledge* (cf.[1], [8]). That is, OM systems should capture all relevant knowledge of an organisation and deliver it to its members whenever needed. Context in terms of an OM is thus restricted to the range of contexts an individual experiences within an organisation and comprises things like roles, tasks, positions, skills, interests, expertise, goals, etc.

2 Information Flow

In a simplified view on the information flow of an OM document ("document" not being restricted to a narrow sense, but comprising all types of information pieces inside an OM) are submitted to the OM and indexed to prepare them for later retrieval. Retrieval is done by matching queries against document indexes resulting in a set of relevant documents. This leaves out representational issues. It also displays an OM as standalone system without its integration in the work environment. People are often unsatisfied using such a system as the delivered retrieval results are often irrelevant and incomprehensible without further (context-) information.

To improve retrieval performance we will especially look at the use of context information to submission, representation and retrieval of documents. Research questions are: How can context be captured, represented and matched? What are the implications if retrieval context and submission context match (or do not match)? In which way should OM updates influence a context model and the context model influence retrieval, submission and representation?

The use of context models changes the information flow. A captured document will be associated with the current context model of the producer, resulting in context-enhanced document and index. Respectively, a query will be extended by the retrievers context adding information to the query. The context-enhanced query will be matched against the context-enhanced document indexes resulting in a set of potentially relevant context-enhanced documents. This match has to be done carefully, as different retrieval goals may be distinguished: a near match of retrievers and submitters context may be as useful as complementary context information.

3 Context Models: Content and Gathering

A useful context model for members of organisations comprises e.g. organisational, personal and situational context. The organisational context describes mostly static information about a person including things like roles, positions, tasks, titles etc. The personal context comprises interest, expertise, skills, experience etc. while the situational context describes the highly dynamic and temporary situation that the person in question is in.

A context gathering agent is responsible for maintaining an up-to-date context model for a person by observing the state of its different constituents. This agent should also stay in contact with the person itself to allow manual control the underlying model.

In order to automatically gather the valid context model for a person the context gathering agent has to be integrated with a number of applications, each of which delivers a piece of the overall image. The *organisational context* is e.g. provided by an employee database providing static information about a person and by a workflow management system which delivers all processes a person is involved with. The information provided by an employee database may be further used to infer relations between people like: "is in the same project as", "is project leader of", etc. The *personal context* can be provided by expertise modelling tools, personalised information retrieval tools, or other user modelling enriched applications. The *situational context* is e.g. provided by a workflow management system delivering information about the currently active process (or the process state). Some information about the situational context may also be provided by the OM system itself: the OM history of recent queries and submissions, assuming they are related to the situational context.

4 Applying Context Models

The submission of a document into the OM (either explicitly by a person or automatically by an integrated application) leads to the following process: the submitted document and the context model will be associated with each other leading to a context enriched document which will be indexed resulting in a context-enriched index. The representation of context-enriched documents and their indexes must allow the separation of documents and their context to enable different retrieval strategies.

Retrieval of documents from the OM follows a similar process: the query will be enriched with context information (keeping in mind the different possibilities of context usage: e.g. similar or complementary match) and the context enriched queries will be matched against the document indexes.

The overall goal of designing a context model is to create an easily extensible framework that allows for adaptations to different types of organisations and their special contextual requirements. It will be one of the goals of further research to identify useful constituents of context models and to define appropriate rules on how to use context information during retrieval.

5 Representational Issues

Various context representations have been discussed in the literature ranging from formal, frame-like knowledge structures (contextual schemas, [7]) and context ontologies (see [1]) to informal representations. For the purpose of OM we can derive a set of requirements that have to be met by context models:

- The comparison of two context model instances has to be possible. A set of meaningful similarity measures has to be applicable to those instances.

- The context models have to be flexible enough to provide a wide range of possible different contents.
- Reasoning has to be possible on (selected parts of) context models.
- Context models have to be indexable and retrievable independently of the information they are attached to.

The different requirements raise a well-known representational trade-off: reasoning capabilities require formal representations that allow the application of some kind of rules whereas the required flexibility and generality may lead to an unmanageable complexity in formal representations. It is therefore very important to identify those elements of contextual information that may be represented formally and those that need informal representations, resulting in context models where formal and informal parts co-exist.

6 Conclusion and Future Work

We have shown the important role contextual information plays in information systems, especially organisational memory applications and presented our ideas on explicit context modelling. These ideas are an attempt to move to a more comprehensive and generally applicable view on context. Even though we restricted our ideas to the area of OM, we believe that information system design in many areas can benefit from these ideas. Research on context is still in its early stages and we want to perform further research in this area, comprising representational issues, reasoning mechanisms and context observing agents.

References

1. A. Abecker, A. Bernardi, K. Hinkelmann, O. Kühn, M. Sintek: Toward a Technology for Organisational Memories. In: IEEE Intelligent Systems & Their Application, May/June 1998.
2. M. Heidegger: Being and Time, Harper & Row, New York, 1962.
3. S. Matwin, M. Kubat: The role of Context in Concept Learning. In: Proc. of the 13th International Conference on Machine Learning, Bari, Italy, 1996.
4. L. D. Murphy: Information Product Evaluation as Asynchronous Communication in Context: A Model for Organizational Research. In: Proc. of the 1st ACM International Conference on Digital Libraries, 1996.
5. P. Y. Raccah: Science, Language, and Situation. In: Proc. of the 2nd European conference on cognitive science, workshop on context (ECCS'97), 1997.
6. K. Srinivas: How is context represented in implicit and explicit memory. In: Proc. of the 2nd European Conference on Cognitive Science, Workshop on Context (ECCS'97), 1997.
7. R. M. Turner: Context-Mediated Behaviour for Intelligent Agents. In: Int. J. of Human-Computer Studies, special issue on Using Context in Applications, vol. 48, no.3, 1998.
8. G. van Heijst, R. van der Spek, E. Kruizinga: Organising Corporate Memories. In: Proc. of Tenth Knowledge Acquisition for Knowledge-Based Systems Workshop, 1996.

The Effect of Context Complexity on the Memorisation of Objects

Séverine Mérand[1], Charles Tijus[1] and Sébastien Poitrenaud[1]

[1]Laboratoire CNRS UPRES A-7021 "Cognition & Activités finalisées"
Université de Paris VIII, 2 rue de la Liberté
93 526 Saint-Denis Cedex 02 - France
severine.merand@univ-paris8.fr
tijus@univ-paris8.fr
poitrenaud@univ-paris8.fr

Abstract. In this article, we present a model of the representation of visual scenes in immediate memory. Our hypothesis is that the structure of this representation is equivalent to the construction of a Galois Lattice which it is based on principles of similarity and differentiation of objects through feature computation. The model allows making precise predictions about the effect of context, defined here as a more or less complex structure of features shared and not shared by an object to be memorized with other objects. We designed an immediate memory task of visually presented objects in which the number of objects and the number of properties remained constant. The distribution of these properties was manipulated. We hypothesized that for the same target object, errors rates as well as response times would prove to be a function of feature distribution. The results of the experimental study are consistent with our predictions and also allow reinterpreting the results of classic experiments in the field.

1 Introduction

Numerous authors working on categorization and memorisation explain the encoding of information in semantic memory through the processing of similarity [2], [4]. Most studies have concentrated on the effect of similarity processing on word memorisation. However, the effect of similarity processing on the memorisation of visual objects is virtually unknown. We present a model of the representation of visual scenes in immediate memory. Our hypothesis is that the structure of this representation is equivalent to the construction of a Galois lattice [1].

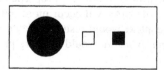

Fig. 1. Example of a visual scene

In figure 1, three different kinds of properties are distributed across the objects : shape (round or square), colour (white or black) and size (small or large). The mental organization of properties is evidenced by the terms that can be used to designate the objects in figure 4. The figure in the center can be designated as "the white one". Likewise, the object on the left can be designated by a single property, either "the circle" or "the large figure". However, distinguishing the figure on the right from the other objects in the context requires using two properties because naming it with any single one of the three properties -- "the black one", "the small one", or "the square"-- would necessarily lead to confusion. Thus, in order to make it clear which object one is talking about, one must say "the black square" or "the little black one". The little black one's particularity is that all of its properties are shared with the other objects in the context and thus it has no property exclusively its own.

Our principal hypothesis is that similarity processing is very much like constructing a Galois lattice, which is to say, constructing a hierarchical network of categories formed by the factorisation of the properties of objects. The Galois lattice corresponding to figure 1 is shown in figure 2.

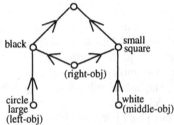

Fig. 2. Galois lattice corresponding to the cognitive arrangement of the properties in figure1

Note that in the Galois lattice, certain properties correspond to more than one object (small, square) and others to a single object (white, see figure 1). The properties corresponding to more than one object are shared properties, they are placed higher up on the network. At the bottom of the network are the properties that are not shared. The object in the center in the figure 1 appears in the lattice (figure 2) on the right-hand side. To "read" the lattice for this object, begin at the bottom and move up: it is white, it is small and it is square. The right-hand object (small black square) in figure 1 does not appear at the bottom of the network. It is found farther up the network because all of its properties are shared properties, it can only be designated by a conjunction of features. In Galois lattice theory, the case of the small black square is a case of multiple inheritance of properties.

We will argue that this way of organizing perceptual information has an effect on the encoding of perceived properties. The Galois lattice enables one to make precise predictions about the memorisation and recall of object properties. So we hypothesized that (i) for a constant number of objects and a constant number of properties of objects, errors rates increase when property distribution becomes complex, (ii) these errors will not be produced randomly: because of the ascending order of access to properties in the lattice (represented by arrows in figure 2), properties that are shared will be less easily accessible in memory and errors will occur more often on this kind of properties and (iii) longer exposure to context would result in better encoding and memorisation, and that the effects of a longer exposure would be more pronounced when the lattice is complex.

2 Method

The objective of our experiment was to test the three predictions expressed above. The material consisted of computer drawings representing 3 objects in a row (left, centre, right). Each of the 3 objects in every drawing is composed of 3 different properties extracted from 3 property pairs (circle/square, crossed/not crossed, alpha/numeric). The properties were distributed across the objects in order to build a simple or a complex lattice (see figure 3).

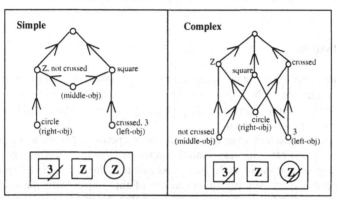

Fig. 3. Example of two drawings and their corresponding lattices, either simple or complex, used in the experiment.

The properties were distributed across the objects in order to build a simple or a complex lattice. There were 12 "simple lattice" drawings and 12 "complex lattice" drawings. The drawings were presented at the rate of either 300 msec or 1000 msec. 48 students (male and female) at Paris 8 University with normal or corrected vision (lenses) were recruited. We propose a property recall task to the participants. The experiment was piloted by a Macintosh PowerPC 7500.

3 Results

3.1 Recall for shared vs. not-shared properties

Recall error rate was significantly higher for shared properties (26%) than for not shared properties (21%) across all conditions ($F(1,44)=12.79$, $p<.001$).

Additionally, in the same experimental condition (simple context, 300ms), the greater the number of shared properties an object possesed, the highter was the average of reaction time: when object had two shared properties (for example, figure 3, simple condition, the object on the right, properties "non crossed" and "letter"), the mean of reaction time was 2.24 sec, when the object had one shared property (for example, figure 3, simple condition, object on the left, property "square"), the mean of reaction time was only 1.91 sec, $F(1,11)=5.23$, $p<.05$.

3.2 The effect of simple or complex context

With a 300 msec S.O.A., participants made more errors on shared properties than on non-shared properties but only in simple context (31% of errors for shared properties against 18% for non-shared properties). In complex context, the same amount of errors was observed for shared and non shared properties (27%), $F(1,22)=8.34$, p<.01.

3.3 The effect of S.O.A. (300 msec vs. 1000 msec)

The prolonged exposure time in 2 out 4 experimental conditions was indeed accompanied by a significant drop in the global number of errors, 29% for 300 msec S.O.A. and 19% for 1000 msec S.OA., $F(1,44)=4.07$, p<.01.

4 Discussion

The results of this experimental study are consistent with the hypothesis. First, as expected, the role of the context on the cognitive processing of objects appears to be sensitive to the delay allowed for processing objects: with a 300 msec S.O.A., properties are less well recalled.

Second, encoding objects with shared properties appears to be more difficult than encoding objects with non-shared properties. Reaction times and percentage of errors were both consistent with the hypothesis that the recall of the properties of an object depends on the sharing of properties of this object with the other contextual objects. Both of this findings seem to indicate that the more an object's properties are shared, more it is difficult to access to these properties.

As expected, the role of the context on the cognitive processing of objects appears to be sensitive to the delay allowed for processing objects: with a 300 msec S.O.A., complex sharing of properties entails more recall errors than simple sharing. However, with a 1000 msec S.O.A., we didn't have the same results. It may be that, having sufficient time to fully process the visual scene, participants try to verbally encode objets, a strategy that they would not use when processing scenes with a complex sharing of properties.

In conclusion, our model does not contradict other theories of feature perception and integration such as Treisman's model [3], with its explanation of the pop-out effect. The pop-out effect is observed when one object differs from others by a single feature; detection is made in parallel. In our model, pop-out is explained as the effect of first processing the only non-shared features of the visual scene. In contrast, sequential processing of conjunctive features corresponds in our model to the detection of one object that has any non-shared property and that inherits properties from superordinate categories.

References

1. Barbut, M., & Monjardet, B. (1970). Ordre et classification: algèbre et combinatoire. Paris: Hachette.
2. Smith, E.E., & Sloman, S.A. (1994). Similarity versus Ruled-Based Categories. *Memory and Cognition, 4*, 377-386.
3. Treisman, A., & Gelade, G. (1980). A feature integration theory of attention. *Cognitive Psychology, 12*, 97-136.
4. Tversky, A. (1977). Features similarity. *Psychological Review, 84*, 327-352.

Effects of Discourse Context on Inference Computation During Comprehension

Yasunori Morishima

Institute of Cognitive Science, University of Colorado, Boulder, CO 80309, USA
and
OMRON Advanced Systems, Inc., 3945 Freedom Circle, Santa Clara, CA 95054, USA
morishima@oas.net

Abstract. This study investigated how discourse context influences the on-line inference process of a high-probability instrument. The experiments showed that such instrument inferences are not computed unless the context provides information that strongly supports the inferences. When the context is compatible with such inferences but weak, the inference is not routinely drawn. However, the reader does generate the inference if motivated to elaborate. A simulation model successfully generated the results that were in agreement with the experiments. The simulations showed that on-line inference processes are affected by the trade-off between construction of a rich representation and the limited capacity of the cognitive system.

1. Introduction

A reader constructs a situation model during comprehension. The situation model is a microworld of agents, objects, and events associated with text elements [1][3]. An important aspect of the situation model construction is that the extent to which the reader actually performs elaboration is subject to a number of influences. This paper investigates such an influence of context on inference generation. To illustrate, consider the sentence, *"Marvin inflated the tire."* It is feasible to infer that Marvin used a pump. Would the inference be drawn if the sentence appears in different contexts? If *"Marvin grabbed the pump in the shed."* precedes the sentence, the context would imply that he took the pump and intuitively supports the inference. If the preceding sentence is *"Marvin looked for the pump in the shed,"* it would not strongly make that implication, but if one assumes a proper sequence of actions, one can reach the implication. It is plausible to assume that the situation model would be built such that a proper event sequence (i.e., finding the pump and taking it) is incorporated, yielding the inference. However, this chain of inferencing would require more cognitive resources. Thus, an alternative hypothesis is that such an elaborated situation model would not be built on-line, and consequently the instrument would not be inferred.

2. Experiments

2.1 Experiment 1

Experiment 1 tested whether, as discussed above, the reader would draw the inference, engaging in elaborations if the context does not readily provide enough information.

Method. The experiment had four levels of context: Strongly Related (*Marvin grabbed the pump in the shed.*), Moderately Related (*Marvin spotted the pump in the shed.*) Weakly Related (*Marvin searched for the pump in the shed.*), and Unrelated (*Marvin grabbed the pump in the shed. He flew to Boston.*). In the related contexts, the instrument use was plausible, but the degree of supporting the implication varied. The participants were 36 native speakers of English. They read the sentence pair at their own pace and had a lexical decision on the instrument (*pump*) and a comprehension question.

Results and Discussion. The summary of the results is presented in Table 1. The participant analysis is reported here as *Fp* and the item analysis as *Fi*. The mean reaction time for the strong context was significantly faster than for each of the other contexts [against Unrelated, $Fp(1, 35) = 19.6$, $p < 0.01$, $Fi(1, 23) = 26.5$, $p < 0.01$; against Weak, $Fp(1, 35) = 13.5$, $p < 0.01$, $Fi(1, 23) = 7.3$, $p < 0.01$; against Moderate, $Fp(1, 35) = 12.3$, $p < 0.01$, $Fi(1, 23) = 5.7$, $p < 0.01$]. The difference between the unrelated context and the weak and moderate contexts combined was not significant. The data showed a priming effect only for the strong context, suggesting that the inference was computed. I argue that this is because the strong context did not require deep processing to generate the inference since information necessary for the inference can be easily retrieved by a text element and can be integrated into the situation model.

Table 1. The results of Experiment 1.

Context	Lexical Decision		Reading Time	
Unrelated	844*a*	(188.7)*b*	1578	(555.0)
Weak	818	(177.3)	1336	(423.1)
Moderate	814	(155.8)	1332	(510.6)
Strong	755	(135.5)	1270	(444.0)

*a*The values are all in msec. *b*The values in parentheses are standard deviations.

The reading time data support this argument. The reading times for the three related contexts were significantly faster than that for the unrelated context [$Fp(1, 35) = 38.4$, $p < 0.01$, $Fi(1, 23) = 9.9$, $p < 0.01$]. The difference between the strongly related context and the other related contexts was marginally significant by the participant analysis [$Fp(1, 35) = 3.2$, $p < 0.082$], but did not reach significance by the item analysis. All related conditions yielded significantly faster reading times than the unrelated condition by both analyses [for Weak, $Fp(1, 35) = 15.2$, $p < 0.01$, $Fi(1, 23) = 6.2$ $p < 0.03$; for Moderate, $Fp(1, 35) = 26.3$, $p < 0.01$, $Fi(1, 23) = 7.1$, $p < 0.02$; for Strong, $Fp(1, 35) = 61.2$, $p < 0.01$, $Fi(1, 23) = 12.3$, $p < 0.01$]. The data showed that the texts in these conditions were processed in a similar manner as in the strong condition, suggesting that the reader integrated only a limited amount of knowledge.

2.2 Experiment 2

Based on the results from Experiment 1, it is hypothesized that if the reader engages in more elaborative processing, instrument inference should be drawn. Experiment 2 tested this hypothesis.

Method. There were three levels of context: Strongly Related, Moderately Related, and Contradictory (*Marvin found the broken pump in the shed.*). The major difference from Experiment 1 was that all comprehension questions were about instruments. The correct answers were to be positive for all but the contradictory context. In the practice session, the participant was given feedback about his/her response. The participants were 36 native speakers of English.

Results and Discussion. Table 2 summarizes the results from Experiment 2. The mean reaction times for the strong and moderate conditions were significantly faster than for the contradictory condition by the participant analysis and marginally significant by the item analysis [$Fp(1, 35) = 8.1$, $p < 0.01$; $Fi(1, 17) = 3.1$, $p < 0.095$]. The difference between the strong and moderate contexts did not reach significance by either analysis. The data for the strong and moderate contexts were compared between Experiments 1 and 2. The interaction between Experiment and Context was significant by the participant analysis [$Fp(1, 71) = 4.4$, $p < .04$]. The results indicate that there was an instrument priming effect for both the moderate and strong contexts as expected. I claim that the training manipulation led the participant to more elaborative processing, resulting in the inference even in the weaker context.

The reading time data provide supporting evidence: no differences among the contexts were significant. The participant spent about the same amount of time on reading the action sentence regardless of context, suggesting that the level of processing for the strong context was as deep as that for the moderate context.

Table 2. The results of Experiment 2.

Context	Lexical Decision		Reading Time	
Contradictory	765a	(210.7)b	1495	(492.5)
Moderate	723	(187.7)	1399	(486.9)
Strong	712	(208.3)	1402	(489.1)

aThe values are all in msec. bThe values in parentheses are standard deviations.

3. Simulation Model

A simulation model has been developed based on the construction-integration theory [1][2][4]. The model processes a text in a number of cycles. A processing cycle consists of a bottom-up construction and a top-down integration. In the construction phase, the model constructs a propositional network by bringing in the information from the knowledge base. The construction is controlled by weak, general rules, resulting in a representation with inferences irrelevant to the context as well as relevant ones. In the integration phase, activation spreads until it stabilizes. The integration process filters out certain elaborations, especially contextually inappropriate ones. It is assumed that the participants adopted an elaborative reading strategy in Experiment 2 whereas they did not in Experiment 1. In the simulation, this assumption is realized by setting an activation threshold that determines which propositions will serve as retrieval cues low and high rspectively. The same set of texts was used for both the high threshold and low threshold simulations. For the strong context, the inference achieved a high activation for both thresholds. For the weaker contexts, while the activation of the inference was low for the high threshold, a higher level of activation resulted when the threshold was lowered.

4. Conclusion

The simulation results are consistent with the experimental results and showed that on-line inference processes are influenced by context. The context effect is due to the trade-off between the demand for constructing a rich situation model and the limited capacity of the cognitive system. On the one hand, the reader tries to activate and integrate as much world knowledge as possible to construct an elaborated situation model. On the other hand, the reader can allocate only limited cognitive resources for the on-line inference processes.

References

1. Kintsch, W.: The role of knowledge in discourse comprehension: A construction-integration model. Psychological Review, 93 (2), (1988) 163-182
2. Kintsch, W.: A cognitive architecture for comprehension. In: Pick, Jr., H. L., van den Broek, P. & Knill, D. C. (eds.): Cognition: Conceptual and methodological issues. American Psychological Association, Washington, D.C. (1992)
3. Kintsch, W.: Comprehension: a paradigm for cognition. Cambridge University Press, Cambridge, UK (1998)
4. Morishima, Y.: Effects of Discourse Context on On-Line Inference Computation. Unpublished doctoral dissertation, University of Colorado, Boulder (1996)

Counterfactual Reasoning by Means of a Calculus of Narrative Context

Rolf Nossum[1] and Michael Thielscher[2]

[1] Department of Mathematics
Agder College, Kristiansand (Norway)
[2] Department of Computer Science
Dresden University of Technology (Germany)

Abstract. The basic Event Calculus is extended by a Calculus of Narrative Context, to allow for reasoning about counterfactuals. Different hypothetical courses of events are distinguished by their narrative contexts. A notion of information transfer between contexts provides a basis for drawing conclusions about counterfactual courses of events.

1 Introduction

The Event Calculus [3] is an axiomatization technique for formalizing, and mechanizing, reasoning about narratives that involve actions and events. A typical axiomatization consists of two parts. Firstly, knowledge is provided about the general effects of the actions and events that might occur in a domain. Secondly, a specific narrative is described, to which the general knowledge of effects is applied in order to draw reasonable conclusions about these particular situations.

As regards this second part, plain Event Calculus only allows specifying events that actually occurred and observations that were actually made during any particular course of events. It does not allow for specification and reasoning about counterfactual courses of events. The lack of support for specification of counterfactual developments of the world in plain Event Calculus distinguishes it from its grand old rival, the Situation Calculus.

In this paper, we propose an extension of Event Calculus which allows formalizing and reasoning about hypothetical courses of events. This is accomplished by formally attaching event occurrences and observations to differing contexts, each of which describes alternative evolutions. The resulting theory inherits the representational merits of Event Calculus as regards reasoning about narratives, and combines it with the paradigm of Situation Calculus which supports reasoning about hypothetical sequences of actions.

2 Example: a Shooting Scenario

Let's enlist an old standby as our running example: a variation on the Yale Shooting Scenario [2]. Suppose we know that, in general, shooting at a vase causes it to shatter, provided the gun is loaded. Likewise, shooting at a turkey with the gun loaded always kills it. Suppose further a specific narrative telling us that initially the vase is in one piece and the turkey is alive. The narrative continues with the information that by shooting at the vase it has been destroyed. A reasonable conclusion here would be that had the protagonist shot at the turkey instead, then the bird would not have survived. For the only explanation of the vase being destroyed is that the gun was loaded to begin with. Hence the supposed death of the turkey in the counterfactual course of events.

In a formalization of the scenario we shall introduce two contexts, in one of which the vase is shot at while the turkey is the target in the other context. Enabling conclusions about counterfactual sequences of events requires a suitable transfer between different contexts: The straightforward conclusion that the gun must have been loaded initially in the context where the vase is destroyed, needs to be transferred to the opposing, hypothetical context.

The solution we propose is to stipulate that two contexts share all temporal conclusions up to the first timepoint at which the two courses of events split. In particular, all contexts agree on the information that holds in the initial state. This will support the expected conclusion as regards the above example.

3 Basic Definitions

- We take actions as atomic, e.g.: *shoot-turkey*, *shoot-vase*, etc.
- Time will be linear, and for simplicity we take the natural numbers as our time domain.
- Events are represented using the predicate $Happens(a, t)$, where a and t are an action and a timepoint, respectively.
- Properties are atomic, e.g. *alive*, *loaded*, *broken*, etc.
- Claims about initial truth or falsity of properties take the form $Initially(p)$, resp. $\neg Initially(p)$ for a property p.
- A (Narrative) Context is a set of $Initially(\ldots)$ and $Happens(\ldots, \ldots)$ atoms.
- A Narrative is a narrative context along with a conjunction of *Initiates*, *Terminates*, and *HoldsAt* formulas (see Section 4).

For a given narrative context N, we define initial segments N^t up to given timepoints t as, $N^t \stackrel{def}{=} N \setminus \{Happens(a, u) : t < u\}$. The latest timepoint at which two narrative contexts N_1 and N_2 agree is,

$$N_1 \uparrow N_2 \stackrel{def}{=} max(\{t : N_1^t = N_2^t\} \cup \{-1\})$$

4 The Event Calculus

A property f being true (resp. false) at some time t is expressed as $HoldsAt(f, t)$ (resp. $\neg HoldsAt(f, t)$). Axiomatizing the general knowledge as to the effects of actions and events is based on two predicates named $Initiates(a, f, t)$ and

Terminates(a, f, t), indicating that action a occurring at time t causes property f to become true (resp. false). For our running example domain, we have

$$HoldsAt(loaded, t) \rightarrow Initiates(shoot\text{-}vase, broken, t) \tag{1}$$

$$HoldsAt(loaded, t) \rightarrow Terminates(shoot\text{-}turkey, alive, t) \tag{2}$$

In addition, the special predicate *Initially*(f) serves the purpose of introducing partial information of the initial state, e.g.

$$\neg Initially(broken) \wedge Initially(alive) \tag{3}$$

The following foundational axioms describe the impact of initiating and terminating properties as a consequence of events happening.

$$Initially(f) \wedge \neg Clipped(0, f, t) \rightarrow HoldsAt(f, t) \tag{4}$$

$$\neg Initially(f) \wedge \neg Declipped(0, f, t) \rightarrow \neg HoldsAt(f, t) \tag{5}$$

$$Happens(a, t_1) \wedge Initiates(a, f, t_1) \wedge t_1 < t_2 \wedge \neg Clipped(t_1, f, t_2)$$
$$\rightarrow HoldsAt(f, t_2) \tag{6}$$

$$Happens(a, t_1) \wedge Terminates(a, f, t_1) \wedge t_1 < t_2 \wedge \neg Declipped(t_1, f, t_2)$$
$$\rightarrow \neg HoldsAt(f, t_2) \tag{7}$$

An instance *Clipped*(T_1, F, T_2) (resp. *Declipped*(T_1, F, T_2)) is true iff an action occurs in the time interval (T_1, T_2) terminating (resp. instantiating) property F. Accordingly these two predicates are defined as follows:

$$Clipped(t_1, f, t_2) \leftrightarrow \exists a, t \, [\, Happens(a, t) \wedge Terminates(a, f, t) \wedge t_1 < t < t_2 \,] \tag{8}$$

$$Declipped(t_1, f, t_2) \leftrightarrow \exists a, t \, [\, Happens(a, t) \wedge Initiates(a, f, t) \wedge t_1 < t < t_2 \,] \tag{9}$$

Suppose given a narrative specification consisting of a conjunction N of *Happens* and *Initially* atoms along with a set of *HoldsAt* formulas and a conjunction E of *Initiates* and *Terminates* formulas. Then the semantics of this axiomatization is given by circumscribing [4] *Happens* in N and, independently, simultaneously circumscribing *Initiates* and *Terminates* in E. Along with the general axioms plus some suitable unique name assumptions, the resulting classical formula is taken as the meaning of the specification.

As an example, let N consist of the atoms in (3) plus *Happens*$(shoot\text{-}vase, 2)$. Circumscribing *Happens* in N yields

$$[\, Happens(a, t) \leftrightarrow a = shoot\text{-}vase \wedge t = 2 \,]$$
$$\wedge \neg Initially(broken) \wedge Initially(alive) \tag{10}$$

Circumscription of *Initiates* and *Terminates* in $E = \{(1), (2)\}$ yields

$$Initiates(a, f, t) \leftrightarrow a = shoot\text{-}vase \wedge f = broken \wedge HoldsAt(loaded, t)$$
$$Terminates(a, f, t) \leftrightarrow a = shoot\text{-}turkey \wedge f = alive \wedge HoldsAt(loaded, t) \tag{11}$$

Let Σ denote the formulas (10) and (11) along with $HoldsAt(broken, 3)$ and the general axioms (4)–(9). Then Σ entails $Declipped(0, broken, 3)$ according to $\neg Initially(broken)$, $HoldsAt(broken, 3)$, and formula (5). Formula (9) in conjunction with (10) then implies $Initiates(shoot\text{-}vase, broken, 2)$. This in turn entails $HoldsAt(loaded, 2)$ following Equation (11). It follows that $Initially(loaded)$ according to (5), provided that $\neg Declipped(0, loaded, 2)$. The latter holds according to equation (9) in conjunction with (11).

5 Counterfactuals by Information Transfer

So far so good. Notice, however, that we cannot formalize an alternative course of events with, say, $Happens(shoot\text{-}turkey, 2)$ instead of $Happens(shoot\text{-}vase, 2)$ without losing the implicitly derived information that $Initially(loaded)$. Hence conclusions about counterfactual events are not supported by plain Event Calculus. In order to facilitate reasoning about hypothetical courses of events, we amalgamate the Event Calculus with a calculus of Narrative Context.

The basic idea is to consider a particular course of events N as a narrative context. That is, formally a Context is a set of formulas of the form $Happens(a, t)$ or $Initially(f)$. E.g., for our key example we use the two contexts

$$N_1 = \{\neg Initially(broken), Initially(alive), Happens(shoot\text{-}vase, 2)\}$$

$$N_2 = \{\neg Initially(broken), Initially(alive), Happens(shoot\text{-}turkey, 2)\}$$

The notation $\mathbf{ist}(c, \psi)$, with the reading that ψ is true in the context c, was introduced in [1], where the application is to localized contexts in the CYC knowledge base. For our purposes here, c will range over narrative contexts.

All foundational axioms, i.e., (4)–(9) are then universally true in any context. The same applies to effect descriptions as in (11).

To see why information transfer between contexts is necessary, observe that in our example we can derive $\mathbf{ist}(N_1, Initially(loaded))$, as shown above. This, however, does not *per se* imply that $\mathbf{ist}(N_2, Initially(loaded))$. The latter is required in order that the intended conclusion $\mathbf{ist}(N_2, \neg HoldsAt(Alive, 3))$ follows.

The crucial connection is this: we demand that for any two narratives N_1 and N_2 we have

$$t \leq N_1 \uparrow N_2 \rightarrow [\mathbf{ist}(N_1, HoldsAt(f, t)) \leftrightarrow \mathbf{ist}(N_2, HoldsAt(f, t))]$$

References

1. R. V. Guha. *Contexts: A Formalization and Some Applications*. PhD thesis, Stanford University, 1991.
2. S. Hanks and D. McDermott. Nonmonotonic logic and temporal projection. *Artificial Intelligence*, 3:379–412, 1987.
3. R. Kowalski and M. Sergot. A logic-based calculus of events. *New Generation Computing*, 4:67–95, 1986.
4. V. Lifschitz. Circumscription. In D. Gabbay etal., editors, *Handbook of Logic in AI and Logic Programming*, volume 3, pages 298–352. Oxford University Press, 1994.

Context and Decision Graphs for Incident Management on a Subway Line

Laurent Pasquier, Patrick Brézillon & Jean-Charles Pomerol

Laboratoire d'Informatique de Paris 6, Case 169, Université Paris 6
4, place Jussieu, 75252 Paris Cedex 05, France
Forename.Name@lip6.fr

Abstract. The management of the incidents on a subway line is a difficult task for several reasons, mainly because parameters that intervene in it are numerous and of various types. Decision trees are structures that permit to model contextual reasoning, but do not take the dynamics of contextual knowledge and proceduralized context into account. Decision graphs get round it and avoid combinatorial explosion often met in industrial applications of decision trees.

Keywords: Decision tree, Decision graph, Context, Incident Management.

1 Introduction

The management of the incidents on a line of subway is a difficult task for several reasons. The SART project (SART is the French acronym for support system in traffic control; general information may be found at http://www.lip6.fr/SART) aims at the development of an intelligent system to support the operators responsible for the traffic and incident management on subway lines at RATP (the French subway company in Paris) [2].

Incidents and their contexts have various natures and their solving are the object of official procedures that are based on the experience acquired by the RATP. The solutions selected by the operators are adaptations of procedures according to the context. As a result, the strategy to solve an incident is different from one operator to another.

The paper is organized as follows. Section 2 presents briefly our views on context that are discussed in a companion paper [1]. Section 3 explains the differences between a procedure and the different operator's practices with regard to context. Section 4 explains how operators' reasoning is modeled and the specificity of this modeling. We propose an alternative operators' reasoning model based on macro-actions, temporal branching and decision graphs.

2 The Contextual Dimension of the Problem

Brézillon and Pomerol [3] define the *contextual knowledge* as all the knowledge that is relevant for one person in a given situated decision problem and can be mobilized to understand this problem. Contextual knowledge is evoked by situations and events, and loosely tied to a task or a goal. Contextual knowledge is considered as a part of the context, the rest of the context, which is not relevant to the situation, is called *external knowledge*.

When an event occurs, the attention of the actors is focused on it and a large part of the contextual knowledge will be proceduralized. The proceduralized part of the contextual knowledge, at a given step of a decision making, is called the *proceduralized context* [3]. The proceduralized context is invoked, structured and situated according to a given focus.

At a given step of the decision making process, one has: proceduralized context which is the knowledge commonly known by the actors of the problem and directly (but often tacitly) used for the problem solving; contextual knowledge which is the knowledge not explicitly used but influencing the problem solving; and external knowledge which is the knowledge having nothing to do with the current decision making step, but known by many actors of the problem.

3 Procedures and Practices

At RATP, most of the incidents are well-known (object on the track, lack of power supply, suicide, etc.). Thus, the company has established mandatory procedures for incident solving on the basis of its experience. For example, Brézillon *et al.* [2] discuss the procedure and the knowledge involved in the incident "Sick traveler in a train." In this case, the driver must stop at the next station because travelers are safer in a station than in a tunnel. At a deeper level, the driver has to avoid stopping the train a long time in a tunnel because some travelers may have behavioral troubles such as claustrophobia and could leave the train to wander about on the railway (and thus may generate another type of incident such as "Person on the track"). These pieces of knowledge, which are not necessarily expressed, result in more or less proceduralized actions that are compiled as parts of the proceduralized context. As such, mandatory procedures are proceduralized contexts.

For simple incidents, a unique procedure is enough for the whole incident solving. However, there is no global procedure for complex incidents, only a set of procedures, each procedure solving a part of the incident. For example, when a train cannot move in a tunnel, there are procedures to evacuate travelers at the nearest station, for clearing the damaged train by another train, etc. Some procedures are sequential, but others may be accomplished in any order. For example, when a train must push a damaged train, both trains must be empty but the order in which travelers of both trains are evacuated is not important and mainly depends on the context in which the trains are. What is important is that the two actions must be accomplished before the damaged train clearing. As a consequence, each operator develops his own practice to solve incidents, and one observes almost as many practices as operators for a given incident solving because each operator structures the set of procedures in order to take the current contextual knowledge into account, which is particular and specific. Thus, cases that are similar in one context may be totally dissimilar in others as already quoted by Tversky [4].

4 Modeling Operators' Reasoning

In operators' reasoning, cases are generally developed into scenarios [5]. The advantage of scenarios and decision trees is to display events and elementary actions. See Raïffa [6] for a simple presentation of decision trees. Contextual elements intervene at various steps of the scenarios (*e.g.*, traffic activity or position of the next train). The operators prefer to take them into account as soon as possible to get a general picture of the best path to choose. At this step, contextual knowledge is proceduralized and in the meantime operators postpone actions. As a consequence of the action postponement, actions are grouped into sequences. Some common sequences may be grouped into macro-actions [5].

In decision trees, it is impossible to model the dynamics of the proceduralization of the contextual knowledge since proceduralized knowledge stays proceduralized up to the end of the procedure. We need to represent the fact that proceduralized context return at a contextual knowledge state when the operator does not focus any more on it. We thus decided to merge the branches when the knowledge piece that introduced the branching is no more proceduralized by the operator. We face no more a tree but a graph, called *decision graph*.

As said in Section 3, the order in which some actions are executed may be indifferent. We thus have added *temporal branching* in the decision graph model. Temporal branching separates action sequences that are independent at a temporal level. Each branch is executed independently from the others, but all of them must be done before the beginning of the next step. This branching is represented by dotted square brackets. Fig. 1 gives an example of the solving of a traction incident represented by a decision graph.

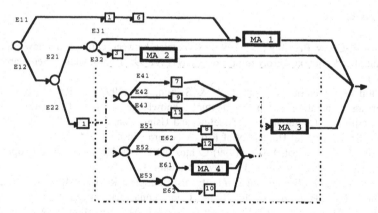

Fig. 1. Decision graph of the reasoning applied in case of traction incident solving.

Indeed, with these new elements (macro-actions, event node branches merging and temporal branching) we enrich our *decision graph* by taking explicitly context and time into account. The decision graph limits the combinatorial explosion in the decision tree. This is particularly interesting when the contextual knowledge represented by the events intervenes only on few nodes.

Operators will have the possibility to modify the structure of a resolution procedure to model their own strategy for solving an incident. However, each procedure and the associated strategies will have the same structure. Concretely, a strategy is a copy of a customized procedure applied for an incident in a given context.

5 Conclusion

In the framework of the SART project, we show that incident solving by an operator, responsible of a subway line, has a simpler representation by decision graph than decision tree. Our representation makes explicit different notions such as contextual knowledge state (contextual or proceduralized) or temporal independence. The representation is adapted to industrial processes in which numerous contextual elements intervene and where different sub-tasks are running in parallel.

Decision graph model has been applied to the procedures of management of the four main incidents encountered in the Parisian subway. Operators and managers at RATP have well accepted our modeling, mainly because of the clarity and comprehensibility of the representation: it is easier to understand a set of decision graphs than the corresponding decision tree, while they represent the same reality.

Acknowledgments:

Grants are provided by RATP and COFECUB in France and CAPES in Brazil. We also thank J.-M. Sieur at RATP, and C. Gentile, I. Saker and M. Secron, Ph.D. students working on the SART project.

References

1. Pomerol, J.-Ch. & Brézillon, P. (1999), Dynamics between contextual knowledge and proceduralized context. Proceedings of CONTEXT-99, Trento, Italy, September (to appear).
2. Brézillon, P., Gentile, C., Saker, I. & Secron, M. (1997) SART: A system for supporting operators with contextual knowledge. First International and Interdisciplinary Conference on Modeling and Using Context (CONTEXT-97), Rio de Janeiro, Brazil, Federal University of Rio de Janeiro (Ed.), pp. 209-222.
3. Brézillon, P. & Pomerol, J.-Ch. (1999) Contextual knowledge sharing and cooperation in intelligent assistant systems. Le Travail Humain, PUF, Paris.
4. Tversky, A. (1977). Features of similarity, Psychological Review 84(4): 327--352.
5. Brézillon, P. & Pomerol, J.-Ch. (1998) Using contextual information in decision making. In: Chapman & Hall. Widmeyer G., Berkeley D., Brézillon P. & Rajkovic V. Eds.: Context-Sensitive Decision Support Systems, pp. 158-173.
6. Raïffa H. (1968), Decision Analysis, Mac Graw Hill.
7. Brézillon, P., Pasquier, L. & Saker, I. (1999) Context-based reasoning and decision graphs. Application in incident management on a subway line. Cognitive science Approaches to Process Control, CSAPC'99, Villeneuve d'Ascq, France, 21-24 September 1999 (to appear).

Using Context to Guide Information Search for Preventive Quality Management

Gerhard Peter[1] and Brigitte Grote[2]

[1] Research Institute for Applied Knowledge Processing
at the University of Ulm (FAW), P.O. Box 20 60, 89010 Ulm, Germany
gerhard@faw.uni-ulm.de
[2] Faculty of Computer Science, Otto-von-Guericke-University,
P.O. Box 41 20, 39016 Magdeburg, Germany
grote@iws.cs.uni-magdeburg.de

Abstract. Preventive quality management (PQM) is a very information-intensive task. Information as diverse as customer requirements, material specifications, and production line characteristics of a product as well as complaints related to similar products have to be taken into consideration when, e.g., predicting and evaluating possible failure modes of a product. However, only a subset of this information is actually relevant in a given stage of the PQM process and for a given person. In this paper, we exploit the notion of context to restrict the number of information sources accessed, make information selection more goal-directed, and finally, to customize system-user interaction.

1 Introduction

The aim of Preventive Quality Management (PQM) is to detect possible mistakes of products *before* these mistakes actually become effective. PQM is a very information-intensive task: Predicting and evaluating possible mistakes or defects (failure modes) of a (still unrealized) product requires access to various information sources such as customer requirements, material specifications, production line characteristics and complaints made about similar products. Matters are further complicated by the sheer amount of data that has to be processed. Yet, only a subset is actually required to answer an information need at a particular stage of a PQM task (such as failure analysis) and for a particular product.

In this paper, we claim that the notion of *context* is essential when aiming at an efficient and effective information system to support the PQM task. The context of an information need is defined by the current stage in the overall PQM task, the product (part) whose failures are analysed, and the role of a user in the PQM process. These contextual constraints guide the information seeking process in several ways: First, the number of information sources accessed can be restricted, second, data selection from these sources can be more goal-directed, and finally, contextual constraints can be exploited in customizing system-user interaction (query formulation and result presentation).

2 Information needs in Preventive Quality Management

Preventive quality management is an information-intensive task, drawing on a vast number of information sources. Information needs that occur during a PQM task are of different kinds, partly interacting with the nature of the information source they address. To illustrate this point, imagine the following situation: A production engineer collects potentially relevant information for the tasks she is involved in, in our case, building a failure structure as part of a specific PQM method, namely failure modes and effects analysis (FMEA), for a newly designed gearbox.

Retrieval queries: Queries where the information seeker (here, the engineer) actively searches the information sources for a specified information need.
Sample query: *Search for all failures that are potential causes of the failure "Gearbox broken".*

What-if queries: Queries where the information seeker actively searches the information sources to support reasoning in a given problem scenario.
Sample query: *Assuming that the gearbox is made from alloy instead of stainless steel, what are the potential failure modes?*

Filter queries: Queries to sort out all irrelevant pieces of information for a given context from a continuous data stream.
Sample query: *Filter all incoming complaints for failures of similar gearbox designs.*

3 Exploiting context in information search

In PQM, the *context* of an information query is defined by the properties of the situation in which an information need is expressed, that is (1) stage in a PQM task, (2) product (part) under consideration, and (3) user profile. Each contextual parameter contributes in a distinct way to processing an information request. In the following, we discuss each contextual parameter in turn with respect to FMEA (see Fig. 1).

FMEA task: FMEA tasks are represented as task-method hierarchies. A task describes the problem type to be solved and a method is a way of accomplishing a task. A fragment is depicted on the right hand side of Fig. 1 (rectangles denote methods and ovals denote tasks). Re-occurring tasks in an FMEA are, among others, failure analysis and function analysis. In failure analysis, potential causes and effects of a given failure mode are searched for. FMEA documents and complaints regarding similar products are a prime information source. In function analysis, the focus is on the realisation of the technical functions of a product. Here, customer requirements indicating important functions are a valuable information source. In short, we observe an interdependency between relevant types of information sources and the task under consideration. The task also influences query interpretation. For instance, in failure analysis type = "cause" is added automatically to the query (see Fig. 1).

Product: Effects on query processing are of three kinds: First, the search space is reduced since a particular product restricts the number of information sources to be accessed. For instance, only those information sources that contain information on gearboxes and similar objects are taken into consideration when searching for potential causes of a broken gearbox casing. Here, the selection is not by type but by content: All information sources that provide particular information are selected, regardless of how this information is represented. Second, interpretation of query terms is constrained by the product under consideration: When expanding a query, the broker selects those terms from the controlled vocabulary that are more general than the product name (or that are more specific in order to make a query more concise). Finally, the product has an impact on query formulation in that the product name is automatically part of the query.

User profile: Currently, we employ the user profile mainly for query term interpretation. That is, in a given stage of an FMEA task, identical query terms are interpreted differently depending on a user's role.

So far, we have only considered retrieval queries. Contextual constraints also apply to filter queries.

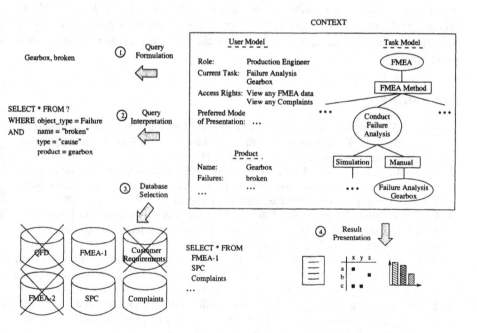

Fig. 1. Impact of context on processing an information request in FMEA

In a nutshell, contextual parameters have an impact on several steps of query processing (see Fig. 1 for illustration). They influence *query formulation* and *result presentation*, and constrain *query interpretation* and *information source selection* (in our case the selection of databases).

4 Discussion

In this paper, we proposed an approach to facilitate information search for preventive quality management.

At present, most information systems for PQM use simple access modes (e.g. [7]), which cannot adequately support the information needs of a user. Our approach is similar to work on the user adaptable graphical user interface [6] of WibQuS [4], an information system for quality management. Here, contexts are defined for roles, topics, methods, processes, customers, and the management; the contexts are implemented as views. However, our work differs in that we employ only one context for each information access that is dynamically constructed from the task at hand, a user's role and the product. The notion of context has been employed in other research on information mediation (e.g., [1], [2], [5], [8]). The main distinguishing feature of our work is that we include an explicit representation of the task at hand and the user profile into the context, thus enabling a more goal-directed search.

In PQM, there exists a huge amount of heterogeneous information in distributed sources that has to be searched, and heterogeneous user groups that require information. We believe that an *integrated filter and broker architecture* as proposed in [3] is a suitable framework for information search in PQM, especially with respect to realizing the contextual constraints mentioned above. An implemention of our approach based on the filter and broker architecture is under way.

References

1. Fensel, D., Decker, S., Erdmann, M., Studer, R.: Ontobroker: Or how to enable access to the WWW. In: Proc. of the Eleventh Workshop on Knowledge Acquisition, Modeling and Management. Banff, Canada (1998)
2. Fikes, R., Farquhar, A., Pratt, W.: Information Brokers: Gathering information from heterogeneous information sources. In: Stewman, J.H. (ed): Proc. of the Ninth Florida Artificial Intelligence Research Symposium. Key West, FL (1996)
3. Grote, B., Rose, T., Peter, G.: Filter and broker: Consumer-producer interactions in the information age. Technical Report. Research Institute for Applied Knowledge Processing (FAW) at the University of Ulm (1999)
4. Jarke, M., Jeusfeld, M.A., Szczurko, P.: Three aspects of intelligent cooperation in the quality cycle. In Proc. of the First International Conference on Intelligent and Cooperative Information Systems. Rotterdam, The Netherlands (1993)
5. Kashyap, V., Sheth, A.: Semantics-based information brokering: A step towards realizing the infocosm. Technical Report DCS-TR-307, Department of Computer Science, Rutgers University. New Brunswick, NJ (1994)
6. Peters, P.: Planning and Analysis of Information Flows in Quality Management. PhD thesis, RWTH Aachen (1996)
7. Pfeifer, T., Reinecke, R., Grebner, H.: FMEA-Wissen transparent machen. Qualität und Zuverlässigkeit **43** (1998) 10 1210–1213
8. Wiederhold, G., Genesereth, M.: The conceptual basis for mediation services. IEEE Expert **12** (1997) 5

The Context-Dependency of Temporal Reference in Event Semantics

Fabio Pianesi[1] and Achille C. Varzi[2]

[1] ITC- Istituto per la Ricerca Scientifica e Tecnologica, 38050 Povo (TN), Italy
pianesi@itc.it
[2] Department of Philosophy, Columbia University, New York, NY 10027, USA
achille.varzi@columbia.edu

Abstract. Temporal reference in natural language is inherently context dependent: what counts as a moment in one context may be structurally analysed in another context, and *vice versa*. In this note we outline a way of accounting for this phenomenon within event-based semantics.

1 Introduction

It is an important characteristic of natural language that temporal relations among events can be refined at will. What counts as a moment at one level of analysis may count as extended at a deeper level:

(1)   John and Mary met last week. More exactly, it was Tuesday. They met at breakfast. John was just having his first sip of coffee . . .

Even if there is a point beyond which refinement is no longer practically feasible, it seems that this is not enough to posit temporal discreteness as linguistically relevant: the underlying model of time is dense. On the other hand, natural language also permits us to discretize time at will:

(2)   That's how they met: *At a certain point*, John asked the waiter to invite her at his table; *the next moment* she was sitting in front of him.

These seemingly opposite phenomena are a fundamental manifestation of the inherent context-dependency of time granularity in natural language: what counts as a moment in one context may be structurally analysed in another context, and vice versa. This is often cited as a source of difficulties for event-based semantics, where models are constructed on the basis of a definite set of events with a fixed structure. In this note we outline a way of refining such models so as to deal with these difficulties.

2 Event Structures

Event-based semantics originated with Davidson [3] and received algebraic formulations in Kamp [5] and Bach [1]. Such semantics are typically based on structures in which a domain of events is associated with explicit temporal relations. In [6] we have shown that such relations can ultimately be construed from some basic ontological properties that a domain of events must arguably satisfy—specifically, mereological and topological properties. The construction is refined in [7], and in [8] it is shown to be especially liable to the sort of refinement that is requiired to account for the context-dependence exhibited by natural language. Here is a brief review of this construction.

The underlying mereotopological machinery is developed within a first-order language with identity and descriptions. The mereological and topological primitives are the parthood predicate (symbolized by 'P') and the closure operator (symbolized by 'c'). As axioms for these primitives we assume those of classical extensional mereology supplemented with the mereologized analogues of the standard topological axioms for closure systems. (See [2] for a full account of the theory defined by these axioms.) Additional derived notions can then be introduced by definition:

$$(3) \quad O(x, y) =_{df} \exists z\, (P(z, x) \wedge P(z, y)) \qquad\qquad x \text{ overlaps } y$$

$$(4) \quad X(x, y) =_{df} O(x, y) \wedge \neg P(x, y) \qquad\qquad x \text{ crosses } y$$

$$(5) \quad C(x, y) =_{df} O(c(x), y) \vee O(c(y), x) \qquad\qquad x \text{ is connected to } y$$

$$(6) \quad \sigma x \phi x =_{df} \iota x \forall y\, (O(y, x) \leftrightarrow \exists z\, (\phi z \wedge O(z, y))) \qquad\qquad \text{sum of all } \phi\text{-ers}$$

$$(7) \quad \pi x \phi x =_{df} \sigma x\, \forall z\, (\phi z \rightarrow P(x, z)) \qquad\qquad \text{product of all } \phi\text{-ers}$$

$$(8) \quad x+y =_{df} \sigma z\, (P(z, x) \vee P(z, y)) \qquad\qquad \text{join of } x \text{ and } y$$

$$(9) \quad x \times y =_{df} \sigma z\, (P(z, x) \wedge P(z, y)) \qquad\qquad \text{meet of } x \text{ and } y$$

$$(10) \quad {\sim}x =_{df} \sigma z\, (\neg O(z, x)) \qquad\qquad \text{complement of } x$$

In addition to the these basic mereotopological notions, the following notions are introduced in [7] with an eye to their use in characterizing event domains:

$$(11) \quad D(x) =_{df} \exists y \exists z\, (y+z = {\sim}x \wedge \neg C(y, z)) \qquad\qquad x \text{ is a divisor}$$

$$(12) \quad d(x) =_{df} \pi z(D(z) \wedge P(x, z)) \qquad\qquad \text{divisor of } x$$

$$(13) \quad S(x,y,z) =_{df} y+z = {\sim}d(x) \qquad\qquad x \text{ separates } y \text{ and } z$$

Intuitively, divisors are distinguished events splitting their complement (the rest of history) into two disconnected parts. The idea is that a divisor comprises all that happens during certain period of time, so that events on one side of it count as past events and those on the other side as future events. On this basis, the construction proceeds as follows.

DEFINITION 1. *An event structure is an ordered pair* $\langle E, \delta \rangle$, *where E is a non empty domain and* δ *a subset of E satisfying the following conditions for all* $x, y \in E$:

$$(14) \quad \forall z \in E(O(z, x) \vee O(z, y)) \rightarrow C(x, y)$$

$$(15) \quad x \in \delta \rightarrow D(x)$$

$$(16) \quad x \in \delta \wedge y \in \delta \rightarrow (x+y \in \delta \leftrightarrow C(x,y))$$

$$(17) \quad x \in \delta \wedge y \in \delta \rightarrow (x \times y \in \delta \leftrightarrow O(x,y))$$

$$(18) \quad x \in \delta \wedge y \in \delta \rightarrow (x-y \in \delta \leftrightarrow X(x,y)).$$

Intuitively, (14) says that E is topologically self-connected and (15)–(18) that δ is an exhaustive set of "coherent" divisors in E (i.e., divisors which cut history into a series of "parallel", mutually disjoint slices).

DEFINITION 2. *An oriented event structure is a triple* $\langle E, \delta, a \rangle$, *where* $\langle E, \delta \rangle$ *is an event structure and a is a distinguished element of E such that*

(19) $\exists x \exists y (S(x,a,y))$.

Intuitively, a is an "anchor" element relative to which every other event can be positioned on the assumption that a covers one of the two sides (intuitively, either the past or the future) of some event x. The positioning is obtained *via* the following:

(20) $f(x) =_{df} \iota z \exists y (S(z,x,y) \wedge (O(x,a) \rightarrow P(z,a)) \wedge (\neg O(x,a) \rightarrow P(a,z)))$
(21) $f'(x) =_{df} \sigma z (P(x, f(z)))$.

(This effectively amounts to defining f and f' as a pair of Galois connections.) We then just stipulate that a represents the past. That is, we treat f as a function of temporal orientation associating each event with the totality of events that precede it; correspondingly, we treat f' as a function associating each event with the events that follow it. This allows us to introduce a relation of temporal precedence by definition:

(22) $TP(x, y) =_{df} P(x, f(y))$

DEFINITION 3. *A refinement event structure is a triple* $\langle E, \{\delta_i : i \in I\}, a \rangle$ *such that (i) for each* $i \in I$, $\langle E, \delta_i, a \rangle$ *is an oriented event structure, and (ii) the family* $\{\delta_i : i \in I\}$ *is closed under meet, i.e., for all* $x, y \in E$ *and all* $i, j \in I$ *there exists some* $k \in I$ *such that*

(23) $x \in \delta_i \wedge y \in \delta_j \rightarrow x \times y \in \delta_k$.

Thus, refinement structures involve not just one divisors class δ, but an entire family of such classes. And condition (23) guarantees coherence among these classes, so that it is only the granularity that may change from one class to another. Indeed, the δ's can be partially ordered in a natural way: a divisors class is a refinement of another iff the former draws at least the same temporal distinctions as the latter (if not more):

(24) $\delta_i \succcurlyeq \delta_j =_{df} \forall x (x \in \delta_i \rightarrow \exists y (y \in \delta_j \wedge P(y,x)))$.

3. Temporal Reference and Context Dependence

Refinement structures allow us account for the effect of context on the granularity of temporal reference. With regard to the phenomenon exemplified in (1), the intuition that time is dense can be accommodated by adding the mereotopological counterpart of the usual axiom for dense linear orders on closed (or, equivalently, open) intervals:

(25) $TP(c(x),c(y)) \rightarrow \exists z (TP(c(x), c(z)) \wedge TP(c(z), c(y)))$.

More generally, in the context of a refinement structure $\langle E, \{\delta_i : i \in I\}, a \rangle$, this corresponds to assuming the following to hold for relevant $i \in I$:

(26) $P(c(x), f_i(c(y))) \rightarrow \exists z (P(c(x), f_i(c(z))) \wedge P(c(z), f_i(c(y))))$.

However this does not fully capture the idea behind (1). The interesting question is what kind of divisors are presupposed by the underlying unlimited refining process. Clearly they must be infinite in number (which in turn presupposes that the domain E

must have infinite cardinality). But, more importantly, they cannot include a minimal element (with respect to the ordering $\succcurlyeq$). This amounts to the following requirement:

(27) For every $i \in I$ there exists $j \in I$ such that $\delta_i \succcurlyeq \delta_j$ but not $\delta_j \succcurlyeq \delta_i$.

This entails that divisors must themselves be infinitely divisible, i.e., there can be no absolute punctual events.

Consider now to the phenomenon exemplified in (2): we can discretize time at will. Intuitively, punctual events are instantaneous, i.e., do not extend over any time *interval*: they are *located in* time but do not *take up* time. Within the present setting, this does not amount to a requirement of mereological atomicity: what counts as instantaneous, as opposed to extended in time, depends entirely on the relevant δ_i. For divisors not only provide the basis for temporal orientation but, in a sense, also for temporal measurement [4]. To see this, define the notion of a *minimal divisor* relative to a divisors class δ_i:

(28) $M_i(x) =_{df} x \in \delta_i \wedge \forall y (P(y, x) \rightarrow \neg y \in \delta_i)$.

In [8] we have shown that the fundamental properties characterizing punctual events according to Kamp [6] hold of minimal—and only minimal—divisors. Accordingly, we can define a punctual events, relative to the granularity set by δ_i, to be exactly those events whose divisors are minimal relative to δ_i:

(29) $PE_i(x) =_{df} M_i(d(x))$.

Thus, punctual events are not merely—and not necessarily—atomic events, i.e., events with no proper parts (although of course every atomic event is punctual, regardless of δ_i). Rather, they are events whose internal structure is irrelevant for the purpose of temporal distinctions. By changing δ_i, events previously treated as punctual may become non-punctual, in that their internal temporal structure is made available, and vice versa. This notion of "change" is purely metalinguistic if we focus on plain structures. But refinement structures can accommodate this variability directly.

References

1. Bach, E., 1986, 'The Algebra of Events', *Linguistics and Philosophy* 9: 5-16.
2. Casati, R., and Varzi, A. C., 1999, *Parts and Places: The Structures of Spatial Representation*, Cambridge, MA: MIT Press (Bradford Books).
3. Davidson, D., 1967, 'The Logical Form of Action Sentences', in N. Rescher (ed.), *The Logic of Decision and Action*, Pittsburgh: University of Pittsburgh Press, 81-95.
4. Giorgi, A., and F. Pianesi, 1997, *Tense and Aspect: From Semantics to Morphosyntax*, New York: Oxford University Press.
5. Kamp, H., 1979, 'Events, Instants, and Temporal Reference', in R. Bäuerle *et al.* (eds.), *Semantics from Different Points of View*, Berlin: Springer-Verlag, 376-417.
6. Pianesi, F. and A. C. Varzi, 1994, 'Mereo-Topological Construction of Time from Events', in A. Cohn (ed.), *Proceedings ECAI-94*, Chichester: Wiley & Sons, 396-400.
7. Pianesi, F. and A. C. Varzi, 1996a, 'Events, Topology, and Temporal Relations', *The Monist* 78: 89-116.
8. Pianesi, F. and A. C. Varzi, 1996b, 'Refining Temporal Reference in Event Structures', *Notre Dame Journal of Formal Logic* 37: 71-83.

How Context Contributes to Metaphor Understanding

Béatrice Pudelko, Elizabeth Hamilton, Denis Legros, & Charles Tijus

Laboratoire CNRS ESA 7021 Cognition & Activités Mentales Finalisées
Université de Paris 8 - 2, rue de la Liberté - 93526 Saint Denis Cédex 02 France

e-mail : bpudelko@univ-paris8.fr - dl@univ-paris8.fr - tijus@univ-paris8.fr

Abstract. The objective of this study is to show how the contextual knowledge about the topic allows choosing one out of the many interpretations possible for attributive metaphors of the form [A (the topic) is B (the vehicle)]. We propose an experiment that shows (i) that the properties of the vehicle that are actually attributed to the topic are the ones that are specified by the context in which the topic appears; and (ii) that conventional interpretations of a metaphor do not predominate unless this context is neutral, i.e. when the attributes of the topic furnished by the context do not belong to the vehicle's category. We interpret these results on the importance of the context in understanding metaphor both in terms of property matching [1, 4, 7] and in terms of categorization [2, 8]. In our approach, understanding a metaphor consists of including the topic in a category specified by the vehicle such that the topic inherits certain of the traits of this category, within a situational object category network.

1 Introduction

A spectator at a one of Shakespeare's plays hears Romeo say "Juliet is the sun", and has no difficulty in understanding that he doesn't really mean that Juliet is a ball of imploding helium molecules. The play-goer understands that for Romeo, the day begins with Juliet. Nonetheless, outside of the context of this particular play, or of lyric poetry in general, the spectator might not interpret this metaphor in the same way. He might think that for Romeo, Juliet is an important person [5]. This example clearly shows that the ambiguity which characterises all metaphors not only concerns the choice between literal and figurative meanings but also between possible figurative interpretations.

The objective of this article is to explain how the choice between different figurative meanings is carried out. To this end, we place the accent on the role of context in everyday situations of metaphor comprehension. We consider that in ecological situations of communication, the context comprises not only knowledge about the world but also new information provided by the situation in which the topic of the metaphor appears. Metaphor disambiguation is based on information furnished by the context which constrains the choice of meanings for the metaphor, and this, even in the case of conventional metaphors.

Most of the cognitive models of metaphor understanding have adopted the approach according to which metaphor is an implicit comparison [1, 4, 7]. From this point of view, understanding a metaphor "X (topic) is Y (vehicle)". consists in converting it into a simile "X (the topic) is like Y (the vehicle)". The mechanism posited by the comparison models is a mechanism of property matching. This is why these models are confronted with the problem of measuring the similarity of properties as well as with the problem of calculating the distance between properties which makes a simile literal or metaphoric. More recently, an alternative categorization approach has been proposed by Glucksberg & al. [2] and Way [8]. According to Glucksberg's class inclusion model, a metaphoric statement of the type "X is Y" is solved by looking for the category, represented by the term Y, which furnishes properties that are potentially relevant for the topic X. The disadvantage of this model is that there is no mechanism for explaining how the relevant properties are selected. From our point of view, this aspect must be adressed if we are to explain how metaphors are disambiguated, i.e. to explain why one property is chosen and not others.

Our general hypothesis is that metaphor understanding consists of including the topic in the category of the vehicle and attributing to it the properties of that category that are compatible with what we already know about the topic. Legros, Tijus & Pudelko [3] have shown that when the context provides specific information about the topic, the selection of vehicle features is compatible with this information. We are assuming that interpretation is constructed on-line and that knowledge about the topic intervenes at an early stage in processing by constraining the selection of features.

2 Experiment

The experiment we report here aims at studying the way in which different contexts providing information about the topic activate features of the vehicle. We opted for presenting 14 metaphors in mini-scenarios in order to make the laboratory situation more like usual conversational situations in which animal metaphors are used. The scenarios were of three types: designed (i) to be compatible with conventional interpretations ("Guy is always joking, he's a monkey"), (ii) to be compatible with one of the actual features of the animal ("Guy likes to climb, he's a monkey") or (iii) to be neutral, i.e. not particularly compatible with conventional or with novel interpretations ("Guy goes to concerts, he's a monkey"). 26 participants were first presented with the context sentence, then with the metaphor, and finally with an interpretation sentence. We tested property transfer by alternately presenting three different interpretation sentences of a given metaphor ("Does this mean that Guy is... funny? agile? likes music?). Participants had to say whether or not they agreed. We predicted that (i) when the interpretation sentence is not compatible with the context, the agreement score would be low; (ii) when the interpretation sentence is both compatible with the context and with a real or conventional property of the animal in question, the agreement score would be high; and, (iii) when the context is neutral, the rates of agreement would be higher in this case for the conventional interpretation which predominates.

3 Results

Table 1. Percentages of "Yes" responses and Reaction Times of "Yes" responses. The 3x3 experimental conditions where, for each metaphor 3 context phrases describing a person in terms of (i) an actual animal trait (e.g. "likes to climb"), (ii) a conventional animal trait ("likes to joke") or (iii) an unassociated trait (e.g. "often goes to concerts") were crossed with 3 target phrases in which a trait is attributed to a person (i) an actual animal trait (e.g. "agile"), (ii) a conventional animal trait (e.g. "funny"), or (iii) a trait not associated with an animal (e.g. "likes music"). Each cell represents 364 data; 26 participants responded to the 9 conditions for each metaphor.

	Target-sentences		
	actual animal "Guy is agile"	**unassociated** "Guy likes music"	**conventional** "Guy is funny"
Context sentences			
actual animal			
"Guy likes to climb"	86% (2.18 s)	5% (3.21 s)	41% (2.65 s)
unassociated			
"Guy goes to concerts"	28% (4.28 s)	35% (3.53 s)	41% (3.36 s)
conventional			
"Guy likes to joke"	36% (3.04 s)	6% (2.46 s)	91% (2.10 s)

4 Discussion and conclusion

Our results show that the context in which the topic appears constrains the selection of the relevant trait to be transferred from the vehicle. Indeed, context can determine the selection of either conventional or novel traits. No effect was observed for kind of trait as long as both context sentences and interpretive sentences were compatible, in either case the metaphor was disambiguated quickly. Neither was kind of trait effect observed when the context sentence was incompatible with the target sentence. Kind of trait only had an effect when the context was incompatible with the metaphor. However, when the context was neutral, agreement rates dropped and reaction times rose significantly when the interpretive sentence was novel instead of conventional. This supports our hypothesis that in the absence of contextual information, conventional metaphors are interpreted conventionally. But when context is supplied, it can overide preference for the transfer of conventional traits and lead to novel interpretations compatible with context.

514

Glucksberg, McGlone & Manfredi (1997) have observed that metaphor comprehension is facilitated when topic's context is irrelevant. They explain this effect by supposing that the topic possesses a single "level of abstraction" : the "concrete" or "literal" level. Our results show that for conventional metaphor, this facilitation only concerns conventional interpretations.

How can the effect of initial knowledge about the topic in the construction of meaning for metaphor be explained, and in particular, how are elements of this knowledge selected? The CADS-T model, a version of the Dynamic Allocation of Meaning Model [6]proposes that the mental representation of situations described using language is composed of the semantic networks for the objects in the situation. Category networks are formed by factorising the properties activated by the context as well as through a property adjustment process. CADS-T enables attributing a meaning to the topic through selecting a vehicle property as a function of the constraints provided by the topic's context. As we see it, the comparison and the categorization approaches are not antagonistic but complementary: understanding a metaphor consists both in (i) including the topic in the vehicle category and (ii) in selecting the properties that are compatible with the context.

References

1. Gentner, D., & Wolff, P. (1997). Alignement in the processing of metaphor. *Journal of Memory and Language. 37,* 331-355.
2. Glucksberg, S., McGlone M.S., & Manfredi, D. (1997). Property attribution in metaphor comprehension. *Journal of Memory and Language, 36,* 50-67.
3. Legros, D., Tijus, C., & Pudelko, B. (1998). The effect of knowledge about topic on metaphorical meaning. In *Proceedings of the 20th Annual Conference of the Cognitive Science Society.* p.1238. Mahwah, NJ: Lawrence Erlbaum Associates.
4. Ortony, A. (1979). Beyond literal similarity. *Psychological Rewiev, 86 (3),* 161-179.
5. Searle, J. (1970). Expression and Meaning. London, Cambridge University Press.
6. Tijus, C., & Moulin, F. (1997). L'assignation de signification étudiée à partir de textes d'histoires drôles. *L'Année Psychologique, 97,* 33-75.
7. Tourangeau, R., & Rips, L., (1991). Interpreting and evaluating metaphors. *Journal of Memory and Language , 30,* 452-472.
8. Way, E.C. (1991). Knowledge representation and metaphor. Dordrecht: Kluver Academic Publishers.

Exploiting Context in Gesture Recognition

Jamie Sherrah and Shaogang Gong

Queen Mary & Westfield College, Department of Computer Science
London E1 4NS UK
{jamie|sgg}@dcs.qmw.ac.uk

Abstract. Recognition of human behaviour is receiving increasing attention in computer vision, and has many useful applications. In this work we investigate how head pose can be exploited to impose contextual constraints for the recognition of gestures. The method is demonstrated in a video conferencing scenario involving three people who use gestures to control the camera and focus of attention.

1 Introduction

Computational modelling of human behaviour is becoming an important area of computer vision. One application is *visually mediated interaction* (VMI), in which the computer acts as an intelligent mediator between two remotely-communicating parties. This requires machine understanding of the visual scene to control an active camera. To perform VMI, *recognition* and *interpretation* of human gestures are required. It has been observed during collection of our gesture database that certain variations in head pose are closely coupled with some gestures. When pointing to the right, for example, subjects often turned their heads and looked to the right. This is an example of how context (*ie:* the subject's gaze) can be used to interpret behaviour. In this work we examine how recognition of gestures can be assisted by the contextual use of head pose.

2 Gesture Recognition and Head Pose

Let us begin with a method for modelling and subsequently recognising gestures. Our models are based on a training database of gestures, recorded with a video camera. The database consists of six gestures: 1) point left 2) point right 3) high wave 4) low wave 5) come here (beckoning) 6) go away (dismissive). Fifteen people performed each gesture four times, resulting in a database of 360 gesture sequences. Each sequence contains about 60 frames. Example frames from some of the gestures are shown in Figure 1.

We adopt a spatio-temporal trajectory approach to gesture recognition, an earlier version of which has been reported in [1]. We model a gesture as a temporal trajectory of motion-based features. To arrive at a feature trajectory from a video sequence, each frame is temporally filtered and thresholded to arrive at a binary motion image. The following six features are then extracted from

Fig. 1. Examples of the gestures collected in the database.

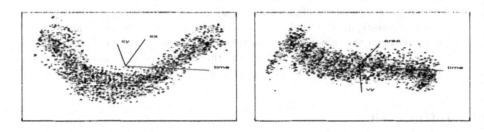

(a) x-y centroid versus time for the point right gesture.

(b) y-velocity and motion area versus time for the go away gesture.

Fig. 2. Examples of feature trajectories for the database of 360 gestures. Only a subset of the features are shown.

each motion frame: area, centroid (x, y), elongation, centroid velocity (v_x, v_y). The features from frame i are collected into a feature vector $\mathbf{z}_{t_i} = [f_1, \ldots, f_d]^{\mathrm{T}}$, where t_i is the time at which frame i was captured, and d is the number of features. The resulting feature vectors are temporally ordered and concatenated to result in a trajectory of features $\mathbf{z} = \{\mathbf{z}_{t_1}, \ldots, \mathbf{z}_{t_n}\}$, where n is the number of frames in the sequence, and $t_n - t_1$ is the duration of the sequence.

The trajectories form structures in spatio-temporal feature space that can be modelled and discriminated. Some examples are shown in Figure 2. In order to perform recognition, gesture models are generated from a database of training sequences, and a Maximum Likelihood technique is used to classify novel gestures. The matching algorithm linearly scales the novel trajectory over time and matches backwards in time to the model using a Gaussian matching function.

To exploit head pose information, the head turning directions were manually extracted from each sequence in the database, and the qualitative associations between gesture and pose were made. As expected, looking left was associated with pointing left, looking right with pointing right, and for the other four gestures people tended to bow their heads slightly. Hence we expect pose to help avoid ambiguities between pointing and the other gestures. Under the Maximum Likelihood framework, each likelihood function is multiplied with a prior which is based on the head pose, $p(\mathbf{m}_i|h)$, where h represents head pose during the gesture. Assuming the models are equally likely in the absence of pose information, we now choose the model that maximises $p(\mathbf{z}|\mathbf{m}_i)p(h|\mathbf{m}_i)$. The priors $p(h|\mathbf{m}_j)$ can be estimated from training examples as co-occurrence frequencies.

3 Interpreting Behaviour of Multiple People

A poignant scenario for VMI is the example of a video conference using an intelligent camera system, as shown in Figure 3. Three people are video-conferencing with their friend overseas. The subjects are labelled A, B and C from left to right. The subject on the far right, C, starts the conversation by waving to attract the camera's attention. C speaks to the camera, then points to the subject on the far left, A, to pass the focus of attention. A also waves to obtain the camera's attention, then speaks. A then points to the middle man, B, who also waves to obtain attention, and speaks. Gesture events are detected separately using the feature and pose trajectories of each subject.

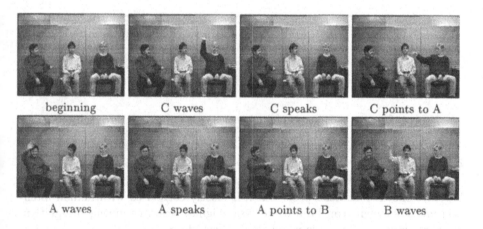

| beginning | C waves | C speaks | C points to A |
| A waves | A speaks | A points to B | B waves |

Fig. 3. A multi-person scenario.

The gesture recognition results without the use of pose are shown in Figure 4(a). Each plot shows the gesture log likelihoods plotted versus time for one of the three subjects. In the first plot, the high wave has the largest likelihood in the first flurry of activity, and then point right has the maximum value. Note that there is considerable confusion between the gestures, and the winner is only best by a small margin. In the second plot, the high wave and then point left are detected. In the third, the single high wave is detected for the third subject.

Figure 4(b) shows the results when head pose is used as a prior for the plotted log likelihoods. When it comes to the pointing gestures, there is considerably less confusion with the other gestures. Note that the plot for subject B has not really changed, since he did not turn his head during gestures.

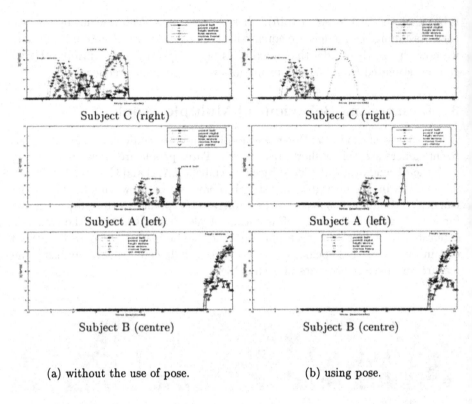

Subject C (right)   Subject C (right)

Subject A (left)   Subject A (left)

Subject B (centre)   Subject B (centre)

(a) without the use of pose.   (b) using pose.

Fig. 4. Gesture Likelihoods plotted versus time for each of three subjects.

4 Conclusion

We have shown that head pose, which is closely correlated with human intention and behaviour, can be used to disambiguate gestures during recognition. Scenarios involving multiple people and a host of gestures and events are much more complex than a setting with a single person in isolation, and provide opportunities for exploiting context. In future research we will use the full temporal dynamics of pose. This information may be useful for determining the urgency of a gesture, and for detecting head gestures such as "yes" and "no".

References

[1] S. McKenna and S. Gong. Gesture recognition for visually mediated interaction using probabilistic event trajectories. In *British Machine Vision Conference*, Southampton, England, September 1998.

The Use of Context in the Analysis of Negative Concord and N-words

L.M. Tovena

ITC - Trento I

Abstract We examine proposals on Negative Concord in Romance, focussing on the use of context in building an explanation, what information is assigned to it, and what is kept in the characterisation of items.

Contexts. The notion of context in linguistics is not too different from that of other fields that make use of formal representations. For instance, a negative context is interpreted as a portion of representation containing an operator characterised as negative and its domain of action. The definition of this type of context—here called type C_1—has two facets, one is the identification of the properties of the operator and the other consists of locality constraints, i.e. a portion of representation is selected as relevant for checking the effect or cashing in the action. There is also a notion of context used for instance to define the environment of a word belonging to a collocation. This is context of type C_2. Particularly in syntactic approaches, generalisations are made on configurations. For instance, government and move α in derivational approaches of GB-style can be perceived as ways to define classes of contexts suitable for given applications. A similar task is carried out by schemata and structure sharing in constraint-based approaches of HPSG-style. From this point of view, context is a configurational constraint enforced on a portion of representation. This is context of type C_3. In some sense, tools of this type give access to 'patterns'. The perception is that reusing the same set of tools in describing different phenomena is a sign that the context is kept stable. The differences are meant to be expressed mainly in the characterisation of single operators with respect to their classes.

Basics on Negative Concord (NC). In (1) *Nobody came*, the occurrence of the negative quantifier *nobody* in subject position has as a consequence that the sentence is interpreted as negated. Its first order logic (FOL) representation would be something like $\neg \exists x Come(x)$, ignoring tense issues. When there are two negative quantifiers in the same sentence, the two expressions of negation seem to cancel each other out, as in FOL. For instance, (2) *Nobody said nothing* contains two negative quantifiers and says that the group of persons who said a null number of things is empty, i.e. everybody said something, a reading called LOGICAL DOUBLE NEGATION. Starting from a FOL formula like $\forall x \neg \forall y \neg Say(x, y)$, one gets $\forall x \exists y Say(x, y)$. Broadly speaking, when the expression of negation works as it does in standard English, it seems possible to rest the analysis on the definition of the properties of certain elements, properties that show up when these elements are considered in isolation and in context. This is because the result of the application of the negative operator seems to be only function of the term to which it applies. A unique function is assigned to an element like *nobody*, and through this function the class of elements called NEGATIVE QUANTIFIERS can be identified. The situation is different in Romance, where the mechanism may be less straightforward to describe. The term NEGATIVE CONCORD is currently used to identify the phenomenon exemplified in (3) *Nessuno ha detto niente* (nobody said anything) from Italian, and N-WORDS are its primary components. Sentence (3) contains *nessuno* and *niente*, that preanalytic intuitions make good candidates for being manifestations of negation. This sentence has only the interpretation whereby there was no saying at all. It can point out that the set of individuals qualifying as speakers is empty. It can also be interpreted as pointing out that the set of things said is empty. In particular, (3) says that the absence of saying event is due to the non instantiation of agent and patient.

Discussion. Fig.1 depicts ways of looking at (3). There are mainly two strands of analysis for NC. First, the contribution of N-words is taken in the flat way cut out by box **A**, which is more in line with FOL and seems appropriate for English. Scholars working in this trend—the majority—follow Labov in striving to eliminate all but one negation in the representation. They disagree on where it is expressed and how many 'manifestations' there are. Basic common steps are the introduction of i) the notion of restricted distribution of the items, ii) a possible lexical split (ambiguity), and iii) licensing, i.e. context modeling. Second, the contribution of N-words is considered with respect to a higher relation that describes the type of eventuality negated in the sentence, as cut out by box **B**. NC is an eventuality level phenomenon. The different manifestations of negation are interpreted as independent and concern the eventuality and the entities that take part in it. N-words block verification via instantiation of the marked arguments in the corresponding predicate.

As for N-words, there is the double issue of identifying the items cross linguistically and characterising them. So far, there isn't an intensional definition. Neither the notion of 'morphologically negative constituent' nor the 'syntactic behaviour' work as consistent membership criterion. Their characterisation also varies. One option is to treat them as negative quantifiers as in English. Invoking the status of NPI is a way of stripping their syntactico-semantic definition of any negative component and to transfer it to the context. In this way, their distribution is constrained more tightly than with indefinites in general. How-

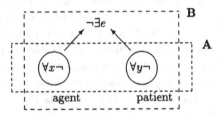

Figure1. Interpreting sentence (3)

ever, this characterisation must be qualified because N-words in Romance require a more restricted notion of negative context than NPIs. Invoking the status of Kamp/Heim indefinite is a way to strip N-words of negative and quantificational force. As a consequence, they can enter unbounded dependencies and do not exhibit scope relations. Yet, they are a special case because the existential closure must be done via a negated existential operator. Note also that when an item seems to have several interpretations, one might say that the same 'designator' is used to refer to different functions, possibly occurring in different contexts. It is not clear whether there is a unique application of type 'N-word', but it is clear is that the phenomenon requires N-words to be looked at in a larger setting.

As for specific proposals on NC, let us start by two analyses that posit a lexical ambiguity for N-words. First, [4] says that the manifestations of N-words in Italian are either instances of negative quantifiers, or existential quantifiers "with peculiar polarity requirements". The two types are assigned different contexts. Here, as in all GB-style analyses, in the description of context one must include the configuration resulting from the movement of elements, in particular the relations the N-word entertains in the position it occupies in the new representation and the relations its trace entertains in the original position. The fact of being in a given configuration that via movement can change into another in which a certain relation holds is a way of legitimising the original structure and a certain interpretation which cannot be paired with it directly. In short, this study proposes a double definition of N-words and uses contexts of type C_1 when talking of quantifiers, C_2 when introducing a rule of negation incorporation, and C_3 when imposing governing constraints on N-words. Possibly, it relies also on extra information about characteristics of the language under examination. Second, in [3] most of the constraints ruling NC in French are stored inside lexical entries. N-words are classified either as negated existential quantifiers or as variables which must be bound with narrow scope and must be collocationally licensed by an affective operator. Technically, the solution consists of making locally available for lexical conditions a portion of the required surrounding structure by adding it under a special attribute inside the attribute-value matrix of words. This is how some N-words become collocations. It is further specified where the 'portion' must be found in the 'syntactic domain', i.e. the larger structure of the sentence. This study makes a massive use of lexical split, for N-words but also the particle ne and many verbs. It uses contexts of type C_2 with respect to the characterisation of N-words, and C_3 for imposing locality constraints.

Then, let us consider analyses that posit a unary nature for N-words. They can be discriminated according to the nature they assign to N-words and to the assumption they make on how many negatives there are in the final representation. First, [2] claims that N-words are special NPIs that have the option of occurring in spec/ΣP, a projection higher than IP that can be interpreted as some sort of syntactic locus for utterance information. It hosts truth-value operators. There, the N-word can get negative meaning via spec-head agreement with an abstract negative morpheme which heads ΣP. Thus, this proposal uses contexts of type C_1 when defining the behaviour of the head of ΣP, and C_3

for locality and structural constraints. It also uses C_2 in the sense that it takes N-words to be a special type of NPI. Second, [6] claims that N-words are negatives. The main components of this analysis are: i) the element *non* (not) heads a functional projection of negative type, ii) postverbal N-words take sentential scope by undergoing raising to spec/NegP-1 at Logical Form, iii) multiple N-words undergo resumptive quantification, so that they merge and create a single negation, and iv) non-negative context like questions involve a negative operator in Comp. The use of an operator expressed via a NegP projection helps in cutting out the relevant portion of representation and gives a space within which to check a relation. Context of type C_1 is used when defining the behaviour of the head of NegP, and C_3 for locality and structural constraints. Extra information on characteristics of the language under examination, e.g. the barrierhood of TP only for negative quantifiers is a use of C_2. Third, [1] hypothesizes that none of N-words nor *non* should be regarded as expressing negation. They are all NPIs, with the negative meaning expressed constructionally. He reshapes the idea of having the manifestations of negation to concord among them via the notion of negative chain. Then, the chain is roofed by an abstract operator in logical form that is triggered by syntactic rules and not by any one morpheme. This proposal uses C_1, C_2 and C_3. It also relies on language specific knowledge for tweaking the theory on cross linguistic data. Finally, [5] says that there can be more than one negative in the representation because NC should be interpreted at the level of the reconstruction of the eventuality described in a sentence. Main points are i) Italian marks all missing participants in an eventuality as negative, ii) if the presence of a participant is denied, it can be inferred that the eventuality is also denied. The reverse does not hold, and iii) a language can choose whether to mark as negative the missing participant(s), the predicate or both. The thematic role discharged by a phrase affects its NC marking potential. This proposal uses C_1 if we assign event descriptions to this type. C_1 are also the notions of thetic and categorical statements.

In short, many analyses add a mark in the representation whose function is to express the sentential reading of negation. Then, negativity and quantificational force are two components that get distributed in various ways among context and application. Taking context to be all the information needed in order to interpret a given operator in a certain way, i.e. for discriminating, then the definitions used in linguistics are relatively underspecified and the information is spread out.

References

1. Ladusaw W.: Expressing negation. Proceedings of SALT II (1992) 237–260
2. Laka Mugarza I.: Negation in Syntax. PhD thesis, MIT (1990)
3. Richter F., Sailer M.: A lexicalist collocation analysis of sentential negation and NC in French. In: V.Kordoni (ed.): Tübingen Studies in HPSG, CSLI (to appear)
4. Rizzi L.: Issues in Italian syntax. Foris (1982)
5. Tovena L.M.: The fine structure of polarity sensitivity. Garland (1998)
6. Zanuttini R.: Syntactic properties of sentential negation. PhD thesis, UPenn (1991)

Aspects of Context for Understanding Multi-modal Communication

Elise H. Turner, Roy M. Turner, John Phelps, Mark Neal, Charles Grunden
and Jason Mailman

Department of Computer Science, University of Maine, Orono, ME 04469

Abstract. Context is important for AI applications that interact with
users. This is true both for natural language interfaces as well as for
multi-modal interfaces. In this paper, we consider aspects of context that
are important in a multi-modal interface combining natural language and
graphical input to describe locations. We have identified several aspects
of contexts in our preliminary study. We describe them here and discuss
plans for future work.

1 Introduction

In this paper, we will discuss contextual aspects which we have identified for
understanding user input in speech and graphics. We consider context to be
anything that is required to understand an utterance beyond syntax and semantics. We call the components of context *contextual aspects* or simply *aspects*. A
distinct aspect was recognized for one of several reasons. First, all of the knowledge contained in the aspect might be connected by a theme. Second, different
aspects would be relevant to, or function differently when, handling different
phenomena. Third, some parts of the context were divided into separate aspects
because they are managed differently. Similarly, some aspects were separated
from others due to the duration of the information in the aspect (i.e., is the
information relevant during a single session or across many sessions?). Fourth,
some aspects have been separated out, for now, because they are well-studied
elsewhere. This is the case for the discourse aspect.

Our work is to be applied to Sketch-and-Talk, a multi-modal interface to geographical information systems that is being created by Max Egenhofer and his
colleagues in the Department of Spatial Information Science and Engineering at
the University of Maine. The system will construct database queries from spoken
natural language and graphical input from the user. Because the implementation
of the initial system has not yet been completed, we have begun our work by
studying ten videotaped examples of members of our research group describing
locations or spatial information. This preliminary work has led us to identify
several contextual aspects that affect the interpretation of multi-modal interaction. These aspects are presented below. More detail can be found elsewhere
[1, 2].

2 Contextual Aspects for Multi-Modal Interactions

Discourse Aspect. The discourse aspect is known in natural language processing as the *discourse context*. It contains all of the entities that are mentioned in the discourse. This context is broken into several subparts, or *discourse segments*. Discourse segments are made up of contiguous utterances that are related to the same topic. Many techniques already exist for creating the discourse context and moving between its segments (e.g., [3, 4, 5]), and any of these could be adopted for our system.

Graphics Aspect. The graphics aspect includes all of the entities that have been drawn and their spatial relations. For our work with Sketch-and-Talk, we will use the entity and relation representations used by that project [6].

We have found that, like discourse, the graphics context should be divided into *graphics spaces*. We have seen indications that users consider the graphics context to be subdivided. Users speak of "the area around *some entity*". They also deviate from their established order of drawing to draw certain related objects. For example, a user who has been drawing entities from left to right may deviate from this pattern to draw all of the outbuildings surrounding a house. Users also draw detailed views of particular regions of the location and move between the overview and detailed views during a session. Entities in a graphics space are often all related to a single entity or function. For example "where we fished" may constitute a graphics space. Also, users can easily refer to a graphics space with a single reference, for example, by pointing or referring to the most significant entity.

Clearly, the graphics spaces and discourse segments will be closely related because users are expected to talk as they draw. For now, we keep the discourse and graphics aspects separate to take advantage of the work that has been done to develop representations and management algorithms for the discourse aspect. In future work, we plan to explore the relationship between these two aspects. This includes determining if they are truly separate. Future work will also include discovering exactly what constitutes a graphics space and how a speaker/drawer moves between them.

Task Aspect. This aspect provides information related to the task that the user is pursuing. For our application, the representation of this aspect will include likely goals of the user as well as procedures for achieving those goals. In addition, we saw evidence of a *social interaction task aspect*, in which users put aside the task of describing a location to interact with or entertain the observers, and a *drawing correction task aspect*. The task context influences the flow of the communication [5], as well as helping to identify important entities and concepts. The information represented for this aspect will vary, depending on the task.

Location Aspect. In Sketch-and-Talk, the kind of location that is the target of the query also constitutes an important aspect of the context. We expect the application to have world knowledge about the location that it can access to build or respond to database queries. The location aspect brings this information into the context. Other types of world knowledge will be needed to understand the speech, and, at times, the graphics. However, we create a separate aspect for location because it is so important for interpreting symbols and for managing the graphics aspects.

Since the identity of the target location often unfolds as the task is being carried out, Sketch-and-Talk must be able to determine the location aspect as it is being discussed. The representation of the location aspect then includes more detail as the location is described by piecing together representations. For example, the current location context may be a forested lot. If picnic tables are added to the sketch by the user, then the current location aspect must be merged with the context of a picnic area.

User Aspect. Knowledge of the user's goals, beliefs, level of expertise, style of interaction, and idiosyncrasies, traditionally stored in *user models* (e.g., [7, 8]), constitute the user aspect. In our application, the idiosyncrasies and style of interaction of the user are particularly interesting. In multi-modal communication, unlike natural language communication, conventions are not necessarily shared by the community of users. Instead, individuals develop their own styles of interacting. Consequently, individual styles of the interaction work like conventions in natural language. Part of our work on the user context will be to better understand particular behaviors of users and the roles they play in interpreting the input.

Temporal Aspect. Locations change over time. While drawing, the user may refer to different features of the location that existed at different times. The system may also be aware of differences in the location at different times. In order to understand what the user is saying and drawing, the interface needs to model and track the temporal context. Thus we have identified a temporal contextual aspect as a separate kind of aspect.

A user's description of a location has a *primary temporal aspect*. If the user has only seen the location at one time, or is describing features of a prototype location that he or she would like to find, this primary temporal aspect will be the only one that is needed to interpret the user's input. Other temporal aspects may be invoked if the user has seen the location at different times.

Legend Aspect. We have noticed that occasionally users provide a legend for symbols that they will use during a particular session. This information also defines the aspect of the context in which those symbols have those meanings. The legend aspect is applicable only during the current session. This distinguishes it from information about what the symbol denotes that can be consistently associated with users, locations, or tasks across multiple sessions.

Environment Aspect. The environment that the user is in also affects the interaction with the system and should be represented separately. The environment aspect includes the user's location, the equipment used, and the presence of observers or other participants in the session.

3 Discussion

Lenat [9] discusses some of the problems with monolithic context representations based on experience with the Cyc program. He delineates twelve dimensions of "context-space" in response, four of which are similar to two of our contextual aspects. His two spatial dimensions, "Absolute Place" and "Type Of Place", are related to our location aspect, and his two temporal context dimensions, "Absolute Time" and "Type Of Time", are related to our temporal aspect. It is difficult to see, however, where the remainder of the contextual aspects we have identified would fit in his framework.

In this paper, we have discussed preliminary work we have done on identifying contextual aspects and contextual knowledge important for multi-modal interfaces. We have so far identified the following aspects, based on examining videotapes of research group members simultaneously talking about and drawing locations: discourse, graphics, task, location, user, temporal, legend, and environment.

4 Acknowledgments

This material is based upon work supported by the National Science Foundation under Grant No. IRI-9613646. The authors would like to thank Max Egenhofer and the other members of UM's Department of Spatial Information Science and Engineering who are developing the Sketch-and-Talk system. The authors also wish to thank Patrick Brézillon for his helpful comment on an earlier version of this paper.

References

1. E. H. Turner, R. M. Turner, C. Grunden, J. Mailman, M. Neale, and J. Phelps. The need for context in multi-modal interfaces. In *Workshop Notes for the 1999 AAAI Workshop on Reasoning in Context for AI Applications*, AAAI Technical Report (ISBN 1-57735-098-7), pages 91–95, Orlando, FL, July 1999. AAAI Press.
2. E. H. Turner, R. M. Turner, J. Phelps, M. Neal, C. Grunden, and J. Mailman. Aspects of context for understanding multi-modal communication. Technical Report 99-01, Department of Computer Science, University of Maine, 1999.
3. B. J. Grosz. The representation and use of focus in a system for understanding dialogs. In *Proceedings of the Fifth International Conference on Artificial Intelligence*, pages 67–76, Los Altos, California, 1977. William Kaufmann, Inc.
4. R. Reichman. *Getting Computers to Talk Like You and Me: Discourse Context, Focus, and Semantics (An ATN Model)*. The MIT Press, Cambridge, Mass, 1985.
5. B. J. Grosz and C. L. Sidner. Attention, intention, and the structure of discourse. *Computational Linguistics*, 12(3):175–204, 1986.
6. M. Egenhofer and J. Herring. Fourth international symposium on spatial data handling. pages 803–813, 1990.
7. C. L. Paris. *The Use of Explicit User Models in Text Generation: Tailoring to a User's Level of Expertise*. PhD thesis, Columbia University, October 1987.
8. S. Carberry. Modeling the user's plans and goals. *Computational Linguistics*, 14(3):23–37, 1988.
9. D. Lenat. The dimensions of context-space. Published on-line at URL http://www.cyc.com/context-space.rtf, accessed March 28, 1999., 1998.

Author Index

Lecture Notes in Artificial Intelligence (LNAI)

Lecture Notes in Computer Science